ENVY OF THE WORLD

ENVY OF THE WORLD

A History of the U.S. Economy
&
Big Business

by

Timothy J. Botti

Algora Publishing
New York

ISBN: 0-87586-431-7 (softcover)
ISBN: 0-87586-432-5 (hardcover)
ISBN: 0-87586-433-3 (ebook)

Library of Congress Cataloging-in-Publication Data —

Botti, Timothy J., 1956-
Envy of the world: a history of the U.S. economy & big business / by
Timothy J. Botti.
    p. cm.
Includes bibliographical references and index.
ISBN 0-87586-431-7 (trade paper: alk. paper) — ISBN 0-87586-432-5 (hard
cover: alk. paper) — ISBN 0-87586-433-3 (ebook) 1. United States—Economic
conditions. 2. Big business—United States—History. 3. Capitalism—United
States—History. I. Title. II. Title: History of the U.S. economy & big business.

   HC103.B77 2006
   330.973—dc22

                        2006010296

Printed in the United States

TABLE OF CONTENTS

Author's Foreword

At time of this writing in 2005, following a Presidential election campaign characterized by harsh criticism of special moneyed interests and foreign outsourcing of labor, many Americans have taken a dim view of Big Business and the federal government's management of the economy. This book does not shrink from pointing out episodes of corporate greed and malfeasance as well as mistakes by Washington both in the recent and distant past. However, the impression is epidemic among the populace that the advances and conveniences of a modern society are the God-given right of Americans. In point of fact, the cornucopia of excellence that exists in food and household products, clothing and consumer durables, housing and motor vehicle transportation, health care and high tech industry, and other goods and services, would not be available to the majority of citizens but for the ambition, effort, and, yes, self-interest of entrepreneurs who founded, grew, and consolidated private enterprise companies. Further, the sometimes contradictory efforts by government officials to balance the interests of corporations, societal groups, and individuals have created by-and-large a most beneficial atmosphere for economic endeavor. Praise of business and governmental leaders in no way diminishes the importance of the exertions, intellectual as well as physical, of working men and women.

Any American who travels abroad for any length of time will recognize that by comparison with the progress and wherewithal of other countries, the United States is most fortunate in its material blessings and accomplishments. Given the number of people from all points of the compass desiring to come to these shores, and conversely the rising tide of hostility toward American economic and geo-strategic hegemony in diverse regions of the world, the majority of foreigners apparently think so too.

However, this book is not about world opinion of the United States. Rather, it is a history of the rise and development of the American economy and Big Business over four centuries and how the individual and collective actions of Americans, native born and foreign, came to create the $11.7 trillion economy of today. Inseparable from the discussion is periodic quantitative summation of gross domestic product, population, employment, company results, and other statistics. Particularly in later chapters, the reader will notice a greater emphasis on numbers. Hopefully, figures will not compromise readability. Because my philosophy continues to be that a picture and a thousand words are better than just the

thousand words, I have made extensive use of graphs, illustrations, industry genealogies, and maps. Updated graphs using current year data will be available on the website Masnapshot.com beginning in autumn 2006. Other analyses of company and industry merger and acquisition activity will also be included on the site.

About the Author

Dr. Botti is an independent American historian without allegiance to any political philosophy or party. As such, he is able in his research and writing to go where the evidence leads. Thorough study combined with inductive, rather than deductive, reasoning is his basic approach. When a reader finishes one of Dr. Botti's books, he or she comes away with a much better understanding of the subject matter than at the start — which should be the result of reading any book but often is not.

Among the areas of Dr. Botti's historical expertise are world empires, American military and strategic studies, ancient Roman history, and the subject of his current work, the US economy and Big Business. He has found that broad knowledge is as important as specialized knowledge in successfully coming to grips with a project.

ABBREVIATIONS

3M	Minnesota Mining and Manufacturing Co.
A&P	Great Atlantic & Pacific Tea Co.
AAA	Agricultural Adjustment Administration
ABB	Asea Brown Boveri
ABC	American Broadcasting Co.
ABF	Arkansas-Best Freight
ACCO	American Clip Company
ADM	Archer Daniels Midland
ADP	Automatic Data Processing
AEC	Atomic Energy Commission
AEP	American Electric Power
AFL	American Federation of Labor
AFLAC	American Finance Life Assurance Co.
AHP	American Home Products
AIDS	Acquired Immune Deficiency Syndrome
AIG	American Insurance Group
AMC	American Motors Corp.
AMCELL	American Cellular Network Corp.
AMD	Advanced Micro Devices
Amoco	Standard Oil of Indiana
AMT	Alternative Minimum Tax
AOL	America Online
ARAMARK	Automatic Retailers of America
ARAMCO	Arab-American Oil Co.
ARCO	Atlantic-Richfield
ARKLA	Arkansas Louisiana Gas Co.
ARM	Adjustable rate mortgage
ARPA	Advanced Research Projects Agency
AT&T	American Telephone and Telegraph
B&O	Baltimore & Ohio

BOF	Basic Oxygen Furnace
BP	British Petroleum
C&O	Chesapeake & Ohio
CAA	Civil Aeronautics Authority
CAB	Civil Aeronautics Board
CAD/CAM	Computer aided design and manufacturing
CAPD	Continuous ambulatory peritoneal dialysis
CBS	Columbia Broadcasting System
CD	Certificates of Deposit; or Compact Disc
CDMA	Code division multiple access
CFC	Chlorofluorocarbons
Chevron	Standard Oil of California
CIO	Committee for Industrial Organizations; or Congress of Industrial Organizations
CLEC	Competitive local exchange carriers
CNN	Cable News Network
CONRAIL	Consolidated Rail Corp.
CPU	Central processing unit
CRT	Cathode ray tube
CWA	Civil Works Administration
DAYCO	Dayton Tire
DEC	Digital Equipment Corp.
DISC	Domestic International Sales Corp.
DNA	Deoxyribonucleic acid
DOE	Department of Energy
DOS	Disc operating system
DOT	Department of Transportation
DRAM	Dynamic random-access memory
DSP	Digital signal processors
DVD	Digital Video Discs
EADS	European Aeronautic Defense & Space Co.
EBASCO	Electric Bond and Share Co.
EC	European Community
EEC	European Economic Community
ENIAC	Electronic Numerical Integrator and Computer
EPA	Environmental Protection Agency
EU	European Union
FAA	Federal Aviation Administration
Fannie Mae	Federal National Mortgage Association
FASB	Financial Accounting Standards Board
FCC	Federal Communications Commission
FDA	Food and Drug Administration
FDIC	Federal Deposit Insurance Corp.
FedEx	Federal Express
FERA	Federal Emergency Relief Administration
FERC	Federal Regulatory Commission

FHA	Federal Housing Administration
FPC	Federal Power Commission
FPL	Florida Power and Light
Frisco	St. Louis-San Francisco RR
FSC	Foreign Sales Corp.
FTC	Federal Trade Commission
GD	General Dynamics
GE	General Electric
GM	General Motors
G-P	Georgia-Pacific
Hasbro	Hassenfeld Brothers
HBO	Home Box Office
HCA	Hospital Corp. of America
HDTV	High definition television
HEW	Department of Health, Education, and Welfare
HFS	Hospitality Franchise Systems
HIV	Human Immunodeficiency Virus
HMO	Health Maintenance Organization
HORC	Home Owners Refinancing Corporation
H-P	Hewlett-Packard
HUD	Department of Housing and Urban Development
IBM	International Business Machines
ICC	Interstate Commerce Commission
IH	International Harvester
ILGWU	Ladies Garment Workers Union
ILWU	International Longshoremen's and Warehousemen's Union
IMF	International Monetary Fund
INA	Insurance Co. of North America
IP	International Paper
IPO	Initial Public Offering
IRA	Individual Retirement Accounts
ISG	International Steel Group
ISP	Internet service providers
IWW	International Workers of the World
J&J	Johnson & Johnson
JDAM	Joint Direct Attack Munition
Jersey Standard	Standard Oil of New Jersey
Katy	Missouri-Kansas-Texas RR
KBR	Kellogg Brown & Root
KFC	Kentucky Fried Chicken
LBO	Leveraged buyout
LNG	Liquid Natural Gas
LOGCAP	Logistics Civil Augmentation Program
LTCM	Long Term Capital Management
MCA	Music Corporation of America
MCCA	Mobile Communications Corp. of America

MCI	Microwave Communications, Inc.
MetLife	Metropolitan Life Insurance
MFN	Most favored nation status
MGM	Metro-Goldwyn-Mayer
MIT	Massachusetts Institute of Technology
MRAM	Magneto-resistive random access memory
MRI	Magnetic resonance imaging
MTBE	Methyl tertiary butyl ether
NAA	North American Aviation
Nabisco	National Biscuit Co.
NAM	National Association of Manufacturers
NAPA	National Automotive Parts Association
NASA	National Aeronautics and Space Administration
NASDAQ	National Association of Securities Dealers Automated Quotations
NATO	North Atlantic Treaty Organization
NBA	National Basketball Association
NBC	National Broadcasting Co.
NCAA	National Collegiate Athletic Association
NCR	National Cash Register
NFAH	National Foundation of the Arts and Humanities
NFL	National Football League
NLRB	National Labor Relations Board
NME	National Medical Enterprises
NRA	National Recovery Administration
NWLB	National War Labor Board
NYSE	New York Stock Exchange
OAS	Organization of American States
OEW	Office of Economic Warfare
OPEC	Organization of Petroleum Exporting Countries
OPM	Office of Production Management
OWM	Office of War Mobilization
P&G	Procter and Gamble
PACCAR	Pacific Car & Foundry
PanAm	Pan American
PATCO	Professional Air Traffic Controllers
PBGC	Pension Benefit Guarantee Corp.
PC	Personal Computer
PCS	Personal communications services
PDA	Personal digital assistant
PDF	Portable Document Format
PET	Positron emission tomography
PG&E	Pacific Gas and Electric
Philco	Philadelphia Storage Battery Co.
PPG	Pittsburgh Plate Glass
PPL	Pennsylvania Power & Light
PSEG	Public Service Electric and Gas Co.

PWA	Public Works Administration
RAM	Random access memory
RCA	Radio Corporation of America
REIT	Real Estate Investment Trust
RFC	Reconstruction Finance Corporation
RISC	Reduced Instruction Set Computer
RLB	Railroad Labor Board
SABRE	Semi-Automated Business Research Environment
SAFECO	Selective Auto and Fire Insurance Co.
SAGE	Semi-Automated Ground Environment
SBC	Southwestern Bell
Socony	Standard Oil of New York
Sohio	Standard Oil of Ohio
SRAM	Static random access memory
Sunoco	Sun Oil
SUV	Sport Utility Vehicle
SWOC	Steel Workers Organizing Committee
TCI	Tele-Communications Inc.
Texaco	Texas Oil Co.
TI	Texas Instruments
TNEC	Temporary National Economic Committee
TVA	Tennessee Valley Authority
TWA	Transcontinental and Western Airlines; or TransWorld Airlines
UAV	Unmanned Aerial Vehicles
UAW	United Auto Workers
UHF	Ultra high frequency
UMW	United Mine Workers of America
UNIVAC	Universal Automatic Computer
Unocal	Union Oil Co.
UPS	United Parcel Service
URW	United Rubber Workers
USPS	US Postal Service
USW	United Steel Workers of America
VCR	Video cassette recorder
VF	Vanity Fair
VHF	Very high frequency
VISTA	Volunteers in Service to America
VOIP	Voice over Internet protocol
WIB	War Industries Board
Wi-Fi	Wireless fidelity
Wobblies	International Workers of the World
WPB	War Production Board
WTO	World Trade Organization

LIST OF ILLUSTRATIONS

(G = Genealogy; GR = Graph; M = Map; P = Picture)

eBay.com (P)
US Internet Retail Companies 2004, Comparison of MC/AR to Employment (GR)
Expedia.com (P)
US Wireless Telecom Services Companies 2004, Comparison of MC/AR to Employment (GR)
Cell phone towers (P)
US Diversified Telecom Services Companies 2004, Comparison of MC/AR to Employment (GR)
Motorola cell phone with AT&T Wireless service (P)
US Electrical Equipment Companies 2004, Comparison of MC/AR to Employment (GR)
US Computer & Peripheral Makers 2004, Comparison of MC/AR to Employment (GR)
HP Officejet (P)
Apple iPod & accessories (P)
Dell Dimension case (P)
Inside a Dell Dimension computer (P)
US Electronic Equipment & Instrument Makers 2004, Comparison of MC/AR to Employment (GR)
US Semiconductor Makers 2004, Comparison of MC/AR to Employment (GR)
US Software Companies 2004, Comparison of MC/AR to Employment (GR)
US IT Services Companies 2004, Comparison of MC/AR to Employment (GR)
HP Easy Share camera (P)
Linksys router (P)
Flat-panel TV (P)
Amtrak high-speed engine (P)
Intel facility in Hillsboro, Oregon (P)
Laptop PC running Windows (P)
Chapter XVIII:
Jack Nicholson (P)
US Multi-Media Companies 2004, Comparison of MC/AR to Employment (GR)
US Other Media Companies 2004, Comparison of MC/AR to Employment (GR)
US Advertising Companies 2004, Comparison of MC/AR to Employment (GR)
Genealogy of US Movie Industry, 1946-2004 (G)
DVD collage (P)
Regal cinema (P)
Tiger Woods (P)
US Print Media Companies 2004, Comparison of MC/AR to Employment (GR)
The Wall Street Journal (P)
US Book Store Chains 2004, Comparison of MC/AR to Employment (GR)
Chapter XIX:
Abbott blood analyzer (P)
Robert Rubin (P)
The Travelers depository receipt (P)
US Health Care Benefits Companies 2004, Comparison of MC/AR to Employment (GR)
US Pharmaceutical Companies 2004, Comparison of MC/AR to Employment (GR)

PART 1. LAYING THE FOUNDATION FOR SUCCESS: 1607-1860

After the fact, the success of any venture that succeeds may appear to have been inevitable. Certainly, the animal, vegetable, and mineral resources extant in the New World continent and the global, regional, and local conditions that prevailed at the outset of the seventeenth century gave colonizing powers an excellent opportunity to establish valuable overseas appendages. However, the outcome as to which colonial empire would emerge supreme in North America depended in no small measure on the economic progress made by each within its sphere of influence and control. In the final analysis, the human and financial resources the British poured into their 13 colonies to develop what nature had provided overwhelmed the productivity and marshal potency of rivals.

On the other hand Parliament, with its not altogether unreasonable expectation that the colonies must share the burden of expenditure as well as the benefits of victory, went too far in expressing London's predilection for keeping tight control of the economic prospects and political aspirations of Americans. Colonial leaders judged, quite rightly as it turned out, that they could better develop the continent's resources and provide for the material well-being of the people than distant overseers. Even so the volume and degree of success, as measured in economic productivity, was in question until the Founding Fathers put the American constitutional house in order and gave the future over to a vision of prosperity founded on manufacturing, industry, and trade rather than farming. Within the *laissez-faire* — which in French means "let alone," in other words the least amount of government interference with private enterprise — environment established by the executive, legislative, and judicial branches of the federal government, the seeds of bigger businesses were planted.

After the British were beaten off again in the War of 1812, the only major impediment to consolidating a material American success story was political division between North and South. Free versus Slave State disputes were submerged long enough to secure wide lands beyond the Mississippi River and render adequate assistance to the transportation and communications network required to bind East to West. Equally important, the American spirit of ingenuity and inventiveness began to gin up the technological improvements needed by agriculture and manufacturing to become more cost-effective and effi-

1

cient. The US was able to support an ever-increasing population of free and slave labor, albeit without as of yet widespread prosperity.

Only because the South envied and feared the North's industrial success did war become a certainty. As with British leaders a century before, Southern statesmen preferred social and political control to maximum material progress. By 1860, Dixie was rapidly falling behind Free State economies even in newly established California. Ironically, after being crushed and laid waste by Union armies, the South rose again — as an integrated part of a mightier economic whole.

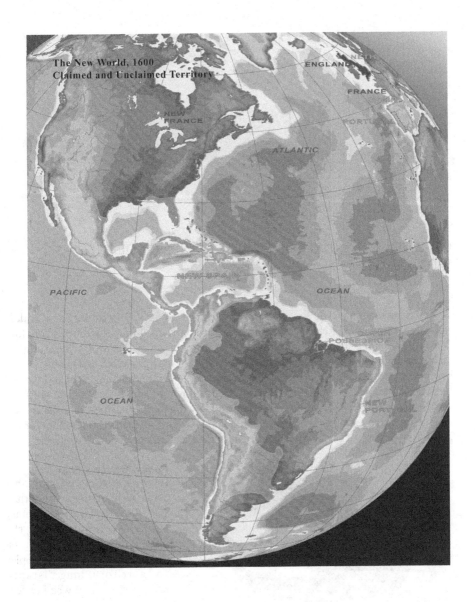

Chapter I. An Irreconcilable Conflict of Interest, 1607-1762

From ancient times, down through the dark ages and back up through the Middle Ages, Renaissance, and Reformation of Europe, the nature and forms of wealth did not fundamentally change. Though a man might be said to be rich in friends, intellect, or good luck, true abundance was measured in quantity of real estate possessed and quality of land byproducts. From nature could be derived stone and lumber for building, animal skins and furs for clothing, and animal, vegetable, and marine life for food. Water from streams and ponds sustained life when game was scarce. In more organized societies, rivers and lakes irrigated soil to raise crops for growing populations. Even in upland pastures of less fertile ground, possession of cattle, sheep, and goats made a man respected and respectable.

Roman Merchant Ship
In the earliest civilizations, goods were bartered rather than sold. Because of the rudimentary nature of trails and roads, the bulk and weight of foodstuffs, and imperfect control of peoples and territory, long distance transport by land was not feasible. By waterway and sea, trade was more facile but risky, given the perils of piracy, war, and natural disaster. Traders had no assurance that what was produced in one region would be received in another, nor that a cargo of equal value would be obtained in return. Thus it became necessary to agree upon a universal medium of exchange acceptable to all peoples. First bronze, then gold and silver mined from the earth, served as surrogates for the necessities and luxuries of life.

Since "precious metals," as they were called, were in themselves of far less practical value than, say, iron and coal used in the forging of steel, this development may in the context of early man's struggle for survival seem odd. However, the aesthetically pleasing quality of gleaming substances convinced farmers, laborers, craftsmen, and governmental leaders that what could be fingered and gloated over was as desirable as what could be eaten, built, shaped, or taxed. At first, metals were melted and cast into heavy bars for storage. To produce "money" light enough to be carried in a purse or pocket, states established mints for stamping coins with the images of leaders and other national symbols.

Throughout the world until the industrial revolution of the eighteenth century, agricultural and food-gathering composed the bulk of economic activity. Lesser but still important forays were made into fashioning household goods, building and ship construction, and metal-working. It was realized by craftsman, ship-builder, and blacksmith that fabrication of saleable goods of specific utility could, by application of knowledge and skill to the process, create value beyond the sum worth of the raw materials. This new kind of manufactured wealth greatly magnified opportunities for trade. Transporting goods — vessels for holding wine and oil, clothing of pleasing color and texture, trinkets and handicrafts of new design, and furniture of exotic wood and delicate inlay — by sea or land, to other markets, made the facilitators of commerce rich. A merchant class sprang up for the exchange of goods between countries and regions.

Some men profited not merely on the sale of cargoes but by charging interest on loans used to finance the transactions of others. By pooling capital, they created a make-shift banking and financial system. Accumulated wealth then permitted larger and more extensive commercial ventures, leading to ever greater concentrations of funds. A financial elite joined the landed aristocracy as possessors of substantial property in society. It was natural, as a consequence, that national leaders should look to them for revenue to run governments. Tariffs on imports, levies against the value of real and moveable property, and confiscated farming production (typically a tenth part, or *tithe*) provided the state with the wherewithal of power. Common people, too, were commanded to contribute to government's resources by handing over a portion of crops and by paying higher prices for taxed goods. When unable to put up tangible assets, they provided labor on public works projects.

If farming, husbandry, craftsmanship, trade, and taxation were the slow, steady paths to wealth and prosperity, war and conquest were the quick ways. Virtually all nations engaged in some form of plundering to expand territorial holdings, seize goods and treasure, and generally take from weaker neighbors what was theirs. The ancient Romans perfected the art and science of national aggrandizement, so much so that in five centuries before the birth of Christ they rose from a tiny collection of villages first to unite the Italian peninsula, next to wrest supremacy in the western Mediterranean from rival Carthage, and finally to smash empires of the eastern Mediterranean and crush barbarian peoples of Europe, Africa, and Asia. Organized mayhem yielded land, goods, gold and silver in abundance.

**Thatched Roof Hut
Roanoke Island Colony,
1584**
But the Romans also prospered from one other asset coveted by predatory nations since the dawn of tribal conflict. They enslaved conquered peoples. Indeed, by making no distinction between defeated inhabitants of the civilized city-states of Greece, Carthage, and the Near East and uncouth marauders of Spain, Gaul, and Germany, they increased the slave population of the empire to over one million by the first second century BC. Not only did they command slaves to perform back-breaking labor in Roman fields, shepherd vast herds in Roman pastures, work and die on labor gangs building Roman roads and aqueducts, but they assembled multitudes of servants to accomplish all kind of menial, skilled, and intellectual tasks in Roman cities. The affluence and ease of the empire's opulent classes grew by leaps and bounds, as a consequence. The labor of free men went begging.

Not only with Rome but with other empire-building states of history, the policy of stripping peoples of their land, wealth, and freedom was most harsh in the immediate aftermath of conquest. To avoid turning valuable real estate into permanent wasteland, the next generation usually followed a more magnanimous approach designed to generate economic activity that could then be heavily taxed. This was the pattern in the seventh and eighth centuries AD when Mohammed's armies poured out of the Arabian Peninsula to impose "the Koran, tribute, or the sword" on much of the Mediterranean world. After the Normans invaded England in 1066 to seize by battle and bloodshed a kingdom contested for centuries by Saxons and Danes, William the Conqueror gathered information about land, crops, herds, and other wealth for a Domesday Book. Likewise, the Mongols of Genghis Khan slaughtered hundreds of thousands of persons from China to Eastern Europe and the Near East in the thirteenth century, only to settle down afterward as fabulously wealthy khans, kings, and emperors. The Spanish followed up Columbus' discovery of the New World in 1492 by organizing a sprawling commercial empire.

A common element in all these episodes was government profit from the confiscation of property and regulation, or at least oversight, of economic activity. The Spanish adopted an even tighter policy of control, called Mercantilism. Not only did the central government in Madrid subsidize and protect important export industries such as the wool trade from merino sheep to create a favorable balance of trade, but it severely restricted the right and ability of foreign merchants to import goods into Spanish-held territory. The belief held sway that a monopoly of trade with dependencies would not only maximize gold and silver in government coffers but prevent an increase of economic and military strength of rivals. Systematically in the sixteenth century Charles V and his son Philip II emptied the New World of wealth to finance a bid for hegemony in the Old; and in fact for several decades, these Hapsburg rulers of Spain and Austria achieved a sizeable strategic advantage. Their heedless exploitation of provinces combined with favoritism toward Spanish agriculture and industry over the interests of other peoples within the empire, especially inhabitants of the Low Countries, engendered poverty and rebellion.

Profits Spanish farmers, herders, and merchants might have reinvested in new enterprises were taxed to fund endless wars and military adventures. When Philip's Great Armada failed to conquer England in 1588, the Netherlands soon gained independence. Spanish weakness then gave opportunity for the Portuguese, French, English, Danes, Swedes, and Dutch to undermine Hapsburg hegemony on the continent even as Spanish treasure ships bringing gold and silver over the Atlantic Ocean were attacked by buccaneers. To gather the more permanent fruits of colonial endeavor, Spain's rivals sent explorers westward to stake a claim to distant lands. They too fell in with mercantile thinking to achieve economic self-sufficiency, larger populations, ballooning national income, and a store of wealth against the uncertainties and vicissitudes of the future. Best positioned in the long run to accomplish these goals were the inhabitants of the British Isles.

Superior sailors, hopeful traders, and aggressive privateers in raiding Spanish commerce, the English attempted to copy Madrid's success in the New World. Although colonies on the Atlantic coast of the North American continent did not take root until a century after Spain's sprawling New World empire, they eventually sprouted healthier trees of economic growth. London dispensed with the immigration restriction that often accompanied Mercantilism to encourage a steady influx of colonists from northwest Europe. As set forth in part I of this history, subtitled *Expansion and Conflict*, English leaders directed action to defeat native Indians as well as the Dutch and French and gather up new territory. Only in the latter stages of the seventeenth century did they progressively constrict the activities of the colonists to serve broader imperial goals. A conflict of interests developed that in the eighteenth century became irreconcilable. Americans, as English colonists came to be known, prized economic liberty and its consequence political freedom as much as their forebears had required the right to worship without persecution. In the New World, they discovered much for which they were willing to fight.

COST AND VALUE OF LAND

When Columbus planted the proud standard of Spain on an island in the Bahamas, he claimed not only that small speck of real estate on the western edge of the Atlantic Ocean for King Ferdinand and Queen Isabella but all the New World. However, because the *conquistadors* moved primarily westward into Mexico and southward, an opportunity remained for other European powers to join the land grab northward. Land there was aplenty, about 3 million square miles, half forested, in the territory that eventually became the lower 48 United States. Beyond that, over four million square miles in what became Canada and Alaska remained to be explored. Initially, vast tracts were covered by impenetrable forest, mountain ranges, desert, and in the far north, ice. Over generations trees would be cleared, peaks surmounted, desert irrigated, and even glacial ice thawed.

The immediate cost to nations of acquiring remote territory was the expense of mounting an expedition. To finally and firmly guarantee title and possession, not only exploration and settlement costs had to be calculated but the drain on government funds

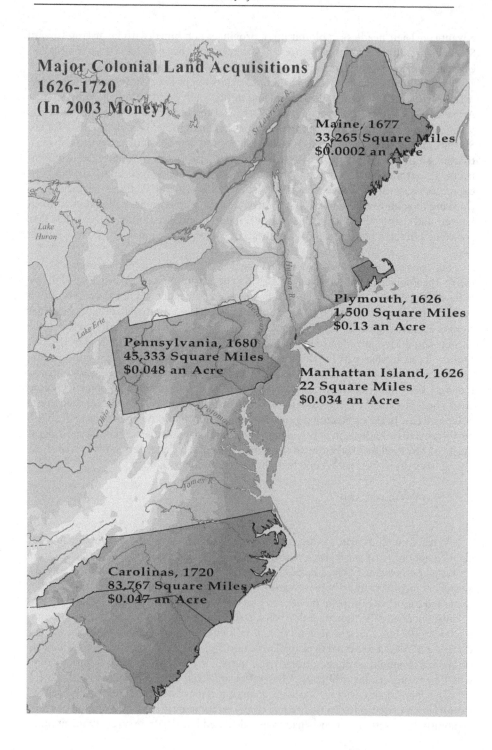

Major Colonial Land Acquisitions
1626-1720
(In 2003 Money)

Maine, 1677
33,265 Square Miles
$0.0002 an Acre

Lake
Huron

Lake Erie

Pennsylvania, 1680
45,333 Square Miles
$0.048 an Acre

Plymouth, 1626
1,500 Square Miles
$0.13 an Acre

Manhattan Island, 1626
22 Square Miles
$0.034 an Acre

Carolinas, 1720
83,767 Square Miles
$0.047 an Acre

of campaigns fought against native peoples, wars between colonizing powers, and compensation paid to the displaced. These expenses might be substantial, as when the British and French battled over decades for control of the Ohio Valley and Great Lakes region. More wars were fought to overawe Indian tribes.

For individuals, the price of land obtained from governments could nominally be as low as nothing. Those with close relationships to rulers, such as English grantees in Maine, the Dutch patroons of New Netherlands, and English proprietors of the Carolinas, became landed nobles in occupation of fantastic holdings. After England conquered New Netherlands, favorites of the newly restored Crown joined Dutch holdovers in privileged possession of estates on western Long Island and along the Hudson and Delaware rivers. It seemed as if the colonies might become another feudal society. But in 1618, to encourage emigration to Virginia, investors hoping to profit from commercial agriculture not only paid the cost of passage for each common man who agreed to join the enterprise but distributed 50 acres free. Eventually, all southern colonies adopted a policy of boosting emigration by assigning similar size plots to each person who emigrated at his own expense.

Many impoverished people did not have the wherewithal to book passage from Europe. Desperate for land, they sold their very freedom and labor for a set period of time as indentured servants to make the crossing. Too often, they discovered upon working off the debt that speculators had accumulated the best land by buying and selling land warrants, which were authorization for an allotment of a certain size but not a specific parcel, and had driven up the price of even basic plots to a level beyond what laborers could afford. Not until 1705 were direct land purchases substituted for the old warrant system, permitting head rights (granted per individual immigrant, including children) to be sold for cash. Just as in New York and New Jersey where ownership of huge estates by a few individuals fostered a system of tenant farmers, in the South settlers who wanted free and clear title to land had to move westward into uncharted wilderness. They used the musket, fort, and homestead to take from Native Americans what governments had yet to assign to their social betters.

Intending to make an immediate profit on investment, London partners in 1620 in the Plymouth Company distributed 100 acres to each adventurer and planter willing to remove to the New World, but charged a perpetual annual quitrent of 2 shillings. In each 36 square mile township, 1,500 acres were reserved for public use but later sold at bargain prices to descendants of the original proprietors. Likewise in Virginia, a 1 shilling quitrent was charged on 50 acres. Over decades, tens of thousands took advantage of this immediate path to land possession.

Parenthetically, the British monetary system was centered on the pound (£). One pound equaled 20 shillings (s.), which equaled 240 pence (d.). In 1776 when the US dollar ($) came into existence, the unofficial exchange rate was about $4.50 to the pound. At present time, the pound trades in the range of $1.25 to $1.90.

A ludicrously low benchmark for the price of land was established by Peter Minuit when in 1626 as agent for the Dutch he purchased Manhattan Island's 22 square miles of unimproved land from natives for beads and trinkets worth the paltry sum of 60 Dutch guilders. That was a bit more than five British pounds. Using the above information about the 1776 dollar to pound exchange rate, historians have extrapolated the 60 guilder price to $24 or, in 2004 money, $0.035 per acre for each of the island's 14,080 acres. Given that four centuries later, the usable size of the area has in effect been multiplied many times by skyscrapers and that prime Manhattan real estate in luxury high-rise buildings sells for thousands of dollars per square foot, Minuit's transaction was almost certainly the most advantageous land purchase in history.

Later in that year, on November 15, the community of Pilgrims bought out the Plymouth Company for £800 and assumption of £600 debt. They obtained that sum (roughly equal to $260,000 in 2004 dollars) by borrowing money from the eight wealthiest colonists in their midst in return for a monopoly of trade and a tax of three bushels of corn or six pounds of tobacco per shareholder until the debt was paid. Settling of accounts turned out to be but a few months away in July 1627. The eight financiers then used the profits to establish trading posts at Kennebec (1628) and Penobscot (1631).

To improve England's position on the continent vis-à-vis the French, His Majesty's government in Virginia emboldened men to move up river valleys into the interior with special grants of 600 acre plots. Settlements and forts established on the western edge of the Tidewater (low-lying coastal plain) in 1646 provided the colony with a buffer zone against danger. These strongholds also served as springboards for expansion into lands beyond the Appalachian Mountains. The process of penetrating the Ohio valley country began even as the spread of inhabited areas and cultivated fields back east drove up land values.

When the Dutch lost New Netherlands to the English in a series of wars 1660-76, frontier land between the Hudson and Delaware Rivers once offered by Dutch patroons to settlers on a quitrent basis was given in grant by the restored Stuart dynasty of King James II and his brother the Duke of York to Sir George Carteret and Lord John Berkeley. Those lords then re-rented the land to the inhabitants, causing considerable uproar and confusion. Outraged by what was considered unfair confiscation and opportunistic extortion, some common men refused to pay new quitrents, and rather rebelled in 1670 in parts of the new colony of New Jersey; two years later they assembled an army at Elizabethport. Although Carteret as governor in 1674 campaigned with military force to compel payment, the value of Berkeley's holding fell so low that he sold his proprietary rights for a mere £1,000.

Where Indian tribes were ousted and productive farming ensued as in the lower Hudson-Delaware lands, the value of real estate ultimately rose. In wilderness areas unsuitable for tillage and still settled by indigenous people, prices remained depressed. Thus in 1677, the colony of Massachusetts purchased title to the territory that became Maine from the heirs of the original grantees for £50. Using the state of Maine's final fixed size of 33,265 square miles, that was equal in 2004 money to about $0.00029 per acre.

Back in England, James II needed money to rule without interference from Parliament. By history, tradition, and law, that legislative body was empowered to vote for or withhold funds for the functions of government. A favorite tactic was borrowing money from wealthy nobles and merchants and making repayment from customs duties on imports. When that source of finance proved inadequate, the Crown in 1680 made more grants of land in the New World to satisfy the king's debts. Quaker merchant William Penn was given a charter for 40 million acres of land west of the Delaware River, extending five degrees longitude between 43 degrees North and 40 degrees Northwest. In exchange, he dropped his father's old claim of £16,000 against the Exchequer.

Even if using the state of Pennsylvania's final fixed size of 29 million acres, on a cost per acre basis in 2004 money under $0.05, Penn's transaction was a brilliant coup. No wonder he resold tracts of 5,000 acres for a price equal in 2004 money to a bit more than 6 cents. However, forty years later, seven of eight Carolina proprietors demonstrated how difficult it was to turn wilderness into riches by selling out their claims to millions of acres for only £2,500 each. Carteret's heir retained his until 1743 when he exchanged it for land just south of Virginia's border.

William Penn

By the mid-eighteenth century, 2.8 million acres had been opened up in the westward regions of Virginia. Land fever carried over to hunger for trans-Appalachian wilderness, which pleased London authorities bent and determined to claim that territory before the French. The Privy Council granted the Ohio Company, founded in 1747 by Thomas Lee, 200,000 acres of land between the Ohio River, Great Kanawha River, and Allegheny mountains. Partially in conflict with this claim, the colony of Virginia granted 800,000 acres to the Loyal Company for territory westward from the recognized Virginia and North Carolina border. Thus, at a nominal cost of zero pounds, but an actual cost of several thousand to mount exploratory expeditions, build forts, and pave the way for settlers, investors received the right to resell or lease homesteads to make a profit. It was well known from the report of adventurers like Daniel Boone that the Ohio country and Kentucky wilderness contained animal and vegetable life of enormous value.

Beaver

BOUNTY OF A NEW CONTINENT

At first, colonists who landed in the New World to plant towns and farms within shouting distance of the sea had only the vaguest notion of the size and abundance of the North American continent. Concerned by harsh winters, Indian attacks, failed crops, disease, and other calamities, many swung around to an opinion that they had exchanged life in a civilized land for bare existence in a godforsaken wilderness. Small consolation to lost colonists on Roanoke Island, the starvelings of Jamestown, and so many others who did not live out a normal lifetime that rays of prosperity would one day warm all the territory between the Atlantic and Pacific Oceans. Although the land overflowed with wildlife and mineral resources, because of hostile local populations, dense forests, and imposing mountain ranges it failed to excite the greed of a miserable and struggling people. Viewed from a greater geographic distance in the capitals of Europe, the enormity and riches of the continent engendered among statesmen excitement and action. After they weighed the human and monetary cost of exploration and settlement against the potential benefit and found the latter heavier, a great competition for domination of the New World began.

Salmon

It turned out that the territory between the Spanish empire and 49th Parallel possessed the most abundant natural resources, raw materials, and potential for profit. Hundreds of thousands of native Indians who might have thrown back the invaders were widely distributed on the continent and disunited. In permanent occupation of only small areas, they preferred a semi-nomadic way of life, hunting in wilderness areas for a few weeks, returning home to family and campfire before moving on again to another village. Teeming wildlife was not seriously reduced by their activity. Thus, at the turn of the sixteenth century into the seventeenth, newly arrived colonists found the tangible bounty of North America at its greatest extent. A simple catalogue of these natural riches explains why, early hardship or not, the colonizing powers coveted the New World.

Even before successful settlement of the colonies, English fishing fleets competed with French for cod, haddock, and mackerel in the waters between Labrador and Long Island. Partly to exploit those fisheries, the Plymouth Company sent settlers to found the Plymouth colony in 1620. Profitable extraction of marine life then ensued not only in coastal waters but inland where trout, salmon, walleye, and other species were caught. Over decades and centuries, lobster from Maine, catfish from Louisiana, shrimp from the Gulf of Mexico, salmon from Washington state, and many other fish products formed the foundation of a burgeoning seafood industry.

Once ensconced on dry land, Pilgrims established a tradition of feasting on wild turkey. Their muskets also brought down pheasant, grouse, quail, geese, and duck. However, the greater proliferation of meaty game was found across the Appalachian Mountains in the wilderness of Kentucky and points westward. White-tail deer, elk, moose, rabbit, and other animals drew hunters ahead of settlers, risking conflict with Indians but providing pioneers with food. Even after the count of wildlife was reduced in trans-Appalachian lands, the continent held one more great animal resource. On the Great Plains, the Sioux, Cheyenne, and other large tribes depended upon a seemingly irreducible population of 20 million buffalo (or bison) for food, clothing, and camp supplies.

Buffalo

Explorers and mountain men who crossed the Plains marveled at the buffalo herds and greatly prized buffalo skins as heavy coats. More valuable in a commercial sense was the fur-trade from bear, fox, mink, muskrat, opossum, otter, raccoon, and squirrel but especially beaver, numbering in tens of millions on the continent. In the seventeenth century, beaver felt hats as well as fur-tipped, lined, and decorated articles of clothing became high fashion in Europe. Even when the population of fur-bearing animals in the East was exhausted, more were found in the Great Lakes region and Rocky Mountains.

A resource infinitely more available and easier to cultivate than fur-bearing animals proved at first more suitable for thousands of small-scale enterprises. Any settler with an axe could chop down trees to build a log cabin. From New England to the Carolinas, hardwood and softwood lumber was in abundance for the construction of houses, barns, schools, stores, and other types of buildings. Byproducts of trees included sap (from maple trees) for syrup, bark (from birch trees) used in canoe construction, dead wood to fuel fire-places, and potash from hardwood ashes as a source of potassium chloride to produce soap to full wool, make glass, and mix saltpeter for gunpowder. More important to London in a strategic sense than wealth accruing to colonists from proximity to forests was naval stores for ship construction. New England white pine built hulls, masts, yards, and bow-sprits for war ships and commercial vessels while pitch and tar, rosin and turpentine, and hemp for rope were exported to England.

Fort McClary Blockhouse
Kittery Point, Maine, 1630

The East also had no scarcity of rivers, streams, and brooks, and also plentiful rainfall to replenish those water courses. However, the greatest fresh water resource in the world waited once the British defeated the French for over lordship of the old Northwest Territory. Five thousand four hundred cubic miles of water filled up the Great Lakes, left behind when glaciers retreated a thousand millennia ago. The Ohio, Mississippi, Missouri, Columbia and other rivers complicated and facilitated the westward movement. But ground water, such as the Ogallala Aquifer beneath the Great Plains, would one day with the Colorado River and other waterways and dams help irrigate 50 million acres of arid land. Average rainfall of 30 inches per year across the swath of the continent that would become the lower 48 states produces nearly five billion acre feet of water, of which one half evaporates, one-sixth runs off, one-sixth seeps down to aquifers, and the remainder feeds lakes, rivers, and streams.

Although the fertile soil of the Great Plains region would one day make the US a food basket for the world, original settlers encountered difficulty in the rockier landscape of the Atlantic coast. A general lack of skill in agriculture combined with a paucity of farm imple-ments and plough animals contributed to periods of starvation. Had Captain John Smith not been given Indian maize as well as peas, beans, squash, and pumpkins, the settlement of Jamestown might have suffered the same mysterious fate as the Roanoke Island colony. Maize or corn eventually became a major feed crop in the Midwest. Likewise, it took cen-turies for Americans to domesticate and turn into profitable industry wild orange trees in

Florida. Farmers had much better and earlier success with wheat, barley, rye, and grasses imported from Europe.

One of the original 13 colonies, New Hampshire became known as the granite state. Granite was also found in Maine, Rhode Island, and Vermont while Massachusetts, Vermont, but especially north Georgia had deposits of marble. Until the coming of canal building and railroads in the nineteenth century, cutting and transport of stone to populated areas did not become feasible. A much more facile material was clay from Maryland baked in kilns to make bricks. Later, in Ohio, surface clays were found to be plentiful, leading to develop of the ceramics industry. Limestone from southern Ohio and Indiana, sandstone from the western slopes of the Appalachians, and slate from Pennsylvania, New York, and Vermont all contributed building materials.

Granite Quarry For preservation of food, seasoning, and health, salt was essential. Establishment of small local salt works such as at Beverly, Massachusetts in the 1640s had to suffice until rock-salt mines were opened in western New York and particularly northern Ohio. Salt domes on the Gulf coast of Texas and Louisiana added to the national abundance. The Great Salt Lake in Utah was a plentiful but more difficult source for extraction.

Likewise, development of the continent's other mineral resources was a matter initially of slow progress. Although charcoal was used for home-heating in New England, the full potential of carbon-based substances did not develop until bituminous coal from western Virginia and Kentucky, then harder, cleaner-burning anthracite coal from the mountains of Pennsylvania was discovered. Smelted with iron ore from Michigan and Minnesota in the nineteenth century, it forged the United States steel industry. Other huge deposits of bituminous coal and iron ore turned up in the Rocky Mountains.

On the other hand, deposits of oil found first in western Pennsylvania in 1859, more abundantly in Texas, Oklahoma, and Louisiana were late in discovery and development, quick to be consumed. Black crude bubbling up from the earth quickly replaced whale-oil in lamps, and then filled the Industrial Revolution's need for lubricants and heating sources. Automobiles and airplanes in the twentieth century would have sat motionless but for petroleum and its byproducts. Natural gas, also plentiful from the Appalachians to the Rockies, became fundamental to the lighting but more especially the heating industry.

Copper was discovered first in New Jersey at the outset of the eighteenth century. Much greater deposits amounting to one-fifth of the world's reserves were found in the Rockies in the latter nineteenth century from Montana to New Mexico. In Florida, huge deposits of phosphate were unearthed in 1881 in the Peace River valley, with North

Carolina sources contributing heavily to the nation's fertilizer and livestock feed industry as well in the twentieth century as chemicals. Magnesium, lead, zinc, bauxite to make aluminum, mercury, nickel and many other minerals were uncovered from Tennessee to California.

Black gold, as oil came to be called, produced undreamed of riches for the country generally and a few individuals personally but never quite displaced in the imaginations of men the allure of real gold. Although small deposits existed in the Appalachian Mountains, nothing major was turned up until the great strike at Sutter's Mill near Sacramento in the Sierra Nevada Mountains of California in 1848. There followed discoveries in the Rocky Mountain states, the Black Hills of South Dakota, and Alaska. Silver, too, was found in great abundance in western Nevada and mountain locations northward. Other mineral deposits that may in hindsight be considered "precious" in the modern industrial age for their rarity and uses in aerospace and high-tech alloy industries included titanium from Florida and Arkansas. Molybdenum, vanadium, and cadmium were mined in the Rockies.

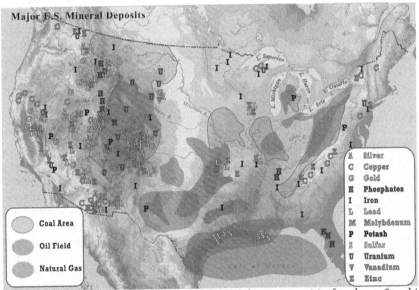

The sole source of diamonds was southwest Arkansas near Murfreesboro. Sapphires were found in Montana, turquoise in the southwest. Generally few mines in the territory of the future United States were remarkable for precious and semi-precious stones. America's bounty was directed more toward practical substances than ornamental.

For example, fur-trading in the Rocky mountains, fertile soil for farming in the Willamette Valley at the end of the Oregon Trail, and lumbering of sequoia and other hardwoods along the Pacific coast were considered for centuries the other natural resources of value in the West. Not until the science of atomic physics was worked out in the twentieth century was it realized that a few pounds of uranium could be transformed into a device both for destructive purposes and limitless energy. Likewise, sand from deserts and ocean beaches was an abundance of waste until the breakthrough of extracting silicon for the semiconductor industry and computers. Hundreds of billions of barrels of oil from shale in the Rockies, difficult and expensive to extract, lie still after a century and a half of American possession almost entirely undeveloped. And under the continental shelf, deposits of oil and natural gas were only tapped by maturing twentieth century technology. There may yet be vast deposits of mineral wealth undiscovered on the continent as well as known resources for which practicable use has yet to be developed.

One example of an underutilized resource is wind power. Although the Dutch brought windmills to New Netherlands, only in the past quarter century on the Great Plains and other places has an attempt been made to turn this omnipresent natural source of energy into electric current. By contrast, human beings have always had an acute appreciation of water power, building dams to drain marshland, free up fertile soil for farmland, and create reservoirs for irrigation and drinking water. Discovery of electricity in the seventeenth century and development of practical applications a hundred years later made possible hydroelectric power from dams and generators. At Niagara Falls, along the Colorado River, and other such places where water crashes over natural cliffs, energy is generated, stored, and distributed. Even the force of waves surging onto beaches and the tides of the sea may some day prove indispensable to industry.

Finally, "air waves" were available for exploitation. Late in the nineteenth century and through the twentieth, scientific and technological knowledge successively made possible broadcasts of radio, television, and satellite communications. The federal government ascertained that frequencies and bandwidth were commodities that could be licensed. Even what could not be seen, smelled, or touched had a value.

POPULATION AND LABOR

It is a true if disturbing statement that human beings have an economic value. When not bought and sold as chattel, people have throughout history by their labor, ingenuity, and skill tended to increase rather than decrease the wealth of nations. A growing population translates into a larger market for goods and services, bringing economies of scale in production, marketing, and distribution. As unit cost declines, the price at which profit can be derived too descends.

In the American colonies, it was a matter of utmost economic urgency and English national policy to boost the labor force and militia reserve as quickly as possible. Particularly since labor shortages drove up wages, contributing to high prices for commodities and resources being exported to the mother country, authorities in London were anxious to find new sources of man and woman power. One possible method was absorption of several hundred thousand Native Americans who lived between the Appalachians and Atlantic into white society, but with few exceptions Indians did not prove adaptable. Although plantation owners in the southern colonies tried to turn the Coosas and Westos into slaves, the experiment was an abysmal failure. Ultimately, the continent's original human inhabitants, east to west, suffered attrition by war, disease, starvation, and neglect. In an economic sense, crude and objectionable though the reference may seem, the human assets of North America were almost entirely wasted.

Such was not the case with immigrants, free and forced, brought in from Europe and Africa. Refugees from political and religious oppression on the British Isles set about improving the land by hard work as soon as they stepped ashore. White indentured servants labored diligently on the promise of eventual freedom, property, and the economic liberty property ownership brings. Black slaves too became productive members of plantation society, albeit in disgraceful conditions. Thus, by fair means and foul, the American colonies of England swiftly became more valuable than French and Spanish holdings because the human contribution to their wealth was as vigorous as resources naturally occurring were plentiful. The Old World tension between those whose labor propelled economic activity and those who directed and profited from it most developed almost immediately.

Slave Market, Charleston

The population of Virginia reached 3,000 persons in 1619 as the Virginia Company organized a regular emigration from England, including maidens as indentured servants for two to seven years but usually four, and orphans as bound apprentices. The maidens were bartered to plantation owners for £120 of tobacco. In fact, indentured servants made up three-fifths to three-quarters of annual immigration to the colonies until 1776. The British also transported 50,000 convicts for sale at a price as little as £15 per head to work seven to 14 year labor terms in various farming, lumbering, and mining operations.

It was the Dutch, not the English, who first brought black slaves from Africa. In 1619, twenty were sold by a ship captain in Virginia. Yet white indentured servants continued to perform most farm labor for the next several decades. There were only 3,000 black slaves in the colonies in 1681.

The first labor strike in the colonies was in the 1630s by fishermen, many of whom had been indentured servants, on Richmond Island off the Maine coast, complaining about low wages. The first guild was established in the colonies in 1644 by master shipbuilders in Massachusetts. The latter were able to sustain themselves against pressure by employers because of a high skill level, irreplaceable in an apprentice system that took years to raise new workers to the same proficiency. A Boston shoemaker guild was founded four years later, then weavers, tailors, carpenters, and other master workers congregated in building trades in Philadelphia and New York in the 1650s and gained footholds for the same reason.

Signaling worsening relations between the English and Dutch, Virginia in 1660 instituted a tax on tobacco grown with labor of black slaves imported by foreigners, i.e. in

Dutch ships. When the English then took New Netherlands by war, twelve years later King James II gave a monopoly on the slave trade to the Royal African Company, which bartered goods worth about £5 to acquire slaves in Africa and then resold them at the going rate for convicts. That slow, single channel of import forced Virginia, with a population in 1670 of 40,000, of whom 6,000 were white indentured servants and only 2,000 black slaves, to seek ways and means of boosting the labor force for the plantation economy. The legislature strengthened codes that prevented blacks from escaping slavery by converting to Christianity. Already in Maryland life slavery had been instituted for blacks, a convention that with Virginia's backing became standard practice in the South. The continuing shortage of black slaves caused the price of a prime West African slave field hand (12–40 years old) to climb to £18, in today's money equal to approximately $1,630.

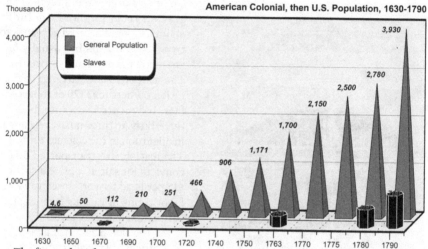

American Colonial, then U.S. Population, 1630-1790

The first colonial government to set wages and prices to prevent high labor costs from stoking run-away inflation was Virginia's House of Burgesses in 1621. All the colonies were forced to resort to that tactic from time to time in the face of persistent labor shortages. The system was tightened in 1690 for towns in which a monopoly was held in such trades as porters, butchers, bakers, innkeepers and even teachers and ministers. Colonies on an individual basis established specific wages, fees, and prices until 1773 when the Continental Congress assumed that power for the duration of the conflict with the mother country.

After a quarter century, the monopoly on the slave trade was taken away from the Royal African Company. Ship masters from Boston, Newport, and elsewhere in New England leaped to engage in the unholy commerce. The result was a surge of black slaves into plantation states, in Virginia alone causing the slave population to soar to 12,000 in 1708, double again by 1715, increase to 42,000 by 1743, and then vault to 260,000 in 1782. Although part of the increase was due to reproduction, average annual imports of 1,000 in 1708, 2,500 between 1715 and 1750, and 7,450 through 1770 meant that blacks died off and were replaced by newcomers as frequently as births yielded American-born substitutes. Meanwhile, colonial legislatures taxed slave importations to build up government revenues. The Crown finally forbade such practice in 1731 to protect the profits of ship-owners.

Even before London's rebuke, a reaction set in against the slave trade. In Pennsylvania in 1712, the clamor of immigrants from Ireland, Scotland, and Germany who feared the depressive effect on wages of competition from slave labor contributed to a ban on impor-tation of slaves. Then slave rebellions in the South, for example one in South Carolina in 1739 that killed 51 whites and dozens of blacks, made even plantation owners think that unrestrained use of slave labor might be a mistake. A decade later, Georgia fixed the ratio of black slaves to indentured whites at four to one, in the hope of preserving a white popu-lation majority. However, attempts to diversify away from a plantation economy dependent upon forced labor were frustrated in the Deep South by a lack of viable alterna-tives as well as interference from London. The South Carolina legislature banned the slave trade, which had been importing 2,800 slaves annually into the colony, only to have the Crown overturn the law in support of English and colonial slave importers.

Meanwhile, the tug of war between colonial governments attempting to control wages and guilds striving to increase them resulted in wide oscillations. Carpenters in Massachusetts earned 2 shillings, 8 pence (the equivalent of 60 cents, but the dollar did not then exist) a day in 1701, 3 shillings, 8 pence (83 cents) a day in 1712, half that amount in 1735, and a more stable 3 shillings (67 cents) a day between 1751 and 1775. Unskilled laborers competing with indentured servants as well as black slaves for the most back-breaking, undesirable work saw their wages fluctuate between the equivalent of 17 and 33 cents a day in the quarter century before the Revolution. Labor protests and disturbances became more prevalent, particularly in the vicinity of New York City. Even in conservative South Carolina, white shipwrights organized as a labor combination to bar blacks from the trade. Very few African-Americans in the South kept their freedom.

Tobacco Production

Boosted by the slave trade but also by a great surge of indentured ser-vants and free immi-grants from Europe as well as natural increase, the population of the American colonies hit 250,000 in 1700, a half million a quarter century later, and one million in 1750. After the British ousted the French from North America in 1763, it stood at 1.7 million, of which a quarter million were black slaves. With Boston, Philadelphia, New York, and Charleston in the tens of thousands of inhabitants, a large regional market for imported British goods was supplemented by potent local economies. Prosperous Americans seemed on the verge of a great escalation in wealth, with concomitant improvements in the lot of white laborers, indentured servants, and even black slaves other than field hands. But the divergence of London's interests from the colonists' became too extreme. The benign brand of Mercantilism imposed by Crown and Parliament had steadily stiffened over time until at last it constricted the ambition of Americans as tightly as the chains the colonists forged bound slaves.

CHANNELING COLONIAL AMBITION

What precisely was the English interpretation and application of Mercantilism? How did it assist or interfere with colonists bettering themselves economically? Unlike Madrid's royal control of New Spain, London did not at first direct the colonial economy of Virginia. That was left to the governing authority, the Virginia Company of London in which merchants bought stock, cumulatively for £200,000, and were jointly responsible for debts. Hoping to emulate the success of joint stock companies then trading in Russia, the Middle East, China, and other settled places, the company's directors wanted to make a quick profit. They hoped in particular to find gold and silver as had the conquistadors in Mexico and South America. For the longer term, they intended to discover a new and easier trade route to China, Japan, and southeast Asia through a guessed at "Northwest Passage." They planned to grow cash crops to feed the growing population of the British Isles where labor would increasingly in the seventeenth and eighteenth centuries be drawn from rural areas to cities for factory work. Pleased by the prospect of both empire and prosperity, the Crown and Parliament expected the Virginia settlements to block permanently any Spanish move up from Florida. Colonial manpower in New England would keep the French and their Indian allies northward confined to the St. Lawrence River valley.

After the ouster of the Dutch from New Netherlands, the middle colonies of New Jersey, Pennsylvania, Delaware, and New York were given over to proprietors with a monopoly on trade. Possession of the majority of land by these New World lords as well as privileges approaching feudal rights in the Carolinas, New York, and New Jersey restricted freedom to diverge from sanctioned economic activities. Except for farming and husbandry, colonists were permitted small scale handicrafts of homespun cotton or woolen cloth, kitchenware, gunpowder, hunting weapons, and other necessities. Whatever disposable income they managed to accumulate was intended to be spent on manufactured goods shipped from England.

While the first and second generations of colonists were busy clearing forests, building up villages and towns, fighting off Indian attacks, and helping English soldiers gain the upper hand on the French, Spanish, and Dutch, there were few complaints about economic restrictions. When, however, the coastal strip was secure and Americans looked to recreate in the New World the creature comforts, conveniences, and prosperity of the Old, a fundamental conflict with authority developed. Particularly after leaders in London gathered to themselves the direct governmental authority initially exercised by joint stock companies and proprietors, friction occurred. Tougher laws prohibiting colonists from developing manufacturing and industry that might compete with English industries impeded efforts by Americans to diversify their economy and build up capital for new commercial activity. Increasingly, the mother country sought to channel colonial energies in a direction compatible with the overall imperial scheme. Colonists began to suspect a deliberate conspiracy to block American ambition at every turn.

Finding no gold or silver to mine, unable to achieve even a subsistence level of agriculture to feed and clothe themselves without re-supply from England, surviving only because of the gift of Indian maize, the Jamestown colonists in 1612 had begun planting and exporting tobacco. However, when eight years later a sizeable crop was in the ground, King James I decided that the practice of taking tobacco snuff was disgusting. Not only did he ban growing tobacco in England, but placed a 1 shilling per pound of weight tax on imported leaf. Yet he failed to snuff out the snuff habit. Following his death, the royal campaign against snuff died as well. Tobacco exports from Virginia exploded by 1627 to 500,000 pounds weight annually (generating £25,000 of annual revenue for the Crown and over time about a fifth of all revenue from the American colonies).

On September 10, 1623, the colony of New Plymouth dispatched a ship carrying lumber and furs to England. Profit from this trade accelerated the process of buying out the ownership stake in the colony of Plymouth Company investors and encouraging a great migration to New England from across the Atlantic through the rest of the decade.

The Pequot Indians in southern New England had long made shell bead money known as *wampum*. Particularly after London prohibited the export of coin from England in 1637, colonists coveted the Pequot specie and went to war to take it as well as Pequot land. To facilitate internal trade, Americans also bartered goods, used paper notes backed by expected profits from tobacco and rice crops, and circulated foreign coins. Bills of exchange eased trade with the British West Indies. Still frustrated at the scarcity of coin in the colonies and recognizing the deleterious impact that shortage had on trade, the Massachusetts General Court defied Parliament to declare itself an independent commonwealth, established a mint, and put out the "pine-tree shilling" until 1684. Paper money as a substitute for coin was not introduced in the colony until 1690 and then only for public payments until 1720.

As Anglo-Dutch rivalry built, Parliament in 1651 passed the first Navigation Act, stipulating that all goods imported into England had to be carried by English- or colonial-owned ships. To further undermine the Dutch merchant marine, no non-European goods could be imported except if shipped directly from their place of production, no fish could be imported by foreigners, and no foreign ships could participate in England's coastal trade whatsoever. Moreover, half of ship crews plus one had to be Englishmen (including colonials). The law was so successful at keeping colonial trade channeled to the mother country and British West Indies that subsequently 55% of colonial exports wound up in England, another 27% went to the British West Indies and 80% of colonial imports came from England. Maneuvered into war the next year, the Dutch were defeated by 1654. English ship-owners and traders moved to tighten their monopoly on colonial trade.

American Brig

War came again with the Dutch over commercial rivalries. Passage of the second Navigation Act in 1660 and third three years later by the Parliament dominated by the newly returned and autocratic King James II seemed to make war as well on American colonial trade. The former act forbade import or export of goods and commodities unless in English-built or owned ships, ruled that three quarters of the crew and the master had to be English, enumerated articles including sugar, tobacco, and indigo that had to be shipped only to England or other colonies, and required that colonial ship owners post bond that cargoes would only be unloaded in imperial ports. The 1663 Act required goods imported into the colonies to be transported in English ships from English ports. Exceptions were salt into New England and the Newfoundland fisheries, wine from Madeira and Azores, and provisions, servants, and horses from Scotland and Ireland. Without competition from Dutch buyers, English and colonial middlemen cut prices paid for Virginia tobacco from 3 pence per pound to 0.5 pence by 1667.

In reaction to the Navigation Acts, colonists began to engage in smuggling. London's response was a fourth Navigation law in 1673 called the Plantation Duty Act that assessed duties at ports of clearance on enumerated products when shipped from one plantation to another. In theory, that prevented avoidance of duties by transshipping through colonial ports. Carolina planters evaded the law by having Massachusetts and Rhode Island traders illegally transship through New England. Although colonial customs commissioners were appointed to collect the duties, they were more sympathetic to merchants than scrupulous about their responsibility. After declining tobacco prices sparked rebellions in Virginia and Maryland, John Culpeper, a customs official in South Carolina, actually led another rebellion for which he was tried and acquitted of treason in London in 1680.

A fifth Navigation Act in 1696 confined all colonial trade, including between colonies, to English-built ships. It also gave colonial customs officers the same power as in England to board ships and enter warehouses by force to collect duties, seize smuggled goods, and compel the posting of bonds on enumerated commodities even where plantation duties had already been paid. Colonial naval officers were delegated to assist customs in inter-cepting smugglers at sea. Parliament declared that any and all colonial laws contrary to the Navigation Acts were void.

Sheep herds having increased over time and colonial cloth manufacturing having expanded during the Dutch war when imports from England were temporarily cut off, Par-liament in 1699 saw fit to pass the Wool Act. In addition to restricting woolen manu-facture in Ireland, the law banned export of wool products from any American colony either overseas or between colonies.

To keep pace in 1705 with expanding colonial production of farm and non-farm products, Parliament added to the list of enumerated articles that could only be shipped to English ports rice from the Carolinas, molasses from the British West Indies, and naval stores from New England. Sixteen years later, London added beaver skins and furs to stop annual pelt exports amounting to 30-40% of the total from New York to continental Europe and cut off as well copper exports from a new mine in New Jersey to the Nether-lands. In 1722 amidst worsening relations with France, all colonial trade was banned with French Canada. The White Pine Act reserved all such lumber from New England for the British navy.

As a further inducement to ship exports in English and colonial ships and obey Navi-gation Act laws, bounties per ton of £4 for pitch and tar, £3 for rosin and turpentine, £6 for hemp, and £1 for masts, yards, and bowsprits were to be paid. Although the bounties were set to expire in 1713, they were extended to 1725, allowed to lapse for four years, then rein-stituted at mostly lower rates. Between 1706 and 1774, London paid colonial producers over £1.4 million in bounties (in 2004 dollars roughly equal to $170 million), adding sub-stantially to government debt.

Besieged by complaints from felt makers about hat competition from France and fearing the same from the American colonies, with beaver felt readily available, Parliament passed the Hat Act of 1732. Specifically, that law banned export of hats from one colony to another, limited hat-makers to those who had served a seven year apprenticeship, restricted the number of apprentices to two per shop, and barred employment of black apprentices. Although enforcement was lax, the fact that the law was on the books and could be enforced at any moment alarmed colonial leaders. They protested to London to no avail.

Meanwhile, New England was plagued by inflation because colonies failed to back up paper money with gold and silver reserves and adequate taxes. Attempting again to make up for a lack of specie, spur trade, and build up a banking and financial industry, in 1740 Massachusetts formed a Land Bank corporation to issue £150,000 in bills secured by mortgages upon which debtors paid 3% interest. Upset that colonial government should control trade, Boston merchants organized a Silver Bank, issuing notes based on silver reserves in their possession. Parliament undermined colonial governments the next year by outlawing the Land Bank and then a decade later prohibiting all New England colonies from forming new land banks and making bills of credit legal tender except during time of war or other emergency. Discouraged from investing in industry and manufacturing and from becoming financiers and bankers, American merchants and traders speculated in real estate, increasingly in the west. A safer investment was British government securities.

Americans Moving West, 1760

With enormous deposits of coal being discovered in Pennsylvania and iron ore at hand from local sources, some ambitious men in the 1740s financed erection in the colonies of rolling and slitting mills, tilt-hammer forges, and steel furnaces. This was a development initially welcomed by London to supply pig and bar iron to England's burgeoning Midlands steel industry. But when colonists advanced to iron-finishing with the prospect of making iron and steel products in direct competition with the mother country's manufactures, Parliament raised its hand. The Iron Act of 1750 forbadee any further construction of iron-manufacturing establishments while still permitting pig and bar iron to enter

England duty free, albeit under special conditions. After in 1757 a second Iron Act lifted all restriction on colonial pig and bar iron export, enterprising Americans violated the ban on further iron-manufacturing establishments. Too many colonists were exasperated by English interference in the American economy to be satisfied with half-measures. Thus, gentlemen from among commercial and entrepreneurial ranks in New England and the Middle Colonies joined landlords and lawyers as well as plantation owners from the South as leaders in the cause for economic and political autonomy from London. A growing number began to contemplate the prosperity that might be achieved by complete independence.

EXPANSION OF AGRICULTURE AND ENTERPRISE

Navigation Acts and other obstacles placed in the way of colonial endeavor did have the desired mercantilist effect of compelling most Americans to concentrate energies and resources upon supplying agricultural products and other raw materials to the mother country while receiving in return English manufactured goods. Particularly as settlers moved up fertile river valleys and cleared forests, production picked up in commercial crops for export, staples required to support more immigrants, and vegetables and fruits for a more varied diet. Local governments took small steps to improve transportation of goods to market by building roads and bridges. A patchwork network eventually made travel possible by land from Boston to Savannah but with no hard-surfaced turnpikes. Then in the 1670s, mail delivery by horse between New York, Boston, and other major cities was instituted. Thereafter came stagecoach lines and boat connections in the Middle Colonies in the early eighteenth century, a full-fledged colonial postal system in 1753 under postmasters Ben Franklin and William Hunter, and regular mail packets in the 1760s from Virginia to New York and Charleston. Distribution of newspapers through the postal system at an affordable fixed rate proved as important for economic development as forging a national identity. Colonists began to think of themselves more as Americans than Englishmen.

Not incompatible with the mission of becoming England's bread basket was expansion of trade with native Indians. In addition to learning from natives how to cultivate maize and other indigenous crops, colonists turned a quick profit trading guns and less lethal items for furs. Both the Dutch in the Hudson and Connecticut River valleys and French along the St. Lawrence River took the fur trade to new heights. Controlling intra-colonial trade as well as the trade in pelts was an important factor in London's decision to make war on rivals. In fact, the British in the eighteenth century built roads westward as much to facilitate east-west trade as for military advantage against the French. Forbes Road from Fort Loudoun to Fort Pitt, Braddock's Road from Fort Cumberland on the Potomac to Fort Pitt, and Gist's Road from Fort Cumberland to the upper Monongahela valley served as arteries of wagon transport of potash for heating fuel, wheat, and household goods.

Because in the long run, farming, herding, and town-building proved more advantageous than fur-trading, the English gained a decisive advantage over the French in the contest to dominate the great middle swath of the North American continent. The steady, sometime surging, increase in population of what came to be thirteen contiguous colonies permitted even greater agricultural expansion inland.

Although famine and starvation were a persistent problem in Virginia, colonists in 1607 were compelled by London Company authorities to concentrate on raising commercial crops for export. They tried West Indies cotton, silk, fruits, and nuts but failed because of the unsuitable climate and back-breaking labor. Greater success was achieved with tobacco after the death of James I made the practice socially acceptable. Profits from tobacco exports came too late to save the company from bankruptcy, leading the Crown to turn Virginia into a royal colony in 1624.

Captain John Smith
Jamestown, 1607

Threats and intimidation to pressure Indians into trading maize provoked a massacre of 347 Virginia colonists in 1622. Only after the government in London encouraged growing wheat for export to fill hungry stomachs in the British Isles did colonists from Virginia to Connecticut concentrate on planting staples. Enriched by fish fertilizer, fields of wheat proliferated over Long Island, the Hudson and Mohawk River valleys, and the Delaware and Susquehanna region. Once hostile Indian tribes had been cleared out, grain was grown in western Massachusetts. Farmers raised as well rye and oats for feed to build up little herds of cattle, horses, sheep, and hogs, imported from Europe. Plough oxen were eventually harnessed in the fields as were Conestoga horses in Pennsylvania a century later.

Apple orchards begun north of Cape Hatteras in the 1620s spread. In Virginia, peach orchards were planted to feed hogs. Indigenous berries and nuts of many varieties sustained settlers in wilderness areas. By the 1640s, barley for beer boosted the tavern trade all over New England.

Larger herds were not possible at first because native rye and broom straw grasses did not provide sufficient nutrition. Many animals had to be turned loose into the wild. But after English grasses were imported in the 1660s, larger herds of cattle, horses, and swine proliferated. Despite a cattle epidemic in Virginia in 1672 that killed off many head and forced grazers to move southward into the unaffected Carolinas, a small livestock industry gained a firm foothold in New England and the Middle Colonies. The migration of hogs and cattle into North Carolina in 1705 made that colony the chief meat-producing colony of the south. Livestock were driven up to Virginia or even Philadelphia to be fattened for slaughter.

Further south, Carolina proprietors warred in 1674 against the Coosa and Westo Indians to protect trappers dealing in furs, deer hides, and—when making captives of the natives—slaves. That martial success opened up a similar barter with Kiowas under the shadow of the Appalachian Mountains. Unlike the St. Lawrence River valley where French power was sufficient to keep control of the fur trade, the Spanish in Florida were too few and weak to interrupt English expansion. Trappers moving south and west were followed in the next few decades by settlers.

More importantly for the colonial economy, tobacco growing in Virginia and Maryland became so successful by the 1680s that an average 28 million pounds weight was produced annually. Unfortunately, such intensive production of one crop exhausted the soil and compelled plantation owners to seek new lands westward. Only after crop rotation techniques that called for substituting wheat grain after three years, use of fertilizer, better control of soil erosion from flooding, and use of legumes were learned from German immigrant farmers in Pennsylvania did production escalate again. By 1750, 50 million pounds of tobacco were exported to England; by 1770 nearly 100 million pounds. Meanwhile, rice seed imported in 1696 from Madagascar to South Carolina gave the Deep South a new and important commercial crop. By the 1760s, 100,000 barrels were exported annually.

Another import planted in New England and New York in the 1740s produced linen for sails and the beginnings of a garment industry in finer cloths. Flaxseed, also known as linseed, was squeezed of its oil to make a high-protein cake meal for livestock. Only in the industrial age was it discovered that linseed oil could be used in paints, printing inks, linoleum, and other products. In the interim, linen's relative importance in making cloths diminished with the rise of the cotton industry.

A disadvantage of linen was that it was difficult to dye. Since wool was more facile in this respect, London in 1748 offered a new bounty of 6 pence per pound to produce indigo needed to make a blue dye for the English woolen industry. Plantation owners irrigated fields in South Carolina and finally Georgia in the mid-1750s to plant indigo. At a cumulative cost to the Exchequer of £185,000 (in 2004 money about $21.5 million), production was made to skyrocket from 100,000 pounds weight to well over one million pounds by 1776.

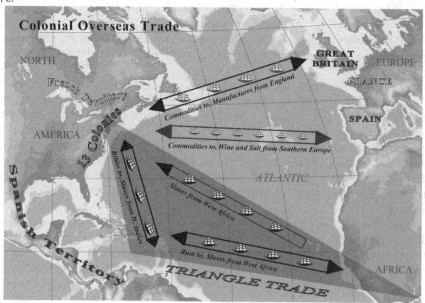

OVERSEAS TRADE

Import-export trade that developed between England and its American colonies was a huge boon to the British empire and benefit to its people. As desired by politicians, statesmen, the Crown and Parliament in London, cheap agricultural products, raw materials, and other natural resources were shipped east in exchange for more expensive manufactured goods. English manufactures having the advantage of government protection against competition as well as higher added value always sold at a premium. American commodities, subject to problems of oversupply and reduced demand, fluctuated sharply in price. Colonials were acutely aware that too often they received the short end of the measuring stick. Navigation Act duties and restrictions imposed to channel colonial ambition only magnified the disparity.

Official figures seem at first blush to bear out the slowly increasing imbalance in trade in the eighteenth century. Although American exports of £395,021 in 1700 exceeded imports from England by over £50,000, both fell in the next decade to an average annual level below £280,000. Then by the 1730s, despite new farm lands opening westward toward the Appalachians and southward into the Carolinas and Georgia, a doubling of colonial exports could not restore a surplus. About midway in the century a dramatic shortfall developed. In fact, between 1700 and 1773 but heavily weighted toward the third quarter of the century, the colonies ran up a whopping shortfall of £20.2 million, imports over exports. British authorities suspected with good reason that much colonial trade was being carried off the books.

What in fact was occurring was elaborate and widespread smuggling as merchants and traders sought to generate off-the-books profits to pay for English cotton goods, hats, hardware, guns, furniture, and other high quality manufactures prized in Boston, New York, Philadelphia, and other large cities. In addition to approved exports to England and the British West Indies of tobacco, rice, cotton, bread, meat, grains, fish as well as iron, paper, glass, and ship supplies, illegal shipments of these commodities were made to ports-of-call in the Caribbean, Africa, and Europe. Export of surplus colonial production brought a measure of prosperity that otherwise would not have existed. It was still far less, argued merchants, ship masters, and plantation owners, than what would have existed had all mercantile restrictions been removed.

The mother country did not object in principle to wealthy colonists. What London frowned upon in the first instance was enriching Americans at the expense of native Englishmen, in the second advancing the commercial interests of French, Spanish, and other colonial trading partners at a time of geopolitical rivalry. Thus, Parliament passed the strangling noose of laws previously discussed. Thus, colonists became increasingly frustrated and angry that their interests were sacrificed for imperial goals. Perhaps officials in London could have headed off much mischief had they prohibited from the beginning all American trade with non-English ports, but then the fledging colonies might never have survived. Colonial merchants realized early on that bartering the natural resources of the North American continent and its surrounding seas for the products of places other than England and English colonies was a path to greater profit.

To fund English imports before agricultural production of tobacco and other commercial crops reached a breakeven point for both plantation owners and middlemen, merchants built up a "Triangle Trade" with the West Indies and England. At first in the 1620s, the practice was purely commercial, exchanging New England fish and lumber and Middle Colonies flour for West Indies sugar, molasses, and rum, then re-exporting the latter commodities to England for manufactured goods. Later, however, Boston merchants sold bibles (and their souls, some argued) in the West Indies for rum, which was then shipped to West Africa to exchange for slaves. The Triangle Trade and colonial exports to England made merchants and middlemen in Boston, Philadelphia, and New York the first class of wealthy Americans.

Singly or preferably in partnership to spread the risk of commercial endeavor, the most successful became general merchants dealing in a wide-range of goods, operating out of counting house offices, and "going on exchange" to deal with each other while delegating responsibility for buying and selling overseas to ship captains and resident agents, oftentimes close relatives. To prosper more than their fellows, some opened wholesale and retail stores, became ship-owners themselves, offered loans at interest to other merchants, insured each others' ventures, bought and sold real estate both in towns and wilderness areas, mined copper and iron, and even established small-scale facilities to manufacture iron goods, paper, and other items not amenable to home handicraft. The most prominent and successful were chosen to sit on city councils, advise royal governors, and represent the people in colonial legislatures. In the process, they crafted laws favorable to their own interests.

For example, prior to London's intervention, no law forbade trading New England cod as near to home as Virginia for flour and tobacco, as far from home as southern Europe for salt and wine. Trade with the Canary Islands and Madeira in Spain helped alleviate an economic downturn in Massachusetts in 1648. But war with the Netherlands soon gave London pause that colonial wheeling and dealing with rivals ought to be curtailed. Because hostilities were largely confined to European waters, colonists in Virginia, Massachusetts, Rhode Island, and Connecticut flouted the 1651 Navigation Act ban on trading with Dutch to continue what had been considered normal internal commerce.

On the other hand, Americans welcomed English intervention to battle the scourge of piracy. British approval and aid was given to colonial naval expeditions, such as the Virginia attack in 1718 on the Bahamas stronghold of Robert Teach, the pirate known as Blackbeard. In fact, many colonial merchants could be legitimately accused of demanding British naval and military protection for trade without being willing to contribute to its cost. In the absence of British control of the seas, many more ships, cargoes, and crews would have been lost.

Timber House
New Hampshire, 1675

Proving that London was not wholly inflexible in application of the Mercantile policy, rice from South Carolina and Georgia was permitted to be exported in the 1730s and 40s to European ports south of Cape Finisterre, Spain. The objective was to woo the Spanish and other southern European nations with trade and in the process lessen their domination by France. Likewise, to strengthen colonial ties with the mother country, regular passenger ship service was established and maintained after the outbreak of the French and Indian War in 1754. Increased spending for military and naval operations and supplies during nine years of conflict produced boom times in America. Moreover, despite Navigation Act controls and other restrictions on colonial economic activity, exports to Britain soared from £1.04 million in 1760 to £1.75 million a decade later. The colonies accepted nearly £1.8 million of imports from England (in 2004 money $185 million). From the British point of view, the trans-Atlantic relationship was highly beneficial to both. From the American perspective, there was so much more that could be accomplished.

MANUFACTURING AND INDUSTRY

Brick house
Delaware, 1728

Not all development of industry by the colonists was incompatible with the Mercantile policy. Endeavors that could not realistically be accomplished in England and exported to America were permitted. The two most essential activities for survival after food-growing were finding shelter and making clothes. Although types of homes and structures varied, almost all women in the New World spun their own garments. The predominance of home-spun production continued for two centuries until technology arrived to make faster factory manufacture possible. In the interim, colonials who wanted finer outfits and could afford them bought imports from England.

Naturally, a people that had just emigrated from merry old England would want to recreate the civilization they had known. They would not only want to look like prosperous subjects of the king but build in the Old World manner. Any building construction on farms, in hamlets and towns increased the value of real estate as surely as tilling the soil. Timber-framed houses New England to Virginia, brick abodes the Middle Colonies to the Carolinas, and even stone structures in New York, New Jersey, Maryland, Delaware, and Pennsylvania all enhanced the long-term tangible wealth of colonists.

A few Americans in the first generation and many more in subsequent eras wanted more than just the rustic beauty and agricultural simplicity of a typical English farm. Men of ambition and energy used knowledge and inventiveness to improve their lot. Thus, here and there from Jamestown to Boston, New York down to Charleston, as villages turned into towns and towns into cities, as wilderness was cleared and the resources of the continent began to be revealed, small-scale economic activity not contemplated for colonials by mercantile thinking popped up. Although America lagged well behind England in joining the industrial revolution, the first bricks of a foundation of an even greater manufacturing base than could ever be developed in the British Isles were laid down.

Perhaps the first industry in America was at Falling Creek, Virginia in 1621. Because of the scarcity of blacksmiths and other metal-working craftsmen, wares produced there were saleable in other towns. In 1643, John Winthrop, Jr., son of the governor of Massachusetts, won the backing of English investors for the Saugus Iron Works near Lynn, Massachusetts to produce from bog iron ore (30-50% purity) heated with charcoal in a blast furnace iron nails, and ax heads, blacksmith tools, and brass. He brought the skilled iron master Joseph Jencks from England to run the shop, and later built a second works at Braintree, Connecticut. Jencks himself in 1654 became notable for building Boston's first fire engine, a pump with a water tank. He was later given a contract for an engine to cut grass more quickly.

The first American-built sloop (of 30 tons) was completed in Boston harbor in 1631. Due to the abundance of cheap lumber, such vessels could be constructed for half the cost as in England. Although New England ships then participated in the Triangle Trade, ship building really took off after the 1696 Navigation Act stipulated that all colonial trade must be carried in English-built ships. Rather than direct profits from the Atlantic carrying trade to English ship-owners, angry merchants and traders put up capital to expand home construction. Thus, New England ships imported French West Indies molasses in 1717 to manufacture rum, incidentally expanding the spirits-making industry beyond beer. Boston led the colonies in volume of coastal trade as well with 11,589 tons, about equal to the cargo shipped from Boston to England.

Massachusetts scored another first when a printing shop opened in Cambridge in 1639. Despite widespread illiteracy in the colonies, particularly among women, the printing of notices, papers, and books expanded over decades into a large industry. Throughout America, colonists read historical accounts, journals of discovery, and religious books and treatises, opened prayer books with psalms and hymns, and entertained their children with books of popular songs and nursery rhymes. In schools, printed material ranged from poetry to medical advances.

Capitol building
Williamsburg, Virginia

When war with the Dutch in the 1660s temporarily cut off clothing imports from England, then the second and third Navigation Acts forbade textile imports from the European continent, Americans founded cloth works to fill the void. That simply meant that a number of women were brought together in one place to do for profit what they had formerly done as a necessity of life at home. The activity was still labor-intensive, however, and only sustainable by turning out higher quality garments. For the first time, style and appearance became marketable commodities.

After 1700, rising prosperity enabled wealthy merchants to have grander houses with double-hung windows (rather than casements), pediments and pilasters to central doorways, and more brick and stone. A style was developed in the following decades called Georgian (in honor of King George I) with two and three story houses, regular-spaced windows, a spacious central hall, and two chimneys. In the South, profits from tobacco, rice, and indigo crops built plantation houses with wide porticoes, stately columns, and wrought-iron stair rails. The increasing authority of royal colonial governments was reflected in larger public buildings as well as churches and the nine colleges, beginning with Harvard in the 1630s, founded before the Revolution. In Boston, Stephen Deblois erected the first Opera Hall in the colonies. Little theaters and hospitals added to the variety of private and public structures.

Construction of more elaborate buildings required the services of stone-masons, bricklayers, and other craftsmen. As in the 1730s furnishings in houses became finer, shops for cabinet making were founded in New York and Philadelphia, and as well clock making establishments in New England. That same decade, silversmiths in Boston and New York catered to the appetite of the upper crust for jewelry. Shoemaking in Lynn, Massachusetts became a wholesale operation.

Related to printing but relying on content to enhance value and boost profits, the publishing industry began in earnest in 1704 with the *Boston News-Letter*, a weekly newspaper that sparked the foundation of many others publications in major cities around the colonies. In 1732, Franklin put out his highly popular *Poor Richard's Almanac* to print proverbs and encourage virtuous conduct. In the 1760s, magazines were attempted but did not take hold until after the Revolution. It was when commentary about hotly debated political issues found its way into print that colonists of all incomes and classes really sat up and took notice.

Benjamin Franklin

In addition to printing, publishing, and civic-minded activities, Franklin was a noted innovator. He adapted a German-built stove to permit ventilation and in 1752 after ten years experimentation proved the electrical nature of lightning with an iron rod connected to a kite. It cannot be said that he profited greatly from this latter innovation, but this advance in scientific knowledge led in the next century to major industry. It was often the case that the lag time between discovery and practical application was decades or more.

On the other hand, three years after the first sperm whale was killed for its oil at Nantucket in 1712, a fleet of six 30-ton whaling sloops hunted the ocean's larges mammal for a whale-oil, candle-making industry in Rhode Island. By 1774, 360 such ships prowled the Atlantic, taking enough whale that year not only for 45,000 barrels of sperm oil but 75,000 barrels of whalebone for corsets. Other products extracted were ambergris for drugs, confectionary for candies, and perfumes. No one really considered at the time that whale and other marine life might be depletable resources.

Meanwhile, small to medium-size iron works proliferated so steadily in the colonies that America produced one-seventh the world output by 1700. After Alexander Spotswood established the Rapidan River Iron Works fourteen years later, even more ironmasters with larger operations appeared. As previously discussed, the British government applauded the production of pig and bar iron for England's use but banned in the 1750s manufacture of finished iron products and establishment of new iron works. Development of a profitable process for smelting iron from black magnetic sand by the Reverend Jared Eliot of Killingworth, Connecticut in 1762 contributed to the law being widely ignored.

Thus, colonial pig and bar production exceeded English and Welsh by 1775. Americans had no lack, at least in potential capacity, of iron to manufacture cannon and other weapons. Already in the 1730s, Pennsylvania gunsmiths had improved on a prototype rifle brought by a German immigrant. When they crafted the Long Rifle with a wood stock and iron firing mechanisms, not only was the American gun industry well launched but the graves of thousands of British soldiers were dug. More than that, the growing American economy, predominately centered on agriculture but broadening into commerce and industry, became a weapon for independence when it might, if more generously handled, have become a permanent asset to the British Empire. Obtuse thinking in London became even narrower once the French in 1763 were ousted from the North American continent.

CHAPTER II. THE STRUGGLE FOR CONTROL: 1763-1783

In the same year as the Declaration of American Independence was signed, a well-educated Scot of middle-class background, former tutor of the children of British political leader Charles Townshend, and a professor at Glasgow University named Adam Smith published *An Inquiry into the Nature and Causes of the Wealth of Nations*. Smith wrote that in the pursuit of their own economic interests men are often and unconsciously "led by an invisible hand" to further the interests of society. Although human nature, specifically a desire for self-improvement, forms the sometimes positive, sometimes negative motivating force of historical development, the competitive struggle of landlords, laborers, and manufacturers results in rents, wages, and profits approximating "natural levels" in correspondence to the real cost of production. If government and society avoids constraints and monopolies inherent in mercantile systems, the marketplace itself corrects divergences from natural levels, direct labor, capital, and resources into more profitable endeavors, and creates a reliable "machine" for economic growth adding annually to the wealth of nations.

In essence, Smith's contention was that economies work best when individuals are given freedom of action to invest capital as they see fit. In the process, they provide a more general stimulant than otherwise is obtainable by government direction. He abhorred Mercantilism because it stifled competition, prevented development of local production (i.e. small business) in favor of government-sanctioned monopolies, and blocked subdivision of labor into specialties. Though he warned against pigeon-holing laborers into repetitive jobs that created boredom, apathy, and long-term inefficiency, his primary concern was with the success of enterprises, not comfort of the working class. Further, he advocated elimination of trade barriers unless for national security reasons because tariffs protected inefficient agriculture and industry. He anticipated the early nineteenth century theory that when nations are permitted to trade freely, they gravitate toward producing what they do best and thereby obtain a comparative advantage over other countries and regions in those niches. Ultimately, all nations are compelled to specialize in activities in which by geography, labor skill, resources, and technological know-how they have inherent advantages. The beneficial consequence for the world is maximized production, expanding exchange of goods, and a broader regional and global economy.

Unfortunately for the British, Smith's publication came too late to influence and remedy policy alienating the colonies. Instead of merely providing security with a constabulary force, the British army and navy, the Crown and Parliament progressively intervened to trample American self-interest in favor of imperial goals. Laws and restrictions impacting economic activities sparked protests and trade boycotts and led to individual citizens and groups taking into their own hands by smuggling, intimidation of officials, and violence the campaign for redress. What began as agitation to institute broad economic liberty blossomed into a full-scale political and military revolution. Thus, when a Continental Congress representing all thirteen colonies, soon-to-be states in the newly declared United States of America, coalesced to direct the war, it was natural for political leaders to move to direct the economy as well. Tension developed between the Congress and states, between government authority and private individuals, to buffet the American economy

TURNING THE FINANCIAL SCREWS

Having spent £140 million to defeat the French in nine years of war in North America as well as finance the improbable survival of Frederick the Great's Prussia against the seven year onslaught of France, Austria, and Russia on the European continent, the British found their national debt in 1763 at over £122 million, paying annual interest of £4.4 million. True, by the Peace of Paris of February 10, they acquired the entire French holding north of the American colonies, including towns and posts along the St. Lawrence River into the Great Lakes and down the Mississippi River, but duties on profits of the fur trade, a £28,000 export business, hardly made a dent in the cost of administering the colonies, including £300,000 annually to maintain nine British regiments. When in spring that year, Chief Pontiac of the Ottawa rallied all the Great Lakes tribes to attack British posts out of anger at not receiving supplies and provisions promised for aid against the French, much of the fur trade was cut off. The British financial crisis worsened.

Times were bad as well in the colonies. A recession that had begun late in 1762 endured into 1765, pushing up commodity prices and reducing American ability to import British goods. Tenant farmers owing rent to proprietors in the Middle Colonies began moving into western Pennsylvania to squat on what they hoped would become freehold land. While beating back Pontiac's attack on Fort Pitt, the British army and colonial militias had their hands full protecting them.

Back in London, the solution to the empire's economic crisis and North America's Indian problem seemed obvious. On October 7, Parliament issued a proclamation banning settlements west of the Appalachian Mountains. The objective was to mollify the Indians and restore the fur trade. The unintended by-product of the policy was great resentment among colonists who believed that their contribution to the victory over the French, including £440,000 chipped in by Pennsylvania for military operations, had earned access to new frontier lands. Therefore, after the defeat of Pontiac, the ban was progressively weakened. A precipitate decline in the fur trade to £19,000 of exports by 1768 convinced London that opening up trans-Appalachian lands to settlement, farming, and other profitable economic activity was a surer way of generating tax revenue than banking on the over-hunted and over-trapped wild life of the region. Promises made to Indians to preserve their land and way of life would not be kept. A calculated risk was taken that over time the tribes would give way before the invaders without starting another major war.

Profit from frontier lands was a long-term prospect, not an immediate balm to the financial wound draining away the empire's life blood. To staunch the flow of red ink, stern and decisive measures were needed. Prime Minister George Grenville analyzed the situation and decided that Americans must pay their fair share of imperial expenses. The only question was what form the exaction should take.

By the American Revenue Act of April 5, 1764, more popularly known as the Sugar Act, Grenville had Parliament raise duties on foreign refined sugar (although duties on raw sugar were lowered to 3 pence per gallon from the 6 pence level of the Molasses Act of 1733), non-British textiles, coffee, indigo, and directly imported Madeira and Canary wines. Duties on foreign goods reshipped in England to the colonies were doubled. Moreover, iron, hides, pearl ash, potash, raw silk, and whale fins were added to the enumerated list of colonial exports that had to be shipped only to England or other colonies. Import of foreign West Indies rum or spirits as well as French wines was banned. One effect of the law was to give British planters in the West Indies a monopoly on the sugar trade. The Exchequer estimated the annual revenue from all provisions to be £45,000.

John Hancock

John Hancock of Boston and other prominent American merchants promptly resorted to bribery of customs officials to avoid paying duties and get around other restrictions. In the colonies, only £2,000 of duties was collected, a quarter of the annual cost of £8,000 of maintaining the customs service and vice-admiralty court in Halifax. So Grenville beefed up its authority and effectiveness by ending the right of colonists to sue for illegal seizures, placing the burden of proof on the accused, requiring that merchants and shippers post bond for the cost of going to trial, and enforcing stricter registration and bonding procedures for ships carrying cargoes. He required customs officials to actually live in the colonies, rather than in England while relying on assistants to perform their tasks.

Even before news of the Sugar Act crossed the Atlantic, Parliament tightened up financial control of the colonies with the Currency Act of April 19. Building on a 1751 law, the members banned further issuance of paper money by all colonies and thereby required the recall of £250,000 of legal-tender paper money issued by Virginia during the late war. To make the point even clearer that ultimate authority emanated from London, they nullified all colonial acts contrary to established British law and fined governors £1,000 if those worthies assented to legislative acts contrary to Parliament's dictates. Because the colonies had come over decades to have substantial autonomy over internal affairs, this last stipulation in combination with Sugar Act provisions so offended Americans that the response was immediate. Lawyer James Otis of Boston raised the now famous cry of "taxation without representation," further whipping up resistance. Boston merchants had no difficulty organizing a non-importation of luxury goods from Britain that went into effect in August, undercutting the Exchequer's revenue projections.

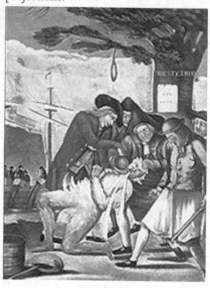

Tar and feathers for a tax official

Howls of colonial protests made barely an echo in far away London. To help pay the cost of maintaining 5,000 British soldiers on American soil, Parliament passed the Stamp Act of March 22, 1765, requiring official stamp on all legal documents, including newspapers, almanacs, pamphlets, broadsides, insurance policies, ship's papers, licenses, dice, and playing cards. Once more Americans were stunned, for the stamp amounted to an "internal tax," breaking tradition that Parliament only passed laws affecting American finances on external trade matters. Projected annual revenue from the Stamp Act was £60,000, which combined with other imposts amounting to £40,000 would produce only one-third what was needed. Thus the same day, Parliament tacked on the Quartering Act, mandating for two years that the colonies provide housing and food for British soldiers and horses. When the New York Assembly refused to comply, British general Thomas Gage suspended its right to meet.

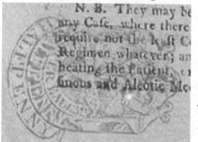

Stamp on newspaper

Although Grenville appointed Americans as stamp tax collectors, he gave jurisdiction over disputes to the admiralty courts, thus threatening the right of colonists as British subjects to trial by jury. Not just merchants and ship-owners but lawyers, printers, tavern owners, land speculators, indeed virtually all Americans affected by the Stamp and Quartering Acts were infuriated. There were riots, assaults on colonial stamp agents, who all subsequently resigned before the effective date of the law of November 1, and an even more thorough non-importation boycott in New York, Philadelphia, Boston, and other cities. British exports to the American colonies declined from £2.25 million in 1764 to £1.95 million in 1765 with some London merchants hurt so badly they went bankrupt.

Because Grenville's policy was an obvious disaster, Parliament repealed the Stamp Act on March 4, 1766. Stubbornly, the members passed the Declaratory Act two weeks later saying they had they right to bind Americans by whatever laws they chose. After Grenville's government fell in August and was replaced by more careful politicians including Smith's patron Townshend as Chancellor the Exchequer, on November 1 they extended a carrot by reducing the duty on foreign molasses imported into the colonies to 1 pence per gallon and removed duties altogether on British West Indies sugar. They brandished a stick as well by requiring that all colonial products shipped to Europe clear through English ports.

In February 1767, landowners who dominated British politics forced through Parliament a measure cutting the British land tax by £500,000 annually. To partially compensate and further provide for colonial defense and administration, Townshend proposed new duties on colonial imports of glass, lead, paints, paper, and tea, estimated to return annually £40,000. Effective November 20, the Townshend Acts also created vice-admiralty courts with broader power to enforce the law and established an American Board of Commissioners of the Customs at Boston, responsible to the British Treasury Board. Townshend believed (quite wrongly in the tense political environment) that Americans would accept these measures because they affected external and not internal trade. Less controversially, he stipulated that all non-enumerated goods being shipped to Europe north of Cape Finisterre had to be shipped first to England. Because most colonial naval stores as well as pig and bar iron went directly to England, because the goods affected amounted to only 4.3% of colonial exports and smugglers got around the restriction anyway, the impact was negligible.

Although Gage's suspension of the New York assembly had been voided by the colonial governor after a June 6, 1767 vote by the assembly appropriating £3,000 to comply with the Quartering Act, further cooperation was not forthcoming. With the cost of garrisoning the colonies now as high as £400,000 and revenue running as low as £80,000, London's mood toughened once more. On May 7, 1768 the Board of Trade ruled all New York legislative acts after October 1 invalid. The stage was set for confrontation.

A month later on June 10, Hancock's sloop *Liberty* was seized in Boston harbor for landing Madeira wine without paying duty. When a crowd assaulted customs officials to free the ship and cargo, the situation became so tense that two British regiments were landed by Gage on October 1 from New York City to keep order, and then reinforced by two other regiments from Halifax. All the New England colonies responded October 28 with a new boycott of British luxury goods. In New York, there were riots in the streets by groups calling themselves the Sons of Liberty. Thus, what had begun purely as a financial crisis had evolved into a political controversy. Meanwhile, the Proclamation of 1763 that had started it all was becoming a dead letter.

WESTERN LAND COMPENSATION

The notion that deliberations and decisions in London, no matter how weighty and well-intentioned, could resolve fundamental conflict between colonists and Indian tribes was fanciful from the start. The entire thrust of British policy had been to populate wilderness areas with settlers and oust Native Americans, not set up an Indian preserve. Virtually unrestricted homesteading had been part of a larger design, now completed, of defeating the French, but the importance of territorial expansion to economic development continued. Banning settlement west of the Appalachians but permitting the fur trade, the Proclamation of 1763 could not forever forestall the westward march of American ambition.

A month before Parliament's statement, a Mississippi Company headed by George Washington, which had purchased military-bounty grants from Virginia militia at a fraction of their value, petitioned the Crown for 2.5 million acres at the junction of the

Ohio and Mississippi Rivers to satisfy the claims. In October, the Proclamation in effect denied that request. But in December, Deputy Indian Commissioner for the northern district George Croghan and other traders aligned with the Pennsylvania merchant firms of Byanton, Wharton & Morgan and Simon, Trent, Levy & Franks asked compensation for losses suffered at the hands of Indians in Pontiac's war. They organized the Indiana Company to promote the fur trade and later in 1766 put together an Illinois Company to penetrate even further into the Indian reserve.

In 1764, the Board of Trade voted to follow a plan by Croghan, his superior Sir William Johnson, and Colonel John Stuart, Indian Commissioner for the southern district, to subdivide the northern and southern districts for trade under Johnson's and Stuart's supervision. However, when Johnson decreed that to curb illegal trapping and stop squatters moving west all Great Lakes trade should be transacted at Forts Detroit and Michilimackinac, the colonial governors refused to cooperate. As a consequence, merchants in New York and Montreal as well as Frenchmen operating from towns near the junction of the Ohio and Mississippi Rivers controlled the fur trade, not Britain's Indian commissioners. When pelt exports declined over the next several years, pressure mounted on London to reexamine the policy of shutting off trans-Appalachian lands to settlement and economic development.

Daniel Boone

On April 17, 1766, the Auditor General of North America Robert Cholmondely rendered a legal opinion that the Proclamation of 1763 did not void prior land grants. With Pontiac's coalition broken up and the Indian threat for the moment reduced, British authorities contemplated three new colonies for the Upper Ohio valley, the Illinois country, and around Detroit. They hoped that by compensating Americans with undeveloped real estate they would mute opposition to the additional duties and taxes then in the process of being levied to alleviate the financial crisis. The only question was how far to go in dispossessing Native Americans.

Parties of frontiersmen led by Benjamin Cutbird and the next year Daniel Boone advanced along the Wilderness Road and crossed the Appalachians through the Cumberland Gap into the Kentucky wilderness to explore, hunt, and trap. Reports they brought back of the region's wildlife and other natural resources whetted the appetite of settlers and speculators to follow. In fall of 1767, Johnson licensed traders to operate north of Lake Superior and the Ottawa River. By reestablishing the fur trade through the Great Lakes region and beyond, he set the stage for the extension of Canada into lands claimed by the colonies.

By agreement between Stuart and Cherokee chiefs in the Treaty of Hard Labor on October 14, 1768, the Proclamation Line was moved west. The Virginia border now ran from Chiswell's Mine to the mouth of the Big Kanawha River on the Ohio River, the South Carolina line was redrawn from Fort Tryon to the Savannah River, and Georgia's western boundary was fixed at the Ogeechee River. With Johnson's help, the Indiana Company on November 3 bought from the Iroquois Confederacy 1.8 million acres southeast of the Ohio River from an extension of the Mason-Dixon Line (the southern boundary of Pennsylvania) to the Little Kanawha River. Two days later, he signed the Treaty of Fort Stanwix, purchasing a vaster tract from 3,400 Iroquois, including territory actually controlled by other Indians. Title was nevertheless acquired for a bit more than £10,000 in trade goods.

Believing because of the Treaty of Fort Stanwix that all land westward would be opened up, settlers in April 1769 besieged the land office at Fort Pitt. Already, the population of western Pennsylvania had reached about 5,000 families and would double in two years. A similar increase was taking place in western Virginia. Authorities feared the squatters would take possession of the choicest part of the territory.

To preempt them, Samuel Wharton of Byanton, Wharton & Morgan formed the "Walpole Group" with Thomas Walpole, a prominent British banker, Lord Hertford the Lord Chancellor, and former Prime Minister Grenville to organize the Grand Ohio Company and receive a crown grant for territory ceded by the Iroquois. They intended to set up a proprietary colony called Vandalia. However, after the arrangement was approved by the Lords of the Treasury on January 4, 1770, and the company paid £10,460, seven shillings, and three pence on August 14, 1772 for 20 million acres, and the Board of Trade fixed final boundaries on April 3, 1773, title was never actually conferred. The Revolution made the attempted land transfer a moot point.

Meanwhile, the "Camden-Yorke" legal opinion by the British Attorney General and Solicitor General stated that authorization by the Crown to purchase lands without an actual patent from the Crown, a practice followed in India, could be applied in North America. The Watauga Association, a squatters' group, promptly on April 9, 1770 leased from Indian tribes a tract covering the northeast corner of what would be the state of Tennessee. Too, Stuart made the Treaty of Lochaber of October 18 with the Cherokees pushing the Virginia border west again by adding another 9,000 square miles to the mouth of the Great Kanawha River, including most land claimed by the Greenbrier and Loyal Companies. In a swindle of Native Americans, a surveyor named John Donelson tripled the ceded territory by running the boundary along the Kentucky River to the Ohio River. Another chunk of Indian land was appropriated in a treaty of June 1, 1773 with the Creeks. Georgia's boundary was moved west from the Ogeechee to the Oconee River.

While in 1774 Wabash and Illinois land companies were organizing to use the Camden-Yorke legal opinion to negotiate with tribes for tracts in the Illinois wilderness, Croghan in partnership with William Trent was accumulating 6 million acres, mostly in western Pennsylvania. Great Lakes Indians finally realized that white settlers and authorities plotted no less than to dispossess them of all their hunting grounds. Although Shawnee and Ottawa warriors had already clashed with hunters in Kentucky, it was the action of Lord John Murray, Earl of Dunmore and Virginia's royal governor that sparked war. Dunmore declared that western Pennsylvania was now part of his colony and sent militia to enforce the claim. After winning the Battle of Point Pleasant on October 10, he forced upon the Indians the Treaty of Camp Charlotte. All Indians had to evacuate Kentucky and allow unmolested transportation of the Ohio River by fur traders and settlers.

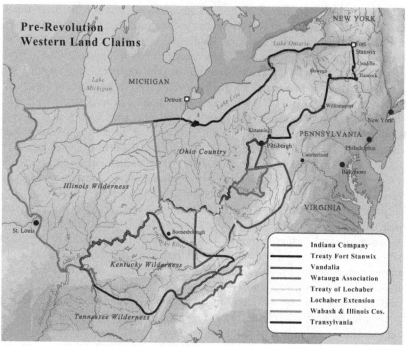

In the space of eleven years since the Proclamation of 1763, British authorities and American colonists had by legal nicety, creeping encroachment, one-sided treaties, and naked force-of-arms appropriated title to tens of millions of acres from Indians for virtually no recompense. Undoubtedly, the hasty aggrandizement would have continued until every tree, bush, hill, mountain, and patch of ground east of the Mississippi River had been acquired had not the Revolution interfered. But hostility was building between the mother colony and her colonies so that Parliament decided to punish Americans by again curbing westward ambition. By the Quebec Act of May 20, authorities in London not only established a permanent civil government for Canada that permitted Roman Catholicism but expanded the borders of that sprawling northern province to include French-speaking settlements in the Ohio and Illinois countries.

In the supercharged atmosphere back east, American land speculators, settlers, and officials decided to take matters out west into their own hands. A Transylvania Company was founded in January 1775 under Judge Richard Henderson and eight other private investors to send Boone through the Cumberland Gap on March 10, make the Treaty of Sycamore Shoals seven days later with the Cherokee to buy for £10,000 land between the Kentucky River and southern border of the Cumberland Valley as well as a strip through the Cumberland Gap, then found Boonesborough on April 6. Soon he was joined by Henderson and many settlers while others founded St. Asaph's Station. However, an attempt to be recognized as a new colony of Transylvania by the Continental Congress was rejected, leading to annexation of what later became the eastern part of the state of Kentucky by Virginia.

Simultaneously, Watauga Association settlements at Watauga and Eaton's Station converted their lease into an outright purchase and were soon annexed by North Carolina.

By end of 1775, a quarter million Americans lived in frontier lands from Maryland to Georgia. They occupied perhaps 20% of nearly 370,000 square miles of wilderness tracts acquired for about one tenth pence per acre but much greater potential because of the mineral wealth and other resources just beginning to be tapped. Thousands of common men and their families now possessed property of real and escalating value.

ECONOMIC TIT FOR TAT

Although the economic and political elite of the colonies undoubtedly led the protest movement against British mercantile restrictions, resistance was strengthened by the adherence of common men. Every tradesman, apprentice, clerk, innkeeper, dock worker, seaman, farmer, farm hand, miner, and trapper felt he had a material stake in the outcome of the struggle, not only because duties, taxes, and restrictions directly or indirectly reduced his income but because the promise of even greater prosperity was implicit in the westward march and development of a free American economy. To the degree that British policy compressed colonists of whatever background into a mass of disgruntled victims, to that degree it negated socio-economic strains between landlord and tenant, merchant and consumer, banker and debtor, even plantation owner and slave that could have provided opportunity for London to split the opposition. By attempting to compel without discrimination all Americans to bear what was accounted a fair share of the financial burden of the empire, the Crown and Parliament again and again stoked the fires of rebellion.

No wonder that a strong and vocal minority of Americans became willing to sacrifice short-term material comfort for long-term economic and political autonomy. Even where conservative thinking ruled, mercantile constrictions choked off the voices of reason. A recession 1768-69 in the larger cities, especially New York and Philadelphia, shoved more leaders of the Middle Colonies toward the radical cause of New England. Only the South remained a bastion of Loyalist sentiment. And yet, the vast majority of plantation owners were medium-size farmers, not landed aristocrats, whose paper-thin profit margins were undermined by levies on imports and exports. Economic imperative, as much as the natural disinclination of a proud people to accept direction and rebuke, shaped a united front against London.

The Townshend Acts, blamed for the recession, provoked Philadelphia (and thus Pennsylvania) and Baltimore (and thus Maryland) to join New England and New York in the non-importation movement by April 1, 1769. In short order, all the colonies joined except New Hampshire. Dissolved by the governor for excessive condemnation of British policy, the Virginia House of Burgesses voted in May to boycott all British goods on which duty was charged except paper. North and South Carolina, Maryland, Delaware, and Connecticut went further by demanding repeal of the Townshend Acts. Altogether, economic retaliation caused British exports to the colonies to fall from £2.16 million in 1768 to £1.34 million in 1769. In New York, the collapse was even more devastating, from over £490,000 to under £76,000.

Violence by Sons of Liberty groups in New York on January 9, 1770 preceded the Boston Massacre of March 5. On that very day and without knowledge of the incident, Parliament repealed the Townshend Acts effective April 12, except the 3 pence a pound tax on tea. When London permitted the aforementioned killings of colonists by intimidated British soldiers to be handled through proper colonial legal means and let the Quartering

Act lapse as well, Americans ended their non-importation movement. Pent-up demand in England for colonial commodities boosted colonial exports to £1.75 million in 1770, of which £900,000 was tobacco, £170,000 rice, and £130,000 indigo. But an increasing percentage of American shipments went to the West Indies. Because the next year British imports leaped to £4.2 million, three times what was shipped from American ports to the mother country, little at first was done about violations of the Navigation Acts.

Burning the Gaspee

Eventually, however, British customs officials began seizing New England fishing vessels and cargo on suspicion of smuggling. That infuriated local merchants, including one John Brown, who led a Sons of Liberty group on June 9, 1772 to burn the British customs schooner *Gaspee* when it ran aground near Providence. Outraged members of Parliament demanded arrests of the guilty for transport for trial in England, but Rhode Island's chief justice Stephen Hopkins helped scuttle the investigation. London considered having colonial judges paid by the Crown, not the colonies, to insure their loyalty, and did begin paying the salary of Governor Thomas Hutchinson of Massachusetts.

Another recession, caused in large part by a British banking crisis that contracted credit and precipitated widespread inventory liquidations, that lasted 30 months into 1775 hamstrung many companies. One such entity in which many important Englishmen had an interest was the East India Company, dealing in tea, cotton, and opium from the Far East. On May 10, 1773, Parliament passed the Tea Act, permitting the company to export tea directly into Boston, New York, Philadelphia, and Charleston instead of the previous rule of selling the commodity at auction in London for transshipment. The members intended to reduce the "mountain of tea" of 17 million pounds weight building up in warehouses and alleviate the company's financial crisis. Moreover, since the 3 pence per pound duty was retained, revenue of £212,500 was expected to flow into government coffers. It was calculated that direct shipment from the Far East to the colonies would not only undercut the price colonial merchants could charge but also put out of business smugglers of tea. But anxious to disrupt trade for political purposes, Samuel Adams and John Hancock sent Sons of Liberty dressed as red Indians to board three East India Company ships in Boston harbor on December 16 and dump 342 tea chests containing 90,000 pounds weight of tea into the harbor. Not only did Sons of Liberty ruffians dump and burn tea imports the next year in New York City, Annapolis, and Greenwich, New York but tarred and feathered British traders and burned their homes.

Boston Tea Party

The campaign of physical violence and economic depredation was too much for London to bear. The government replaced Hutchinson with General Sir Thomas Gage, Parliament passed the Boston Port Bill on May 20, 1774 closing the port (except for military supplies and approved shipments of food and fuel) until compensation was paid for the destroyed East Indies tea, and all Massachusetts representatives and officials were made appointees of the Crown. After a Boston town meeting called for new economic sanctions and an inter-colonial congress in Philadelphia, town meetings were banned unless approved by Gage. Reactivation of the Quartering Act on June 2 placed the burden on colonists of putting up and provisioning troops in unoccupied houses, barns, and other buildings.

Colonial representatives convened in Philadelphia in September to affirm the American right to "life, liberty, and property." After declaring the Boston Port Bill, Quartering Act, and other so-called Coercive Acts unconstitutional, the representatives (as well as local committees around the colonies) began setting prices for scarce commodities and recommended an even more stringent economic boycott than before. To that purpose on October 18, Congress formed the Continental Association, ceasing all import of British goods, discontinuing the slave trade to injure British traders, calling for non-consumption of all foreign luxury goods, and imposing an embargo on exports to the British Isles and West Indies including badly needed tobacco, cotton, naval stores, and wheat. Economic warfare had begun.

Thus, on April 13, 1775, British Prime Minister Lord Frederick North decided to bring the matter to a head by extending the New England Restraining Act to include the Middle and Southern colonies. However, by stipulating that trade with countries other than Britain and Ireland was illegal, he provoked greater sympathy for the idea of independence on the eve of clashes between British soldiers and American militia at Lexington and

Concord. With Continental Association rules under enforcement by all colonies that year, British exports were squeezed down to only £196,000 of value. Merchants and smugglers continued to send commodities the other way, ringing up £1.92 million of exports to England.

FIRST US WAR ECONOMY

Although for the Declaration of Independence, Thomas Jefferson change the phrase "life, liberty, and property" to "life, liberty, and the pursuit of happiness," it was well understood by the founding fathers that the Revolution was as much about material wealth, general prosperity, and economic self-sufficiency as political independence. They signed off on July 4, 1776 in that document on the assertion that economic repression and cutting off of American trade with the rest of the world was a major cause of the rebellion. Moreover, to defeat the British in battle and survive as a new nation, the wherewithal to field and pay armies, send out privateers on the high seas, and sustain a governing administration had to be acquired. Upon becoming sovereign entities, the states resisted the idea of a central government assuming so much authority that it would replace one tyranny with another.

Therefore, both the fight for Independence and supervision of the war economy became fragmented efforts. Aside from military matters, issues that divided Congress from states and states from each other included conflicting claims to western lands, regulation of trade, organization of a new financial and banking system, and taxing power. Uncertain whether to follow the lead of Congress in pledging "lives, fortunes, and sacred honor" for the new republic, many Americans even among supporters of Independence carried on trade with the enemy. Because London too conceived of America as an essential market for British goods and not as an irreconcilable nation to be pillaged and looted, a substantial measure of prosperity maintained. In fact, the British army and navy's failure to attack the US economy the way Abraham Lincoln's Union nine decades later savaged the Confederacy probably was decisive in permitting the rebellion to succeed. The age of total warfare, in which not merely an adversary's military forces but property, resources, and civilian population were targeted, had fortunately not yet arrived.

The fighting was brutal enough for the times, however. Using fire and traitor Benedict Arnold's raids as their tools, the British finally got around to burning New England and Virginia towns too late in the war to make a difference. As well, they looked the other way at depredations by their Indian allies. The British navy intercepted American exports not bound for England as did American frigates prey upon British shipping. But the fact remains that the core economy of the United States was not struck in any systematic manner. Spending with borrowed money by Congress and state legislatures pumped up businesses supplying the Continental army and state militias; domestic production increased to replace English cotton textiles and iron goods.

A symbolic move by Congress in July 1775 to claim a central governing role was to make Franklin postmaster general of a united postal system for the colonies and supplant the British system by December. With the British ousted from Boston in March 1776 only to invade New York and New Jersey, rates soared.

US Continental Six Dollar Bill

Denied taxing power by the colonies, dreading economic collapse as exports that generated hard British currency were interrupted, Congress resorted to issuing paper money denominated as *dollars* (worth roughly $4.50 to £1) to keep the economy above water. Through 1779, currency valued nominally at $191.5 million was issued as well as millions more in quartermaster certificates to pay for requisitioned supplies from the states for Washington's Continental Army. Including loan-office certificates paying 6% interest and debit certificates given soldiers for later redemption for back pay, total cost of the war with interest amounted to more than $300 million. Despite congressional borrowings from wealthy citizens, for example $5 million on October 3, 1776, paper currency rapidly depreciated in value. Typically, it traded for specie at only 8 to 1, only 40 to 1 by end of 1779. When in March 1780 Congress finally retired $120 million of currency by accepting payments due from states in specie at one-fortieth face value, or $3 million, the remaining $71 million outstanding of Continental bills was worthless.

US Continental Dollar

With finances shaky at home, foreign assistance became essential for the war effort. Fortunately, both the French and Spanish were amenable to injuring Great Britain by aiding the American rebellion. On May 2, 1776, King Louis XVI of France ordered 1 million *livres* of munitions shipped to the Americans through front company *Roderique Hortalie et Cie* set up in Spain for that purpose. Franklin arrived in Paris December 31 with orders to negotiate a military alliance, which was accomplished February 1778 after news of victory in the Battle of Saratoga. Not only did the French and Spanish ultimately provide war loans totaling $9 million but the Dutch too chipped in $2 million in the last year of the war to retire part of the earlier debt. The American-French alliance set a precedent for the future by establishing most favored nation trade status for each other.

Foreign assistance took months and years to arrange. For the immediate future, Congress buttressed the economy and customs receipts by opening American ports in April 1776 to trade of all nations of the world except, of course, Britain. On another front, the members voted in August grants of 100 to 500 acres of western land to British military deserters (depending on rank up to colonel) who would serve in the Continental Army to the end of the war. Later in August 1780, after Arnold's treason, they offered 850 to 1,100 acres to British generals on the same conditions.

Meanwhile, individual states dangled even larger grants before the eyes of deserters. The problem was that land assignments as well as previous grants and purchases from Indians sometimes overlapped or were confusing. Congress attempted to persuade all parties to drop claims to 236.8 million acres of western land and let the central government decide policy. Wrangling over the issue held up agreement to an Articles of Confederation binding the states together within the United States of America until 1781.

To facilitate confiscation of Loyalist estates and make ownership of land more wide-spread among the populace, states began to change age-old laws brought over from England. In 1776, Virginia abolished entail, which limited the passage of an estate to a designated line of heirs to prevent its future sale, bequeathment, or other disposal. The next year, states began ending primogeniture, requiring that the eldest son inherit all land, prompting all states to follow suit over the next twenty years. New England and Pennsylvania did away with laws granting the eldest son a double portion. The effect of these changes was to carve out moderate land holdings, distribute wealth more equitably, and strengthen the allegiance of people to the new country.

In control of New York City from 1777 and Philadelphia more briefly 1777-78, the British dumped manufactured goods in those places to reduce warehouse inventories at home. Nevertheless, imports were down 90% from pre-war levels. Because the British did not retaliate against trade going the other way, American exports only diminished 50%. New England ships regularly ran the enemy blockade for Europe and the Caribbean.

Morris House, Built 1765 George Washington's New York HQ, 1776

After the British captured Charleston on May 12, 1780, they repaired the Triangle Trade by taking away southern cotton, tobacco, and sugar to England for textiles, hardware, rum, and trinkets, then sailing to West Africa for slaves to transport back to the southern colonies and the Caribbean. In fact, the renewed slave trade became so lucrative at 100,000 persons a year crammed into the holds of cargo ships that Americans continued the high volume flow after winning independence. In 1782, the Virginia legislature made the emancipation of slaves completely illegal. Plantation owners knew that their prosperity would collapse without a cheap labor force.

During the war, Americans were fending off British invasions and confiscation of land and property. However, at sea American privateers ravaged British commerce and raided British ports. From only six dozen ships at the outset, 449 privateers prowled the Atlantic and Caribbean in 1781, capturing 600 British ships, with cargo worth $18 million. The Continental Navy destroyed or seized another 196 ships.

Ratification of Articles of Confederation basic rules for a new and more unified American government on March 1, 1781 should have been a cause of great celebration. Many in Congress did not applaud because they still lacked taxing power independent of state approval and could not regulate commerce, traditionally the greatest source of revenue for governments. A request to the states in October for $8 million yielded only $1.49 million through 1783. Congress' inability to enter into commercial treaties with foreign nations because every state had an absolute veto frustrated trade. Even the postal system, reorganized late in the war, was affected by the weak central government. After termination of hostilities, mail sent overseas had to be carried by British and French packets.

Even after Washington effectively won the war by trapping and compelling the surrender of the army of Lord Charles Cornwallis at Yorktown in October, the country still had a huge war bill to pay. To deal with that problem, Congress named Robert Morris of New York Superintendent of Finance on February 20. He proposed a charter for a private commercial Bank of North America, which Congress granted on December 31, to receive government deposits, make loans, and generally facilitate financial transactions. A new subsidy from France as well as a loan from Netherlands (received November 5) helped Morris make progress returning the country to a sound specie-based financial system.

On the other hand, those persons stuck with worthless paper currency suffered. Many waited years for settlement, which sometimes never came. On March 15, 1783, Continental Army officers based at Newburgh, New York revolted over back pay, only desisting after a personal appeal by Washington and a vote by Congress to compensate them for five years war wages. Morris was forced to overdraw the country's account in the banks of Europe to demobilize and pay off thousands of regular soldiers.

What really compensated for seven years of war, destruction of property, and loss of life was the spoils the country received in the preliminary peace treaty signed November 30, 1782 and final Treaty of Paris, September 3, 1783. By the former, the United States gained the right to fish off Newfoundland and Nova Scotia, dry and cure fish on any unsettled shore in Labrador, the Magdalen islands, and Nova Scotia, and receive payment for debts due its citizens from British subjects; by the latter, the country acquired title disputed only by scattered Indian tribes to 846,000 square miles or 542.4 million acres of territory between the Appalachian Mountains and Mississippi River. Although Congress pledged to recommend to state legislatures full restoration of rights and property taken from Loyalists, the states passed confiscatory laws instead, resulting in seizure of $16.5 million worth of property. The British government ultimately compensated Loyalists for the damage. But 100,000 Loyalists still on American soil departed forever, most for Canada, some like Arnold for England. Their numbers were swiftly replaced by a new influx of refugees from northwest Europe.

Chapter III. Independence with Material Advantage: 1783-1815

Proof came swiftly that a liberated American economy was superior to one chained to British Mercantilism. Despite a postwar recession caused by heavy import of goods, unstable currency, and scarcity of coined money, gross domestic product (GDP) of about $150 million in 1783 became $210 million seven years later, $520 million by end of the eighteenth century, and $810 million on the eve of the War of 1812. As the population nearly doubled to 7.43 million, *per capita* GDP increased 80% to $109, equivalent to $1,290 in year 2004 money. Given the modest needs of early citizens of the republic and the abundant land available for settlement, most Americans looked forward to a brighter future. Thus, after Loyalists departed for Canada and Britain, emigration dwindled to a tiny trickle. The flow of refugees from Europe quickened.

**Lincoln birthplace
Kentucky, 1808**

Why? Land title by purchase, homesteading, and even squatting not only offered status in society and a standard of living unattainable in the Old World but conferred voting rights. As states completed the process of eliminating entail and primogeniture and abolished quitrents—90 cents per 100 acres in Pennsylvania—the percentage of white males who owned land and could visit polling booths mounted. Their electoral clout pushed laws through legislatures restricting the slave trade in all but Georgia and South Carolina. Protection from African labor competition permitted free laborers with skill in a trade in New England and the Mid-Atlantic states to accumulate enough wealth to break permanently out of the bonds of poverty. Property still mattered. In Virginia voters had to possess 25 settled or 500 unsettled acres and all states required proof of material wealth for office-holders. The unmistakable trend was away from linking suffrage to property and toward insuring that common men could possess both political and economic liberty.

At the other extreme of wealth, men of ready capital and perceptive vision now had latitude to invest in whatever fruitful endeavor attracted. With the defeat of Mercantile thinking, they considered collaboration with inventors and innovators to produce the kind of finished goods British importers had so long monopolized. To sweep away state tariffs and restrictions, the founding fathers and a new generation of leaders debated provisions for a stronger federal government. The states moved on a somewhat parallel track toward developing the country's communication and transportation system. However, the country was not and would not be for decades formidable enough to chart a course independent of European conflicts. The rivalries of great powers entangled the geopolitical and economic interests of the United States.

A FITFUL START

If the Revolutionary War had compelled a measure of cooperation between Congress and the states, peace and its aftermath removed the imperative for state legislatures to defer to central government leadership. In fact, the feeling was widespread that each of the thirteen former colonies was now sovereign to pursue parochial interests. Instructions given representatives sitting in Congress under Articles of Confederation authority emphasized state interests over national consensus on foreign trade, western land claims, finance and taxation. Because most delegates sent to Philadelphia were well-to-do merchants, lawyers, and plantation owners, their personal economies were caught up in the debate. Had they been elected directly by the people, possibly their will and inclination to act for the general welfare might have been stronger. Even the most submissive to the dictates of home legislatures saw plainly that chaos and fragmentation would result should common sense and compromise not begin to supercede state and individual biases.

In the 1780s, deliberations by Congress and state legislatures produced disjointed, overlapping, and abortive solutions for the country's problems. States chartered corporations to build roads, canals, and bridges within their boundaries even as Congress imagined a grander scheme of internal improvements to create a nation-wide transportation and communication network. Whereas the former projects were financed by construction bonds backed by tolls, fees, and other levies on commercial and passenger traffic, the latter depended on uncertain funding by the national treasury. Representatives from Rhode Island, Delaware, Connecticut, and other states whose towns and farms did not touch frontier lands blocked plans by Virginia, Pennsylvania, New York, and the rest to connect wilderness areas with eastern cities.

So too policy governing foreign trade perplexed statesmen in the City of Brotherly Love. Even before the final peace treaty with the mother country was signed, the British Admiralty on July 2, 1783 imposed an order-in-council banning importation of meats, fish, and dairy products from the US into the British West Indies and closing all other trade from the former colonies unless carried in British ships. Because Congress had no authority to retaliate in kind, surpluses built up in warehouses and commodity prices dropped 30%. Small farmers who could not afford the higher shipping charges imposed by British traders were badly hurt. Fearing that too restrictive a policy would infuriate Americans into organizing an embargo such as preceded the Revolution, London on December 26 issued a second order-in-council permitting most US manufactured goods into British territory on the same favorable terms as in colonial days. Since the volume of trade in finished goods

Early stage coach travel

transported eastward across the Atlantic was negligible, in the first full year of peace, $16.5 million of British imports into the US was balanced by only $3.4 million of US exports to Britain.

Losing preferential treatment for exports to the mother country, facing restrictions on the West Indies trade that smuggling could not entirely alleviate, restless to restore pre-Revolution prosperity and climb to even greater economic heights, Americans looked to other markets. Merchants from Boston, New York, Philadelphia, and other seaboard cities sent ships to trade in the ports of continental Europe. They also dispatched expeditions to circumnavigate South America to look for fur in the Pacific Northwest and exchange goods in China. The inability of Congress and the states to agree on tariff policy thrust responsibility for developing this sector of the American economy entirely into private hands. Only in the areas of national finance and western land policy did Congress overcome parochialism and make progress. That success was enough to suggest the benefits of an even stronger central government.

The Bank of North America chartered by Congress in 1781 was followed three years later by state-chartered banks in New York and Massachusetts. Both were private commercial entities, albeit intended as depositories of government funds. As governor of Massachusetts in 1792, John Hancock signed the charter for Union Bank. That was the first founding of a financial institution that would become part of today's State Street.

Meanwhile, superintendent of Finance Morris crowned a successful tenure by using a Dutch loan arranged by John Adams to pay off $230,000 in notes. Although the country still owed France, the Netherlands, and other countries several million dollars, the US Treasury ended the fiscal year with $21,000 surplus. But the New Yorker was replaced by a board of three commissioners on November 1, 1784. He soon got into personal financial difficulty.

With Congress still at an impasse over internal improvements, George Washington led a non-federal movement to connect the Potomac valley to trans-Appalachian lands. He raised $181,000 from private sources to build a route from the headwaters of the Potomac to the Cheat or Monongahela Rivers. Then the Potomac Company chartered jointly by Maryland and Virginia was granted $30,000 each by the thirteen states for the same purpose. This road was intended to compete with older roads built east to west in Pennsylvania.

Robert Morris

Simultaneous with resumption of westward exploration, the first US trading ship to journey to China was the *Empress of China* under Captain John Green of New York. Green sailed around South America's Cape Horn to reach Canton on August 30. After he returned the next year with tea and silks, many merchants financed similar expeditions. Although only a slight percentage of US trade activity, the China connection and other overseas ventures set a precedent for future American risk-taking to obtain profits.

Congress came to agreement about what to do with the Northwest Territory on May 20, 1795. In the Land (or Northwest) Ordinance, the members divided the region north of the Ohio River, east of the Mississippi River, and south of British Canada into six mile square townships. Each township was subdivided into 36 lots of 640 acres with one lot set aside for public schools. The others were to be sold for $1 an acre. Because most Shawnee, Miami, Delaware, and other Indian tribes inhabiting the region had not been party to treaties made by chiefs of dubious authority signing away the collective birthright of Native Americans, because the British, illegally in possession of Fort Detroit and eight other posts on US territory, traded guns and supplies to their warriors, American fort-building and homesteading precipitated hostilities. Settlement and economic development of the region was decades delayed.

In 1785, the balance of trade with Britain was approximately $4 million of US exports and $10.4 million of imports. The improvement over the previous year was occasioned by duties and restrictions placed on incoming goods by individual states. For example in June, Rhode Island instituted a strong protective tariff to encourage domestic industries. Massachusetts retaliated against the British order-in-council of July 1783 by banning export of US goods unless carried in US ships and doubled tonnage duties on imports not carried in same. Although these measures failed to effect any improvement in exports — $3.8 million in 1786 — British imports fell precipitously to $7.2 million. A continuation of depressed prices for commodities also inhibited American ability to pay for finished British goods.

The better prospect for long-term appreciation of wealth was still real estate and speculators knew it. Boston merchants and financiers who formed the Ohio Company on March 1, 1786 issued $1 million in stock to exchange for depreciated Continental certificates they planned to persuade Congress to redeem for public lands at par value. Cleverly, they recruited Arthur St. Clair, former president of Congress, to become president of the company. His influence behind a July 1787 petition by the Scioto Company, whose agent the Ohio Company became, for at least 1.5 million acres north of the Ohio River tipped the Board of Treasury to sell that entity 1,781,760 acres for $1 million with an option for another 5 million acres at a similarly discounted price. However, because of Indian trouble, auctions of surveyed land in Ohio yielded only $176,090 in the depreciated certificates. The Ohio Company pressed on by sending settlers in April 1788 to found Marietta on the Ohio River.

The course of the war against the Indians of the Northwest Territory and ultimate triumph of American arms is discussed in Part 1 of this history. Fortunately for the westward march of the new nation, even relatively modest applications of military power sufficed to clear a path through native peoples. On the other hand, unable to persuade states to finance a potent ocean-going navy, Congress had little sending power to deploy against Barbary Coast raiders who from 1786 onward seized ships and cargoes headed for Mediterranean ports. To stop this scourge and prevent the selling of American captives into slavery, Congress had no recourse but pay Morocco "gifts" amounting to $10,000. Later in the middle 1790s, the administration of George Washington paid tribute as well to Algiers, Tripoli, and Tunis to protect American commerce. A September 1804 land and sea attack on Tripoli by Lieutenant Stephen Decater and Commodore Edward Preble to free the crew of the captured US frigate *Philadelphia* and destroy the pasha's fleet ended payments to the Barbary pirates.

National weakness in the face of international piracy was humiliating to Americans, as was failure of the Articles of Confederation government to resolve issues of fundamental economic, political, and social importance. Therefore, US leaders agreed to congregate in Philadelphia to write a new constitution. While deliberations were ongoing, the Congress still in session passed on July 13, 1787 a second Northwest Ordinance, providing for division of the region into three to five territories that ultimately became the five states of Ohio, Indiana, Illinois, Michigan, and Wisconsin. They banned slavery to encourage homesteading by free settlers without fear of competition from plantation-size enterprises.

The *quid pro quo* for Southerners displeased that slavery was to be kept out of such fertile farmland was silence about the "peculiar institution" in the new constitution even while counting slaves as three-fifths a person for census purposes. A Great Compromise then forged three branches of government—an Executive headed by a President picked by electors chosen by the people, a bicameral Congress divided between House of Representatives and Senate, and a Judicial topped by a Supreme Court. House members, proportioned to the states according to population, had the power to propose money bills for revenues and expenses in which the Senate then concurred or did not. The Congress retained authority to provide for the "general welfare" of the people, a clause little considered at the time but important for economic, political, and social change in the twentieth century.

It took nearly two years for the states to ratify the Constitution and hold an election for the first President and Congress. In the interim, state legislatures continued to wield unfettered power within their borders, even to the extent of causing complications for the country as a whole. For example, Georgia granted 25.4 million acres along the Yazoo river to the Yazoo Company. Not only did the Spanish in Florida claim the same territory but

Indians of the old Southwest prepared to resist encroachment of fur-trappers and plantation owners. But very soon, the enemies of the republic would face not merely militia armies of a few hundred frontiersmen but the resources of an entire nation. Regardless of the political and social philosophy advocated by individual congressional and state leaders, they all agreed that conquest of the continent's interior was vital for the American economy.

HAMILTON'S ECONOMIC SYSTEM

In possession of an extensive library of books, with knowledge of both ancient and modern history, Thomas Jefferson knew that in both European and American societies, property was and had always been the cornerstone of political power. It followed, therefore, that if the new US government was to avoid the tyrannical blundering of the Old World and institute a polity reflective of the people's will and interests, a leveling of economic circumstances must take place and be maintained. Key to his thinking was the presumed fact that inexhaustible land for farming existed toward the Appalachian Mountains and beyond. Once resistance by Indian tribes was overcome, the wilderness transformed into productive real estate, and an equitable distribution of the natural bounty mandated by government fiat, a nation of small free holding farmers would be created. Their combined economic power would coalesce into a majority voting bloc to frustrate forever the ascendancy of an ambitious few. Both political and economic equality would be guaranteed.

Thomas Jefferson
After the experience of bullying and repression by the British Crown and Parliament, Jefferson trusted the revolutionary war ally France more than the mother country to be a reliable trading partner for the American farmer. Moreover, he considered individual states best positioned to protect the political and economic rights of citizens from a power-grasping Congress. He miscalculated in the first instance in that only England had advanced so far in the Industrial Revolution as to offer a sizeable market for American wheat, cotton, rice, indigo, and other exports. For citizens in an agricultural economy to obtain the creature comforts desired, imported British goods were essential. As to the question of state versus federal authority, how could an effective economic policy favoring common men be implemented over local opposition except by a strong central government commanded by electoral assent? The power of property in state legislatures, Jefferson failed to consider, was too formidable and entrenched to be surmounted in any other way.

The Virginia patrician's critics had a deeper and more fundamental reason to mistrust his scheme. The irony—some said hypocrisy—of his concept was that he himself was a plantation owner in possession of many dozen slaves. True, he made provision in his will to free some after his death, but his past conduct hardly bespoke a man overly concerned with raising up common men, or climbing down himself, to middling ground. When he did passionately champion their cause, for example to propose a lowering of the tariff to keep down prices to protect the standard of living of Americans of modest means, his own self interest ran parallel. Lowered tariffs would encourage similar restraint by European countries, it was believed, permitting continued profitable export of plantation commodities. Home-grown industry in New England and New York attempting to achieve size and stability to compete with imported goods would shrivel.

Had merchants, financiers, land-speculators and other conservative interests merely opposed what Jefferson championed, they would have been hard-pressed to counter charges by James Madison and others of his supporters in the Constitutional Convention that their design was to replace the Articles of Confederation government with one they could dominate then proceed with an avaricious partition of western lands. In fact, they went far beyond the Old World practice of feudal estates, monopolized industries, and directed economies to a model merging elements of Adam Smith's theory with hard-headed pragmatism. For they pointed out that from ancient Egypt to the present day (1789) societies that relied primarily upon agricultural endeavors to feed, clothe, house, and employ their people had suffered from periods of drought, famine, starvation, military weakness leading to invasion, and other calamities. The most successful nation-states in history had looked beyond their own shores for trade, investment, and yes conquest. Not that they intended to launch wars of aggression and build up an overseas empire, rather they merely wanted to acquire the wherewithal to compete in world markets with the British. The best way to beat John Bull at his own game was to leap head-first into manufacturing of finished goods.

To protect embryonic industry even at risk of retaliation against farm exports, it would be necessary (and contrary to Smith) to raise tariffs. The strongest central government possible was required to create a navy to protect American trade, regulate commerce between quarreling states, protect settlers surging into the Northwest Territory, push development of a larger home market for the products of industry, and gain leverage to deal with the British as equals. Although it was not yet clear that the deteriorating political situation in France would lead to a quarter century of revolution and war convulsing the continent of Europe, the conclusion was yet inescapable that for the immediate future, American prosperity could only be secured by restoring commercial ties with London. Allegiance to the new government would be undermined if policies were not instituted to make citizens better off than before the Revolution.

The greatest proponent of this Federalist point of view was Alexander Hamilton. Born in the British West Indies as the impoverished son of a Scottish trader who abandoned the family but grandson of a Scottish lord, he saw merit in individual initiative while working as a bookkeeper in St. Croix for New York merchants as well as after emigrating to the United States. Serving under Washington in the Continental Army, winning election to the Congress, and building a small fortune as a lawyer in New York, he recognized that the new nation possessed in land, natural resources, population, and entrepreneurial spirit the building blocks of an industrial revolution overawing what had occurred in England. What was required was construction of an environment by government in which vigorous economic development could take place. Thus, while he collaborated with Madison and the more conservative John Jay in a series of 85 essays published in newspapers and then books, called now the *Federalist Papers*, that a republican form of government with representatives chosen from among the people, as opposed to true democracies such as had once existed in the city-states of classical Greece where citizens voted by plebiscite on all issues of importance, should be installed, he considered Jefferson's idea of eschewing manufacturing and industry to avoid imbalances in wealth and therefore political influence of citizens not only ridiculous but suicidal. Once he gained as Secretary of Treasury a leading position in the administration of his old commanding general and now first President George Washington, he moved to make American production of iron goods, household products, textiles, and other manufactures the linchpin of economic success.

Alexander Hamilton
In actual fact, the Constitution provided that Congress, not the Executive Branch of government, was vested with the power to make law for the collection of taxes and regulation of trade. The Executive Branch must merely administer the law. However, using allies in the House of Representatives as conduits, Hamilton and Washington proposed revenue and spending bills. Their assertiveness began a tradition of Presidents submitting annual budgets for congressional approval.

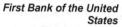

First Bank of the United States
On January 14, 1790, the 33 year old Hamilton delivered to Congress a "Report on Public Credit." In that document, he proposed paying off with available capital foreign loans from France, the Netherlands, and other countries amounting to $11.7 million. Additionally, he wanted to eliminate domestic debt of $40.4 million and state debts of $25 million, including $21.5 million arising from Revolutionary

War expenses. The method would be to exchange previously issued securities, even those that had severely depreciated, with new interest-bearing debt of equal face value backed by the federal government. Since after the war's end, farmers and other debtors had been forced to sell off depreciated securities at few cents on the dollar to creditors and speculators who would now reap a windfall, Jefferson, Madison, and other so-called anti-Federalists were outraged. Southern states had already funded most outstanding debt and would not, therefore, benefit equally with New England and Mid-Atlantic states from Hamilton's scheme. Madison garnered substantial backing for a proposal to provide full compensation only to original holders of securities, give a discounted amount to subsequent holders, and as a short-term measure to stabilize prices and wages have Congress (on March 18) fix the value of Continental bills at not more than one fortieth face value. Hamilton, however, stood firm.

Matters remained at an impasse until Jefferson in the spirit of compromise mediated a plan to exchange acceptance of Hamilton's plan for approval of a new capital on ten mile square Maryland land on the north bank of the Potomac River across from Virginia. It would be called the District of Columbia (after the first President's death in 1799, Washington in the District of Columbia or Washington D.C.). That cleared the way for the Treasury to issue new bonds with principal and interest paid by revenues from import duties and excise taxes. The administration's financial program was well launched.

Hamilton also won Jefferson's grudging support, more importantly Washington's sanction, for a policy of strengthening the nation's economy by reinvigorating trade ties with the British empire. The decisive statistics were that 90% of the nation's imports still came from the mother country and its dependencies in the West Indies and elsewhere while 75% of exports went back the same way. However, the secretary of state called it a mistake when trade preferences for France, now in the throes of revolutionary upheaval, were considered and denied. The bloodletting by guillotine in Paris had not yet progressed so far as to testify to the complete breakdown of civilized conduct.

Jefferson broke finally and completely with the Federalist program over Hamilton's proposal to create a Bank of the United States in Philadelphia to facilitate placement of the bonds and control of government accounts. Nothing in the Constitution permitted such an agency to monopolize fiscal affairs, protested the Virginian, and the degree to which New England and New York financiers were profiting by buying up old bonds at depressed prices and receiving in exchange new bonds at par value was outright theft. Hamilton countered that the ends set forth in the Constitution permitted a "loose construction" of its clauses to acquire the means for their accomplishment and that no one had forced southerners and westerners to unload their wartime bonds. His interpretation of the implied powers of the Constitution was accepted by Washington, who signed the bill that came out of Congress on February 25, 1791, and was later endorsed by Chief Justice John Marshall in an 1819 Supreme Court decision in *McCullough v. Maryland*.

In a hurry to close the books on old foreign loans, Hamilton pushed through Congress on March 3 an excise tax on distilled liquors, particularly whiskey, as a supplement to duties on imported wines, spirits, coffee, and tea. Protests over the imposition in frontier lands eventually erupted June-November 1794 into rebellion in the Monongahela valley of western Pennsylvania. Washington was so indignant at this revolt against lawful authority that he briefly took the field with an army of 12,900 men. When no battle took place, he pardoned two men convicted of treason.

Meanwhile, the secretary of the treasury bulled ahead with his design to make over the American economy. On December 5, 1791, he presented to Congress a "Report on Manufactures." Therein, he called for high tariffs to protect American industry, bounties for agriculture to encourage more exports, and a favorable balance of trade until manufactured goods in quantity were ready for overseas markets. He proposed federal funding of road, bridge, and canal construction to facilitate trade within the domestic market as well as harbor improvement to promote external commerce and trade.

Outmaneuvered at every turn by Hamilton, fearful that a central government dictating the course of economic development would sooner or later trample the rights of citizens and transform the republic into an entity more closely resembling Old World autocracy, rebuffed by Washington's decision April 21, 1793 to declare a Neutrality Policy that favored Britain rather than a French alliance during the European war, Jefferson resigned as secretary of state before the end of Washington's first term. Hamilton's blueprint for an industrial revolution in the United States was now unopposed within the cabinet.

With Jefferson gone, Washington sent Supreme Court Chief Justice Jay to London to negotiate what came to be called Jay's Treaty. This important document settled the issue of debts owed by US citizens to British creditors by establishing a joint Anglo-American commission to sort through claims (and eventually in 1802 decide that about £600,000 equal to $2.7 million should be paid) but did nothing to satisfy claims by Loyalists for seized property. It also established most favored nation trade status for the mother country, giving British importers the lowest tariff rates available to any other country. It provided for the evacuation of nine forts still held by the British on US territory by June 1, 1796. Not only were British East Indies ports in the Far East to be opened to American vessels, but British West Indies ports in the Caribbean had to receive US cargoes if ships were under 70 tons except that cotton, sugar, and molasses had to be carried in non-US ships. Because nothing was mentioned about British practices of impressing US citizens by force into the British Navy, removing slaves from American ships, and rendering aid to Indians on American soil, almost all members of Congress and the state legislatures had some complaint. Still, after invalidating the West Indies clause out of indignation US ships would not be permitted to carry all American commodities, the Senate ratified the treaty on June 24, 1795. An attempt by the House of Representatives also to review the treaty was rejected by the President as unconstitutional, establishing a precedent for the future.

DEVELOPING THE INTERNAL MARKET

In 1788, settlements called Columbia and Losantiville were made near the mouth of the Little Miami River where it spilled into the Ohio River. After Fort Washington was constructed nearby to serve as a base from which to campaign against Indians, in 1790 Governor St. Clair renamed the latter town Cincinnati after an ancient Roman farmer-general and a Revolutionary War officers society of which he had been part. Following General Anthony Wayne's victory over the hostiles at Fallen Timbers four years later, farmers from the surrounding countryside brought hogs in increasing numbers for slaughter and river shipment to towns and cities along the Ohio River, swelling the city's size eventually to 150,000 persons. Over decades, Cincinnati became "Porkopolis," the leading center for packing not only pork but beef, chicken, and other livestock for market.

Cotton loaded on Mississippi steamboat

The spread of agriculture into the continent's interior is what Jefferson desired. The rise of food processing and other industries servicing the nation's farmers pleased Hamilton. But in order for the Northwest Territory, indeed all lands west of the Appalachians, to become fully integrated economically with the eastern seaboard, better transportation and communication routes were required. A start was made with locally important initiatives such as the Philadelphia to Lancaster turnpike and Knoxville Road linking the Wilderness Road to Cumberland Gap settlements. In the early 1790s, toll roads appeared all over New England and the Middle States. Once Congress took the lead with internal improvements during Washington's second administration, the patchwork of highways slowly became a national network.

The House and Senate agreed in 1794 to build more post roads, tripling miles covered to 16,000 by the new century and extending mail delivery and stage transportation into Vermont, Kentucky, Tennessee, and other western places. Congress established the US Postal Service on May 8, 1795. As well, that body funded Zane's Trace, the first road extending into Ohio. When completed, it connected Wheeling, West Virginia on the Ohio River with Limestone (later Maysville, Ohio).

Federal activism did not still private enterprise. The Western Inland Lock Navigation Company, chartered in 1792, opened a canal that circumvented the Little Falls of the Mohawk River. Other such projects made it possible for farmers in central New York State to ship commodities back to Albany. The Hudson River completed the water course to New York City.

Meanwhile in 1796, the British evacuated forts on US soil per the Jay Treaty, creating an opportunity for John Jacob Astor, a German immigrant, to move in on the fur trade. His trappers and agents were so successful at dealing with the British North West Company that he became a very rich man. His personal fortune of $250,000 by 1800 was equivalent to $3.6 million in 2004 dollars. It financed trading ventures to the Far East, real estate purchases in New York City, and middleman buying and selling in cotton.

With the Indian threat reduced in the Northwest Territory, speculators would have dominated western land purchases had not Congress established law as well as land offices in Cincinnati, Chillicothe, Marietta, and Steubenville. Although the May 18, 1796 Land Act doubled the minimum price per acre to $2, a provision delineating township units as six mile square areas with half divided into single sections of 640 acres (1 mile square), and half disposed of as eight section entities permitted purchase of homesteads by men of modest means as well as acquisitions by wealthier investors of larger tracts. Four

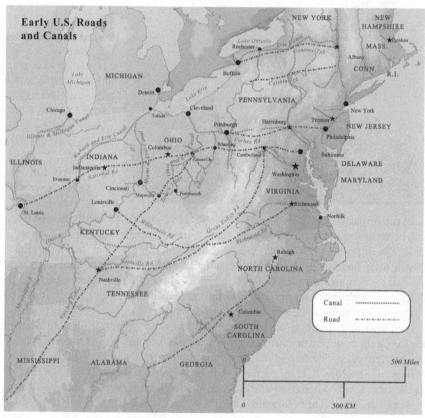

Early U.S. Roads and Canals

years later, the Harrison Land Act of May 10 attempted to generate more revenue for the federal government by extending credit over four years or offering an 8% discount for full cash payments on a minimum purchase of 320 acres. Encouraged by this arrangement, buyers in 1801 snapped up nearly 400,000 acres. Congress sweetened the pot for what remained in the Land Act of March 26, 1804. The minimum price was reduced to $1.64 per acre and the special deal's minimum quantity was halved to 160 acres.

Land policy applied to the Mississippi Territory as well. On March 3, 1803, Congress provided for the survey and sale of ungranted lands in that region, encouraging plantation owners looking for fertile soil to move west. Because Eli Whitney's cotton gin invention made growing cotton on a large scale economical and profitable, production hit 171,000 bales by 1810. Cotton swiftly became the nation's largest export crop.

Land sales continued to supplement customs duties after Jefferson as President purchased the Louisiana Territory's 828,000 square miles (530 million acres) in 1803 from Napoleon Bonaparte of France for $15 million in cash and assumption of debts owed by US citizens, a cost per acre of about 2.8 cents. Once Congress passed a March 2, 1805 law mandating land surveys of the vast region and penalties for squatters, profit for government coffers was guaranteed. For political purposes, Federalists turned around 180 degrees on the issue of strict versus loose construction of the constitution to complain that Jefferson's acquisition violated basic law. Because most Americans wanted the land, the Democrat-Republican party gained at the voting booth.

Whitney's cotton gin
It was one thing to explore the former French holding to the Pacific Ocean as the Louis and Clark Expedition did and catalogue its natural resources. It was another to actually extract wealth in the face of the continent's most hostile and powerful tribes, the Great Plains Indians. But with the fur trade playing out around the Great Lakes, Astor in 1807 sent trappers up the Missouri and Yellowstone Rivers into the virgin forests of the Rocky Mountains. He established the American Fur Company for that purpose. In 1810, he also founded the Pacific Fur Company to build a trading post called Astoria at the mouth of the Columbia River. He evaded US customs duties by funneling furs through the British in Canada.

Eli Whitney
Back east, road and canal building began to have the desired effect. As settlers cleared land for farming in the Hudson-Mohawk river valleys and eastern Pennsylvania, wheat production increased. Then the Genesee River country was opened for agriculture and homesteaders filled up all the land on the near side of the Appalachians. The time had come to spill over to the other side.

Under an 1806 law, Congress let contracts amounting to $1.7 million to build a paved National Road connecting the east with the Northwest Territory. It was called the Cumberland Road after construction was started 1814 at Cumberland, Maryland. Had the War of 1812 not intervened, horse, wagon, and stage would soon have carried passengers and mail from the capital to Wheeling. Not until 1818 was the terminus reached, then later in the 1830s extended successively to Columbus, Ohio and Vandalia, Illinois (near St. Louis) so that by mid century an American could travel the entire route from the Potomac to the Mississippi River in four days.

EXPANDING THE FINANCIAL SYSTEM

Colonial merchants became the country's first bankers after independence. By prospering with imports and exports, they accumulated sufficient capital to finance other ventures and loan money. Such men were the primary shareholders of the first Bank of the United States founded in Philadelphia on December 12, 1791 with eight branches in other large cities. That institution issued notes backed by gold and silver reserves, acted as clearing house for transactions, and provided loans for trade, manufacturing, and other profit-making enterprises.

A relative scarcity of specie and a hodgepodge of coins dating from colonial days motivated Congress on April 2, 1792 to create a decimal system of coinage. The United States dollar was valued at 24.75 grams of gold and the silver to gold ratio was fixed at 15 to 1. The country's first mint struck both silver dollars and gold coins by authority of the Bank of the United States. Shortages in Philadelphia of both metals limited the number of coins in circulation until new deposits of silver were discovered in Mexico, but silver then became overvalued.

John Jacob Astor

The American financial system began slowly to broaden out. The success of Hamilton's plan to reestablish close economic ties with the British built up even more capital and wealth among the nation's commercial elite. Once again, as before the Revolution, men got the urge to replicate what the mother country possessed in great banking houses, stock exchanges, and insurance. The first American stock exchange was established in Philadelphia, easily the financial center of the country for the next three decades. But the next year, 24 merchants and brokers set up the New York Stock Exchange (NYSE) on Wall Street. The NYSE was destined to eclipse all rivals.

Although British merchants financed most foreign commerce on generous terms, wealthy US merchants founded companies to insure cargoes and ships. Forty such entities came into existence by 1807, including the Insurance Company of North America (INA) founded in Philadelphia in 1792 to provide marine and fire insurance, then life insurance for sea captains. By 1808, INA marketed fire insurance west of the Appalachians. Several years after the War of 1812, it moved into Montreal, Canada.

In New York in 1799, the legislature chartered Aaron Burr's Manhattan Company to provide water in New York City. Burr secured as well the right to make loans to merchants and other reputable men of property, a unique arrangement in an era when banks usually had a strictly circumscribed role in the economy. The fact that he was a former senator with influence enough to have defeated Hamilton's father-in-law for the high office accounted for his coup. The next year, he nearly maneuvered his way into the White House before settling for the vice presidency.

However, position and notoriety did not always guarantee financial success. Former Superintendent of Finance Morris went bankrupt and was put in jail for failure to pay debts. To get him out in 1800, friends and supporters in Congress passed the country's first federal bankruptcy law. Only those like Morris who were merchants and traders could make use of its provisions to protect assets from seizure.

As the new century began, farmers and merchants had a crying need for credit to plant crops and finance trade opportunities. Vermont responded with the first state-owned bank, followed by Indiana, Ohio, and Virginia. Although private banks then proliferated by the hundreds and thousands and owned stock in state banks, only the latter had the right to issue bank notes. All such paper documents became part of the nation's money supply and were redeemable in gold or silver.

Jefferson's advent into the White House worried the financial community, but new Secretary of the Treasury Albert Gallatin instituted a fiscally conservative policy. Economies were necessary because a Direct Property Tax passed by Congress in 1798 had failed, largely because no central agency with sufficient resources existed to collect the tax and penalize cheaters. His target of cutting the $83 million national debt in half was 60% achieved by the time the Virginian left office, in part by slashing the War and Navy department budgets. To increase money in the hands of common Americans he had Congress repeal internal excise taxes, lastly on salt in 1807. Democrat-Republicans installed a system in Congress of making appropriations for specific purposes, rather than a general grant of spending authority. Tighter control of the federal budget was achieved.

One change Gallatin did not want but which was insisted upon in 1811 by members of the House was letting the charter of the Bank of the United States lapse. Aside from the fact that government deposits could then be directed to 88 state banks in their own constituencies, the people's representatives were outraged that on the eve of the War of 1812, two-thirds of stock in the national bank was owned by Britons. Therefore, the national bank did lose its charter and the nation went into that second conflict with the mother country without an institution to coordinate and facilitate government borrowing of funds. When banks in New England, New York, and Philadelphia proved lukewarm toward assisting the public subscription of government bonds, the war effort was hampered.

To pick up the slack, states chartered another 120 banks during the war. Two innovations that came too late to finance armies but which facilitated accumulation of capital for investment in manufacturing and other commercial ventures afterward were life insurance companies and savings banks. The first of the former institutions was the Pennsylvania Company for Insurance on Lives and Granting Annuities in Philadelphia. New York Life, Mutual of New York, and Equitable Life of New York quickly followed. Thus, Philadelphia and New York consolidated their domination of finance in the country. Political and economic developments in the next two decades would bring about the permanent ascendancy of the latter.

INNOVATION, INDUSTRY, AND LABOR

By the 1780s, the Industrial Revolution was going full-bore in Britain. Steam engines perfected by James Watt pumped water from mines to make the extraction of coal cheaper and easier, coal replaced charcoal in continuous operation blast furnaces for manufacture of stronger steel, and better steel went into the ties, rails, and spikes that soon connected British cities in a massive railroad network. As well, steam engines replaced human labor driving spinning and weaving machines in the textile industry, turning out paper and flour in mills, and brewing beer. Increased production in factories of all kinds made piece-meal work in rural cottages obsolete. Thus, more people congregated in London and the Midlands region for industrial work. The ultimate outcome was a larger economy, a growing population, and accumulation of capital for investment in manufacturing and trade.

Excess profits were available, as well, for seed money in American enterprises. Despite hard feelings lingering from the Revolution, US entrepreneurs, financiers, and merchants did not turn down a helping hand. However, London clung to the old idea that British manufactures and American commodities made a perfect match, not vice versa. Export of technological know-how and immigration of skilled tradesmen remained illegal. Nevertheless, ways and means were discovered for smuggling out the knowledge and machinery necessary to set up manufacturing facilities on US soil. Political independence and economic liberty stimulated native American ingenuity to expand upon the industrial success of the mother country. Then the growing republic provided a home market capable of absorbing the output not only of US factories but British imports. To the already established industries of home-building, clothes-making, and ship construction would be added food processing, cotton-spinning, firearms manufacture, and finished household goods.

Oliver Evans

It was wheelwright Oliver Evans of Delaware who in 1784 jumped a generation ahead technologically to build a factory powered by waterwheels on the Patapsco River near Philadelphia to process grain into flour with an automated production line. Grain was transported along conveyor belts and chutes for milling and refining at half the cost as done by hand. Three years later, it occurred to Evans that by improving the design of steam engines, he could dispense with water power entirely and permit factory locations anywhere. Non-condensing, high-pressurized engines might also propel vehicles on roads and rivers. However, it was John Fitch who launched the first steamboat on the Delaware River and James Rumsey who succeeded with the second on the Potomac. Evans continued working on his version for several years.

Recognizing that inventors must be encouraged, Congress passed a patent law on April 10, 1790 giving them the exclusive right to make, sell, or use their inventions for 14 years but copyrights for twice as long. The first patent issued on July 31 by a board composed of the secretaries of state and war as well as attorney general went to Samuel Hopkins of Pittsford, Vermont. He had devised a process for extraction of higher concentrations of potash and pearl ash from hardwood ashes by burning raw ashes in a furnace prior to leaching. His innovation reinvigorated the potash industry, generating at up to $300 a ton annual revenue approaching $2 million, which made the US the world leader until the 1860s.

In the first three years of the patent law, 47 were granted. Evans claimed two, including for the Evans straight-line linkage. That innovation made feasible his steam engine design by installing both cylinder and crankshaft at the same end of a beam instead of opposite ends. The weight of both beam and engine was greatly reduced, creating the possibility that a steam-powered vehicle might be invented.

Slater's mill at Pawtuckett
The British had patent law too, of course, but no reciprocal agreement with the US to respect each others. Therefore, when an Englishman named Samuel Slater who had been appren-ticed to Richard Arkwright, inventor of the water frame, heard that bounties were being offered by state legislatures to persons with manufacturing and technological know-how, he broke British law to leave England and emigrate in December 1790 to Rhode Island. There he won the financial backing of a Quaker merchant named Moses Brown to set up a cotton mill at Pawtucket with 250 spindles powered by water and operated by children. In 1793, he partnered in the firm of Almy, Brown & Slater. Five years later, he established the Samuel Slater & Company partnership. The result was six more Arkwright mills con-taining 2,000 spindles in Pawtucket, Smithfield (later Slatersville), Rhode Island, East Webster, Massachusetts, Oxford (later Webster), Massachusetts, and Amoskeag Falls, New Hampshire.

The reason Slater's mills had ample cotton to spin into cloth was that young Eli Whitney, son of a metalworker and a Yale graduate, built a cotton gin in Georgia in 1793 to extract seed from short-staple cotton by machine instead of hand. This device boosted the daily output per slave from one to 50 pounds of cleaned cotton. Moreover, it encouraged the development of other inventions, including the cast-iron plow of Charles Newbold in 1797 and seeding machine of Eliakim Spooner two years later. Ever larger cotton planta-tions spread across the South. But Whitney did not receive a patent until 1794; thus it took another 13 years to win all the infringement suits he filed. Legal fees consumed most profits from selling cotton gins.

On the other hand, factors who bought raw cotton from planters and merchant firms in New York, Boston, Philadelphia, and New Orleans profited enormously from the cotton trade. Most prominent among the latter was the Boston Associates, including in part-nership the Cabot and Lowell families. These cotton houses, as they came to be known, took no ownership, rather received cotton on a consignment basis, sold the bales to Liv-erpool factories, then returned the proceeds less a 5% commission to the factors. The factors then paid off the planters.

Meanwhile Whitney, frustrated at the intractable legal proceedings that kept him from becoming a wealthy man, won a contract in 1798 to manufacture 10,000 muskets for the government. In 1800 in a factory near New Haven, Connecticut at present-day Whit-neyville, he attempted to develop machinery and a system for producing interchangeable, precision parts. Shortly thereafter, gunsmith Simeon North of Connecticut did the same for the production of pistols. Eli Terry of Plymouth then used interchangeable parts in clock manufacturing.

Eli Terry clock

At last in 1801, Evans rolled out an ungainly steam-powered vehicle to startle pedestrians and horses on the streets of New York. Because the National Road and most state turnpikes not only included very steep gradients and other impediments but were indifferently maintained, cross country operation of such a machine was not practicable. Nevertheless, he persevered to build steam engines that drove a dredge in the Philadelphia harbor, sawmills, and boring machines. For over a decade in his Mars Iron Works, he manufactured steam engines to power screw presses for the processing of cotton, paper, and tobacco as well as high-pressure engines for water works.

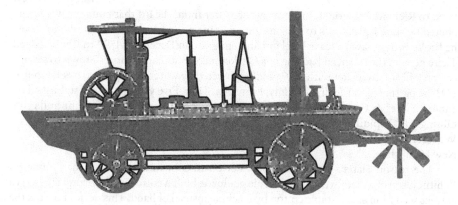

Evans' amphibious steam dredge

While innovators and men of affairs followed the footsteps of the mother country toward industrialization, common people were suspicious of regimentation. On the one hand, the colonial legacy of indentured servitude prepared the way for docility toward employers, particularly among women and slaves; on the other, the recent Revolution with its inherent theme of rebelling against authority — albeit London's and not that of American elites — indicated that craftsmen would not take kindly to having their trades undermined by factory manufactures. Nor would farmers and freedmen readily assent to give up hard scrabble but independent ways for steady wages but industrial servitude. In the slave-holding South, even the meanest white farmers and laborers rested content with an impoverished place in society because the psychological satisfaction of lording it over a suppressed race made inferiority to a patrician, propertied class bearable.

Likewise, the leadership of the nation was disunited about whether to move with vigor toward industrialization. The South with its docile, plentiful, and cheap labor force would have been well positioned to maximize profits, but even after Maryland in 1783 joined northern states in banning the slave trade, Southern plantation owners refused to countenance an adjustment to their economy. Nor did Washington's appeal in 1786 for the outright abolishment of the infamous institution impress his fellow patricians. For all his land holdings, the Virginian was known to be "cash-poor," so much so that before setting out for his inauguration in New York City as first President on April 30, 1789, he had to borrow money to pay travel and lodging expenses. But of course, Whitney's cotton gin four years later decided the South once and for all to eschew manufacturing and worship King Cotton. Even marginal lands went under the plough.

In 1795, the price of a prime field hand was $300. The cost came down with acceleration of the slave trade from Africa. Rising demand from New England textile mills, employing farm girls rather than boys, as well as the British textile industry provoked expansion of plantations from soil-depleted areas into the Mississippi Territory. Even after enough votes were gathered in Congress in 1808 to outlaw the importation of slaves, the buying and selling of human beings in Richmond, Charleston, Mobile, New Orleans, Louisville, and even Washington D.C. proceeded apace. Though over time the cost and feeding of slaves as well as other expenses related to running plantations began to rise again to squeeze profits, still there was only isolated movement in the South toward industry. In 1800, for example, slaves were hired out by their masters for seasonal use in iron, lead, and coal mines and earned about $100 a year in textile and tobacco mills.

Another factor militating against Hamilton's plan on manufactures was his own acknowledgement that the average US wage for skilled labor was twice that of Britain's and the unskilled wage rate, below 40 cents a day, 50% greater. As well, the national policy of keeping land cheap and assisting homesteading in the West might deprive factory managers of the strongest backs. That was why the open door the government kept for new immigrants was so critical. The fact that life expectancy at birth was only 35 years also mandated a constant introduction of fresh flesh and blood.

From a population of 3.9 million at the first census of 1790, including 697,000 slaves and 59,000 free blacks, with only 3.3% living in cities of 8,000 or more and the Ohio and Mississippi valleys already boasting 150,000 settlers, the republic grew by 1800 to 5.3 million and by 1810 to 7.2 million. Although Philadelphia with over 42,000 people was at first the largest city, New York with over 33,000 soon outpaced it. Boston, Charleston, and Baltimore were the other major concentrations of people. It was in the cities where owners of manufacturing establishments and their employees first butted heads.

In point of fact, strikes were a common tactic of tradesmen. In 1785, New York City shoemakers refused to work until wages were raised; the next year Philadelphia printers stopped the presses. But the most serious disturbance during the recession of 1786 was a rebellion by 1,200 farmers and field hands in western Massachusetts led by Daniel Shays protesting farm wages depressed by 20% and seizure of farms, livestock, and household goods for non-payment of debts. When Shays and his men unsuccessfully attempted to seize the arsenal at Springfield, they were dispersed by artillery. The state government later pardoned everyone and lowered taxes and fees. Clothing, household goods, and tools of one's trade were henceforth exempted from debt confiscation.

A new era of labor strife began in 1794 with a series of strikes by various trade unions, including printers and cabinetmakers in New York, to win higher wages, shorter hours, union control of apprenticeship, and closed shops in which only union workers could be employed. A Federal Society of Journeymen Cordwainers (shoemakers) was begun in Philadelphia that in 1799 won concessions after a nine day strike. Seven years later, however, employers there finally had enough of such disturbances, had strikers prosecuted for joining in an illegal conspiracy at common law, and destroyed the union. The same charge was levied to break strikes of shoemakers in New York City and Pittsburgh in 1809 as well as Boston printers.

Fulton's Clermont

More positively in 1807, after two decades of development, steamboats came into their own because of the efforts of an ex-patriot American named Robert Fulton who returned to US soil after trying unsuccessfully to interest first Napoleon Bonaparte, then the British government in submarines and torpedoes. Fulton designed the *Clermont*, a two paddlewheel boat to travel from New York to Albany and back over five days in 62 hours of actual operation. In short order, John Stevens' *Phoenix*, using a screw propeller device, steamed over open sea from New York to Philadelphia. The steamboat *New Orleans* built at Pittsburgh steamed all the way to New Orleans in 1811, making feasible water shipment of grain and hogs from Cincinnati and tobacco from Louisville, Kentucky to cities back east.

First US Patent

While food processing, textiles, and steam engines for various applications were making great strides, the iron industry remained a collection of small, unintegrated companies, either smelters, iron foundries, or iron finishing works but not all together in the same factory. Therefore, a basic problem was moving iron from one operation to the next

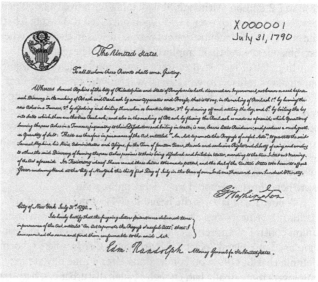

step of manufacture as needed in the right quantity, at a mutually acceptable price. Iron dealers known as jobbers arose to facilitate the process. Like the cotton houses, they took possession of product on consignment and profited by commission. Larger, more profitable operations awaited on the one hand an upsurge in demand such as was provided in Britain by development of the railroad network, on the other investment of American and British capital in a similar US system. First, however, Britain's death struggle with revolutionary France had to be settled and collateral conflict between London and Washington resolved.

ECONOMIC CAUSES AND CONSEQUENCES OF THE WAR OF 1812

Virtually all wars can be said to have an economic cause. Throughout history, invasion and confiscation of territory, destruction of property and lives, enslavement of people, or interruption of trade and commerce have provided ample justification for tribes, nation-states, and empires to assume the offensive. Certainly all these grievances were present in the Revolutionary War. Continued reliance on trade with the mother country and British willingness to use that leverage in the context of the great campaign to prevent France from dominating Europe kept alive the potential for conflict.

When Washington took office in New York City in 1789, American manufactures were still small scale and posed no economic threat to Britain. To maintain access to the growing US market for goods, British merchants were willing to pay the tariffs instituted by Congress on July 4, 1789. Specific duties of 8.5% were imposed on 30 commodities including molasses, hemp, steel, and nails. All other goods were taxed at 5%, then 7.5% in 1792. However, articles imported in US-built or owned ships earned a 10% reduction in tariffs. A July 20, 1789 Tonnage Act also discriminated in favor of Americans by taxing US-built and owned vessels at 6 cents a ton, US-built but foreign owned ships at 30 cents a ton, and foreign-built and owned ships at 50 cents a ton.

The President's decision on April 22, 1792 in advance of the coming Anglo-French war to maintain neutrality pleased the British. The official declaration on April 21 the next year facilitated negotiations leading up to Jay's Treaty. That agreement guaranteed accelerating US exports to Britain of plantation commodities but especially cotton, rising from 10,000 pounds weight in 1789 to 8 million pounds twelve years later, or 20% of the country's production of 100,000 bales (400 pounds each). Cotton surpassed tobacco in 1803 with $15 million worth of exports. After London in 1796 ordered evacuation of the nine frontier posts on US soil, tension in the Great Lakes region and along the US-Canadian border was greatly reduced. Trade with the mother country boomed.

However, new trouble was brewing on the high seas. In June and November 1793, the British Admiralty invoked the Rule of 1756 that if a European nation forbade commerce by third parties with its colonies in time of peace, it could not open them to neutrals during war. That order-in-council authorized His Majesty's sea captains to seize US vessels sailing for French ports. Often, they impressed into the British Navy American seamen, usually British-born.

Although interference with US exports worsened a recession that lasted 36 months into 1798, high European demand for US farm commodities and shipping pushed up prices, justifying losses in ships and cargoes. Washington refused to retaliate for fear of reducing British imports, the single largest source of tariff revenues and funding for his government. However, successor John Adams took umbrage at French attacks on American merchantmen visiting British West Indies ports in 1797 as well as an attempt by the French Directory government to blackmail the US. A war scare amid clashes between US and French ships in the Caribbean, such as the victory of the *USS Constellation* over the French *Insurgente* in February 1799, prompted Congress to authorize a fleet of fast frigates to protect US shipping.

Even after Napoleon Bonaparte took over the French government in 1798, declared himself emperor three years later, and raised the conflict in Europe to another level, US exports increased. They hit a peak of $94 million that year before dipping 1802-04 during the Peace of Amiens. Spain's decision to close the port of New Orleans and its warehouses October 16, 1802 to US goods shipped down the Mississippi gave way before US diplomatic pressure and implied threat of war. Shortly after the port was opened again April 19, 1803, Jefferson moved to negotiate the purchase of Louisiana and New Orleans from Napoleon. Plotting new war with the British, the French dictator wished to create in the US a formidable threat to British Canada and an economic ally for France. When hostilities did resume in 1805, American exports surged.

That year, the British Admiralty instituted a new policy to destroy neutral commerce shipping commodities produced in French and Spanish colonies in the West Indies needed by Napoleon's armies. The Lords of the Admiralty ruled in the *Essex* case that broken voyages were illegal because the US shipper in question could not prove he intended to terminate his voyage in an American port. In fact, a "continuous" voyage to an enemy port was planned. The ship and cargo could be lawfully seized.

Congress eventually retaliated on April 18, 1806 with the Nicholson or Non-Importation Act, prohibiting a list of British imports including hemp, flax, tin, brass, and woolens, items which could be produced in the US or imported from other countries. But after only one month of operation, Congress listened to Jefferson and suspended the law. The President feared further British measures attacking the vulnerable American economy.

For example, of $138.5 million in US exports in 1807, $60 million were re-exports of French and other European goods shipped to US ports, passed through customs, and sent on in US vessels to prevent British seizures and sinkings. Despite Jefferson's conciliation, London not only cracked down hard on this type of "broken voyage" but reacted to Bonaparte's Berlin Decree of November 21, 1806 blockading the British Isles by closing French waters and French-allied ports to commercial shipping, seizing cargoes bound for France and French-controlled ports, and impressing US seamen into the British navy. After the British *Leopard* broadsided the *USS Chesapeake* and impressed three seamen, Congress retaliated with the Embargo Act, halting all trading with Britain and France in an attempt to force combatants to give in and respect neutral rights. Exports plummeted six-fold to $22 million. Too, the British abolished the slave trade on March 25. Since Congress at Jefferson's urging had already banned on March 2 the import of slaves as of January 1, 1808, the action did not engender official US protest. But then Napoleon ordered all US ships appearing in French ports to be seized. He reasoned cynically that because the US Embargo Act forbade trade with France, all such vessels must not be US ships, rather British.

Overall, the Embargo Act badly wounded the New England and New York shipping industry, caused a recession in those areas that spread inland, and sparked talk of secession. Congress attempted with Macon's Bill Number 2 on May 1, 1810 to get satisfaction from the British and French by authorizing the President that if either country ceased violating US shipping by March 3, 1811, the US would reopen trade with that party and prohibit it with the other. The law backfired when Napoleon duped President James Madison into believing he accepted, then seized more US ships and cargoes. A year passed before Americans tumbled to the deception.

As the British turned the screws even tighter by blockading New York City and impressing more US seamen, the country received some compensation for the collapse of imports and exports in development of industry. By 1811, 14 new woolen and 87 new cotton mills were founded. Having to replace British products, Americans invented a screw-cutting machine, a circular saw, and tacks. It was the beginning of US innovation and world leadership in machine tools.

Even so, the country was scarcely prepared when on June 19, 1812 War Hawks in Congress mustered enough votes to declare war on Britain to settle all outstanding grievances with the mother country by force-of-arms. Ships in Chesapeake Bay carried giant flags reading "Free Trade and Sailors' Rights." In fact, because the British economy had been badly hurt by a combination of Napoleon's continental system excluding British commerce and the US non-intercourse policy, London had a few days earlier revoked the offending orders-in-council. News did not travel fast enough across the Atlantic to permit cooler heads to prevail.

Demand for iron and steel in great quantities would not occur until the railroad era began in the 1830s. Although the War of 1812 did stimulate a need for cannon and other metal armament, even after Stevens built the first ironclad vessel and the first steam-engine warship the *Fulton* left New York City in 1814, ships were still constructed primarily of wood. However, Eleuthere Irenee Du Pont, a French immigrant, did well selling gunpowder from works on the Brandywine River near Wilmington, Delaware. His E.I. Du Pont de Nemours & Company became the principal supplier of that explosive substance to the US government and also exported gunpowder to South America.

Whitney musket

Unimpressed with American armaments, the British reacted to the US declaration of war by blockading the Chesapeake and Delaware bays with warships, then extending the blockade to New York City and New Orleans. Only New England ports remained open until April 25, 1814 to provide beef, flour, and other provisions to British armies in Canada and enemy vessels off the coast (which trade by a December 17, 1813 embargo act was rendered officially illegal). Exports plunged to only $7 million in 1814, driving the US Treasury almost into bankruptcy. While nominally the overall economy rose from $810 million of GDP in 1811 to $1.15 billion in 1815, *per capita* GDP swung violently, as measured in 2004 money plunging from a pre-war level of $1,650 to 1813's bottom of $1,285 before recovering in 1815 to $1,625.

What brought the economy back was a US manufacturing boom stimulated by a need to replace British imports combined with Congress' repeal in April 1814 at Madison's urging of all Embargo and Non-Importation Acts. The House and Senate then boosted tariff rates and doubled property taxes on land, dwelling houses, and slaves to obtain new revenue to fight the war. Heavy government borrowing of funds boosted the national debt from $10 million to $127 million. This was an early, *ad hoc* implementation of the strategy of deficit spending adopted twelve decades later to cure the Great Depression.

One great success story was in textiles. Francis Cabot Lowell of the Boston Manufacturing Company, formerly the Boston Associates, used profits accumulated in the cotton trade to build a large factory in Waltham, Massachusetts to house all operations for converting cotton to cloth. Combining machinery and innovations developed in the past three decades, the firm employed New England farm girls to produce standardized coarse cloth in a fully integrated process. Called the Waltham System, it justified a large capital investment with steady profits and made New England for decades the center of the US textile industry.

With interest, the war cost the government $250 million, including $1.5 million to repair damage and destruction by the British burning of Washington's public buildings and the Navy Yard, or nearly $3 billion in 2004 dollars. By the Treaty of Ghent of December 24, 1814 officially ending the conflict, the US obtained neither immediate gain in territory nor indemnity for impressments, cargo and ship seizures and destructions nor compensation for blockade reduction of trade, lost trade contacts, and other economic impairments. However, Andrew Jackson's victory in the Battle for New Orleans in early January 1815 gave confidence that the British would at last respect American national independence. With elimination of the Indian threat east of the Mississippi River and west of the Appalachians, large-scale expansion and settlement resumed.

CHAPTER IV. MANIFEST ECONOMIC PROGRESS: 1816-1860

Because of the period of external and internal peace the US enjoyed after the war of 1812 as well as an absence of rancorous political quarrel, the latter 1810s and early 1820s has been called an Era of Good Feeling. Steadily improving relations with the British in Canada, diminishment of the Indian threat east of the Mississippi River, and American sympathy for the rebelling peoples of Central and South America fostered an atmosphere of security against physical attack. On the other hand, a surge of postwar prosperity was more than offset by a bout of economic depression beginning in 1819 that reduced current dollar per capita income by over 25% to below $90 in 1823 (calculated in 2004 money, from $1,800 to $1,340). The boom-bust cycle was repeated with an 1824-36 upswing and 1837-43 plunge so that nearly three decades after Jackson defeated the British at the gates of New Orleans, Americans on an individual basis were no better off than before.

Why with peace and physical security insured did it take so long to fulfill the plan of

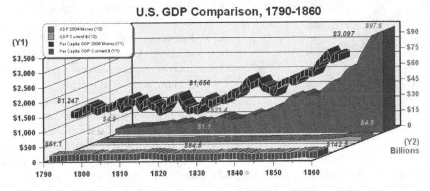

Hamilton for a prosperous economy stiffened by manufacturing and industry? As in the aftermath of the Revolution, capital for investment was sorely lacking and the US banking and financial system needed strengthening. Although merchants and manufacturers rees-tablished trade relationships with London, sufficient funds were scarcely available for internal improvement projects. Agricultural production continued to be the lifeblood of the vast majority of the American people. Only after invention and technological innovation shoved the Industrial Revolution into higher gear was a better balance achieved. By 1860, agriculture and manufacturing each accounted for roughly 42% of the nation's gross domestic product (GDP) of $4.5 billion.

At times, the nation appeared more prosperous than it really was. Spurred in the first instance by natural re-production, in the second by new waves of immigrants, overall GDP rose without advancing *per capita* income. Old World revolutions in 1830 and 1848 as well as famine, oppression, and wars of rebellion caused tens and then hundreds of thousands of discontented Germans and Irishmen, Frenchmen and Greeks to cross the Atlantic. Census figures swelled from 9.6 million in 1820 to 17.1 million in 1840 to 31.4 million in 1860. In the South, the plantation economy could not support immigrant labor, thus the region fell steadily behind in population. Only 9 million people including 3.5 million black slaves lived in Dixie on the eve of the Civil War. Moreover, the institution of black slavery became not just a prerequisite for a marginally profitably plantation economy but a psychological crutch for a landholding aristocracy falling behind northern rivals in resources, adaptability, and willingness to change. The South's position on government funding for internal improvements, tariffs, and the balance of power between federal and state authority revealed an obstructionist mentality laced with concern about the long-term political implications of relative material decline. Certainly, southerners joined in the westward movement, but the conquest and clearing of the lower Mississippi Valley for King Cotton merely replicated what already existed rather than added to the national diversity. Failure to move beyond the plantation ideal, as the West began to move into manufacturing and urbanization as a complement to King Wheat, not only proved a drag on the economy but deprived the region of the wherewithal to win a separate existence.

Nicholas Biddle

As French traveler Alexis de Tocqueville discovered in the 1820s, Americans north of the Mason-Dixon line were frenzied in their desire for wealth and social-standing but mostly interested in economic and business activities. Among well-to-do and common folk alike, not a few were curious and energetic, pragmatic and innovative, and constantly striving to discover the invention that would make a material fortune. Westward, the same profit-oriented thinking proliferated among farmers and trappers. The land and its resources of lumber, coal, wildlife, and pasture were viewed by the General Land Office, established within the Treasury Department on April 25, 1812, as a means to greater riches. Nineteenth century thinking favored rapid expansion and economic development over consolidation and conservation. Even when from time to time government leaders did not actively encourage precipitate exploitation of the continent's assets, they certainly did not stand in the way.

Despite sectional differences and wistful nostalgia about virgin wilderness, no one seriously proposed that the juggernaut of commerce and manufacturing gathering steam in the North be slowed. Suddenly, a confluence of events — repeal of protectionist British corn laws in 1846, victory over Mexico in war 1846-48, discovery of gold in California — produced the first American boom economy. Railroad building east of the Mississippi crossing west spurred expansion of the iron and steel industry even as textile production and food processing supplied clothing and nourishment to the country's millions. Farms spread over the Midwest and onto the Great Plains.

Thus, in the last 17 years before the Civil War, GDP of $1.45 billion tripled to $4.5 billion. *Per capita* income recovered to $140 prior to the Panic of 1857 before settling three years later at $126. Calculated in 2004 money, real GDP vaulted from $35 billion to $98 billion while *per capita* income broke the $2,000 barrier permanently and rushed to $3,100. Even the standard of living of skilled and semi-skilled workers began to advance. But comparable progress had not taken place among black slaves in the South nor unskilled laborers in the North. As American industry surpassed production in Britain, Jefferson's ideal of a nation of farmers with equal economic and political power gave way forever to Hamilton's conception of a capitalist society dominated by manufacturing and industry.

DEVELOPING A MODERN FINANCIAL SYSTEM

In 1816, youthful leaders of the House of Representative John C. Calhoun of South Carolina and Speaker Henry Clay of Kentucky backed the plan of Secretary of the Treasury Alexander J. Dallas to reorganize the nation's currency by bringing into existence a second national bank. During the war, a hodgepodge of notes issued by state banks of varying reliability had forced a suspension of specie payments, further bringing into question the soundness of the banking and financial system. After overcoming opposition by President James Madison and others who feared placing power to control the currency outside government, they pushed a law through Congress that Madison signed. Capitalized at $35 million, including 20% from of the federal government, the second Bank of the United States came into existence like the first with headquarters in Philadelphia and branch offices, 25 this time, in other cities. Acting as a depository for government funds, the national bank received the benefit of not having to pay interest. That was only one reason why the institution and its officers became both controversial and dominant in financial matters for the next two decades.

Second Bank of the United States

Genealogy of Large Banks & Investment Houses, 1784-1945

Simultaneous efforts were made to concentrate capital in private banks. The first incorporated savings bank opened its doors in Boston in 1816. Three years later, banks in New York (including City Bank, founded 1812), Philadelphia, and Baltimore also attracted deposits by paying interest. They and other state banks, most notably the antecedent, of J.P. Morgan & Company and Chemical Bank of New York, that popped up in the ensuing decades profited by making loans to persons buying land or financing trade, then collecting principal and interest on debt or foreclosing if obligations were not met. However, the scale of lending operations was curtailed by a law requiring redemption after February 20, 1817 by specie rather than bank notes of legal currency and bank notes of other entities used for payment to the government of taxes and other public dues. Eventually, bank managers hit upon the idea of minimizing that disruption by locating the legal offices for redemption known, as "wildcat banks," in inaccessible places.

A sharp economic downturn struck the country in 1819. Its financial causes were mismanagement of the second national bank, contraction of credit forced by the specie redemption law, overextended investments in manufacturing that did not produce expected returns as well as commodity inflation, wild speculation in Western land that collapsed when credit dried up and prices fell, and foreign economic troubles that reduced American farm exports and hurt the South and West. With customs and land sale receipts down, the federal government ran budget deficits through 1821. Many in Congress demanded that the charter of the national bank be revoked.

But reorganization of the bank and accession to its presidency four years later by strong-willed former diplomat, editor, and Congressman Nicholas Biddle of Philadelphia helped end the depression. Biddle not only issued $4.5 million of notes expanding to $19 million by 1831 but made timely loans to the US government to cover deficits and created an "elastic currency" of documentary bills acting as short-term commercial paper to facilitate business transactions. Once credit and currency became more available in agricultural regions, the economy recovered. As land sales picked up and the federal government enjoyed surpluses that cut the national debt to $7 million by 1829, public and private funding for large-scale internal improvements resumed.

Earlier in 1815, Calhoun had pushed the idea of a $1.5 million payment by the second national bank to the government for its charter, that money to be used for internal improvements throughout the country. Madison had vetoed the appropriation in the last act of his presidency on March 3, 1817. His decision motivated New York banks to pool enough capital to float bonds for a canal across upper New York State to connect the Hudson River to Lake Erie. Profits from the bond placement and the eventual completion of construction in 1825 advanced the prestige and power of New York City's financial institutions. More canal projects backed by state banks of the old Northwest Territory followed. What finally undercut Philadelphia's domination of finance was reaction against Biddle's active campaigning in 1832 for early re-charter of the national bank prior to its scheduled termination of March 1, 1838. He thereby locked horns with President Jackson, who despite being a "hard money" man who disliked paper currency and bank notes as inflationary, wanted looser credit to help Democratic party political supporters' re-election prospects in the South and West. Not only did Jackson veto the re-charter bill on July 10, 1832 but with encouragement of Vice President Martin Van Buren, closely connected to New York banking circles, removed government deposits from Biddle's bank in favor of 23 state banks, called "pet banks," as of October 1, 1833. Biddle's retaliation of using the national bank's still formidable financial clout to tighten credit caused a short recession in 1834 but failed to dissuade the stubborn Indian-fighter and war leader to relent. Thus, Biddle's bank lost its federal charter and was reorganized March 1836 as the Bank of the United States of Pennsylvania with a state charter. Five years later, it collapsed after an attempt to sustain cotton prices to protect loans to cotton factors (middlemen) failed.

Genealogy of Insurance Industry, 1810-1945

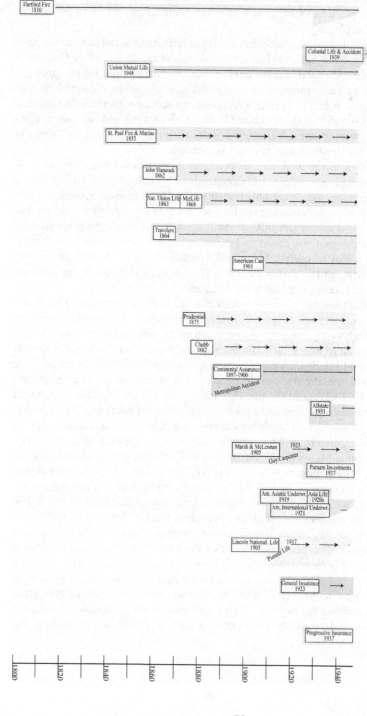

Biddle's Whig supporters in Congress, including Clay and Calhoun, rallied enough support to censure Jackson, but economic recovery spurred by easier credit and land speculation boosted government revenues and made the President look like an economic genius. Fearing a political windfall for Democrats from Jackson's pet bank scheme, Whigs backed the Deposit Act of June 23, 1836, requiring at least one bank in each state and territory to be a federal deposit bank and distributing Treasury surplus in excess of $5 million as a loan to states subject to recall. That year, the government sold $25 million in land, more revenue for the first and only time than generated by customs duties. As the surplus mounted to $40 million, the government began distributing an amount that eventually reached $28 million.

Opposed to this incautious and excessive dispersal of Treasury funds to the states, worrying about rising inflation and land speculation caused by issuance of so much paper money, including "land-office money" based on speculators' notes, Jackson waited until Congress recessed, then ordered the secretary of the treasury to issue the Specie Circular on July 11, 1836. That document mandated with few exceptions that after August 15 only gold and silver be accepted by the government as payment for public lands. Because beginning January 1, 1837, pet banks were required by the Deposit Act to distribute the federal surplus to the states, not only were western land sales knocked down to a low of $3.5 million by 1838 but gold and silver was drained out of eastern banks. The consequence was a credit crunch more severe than Biddle had precipitated five years earlier.

Suddenly, commodity prices collapsed. The republic's most important crop cotton fell from 18.75 cents a pound to 5 cents by 1842. Crop failures made farmers desperate for new loans to replace old obligations coming due. They were met by demands from creditors, themselves under pressure from British bankers whose net investment in the US had grown from under $90 million in 1831 to three times as much, for full repayment or foreclosure. When interest rates soared and a worsening balance of trade drained more hard money from the economy, Congress on May 21, 1838 repealed the Specie Circular by joint resolution, permitting banks to suspend payments in gold and silver. Many banks failed and a full scale depression occurred. Through 1843, the federal government accumulated deficits of $46 million that had to be covered by Treasury notes. Individual states repudiated maturing debts, doing damaged to American credit overseas.

Far back in 1821, Kentucky had been the first state to abolish imprisonment for debt. Other states followed sporadically over the next three decades, but still in 1829, 75,000 people were in jail for failing to meet financial obligations. The depression of 1837-43 might have produced even greater criminal prosecutions had not Congress passed a second federal bankruptcy law on August 19, 1841. Before repeal 19 months later, over 33,700 debtors declared voluntary bankruptcy to cancel $440 million of debt while less than $47 million in assets was surrendered by debtors to creditors.

As the depression deepened, the political parties fragmented. Calhoun and southern Whigs joined the Democratic Party to push for an Independent Treasury Act to remove deposits from pet banks and place them in sub-treasury offices in New York, Boston, Philadelphia, St. Louis, New Orleans, Washington, and Charleston. Passed July 4, 1840, the law gradually transitioned from acceptance of notes from specie-paying banks to acceptance only of government legal tender. After Whig military hero William Henry Harrison led his party to victory in the presidential election that fall, his backers in Congress mustered strength for repeal on August 13, 1841. Thus, for a few more years, the federal government used pet banks as depositories. The sudden death of Harrison a month after inauguration, the political isolation of his successor John Tyler, and the recovering economy permitted Democrats to pass a second Independent Treasury Act on August 6, 1844 with the same provisions as before, putting in force an Independent Treasury system that endured for seven decades.

If the fall of the second national bank leveled the financial playing field between Philadelphia and New York City, a 1838 New York law requiring specie reserve for banks of 12.5% against note issues gave the latter the upper hand. By 1840, New York City banks held $8 million of bankers balances, which were funds from small banks held at large banks to insure their notes. In ensuing decades, half a dozen new institutions, including Metropolitan Bank, came to dominate the field and concentrate bankers' balances of $30 million by 1857. New York City also benefited from development of the credit rating Mercantile Agency in 1841, which later in 1859 became Dun & Company, Bradstreet's in 1855, and life insurance companies that by 1860 grabbed a sizeable share of the nation's $160 million of policies in force.

Most prominent in the insurance field outside of New York were INA, Hartford Fire Insurance Company (1810), Aetna Insurance Company (1819), and Aetna Life Insurance Company, spun off from the entity doing property and casualty in 1853. The original Aetna established in 1858 a reserve fund in case of catastrophic fires and big losses, inspiring over time states to pass laws requiring such a reserve by all companies. In Minnesota, bankers and other prominent persons exasperated by slow communications with eastern insurance companies founded the St. Paul Fire and Marine Insurance Company in 1853. Although the firm barely survived the financial panic four years later as well as the Civil War, afterward it gained strength by underwriting insurance in Canada.

War with Mexico in 1846 required heavy borrowing by the federal government through the Washington D.C. bank of Corcoran & Riggs. Deficits through 1848 amounting to $53.2 million provided another unintended wartime stimulus for the economy. But what really compensated many times over for the war cost with interest of $220 million was the huge gain in territory and resources secured by the Treaty of Guadalupe Hidalgo. Gold discoveries in California attracted British capital to help finance railroads and iron production of engines, rails, and spikes. Net liabilities to foreigners grew from $188 million in 1849 to $384 million a decade later. As the federal government ran up large surpluses through 1857, the US became once again a good investment for overseas capital.

Too, westward expansion, railroad building, and the climb of manufacturing to an equal prominence with agriculture built up domestic sources of capital. Seven million dollars of bank deposits in 1835 became $43 million by 1850 and $150 million in 1860 in 278 savings banks. More important for railroad and manufacturing expansion, corporate securities escalated to $2 billion, of which $500 million was held by foreigners, mainly British. Investment houses in New York City placed the securities, the New York Stock Exchange dominated trading in stocks, and brokerage firms sprang up to handle investment by wealthy individuals.

However, a financial panic resulted from the bankruptcy of the New York branch of the Ohio Life Insurance and Trust Company on August 8, 1857. As banks hastened to pull balances out of New York City banks, most others around the country suspended specie payments and called in loans. A sharp economic downturn then claimed over 4,900 companies, including many western railroads. From 1858 through 1860, the federal government went into deficit spending. However, the real danger for the American economy was the fact that the political struggle of North versus South was moving toward violent confrontation. Westward expansion and the purposeful exploitation of the republic's natural resources would temporarily have to cease.

TAPPING A CONTINENT'S NATURAL RESOURCES

The Missouri Compromise of 1820, followed by Jackson's hard-line stand against South Carolina's effort to nullify the protectionist tariff of 1832 and thereby reassert its absolute sovereignty to secede, gave Americans a precious generation to seize control of all territory that would become the continental US Already in 1817, the republic had bullied Spain into selling Florida and all it contained including myriad animal and vegetable life for 13.3 cents an acre. Wild orange trees would one day be cultivated into groves and fruit farms. Sunshine and sandy beaches for a tourist industry became a phenomenon of the twentieth century.

Likewise in the war with Mexico, 1.2 million square miles of land annexed at final cost of 2.1 cents an acre contained a treasure trove of mineral wealth, fertile valleys, and tourist industry possibilities. The Gadsden Purchase of December 30, 1853 added another 29,640 square miles at 52.7 cents per acre, securing a southern railroad route to California. Temporarily, Indian tribes and the rough environment of mountains and desert impeded Americans from cataloguing and developing what the earth had to offer. Nevertheless, the policy of the federal government was to encourage citizens to move west, buy land, and uncover the continent's hidden wealth.

In 1819, Secretary of the Treasury William H. Crawford reported that since 1789 the government had sold $44 million worth of land. Although actual payment had only been received for half that amount, Congress had been so anxious to forward continental expansion that it had passed a series of 12 relief acts for land purchasers who were unable to meet their financial obligations. Reasoned largesse toward its citizens continued with the Land Act of April 24, 1820. That legislation reduced the minimum price per acre to $1.25 and the minimum purchase amount to 80 acres. However, the possibility of buying on credit was eliminated, giving rich speculators with ready cash a decided advantage in obtaining prime real estate. A provision of the Missouri Compromise banning slavery in Louisiana Purchase Territory other than the new state of Missouri prevented plantation size operations from muscling out free homesteaders.

Therefore, common folk began to cross the Mississippi River in numbers. In 1824, Senator Thomas Hart Benson of Missouri began introducing bills to price land below the official $1.25 per acre minimum depending upon location and quality and then give it away if within a certain time frame it did not sell. Widespread squatting moved Congress on May 29, 1830 to pass the Pre-emption Act, allowing settlers who had squatted and cultivated public land the year before first right to take legal title to as many as 160 acres for the minimum price. The Distribution and Pre-emption Act of September 4, 1841 confirmed the right to stake a claim to most surveyed lands excepting alternate sections of grants made to canals and railroads, which could only be pre-empted for $2.50 per acre. Under the Distribution part of the law, Congress granted 500,000 acres of public land to each new state for construction of internal improvements with 10% of the proceeds being apportioned to states in which lands were located and the remainder less administrative costs being divided among all states according to representation in Congress. The effect of the act was to make Pre-emption the permanent policy of the republic and give Western squatters an advantage over late-coming speculators who might pay more.

Southerners inserted a clause in the 1841 law that if the general tariff rate was raised above 20%, apportionment would be repealed and money from the sale of distributed acres would be directed into the Treasury rather than state coffers. Desiring protection for American industries, fretting at the mounting federal deficit caused by the ongoing depression, northern politicians agreed the next year to repeal the Distribution provision. Renewed pressure for change did not occur until the defeat of Mexico and creation of more territories and states brought the western half of the country into prominence. In 1849 an Interior Department was established to take over duties of the Treasury Department's General Land Office. Finally on August 3, 1854 with the backdrop of Senator Steven A. Douglas' Kansas and Nebraska Act for a transcontinental railroad across the Great Plains forwarding western development, politicians from the North and Midwest united to defeat southern opposition to a Graduation Act to sell public land at a declining price depending upon time on the market. After ten years, land would be sold for $1.00 per acre, after 15 years for 75 cents per acre, after 20 years for one-third that amount, and after 30 years for 12.5 cents per acre. Furthermore, Pre-emption applied at all times to these graduated lands but not to mineral lands and grants for internal improvements made to canal and railroad companies. Every year until the Homestead Act of June 2, 1862 made land free for squatters, 30-40 million acres were sold in this manner.

Once settlers gained possession of western land, they were free to cut timber, shoot wildlife, farm, fish, and pan in rivers for gold, or take whatever other action might improve their circumstances. General Land Office and Interior Department officials expected a cornucopia of new wealth for the country. But discovery and development of natural resources took time, particularly of substances mined underground. Not all hidden treasures were found in the West.

Hotel Astor, New York City

For example, the nation's first natural gas was well was dug at Fredonia, New York in 1821 near Lake Ontario. For the future, a cleaner, more efficient heating and cooking source than charcoal and coal-fired ovens as well as an economical fuel for lighting would be developed. The next year when explorers entered the forested wilderness that would become Yellowstone National Park, they came upon gas geysers, including Old Faithful. No one had any idea, however, how much fossil fuel would be found in the West.

For the moment, however, trappers sent up the Missouri River to the Yellowstone country by John Jacob Astor's American Fur Company Western Department and the Rocky Mountain Fur Company of William H. Ashley were looking for fur-bearing animals and hides to ship back east. Mountain men and fur traders also penetrated the Rockies by South Pass in what became the state of Wyoming. By absorbing in 1827 the Columbia Fur Company, Astor's firm came to dominate the upper Missouri River and northwest trade. Annually from 1815-30, the American Fur Company shipped an average of 26,000 buffalo hides, 37,500 muskrat skins, and thousands other pelts. Astor used profits to expand into other economic activities in New York and retire early from business. At his death in 1848, his net worth was $20 million.

Eviction of Indians from territory east of the Mississippi opened up Wisconsin and Minnesota forests for heavy lumbering. Floated down river, logs were prepared in saw mills for railroad ties and telegraph poles. From 1837 to 1840, so much land was cleared that Scandinavian immigrants poured in to farm. The region's growing population, including in Chicago and other Midwest cities, boosted demand for foodstuffs.

Heretofore, charcoal had been used to smelt iron. Now technological improvements including the hot blast furnace permitted harder, cleaner burning anthracite coal from the Susquehanna River area of eastern Pennsylvania to be fully developed. Production shot up from 215,000 tons in 1830 to one million in 1837 and then 8.5 million tons in 1859. Mining of softer, dirtier burning bituminous coal was eclipsed.

Likewise, quality of iron was improved by better iron ore from near Marquette, Michigan. This was the first of several Lake Superior iron ore finds that culminated in discovery and development of the Mesabi, Vermilion, and Cuyuna ranges in Minnesota over a 110 mile square area just prior to the Civil War. Peak production of high-grade hematite ore with up to 95% iron content was not achieved until 1892. Exploitation of lower-grade taconite ore with 50% iron content was not economically feasible for another six decades.

Gold nugget

On January 6, 1848, a mechanic from New Jersey named James W. Marshall who was building a saw mill for Johann Augustus Sutter on land Sutter owned at a branch of the American River in the lower Sacramento Valley discovered gold. Within weeks a movement of prospectors into the area began that became a gold rush of 80,000 people by wagon trail and ship around Cape Horn or across the Panama Isthmus or Nicaragua as well as from China and Australia. California's population exploded to 100,000 by end of 1849 with San Francisco booming from a few hundred inhabitants to 25,000. Congress established a mint in that city to coin a gold dollar and the $20 double eagle. By 1851, the annual production of gold hit $55 million, about the same as federal spending. With major strikes seven years later in Colorado, Nevada, and British Columbia, great fortunes were made that advanced the economic development of Rocky Mountain states. For example, the Comstock Load near Virginia City, Nevada yielded $300 million in gold and silver over 20 years. Peak regional gold and silver production was not attained until 1880-93.

First oil well

Back east there were no gold or silver mines, rather something in the long run far more valuable. On August 28, 1859 in Titusville, Pennsylvania in the Allegheny Valley, a former railroad conductor named Edwin L. Drake used the same technique developed for drilling salt wells to bore down 69 feet and strike oil. Initially, his well produced a daily flow of only 25 barrels, each of 42-gallon

capacity. Industrialists quickly realized that crude oil could be refined into a kerosene product of superior efficiency and cost for heating and lighting. Within one year, oil production from 1,500 wells reached 500,000 barrels. Selling for $9.59 a barrel, well-owners raked in $4.8 million of revenue. Each year with new discoveries in Pennsylvania, Ohio, and western Virginia the take increased but slowed because of the Civil War. Not until the invention of the internal combustion engine and automobile in the 1880s did it became imperative for producers to look out west for more.

Overseas Trade Advances

For a century after the War of 1812, with the sole exception of the 1830s land sale boom, customs duties provided 80-90% of government revenues. In the *laissez-faire* atmosphere that prevailed prior to the Civil War, half of federal expenditures went to the War and Navy Departments, virtually none for public relief and welfare. Thus, as late as 1860 rural Americans accounting for 84% of the population and farm workers at three-fifths of the labor force required export of agricultural products to generate enough income above domestic trade to pay for imported manufactured goods. Despite progress on Hamilton's plan for a larger home market powered as much by industry as agriculture, chief export items remained as they always had been tobacco, sugar, coffee, cotton, indigo and other crops required by British consumers and the mother country's textile industry.

Demonstrating that Jackson's rout of the British army at New Orleans punctuating the end of the War of 1812 mattered not one iota where American economic grievances against Britain were concerned, Parliament on March 23, 1815 passed a Corn Law placing a high duty on foreign grain imports, waveable only when the price rose to 80 shillings a quart (at 8 bushels per quart, 10 shillings per bushel). American farmers in states of the

Old Northwest Territory hoping to ship wheat and commodities down the Ohio and Mississippi Rivers through New Orleans to the mother country were forestalled. The US bargaining position was so weak that the Madison administration could win no more concession in a Commercial Convention signed with London on July 3 than to end discriminatory duties on American shipping to British holdings in the East Indies. Nothing was said about the more lucrative Caribbean market of the British West Indies.

Nor did the US make more than sketchy progress expanding trade with continental Europe. An 1826 treaty of friendship and commerce with Denmark was more symbolic than lucrative. Better prospects were offered by a trade treaty of December 25, 1825 with the Central American Federation and a later 1836 treaty of commerce and navigation with Venezuela. Although the Monroe Doctrine of 1823 warning Europeans against meddling in the Western Hemisphere had been intended to prevent military interventions and interference in political affairs, economic exclusion was a long-term possibility.

Meanwhile, a new tariff debate erupted over the desire of New England and New York wool and textile manufacturers to eliminate British competition. When Vice President John C. Calhoun of South Carolina used his constitutional prerogative to break a tied vote in the Senate with a negative ballot, protectionists only hollered louder for high tariffs on hemp, flax, hammered bar iron, and steel. Secretly in 1827, Calhoun wrote the *South Carolina Exposition and Protest*, urging his state legislature to "nullify" the tariff with its state sovereignty powers. Openly Jackson as senator from Tennessee and other southerners proposed duties twice the prevailing 25% rate as a tactic to make protectionists back down and damage his opponent for the presidency in 1828 John Quincy Adams. A majority in Congress stunned anti-protectionists by accepting the Tariff of Abominations on May 19, 1828. Ironically, it was Jackson as President in 1832 who had to defend a somewhat milder tariff that retained the 50% rate only on manufactured cloth and iron against South Carolina's Nullification attempt, threatening use of force until a compromise tariff of 1833 with provision for automatic cuts toward 20% over a ten year period let the nullifiers save face.

Protective tariffs naturally elicited bitter complaints by southerners about the danger of retaliation by foreign governments. If the republic had to take a strong stand on trade, they preferred the Reciprocity Act of May 24, 1828 promising to eliminate discriminatory import duties for countries that did likewise for American exports. In fact, President Jackson used it in 1830 negotiations to persuade London to open up the British West Indies to US trade. He also had the leverage of John Bull's desire to invest in the coming American railroad boom, a far more valuable carrot at hundreds of millions of dollars than was the reciprocity stick at tens of millions.

Back in 1765, American ships had accounted for one-third the British total shipping tonnage of 398,000. Because cost of ship building in Boston, New York, Charleston and other cities had been 20-50% below cost in Europe, colonists added 25,000 more tons of shipping a year. However, exclusion from British markets after the Revolution, problems on the high seas contributing to the outbreak of the War of 1812, and difficulties finding other overseas markets to expand exports caused the American shipping industry to stagnate. Although in 1818, transatlantic ship service was established between New York and Liverpool, US owned shipped tonnage grew from only 750,000 tons to 1.6 million tons 22 years later. Pride was taken that in 1841 the American steam ship *Savannah* was first to

The Savannah

cross the Atlantic, cutting eleven days off the average sailing ship's time of 38 days. Two years later, Americans again caught the attention of Europe with fast clipper ships.

As sailing ships of small cargo capacity, the clippers were more important for sea trade between the west and east coasts than for crossing the Atlantic. Sailing time from San Francisco around South America to Boston was cut to three months, encouraging many easterners to join the 1848-49 gold rush. Travel time the other direction, from San Francisco to the Orient by way of Hawaii, was also reduced to a month. The sudden ability of American merchants to transport goods in a timely fashion across the Pacific helped motivate the State Department to pressure China to sign the Treaty of Wang Hiya (or Wanghia) on July 3, 1844, opening five ports to US trade under the same most-favored-nation status as compelled by Britain after the Opium War of 1839-42.

Two years later, American trade was given a tremendous boost by repeal of the British Corn Laws. That decision by Parliament not only led to more trans-Atlantic trade between the mother country and its former colonies but a general upsurge in global economic growth.

Particularly as cotton production proliferated in the Mississippi Valley to 2.2 million bushels in 1859 or 40% of the US total, the port of New Orleans benefited. Annual receipts in New Orleans of $22 million in 1830 climbed to $50 million a decade later and $185 million on the eve of the Civil War. The other half of US exports was channeled predominately through the port of New York. Because of close proximity to Europe and burgeoning east-west railroad lines, New York handled 70% of imports as well.

The boost in trade permitted specialization on the part of merchants. No longer did they have to have a hand in all activities to remain profitable. Rather they could segregate exporting from importing, wholesaling from retailing, and leave manufacturing and mining

Cotton season in Georgia

operations to domestic businessmen. As cotton houses grew up to specialize in that trade, so did other merchants narrow their focus solely to tobacco or wheat or iron products.

In the 1830s and 40s, and partially because the Depression of 1837-43 removed the wherewithal from so many Americans to buy imported goods, the republic enjoyed a favorable balance of trade annually in the millions then tens of millions of dollars. Only when the country became prosperous enough after the War with Mexico and California gold rush to afford quality woolen and cotton manufactures from Europe as well as other pricey items did Americans again begin to splurge. In 1851, $174 million of imports swamped $144 million of exports (about half cotton). The overall balance of payments including financial transactions and services was even worse by $10 million. That decade, however, the flow of money and investment, including foundation of a Colt gun factory in England in 1852, was reversed. By 1860, despite exports of $316 million falling short of $354 million of imports, the overall balance of payments was nearly level.

1847 Colt revolver

Americans tried to diversify exports as well as markets. Successive administrations concluded commercial treaties with countries in many regions. But US textiles and other manufacturers suitable for export could not yet compete on a quality basis with those made in the mother country and the American shipping industry lagged behind European. Even with cotton exports amounting to over half the total by the end of the period, overseas trade fell to only 7% of GNP, one-third the 1807 figure.

On March 3, 1845, a Postal Act by Congress reduced the rate charged for a half ounce letter transported up to 300 miles to only five cents. Another provision authorized subsidies for steamers carrying mail across the Atlantic. The combination of these two changes created favorable economics for the Collins Line two years later to open regular steamship service between New York and Liverpool as well as the Ocean Steam Navigation Company to connect New York to Bremen. Because subsidies paid to US shipping lines by Washington were always less than paid by London to Cunard, because iron frames and steam engines produced by US industry were inferior in size to rivals, even shipping magnate Cornelius Vanderbilt had difficulty in the 1850s challenging European domination of ocean steam-powered shipping. Still, on the eve of the Civil War, US shipping tonnage cleared to carry exports amounted to 4.2 million out of the national total of 5.9 million tons. Annual shipyard capacity approached 200,000 tons a year.

American Clipper Ship
Wounded by the Panic of 1857, American transatlantic steamship service was abandoned two years later. Nevertheless, Cyrus W. Field, from an enterprising family that included Supreme Court Justice Stephen J. Field and department store owner Marshall Field, organized two unsuccessful attempts that difficult economic year to lay a transatlantic cable between the US and Britain via Newfoundland. A third attempt in 1858 with $1.5 million dollars from manufacturer Peter Cooper in their New York, Newfoundland & London Telegraph Company briefly succeeded. On August 16, Queen Victoria sent the first transatlantic cable message to President James Buchanan, saying "Glory to God in the Highest, peace on earth, good will to men." But the cable went silent September 2 and the Civil War delayed Field's ultimate triumph with a cable laid by the *Great Eastern* steamboat until July 1866. Unfortunately, he later lost his fortune in failed railroad and elevated railway stocks. Field's up and down career and the fulfillment of his dream was paralleled within the country by other ambitious men. The willingness of individuals to risk all on schemes, sometimes fanciful, sometimes practical, always daring, moved the country forward.

INTERNAL IMPROVEMENTS

With overseas trade a building disappointment, it became imperative for the US to develop its internal trade, north and south but especially east and west. Prior to the War of 1812, poor communication and transportation inland had limited commerce to coastal shipping, river traffic up the Hudson and other major waterways, wagon freighting between cities, and short hauls not exceeding 100 miles from population centers. The next steps had to be improved roads and turnpikes toward the Appalachian Mountains and beyond, canals linking rivers for bulk water transport over longer distances, and railroad lines such as were creating a powerful passenger and trade network in Britain. Bringing New England, the South, and the West into closer economic harmony would permit, as Adam Smith had hypothesized, regional specialization, more efficient use of resources, and a rising standard of living. Particularly railroads, with advantages of speed, dependability, and track laid to go in different directions, would be essential for this transformation. Finance would come from federal and state government as well as private capital, American and foreign.

Genealogy of the Railroad Industry, 1827-1860

Even in the Era of Good Feeling, there were constitutional and legal barriers to overcome. Many in Congress and particularly southerners were sorely vexed over the issue of whether Congress had the right to appropriate money for roads, bridges, canals, and harbors within states. In 1824, the constitutional question was finally decided by the Supreme Court decision in Gibbons v. Ogden voiding an 1808 monopoly granted by the New York legislature for operation of steamboats in state waters as violating congressional power to regulate interstate and foreign commerce. The political debate was only sharpened by Speaker of the House Clay's speech March 30 calling for an American System combining a protective tariff and a national program of internal improvements as a means to expand the domestic market and lessen US dependence on imports averaging $100 million annually. His influence was sufficient to pass a General Survey Bill, empowering the President to initiate surveys and estimates of roads and canals required for national military, commercial, or postal purposes. Although he intended to ride the plan to victory in the 1824 election, it was John Quincy Adams who, after neither he nor Clay nor Jackson won a majority of electoral ballots, deftly obtained Clay's support by getting behind the American System for a deciding vote in the House of Representative.

Jackson's bitterness as well as stiffening southern opposition to seeing federal funds benefit the North and West hindered Adams' recommendations the next year for a federal program not merely of road and canal building but standardization of weights and measures, exploration westward, promotion of agriculture, commerce, and manufacturing, and other ideas. Bereft of federal leadership, states decided to emulate New York's success with the Erie Canal by borrowing to spend $125 million on canals over the next 15 years. That

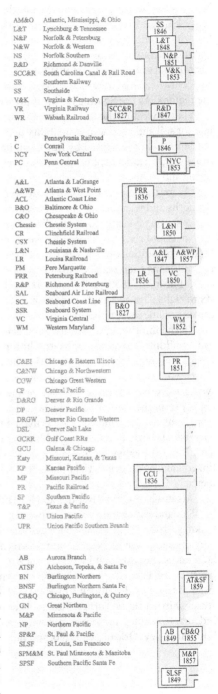

AM&O	Atlantic, Mississippi, & Ohio
L&T	Lynchburg & Tennessee
N&P	Norfolk & Petersburg
N&W	Norfolk & Western
NS	Norfolk Southern
R&D	Richmond & Danville
SCC&R	South Carolina Canal & Rail Road
SR	Southern Railway
SS	Southside
V&K	Virginia & Kentucky
VR	Virginia Railway
WR	Wabash Railroad
P	Pennsylvania Railroad
C	Conrail
NCY	New York Central
PC	Penn Central
A&L	Atlanta & LaGrange
A&WP	Atlanta & West Point
ACL	Atlantic Coast Line
B&O	Baltimore & Ohio
C&O	Chesapeake & Ohio
Chessie	Chessie System
CR	Clinchfield Railroad
CSX	Chessie System
L&N	Louisiana & Nashville
LR	Louisa Railroad
PM	Pere Marquette
PRR	Petersburg Railroad
R&P	Richmond & Petersburg
SAL	Seaboard Air Line Railroad
SCL	Seaboard Coast Line
SSR	Seaboard System
VC	Virginia Central
WM	Western Maryland
C&EI	Chicago & Eastern Illinois
C&NW	Chicago & Northwestern
CGW	Chicago Great Western
CP	Central Pacific
D&RG	Denver & Rio Grande
DP	Denver Pacific
DRGW	Denver Rio Grande Western
DSL	Denver Salt Lake
GCRR	Gulf Coast RRs
GCU	Galena & Chicago
Katy	Missouri, Kansas, & Texas
KP	Kansas Pacific
MP	Missouri Pacific
PR	Pacific Railroad
SP	Southern Pacific
T&P	Texas & Pacific
UP	Union Pacific
UPR	Union Pacific Southern Branch
AB	Aurora Branch
ATSF	Atcheson, Topeka, & Santa Fe
BN	Burlington Northern
BNSF	Burlington Northern Santa Fe
CB&Q	Chicago, Burlington, & Quincy
GN	Great Northern
M&P	Minnesota & Pacific
NP	Northern Pacific
SP&P	St. Paul & Pacific
SLSF	St Louis, San Francisco
SPM&M	St. Paul Minnesota & Manitoba
SPSF	Southern Pacific Santa Fe

heavy debt and the Panic of 1837 caused a backlash among voters, forcing legislatures to adopt balance budget laws and limit states' ability to fund new projects. Withdrawal of British finance crimped railroad projects until state land grants to railroads, laws for making the buying and selling of land cheaper and easier, and incorporation laws for limiting liability assured investors that railroad companies would go on even if catastrophic accidents occurred. Gradually, economic specialization did deepen the fissures between the regions. As the South gave itself up wholly to slave-worked plantations and rich new farm lands west of the Appalachian mountains gained a comparative advantage over the inferior soil and productive capability of New England agriculture, displaced farm workers in the East supplemented by European immigrants flocked to factory work in cities and provided a cheap, surplus labor force unavailable elsewhere for the growth of manufacturing and industry.

As for the transportation revolution gripping the country, eventually the comparative strengths and weaknesses of the various modes became well known. Wagon freighting on turnpikes moved cargoes in any direction but cost 15 cents per ton-mile. Water transport on canals and rivers provided at 1/4 to 1 cent per ton-mile the cheapest method of moving bulk commodities but took 18 days from Cincinnati to New York, 28 if heading south to New Orleans then transferring cargoes to a ship for the trip around Florida up the east coast. But in the 1850s, rail transport yielded an optimum combination of speed and price, six to eight days at 2 cents per ton-mile for the Cincinnati to New York run. Wagons and canals became less important.

In the interim, however, Americans moved ahead with road, turnpike, and especially canal building. Governor De Witt Clinton's influence, capital from New York banks, and Irish immigrant labor built the Erie Canal between 1817 and 1825. New York City was thereby linked to the Great Lakes by the Hudson River and the canal. At first, grain from western New York State was the primary cargo, then in the 1840s pork, lumber, and copper from the states of the old Northwest Territory, then in the 1850s iron. West of the Appalachians, the Ohio and Erie Canal connected Portsmouth and Cleveland by 1827, the Wabash and Erie Canal struggled for two decades through financial difficulties to bridge Toledo with Evansville, Indiana on the Wabash, and the Illinois and Michigan Canal linked Lake Michigan to the Illinois River. By 1848, Chicago was the hub of Midwest commerce.

Meanwhile, Ohio River flat and keel boat operator Henry M. Shreve opened a new era in US inland water transportation by launching the steamboat *Washington* at Wheeling and making a round-trip voyage between Louisville and New Orleans. Soon, steamboats not only carried passengers and grain down the Ohio and Mississippi Rivers at 25 miles per hour and sugar, flour, and whiskey back up again at 16 miles per hour but crisscrossed the Great Lakes. Fare per person for the river run fell 85% to $20 by the 1830s. Control of Mississippi trade made a fortune of $500,000 for Cornelius Vanderbilt. In the 1830s and 40s, steam ship salvaging turned into another lucrative business for James Buchanan Eads of Indiana. River city and pork capital Cincinnati hit 115,000 people by 1850 with St. Louis, Louisville, New Orleans, Chicago, and Buffalo also rising up to become major metropolises.

Cincinnati "Porkopolis" 1835
Cities and states had far more success with improvement of local roads and bridges than the federal government had creating a national road network. After the Panic of 1819 stopped the Cumberland Road at Wheeling on the Ohio River, a plan for its repair and further extension by self-funding toll gates was vetoed by President Monroe on May 4, 1822 on the grounds that Congress did not have the constitutional right to construct an interstate road. Eight years later on May 27, Jackson used the same logic to block the Maysville Road Bill for a 60 mile turnpike from Maysville to Lexington in Kentucky, desired by Clay and the Whigs. The President's deeper motive was to head off any program that would accrue to Clay's credit and gain votes himself by distribution of the federal surplus to the states. He did, however, sign a new Cumberland Road Bill on May 31 that year. Congress turned over the National Road to the states to institute tolls and effect repairs.

The Tom Thumb

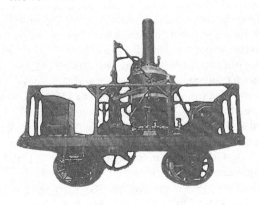

On the frontier, of course, there was no organized effort to build roads. Aside from river transport, arteries for travel and transport through forests consisted of old Indian trails, on the plains and mountains of whatever path proved easiest. Missouri trader William Beckness found the best route across the southern Great Plains to Santa Fe in Mexican territory in 1821, opening the territory for wagon caravans carrying trade goods. In 1830, the first wagon train carrying settlers crossed the barrier of the southern Rocky Mountains into California. Then in the 1840s, "prairie schooners" left Independence, Missouri for a 2,000 mile journey along the Oregon Trail. After crossing through

Indian territory on the Great Plains, they climbed through South Pass bound for the Willamette valley.

If canals were first conceived for transport of bulk agricultural commodities to market, railways were required to move heavy rock and stone to waterways. Thus on October 7, 1826 the Granite Railway Company (first predecessor to Conrail) opened at Quincy, Massachusetts to transport granite to the Neponset River; the Mauch Chunk railroad at Carbondale, Pennsylvania soon carried coal to the Lehigh River. Despite the fact that in 1783 John Stevens had taken out a patent on a multi-tubular steam engine, until Peter Cooper at his Canton Iron Works in Baltimore built the first US locomotive, the *Tom Thumb*, in 1828, British models had to be imported. The next year on December 22, 1829, the ambitiously named Baltimore & Ohio (B&O) became the first long-distance passenger railway company, intending to carry fare-paying citizens from Baltimore to Wheeling. Not until 1853 was the line completed. Major reasons for slow progress in connecting East to West were inefficient steam engines that could not generate enough speed, the high initial capital cost of acquiring railroad locomotives and cars and laying track, incompatible equipment between railroads, and financial difficulties brought on by the Panic of 1837. Well into the 1840s, most successful railroads remained like the Mohawk and Hudson Railroad between Albany and Schenectady intrastate lines. Even so, the republic had 3,300 miles of railroad track by 1840, nearly twice as much as continental Europe.

Intrastate rail connections and systems within the Northeast, the South, and Ohio beefed up in the 1840s with expansion of the B&O, foundation in 1846 of the Pennsylvania Railroad, and extension of what became the Virginia Central (forerunner of the Chesapeake & Ohio) in 1850. What transformed this regional hodgepodge into a continuous network was advances in railroad technology and intervention by the federal government to facilitate commodity, passenger, and mail service. On September 20, 1850, Congress authorized land grants to the states of Illinois, Mississippi, and Alabama for construction of a railroad line connecting Chicago to Mobile and as well grant by the states of tracts of public land in alternate sections not exceeding six square miles to the railroads. Through 1857, grants totaling 21 million acres (32,815 square miles) turned the Illinois Central, Pennsylvania Railroad, Southern Railway, and other railroad companies into the republic's first big businesses. But most of the $1 billion in private capital invested by American and British sources including Baring Brothers in the two decades prior to the Civil War in 28,000 miles of track ($35,714 per mile) went to connect New York and other cities in the Boston to Washington D.C. corridor with Chicago on Lake Michigan and St. Louis on the Mississippi River. In the South, only one line from Norfolk, Virginia to Memphis, Tennessee connected the Atlantic with the Mississippi. Worse, there was no direct rail connection between the nation's capital and Charleston and Savannah. Greater national urgency was given to a Chicago and Rock Island Railroad to bridge the Mississippi and a Missouri Pacific Railroad to push into the Great Plains from St. Louis to Kansas City by 1856 than to provide the South with equivalent arteries of economic development.

Railroad connections permitted Henry Wells and William G. Fargo and their American Express Company to provide complete mail service to the eastern half of the country. In 1852, they started the Wells-Fargo Company to do the same for the western half of country. Because prior to the Civil War, no rail line crossed the Great Plains, the only connections were regular stagecoach service begun 1858 by the Overland Mail Company between St. Louis and Los Angeles — a jarring 20 day, 2,600 mile day and night journey — and the next year Pony Express service of the Central Overland Company nearly 2,000 miles from St. Joseph, Missouri to Sacramento carrying letters and newspapers in 11 days. Despite successful transport in 1859 of mail from St. Louis to Henderson, New York in 19 hours and 40 minutes over 812 miles by John Wise and three others in the balloon Atlantic, air transport relying on fickle wind currents was not a practicable alternative.

Hoe's 1846 cylinder press
What was both revolutionary and viable was the quantum leap in communication technology achieved on May 24, 1844 by former professor of painting and sculpture at New York University Samuel F.B. Morse. Using a telegraph he had invented in 1832 (that adapted Joseph Henry's intensity magnet), a system of electromagnetic renewers, the Morse code he devised in 1838, his wealthy partner Alfred Vail's printing technique, and a $30,000 Congressional appropriation, he sent the first telegraph message "What hath God wrought?" along wires strung 40 miles between Baltimore and the nation's capital. When the government balked at buying the rights to the system, Morse and Vail formed their own company. By 1855, the American Telegraph Company controlled all telegraph lines marching alongside railroad lines in the eastern half of the country. The next year, the New York & Mississippi Valley Printing Telegraph Company was renamed the Western Union Telegraph Company to do the same beyond the Mississippi River. Thus by 1861, Americans had undisputed visual evidence sea to sea of their fellow citizens ingenuity and drive. In actual fact, invention and innovation had been making its mark on the economy for decades.

INNOVATION FUELS ECONOMIC EXPANSION

It was quite natural that a desire to improve agricultural output, still in 1839 accounting for 70% of GDP, should spur invention and innovation. The opening up and clearing of fertile land in the Midwest and growing domestic population created an obvious supply and demand. The potential need of overcrowded Europe for US foodstuffs and the possibility that the British Empire would renounce protectionism, which it did in 1846, promised at some point an explosion of commodity exports beyond cotton. Whitney's gin inspired a generation of American mechanics to design machines and implements to make planting and harvesting of other crops easier. But US manufacturers also got the idea from textile spinning of wool and cotton goods that machinery and factories could be adapted for food processing. Meatpacking turned Cincinnati, with 500,000 hogs handled in 1848, into the first major metropolis west of the Appalachians. Chicago equaled Porkopolis in that industry by 1860 and shipped as well over 20 million bushels of grain. The previous year and only five years after the first commercial flour mill was established in Minneapolis, flour milling became the largest single component of US industrial production.

Next in dollar value but perhaps first in psychological importance was the iron and steel industry. The typical one or two decade time lag in acceptance of new technology that delayed replacement of New England waterwheels with water turbines and wood as fuel for steam engines with coal also delayed the switchover from charcoal for iron-smelting to coal, especially anthracite. It was to encourage more rapid adoption of technology that Congress on July 4, 1836 created the US Patent Office with a commissioner of patents within the State Department. A provision requiring examination of any submitted patent for novelty and usefulness was designed to provide protection for the rights of original innovators but was later dropped as too restrictive of add-on inventions.

By 1840, cumulative capital investment provided by US and British sources of $50 million had propelled industrial production to a value of $200 million, a bit less than 10% of GDP. By 1859, net investment had jumped 20 times to $1 billion and industry and manufacturing had expanded nearly ten times to $1.9 billion. In addition to cotton and woolen textiles, iron goods, flour and meal, American factories turned out lumber products for building construction, boots and shoes, carriages and wagons, leather goods, and machinery. The Middle States at $800 million of production and New England at $470 million accounted for two-thirds as well as nearly 70% of investment. Demonstrating just how explosive economic development was in the Midwest, that region's $380 million of production was 2.5 times as much as in the South while $190 million of investment was twice as much. Most efficient region of all was California and the Pacific where $23 million of investment generated $71 million of industrial and manufacturing production.

It cannot be forgotten that a sizeable portion of US manufacturing went to produce farm machinery, $152 million worth by 1850 on 1.45 million farms with 293 million acres. Nine years later, the figure was $246 million of farm equipment on 2.04 million farms and 407 million acres. If Whitney's cotton gin was primarily responsible for cotton production rising from 731,000 bales in 1830 to 5.4 million in 1859, other mechanical devices and innovations lifted corn production to 840 million bushels with huge increases in wheat, rye, oats, sugar, tobacco, dairy products, and livestock. Improved agricultural yields reliant on machinery turned out by US manufacturers buoyed the fortunes of millions of Americans. When finally, the industrial revolution in heavy industry, transportation, textiles, and food-process got going full bore, farm equipment inventions and innovations had already proliferated. American mechanics had decades of experience making machines.

In 1819, Jethrow Wood of New York introduced the cast-iron plow with three-piece standardized, interchangeable parts as a replacement for wooden moldboard plows. Three years later it was improved by John Conant of Vermont with the lock colter device. In 1837, Conant's model was itself superceded by the steel plow of John Lane and John Deere. Deere was so confident that he had a permanent answer to the farmer's spring planting problem that he starting making plows even before he had orders. Eventually, he founded a factory in Moline, Illinois and used special rolled steel brought across the Atlantic from Britain and up the Mississippi River on steamboats to make one-horse models costing as little as $6 and big breakers selling for as much as $23. Exceeding 1,000 plows of annual production in 1846, he was eventually able to pay his most skilled employees $1.50 a day, his least skilled about one-third that wage.

Deere plow with cutting blade
During the same time period, the cradle costing no more than $5 and permitting harvesting of two acres of wheat per day replaced the sickle for reaping, and then was overtaken in 1831 by Cyrus H. McCormick's reaper-harvester. Drawn by a two-horse team, that device featured a reel to gather grain, a vibrating blade to cut it, and a platform to collect it. Once again the time lag between invention and full development and production prevented McCormick's device, which harvested at three times the speed and six times the capacity of the cradle, from achieving substantial acceptance. A critical problem was making reapers with standardized parts in a high volume, low cost process, which McCormick finally did with a factory in Chicago in 1846. Thereafter, the technique was applied to plows, threshing machines, harvesters, stoves, metal clocks, and sewing machines. Samuel Colt used interchangeable parts for production of his Colt revolvers as early as 1833.

Cyrus H. McCormick
Not until 1860 did the reaper-harvester as well as mowing, threshing, and haying machines, seed drills and cultivators, and grain elevators come into nearly universal use. However, because of cheap slave labor in the South, that region lagged far behind in switching over to new machinery. More narrowly focused agricultural improvements, including the revolving disc harrow, the agricultural binder, the chilled plow, and the twine knotter rarely found their way south of the Mason-Dixon Line. Manufacturers of farm machinery had neither financial nor social incentive to open factories in Dixie.

In the Midwest and North, wheat could be stored, particularly in elevators, until ready for processing into flour. Livestock carcasses could be packed and preserved in refrigerated compartments until shipment to market. But dairy products were too susceptible to spoilage until a knock-about New Yorker named Gail Borden came up with a process to condense milk in 1856. Taking out US and British patents, he founded the Borden Company and in 1861 set up a condensing plant to supply product to the Union army. Thereafter, methods to freeze, dry, can, salt, and concentrate foods to prevent deterioration led to rapid expansion of food processing in major cities, not always in the most wholesome of circumstances. More careful techniques to expand and protect the food supply would have to wait the twentieth century.

Meanwhile, in the 1830s and 40s, the mass production of newspapers was made possible by a series of technological innovations, in particular by Richard M. Hoe of New York. The Hoe Company developed in succession the single small cylinder press, double small cylinder press, single large cylinder press (the first in the US to use a flat bed and cylinder press in combination), and in 1846 the rotary press for printing on both sides of the paper. The latter machine, installed the next year by the *Philadelphia Public Ledger*, was capable of printing 8,000 newspapers an hour while Hoe's cylinder press of 1853 performed even better. Other inventions, such as Thomas Davenport's electric printing press, had to await even more advanced technological times. Nevertheless, production runs could now keep up with increased circulation sparked by Benjamin H. Day's innovation of the penny-press daily *New York Sun* on September 1, 1833 and sensational articles such as the August 25, 1835 claim that vegetation grew on the moon. Politically active men such as Horace Greeley and his Whig-leaning *New York Tribune* of 1841, founded newspapers to advance the westward movement, abolitionism, and political parties.

Edgar Allen Poe
Increased newspaper circulation as well as book manufacturing for 1840s bestsellers (Edgar Allen Poe's *The Murders in the Rue Morgue*, Henry Wadsworth Longfellow's *Ballads and Other Poems*, and James Fenimore Cooper's *The Deerslayer*, culminating with Harriet Elizabeth Beecher Stowe's anti-slavery novel *Uncle Tom's Cabin* that sold 300,000 copies in 1852 and 1.2 million ultimately) required much larger quantities of paper. Back in 1817, Thomas Gilpin near Wilmington, Delaware had produced the first machine-made paper. Introduction of the *Fourdrinier* process of paper manufacturing, originally invented by British inventors for a French company, in the mid-1820s greatly speeded up paper production. However, not until lumbering operations reached a commercially-profitable size in the 1840s and 50s could the Parson Paper Company of Holyoke, Massachusetts have an ample supply for the first large-scale paper manufacturing operation in the country.

Although the South was severely negligent in failing to take advantage of nineteenth century industrial and technological development, the eighteenth century cotton gin was still sufficient to ship increasing quantities of cotton northward. By 1830, dozens of textile works supplied with machinery by the Merrimac Company of Lowell and other textile machinery manufacturing companies sprang up in Massachusetts, including nine in Worcester, large establishments in Lawrence, and several others in Lowell. After adapting the Waltham System of cotton manufacturing for wool, the latter town became known as the "Manchester of America." The final turning point in eliminating the livelihoods of women who home-spun clothing came in 1840 with William Crompton's invention of a loom for manufacture of figured woolens. The number of textile spindles in the country leaped from 1.1 million in 1830 to twice as many in 1850 to 5.2 million a decade later. Seventeen thousand New England women in 1840, 23,200 in 1850, and 31,400 in 1860 could only produce clothing worth $1.70 *per capita* ($29 million in total) then $1.18 *per capita* ($27.4 million) and finally $0.78 *per capita* ($24.5 million). Factories using belt transmission of power and finally steam power brought the price of basic textiles lower and lower until home-spinners produced for their own families and no one else. A simpler, more self-reliant way of life was lost.

Howe's lockstitch sewing machine

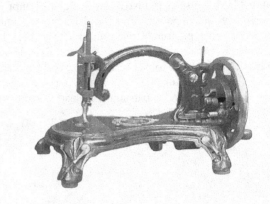

But then in 1846, Elias Howe of Massachusetts patented a sewing machine. Although he had learned about machines and sewing in a Lowell textile plant, his ability to sell was small. Thus, after failing to interest investors in the US, he sold patent rights in England for only £250 pounds and moved there to work for £1 a day for a British partner interested in a sewing machine for leather. After a falling-out, he returned to the US only to discover that several men had made unapproved improvements on his patented design. Powered by a treadle and featuring a lock stitch, toothed wheel, foot-pedal and standardized parts, the machine of Isaac Merritt Singer of Pittsburgh proved best. In 1853, he opened a factory in New York for volume production of the Singer Sewing Machine, priced above $65. Although Howe's suit for violation of his patent was ultimately successful, tens of thousands of Singer's machines stitched the uniforms worn by Union armies in the Civil War. As for Howe, he eventually received royalties up to $4,000 week, established the Howe Machine Company of Bridgeport, Connecticut, and two years later won vindication with a model that won the Paris Exhibition award.

Singer's machines brought about a remarkable revolution in cost and capability in the manufacture of clothing. Rather than being restricted to a choice between basic garments of rough fabrication and high-priced imports of European fashion, Americans now had an opportunity for better quality clothing at an affordable price. Moreover, items of specific utility, such as Walter Hunt's safety pin in 1849 and Bavarian immigrant Levi Strauss' brown and blue indigo-dyed "jeans" for California miners in 1853 broadened out the consumer market. It was only the very beginning of a transformation in the American economy that would create myriad kind of mass-produced goods in the twentieth century.

Although the country's population was still overwhelmingly dispersed in rural areas, the growth of cities and concentration of money in cities permitted opening of the first department stores. Most notable were Shillito's in Cincinnati as early as 1830, Jordan Marsh in Boston in 1841, and F&R Lazarus in Columbus, Ohio a decade later. Later in 1858, R.H. Macy and Company opened as a dry goods store in New York City, ringing up

$85,000 in sales the first year. All these companies as well after the Civil War as Wechsler & Abraham in Brooklyn, Rich's in Atlanta, Goldsmith's in Memphis, and Bloomingdale Brothers in New York became large local retail operations.

Invention and innovation was initially more important for iron production than size of operation. In 1817, puddling and rolling as a continuous process was begun at Plumstock, Pennsylvania and soon spread to Pittsburgh. Although Frederich W. Geisenheimer successfully smelted iron ore with anthracite coal in 1830 and the hot blast furnace was first tested in 1834 as an improvement on the open forge, charcoal remained the sole practical fuel for large-scale industrial smelting until improvements in puddling and rolling required more steam power. After David Thomas of Connecticut made the first successful production run of pig iron by using anthracite coal in a hot-blast furnace at Lehigh Crane Ironworks in Catasauqua, Pennsylvania on July 4, 1840, mine output of anthracite was quadrupled to 4 million tons. The anthracite coal breaker, the roller and crusher for coal, as well as further refining and rolling improvements permitted production of stronger, heavier rails by 1845 and expansion of the nation's railroad system.

Locomotive factory, New Jersey

In 1851, William Kelly of Kentucky converted pig iron into steel by directing a current of air upon the molten metal. Five years later in England, Henry Bessemer used the same method for what came to be called the Bessemer Steel Process for producing very rapidly in a 20 foot tall pot purified ingots, hardened by carbon, in quantity for forging or rolling mills. Cooper at his Trenton, New Jersey rolling mill was first that year to use a Bessemer converter in the US With the spur of railroad locomotive production, then Civil War armament production, the steel industry began to replace iron.

Particularly important for the early expansion of railroads and thus the iron and steel industry was fabrication of more powerful locomotives. In 1832, the Baldwin Works was opened for specialized locomotive development in Philadelphia, then two years later the Norris' Forge of the same city. However, not until George H. Corliss opened his Corliss Works in Providence, Rhode Island in 1846 to produce a locomotive with a four valve control system featuring a valve gear and drop cut-off to reduce condensation and provide better fuel economies in operating reciprocating steam engines were general machine shops eliminated from locomotive manufacturing. Railroads switched over to Corliss' standard steam engine.

Rapid expansion of rail lines was matched by critical improvement in bridge construction to bear the weight of iron and steel locomotives and cars carrying full loads at vigorous speeds. In 1841, John A. Roebling, a German immigrant, opened a factory in Saxonburg, Pennsylvania that was later moved to Trenton, New Jersey to fabricate steel wire ropes for use in suspension bridges. The first such bridge spanned the Monongahela River at Pittsburgh in 1846. The first railroad suspension bridge carried trains over the Niagara Falls in 1855.

Use of the Bessemer converter helped Cooper make the first structural iron for fire-proof buildings in 1854. Mechanic and manager of a bedstead factory in Yonkers, New York Elisha G. Otis had already in 1852 built a "safety hoist" equipped with an automatic device to keep an elevator from falling if the lifting chain broke. Opening his own elevator factory, Otis obtained an order in March 1857 to install the first passenger elevator in New York City's E.V. Haughwout & Company Department Store. After on January 15, 1861 he patented a steam-run elevator, not only could architects now plan buildings that rose dramatically into the sky, but contractors could dream of fantastic profits from construction of sky-scrapers whose real estate value soared with their height.

Across the Atlantic in May 1851, the British opened a Great Exhibition in a Crystal Palace built in Hyde Park in London to show off the technological achievements of the world and in particular Great Britain. In point of fact, American industrial production caught up with the mother country's that decade and raced past. One reason was more rapid adaptation of innovations to cut the lead time between invention and practical application. An important example was the *Vernier Caliper* by J.R. Brown of Providence (later Brown and Sharp Manufacturing Company), a device that made measurements accurate in thousandths of an inch and led to true precision manufacturing. Within a few years, the US became by far and away the world leader in machine tool making, producing machines to make other machines. Having relied on narrowly-trained artisans to advance the original Industrial Revolution, the British now swallowed their pride to cross the Atlantic and study the "American System" of producing durable, cheap, and plentiful goods. In 1854, the US held its own Crystal Palace exhibition in New York City. Critical inventions such as the turret lathe by Robbins and Lawrence Company of Windsor, Vermont, essential for mass production techniques, were shown.

LABOR AND POPULATION

The Industrial Revolution in the US was a double-edge sword for American workers. One the one hand, the development of heavy industry opened up employment opportunities for tens of thousands of urban poor, displaced farmers, and immigrants. On the other, the innovation of interchangeable, standardized parts permitted employers to substitute semi-skilled wage-earners for higher paid, skilled mechanics. Although the accumulation of revenue and profits by railroads and iron manufacturers, textile companies and farm implement makers stimulated hope in the 1840s that real wages would continue to rise by that decade's 17% clip, replacement of labor with machinery in capital-intensive operations as well as population soaring above 30 million by 1860 caused the wage to cost of living ratio to reverse course. The law of supply and demand hurt workers just at a time when the economy was enjoying ten years of almost unbroken prosperity.

As in colonial and early national times, tradesmen and common laborers tried to unite to improve working conditions and wages but lacked resources to sustain the fight. In the main, they used strikes to pressure employers for concessions as well as limited appeals to state governments and legislative bodies and, when truly desperate, resort to force. The fact that city populations were riven by ethnic, religious, and racial differences made the fight more difficult. As the work force climbed from 3.2 million in 1820 to 5.7 million in 1840 to 10.5 million in 1860, 40% concentrated in manufacturing and industry, New York City with more than one million persons, Philadelphia with 565,000, Baltimore, Boston, and other cities with lesser amounts became major metropolises wherein the standard-of-living for wage-earners fell even further behind that of the middle and upper classes.

Boys breaking up chunks of coal in Pennsylvania mine

The struggle of working men and women for a measure of material prosperity and personal dignity took place largely in the Northeast and Middle Atlantic states. In the Midwest, manufacturing and industry had not yet progressed to the point where labor had the numbers and potency to challenge employers. In the South, the plantation economy surrounded the few enclaves of industry with a social order bordering on repression. Black slaves rattled the chains of degradation only at risk of their lives. In the absence of more mechanization, a better and more extensive transportation system, and improved farming techniques combining crop rotation, fertilizers, and other advanced practices, the profitability of cotton plantations depended absolutely on cheap labor costs. Even in northern states, the prosperity of hundreds of thousands could not have been maintained except at the economic expense of millions.

Ante-bellum mansion, Birmingham, Alabama

An alternative for the country that would have sustained even at subsistence levels so many people and given hope of a more general prosperity did not then exist. In the 1840s, dozens of experiments from Massachusetts to Wisconsin in Fourierism, setting up "phalanx" communities of approximately 1,500 people to produce agricultural-handicraft goods that were the property of the phalanx while protecting private property and inheritances, as well as Owenist Societies, that combined agriculture with factory production and took even more control of individual's lives, proved impractical and an aberration to American life. As Jefferson's ideal of a nation of farmers with approximately equal prosperity and political power steadily slipped away, a muscling, driving capitalist economy came to the fore. It looked increasingly from the bottom up as if the McCormicks and Coopers, Colts and Singers were riding the engine of industrial progress while American labor was crammed inside the box cars.

Shirt factory, Salem, New York

America's first industrial workers were New England farm girls brought together in Waltham System factories by the Boston Manufacturing Company to convert cotton to cloth. After a decade of regimentation without reward, female weavers in Pawtucket, Rhode Island struck in 1824 to prevent wage cuts. Lacking suffrage and composing a much smaller percent of the workforce, they achieved little and subsequently suffered in silence. Not until a woman's movement for political and economic rights was begun July 1848 in Seneca Falls, New York by Lucretia Mott and Elizabeth Cady Stanton was there some hope of what in the late twentieth century came to be called gender equality. The Married Women's Property Act championed by Mott and Stanton through the New York legislature, permitting divorced women to keep some possessions, did not help the vast majority of working women living with their families sometimes hand to mouth. Aside from widows such as Rebecca Webb Lukens, who took over management of a Brandywine River Pennsylvania boiler-plate mill on the death of her husband in 1825, women in the work force continued to be poorly paid and ill treated.

For one thing, with the decline of home-spun cloth, they were usually not skilled at a marketable trade and therefore had no leverage with employers to effect beneficial change. Rather, it was the Workingmen's Party of craftsmen and artisans in 1828, under pressure as larger operations put smaller shops out of business, that won 30% of the vote in New York state and used that electoral clout to put forward a reform program calling for a ten hour work day, abolition of imprisonment for debt, regulation of banks and other monopolies, free education, and free public land. A series of strikes in the 1830s made progress on the first two measures, but the Panic of 1837 and high unemployment forced labor groups to merge into the major political parties. More radical demands for economic and social reform were dropped or moderated.

The reason that some employers, including textile manufacturers in Massachusetts, could resist the 10 hour work day and higher wages was that the US permitted virtually unrestricted immigration from Europe to swell the labor force. The Old World's economic problems, ethnic rivalries, and environmental disasters produced notable surges in 1827-

28, 1832, 1842, 1846-51, and 1854, pushing up annual arrivals from 10,000 to 27,000 to 60,000, and then 104,000, and then 221,000, and finally 427,000. Most were from Germany and Ireland with significant numbers of Scandinavians. The amazement for native born citizens was not that there were ethnic clashes in the cities but that there were not more. Certainly, the westward outlet drew away many of the restless and dampened tensions. However, when race entered into the picture, as in Philadelphia in summer 1834 when 500 unemployed whites rampaged in black sections of the city over job competition, dangerous conflict was possible.

No surprise to local constables, riots, damage to property, and homicide peaked in time of economic distress. In 1839 around Albany, tenant farmers took up arms over an attempt by the heirs of Stephen Van Rensselaer to collect $400,000 in back rents. The rebellion against patroonships that were a legacy of Dutch colonial times required a call up of the New York State militia to suppress. Not until 1846 when adoption of a new state constitution replaced the system with fee-simple tenure which allowed a person to sell or will his holding to his heirs were secret societies resisting authority disbanded and the situation pacified.

Larger manufacturers began to make money hand over fist in the decade before the Civil War. Ruthlessly taking advantage of the abundant labor supply, they paid wages that rose only 4% from 1851 to 1860 to an average 80 cents a day, in 2004 money equal to annual earnings of $5,200, while the cost of living escalated 12%. In industry after industry, trade unions were formed to battle for higher pay and better working conditions. Although the National Typographical Union in 1852, Hat Finishers in 1854, Journeymen Stone Cutters Association the next year, United Cigarmakers in 1856, and both Iron Molders and Machinists and Blacksmiths in 1859 took hold, the Panic of 1857 undermined dozens of others. But then on January 10, 1860, a textile factory collapsed in Lawrence, Massachusetts, killing 77 workers. Anger sparked strikes by shoemakers on February 22 in Lynn and Natick that spread throughout New England. Soon, 20,000 workers, including women, were involved. Fearful of social upheaval, employers caved in on pay and other major demands. Now the possibility existed that manufacturing and industrial workers elsewhere might demand concessions, possibly even pressing federal and state government for elements of a social-welfare state such as would soon be conceded in Germany. Before unions could take the next step, the American Civil War superceded all other problems.

In point of fact, the South's political troubles vis-à-vis the North and Midwest were a product first and foremost of economic backwardness. A veneer of big plantation prosperity in which 2,292 planters owned more than 100 slaves and only 7,600 owned more than 50 obscured a crisis of revenues and expenses for the other 375,000 slave-owners. Although 400 pound cotton bales commanded prices on the eve of conflict as high as 16 cents per pound, inflated land prices on the order of $40 per acre and slave costs as high as $1,500 per prime field hand drove return on investment for a typical 1,600 acre cotton plantation to a miniscule 1-3%. Return on investment for northern farm land, by comparison, was 8-12% and as high as 30% while land value was $35 per acre.

Caught in a vice wherein slavery was essential for the economy and social structure yet did not produce the population and wherewithal to match northern progress, the South was maneuvered into a position of escalating political inferiority and bitterness. Leaders in Georgia and South Carolina, Virginia and Alabama concluded that a policy of inaction would only lead to stronger Free State legislation in Congress to destroy the plantation slave system. Therefore, they pondered the disagreeable choice between radical economic change to promote manufacturing and free agriculture or secession and Civil War to establish independence. Because economic reform would have undermined southern society, because exploitation of black labor in the guise of slavery was the sinew and soul of southern self-worth, they opted for the latter.

Picking cotton

PART 2. BIG BUSINESS AND GOVERNMENT VIE FOR SUPREMACY: 1861-1945

Every action has an equal and opposite reaction, physicists say. The same reciprocal relationship did not apply to Economics in the US nineteenth century. After victory in the Civil War, the Republican Party gave captains of industry unfettered ability to gain monopoly power over railroads and finance, oil and steel, and other sectors of the economy. Farmers, laborers, immigrants, and consumers did not have the cohesion and clout to balance the scales. Therefore, the country divided between those who considered themselves well-off and those who did not. The surge westward to subdue the Plains Indians as well as wonderment at inventions brought forth by Bell, Edison, and others provided enough gratuitous satisfaction for most have-nots to wait for better times.

Finally, however, the government had to intervene to curb Big Business power. Competition became the watchword as much as regulation to insure that consumers got a fair shake on the price of goods and services. The Progressive Era dawned just as a proliferation of food, drug, and household products required safeguards on quality and safety. New industries centered on electricity, telephone service, and motor vehicle transportation required scrutiny to insure that financial interests did not cobble together even bigger holding companies and trusts than before.

Washington also assumed a bigger role in national economic life by advancing trade abroad and acquiring more territory, by means peaceful and otherwise. In the last analysis, a President with the ego and drive of a Teddy Roosevelt could, after the federal government acquired the administrative tools and legislative authority, direct the nation's material destiny to a substantial degree. A temporary apogee of federal intrusion into areas that previously had been governed by *laissez-faire* thinking was reached with American participation in the First World War. Briefly, the government took control of the US economy to mobilize for military conflict, in the process commanding Big Business acceptance of unions.

Both political parties placed the public interest above purely economic considerations for a generation. Republicans gave Big Business its head again in the 1920s to take full advantage of consumer demand for cars, appliances, leisure time entertainments, and even

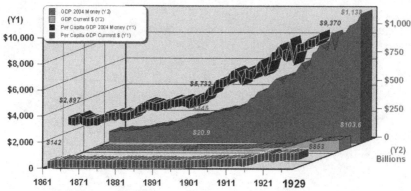

U.S. GDP Comparison, 1861-1929

Legend:
- GDP 2004 Money (Y2)
- GDP Current $ (Y2)
- Per Capita GDP 2004 Money (Y1)
- Per Capita GDP Currrent $ (Y1)

(Y1) axis: $10,000; $8,000; $6,000; $4,000; $2,000; 0

(Y2) Billions axis: $1,000; $750; $500; $250; 0

X-axis: 1861 1871 1881 1891 1901 1911 1921 **1929**

Data labels: $142; $2,897; $5,732; $9,370; $1,138; $20.9; $103.6; $853

stocks. Although higher wages and salaries gave more citizens the wherewithal to make purchases beyond just the necessities of life, wealth and income were highly concentrated in the richest 5% of households. To keep up with their economic betters, Americans of marginal means had to buy on credit. However, without the tangible and intangible assets to support such spending, they became vulnerable to the naturally occurring turn in the business cycle. When a decade of prosperity came to an end with a disastrous stock market crash, tens of millions of Americans lost everything.

Not for the first time in US history, the economy suffered a severe depression. The difference with past downturns was that the westward outlet for frustration and failure was no longer available, nor did a fortuitous event such as discovery of gold in California or Alaska relieve the gloom, nor did the business cycle swing up again with sufficient momentum to relieve the misery. As citizens lost faith in Big Business leaders, they turned to an aggressive politician. Franklin Delano Roosevelt may not have known at first how to solve the nation's economic ills, but optimism and willingness to experiment tided people over until he listened to the right adviser. Ironically, by borrowing against future income for present prosperity, the very strategy employed with such calamitous consequences by individuals and households, Washington broke the economic slump. Pump-priming the economy with massive deficit spending on military hardware and personnel to fight the Second World War achieved its greatest triumph.

This time, it was the Democratic Party that used a national emergency to adjust the political landscape. Roosevelt installed the social-welfare system that insured to this day a major role for government as guarantor of prosperity and counterweight to Big Business. Global American responsibility also required Washington to flex its muscles to keep open overseas markets and begin a push for freer world trade. However, the domestic mass market remained by far and away the greatest focus of corporations.

CHAPTER V. RISE OF BIG BUSINESS: 1861-1890

The revolution in American economic thinking heralded by Adam Smith's *Wealth of Nations* put an end to Mercantilism. It did not dispense with political interference in economic affairs. On the contrary, the national financial system, tariffs, and internal improvements pushed by Hamilton opened a new era of government involvement. US federal, state, and local laws and initiatives created an environment less intrusive and coercing than British colonial policy but still far short of Smith's ideal of an Invisible Hand of market forces alone directing the fortunes of men.

Alexander Graham Bell

Given the tenor of the times, in which North-South and East-West differences as well as Free Labor versus Slave-based society exercised a destabilizing influence on the body politic, a tug of war over government economic policy was certain. Ironically, the side that put chains on three and a half million people usually favored a hands-off approach. Not only did Southerners insist on the spread of slave plantations to preserve the political balance in Congress but preferred low tariffs to generate needed federal revenue without risking foreign retaliation against cotton exports. They believed the surest way to guarantee a *laissez-faire* attitude in Washington was to buttress states rights against federal interference and permit state bank notes to grease the economy rather than a national bank monopolizing credit.

On the other side of the Mason-Dixon Line, not only was there an urgency to position the federal government as the champion and protector of a tightly controlled financial system in which manufacturing and industry benefited as much or more than agriculture but an implacable determination to set aside virgin territories for Free Land and Free Labor. Northern businessmen and western expansionists realized that market forces alone could not open world ports to American trade, nor swiftly allocate land and resources for efficient development of the transportation and communication system, nor conquer and remove wild Indians. Rather, those beneficial ends could only be accomplished with substantial assistance and direction by government. Capitalists and would-be capitalists appealed for a *Visible Hand* in Washington to direct American economic destiny. When a clamor was added in the 1850s for emancipation of the slaves, a Republican Party coalesced across the North to push a platform emphasizing high tariffs to force reciprocal free trade from other nations, financial and land grant support for railroad construction to link East and West, and free land for settlers in western territory kept free of slavery. The secession of southern Democrats from Congress made swift and complete adoption of this plan a foregone conclusion.

Hamilton's original idea had been to protect nascent American industry against foreign competition until it acquired sufficient strength to stand on its own. After losing all hope of winning back the colonies, British investors adopted an "if you can't beat 'em, join 'em" philosophy and poured hundreds of millions of dollars into US canal and railroad construction. Now in the early 1860s the imperative of winning the Civil War provided a third impetus to US manufacturing. To insure that rifles and cannons, uniforms and shoes, gunpowder and bullets, and all the paraphernalia of war were readily available for Union armies, the Republican Party forged close associations with captains of industry. The success of that relationship led naturally to continued cooperation after the war. The fact that the Democratic Party was for a decade kept powerless in the capital by the political restrictions imposed on southerners by Reconstruction not only permitted a willful arrogance to grow in the minds of ruling politicians but created an atmosphere of greed in which abuses and corruption flourished. That is to say that those self-made men of iron and steel, railroads and oil, banking and commerce directed a not inconsiderable portion of their profits into the pockets of political allies eager to receive them. They insured that Washington's good will would remain long enough to make their economic position virtually unassailable.

Under an umbrella of government approval and support, captains of industry transformed themselves into robber barons who routed out smaller rivals, stifled competition, and created business monopolies. Powerful banking interests in New York engineered mergers and trusts to minimize the role of market forces and further maximize the control of an oligarchy of wealth. The Visible Hand of government not only clasped in friendship the Mailed Fist of Big Business but in some ways superceded it. By the time in the late 1870s that Reconstruction ended and the return of southern Democrats to Congress restored balance to American politics, the competitive maelstrom of small and medium size entities that had existed before and during the Civil War in railroads, banking, steel, oil, and agricultural commodities had ceased to exist.

With the exceptions of farmers buffeted by tight money policies and arbitrary railroad rates and working men oppressed by immigrant labor competition, low wages, and unsatisfactory factory conditions, the public was late in coming to an appreciation of the new state of affairs. The winning side in the Civil War generally approved fulfillment of the Republican platform and benefited from national economic growth. Moreover, the escalating ascendancy of organization over individual was temporarily obscured by the notoriety achieved by Bell, Edison, Tesla, Eastman, and other inventors who carried on the tradition of ingenuity established by Franklin, Evans, and Whitney. The fact that the encroachment of Big Business and Finance was required to translate the blessings of electricity, telephones, photography, and other technological innovations into new industries did not at first dampen the enthusiasm of the public for progress. In fact, caught up in the euphoria that anything was possible in this American Industrial Revolution, citizens who were prospering and expecting to prosper not only applauded the innovations that improved civilization but so wished to emulate rags-to-riches success stories that they little contemplated the control over their lives conceded to massive new institutions. Those who harbored nostalgia for the familiar, disdain for the greedy, and fear that change would undermine society were in a decided minority.

CIVIL WAR ECONOMIC STIMULUS

The Civil War not only bloodied the republic from Pennsylvania to Georgia and the Mississippi to the Atlantic but temporarily interrupted the westward movement. Governor of California Leland Stanford and merchandiser for gold miners Colis P. Huntington pressed on with organization of a Central Pacific Railroad, but human and material resources that might have been directed toward an early conquest of the Great Plains were reallocated back east for marshal endeavor. Within both the Union and Confederacy, the immediate urgency was moving men and supplies to theaters of war. Because North and South had to make due in the short term with what railroads and rolling stock already existed, the former had a large strategic advantage.

Another difference between North and South was that in the former war-spending was as much industrial as military, in the latter resources had to be directed toward battles and campaigns to fend off Union invasion without providing any economic stimulus for the future. While the Union spent $17.1 billion dollars to defeat secession, much  on manufacturing facilities that were shifted after victory to domestic production, the small Confederate infrastructure for munitions production was ultimately destroyed. The North's burden was financed in a way that did not bankrupt the republic. After a fifth was raised by the first federal income tax on incomes in excess of $800, 23% came from a manufacturers' tax and a sales tax, and another $450 million was printed as greenback paper money, national debt rose to a peak of $2.85 billion in August 1865. Over a billion dollars of Confederate securities, by contrast, whose value had been supported by expectation of profits from restored cotton exports, became in the throes of defeat worthless.

To make matters worse for the postwar future of Dixie, northern Democrats who remained loyal but did not join Republicans in the Union Party were unable or unwilling to stop passage of major planks in the Republican platform. That meant that once defeated, the South would face an economic reality of high tariffs, government subsidized internal improvements, and land grants redounding to the benefit of the North and West. A surge of railroad building in the latter stages of the war permitted rapid shipment of western produce and raw materials to eastern cities and industry. Whereas prior to the outbreak of hostilities only 132 tons of Minnesota iron ore carried on barges to Cleveland was being shipped by rail to Pittsburgh, by 1863, 235,000 tons went into thick, rolled-iron plates to make cannon barrels as well as steel for rails, locomotive castings, mine equipment, and oil refining machinery. Heavy industry then generated spin-off production, for example of wooden cross-ties for railroad tracks, to create national enterprises from ones that had previously been local and regional. In October 1861, a telegraph line with tens of thousands of wooden poles carried the first message between San Francisco and Washington D.C.

It was government favoritism to private firms that could turn out war munitions and supplies that really gave an indispensable stimulus to small and medium-size businesses. Profits the E.I. DuPont de Nemours & Company earned producing gunpowder for bullets, cannonballs, and artillery shells laid the foundation for a twentieth century business empire diversified into non-explosive chemicals with sales by 2004 exceeding $27 billion. No matter whether products were bullets or buttons, all required new and larger facilities to house the surge in production. Twenty-four packing houses opened in Chicago alone during the war while dozens of factories went up in each major eastern city each year.

So important was federal wartime largesse for later peacetime success that in 1862, the Philadelphia banking house of Jay Cooke & Company offered to become the agent for $2.5 billion in bond issues for military purposes at almost no profit. In a break from previous practices, the firm appealed to individuals of all economic backgrounds on patriotic grounds to buy the bonds rather than place them more privately with wealthy investors and large institutions. That generosity led to its appointment as the financial agency for the Northern Pacific Railroad. A June 20, 1863 National Currency Act that permitted 450 banks, including 150 state entities, to turn their institutions into national banks further established Cooke's position as a leading banking house. By subsequent legislation in 1864, all national banks were required to have one-third their capital invested in US securities and authorized to issue notes up to 90% of the value of such holdings. After a 10% tax on state bank notes imposed on March 1, 1865 forced an additional 700 state banks to become national banks, these restrictions created in effect a system of reliable national bank notes. Another consequence of Washington's actions was to encourage new bank charters. Three banks that merged into Rockland-Atlas, component of what became a century later the State Street Bank and Trust Company, thus came into existence.

Meanwhile, Huntington's lobbying effort in Washington paid off in the Pacific Railroad Act of July 1, 1862, authorizing the Union Pacific Railroad to build a line from Nebraska to Utah to meet the Central Pacific line coming east from California. Land grants of 10 alternate sections per mile on both sides of the entire distance was doubled July 2, 1864 to 20 sections per mile while the federal government agreed to take the second mortgage on railroad property instead of the first greatly facilitated progress. Ultimately, Washington granted 13 million acres and loaned $65 million to six railroad companies to link the Pacific region with the rest of the country. The loans were repaid with interest by 1899. Additionally, the land grants sold for an average of $3 per acre, but the railroads were burdened with a requirement to transport US property and the military free of charge. That stipulation was later reduced to 50% of normal rate until October 1, 1946.

The railroad building boom came at the right time for Frederich Weyerhaeuser, a German immigrant in Rock Island, Illinois. Buying tracts of virgin forest northward into Wisconsin and Minnesota that by 1880 amounted to half a million acres, he built up a lumber and sawmill empire by supplying wood not only for gun stocks, wagons, caisson carriages, bridges, and ships at prices three times peacetime rates but cross-ties for railroad track. Since each mile of track required 2,500 cross-ties made from 12.5 acres of timber, his business exploded. After the war, the innovations of vertical gang saws and circular saws powered in saw mills by water power, then steam power, facilitated the cutting of 195,000 acres of timber for 39 million cross-ties in 1870 alone

Genealogy of Railroad Industry, 1861-1930

With exports of Confederate cotton reduced by blockade to only 300,000 bales, one fifteenth the prewar total, northern wool manufacturers expanded annual production to 200 million pounds to meet government contracts for uniforms. Textile plants stocked with Singer sewing machines not only employed hundreds of thousands of persons but generated annual export of $800,000 worth of wool to England. Likewise, boot and shoe manufacturers marched with the Union Army into national prominence. The Blake-McKay machine for sewing soles to uppers accelerated production at a time when Confederate soldiers increasingly went barefoot.

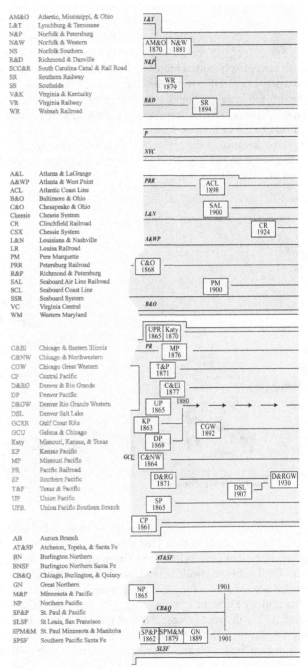

AM&O	Atlantic, Mississippi, & Ohio
L&T	Lynchburg & Tennessee
N&P	Norfolk & Petersburg
N&W	Norfolk & Western
NS	Norfolk Southern
R&D	Richmond & Danville
SCC&R	South Carolina Canal & Rail Road
SR	Southern Railway
SS	Southside
V&K	Virginia & Kentucky
VR	Virginia Railway
WR	Wabash Railroad

A&L	Atlanta & LaGrange
A&WP	Atlanta & West Point
ACL	Atlantic Coast Line
B&O	Baltimore & Ohio
C&O	Chesapeake & Ohio
Chessie	Chessie System
CR	Clinchfield Railroad
CSX	Chessie System
L&N	Louisiana & Nashville
LR	Louisa Railroad
PM	Pere Marquette
PRR	Petersburg Railroad
R&P	Richmond & Petersburg
SAL	Seaboard Air Line Railroad
SCL	Seaboard Coast Line
SSR	Seaboard System
VC	Virginia Central
WM	Western Maryland

C&EI	Chicago & Eastern Illinois
C&NW	Chicago & Northwestern
CGW	Chicago Great Western
CP	Central Pacific
D&RG	Denver & Rio Grande
DP	Denver Pacific
DRGW	Denver Rio Grande Western
DSL	Denver Salt Lake
GCRR	Gulf Coast RRs
GCU	Galena & Chicago
Katy	Missouri, Kansas, & Texas
KP	Kansas Pacific
MP	Missouri Pacific
PR	Pacific Railroad
SP	Southern Pacific
T&P	Texas & Pacific
UP	Union Pacific
UPR	Union Pacific Southern Branch

AB	Aurora Branch
AT&SF	Atcheson, Topeka, & Santa Fe
BN	Burlington Northern
BNSF	Burlington Northern Santa Fe
CB&Q	Chicago, Burlington, & Quincy
GN	Great Northern
M&P	Minnesota & Pacific
NP	Northern Pacific
SP&P	St. Paul & Pacific
SLSF	St Louis, San Francisco
SPM&M	St. Paul Minnesota & Manitoba
SPSF	Southern Pacific Santa Fe

Union Army shoes made with Black-McKay machine
Wool exports were insufficient to replace cotton and other southern commodity shipments. From $400 million of exports in 1860, the republic dropped to an average annual wartime level of less than $250 million. The Morrill Tariff of March 2, 1861 that doubled duties to 10% with further substantial increases July 16, 1862 and June 30, 1864 (that moved toward a postwar peak of 47% on February 24, 1869) shattered imports as well. Not only did imports fall from $362 million in 1860 to an average of $275 million, but privateer attacks on northern commerce dropped the net tonnage of US vessels entering US ports from 5 million to 2.9 million by war's end. Foreign tonnage rose 53% to 3.21 million to compensate. Because of the high cost of building new ships domestically, the effect of this catastrophe on the US Merchant Marine undermined the American shipping industry until the First World War.

Logging in Wisconsin

Likewise, the long-term impact on the standard of living of American workers of the Civil War was not favorable. That was principally due to the arrival of 800,000 new immigrants by boat at fares as low as $35 from the British Isles. Eighty percent had been forced out of Ireland by consolidation of small farms into larger entities. They competed with native-born workers for jobs in armament factories as well as western railroad construction. By 1865, the growing surplus of unskilled labor drove basic wages down one-third. Although overall wage rates that included skilled tradesmen rose 43%, prices during the war jumped 117%, making the working man's plight quite grim. But focused on recruitment for Union armies to bear down the South by numbers and pleased that each immigrant brought on average $50 of cash and valuables to American shores, Congress established on July 4, 1864 the Office of Commissioner of Immigration to admit contract laborers willing to trade a maximum of 12 months labor for the cost of passage. The American Emigrant Company organized to bring in even more men and families than otherwise would have come. Too, Lincoln's emancipation policy liberating by war's end all 3.5 million blacks enslaved in the Confederacy proved a boon for businessmen, a burden for other working men. Citizens who could not find a way to rise above the crowd regularly sank into oblivion.

STRUGGLES OF FARMERS AND WORKING MEN

Perhaps in no other period of American history was government regulation and control of business so weak. For more than two decades after the Civil War, industrialists and manufacturers had virtually free rein to maul competitors, establish monopolies, set wages and prices, and rake in profits. Fortunes made by the top tier of business leaders ushered in what has been described as a Gilded Age of luxury and leisure time for the elite. An enormous gap in wealth between the Astors, Vanderbilts, and others who built homes along the cliffs at Newport, Rhode Island was framed in sharp contrast against the misery of the working poor, increasingly foreign born, who scraped out a meager existence in big cities.

Government passivity in the face of what today some would call social and economic injustice can be explained in several ways. The rapidity of industrialization gave political leaders little time to understand the ramifications of the transformation washing over the republic and less to craft solutions. Even if early consensus could have been reached that monopolistic tendencies should be nipped in the bud, the prevailing *laissez-faire* attitude coupled with a traditional notion that individualism should be encouraged among the populace rather than dependency on government would have restricted the remedial choices available. Close and corrupting contacts between monopolists and the Republican Party would have stalled reform for a few more years. Too, Washington politicians were distracted by revisited issues of monetary policy, tariffs, and trade as well as by imposing a punitive Reconstruction on Dixie. They engaged in legislative battle-royals not warranted by the nature of the disputes. Not until scandal undermined the Grand Old Party's fiat to wave the "bloody shirt of rebellion" at Democrats and forced restoration of full civil and political rights for white southerners were they compelled to focus on matters of central economic importance. When Grover Cleveland broke the Republican lock on the Presidency in 1884, when Mugwump Republicans pressured the conservative majority of their party for reform, a coalition formed to put brakes on the run-away train of Big Business.

Meanwhile, the policy of welcoming immigrants with open arms continued after the war so that French historian Edouard de Laboulaye was encouraged to suggest fabrication of a Statue of Liberty in 1885. The effect of transporting to America the "huddled masses" of Europe "yearning to breathe free," as Emma Lazarus put it, was to swell the industrial labor force and suppress wages. From 1866 through 1869, 1.1 million persons fled poverty, overcrowding and war in Europe for a safer but not necessarily more comfortable existence in the New World. Because the South held on to most of its freed black labor force, almost all the newcomers spread across the North and West. And since the first wave of immigrants originated in northwest Europe, they encountered less resistance that might have been expected from native-born white Americans already accustomed to accented Germans and Scandinavians, Scots and Irish. Working men with Old World skills gave renewed impetus to trade union organization. In fact, by 1873 twenty more unions were added to the six that had formed prior to the Civil War with a membership by 1870 of 300,000. Although as a percentage of 12.9 million workers counted in the census, that figure was not very great, the share of the industrial labor force was 14.3%. Heavy concentration of union members in eastern cities boosted the figure to 50% or more in some locales, enough to contemplate strikes and other job actions to boost wages, shortens hours, and improve factory conditions. Some labor leaders formulated more ambitious agendas for social change.

Statue of Liberty

Had organized labor continued to add to its homogenous strength, a time might have come sooner rather than later of decisive confrontation — or compromise — with business and political leaders. After all, the industrial revolution in Great Britain had been attended by violent conflict, the Germany of Chancellor Otto von Bismarck had been forced to buy peace at home by conceding a social-welfare system, and backward Russia was even then lurching toward modernity and revolution by failing to do the same thing. But the westward outlet for angry American passions boosted the population beyond the Mississippi River by 7.5 million through the 1880s and the character of immigrating peoples changed. Of the 2.7 million foreigners who crossed the Atlantic in

the 1870s and 5.2 million who followed in the 1880s, the vast majority came from Italy, Austria-Hungary, the Balkans, Poland, and Russia. To aggravate still further the sensibilities of native-born white Americans, Chinese immigrants flooded into the country to work on western railroad building and mining operations. For the second time in the republic's history — repeating the Know-Nothing, anti-Catholic, anti-Irish nativism of the 1840s and 50s — a significant xenophobic reaction took hold.

Log buildings on Ohio farm

It was felt as intensely by trade unionists worried about wage rates and employment security as by middle and upper class citizens shocked by the wretched condition of the oftentimes unintelligible foreigners in their midst. When immigrants congregated in New York, Philadelphia, Baltimore, Boston and other eastern cities, they turned many an apartment block and neighborhood into ethnic ghettoes. When they then went looking for work, a lack of job skills and English-language ability kept them in the most menial positions or chronically underemployed. They were viewed by most labor leaders as a despised burden, not an asset. Consequently, skilled working men composed an important element in nativist organizations such as the American Protective Association of 1887. Although the work force in 1880 amounted to 17 million persons in a population of 50.1 million and ten years later hit 21 million people, including 3.7 working women, in a population of 62.9 million, the labor movement was divided between native-born Americans and immigrants, between trade unionists and the unskilled.

Census figures through 1890 showed that the Homestead Act did its work well in propelling millions of families westward and making property owners of the landless. The number of farms increased 80% to 4.6 million with acres under production up 26% to 623 million. Manufacturers geared up to provide farmers with all manner of machinery and equipment. By becoming centers for processing commodities and livestock, Chicago, Cincinnati, St. Louis, and Kansas City grew into larger metropolises. But as the Great Plains was conquered, it became instead a vast belt for raising wheat, corn, hogs, cattle, and other agricultural products. Congress signaled that farming was and would continue to be of cardinal importance to the economy by establishing the US Department of Agriculture on May 15, 1862 and passing the Morrill Act on July 2 granting loyal states 30,000 acres for each senator and representative then in Congress for the purpose of endowing at least one agricultural college (70 were so established). However, the industrial surge caused a relative decline in agriculture's importance through the 1880s even as the dollar value of farm production doubled. Destruction of the South's cotton plantation society and its military occupation under Reconstruction helped hinder rural America's ability to organize and respond to the encroachment on its traditional economic and political clout of big railroad interests.

On December 4, 1867, the Patrons of Husbandry, more popularly called the Granger movement, came into existence in Washington D.C. to fight a rear-guard action for the survival of farmers. It not only rallied homesteaders but gained support from small town merchants and businessmen for opposition to state chartered monopolies and for laws fixing reasonable maximum rates for freight and passengers. The inherent difficulty in an era prior to the age of mass communications of organizing millions of widely dispersed persons for collective action as well as the instinctive reluctance of independent-thinking men and women to equate their problems with the plight of urban poor forestalled creation of an effective counterweight to the burgeoning economic resources and political influence of captains of industry. When Grangers did succeed in pushing through laws in some states to curb the power of middlemen and railroads, they ran afoul of the constitutional requirement that Congress alone could restrict interstate commerce.

Supreme Court decisions reflected the opinion of only one of three branches of the federal government. Officials elected directly or indirectly by the people had to pay closer attention to the clamor of constituents. Thus, the Congress became the instrument of last resort for a generation of farmers and working people to regain control of their fate. Even when Washington got around to crafting legislation to relieve the economic pressure on the republic's have-nots, the result was scarcely satisfactory.

DISTRACTED, RELUCTANT GOVERNMENT

After the Civil War, American industrialists and manufacturers could rightly claim partial credit for defeating the Confederacy. Because of success placing into the Union Army's hands the tools of victory, there was no longer any question that government should be an ally of business and craft policies, such as subsidization of transportation and other internal improvements, such as open immigration for a surplus labor force, to its advantage. Particularly after Lincoln's assassination, Republican politicians busied themselves with hammering into place the fences of Reconstruction to keep the South in its place and Democrats weakened. The legitimate function of Congress was defined as putting the republic's fiscal house in order, not keeping an eye on what the Rockefellers, Goulds, and other would-be monopolists of the republic were about. For war debt of $2.85 billion had to be paid down, $450 million of inflationary paper money retired or reduced, and the budget balanced. A start must be made on recovering American export markets from foreign competition.

Overseas trade would be particularly important, economic thinkers believed, to pay for a backlog of imports shunned during the war. As industrial activity picked up, manufacturers needed raw materials not readily available at home. Government officials were pleased that in the first full year of peace, exports accelerated 260% to $434 million, covering all but $11 million of imports. High customs duties and continuation of the wartime income tax produced revenue the next year $133 million in excess of expenditures. Although exports then fell by 1870 below $400 million while imports remained fairly level and the overall balance of payments when including financial transactions was negative at $101 million, Congress was able to remove most excise taxes and let the inheritance tax expire. Much to the delight of prosperous Americans, the income tax was dropped altogether in 1872.

US Mint, San Francisco
During the election campaign of 1868, the Republican nominee for President Ulysses S. Grant had the full backing of

his party for paying off the national debt in gold. Although some Democrats from Ohio and other farm states advocated using greenbacks instead to promote inflation that would help indebted farmers, the Democratic nominee Horatio Seymour — former wartime governor of New York and dutiful if unenthusiastic supporter of conscription and other necessary war measures — was a conservative, hard-money man concerned about the purchasing power of urban-dwelling easterners. Thus, from the perspective of rural Americans and westerners there was little advantage to voting Democratic. Because of near unanimous support from half a million freed slaves in the six southern states permitted to vote, Grant won by 306,000 out of 5.7 million ballots but a more impressive 214-80 electoral advantage.

Arguably a great general, as 18th President Grant was detached from the administration of government and too trusting of cronies and subordinates. The good his policies did was almost always overshadowed and overwhelmed by scandal. For example, on March 18, 1869 Congress passed the Public Credit Act agreeing to pay off the national debt in gold. Since that was a major plank in Grant's program, he and his party could have expected to benefit handsomely. But on "Black Friday" September 24 Jason Gould and James Fisk attempted to corner the gold market and profit by inducing Grant, through his brother-in-law lobbyist Abel R. Corbin, to stop the government from selling gold, constrict the supply of that precious metal, and thus drive up the price. Although the President did the opposite by approving Treasury sale of $4 million worth of gold, causing the price to plunge from $162 to $135 an ounce, ruining many speculators, and making Gould's financial position precarious, the taint of impropriety permanently stained his administration.

The President's troubles left it to Congress to take the lead in selectively dismantling the high tariff policy inherited from the Civil War. On July 14, 1870, Republicans in control of the House and Senate placed dozens of raw materials important to industry on the free list and slightly reduced duties on other commodities. Two years later on June 6, duties on imported manufactured goods were cut 10% to encourage reciprocity by foreign governments and make more affordable merchandise such as luxury clothes Americans desired. Because US factories then moved with celerity to turn out similar high quality goods, the reduction only endured until March 3, 1875. In fact, for the first time, the republic became a net exporter of manufactured goods. These higher value exports boosted the total to $836 million by 1880, versus $668 million of imports, and produced an overall favorable balance of payments of $114 million.

Meanwhile, Grant's political position and authority to direct economic policy was further undermined by scandal. On September 4, 1872, the *New York Sun* newspaper charged that Grant's running mate that year Henry Wilson, the current Vice President Schuyler Colfax, Representative James A. Garfield (R., Ohio), and other prominent politicians had accepted stock in the Credit Mobilier construction company. That entity had been organized in 1864 by promoters of the Union Pacific Railroad as a method of diverting profits of railroad construction to themselves. Although not directly implicated himself and thus able to defeat Democratic publisher Horace Greeley (of "Go west, young man" fame) for a second term, Grant fell under a dark political cloud from the censure of Colfax and two lesser congressmen.

The President might yet have regained the political initiative had not railroad construction over-speculation, overexpansion of industry, and the planting of too many acres combined to boost inventories at a time when European demand for US products was undermined by a generation of peace on the Old Continent following a quarter century of abortive rebellion and war. High gold prices encouraged by Congress' passage of the Coinage Act on February 12, 1873 omitting the silver dollar from coinage caused an inadequate supply of circulating specie that also helped precipitate a September panic on the New York Stock Exchange. Grant's response was to use authority granted by Congress in 1871 to convert $26 million of long-term bonds into greenbacks and boost the paper money supply. That inadequate measure failed to prevent a recession deepening over 66 months into depression. Not only did Cooke's banking firm go under because of the inability of the Northern Pacific Railroad to pay principal and interest on loans but all railroad construction on the Great Plains was arrested. Instead of putting liquidity into the money supply, out of fear of runaway inflation Congress capped greenbacks at $382 million on June 20, 1874.

1881 Morgan Silver Dollar
Angry farmers, working poor hurt by rising unemployment, and silver miners damned the Coinage Act as the "Crime of '73" or the "Gold Conspiracy." New discoveries of silver in Nevada, Colorado, and Utah in 1876 increased the political pressure on Washington for unlimited coinage of silver at a 16 to 1 value ratio to gold. Although the Republican Presidential candidate Rutherford B. Hayes of Ohio, a hard money man, ultimately won an acrimonious and disputed election (not finally decided until early 1877 by an Electoral Commission) over New York Governor Samuel J. Tilden, Tilden's popular-vote victory of 250,000 persuaded leaders of the GOP that more attention had to be paid to the complaints of common citizens. It was fortunate that increased customs duties (producing Treasury surpluses from 1875 to 1893 and steadily reducing the national debt to $839 million) were available to buttress government finances. National affluence convinced even hard money men to vote in the affirmative on February 28, 1878 for the Bland-Allison Act requiring the secretary of the treasury to purchase each month a minimum of $2 million, a maximum of $4 million worth of silver at market prices and mint that much-

maligned commodity into standard silver dollars. Still obsessed with inflation, Hayes' Treasury Department bought and minted each year only the minimum.

Meanwhile, the Granger movement achieved a significant success by persuading the Illinois legislature in 1873 to fix maximum rates for grain storage charged by middlemen prior to rail shipment to market. Wisconsin and Iowa followed Illinois' lead the next year in establishing regulatory commissions overseeing not only warehouses but railroads. After the Supreme Court held in 1877 in *Munn v. Illinois* that states did indeed have the right to fix maximum rates for grain storage, Grangers believed they could move ahead with state regulation of railroads within their borders. A problem developed when they began to scrutinize carriers operating across state lines.

The depression finally ended in 1878, but passions did not cool for easier money and credit in the economy. A Greenback Labor movement begat a Greenback Party, which then polled one million votes across the country and sent 14 representatives to Congress. Because its program of reform included women's suffrage and a graduated income tax that seemed radical for the times, its candidate in the 1880 Presidential election James B. Weaver garnered only 308,000 votes out of over 9 million cast. Its more popular planks such as federal regulation of interstate commerce were soon co-opted by reforming wings of both the Democratic and Republican parties. In the interim, Garfield won a narrow victory over Civil War hero Winfield Scott Hancock. Already on January 1, 1879, Congress had snubbed the Greenbacks by passing the Specie Resumption Act, ordering the national debt paid down with gold and silver, and greenbacks in circulation reduced to $300 million.

The conservative fiscal reaction against mollycoddling have-nots did not extend to supporters of the Republican Party. Pressured by Civil War soldiers who styled themselves veterans of the Grand Army of the Republic, Congress passed the Arrears of Pension Act in 1879 to draw upon the Treasury for veterans' benefits. By 1885, pension payments amounted to $56 million, then $80 million in 1888. Although the Treasury was still running a surplus, the drain was severe enough for President Cleveland to veto new pension requests, including an 1887 Dependent Pension Bill.

Cleveland had his hands full with another political hot potato. In 1886, the Supreme Court ruled in *Wabash, St. Louis & Pacific Railroad. Company v. Illinois* that state regulation of railroads was unconstitutional because the Constitution had specifically delegated power to Congress to oversee interstate commerce. The outcry and protest against leaving railroads unregulated was so great that on February 3, 1887, Congress passed the Interstate Commerce Act declaring that all charges by railroads had to be "reasonable and just." The law created an Interstate Commerce Commission (ICC) with authority to investigate railroad company management, call witnesses, look at accounting books and papers, and make railroads file annual reports of operations and finances according to a uniform accounting system. Pools, which were combinations of business units to control prices by apportioning markets, were made illegal. Also banned were rebates, drawbacks, and discriminatory rates, the practice of charging more for a short haul than a long one over the same line. Railroads had to give a ten day public notice before changing rates.

However, Congress gave the ICC neither enforcement powers nor ability to fix or cap prices. Since the Commission had to get court orders to make railroads toe the line, it could respond in neither a timely nor effective manner to abuses. Making such high profits that they attracted hundreds of millions of dollars more in British investment, the railroads soon just ignored the ICC or paid lip service to its authority. The ICC degenerated swiftly to an agency that merely collected and published railroad business data.

Chicago & Northwestern train station De Kalb, Illinois Although nine decades had passed since Hamilton put in place a system of protection for nascent American industry, despite the fact that US manufacturers now had size and strength to fend of foreign competition, Congress reduced customs duties only 5% on March 3, 1883. The Cleveland administration wanted to do more, but was blocked by Republican strength in the House and Senate. In fact, in the election of 1888, the GOP attacked the incumbent on the issue of preserving a high protective tariff, as well as vetoes of veteran pension increases. Although Cleveland led by 6,000 votes out of 11 million cast over Civil War veteran and former senator from Indiana Benjamin Harrison, he lost Irish-American support in his home state of New York over alleged sympathy to the British empire. That put the Republican Harrison in the Executive Mansion with an Electoral College victory of 233 to 168 but without a mandate to move very far on economic policy. In order to insure passage of the McKinley Tariff on October 1, 1890 establishing a high average 49.5% duty on imports and right of the administration to raise rates even further if foreign governments charged higher duties on US exports, he and his hard money supporters had to agree to the Sherman Silver Purchase Act, discussed below. Although duties that year on $789 million of imports provided nearly 62% of federal revenue, foreign investment of nearly $3 billion was five times US investment abroad. The republic's overall balance of payments fell to $150 million in the red.

Decades before being tagged irrevocably with the opprobrium "party of Big Business," Republicans signaled their compassion for have-not Americans by reversing Cleveland on pension policy. The Dependent Pension Act of June 27, 1890 boosted the number of persons on the pension roll in five years by 44% to 970,000 at annual cost to the Treasury of $135 million. Further, they voted for the Sherman Silver Purchase Act of July 14 as a way of securing reciprocal support for the McKinley Tariff as well as fighting a recession that lasted nine months into 1891. The Treasury was required to purchase at market prices 4.5 million ounces of silver each month (the total US production at that time) and issue in payment for same legal tender notes redeemable in gold or silver at option of the Treasury.

Afraid on the one hand to tamper with the engine of manufacturing and industry that had boosted US GDP to $13.4 billion but afraid on the other not to take steps to bring relief to millions of farmers and workers adversely impacted by business monopolies, Congress compromised with the Sherman Anti-Trust Act of July 2, 1890. Although contracts, combinations, trusts, and other organizations in "restraint of trade" became illegal and the government could bring suit in federal court for relief, authors of the law never made clear just what constituted trusts and restraint of trade. In particular, it was not certain whether railroad combinations could be attacked nor what specific practices should be outlawed. The fecklessness of the law resulted in action against only a handful of lesser trusts. To the outrage of working men, four unions were prosecuted as combinations in restraint of trade. Embittered farmers and workers felt vindicated in their belief that the politicians occupying positions of power in Washington would never serve their interests. Thus, the social, political, and economic solutions to the nation's ills they supported became more radical in the next decade. Party leaders and candidates had eventually to respond to the pressure.

RECONSIDERING LAND USE POLICY

It is not perhaps too simplistic to state that national land policy prior to the Civil War was to acquire territory by hook or crook, encourage settlers to move into frontier districts, and permit individuals to clear forests for farming without consideration for the effect on native peoples and the environment. The culmination of this strategy was the Homestead Act of May 22, 1862. Offering 160 acres of public land free to every head of a family over 21 years of age, the government wound up giving away tens and hundreds of millions of dollars in real estate. Final title and ownership was guaranteed after five years continuous residence and payment of a registration fee averaging $30. Alternatively, recipients could acquire the land outright after six months residence by paying the old minimum price of $1.25 an acre. To insure that new property owners did not swiftly squander what had been granted, homesteads were exempt from attachment for debt. Although with men between ages 20 and 45 being drafted into the army under the Conscription Act of March 3, 1863 the intended impact of the Homestead Act was delayed, once Union forces turned the tide at Gettysburg and Vicksburg, Congress voted on March 21, 1864 a Homestead Land Bonus to soldiers with two years military service. Recipients had to remain only one year continuously to confirm title and ownership.

By 1865, family farms exceeded the prewar peak of 2.5 million. The economy received an additional stimulus from expanded production and sale of reapers, mowers, revolving horse rakes, two-horse cultivators, rotary spaders, and grain drillers until farm machinery value surpassed $270 million. Despite Union Army devastation of large plantation operations in the Deep South, the Shenandoah Valley, and elsewhere, total acres under production rose in the republic to 493 million. That increase in farm land came back to the nation in booming harvests of corn, wheat, oats, and hay as well as larger flocks and herds.

Although in addition to farming the land, the government wanted Americans to discover and extract mineral wealth, the California Gold Rush was more the product of luck than deliberation. Individual initiative rather than master strategy caused the strikes that produced gold finds in Rocky Mountain locales 1861 to 1864 and boom mining towns of Humboldt and Esmeralda in Nevada, Idaho City in Idaho, and Virginia City and Helena in Montana.

After the war and particularly as 600,000 square miles (384 million acres) were conquered from Great Plains Indians, government land policy became more purposeful. Specific legislation was designed to forward extractive industries. Only belatedly in the 1870s did the idea of conservation to preserve natural resources and wilderness beauty begin to compete with all-out development of mines for precious metals, other minerals, and stone as well as the cutting of timber. It came much too late to spare old growth forests in the East that accounted for a large part of the 200 million acres cleared in the country between 1800 and 1880. Because of the remoteness of wilderness areas, the size and expanse of the Rocky Mountains, and the unsuitability of desert (prior to twentieth century irrigation techniques) for cultivation and town-building, the West avoided in part the deforestation, over-hunting and over-fishing of wild life, and soil depletion that had scarred the East. The shift away from unrestricted development and toward balancing the wants and needs of individuals and industry for land and raw materials with environmental concerns achieved some success in preserving pristine, wilderness areas.

A homestead on the Great Plains

Moreover, Seward's purchase of Alaska from Russia in 1867 seemed to insure that the republic would always have abundant wilderness. For a price of $7.2 million, he acquired 589,757 square miles or 377,444,480 acres at 1.9 cents per acre. That was hundred times the bargain as the average price of $2.17 an acre paid (sometimes to white trader creditors of the Indians) for 86 million acres of Indian land between 1784 and 1880. Seward's Icebox turned out to be a treasure trove of mineral wealth.

It would be another quarter century before citizens got around to exploiting Alaska's gold. On July 9, 1870, Congress decided to catalogue what remained of mineral wealth in the contiguous US The House and Senate authorized a survey of lands potentially containing deposits with the objective of selling what the government owned at $2.50 an acre. Subsequently, the price was raised to $5 an acre, except that iron mining areas were offered at $1.25 an acre to encourage extractions for the rapidly growing steel industry. Since the government gave no guarantee that significant, recoverable deposits would be found, the program initially favored investors with deep pockets. However on March 1, 1872, Congress passed a law providing that prospectors who discovered gold, silver, iron, and certain other ores on public land could stake a claim, open a mine, and ultimately obtain title for the land and all surface and subsurface rights. Individuals also received the right by the March 3, 1873 Coal Lands Act to purchase 160 acres of highly sought-after plots with coal deposits at $10 to $20 an acre, depending on distance from railroad lines. Associations of more than one person could obtain 320 acres.

For the first time on March 1, 1872, Congress moved to preserve a portion of the republic in its original state. An area of mountain plateaus covering 2.2 million acres in contiguous parts of Wyoming, Montana, and Idaho famous for 10,000 hot springs and 200 geysers, including Old Faithful, was designated the Yellowstone National Park. Washington knowingly abjured a rich harvest of old growth pinewoods, bighorn sheep, elk, deer, moose and other species in favor of environmental beauty. That altruistic abstention would decades hence create a multi-billion dollar national park tourism industry promoted by Rockefeller, President Theodore Roosevelt, and other notable, nature-loving citizens.

Yellowstone National Park However, at that time the Yellowstone preserve was the exception, not the rule. A year later, Congress tried to strike a balance between protecting the nation's forests and increasing the supply of timber for building by authorizing in the Timber Culture Act of March 3, 1873 grants of 160 acres to persons who kept one quarter in good forested condition. Equilibrium lasted only five years until the requirement was reduced to only 10 acres of the total and the House and Senate passed on June 3, 1878 both the Timber Cutting and Timber and Stone Acts to accelerate development. By the former law, *bona fide* settlers and miners were permitted to cut timber on public land needed for homesteading and mining free of charge; by the latter, land in California, Oregon, Nevada, and Washington (and later public land in all states) valuable for timber or stone but unfit for cultivation was offered at $2.50 an acre up to an 160 acre limit. Ultimately, 25 million acres of public land was so distributed, raising in excess of $60 million in revenue. Only when Congress effectively repealed the old laws by passing the Forest Reserve Act in 1891 was the depletion of the national birthright of old growth forests slowed.

Meanwhile, the first gold rush in a decade brought 15,000 prospectors into the Black Hills of the southwestern Dakota Territory. Boom towns Custer City and Deadwood sprang up overnight, as did war with the Sioux and Cheyenne. Custer's Last Stand on June 25, 1876 barely caused a pause in the pace of development and rounding up of free Indians. The Homestake Mining Company eventually gained control of most operations in that formerly sacred ground to Native Americans.

In anticipation of vanquishing the Apache Indians of the southwest and opening for settlement another 160 million acres, Congress provided in the Desert Land Act, March 3, 1877 for the sale to each individual who applied of 640 acres of desert land at 25 cents an acre, provided the land was irrigated for cultivation within three years. Nearly 11 million acres were ultimately sold, netting the Treasury $2.7 million in revenue. The Apaches fought on well into the 1880s, however.

The clearing out of hostiles from the northern Rockies also rebounded to the economic benefit of the republic. A major gold strike was made in 1883 at Coeur d'Alene in Idaho followed by discovery of silver and lead at the Bunker Hill and Sullivan mines two years later that ultimately yielded $250 million of ore, in 2004 money worth $5 billion. Not for the first time, claim jumping, homicide, and other disturbances interfered with the efficient extraction of mineral wealth. Although Land Commissioner William A. Sparks suspended all titles in the country where fraud was suspected, his firing in November 1887 put back into production mines on 2.75 million acres.

Besieged by complaints from settlers and miners, railroad men and land speculators that land for development was running out in the West and that what was left should be opened for immediate exploitation, Congress passed in 1887 the Dawes General Allotment (or Severalty) Act. That measure dissolved Indian tribes as legal entities but divided tribal lands into 160 acre holdings for each head of family with an additional 80 acres handed over to each adult single person. A portion of the 52.7 million acres composing 118 Indian reservations was thereby declared surplus and opened to non-Indian homesteaders. Because the federal government retained a trust patent on Indian land for 25 years, Native Americans could not receive full ownership and US citizenship until then.

Particularly desired by homesteaders who had previously been rousted out by the US Army was fertile land in the midst of the Oklahoma Indian Territory. When on April 22, 1889, all barrier to settlement to non-Indian lands in the Territory was dropped, 10,000 people — including railroad men, real estate agents, and cattle barons interested in water rights — snapped up 1.92 million acres by nightfall. This mad rush in covered wagons and on horseback increased pressure rather than relieved it for new cessions. Another 10 million acres of Indian land was opened and claimed through 1893, dispossessing 75,000 natives to the advantage of 200,000 Americans.

Altogether in the quarter century since the Civil War, approximately 400 million acres were settled by Americans. About half that bounty was cultivated, mined, and otherwise utilized. However, in 1890 the Bureau of Census suggested that the frontier had ceased to exist in the area that would become the lower 48 states. The sudden realization that open spaces and wilderness areas would now be yearly reduced finally caused a backlash at the turn of the century against unrestricted development and the first sustained environmental movement in the country's history.

EXPANSION BUT RELATIVE DECLINE OF AGRICULTURE

The year 1866 was a golden harvest for farmers and ranchers. Although predictably the nation was hit by a postwar recession of 18 months, the region that suffered most was the war-torn, drought-afflicted South while the North was generally prosperous and the West boomed. Already wartime railroad building had boosted track to 36.8 million miles. Demand in connected cities created profitable incentive for cattle drives that brought herds from Texas to Kansas and Nebraska for shipment by rail to Chicago slaughterhouses. Through 1879, four million head were moved, encouraging the foundation of cattle towns such as Abilene (1867) and Dodge City (1875) along the way. With commodity prices at a peak and shipping rates reasonable, not a few cattle men got rich.

Chicago's Union Stock Yard

Some farmers did too but the very success of homestead grants caused a rapid build up of farm production and surplus that threatened to drive down prices. Although immigration increased the domestic market for food products by millions of mouths, when farms failed rural boys and girls could no longer count on the availability of factory jobs in big cities for a better living. Thus, the rise in industrial production 1866-78 that buoyed the economy was offset by increasing hard times in agriculture, causing GDP to remain flat in the $8.2 billion to $9.2 billion range while *per capita* income fell steadily to $180. Very low inflation boosted GDP as calculated in 2004 dollars by 55% to over $155 billion while *per capita* income in 2004 money climbed more modestly by 17% to $3,270.

By 1870, commodity prices were still at an acceptable level for family farmers to make a profit. The crunch came over the next ten years as they fell 40% from the immediate postwar peak and after brief rebound to 1882, dwindled another 15% by 1886. A concomitant rise in shipping rates forced farmers to borrow more with a consequence that their equity in land declined to only 62% by 1880 and kept falling 4% each decade until a rock bottom 38% in 1935. Farm failures, foreclosures, and dislocations became all too common. Nor did southern agriculture recover as quickly as hoped from the effects of Union blockade and Sherman's scorched earth policy. The English textile industry and other overseas markets that had turned during the war to Indian and Egyptian cotton did not switch back.

Reduced dependence on King Cotton forced the South to diversify its agricultural base and adopt better farming techniques, especially crop rotation and fertilizing to replenish the exhausted soil. Desperate for industry, southerners discovered that rivers flowing down from the Appalachians could provide in water mills power to replicate New England's success with textiles. By 1880, 542,000 cotton spindles were in use, by 1890 over 1.5 million. Dixie's textile industry amounted to one quarter the nation's total.

But it was agriculture Republicans in Congress wanted to reform when on June 21, 1866 they passed the Southern Homestead Act, allocating 160 acres of land in five southwestern states to former slaves. They intent was not only to free black Americans politically but prevent their return to subservience as menial laborers. However, most freedman had neither the capital for starting up a farm nor confidence after a lifetime of slavery to consolidate what they were given. When the law was repealed in 1872, only 4,000 black families had succeeded in carving out an independent existence.

The policy of military occupation, extended disenfranchisement of ex-Confederates, registration of former slaves and northern carpetbaggers to vote, and high state government spending on rebuilding projects as well as new public services such as tax-supported free public schools not only for whites but blacks, hospitals, and asylums was crafted in part to punish the South, in part to give blacks a chance to establish themselves in southern society. It backfired disastrously. Not only did spending and high taxation by Republican-controlled state governments boost the South's debt five fold but drove down property values and undermined economic recovery. When blacks failed to succeed as viable small farmers and had to sell out, they were forced into a sharecropper system in which white landlords determined which crops they planted. Proceeds from sale of commodities were divided one-third to landlords, one-third for black tenants, and one-third for reinvestment in farm implements, seed, fertilizer, and other necessary expenses. Even those blacks as well as poor whites who kept ownership of their land succumbed to an equally odious crop-lien system wherein the farmer borrowed from a merchant and used as collateral his crops, which were then sold to the merchant at low prices and the loan repaid. Although in the late 1870s, thousands of blacks began to migrate from the South to the Midwest, those that remained were little better than economic serfs. Millions remained in that state until the Civil Rights reforms of the 1950s and 60s.

The sharecropper system as a replacement for slave-worked plantations on about 9 million acres only brought the South's production of cotton back up by 1870 to 2.3 million bales, just 51% of the prewar total. The number of cattle and pigs was about 60% what it had been, sugar cane about 50%, and rice 40%. Although average farm size too was down to 230 acres from the 400 acre average before the war, tenant holdings were segregated in the accounting. The fact that sharecroppers answered to landlords meant that fragmentation was not as great as it seemed.

Cattle Drive

Southern difficulty notwithstanding, two trends became apparent for the nation's agricultural sector. One was a general increase in production in crops and livestock; the other was increasing specialization by region. Only a decade after the surrender of the Confederacy, 40 million acres of corn were planted, 22 million of wheat, 20 million of hay, and 11 million of oats. Farmers and ranchers counted about 30 million pigs, 30 million head of cattle, 12 million milk-cows, 9 million horses, and over a million mules. If the South was still known for cotton, tobacco, and rice, the north central states of the Midwest and Great

Plains were well on their way to becoming the republic's great breadbasket for wheat, corn, barley, oats, and other staples. Only in buckwheat, milled into flour for pancakes, did Pennsylvania and New York retain their former ascendancy. The latter state as well as Wisconsin, Iowa, and Illinois produced half the nation's whole milk. In addition to wheat Texas and Oklahoma grew cattle and sheep, but sheep herders lost range wars and had to re-concentrate in mountain states.

The Panic of 1873 was followed by dramatic changes on the Great Plains that had as much to do with nature as economics. In 1874, a severe drought and a plague of grass-hoppers from north Texas to the Dakotas ravaged the land. Aside from making it easier to conquer starving Indian tribes, the devastation also encouraged cattle barons and sheep farmers to fight amongst themselves for water rights and grazing land. Range wars, killings, and confusion endured another decade until barbed wire, invented in 1874 by Joseph F. Glidden, was mass produced by the American Steel and Wire Company to fence in pastures. Another drought 1885-87 and cold winters not only forced the last free Indians onto reservations but promoted consolidation in the cattle industry where too many head had a couple years earlier caused prices to crash. Survivors bred better cattle that could be fattened up in fenced pastures before being shipped to market.

If cattle dominated the southern Great Plains, grain farming spread across the north. Particularly in the Dakotas, railroad lines facilitated an influx of tens of thousands of homesteaders who boosted the territory's population to 540,000 by 1890. Millions of acres were put into production even before the US Army defeated the Plains Indians, but afterward tens of millions of acres were ploughed. A proliferation of machines, including twine binders (1878), spring-tooth harrows (1878), centrifugal cream separators (1879) in dairy regions, and giant combine harvester-threshers increased the value of farm machinery to $110 per farm and the speed at which farmers could work the land many fold. While producing models maimed veterans could operate, Deere sold 224,000 *Walking Culti-vators* to able-bodied men between 1868 and 1883. The *Gilpin Sulky Plow* of 1875 that let farmers ride instead of walk as well as plows, harrows, drills and planters, and after 1880 wagons and buggies made the company an industry leader.

In relative terms, agriculture declined by 1890 to only 49% of GDP, the first time in history it had not provided most of national economic production. The fall would have been much more pronounced had not farming in Pacific Coast valleys, the South, and even Rocky Mountain States added to the republic's total. The use of 1.5 million short tons of fertilizers by 1890, up from only 321,000 in 1878, also greatly increased yield per acre. The last decade of the century witnessed a near doubling of that figure while the introduction of even more farm machines, including the disc harrow (1893), brought the average value of equipment per farm to $130. However, commodity prices that held up initially during a recession that lasted 36 months from 1882 into 1884 finally collapsed because of overpro-duction and competition from foreign wheat in European markets. When state and local Granger cooperatives failed, desperate farmers finally sought regional solutions for their problems by forming in the late 1880s the Southern Alliance and National Farmers' Alliance of the Northwest.

As previously discussed, the federal government's weak efforts to relieve the debt-burden of farmers and curb monopolies cast a pall on what otherwise would have seemed by 1890 and the closing of the frontier the partial fulfillment of Jefferson's dream of a nation of small farmers. The total of 4.6 million farms would increase another 1.2 million over the next decade but without any guarantee that possession of land alone would bring perpetual prosperity. Rather, the near or distant future belonged to ambitious men such as John Duke of North Carolina who founded the American Tobacco Company on January 31, 1890 to combine the operations of the South's largest tobacco producers. When hundreds of thousands, then millions of Americans discovered that they enjoyed the practice of smoking new, slim cigarettes rather than traditional cigars, tobacco became the foundation of a much larger industry.

Less imposing and ostentatious but destined for equal success was the burgeoning business of W.W. Cargill, owner of grain flat houses and elevators in his native Wisconsin, Iowa, and Minnesota. After a quarter century of effort, Cargill owned 71 such storage facilities as well 28 coal sheds and two flour mills. Moreover, he had just begun building barges and ships in La Crosse, Wisconsin to transport his commodities. Over the next century, he and his successors would steadily expand their holdings to construct the largest privately held company in the US.

However, these were just two of the companies, and not in this era the most famous, that would become major US enterprises. The rise of Big Business as a collective economic force in the life of the nation began with a dream.

MYTH AND REALITY OF THE SELF-MADE MEN

Horatio Alger, Jr.

In 1867, Horatio Alger, Jr., a graduate of the Harvard Divinity School, published in New York City in serial form *Ragged Dick*, a story of an shoeshine boy who rose from obscurity to wealth and fame. To his astonishment, the serial proved so great a success that his publisher encouraged him to follow up in 1869 with another series called *Luck and Pluck*. Altogether over a career that stretched into the 1890s, Alger wrote 135 novels along a similar model of an impoverished boy moving from farm or small town to big city and achieving all he desired. He eventually sold 20 million books.

Although Alger's standard story line appealed to the public, it was his own personal biography that was most telling. This one-time minister in Brewster, Massachusetts, disgraced for illicit relationships with boys, made the most of a unique opportunity to become one of the most influential writers of the era. His rise was paralleled by other flawed but persistent self-made men who scratched and clawed their way to the highest pinnacles of business, manufacturing, and industry. The American Dream he inspired of reaching the top rung of society in one lifetime and claiming all material and intangible benefits accruing thereto kept hope alive for millions of working men, immigrants, and farmers' sons. Though in fact the vast majority of "self-made" men were born to middle or upper class families and had fathers who already had established a foothold in business or the professions in big cities, such fairy tale success stories did occur. They became less likely each decade as business organizations became more complex and closed down existing windows of opportunities for ambitious young men.

For example, in 1870 the Pennsylvania Railroad formed a holding company to control stock of other corporations and lease rail lines to Pittsburgh, Cincinnati, Chicago, St. Louis, Baltimore, and Washington. A new decentralized organization modeled on the Union Army with a corporate headquarters overseen by a president and several vice presidents and supported by a staff for general policy making, monthly and weekly financial calculations, legal affairs, and other matters as well as three major operating divisions run by line officers called general managers was put into place. Each division was divided into subdivisions and sub-subdivisions with men of manager rank in charge. Managers reported up a chain of command and received orders down that chain, preventing the possibility of freelancing and discretion in decision-making.

Granted, the basic holding company model in which many shareholders owned preferred stock, receiving annual dividends, while others held common shares and retained full operating control, was largely unique. Still, the trend toward more complicated corporate structures and proliferation of bureaucracy was clear. Moreover, getting to middle manager status was yearly becoming more difficult. Already by 1870, 2.1 million people labored in factories with another one to two million being added each decade. Even if a young man aspired to do what John D. Rockefeller of Cleveland did in 1862 by investing $4,000 in an oil refinery to make kerosene as a replacement for whale oil and building up a wheeler-dealer business empire, there were only a few industries with fundamentals that lent themselves to similar success. Competition to carve out an exceptional niche was both ruthless and intense. Rockefeller himself left dozens of ruined oil men in his wake and a legacy of bitterness that dogged him to his death in 1937. To rule his kingdom with an iron hand, in 1886 he established a centralized management structure with corporate headquarters being served by an executive committee of department heads overseeing production, transportation, sales, and finance as well as a large staff.

Another trend that made it difficult for late-comers to rise to the top of established industries was vertically integrated production, distribution, and sales. Among industries that became consolidated that way were beer, meats, and citrus fruits that required rapid transport of perishable product to market. Too, technologically sophisticated goods made of steel like sewing machines and reapers for which the existing merchant network could not adequately provide demonstrations, finance, and service to customers established internal wholesale and retail networks against which segmented operations could not compete. Rockefeller's way was horizontal integration by buying up oil refineries and wagon transport. Further, any patent control of innovation gave ambitious men a leg up over competitors. Sometimes just acting first led to an insurmountable lead.

Sometimes it did not, as with Cyrus Field's breakthrough success of laying an inch thick trans-Atlantic cable 2,500 miles from Newfoundland to Ireland in July 1866. Not only did he have competitors within three years who undermined his business, but another firm completed an undersea cable connecting San Francisco to Shanghai, China on June 3, 1871. Rather, the merger in 1866 of the American Telegraph Company and Western Union Telegraph Company made the field of long distance communication within the US the first to have a national consolidation. Running alongside the telegraph, of course, was the railroad.

Chicago, Burlington, & Quincy railroad bridge

Emerging in the East from the railroad building boom that began in the 1850s was a patchwork network of dozens of independent companies and lines. It became the purpose of ruthless competitors to gobble up as many as possible to achieve a sustainable size. Gould, Fisk, and Daniel Drew won a power struggle with Vanderbilt in 1866 for control of the Erie Railroad by issuing fraudulent stock securities and bribing members of the New York legislature. Vanderbilt used extra-legal means himself to combine the New York Central & Hudson River Railroad with the New York West Shore and Buffalo Railroad and amass at his death on January 4, 1877 at age 83 a fortune of $100 million.

Meanwhile, great notoriety attached to completion of the transcontinental railroad on May 10, 1868 at Promontory Point, Utah. Hammering of a golden spike joined 1,776 miles of track laid by the Union Pacific and Central Pacific Railroads over three years at average cost, excepting mountainous terrain, of $16,000 per mile. But after the Panic of 1873 exposed the US transportation network as overbuilt and caused 20% of railroad companies to fold, Gould gained control of the Union Pacific and by 1881 built up the largest railroad empire in the country, 8,000 miles of track. His holdings included the Texas & Pacific Railroad running west from New Orleans to meet Huntington's Southern Pacific coming east from California, much of the way along the 32d Parallel.

In 1878, James J. Hill, a Canadian immigrant who had lost an eye in a childhood accident but not perspicacity that fame and fortune was still possible in the railroad industry, seized the bankrupt St. Paul and Pacific Railroad and created with his steamship line and Canadian Pacific Railroad a burgeoning business empire. Eventually in 1889 with pacification of the Plains Indians, track of the renamed Great Northern Railroad reached Seattle. Four years later, the line ran from Lake Superior to the Puget Sound. Hill not only profited enormously from rail operations but facilitated farm settlements, lumbering operations, and mining along the route.

Government contacts had made Jay Cooke & Company the leading investment banking firm during the Civil War. However, the Panic of 1873 extending 66 months into 1878 struck Cooke's interest in the Northern Pacific Railroad so hard that the firm went bankrupt. Although having worked his way up through the banking business from humble beginnings Cooke paid off personal debts and became wealthy again, John Pierpont

Morgan of a well-established international banking family seized the opportunity of the Philadelphia competitor's fall to place Drexel, Morgan, & Company (later in 1895 J.P. Morgan & Company), the New York branch of his father's London banking house, at the top of the investment banking heap. His standard policy after wresting control of the Albany & Susquehanna Railroad from Gould and Fisk in 1871 was to demand participation in management before extending credit as a method of preventing poor financial decisions. In 1879, he and a consortium of banks did just that with the New York Central Railroad, pushing the railroad company of the late Vanderbilt to add the Michigan Central and control the so-called "Big Four" system of Cleveland, Cincinnati, Chicago, and St. Louis. The increased financial leverage resulting from large positions in railroads permitted Morgan's bank, the National City Bank of New York (later Citibank), and a few other New York City banks to further concentration bankers' balances in their hands.

Railroad company success in uniting east and west coasts inspired merchants who had in 1859 founded a mail order business specializing in $1 per pound tea and spices to rename their company The Great Atlantic & Pacific Tea Company. With 100 stores a half dozen years later, A&P, as it came to be known, emerged as the country's first substantial grocery chain. Peddler wagons delivered products, including *Eight O'clock Breakfast Coffee*, made by the company to stores. Selling its own brands cut as much as 30% off the cost, boosting profits.

A new industry that could not have been possible without railroad expansion was begun by a traveling salesman working for the wholesale dry-goods firm of Marshall Field, brother of Cyrus. Having grown up in rural Niles, Michigan, Aaron Montgomery Ward realized that millions of Americans in small towns and farming areas now had enough money to purchase items of practicality and interest. Thus, in 1872 he pooled $1,600 of his own money with an additional $800 investment from a partner to start the Montgomery Ward mail-order company. Only after he made arrangements to distribute products by rail did the price-list become by 1884 a catalogue containing 10,000 items and generate four years later $1 million in sales and $40 million by his death in 1913. Similarly, a station agent in North Redwood, Minnesota who sold watches part time to supplement his income named Richard Sears discovered the benefit of mass mailing. Although the first catalogue he and watch making partner Alvah C. Roebuck put together in Chicago in 1888 featured only watches and jewelry, the next decade he expanded his list to become Ward's biggest and most enduring competitor.

A Montgomery Ward Hat that becomes nearly every woman

Y 9743—VIRGINIA—$4.89

A style that pleases because it is attractive, dressy, stylish and becoming. The hat is constructed of navy blue satin braid, hand sewed over a medium sized mushroom wire frame. Trimmed with American Beauty Roses, with buds and foliage, and wide pink satin taffeta ribbon rosette at left of crown. Hat can also be ordered in black, white or brown. Mention your choice of color.

Each......................................$4.89

We solicit your order for either hat shown. Or we will on request send you free our New 1908 Spring Fashion Book, showing all the season's modes; also gowns, wraps, suits and everything for women, misses, girls and children, all at economy prices for latest, most becoming and attractive styles.

We are headquarters for the world in Women's apparel.

MONTGOMERY WARD & CO.
Michigan Ave., Madison and Washington Sts., Chicago
Nineteenth and Campbell Sts., Kansas City   OVER

Despite Ward's and Sears' successes, most Americans still bought through general stores. A number of inventions and innovations made even larger department stores that already existed in big cities with higher turnover of inventory possible. First came the cash register patented by James Ritty in 1879, then wholesale purchases of the entire output of factories by Marshall Field two years later in anticipation of customer demand. By establishing his own manufacturing plants and buying agencies, Field controlled the entire process of making goods, distributing and selling them to customers. Moreover, advertising agencies sprang up in big cities to stimulate even greater demand for goods of department stores such as Macy's in New York City with notices in newspapers and hoardings on streets. An era of vertical integration in merchandising had begun.

Meanwhile in Lancaster, Pennsylvania in 1879, the type of store that would most benefit from higher volume sales and reduced purchasing costs opened. Frank W. Woolworth opened what he called a Five and Dime in which every item literally sold for five and ten cents. Little noticed at the time, it was the beginning not only of off-price or discount stores but chain stores. The next decade, Woolworth built more such establishments to cater to the simpler needs and wants of the vast majority of Americans.

Bessemer converter

Feeding off the railroad expansion was iron and steel. Although the latter made inroads in locomotive and car construction, the former was used exclusively for rails until a plant in Troy, New York installed a Bessemer converter to gear up production of steel rails. From a negligible amount in 1864, 115,000 tons were turned out nine years later, albeit one-seventh iron rail production. Foundation of the Bessemer Steel Company and Edgar Thompson Steel Works in Pittsburgh in 1873 boosted Bessemer steel production to 1 million long tons of steel ingots and castings by 1880 and 3.5 million tons five years later. Already, however, a new and better process had been adapted in 1868 by Abram S. Hewitt in Trenton, New Jersey from a process devised overseas by a German William Siemens and two French brothers Pierre and Emile Martin. What came to be called Open-Hearth used air and oil or natural gas fuel to heat iron ore, limestone flux, and steel scrap in larger capacity furnaces. Sulfur and phosphorus impurities difficult to eliminate by the Bessemer process were thereby removed, making more usable iron ore reserves in Alabama and the Lake Superior area that by 1890 produced annually 16 million tons. Open Hearth caught up to Bessemer steel production by 1885. Thereafter, it became dominant in structural frames for bridges and buildings, wire, pipe, tubes, and armored plate. Blast furnaces got larger and larger so that the total number in 1890 had fallen to 211 from 269 a decade earlier.

At first, men like Andrew Carnegie, a Scottish immigrant and former head of the Pennsylvania Railroad's Western Division who had founded the Union Iron Mills in Pittsburgh in 1868 and the Carnegie Steel Company five years later, were natural allies of the railroads. In the 1880s with consolidation of rail networks leading to higher shipping charges for iron ore, limestone, and coal, he lost patience. Not only did he buy the Frick Coke Company, Rockefeller Mesabi Iron Ore range, and limestone deposits to control necessary raw materials but built a fleet of iron ore ships to carry same to Pittsburgh by way of a Conneaught pier he had built on the shores of Lake Erie. When he then failed in an attempt to bribe the Pennsylvania legislature to force the Pennsylvania Railroad to cut its charges, he built his own railroad. By opening sales stores in every major city, he completed the vertical integration of his business. Taking over the Homestead Steel Works in Homestead, Pennsylvania in 1888 and switching over to Open-Hearth Production, he turned a net profit by 1899 of $40 million.

Andrew Carnegie

A similar commitment to state-of-the-art technology and self-sufficiency attended Rockefeller's rapid rise in the oil industry. By 1865 with foundation of the Standard Oil Works in Cleveland, he gained the upper hand in the oil refining industry along the Cuyahoga River. When the next year the first oil pipeline from Pithold, Pennsylvania made possible a steady half decade rise in pumped crude from about two million barrels a year to 5.26 million barrels (worth at the well head $20 million), he used Samuel Andrews' breakthrough of heat generated by burning anthracite coal to evaporate oil in a distilling drum to take off refined products more efficiently in much larger refineries. On January 10, 1870, he and brother William incorporated the Standard Oil Company of Ohio to attract an additional $1 million of capital to boost refining capacity yet again and gain leverage to negotiate a special rate agreement with eastern railroads.

In 1879 with the Standard Oil Trust agreement, he brought 90% of US production of refined oil under his control. Well-head production of 26.3 million barrels the next year at $0.94 per barrel was magnified in worth by value-added refining of kerosene, distribution, and sale. Not only would a regional search for oil in Ohio and West Virginia raise production 75% to 45.8 million barrels and lower prices to below $0.80 by the end of the period, but invention of the internal combustion engine for installation in automobiles would provide a sudden and escalating need for a substance heretofore considered a waste product of the refining process. Gasoline, amounting to 40% by volume of a barrel of crude oil, had previously been dumped into rivers.

Shrewd men knew a good thing when they saw it. Rockefeller's success with the Standard Oil Trust was copied in the 1880s by captains of industry in cotton, whiskey, sugar, lead, beef, linseed oil, wheat and others. Finally, the power of monopolists to set prices too high and wages too low provoked widespread alarm among the public. Congress passed the Sherman Anti-Trust Act on July 2, 1890 to ban trusts and similar conspiracies that dominated commerce in one industry and restrained trade among states. Through 1900, the federal government brought 14 suits to break up the trusts. Substantial success was not achieved until the first decade of the twentieth century.

Genealogy of US Steel Industry, 1810-1945

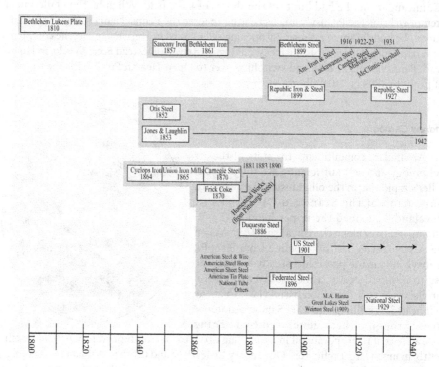

INVENTION OF NEW PRODUCTS AND SERVICES CREATES NEW INDUSTRIES

Not surprisingly, monopolistic tendencies were greatest in industries with the highest profit potential. An alternative way to rise from humble origins to wealth and fame was invention of some technological device spawning an entirely new industry. The most famous of the many mechanics and scholars, farmers and tradesmen who labored decades to make the one breakthrough that would seal their fame turned out to be Thomas Alva Edison. Born in Milan, Ohio, he found employment in Boston with the Western Union Telegraph Company. When his first substantial attempt in 1869 at innovation with an electrographic vote recorder failed to produce (until 1892) a workable machine, he moved to New York City to become a partner in the Pope, Edison, & Company electrical engineering firm. After the firm was bought out the next year, he received $40,000, with which he started his own business working on telegraph improvements.

Thomas A. Edison

By 1876, Edison had accumulated enough fortune and success to build an industrial laboratory in Menlo Park, New Jersey. Staffing it with talented assistants, he and his working group turned out over 1,000 patented inventions, one of which was the first crude phonograph, recording the words "Mary had a little lamb" on a wax disc. Only after another decade of improvements was a practical phonograph sold to the firm of Bell and Tainter for distribution to the general public. The lesson he learned was that an idea was one thing, pragmatic application another. At some point in time, cooperation with investors with deep pockets was necessary to achieve great commercial success. To maximize profits, care had to be taken to secure patent and contractual protections against the encroachment of competitors.

Edison's incandescent bulb

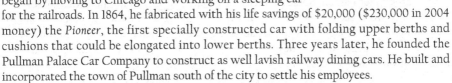

One good thing for American inventors was that government policy had consistently since the first patent law in 1790 placed the interest of legal owners of technology above the welfare of society at large. In effect, patent protection afforded time to turn invention into money rather than create a situation in which early competition forced down prices and permitted the public to enjoy the fruits of progress at low cost. If development was rapid enough, shutting out rivals not just for the term of the patent but into the foreseeable future was possible. For that reason, some of the nation's largest business empires were forged in a relatively short period of time in the 1860s, 70s, and 80s.

New Yorker George M. Pullman got started building up his business fiefdom even before the North-South conflict began by moving to Chicago and working on a sleeping car for the railroads. In 1864, he fabricated with his life savings of $20,000 ($230,000 in 2004 money) the *Pioneer*, the first specially constructed car with folding upper berths and cushions that could be elongated into lower berths. Three years later, he founded the Pullman Palace Car Company to construct as well lavish railway dining cars. He built and incorporated the town of Pullman south of the city to settle his employees.

Henry A. Sherwin of Cleveland, a banker and wholesaler somewhat better off to invest money than Pullman, bought into the Truman Dunham & Company's business selling colors, brushes, linseed oil, and painter's pigments in 1866. Four years later, he partnered with Edward P. Williams, formerly invested in a glass company, to found Sherwin-Williams. Not for another decade did they make the breakthrough that would establish their company as national leader in paints. Finally, their ready-mix paint formula that suspended fine paint particles in oil permitted homeowners to forego the tedious and time-consuming process of mixing their own ingredients. Sales mounted after the company opened a plant in Chicago in 1888 to supply finishes and paints to Pullman as well as farm equipment and carriage manufacturers. In the twentieth century, Sherwin-Williams built up a retail chain of 2,600 stores to sell brand names including *Dutch Boy*, *Krylon*, and *Minwax*.

George Westinghouse

Pullman and Sherwin-Williams never branched out beyond their main businesses. One entrepreneur who did was a Union army veteran, college drop-out, and inventor from New York City named George Westinghouse who in 1869 patented an air brake, subsequently improved in 1872, to permit rapid stopping and safe high-speed travel. That was merely the first step in creating a diversified business empire, for after setting up the Westinghouse Air Brake Company in Pittsburgh and manufacturing automatic air brakes for long freight trains, in 1882 he organized the Union Switch and Signal Company for railroad signaling by electrical controls. Once Congress the next year passed the Railroad Safety Appliance Act, Westinghouse's air brakes as well as automatic couplers became standard railway equipment.

One industry that did not succumb to regional and national consolidation was printing. The web printing press using a continuous roll of paper invented in 1865 by William A. Bullock but improved in 1871 by venerable printing genius Richard Hoe and Stephen D. Tucker was marketed to individual newspapers in big cities. The *New York Tribune* immediately installed one to turn out 18,000 newspapers per hour. In combination with a better rotary printing press by Tucker and Andrew Campbell in 1875, Hoe's triangular form folder (1881), the curved stereotype plate, and Ottmar Mergenthaler's linotype machine (1884) for stamping and casting of type metal in a typesetting machine, web printing made modern, large-scale, high speed newspaper production possible.

On the other hand, the typewriter invented and patented by Wisconsin newspaper editor Christopher Latham Sholes and two others in 1867-68 did not immediately revolutionize office work because of the difficulty of raising capital. Sholes sold patent rights to the Remington Arms Company in 1873 for $12,000. Only then did the Remington Typewriter Company begin to turn out production models that Sholes helped improve until his death. Not only clerks but famous novelists such as Mark Twain (real name Samuel L. Clemens) made use of these devices to speed paper work and creative writing.

Similar difficulty turning consumer goods into personal fortune plagued inventors throughout the period while improvements made by second comers often did better. For example, the first suction type vacuum cleaner was credited to I.W. McGaffey in 1869, but the first practical carpet sweeper brought longer-lasting fame to Melville R. Bissell. Likewise, the Kampfe brothers of New York came up with the first safety razor, but it was

King C. Gillette's modern, throw-away razor blades in 1895 that produced a twentieth century business success story. On the other hand, John Harvey Kellogg's flaked cereal (to curb sex drive, said this Seventh Day Adventist) and Henry J. Heinz's tomato ketchup in 1875 are still associated with their names. If only pharmacist Dr. John Styth Pemberton's 1886 concoction of coca leaves, water, and sugar had caught on sooner, he and not pharmacist Asa Briggs Candler of Atlanta who bought the rights for $2,300 on May 1, 1889 might have profited from Coca Cola.

Bell's 1876 telephone

In the early 1870s, Scottish-born professor of vocal physiology and mechanics of speech in the school of oratory at Boston University Alexander Graham Bell attempted to bring hearing to the deaf as well as transmission of multiple telegraph messages over the same wire. In the process of working on the latter, he came up with the idea for a magneto-electric telephone to transmit the human voice. On March 10, 1876, he proved the concept by calling "Watson, come here! I want you!" over a prototype to assistant Thomas Watson after spilling acidified water on himself. Demonstrating the success to the emperor of Brazil in June at the Centennial Exhibition in Philadelphia over 150 yards of wire with the Shakespearean words "To be or not to be," he soon had sufficient investment dollars to incorporate the Bell Telephone Company on August 1, 1877. But even as Bell workmen strung the first telephone wires on poles from Salem to Boston, Western Union used patents from Edison and Bell's competitor Elisha Gray, an Oberlin College physics professor and half owner of the Western Electric Company of Chicago, to plan a Chicago to Milwaukee system. Although Western Union quickly gave up the struggle to supersede Bell's claims (and concentrated more heavily on telegraph operations, money escorting, and other lucrative activities), 146 other companies did not. Only after Bell took over Western Electric in 1881 and an 1893 Supreme Court decision established the preeminence of his patent beyond question could Bell and his partners begin the process of unifying a national telephone system under the banner of the American Telephone and Telegraph Company (AT&T). Hundreds of thousands of miles of wire were strung across the land, connecting millions of telephones.

Meanwhile, in 1878, Edison's experiments and labors finally produced a commercially pragmatic incandescent lamp burning a filament of sewing thread converted to carbon by baking. On October 15, he established the Edison Electric Light Company in New York City. While defending himself in court battles on charges of patent infringement by Joseph Swan of Newcastle, England who allegedly had preceded Edison with a filament lamp, the next year his company installed electric arc lamps in Philadelphia and Cleveland, then opened a factory in 1880 at Menlo Park to produce incandescent bulbs. An even bigger business breakthrough came on September 4, 1881 when a lighting system powered by the first successful operating dynamo turned on lights for 85 paying customers in New York City. Within a year, he was producing electric power for the entire city. It seemed that his company would eventually energize the entire nation and in the process undermine Rockefeller's kerosene oil for the lamp lighting business as well as gas lighting of city streets.

The latter industry had risen up before the Civil War. It included companies in smaller towns such as Fort Wayne, Lafayette, South Bend, and Elkhart in Indiana that would one day be part of CenterPoint Energy. Following termination of hostilities, firms that would one day form part of Sempra Energy, most prominently the Los Angeles Gas Company, Houston Gas Light Company, founded 1866 to make manufactured gas from oyster shells and coal, and the Minneapolis Gas Company, begun in 1870 to do the same from coal and oil, swiftly established themselves in their communities. In the 1880s, they were all threatened with extinction by electricity.

Although many Edison power companies were formed, including Edison Electric of Detroit in 1886, his system relied upon direct current, an electrical charge that does not change direction and loses potency over long distances. That delayed for a decade the replacement of kerosene city lamps and gas lighting by electricity and opened the door for a Hungarian immigrant and naturalized US citizen of genius named Nikola Tesla. After arriving in the country virtually penniless in 1884, he worked briefly for Edison and then on his own to invent an alternating current system. Unlike direct current, alternating did change direction many times per second and was transmittable at steady power over long distances.

Niagara Falls electric power plants Tesla sold patents for motors (perfected 1888), high frequency generators (1890), and the *Tesla* coil or transformer (1891) to the Westinghouse Electric Company. In 1893, Westinghouse put an alternating current system together to light up the World's Columbian Exposition in Chicago. That was the breakthrough that won a contract to install Tesla's system and not Edison's at Niagara Falls. The plant transmitted hydro-electric power 22 miles over high-tension wires to Buffalo, New York.

The success of Edison and Tesla permitted the Westinghouse Company to branch out into trolley car motors, electrical brakes for subway cars, and consumer electronics products. The 1880s also saw an electric fan by Schuyler Skaats Wheeler, an electric flatiron by Henry W. Seely, an electric welding machine by Elihu Thomson that would soon have a use in the auto construction industry, an electrolytic process for refining aluminum by Charles Martin Hall that led in 1888 to foundation of the Pittsburgh Reduction Company (later Alcoa) and an 84% reduction in five years in the price of aluminum ingots to $0.78 cents a pound, and in 1889 an electric sewing machine by the Singer Manufacturing Company. All these inventions required real-time generation of power through electrical outlets. In 1890, the National Carbon Company marketed the first commercial dry-cell battery under the brand name *Ever Ready* which launched a perpetual search for devices that could store and transmit ever greater wattages of power.

***Roebling's Brooklyn Bridge,
Constructed 1870-1883***

In addition to telephones and electrical power, the other new novelty of the time that would result in a far-flung business empire was the camera of George Eastman of Rochester, New York. In 1880, the 26 year old inventor patented a dry-plate process for capturing photographic images on film. Four years later, he came up with a paperback flexible roll film and incorporated the company with 14 shareowners contributing $200,000 in capital. Four years after that, he produced the first *Kodak* hand camera, assuring customers that "you push the button, we do the rest."

With far less fanfare than the breakthroughs of Bell, Edison, and Eastman, new techniques for large batch and continuous processing began to boost manufacturing productivity. In 1884, chief engineer of the Midvale Steel Company Frederick W. Taylor developed what he called "scientific management" practices for the minute subdivision of labor into single specialties on the factory floor, strict record keeping to speed the flow of materiél through plants, internal cost accounting to determine where efficiencies and inefficiencies in production existed, and plant layout to eliminate bottlenecks. His improvements were so successful that Midvale boosted output 300% by 1890, permitting pay raises for workers ranging from 25% to double previous wages. Not only did he design and have constructed the largest steam hammer to that time but came up with over 100 other useful inventions. Afterward in 1893, he became a consultant for the Bethlehem Steel Company. He published books on scientific management and other topics until his death in 1915.

Interior of a power house

Equally as unheralded as factory innovations, the insurance industry grew into a more important sector of the economy by making Americans of various status and wealth realize that they now had much more to lose. The expansion of railroads, factories, and big businesses had created hun-

dreds of millions increasing into billions of dollars in fixed asset wealth while profits in key industrials were producing substantial financial assets. Naturally, there had always been fear that fire such as had burned out 52 acres and 700 buildings in lower Manhattan on December 17, 1835 at cost of about $20 million in property damage (14% of the total in the district) and 4,000 jobs would turn budding prosperity to ashes. The accelerating human cost of the Civil War gave a new impetus to life insurance. Opportunely in 1863, New York businessmen pooled $100,000 to start the National Union Life and Limb Insurance Company to insure Union soldiers and sailors against disabilities from accidents, disease, and war wounds. That was the beginning of the institution that became Metropolitan Life Insurance (MetLife), focusing on life insurance policies in 1868.

The great Chicago fire of 1871 destroyed 2,000 acres and property worth $200 million, rendered 100,000 persons temporarily homeless, and weeded out three-quarters of the 200 insurance companies legally obligated but financially unable to cover losses. The Panic of 1873 bankrupted three dozen life insurance companies in New York State. But within six years Met Life was able to recover sufficient strength to offer workingman's insurance, an idea imported from Britain. Five and ten cent weekly premiums to protect life and limb made so much sense to American industrial workers that by 1880 the company exceeded a quarter million such policies, bringing in nearly $1 million in premium.

General prosperity in the decade of the 1880s caused a new surge in interest in life insurance. Two other companies founded during the Civil War, John Hancock Mutual Life Insurance Company of Boston and Travelers Life & Annuity of Hartford, contended with MetLife, Prudential Insurance of Newark, New Jersey (1875), and others for the growing pie. Travelers was particularly innovative, coming up with a retirement income contract in 1884 and employers' liability insurance, an early form of workman's compensation, five years later. The company subsequently offered a double indemnity life insurance contract that paid double the face amount for death by accident. Too, there was Chubb & Son, capitalized at $100,000 by Thomas Caldecot Chubb, his son Percy, and 100 merchants that in short order became the most successful marine underwriters. The primary business was insuring ships and cargoes sailing out of New York harbor.

Even greater gains were ahead for the insurance industry as the republic reached a population of over 63 million and the larger pool of policies spread the risk of promising millions of dollars in benefit payments. New types of insurance would be offered as inventions created the need, and broader prosperity for the people created the wherewithal, to pay for more protection. Naturally, insurance companies became increasingly concerned that customers make a maximum effort to avoid taking actions leading to the filing of claims. Specifically where life insurance, health, and accident policies were concerned, they desired the very best medical care for citizens.

In point of fact, the American health care system was woefully inadequate. Although both the first general hospital begun way back in 1752 by Thomas Bond and a medical college thirteen years later had been located in Philadelphia, sanitary conditions in the nation's first capital had been so appalling that a severe yellow fever epidemic had swept away thousands in 1793. Foundation between 1783 and 1810 of the Massachusetts Medical School and several other such institutions as well as the arrival from England of Joseph Priestley in 1795 to chair the department of chemistry at Princeton stimulated medical advances, but improved knowledge, training, and techniques were slow to catch up with the march of Manifest Destiny westward. During the Civil War, medical care was still so poor that two-thirds of the 618,000 men who died were killed by disease.

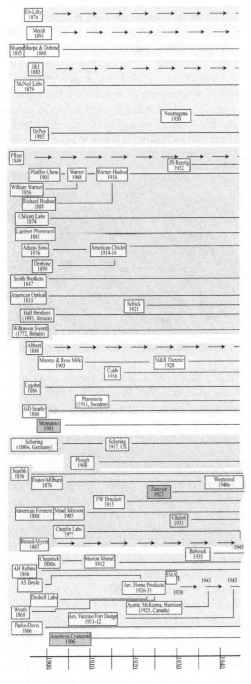

Genealogy of US Pharmaceutical Industry, 1845-1945

After the Panic of 1873 and shuttering of so many insurance companies, state governments and private educational institutions finally realized something must be done. Over the next 17 years, they financed the opening of 112 more medical schools. Simultaneously, a small pharmaceutical industry took root. Chemical makers Pfizer of New York City (1849), John Wyeth & Brothers of Philadelphia (1860), and Eli Lilly, founded in Indianapolis in 1876 by Colonel Eli Lilly, a Civil War veteran who had witnessed the North-South bloodletting firsthand, all concocted and manufactured medicinal drugs. In 1886, Lilly even hired a full-time scientist for research of new pharmaceuticals. Another specialist, Dr. Wallace C. Abbott, founder of Abbott Laboratories, began making dosimetric granules in his north side Chicago apartment in 1888. Except for Pfizer's non-pharmaceutical breakthrough of importing concentrated lemon and lime to make citric acid for soft drinks, companies involved in health care by-and-large did not yet become great commercial successes. They prepared the ground, nevertheless, for the flowering of yet another big American industry.

EMBATTLED INDUSTRIAL LABOR

For a time, Homestead Act giveaways of tens of millions of acres of land persuaded farmers that the federal government had their best interests at heart. Building agricultural production sustained that illusion until the failure of the Interstate Commerce and Sherman Anti-Trust Acts to reign in big business monopolies proved it was not so. Working men in eastern cities, by contrast, had always understood the bias of Washington in favor of captains of industry. They muted their protests during the Civil War because government contracts for war matériél, clothing, and supplies kept production humming and themselves employed.

On the other hand, the flood of immigrants that began in the 1860s was ominous as was the appearance of newly freed slaves. Once conscription ended, war dead were buried, and no more young men had to be sent into battle, a surplus of unskilled labor rapidly mounted. That was why leaders of trade unions moved with dispatch to secure as many wage and job improvement concessions as possible. While they had the leverage of a finite number of skilled workers with which to pressure employers, they wanted to take advantage.

Railroad car work shop Unfortunately for
trade
unionism,
manufac-
turers found
a quicker
way to
replace
skilled
workers than

training the unskilled. The adoption of machinery, new production techniques, and better technology boosted output 6% annually between 1865 and 1880. Because the labor surplus enabled employers to keep wages flat, prices passed along to consumers dropped by an average 3% a year. Those workers who had jobs gained a minor measure of affluence. Yet even the skilled had to work long hours to feed their families and obtain a few luxury items. It was clear that in the long term open immigration and mechanization would undermine the standard of living of working Americans.

That was why a Boston machinist named Ira Stewart and author George E. McNeill formed the National Labor Union in Baltimore in August 20, 1866. They wanted to secure an eight hour day for the same daily wage goal that had yet to be obtained for 10 and 12 hour shifts. By contrast, a second national organization called the Order of the Knights of St. Crispin (an ancient Roman shoemaker) was formed in Milwaukee on March 7 the next year by skilled shoemakers angry had being precipitously replaced by apprentices and unskilled workers trained to operate Blake-McKay machines. It grew steadily over the next three years to 50,000 members in a vain attempt to save an old craft from the technology of a more modern era. Only US government mechanics and laborers had their daily hours cut to eight by an 1868 act of Congress. Bitter and frustrated at industry resistance, Stewart and McNeill shifted from specific wage and hour-related issues to an overall program of political reform.

Hard economic times tend to boost interest in unions, but Labor organizations are like any other going concern in that they must have revenues to survive. Thus, the Panic of 1873 collapsed in four years 21 of the 30 unions then in existence and cut cumulative membership by five-sixths to 50,000. Labor's image with the public was badly damaged by a riot in New York City's Tompkins Square on January 13, 1874, in which 10,000 people marching for public works programs were routed by mounted police, and the violent reactions of Irish coal miners in eastern Pennsylvania against low wages, high company store prices, and dangerous work. A secret miners organization there called the Molly Maguires destroyed property, committed homicides, and generally conducted a minor reign of terror. Ten members were eventually hanged in 1877 for murders of Lehigh Valley Railroad agents and two coal mine bosses.

The nation's railroads were a particular target of organized labor for relying heavily on immigrants. For example, importation of Chinese coolies to work on the Central Pacific led to bloody conflict with Irish laborers on the Union Pacific. But when in the trough of economic depression in 1877 railroad management collectively cut brakemen pay around the nation 10 cents to $1.75 a day for 12 hours of work, equal in 2004 money to an annual income of over $9,000, railroad workers not only walked out but called for a national strike of all workers for July 17. Riots broke out in Baltimore, Chicago, St. Louis, and Pittsburgh in response. In fact, strikers temporarily took the B&O station in Martinsburg, West Virginia and beat off state militia at cost of nine persons dead. In Pittsburgh on July 21, militia from Philadelphia fought a pitched battle with a mob that tore up tracks, burned a machine shop, destroyed the Union depot, and caused nearly $10 million property damage and another 26 deaths. The Martinsburg eruption prompted President Hayes to send in federal troops. Several state legislatures revived old conspiracy laws to prosecute strikers.

Because in January 1878 the time was right for formation of a national union, a secret tailors' group in Philadelphia went public to make the attempt. This Knights of Labor organization hit its stride the next year after railroad worker and mayor of Scranton, Pennsylvania Terence V. Powderly took over leadership with a program of using boycotts instead of strikes and demand for arbitration of grievances rather than violent protest. By championing an eight hour day for all Americans and admitting unskilled as well as skilled workers, the Knights soared to 750,000 members in 1886. Their greatest successes came in 1884 when blockage of Gould's Union Pacific Railroad and Southwest System freight trains at St. Louis over firing of a foreman won a reversal, and the next year after another boycott by shop mechanics compelled his Missouri Pacific and Wabash Railroads to reverse a wage cut of 10% and give more consideration to Knight's members.

Meanwhile, the livelihoods of skilled shoemakers suffered a fatal blow in the merger of shoe manufacturers Charles Goodyear and Gordon McKay. By committing fully to machine sewing or welt manufacture shoes and unskilled labor, the Goodyear Shoe Machinery Company upped production to 12 million pair by 1890 at affordable prices for consumers. Too, in the clothing industry, installation of cutting machines and mechanical pressers dramatically boosted volume. A system of subcontracting sewing work to independent producers paying immigrant women minimal wages on up to 16 hour shifts created "sweat shops" with terrible conditions in tenement buildings.

As usual, Congress was slow to react to changing conditions. The House and Senate finally moved as part of an anti-Chinese coolie movement to forbid with the Contract Labor Law, February 26, 1885 import of contract laborers except for professional, skilled, and domestic labor. That did nothing to slow the pace of European immigration and alleviate worsening conditions in eastern cities. In the midst of generally good economic times, the anger of working men became red hot.

Powderly's ambition was not merely improvement of the working man's lot but a broad political reform including a graduated income tax, consumers' and producers' cooperatives for ownership and operation of businesses, and other notions considered highly radical for the times. However, he always emphasized non-violent methods for achieving change and a willingness to be patient. That wisdom was lost on other Knights of Labor leaders who called a national strike for May 1886. In 1,600 different locations, 600,000 people walked off their jobs, most on May Day (May 1). But that impressive display of union solidarity backfired after a mass protest on May 4 at the McCormick Haymarket Square plant in Chicago turned into a riot. A bomb was thrown, seven police officers were killed, and 70 other persons were wounded.

Samuel Gompers

The impact on the Knights of Labor of the Haymarket outrage and the consequence for the idea of a national union of skilled and unskilled workers was catastrophic. Over night, they lost all public sympathy and became the target for vigorous government harassment and prosecution. Rather, the American Federation of Labor (AFL) of skilled workers organized December 8, 1886 in Columbus, Ohio with 25 trade unions and 150,000 members became Labor's best hope for acceptance and success. Headed by British immigrant and cigar factory worker Samuel Gompers, the AFL focused pragmatically on shorter hours, better wages, and integration into the Capitalist system.

Not until the Progressive Era began in the twentieth century would exposure of the plight of sweat shop workers again soften the public's mood toward organized labor. Not until the First World War, would Labor gain by cooperation with government and business the respectability it needed to gain a firm foothold in the American economic system. In the interim, the AFL survived by carefully eschewing radical proposals and violence. Although after the Supreme Court's *US v. Debs* decision in 1894 the Sherman Anti-Trust Act was used as a weapon not only against business monopolies but labor unions, Gompers organization was not targeted.

CHAPTER VI. CAPITALISM WITHIN A PROGRESSIVE ENVIRONMENT: 1890-1913

The year 1890 was a natural moment for leaders of the American Republic to take stock. With the collapse of Indian resistance to white encroachment, the full resources of the country lay open to economic exploitation. However over the previous century, the clearing of forests, hunting of game, and mining of minerals had so depleted trees, animals, and even earlier discovered deposits of ore that announcement by the Census Bureau that a definable frontier no longer existed made citizens realize that the nation's bounty was not inexhaustible. More careful planning was required to insure that production of lumber, meat, furs, staples, and other agricultural products continued at a sustainable and increasing pace.

Farming was still of vital importance to the economy and livelihoods of Americans. One-sixth of the nation's 63 million people worked on 4.6 million farms, generating directly from production of wheat, cotton, corn, and tobacco, herds of cattle, hogs, and sheep, and indirectly through food processing and farm machinery a substantial portion of the country's $13.4 billion in gross domestic product. Agricultural products made up the vast majority of the nation's $858 million in annual export. Over 620 million of the nation's 1.97 billion acres were under cultivation. That figure would climb to 878 million cultivated acres by 1910 and just over 1 billion in the 1930s. Although the mechanization of farms and use of fertilizer, crop rotation, irrigation, and other techniques boosted production again and again, large surpluses not exhausted by domestic need and foreign demand suppressed prices and profits. As agriculture became less manpower intensive, farms could no longer sustain an increasing population. Yet number of farms continued to increase throughout the period.

Thus, the manufacturing sector of the economy had increasingly to carry the material fortunes of the country. Hamilton's plan and the energies of succeeding generations had raised up major industries in construction, textiles, iron and steel, transportation, and food processing. Domestic capital available for investment had now reached a level sufficient to spawn new industries and plant construction without infusions of foreign capital. Prototype machines for ground and even air transportation would be built or bought for as little as a $25,000, about $515,000 in 2004 dollars. Equally prideful, special areas of American know-how provided an additional boost to manufacturing efficiency. After the turn of the century, the US machine tool industry vaulted to undisputed world supremacy with electrically driven, high-speed cutting tools, power presses, heavy portable machine tools, and improved pneumatic (compressed air) tools.

George W. Carver

The manufacturing bug lifted even the impoverished South out of the wreckage of Civil War destruction. New textile factories powered by hydro-electric power brought a measure of prosperity to piedmont towns. The amazing innovations of George Washington Carver, born the son of black slaves in 1860 and illiterate until age 20, brought credit to Dixie, though southern whites still looked down on African Americans. As director of the department of agricultural research at the Tuskegee Institute in Alabama, he conducted chemical experiments with peanuts, sweet potatoes, and soybeans that over time helped diversify the South's economy into other industries. For example, he discovered that derivatives of sweet potatoes could be used to make flour, glue, ink, molasses, rubber, and vinegar. From peanut oil he produced cosmetics, dyes, linoleum, medicines, plastics, soap, and wood stains. Indeed, because of Carver's ingenuity the South's peanut crop sprang up from nearly no harvested value in 1900 to the region's second cash crop in 1940. Five million acres of this nitrogen-restoring wonder were planted during the Second World War.

For all the country's progress in the last decades of the nineteenth century, the standard of living of most citizens had not risen very high. Not only did the top 1% of households control 50% of private wealth but blacks in the South, Indians in the West, and immigrants still crossing the Atlantic annually in record numbers had little or no net worth. The disappointed expectation of the latter group, boosted by another 17 million persons between 1890 and 1914, at not finding eastern cities paved with gold worried politicians, business leaders, and military thinkers. Some feared a revolution in which newcomers with radical ideas would make common cause with disaffected farmers and native-born laborers to overthrow the republican form of government.

Solutions were sought that would not only double the nation's overall economy but improve standards of livings. Although GDP had increased threefold since 1860, *per capita* GDP had only ascended as a percentage by half as much. A sharp depression that bottomed out in 1894 reduced *per capita* GDP below $200 for the first time since 1879, in fact descending to only $194, the same level attained in 1863. A majority of citizens feared that they would slide back toward the general poverty of the pre-Civil War era.

To prevent dislocation and upheaval, American strategists headed by naval Captain Alfred T. Mahan came to the conclusion and convinced political leaders that an imperial push to secure overseas colonies and markets for surplus American production was required to restore the economy. The difficulty lay in the fact that European Great Powers had already in preceding decades seized the choicest real estate in Africa and Asia. The US was left with no better alternative than to confront and overwhelm in 1898 the weak Spanish empire for control of unstable Cuba, Puerto Rico, the Philippines and Guam. Hawaii was opportunistically annexed to form an American island empire across the Pacific.

Scattered possessions were more of a burden economically than an asset. When Americans recoiled at assimilating and granting citizenship to "little brown brothers," statehood for the islands was rejected. Fortunately, a more peaceful remedy for American economic ills than further territorial conquest was at hand in the amazing aggregation of inventions and technological advances perfected by Bell, Edison, Tesla, Eastman, and others. The new industries they championed as well as advances made in Europe toward a workable steam-powered vehicle for transportation over dirt and paved roads inspired the imaginations and energies of thousands of citizens. In the process, American mechanics backed by entrepreneurs and financiers jump-started an industry that would maximize the potential of Rockefeller's oil and Carnegie's steel. Profits from mass production of automobiles eventually made possible not only employment for tens of thousands but "living wages" with which working men could for the first time take a share in the material American dream.

Cotton mill Rocky Mount, North Carolina Evidence of an up-tick in the general standard of living shows up in broad statistics for the period. The expansion of new US industries between 1890 and 1914 lifted GDP another 255%, providing to be sure a disproportionate windfall for the wealthy but boosting as well average *per capita* GDP by nearly 165%. With the determination of progressive-minded politicians to regulate business practices and monitor societal conditions with a more discerning eye, life expectancy at birth for women at the turn of the century reached 48 years and men 46, not impressive by current standards but significant for the times. The promise of America's new industrial might was better housing, more and better food, a diversity of labor-saving products, further real and significant gains in living standards, and longer and more fruitful lives for citizens.

DEVELOPING A REGULATORY ENVIRONMENT

At first in the 1890s, it did not appear that the alliance of conservative politicians and aggressive businessmen that had controlled the country and economy since the Civil War could be shaken. A November 1890 failure of the British banking house Baring Brothers caused London investors to redeem US securities for gold but did not cause undue concern in American financial circles used to boom and bust cycles. However, after both the Philadelphia and Reading Railroad and the National Cordage Company went bankrupt over the winter of 1892-93 and the Treasury's gold reserve plunged to $100 million by April 21, 1893, stock values on the New York Stock Exchange, that had witnessed its first one million share trading day only seven years before, plummeted on May 5. In the ensuing business panic, no fewer than 600 banks, 74 railways, and 15,000 other firms failed, rendering 20% of the nation's 24 million workers unemployed.

To stem the drain on the Treasury's reserve, Congress repealed the Sherman Silver Purchase Act requiring the government to redeem treasury notes with gold. However, passage of the McKinley Tariff with general duties at 49.9% discouraged foreign imports and caused retaliation against US exports. Escalating pension payments to aging veterans of the Civil War made the situation worse. In 1891, the government faced a $61 million deficit, its first shortfall in 26 years. Thus, when Congressman William Jennings Bryan (D., Nebraska) rose up to demand free and unlimited coinage of silver at a 16 to 1 ratio with gold, pressure from a coalition of angry farmers and laborers motivated Congress in 1894 to pass as part of the Wilson-Gorman Tariff a small income tax. The legislation was promptly on May 20, 1895 voided by the Supreme Court in *Pollock v. Farmers' Loan and Trust Company* as a direct tax that per the Constitution had to be levied by apportionment among the states. Even had the government acquired at that time more revenue, no consensus existed among fiscally conservative Democrats led by President Grover Cleveland and Republicans adamantly opposed to anti-business legislation to use the windfall for a silver purchase plan or any other inflationary stimulus for the economy. Firmly committed to the frontier philosophy that individuals should pull themselves up by their own bootstraps, political leaders would not contemplate government largesse for needy citizens who, unlike civil war veterans, had not performed distinguished national service.

Without the wherewithal to fight the depression, Cleveland concentrated on financial manipulation to boost the gold reserve from its nadir of $41 million in February 1895. For a fee of $1.5 million and collateral of 3.5 million ounces of gold (which had been purchased by US bonds), he persuaded J.P. Morgan's banking establishment to loan the government $62 million. When the gold reserve fell again in December to $79 million, he had the Treasury offer $100 million in bonds to the public. That infusion tided the government over until the natural business cycle ended the depression.

Anvil gold mine, Alaska

But Bryan split the party and won the Democratic nomination for President with a July 8, 1896 "Cross of Gold" speech urging free coinage of silver to make repayment of debts easier. He was successfully opposed by Republican candidate William McKinley, who rode news of an August 16 gold strike near Dawson in the Klondike Creek tributary of the Yukon River of Canada, 50 miles east of the border with Alaska, as well as public fear of the inflationary effect of Bryan's plan to victory in the November election. Subsequent gold discoveries in Alaska simultaneous with a new process that dramatically boosted gold extraction from ore caused US production of the precious metal to peak in 1900 at 120 metric tons, 31% of the world total, worth $73 million equal to over $1.5 billion in 2004 money. By the Currency Act of March 14, the US went on the "gold standard," an international system pushed by the British to stabilize currencies and exchange rates. Accordingly, the dollar's worth was tied to a gold dollar of 25.8 grains, nine-tenths fine while the Treasury established an official gold reserve of $150 million paid for by bonds to redeem legal-tender notes. More national banks with capital not less than $25,000 in towns of at least 3,000 persons were authorized.

Meanwhile, the Supreme Court, led by conservative chief justice Melville W. Fuller, eviscerated part of the weak regulatory power of the federal government put in place in the Sherman Antitrust Act to scrutinize industry. In the 1895 *US v. E.C. Knight Company* case, the justices held that the law only applied to manufacturing combinations engaged in interstate commerce, not other businesses whose manufacturing operations were intrastate. Since at the time most US industry was limited to the latter, the Sherman Anti-Trust Act could not be used to break them up. Only the largest trusts and monopolies with interstate operations need be wary. Moreover, with the pro-business administration of McKinley firmly ensconced in Washington, ICC regulators were disinclined to investigate the predatory practices of Carnegie, Rockefeller, and other overt monopolists. Reform on a national basis was effectively squelched.

Rather it was at the state and local level that Progressivism sprang up. Future President Teddy Roosevelt carried a reforming banner into the New York legislature 1882-84 to fight corrupt city governments, cronyism, and vote buying, then brought his impeccable reputation for honesty to the newly depoliticized US civil service commission 1889-95. What the impending movement needed more than piecemeal success was broad public exposure of and outrage over economic, political, and social inequities. The instruments of that publicity became at first not politicians but the press.

William R. Hearst

In the 1890s, newspaper tycoons William Randolph Hearst with his *New York Journal* and Joseph Pulitzer and his *New York World* seized upon Spanish repression of Cuban rebels to invent what came to be called "yellow journalism." Sensationalized reporting highlighted by photographs, inflammatory cartoons, and manufactured facts pressured McKinley to intervene with diplomatic initiatives and finally military force. Damage to US business interests on the island contributed to the President's reluctant decision. The real beneficiary was Hearst, expanding his media empire by 1934 to

include 30 papers, two wire services, the *King Features* syndicate, six magazines, and the *American Weekly Sunday* supplement. Along the way, he used his clout to advocate the eight hour work day, public ownership of utilities, and popular election of US senators. Other newspaper chains joined the Progressive bandwagon to take advantage of the aroused public mood.

Robert La Follette

Thus after the Spanish-American war ended in just a few months, reporters hit on the idea of writing what Roosevelt later called "muckraking" stories about domestic ills. Specifically, they revealed the abuses of sweat shops in the garment industry, long hours and mistreatment of child labor, unsanitary conditions in the food processing industry, unabated monopolistic practices in business, and corrupting connections between businessmen and politicians. Opinions and many votes were swayed, for example to elect in 1900 on a third attempt Robert M. La Follette governor of Wisconsin. La Follette's program centered on sweeping regulation of railroads and utilities, regulation of working conditions, establishment of workers compensation for those injured on the job, substantial taxes on business profits, and graduated taxes on inherited fortunes. Although business men could count on McKinley not to upset the national economic applecart, to insure reelection the President was compelled to accept Roosevelt as vice presidential running mate. McKinley's assassination in Buffalo in the late summer of 1901 put T.R. — "that damned cowboy," McKinley's Ohio political handler Marcus A. Hanna called him — into the White House.

Without that accident of history, the Progressive movement and its impact on business and the economy would not have been so striking. Simultaneous with a Big Stick policy of building the Panama Canal (with Ingersoll-Sergeant drills supplementing the labor of 34,000 West Indians) and dominating the Caribbean, the young President ordered Attorney General Philander C. Knox to bring suit in federal court on March 10, 1902 to break up the Northern Securities holding company. Put together by Morgan, Hill, and Harriman, the monopoly dominated railroad shipments of farm products, coal and steel, oil, cotton, and flour from the Great Plains to the Northwest. By a 5-4 decision in 1904, the Supreme Court, still led nominally by Fuller but increasingly under the influence of his more progressive successor Edward D. Douglas, dissolved the entity as an illegal combination in restraint of trade. Emboldened by that judgment and encouraged by the President, the ICC then used powers granted under the Elkins Act of February 19, 1903 to ban railroad rebates as a deviation from published rates and appeal to federal courts for injunctions. After Roosevelt's overwhelmingly popular election as President in his own right in 1904, the Hepburn Act of June 29, 1906, gave the ICC power to fix just and reasonable maximum railroad rates and set uniform accounting methods.

In fact, the commission's jurisdiction was broadened to include sleeping-car companies, oil pipelines, ferries, terminal facilities, and bridges. Its orders were binding pending a court hearing. Although the burden of proof was placed on carriers, the ICC could not investigate railroad actions until rate increases actually took place. That limitation gave companies enough wiggle room to perpetuate abuses. On the other hand, per the Hepburn Act, railroads were no longer permitted to own or have any interest in the commodities they shipped. That provision was designed to prevent discrimination for or against customers.

The power of government to regulate business appeared to be waxing, but Roosevelt's Progressive juggernaut was brought up short by a sharp business panic in 1907. Ten years of general prosperity that had doubled bank deposits to $14 billion and circulating currency to $3 billion ended abruptly on March 13 with a stock market plunge, business failures, and over 200 bank suspensions, including on October 22 the Knickerbocker Trust Company of New York. Even Westinghouse Electric fell into receivership, causing George Westinghouse to lose control of the company that continued to bear his name and much of his fortune. To buttress the steel industry, the President was forced to let US Steel buy the Tennessee Coal and Iron Company. More humbling, he had to ask Morgan to use his influence to have banks loosen credit to stabilize financial conditions. To make it easier for financial institutions to inject money into the economy in an emergency, the Aldrich-Vreeland Act of May 30, 1908 authorized national banks to issue circulating notes based on commercial paper as well as state, county, and municipal bonds for six years, but applied a 10% graduated tax on such notes to prevent excesses. By 1910, bank deposits totaled nearly $17 billion and circulating currency approached $3.5 billion. Translated into 2004 money, the amount available for loans and investments equaled $325 billion with $67 billion of liquidity, or about $4,225 in aggregate per American.

Congress also included in the Aldrich-Vreeland Act a provision setting up a National Monetary Commission to study banking systems in the US and Europe. Nine senators and nine representatives periodically went about the work over the next three years.

Lucky Strike plant Durham, North Carolina
Altogether, Roosevelt's administration filed 44 anti-trust cases. His vice president and successor, William H. Taft of Ohio, although touted by Republicans as staunchly pro-business both at home and abroad with a Dollar Diplomacy push of American investment into Latin America and the Far East, wound up filing 90 cases in just four years. Most important was the Standard Oil Trust decision of 1911 in which Supreme Court justices used the "rule of reason" (first enunciated in a 1897 opinion that only those combinations in unreasonable restraint of trade are illegal) to break up Rockefeller's empire. They justified the move by observing that, although Standard Oil controlled only 35% of the country's crude oil supplies, it dominated 90% of refining, shipping, and marketing. On the other hand, the rule of reason permitted the American Tobacco Company to continue after reorganization to reduce monopolistic practices, which limitation was sufficient to open

the door in 1913 for the R.J. Reynolds Tobacco Company, originally founded in 1875 as a chewing tobacco producer, to compete for the industry lead in cigarettes with its *Camel* brand, combining several different kinds of tobacco in an "American blend," sold in 20-cigarette packs and 10-pack cartons. The American Smelting and Refining Company, the mining trust of metal processing plants belatedly put together in 1901 by the copper magnate and Swiss immigrant Meyer Guggenheim and son Daniel, survived too, expanding overseas to include nitrate from Chilean fields, tin from Bolivia mines, and rubber and diamonds from Belgian Congo plantations and mines.

Paper and fiber plant, North Caroline

As for the forest and lumber empire of Weyerhaeuser, it not only escaped destruction but expanded many times from the 400,000 acres cut in 1890. In 1900, he purchased 950,000 acres of forest land from Hill of the Northern Pacific Railroad at $6 an acre. Since most remaining virgin forest was located in the Rocky Mountain and West Coast regions, he moved his headquarters from St. Paul to Tacoma, Washington. It soon came out that 36% of the nation's original timberland, and an even higher percentage in the over cut East and Great Lakes region, had over the past century been harvested without having grown back. Moreover, as newspapers increased circulation, demand for paper escalated. The International Paper Company was founded in the Northeast in 1898 by merging 17 pulp and paper mills. Prior to the 1913 elimination of tariffs on low-cost Canadian imports, it supplied 60% of newsprint in the country. Increased business accounting, secretarial, and other paper-intensive activity also increased demand for paper and lumber.

No wonder that Roosevelt, New York born and raised but an environmentally conscious cattle rancher from having spent 1884-86 in the Dakotas bad lands recovering from the tragic loss of his first wife and mother on the same day, launched a major push to preserve what remained. He knew and deplored the fact that by 1892 buffalo herds that once had numbered 20 million head were near extinction at less than 1,000 and that white-tail deer were down to half a million from an original population in 1607 of well over 30 million. McKinley's reversal in 1897 of Cleveland's decision seven years earlier setting aside 21 million acres of forest in national parks as well as the opening on September 16, 1893 of six million more acres of Cherokee lands in Oklahoma to settlers made the situation worse. The Carey Act of August 18, 1894 authorizing the President to grant each state with public land up to 1 million acres for irrigation, reclamation, settlement, and cultivation and letting states use revenue from the sale of such land to reclaim other lands in that state had not been fully implemented.

The situation turned around 180 degrees in a very short time after Roosevelt's rise. In July 1902, he created the Division of Forestry within the Department of Agriculture and placed in charge the dedicated environmentalist Gifford Pinchot to implement a comprehensive program reclaiming arid lands for agriculture and conserving and restoring others in national parks. Under the National Reclamation or Newlands Act, almost the entire proceeds of public land sales in 16 western states were set aside for use by a Reclamation Bureau within the Department of the Interior to finance the construction and maintenance of irrigation projects in arid states. The next year, the Department of Agriculture was enlarged to give active help to farmers to defeat insects, match crops to soils, develop better seeds, circulate helpful information, allocate federal land grants, and give subsidies for the establishment of agricultural colleges in the South and West.

Some lands were still available for settlement. The Kinkaid Home Act of 1904 awarded 640 acres of desert land in Nebraska to anyone who maintained a residence for five years and made improvements worth $800. On June 11, 1906, the Forest Homestead Act permitted the Secretary of the Interior at his own discretion to open forest lands with farming possibilities for settlement. After Western grazing interests organized a protest in Denver a year later against new restrictions on use of public land, Congress added a rider to an appropriation bill repealing the Forest Reserve Act of 1891. However, Roosevelt withdrew 21 forest reserves before the effective date, diminishing the importance of the measure. He had already on June 29, 1906 withdrawn by Executive Order all coal lands owned by the federal government for appraisal, permitting them to be offered again for sale at prices ranging from $35 to $100 acre, quite an increase from the 1873 legislation setting a $10-20 range.

Oil wells in California, 1913
The culmination of Roosevelt's environmental policy came on June 8, 1908 with appointment of a National Conservation Commission

chaired by Pinchot to study mineral, water, forest, and soil resources. Its report on January 11 the next year not only inventoried existing US natural resources but urged Congress to repeal the Timber and Stone Act of 1878 so that land could be valued at its title value rather than the prescribed $1.25 an acre. However, Congress chose to offer for sale the entire inventory of public desert land per the terms of Kinkaid Home Act. Pinchot subsequently ran afoul of the new Secretary of the Interior under Taft and was forced to resign. Nevertheless, Roosevelt and Pinchot had succeeded in setting aside 148 million acres in national parks and withdrawing from sale 80 million acres of mineral lands and 1.5 million acres of potential water-power sites. Sensing which way the winds of change were blowing, Weyerhaeuser was persuaded to jump on the reforestation bandwagon and participate in the First National Conservation Congress in Seattle on Aug. 25, 1909.

The Taft administration swung back partly the other way on the fundamental question whether to exploit American natural resource wealth to the fullest in the shortest period of time or actively preserve them for future generations. To satisfy western ranchers, the Enlarged Homestead Act of February 19, 1909 increased the maximum size of homestead grants to 320 acres in parts of Colorado, Montana, Nevada, Oregon, Utah, Washington, Wyoming, and Arizona. One quarter of the grant had to be cultivated, however. All timber and mineral land was kept at the old 160 acre limit. But the salient fact was that a process had been put in place that would by the twenty-first century achieve the goal of restoring much of the animal and vegetable resources of the country. Numbers of white-tail deer, beaver, and other species hunted for meat and fur came by 2000 to approach 1607 levels and over 70% of the 1 billion acres originally covered by virgin forest or nearly three times the level of 1880 were reforested.

Federal Reserve, New York City

Congress came round the last lap of the Progressive period with new legislation to strengthen the federal government's hand in the burgeoning communications industry as well as transportation. On June 18, 1911, the Mann-Elkins Act placed telephone, telegraph, cable, and wireless companies under ICC jurisdiction so that the commission could suspend new rates pending a court hearing. The Radio Act on August 13 the next year gave authority to the Secretary of Commerce and Labor (the Secretary of Commerce after the departments were split in 1913) to assign operator and station licenses as well as wavelengths and time limits. The Physical Valuation Act of 1913 granted the ICC power to investigate the value of property held or used by railroads so that cost and physical valuation could be established as basis for rate making and fixing reasonable profits.

More importantly for government's ability to influence the economy directly, the commission set up by the Aldrich-Vreeland Act handed in its report on January 8, 1912. It recommended a reform of the financial system that led to the Federal Reserve (Owen-Glass) Act of December 23, 1913 that has remained the basis of the banking system to present time. Per the legislation, 12 Federal Reserve banks were set up in New York, Philadelphia, Boston, Richmond, Atlanta, Dallas, Kansas City, St. Louis, Chicago, Cleveland, Minneapolis, and San Francisco to act as "lenders of last resort" or bankers' banks. National banks were required to keep 6% of their capital as reserves in these centers while state banks could do so voluntarily. A Federal Reserve Board of 7 (later 8) members, including the Secretary of the Treasury and Comptroller of the Currency, was installed in Washington D.C. with power to adjust rediscount rates at the 12 district banks for direct control of the nation's credit supply. Federal Reserve notes backed by a gold reserve of 40% at each bank were issued to make it even easier for the government to move money around quickly to head off panics and smooth out boom-bust cycles.

The final chapter of the Progressive era was written by Democrat Woodrow Wilson, former governor of New Jersey. Elected to the White House when Roosevelt as a Bull Moose Progressive angry at Taft's abandonment of his legacy split the Republican vote with the incumbent, he took up the cause with a passion. Happily, he signed the Smith-Lever Act passed by Congress May 8, 1914 replacing the Bureau of Corporations with a Federal Trade Commission or FTC which had the power to obtain annual reports from public corporations and investigate unfair competition. The commission was also instructed to attack trade boycotts, the mislabeling and adulteration of commodities, false claims to patents, and other abuses. Wilson also approved the Clayton Antitrust Act of October 15, under which the FTC obtained broader discretion to investigate price discrimination, tying contracts, and interlocking directorates controlling business that exceeded $1 million, a fairly low standard. Its remedies included suing individual corporate officials as well as trusts, triple damages from such suits, and court injunctions to protect the rights of workers to strike, picket peacefully, and organize boycotts unless such injunctions would result in irreparable injury to property. Although federal court opinions subsequently weakened parts of the legislation, AFL leader Gompers called the act labor's *Magna Carta*. The last provision was an important loophole that business used for another two decades to hold off effective mobilization of union power.

Rising Might of Industry and Finance

In 1911, the unrepentant Rockefeller, greatest captain of industry of the era, was so disgusted by Washington's trust-busting and regulating of the golden goose of *laissez-faire* enterprise that he retired. Leaving operation of his still substantial oil holdings to son John Jr., he busied himself until his death in 1937 with philanthropic giving through the Rockefeller Foundation. Carnegie had already in 1901 sold Carnegie Steel to the US Steel consortium headed by Morgan for $480 million and established the Carnegie-Mellon University in Pittsburgh, the Carnegie Institution of Washington (1902), the Carnegie Foundation for the Advancement of Teaching (1906), and Carnegie Endowment for International Peace (1910). Even Morgan, whom Roosevelt had called with a mixture of derision and admiration the greatest pirate of them all, softened posthumously his public image by bequeathing in 1913 a private collection of books, manuscripts, and art objects to the Metropolitan Museum and Pierpont Morgan Library in New York City. The reason the titans of industry were able to afford both opulent retreat and generous charity was because their business monopolies consistently reaped huge profits. While Carnegie's fortune at death was estimated at $250 million and Weyerhaeuser, who passed in 1914, owned 3 million acres and total net worth of $150 million, Rockefeller was reliably said to possess assets topping liabilities by $1 billion, in 2004 money equal to $18.75 billion.

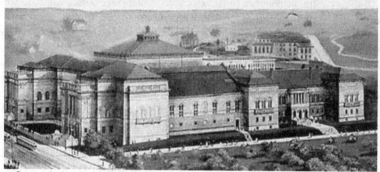

Carnegie Institute, Pittsburgh

It was only the beginning of a century of wealth accumulation. The inventions of the 1870s and 80s were crystallizing into industries that would overawe the business empires of the past. However, a novelty of the era was that revenues and profits from new enterprises promised to spread wealth beyond the upper crust of society. Rapidly, they achieved the size and strength to do so.

In 1892, Edison General Electric merged with Thomson-Houston Electric to form the General Electric Corporation (GE) in a deal backed by J.P. Morgan. GE continued to expand over the years but also sold the right to use Edison patents to more local companies such as Los Angeles Edison Electric Company in 1894. Although some of Edison's thunder was stolen the next year by the success of Westinghouse and Tesla installing huge steam turbines to drive dynamos to generate electric power in the first hydroelectric plant at Niagara Falls on August 26, 1895 for transfer by improved copper wire to Buffalo, New York, many Edison systems survived and prospered by switching over to alternating current. In 1903, for example, Edison Illuminating of Detroit and others combined into Detroit Edison Company, the forerunner of DTE Energy, and discovered new demand for electricity from the Cadillac Motor Company as well as other automobile manufacturers that boosted Detroit's car and truck production from 9,125 that year to 443,000 in 1915, 78% of the American total.

However, it was GE itself that in the long run would become the nation's greatest business powerhouse. The company set up an impressive R&D department that came up with improvements of existing products such as the ductile tungsten filament for light bulbs in 1909. Operating out of Fairfield, Connecticut, the GE empire branched out beyond power and lighting systems to electrify city railways, produce myriad electrical and household appliances, and as the new century progressed diversify into non-electricity based fields such as aeronautical systems, medical instruments, insurance, and other financial services. By the twenty-first century, the conglomerate operated domestically and internationally with annual sales of $130 billion and market value of $240 billion. As for the nation's electric power system, it continued to proliferate from 2,800 private companies in 1920 to 6,500 by 1920. Electric utilities combined with gas and water companies in many places for monopoly strength.

Nicola Tesla

Most successful of the little competitors that tried to take on GE and Westinghouse in household appliances was Emerson Electric Manufacturing Company of St. Louis. Two years after its founding in 1890, it was first to produce electric fans. Gradually, it built on this foundation to turn out electric motors for dental drills, player pianos, power tools, and sewing machines. Its strategy evolved over time to make components for electric devices rather than end products.

Likewise, Bell's American Bell Telephone Company achieved success wiring cities for local phone serve and absorbing competitors. On March 27, 1893, the headquarters in New York City placed its first long-distance call to a branch office. Reorganizing in 1900 as AT&T but known as Ma Bell, it benefited from the experienced leadership of Thomas N. Vail. As a monolithic communications giant selling, installing, and providing phone service, it was granted government recognition in 1913 (confirmed by the Graham-Willis Act of 1921) as a "natural monopoly." The ICC then permitted the company over time to buy out most independent telephone companies and provide long distance service for the entire country. It established a steady and reliable flow of revenue for the next seven decades. Before a court-ordered breakup in 1982 sheared AT&T of seven regional Bells providing local service, monopoly power produced $200 billion of sales and employment for 1 million people. Ma Bell's children in aggregate came to exceed many times the financial and business strength of the surviving long-distance company.

Brownie camera

Eastman too made his invention of the camera pay off big in 1892 with establishment of the Eastman Kodak Company to market as well motion-picture film. While the *Brownie* folding pocket camera of 1900 sold for $1, a roll of film cost 15 cents and produced negatives still standard at 2 1/4 inch by 3 1/4 inch. The huge industrial plant he built to produce these and other photographic supplies generated a fortune for himself that exceeded $100 million by his death in 1932, most of which was then distributed in philanthropic grants and bequests. The company's employment rolls hit the 5,000 mark in 1907 with thousands more to come over the next decades as new plants were built as far away as Australia.

Meanwhile, older American industries had a bumpy, downhill ride through the Panic of 1893. The September 18, 1893 completion of the Great Northern Railway was followed swiftly the next spring by failure of so many railroad companies that within five years 27,000 of the nation's network of 190,000 miles was in court receivership and another

40,500 miles had been sold at foreclosure sales. Entities temporarily in receivership included the Union Pacific and B&O. In 1897, president of the Illinois Central E.H. Harriman joined a group of investors to buy the former for $110 million while Alexander Cassatt, president of the Pennsylvania Railroad, bought a block of B&O stock cheap when it came out of receivership in 1899. The B&O got back on its feet by taking over smaller railroads east of the Mississippi River. The Chesapeake & Ohio, shipping bituminous coal out of West Virginia and eastern Kentucky, became a main competitor. Further consolidation of the railroad network into powerful national and regional lines would have continued had not the Supreme Court broken up Morgan's, Harriman's, and Hill's Northern Securities holding company. In 1913, the justices also ordered the revived Union Pacific to divest itself of a 46% share in the Southern Pacific Railroad. Still, the industry grew from under $500 million of annual revenue at turn of the century toward $1.4 billion in 1914; owning and operating a railroad company was still considered a high prestige business.

Somewhat less well known than Morgan's steel and railroad deals was the consolidation he engineered in farm machinery manufacturing. Although a proposal to combine 20 companies, headed by Deere with $2 million of annual sales, fell through, a merger of the McCormick Harvester Manufacturing Company and Deering Harvester Company succeeded in 1902. Because McCormick-Deering was a full line producer of farm machinery including tractors and four years later *Famous Engines* to power friction drive tractors to pull large plows and for belt work on threshing machines, Deere was forced to innovate. Its gas-type tractor of 1906, competing with John Froelich of Waterloo, Iowa's original *Waterloo Boy* model, as well as acquisitions after 1911 of six smaller competitors put it in position to survive.

In addition to funding and taking positions in railroad mergers, US banks broadened the scope of their activities. Some of the most innovative were smaller financial institutions destined to grow into industry titans. Up in Seattle in 1890, the building and loan investment association that would become Washington Mutual made the first monthly-installment home loan on the west coast. Eight years later, Household Finance Corporation of Minneapolis demonstrated that innovation could make a large national bank out of a small local one by becoming the first consumer finance company to offer loans to former customers through the mail, and then added a monthly payment plan in 1905. Likewise in San Francisco, Italian immigrant Amadeo P. Giannini began building the Bank of Italy, founded in 1904 with $150,000 borrowed from his father-in-law and ten friends, into the company that would one day gobble up and assume the name of Bank of America. In addition to soliciting business door-to-door and extending credit after the great earthquake of 1906 "on a face and a signature," he pioneered risky but ultimately successful loans to California wine growers and the movie industry.

However, it was still the big eastern banks and insurance companies that had the financial clout to mix with captains of industry. The republic had a growing core of wealthy individuals with financial assets that required advice and management. Thus in 1894, American Express added a Financial Advisors division. The expanding network of brokerage firms would two decades later persuade Charles E. Merrill to open an office on Wall Street to cater to the individual needs and desires of investors. Also in the forefront of financial innovation were the two major entities that would one day combine to form Citigroup. In 1897, National City Bank of New York added a foreign exchange department, five years later opened offices in Asia, Europe, and India, and in 1904 copied Wells Fargo's innovation of traveler's checks.

Meanwhile, Travelers Insurance added to its product line with automobile insurance in 1897 and health insurance two years later, to compete with Aetna, also branching out into health that year but car insurance only in 1907. The former reinforced its image as an industry leader with higher rate policies for substandard applicants and lower rate policies for group life insurance. Connecticut General, founded in 1865, stole a march on the industry by establishing a bureau of financial statistics to advise on investment of premium dollars to boost profits. In 1913, it joined Aetna in competing for group life insurance contracts, while the much smaller Lincoln National Life Insurance Company, founded only eight years before in Fort Wayne, Indiana, suddenly distinguished itself by offering reinsurance for 14 other life insurance companies.

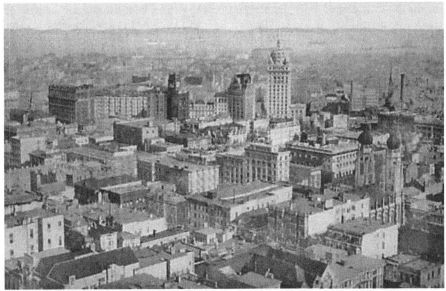

San Francisco before the 1906 earthquake

The world's largest insurance company became Burrows, Marsh & McLennan (later Marsh & McLennan) of Chicago with annual premium in 1905 of $3 million. The firm achieved that status through research in risk management for US Steel and major railroads. A wider net was cast by the Continental Assurance Company of North America (later CNA Financial) founded in Detroit in 1897. Focusing initially on accident and health insurance for railroad workers costing $1 per month, the company swiftly expanded throughout the Great Lakes region by offering coverage against fire and natural calamities, marine insurance policies, and mergers. Finally, in the last few years before the First World War, Continental joined Travelers, Hartford, Aetna, and other companies in the rapidly growing field of automobile insurance. Together with life and fire insurance, property and casualty would be the other pillar holding up the insurance industry in the early part of the century.

After the Pure Food and Drug Act of 1906, not only pharmaceutical company Eli Lilly but Squibb, a Brooklyn producer of ether and other pure medicines, benefited. The latter had been founded in 1856 by Edward R. Squibb who insisted that the "priceless ingredient in every product is the honor and integrity of its maker." Abbott Alkaloidal Company saw its fortunes rise as well. Best positioned of all to profit was McKesson and Robbins, founded in 1833 in New York City as an importer of therapeutic chemicals and drugs, that proceeded after the turn of the century to solve the problem of falling drug prices by buying up rival wholesalers and becoming a nationwide distributor and middleman.

Companies that emphasized personal products did better commercially than those that remained strictly speaking pharmaceutical. In 1903, the Bristol-Myers Company founded in 1887 when William M. Bristol and John R. Myers used $5,000 to buy out a failing drug manufacturer in Clinton, New York suddenly vaulted into prominence with its eight year old *Sal Hepatica* laxative mineral salt that tasted like mineral water from Bohemia. Next, it offered *Ipana* disinfectant toothpaste for protection against bleeding gums. Most successful of all was still Pfizer, raking in $3 million in sales from citric acid for soft drinks.

Another established industry that needed a boost from new innovation and products was textiles. Although the improved *Northrop* loom quickened the production of cotton clothing and boosted bales of cotton consumed in 1895 to 3.5 million, nearly 40% of that amount went to the South's expanding mills, eventually by 1914 accumulating 13 million spindles to the north's 11 million and producing cheaper, coarser cloth. What was lacking was diversity of fabric to manufacture higher value garments. That finally became possible in 1902 with invention and patent of rayon and artificial silk by Arthur D. Little, William H. Walker, and Harry S. York. Although commercial production of the former by the American Viscose Company of New York did not start for another seven years, by 1914 US silk production reached a quarter billion dollars. The moment of glory for rayon arrived after the First World War when production shot up from 3 million pounds in 1919 to 33 million pounds a decade later.

In the 1890s, the steel industry too appeared briefly to plateau because of the woes of the railroad industry. But the success of architect Louis Sullivan constructing the nine-story Wainwright building in St. Louis around Bessemer steel I-Beams forged in Pittsburgh factories resulted by 1896 in the volume of structural and other rolled steel products exceeding steel rail production two to one. Moreover, a steady replacement of Bessemer steel converters by more efficient Open Hearth furnaces caused national production of steel to reach 12.5 million tons by 1900 priced above $20 a ton. When Carnegie sold out to Morgan's consortium then next year, combining Carnegie Steel with Federal Steel, the new US Steel Corporation's capitalization was $1.4 billion and its market share over 60%.

The use of steel in building construction as well as the innovation of arc welding — using a disposable electrode of coated wire to transfer heat and melt metal — that slowly replaced riveting, began to transform the skyline of American cities. Skyscrapers climbed ever higher until in 1931 the Empire State Building in New York City rose 102 floors and 1,250 feet off the ground. "Form follows function," Sullivan liked to say, and within sky scrapers wide floor areas, bright interior lights, windows from the Pittsburgh Plate Glass Company (later PPG Industries), and air circulation systems first offered by the McLeod American Pneumatic Company for warmth in winter and cool air in summer, that gave the Johnson Service Company (later Johnson Controls) a market opportunity in 1903 to make humidostats, created an attractive, pragmatic environment for hundreds, then thousands, then legions of office workers. They used improvements on Sholes' typewriter and adding machines first invented by Edmund A. Barbour in 1872 as well as myriad office supply products such as the 1904 ring binders of the Clipper Manufacturing Company (later renamed the American Clip Company or ACCO) to bring new efficiency to accounting and secretarial positions. Business staff positions grew steadily into a salaried "white-collar" work force that would expand the American middle class. The purchasing power of this segment of the population was critical in the next generation for the development of the consumer durable industry.

Wainwright building, St. Louis
Real estate values in city centers vaulted to the clouds with realization by landlords that potential square footage for rent and lease had just been multiplied by the vertical limit of high-rise buildings. Construction of large steel, stone, brick, and glass structures boosted the fixed asset value of nonresidential buildings excluding utilities to $38 billion on the eve of the First World War from $28 billion in 1900. That was 40% of the fixed asset value of all non-residential structures, dominated by utilities, chiefly railroads. Even more wealth was tied up in residential buildings, worth about $80 billion dollars at turn of the century and rising to $90 billion in 1914. Adding $29 billion in federal, state, and local government owned structures and equipment and $4 billion in private owned equipment, including desks, chairs, carpets, typewriters, and other furniture and fixtures going into sky scrapers, the nation in 1900 boasted over $180 billion in fixed assets. Through the generally prosperous decade and a half to come, that figure would swell another 25%.

A small but increasingly important part of wealth creation was due to innovation in building construction. In 1894, Frank Lloyd Wright of Oakpark, Illinois began a decades-long career as an architect with a desire to integrate in homes form, function, building site, and materials to satisfy the needs of occupants, not merely showcase style. His conception gave birth to dozens of houses and other buildings of unique design. He began an era in which tangible structures acquired because of aesthetic reasons a perceived worth higher than what the market would otherwise bear.

Wall phone

Beauty and comfort played a role in the value of some commercial properties as well. In a residential neighborhood in New York City, John Jacob Astor IV broke ground on the St. Regis hotel in 1902. With telephones in every room, central air cooling and heating, mail chutes on each floor, and electric sockets for vacuum cleaners, the hotel after its completion in 1904 quickly rivaled Europe's finest. Other luxury hotels with similar amenities attracted clientele willing to pay many times the cost of simpler institutions' room and board for a night or an extended stay.

Artistic creations had always benefited, of course, from "beauty being in the eye of the beholder." Similarly, Wright's structures escalated in value whenever someone bid up the price. As the twentieth century began, luxury items were the exclusive province of the very few, very wealthy. The complete lack of savings and capital for most American families showed up in the fact that only $1.4 billion of consumer durables then listed were spread among 76 million people, or about $18 per head, in 2004 money equal to $385.

Although many households had cooking stoves, most were wood or coal fired. The first electric model by William S. Hadaway was far too expensive. Not until 1890 did the Columbia Phonograph Company begin making non-electric acoustic phonographs with a protruding sound horn and build up a catalog of cylinders, costing around 50 cents, recorded with John Philip Sousa's military marches, other popular songs, and speeches. Not until the mid-1890s did GE make electric fans in Fort Wayne, Indiana. On the contrary, when most Americans sought to improve their living standard, it was with investment in housing, including new single family dwellings with a median price of $2,225. In 1900, $837 million was put into residential fixed assets while only $462 million went into consumer durables.

Victor Victrola

All that began to change with proliferation of less expensive household appliances. In 1906, the Victor Talking Machine Company improved on Columbia's phonograph with its *Victrola*, featuring an inverted horn, enclosed in a box, that sold 2,500 machines annually rising to 573,000 in 1917. Two years later, an electric iron was patented; the year after that, Albert Marsh's Nichrome heating element alloying nickel and chromium was used to make the first successful electric toaster. While small appliances were within the wherewithal of millions of households, suction vacuum cleaners as well as the *Thor* self-contained electric washing machine from the Hurley Machine Company of Chicago became wide-spread only in finer residences.

The Second Transportation Revolution

Exclusivity in expensive consumer durables was about to end because of the aspirations of a little known farmer's son from Michigan named Henry Ford. Leaving home in 1879 at age 16 to apprentice in a Detroit machine shop, he worked part-time in the middle 1880s for the Westinghouse Engine Company, then eventually in 1893 become chief engineer for the Edison Electric Company's Detroit plant. Along the way, he dreamed of emulating the success of German manufacturer Gottlieb Daimler, who invented the internal combustion engine in 1884 and Karl Benz, his countryman who made the first automobile the next year. Dozens of mechanics and engineers had the same aspiration.

In actual fact, the first gasoline powered automobile in the US was driven around Springfield, Massachusetts by Charles E. and J. Frank Duryea on September 21, 1893. The first gas powered automobile patent was issued to George B. Selden of Rochester, New York in 1895. Invention of pneumatic tires in 1892, use of Portland cement two years later for paving, rapid increase in smooth-paved roads to 160,000 miles by 1905, and improvements on the internal combustion engine such as utilizing Charles B. King's pneumatic hammer for improved engine pistons that produced 36,000 watts of energy from one gallon of gasoline prepared the way for the coming transportation revolution. Packard Motor Company's 1902 *H* slot sliding gearshift that became standard in US cars, Sterling Elliott's steering knuckle that let front wheels turn while the axle remains stationary, permitting replacement of turning tillers with steering wheels, and the universal joint of Charles Spicer that facilitated power transmission by cleaner attachment of propeller shafts to the engines and rear axles all made the driving experience progressively safer and more enjoyable. Other dramatic and incremental design improvements in the ensuing decade included quick-demountable tire rims, automatic lubrication, front bumpers, non-skid and cord tires, and the 1907 *V-8* engine by Hewitt Motor Company of New York City. Positioning the steering wheel on the left side of the car permitted a much better view of oncoming traffic while driving on the right.

What Ford added was not better technology but, as his successors claimed decades later, a better idea. He wanted to build low-cost automobiles from strong, cheap metal that average-earning men by the thousands, then hundreds of thousands could afford. However, his first effort in 1896, a *Quadricycle* based on a buggy frame and bicycle wheels, as well a subsequent rudimentary models did not sufficiently impress J.P. Morgan or any other large financier to lend support. Investors in his Detroit Automobile Company, founded 1899, forced him out three years later because he refused to concentrate on producing luxury passenger cars. The fact that some prominent financiers were of Jewish ancestry may explain the darker side of Ford's personality as a virulent anti-Semite. Investors of whatever race and creed tended in the era to play hard-ball with entrepreneurs and inventors.

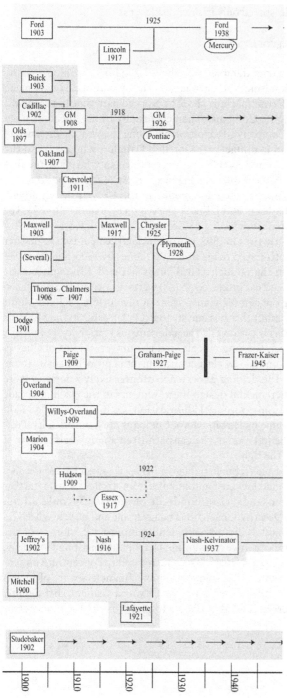

Genealogy of US Auto IndustryMain companies, 1897-1945

In point of fact, motor vehicle companies churned out only 4,192 autos in 1900, nearly doubling licensed cars. Fifty companies, led by short-lived Columbia and Locomobile, vied for a share of the slowly expanding pie. Surging to prominence over the next few years were Lansing, Michigan's Olds Motor Works, Jeffrey's with its Rambler model, the Maxwell-Briscoe Company, which turned out 532 cars in just seven months in 1904, and the Buick Motor Company led by William C. Durant. Durant would ride Buick to an industry leading 8,820 cars manufactured in 1908, then buy out in succession Oldsmobile, the Oakland Motor Company, and finally for $5.5 million on July 29, 1909 Henry M. Leland's Cadillac Motor Company, successor of the Detroit Automobile Company, to form General Motors (GM). No fewer than 5,903 of Cadillac's high end car were bought that year with a base price of $1,400 and options costing another $550, altogether about 80% of the cost of the median-priced home. GM appeared to have an insurmountable lead.

164

Ford Model T

Meanwhile, Ford persisted to open the Ford Motor Company in 1903 in a Detroit shed with $28,000 scraped together from non-wealthy investors. His enterprise was immediately threatened by a law suit by the Association of Licensed Automobile Manufacturers, holding Seldon's 1895 patent purportedly applying to all gas powered automobiles. The long and bitter fight was not resolved in his favor until 1911. In the interim, he turned out on average a new model a year and on August 12, 1908 made his great breakthrough, the *Model T Flivver* with standardized parts, "a motor car for the multitude." The next year, he installed a mass-production assembly line to boost annual production to 17,771 and begin dropping the price from $950 to $360 by 1916. GM was so threatened by Ford's surpassing Buick's 14,600 turn-out that Durant attempted in 1910 to assemble $9.5 million in bank financing to buy out his competitor. However, he failed and was ousted himself in a reorganization. By 1912, Ford was producing over 78,000 cars or 22% of the market.

Henry Ford

To the chagrin of minority stockholders, he decided to concentrate solely on *Model T* production. When on October 7, 1913, he opened a new plant in Highland Park, a suburb of Detroit, the main 250 foot long assembly line fed by subassembly lines cut 87% off the 12 hour time previously required to turn out a complete chassis. Thus, *Model T* production soared in 1915 to 501,000, accounting for 56% of the industry total. By 1920 when production approached 1 million, the Ford Motor Company was worth $300 million.

1904 Cadillac

An industry that climbed on the back of, or rather supported, automobiles was rubber. B.F. Goodrich, founded in 1870, the US Rubber Company (later Uniroyal), beginning in 1892, and many smaller shops all centered on Akron, Ohio prospered making rubber tires for the bicycle craze of the 1890s. In 1898, Frank Seiberling, David Hill, and other opportunistic investors put up $100,000 to capitalize on Goodyear's fame and name by expanding from making bicycle and carriage to automobile tires. Goodyear soared during its first two decades of operation with innovations of tubeless tires, all-weather, non-skid tread, rubber flooring, pneumatic airplane tires, and in 1912 the first Goodyear blimp, subsequently in the First World War sold to the US Navy. Competitors included Firestone Tire and Rubber Company, which won the contract to provide tires for Ford's

Model T and the first Indianapolis 500 in 1911, as well as Dayton Rubber Company, originally specializing in garden hoses and fruit jar sealing rings but leaping on the automobile and truck bandwagon with rubberized hoses and belts for motor vehicles. None could match Goodyear's annual sales on the eve of US entry into the war of over $100 million, permitting the company to claim rightly that "more people ride on Goodyear tires than any other kind."

Studebaker car plant, 1908

Although the *Model T* did not contain such cutting edge advances as founder of the Dayton Engineering Laboratories (Delco) Charles F. Kettering's electric self-starter, installed in Cadillac's 1912 model, the simplicity of Ford's design and efficiency of his production line generated huge profits. So successful did the firm become in using operating income rather than borrowed funds that required burdensome interest payments for expansion that he was able to make the eight hour day and a minimum daily wage of $5 standard in his plants. He was first, as well, to install a profit-sharing plan. As he had hoped, the increasing financial wherewithal of his employees and other Americans enabled many to buy *Model T* cars. Partly as a consequence, the annual investment by citizens in consumer durables rose to $1.92 billion in 1914 while total consumer spending that year was $33.4 billion. Investment in housing was only 72% of the consumer durable amount, a reversal of the situation in 1900.

In addition to rubber tires, the 1.4 million vehicles produced in the US prior to 1914 required quantities of paint for external parts and glass for windows, much to the advantage of Pittsburgh Plate and Glass, metal alloys for specialized heat-resistant parts, but especially steel for body frames and petroleum products for lubricating oil and fuel. Steel production soared to 24 million tons by 1909, of which 14.5 million was Open Hearth. Quality was further improved by iron ore of the Mesabi Range, a 100 mile long deposit in northeast Minnesota of superior content that by 1914 dwarfed Wisconsin and Michigan deposits in importance. At turn of the century, Great Lakes ships weighing 1.45 million tons, which was nearly 34% of total US shipping tonnage, carried iron ore, copper, grain, and other cargoes to Chicago, Detroit, Cleveland, Pittsburgh and other industrial cities.

As important as was Ford and other automobile companies to the steel industry, the jolt given by oil to automobile engines and the American economy was even more impressive. The fact was that in 1890, only a tiny portion of the country's original energy reserves of 221 billion, 42 gallon barrels of light medium oil, 52 billion barrels of heavy oil, 1.7 trillion barrels (626 billion recoverable under technology known in present day) of shale oil, and 44 billion barrels of oil in tar sands as well as 41 trillion cubic meters of natural gas had been used up or burned off after coming to the surface. Annual production of oil for kerosene (75% of the total), heating oil, and other purposes was only 45.8 million barrels, valued at $0.77 per barrel at the well head or $1.49 billion. Ten years later, 63.6 million barrels of oil was being pumped, half for kerosene, at $1.19 per barrel. Suddenly, dramatic new oil finds in Texas and Oklahoma permitted foundation of the Texas Oil Company (Texaco) and Gulf Oil in 1901, Getty Oil two years later, and Phillips Petroleum in 1905, kicking up production from 300 million gallons of fuel oil to 1.7 billion by 1910. That was 20% of all oil pumped.

Oil well strike in Texas

Although prices at well heads, in part because of innovation in drilling equipment by companies such as headed by Reuben C. Baker and Howard R. Hughes, Sr. that would decades later merge into Baker Hughes, fell to an average $0.61 a barrel, Standard Oil Company refineries became far more efficient at separating crude oil into different, higher value products with installation of fractionalization towers or columns, each handling 400,000 gallons of oil a day. From light or low carbon atom content to high, these were propane, butane, gasoline, kerosene, diesel fuel, lubricating oils, paraffin wax, and tar. Equally beneficial, the heating process boosted gasoline to a higher octane rating from the 20% originally secured from old-fashioned distilling. In 1911, William Burton of Standard Oil Indiana came up with a "thermal cracking" process to extract an even better gasoline from crude. Not only did he heat the heavier by-products of fractionalization at 700 degrees Fahrenheit but applied high pressure above one atmosphere to boost octane rating to 70. This so-called "cracked gasoline" was then mixed with distilled to get an octane rating of 40-50, the level usable in that era's engine technology.

Right from the start, oil companies had to solve the problem of transporting gasoline to car-owners. As hundreds of thousands then millions of *Model T*s and other cars took to city streets and country turnpikes, Rockefeller's old system of horse-drawn wagons carrying huge barrels would not suffice. After the invention of leak proof couplings in pipelines made transfer of natural gas feasible in 1890, a similar system was adapted to distribute oil from refineries to regional storage facilities. Tanker trucks then carried gasoline to gas filling stations. The first such station was improvised by a farmer in Indiana in 1905. The first drive-in station was opened in Pittsburgh by the Gulf Oil Company in 1913. The struggling Union Oil Company of California followed swiftly with one in downtown Los Angeles. Thus, the company that became Unocal staked an early claim to what would become over decades one of the nation's largest driving markets.

Discoveries of new oil deposits by individual wildcatters and larger operations continued as demand picked up. Gasoline for automobiles swiftly replaced kerosene as the dominant product of refineries. Simultaneously, drillers found that oil was often combined with deposits of natural gas or that wells turned up the latter and not the former. In 1909, for example, a major natural gas field was discovered near Taft, California by the Southern California Gas Company. Because natural gas produced twice the heating value as manufactured gas, the company moved swiftly to expand its natural gas pipeline facilities. That was a boon for Miller and David Williams of Fort Smith, Arkansas who began a successful construction company for cross country natural gas and petroleum pipelines.

Meanwhile, demand for gas received another incremental boost in 1903 after bicycle mechanics Wilbur and Orville Wright of Dayton, Ohio flew the first airplane at Kitty Hawk, North Carolina on December 17 for 12 seconds. A contract from the US Army for reconnaissance aircraft permitted the Wright Company to begin commercial operations of a patented model in 1909. Although other competitors came into the field to push improvements and innovations, planes remained too small and fragile to carry numbers of fare-paying passengers until the 1920s. Ground transportation continued to dominate the field for decades to come

Mesabi open pit mine

On the other hand, the advent of flying machines was a boon for the Pittsburgh Reduction Company. The Wright brothers' first plane included a crankcase cast from aluminum. Desiring stronger, more durable, less flammable materials for military planes, designers moved away from wood to metal. The fact that aluminum was much lighter than steel made the former an attractive alternative to the latter. As a consequence, US demand for aluminum surged to 16,500 tons by 1909, up from only 125 pounds in 1884 when Hall, as a chemistry student at Oberlin College, first became interested in the substance. His renamed Aluminum Company of America (Alcoa) came up the next year with an aluminum alloy for propellers, wings, and aircraft skin, including the covering for dirigibles.

CONSUMER SPENDING GRAVITATES TOWARD BRAND NAMES

Like airplanes, the germination period of other key inventions would be extensive. In 1903, DuPont opened an experimental laboratory near Wilmington, Delaware to facilitate its transformation from a producer of explosives to a manufacturer of chemical products including paints, synthetic textile fibers, and varnishes. But it was a Belgian-born chemist named Leo H. Baekeland who in 1907, while failing to make an improved electrical insulating material, came up with an even more promising product. His oil-based *Bakelite* substance, patented two years later as the first plastic, was used in billiard balls, buttons, valve parts, electric plugs, and other applications requiring a cheaper but still hard and durable replacement for aluminum, tin, and other light metals. However, it was DuPont with its deeper pockets, Dow Chemical switching over from the production of chlorine bleach to using chlorine as a raw material in a variety of products, and Union Carbide building on its original business of manufacturing calcium carbide for acetylene lighting that came to dominate the chemical industry. The only setback to industry concentration came in 1912 when DuPont was compelled by court order to spin off 50% of its black powder monopoly controlling 42% of the country's dynamite production to create competitors the Hercules and Atlas Powder Companies.

Meanwhile, overlooked because of developments with heavy industry and new technology, a number of companies had taken root to bring American consumers myriad non-durable goods for personal and household use as well as food and beverage. These included Procter and Gamble (P&G), founded as a soap and candle making company in Cincinnati in 1837, its competitor Colgate started in New York City in 1857, and paper product manufacturers Kimberly Clark of Neenah, Wisconsin and the Scott Paper Company of Philadelphia, the latter becoming the leading producer of bathroom tissue. Additionally, Anheuser-Busch of St. Louis turned a local brewing company into a national business by constructing a fleet of refrigerated freight cars as well as a network of rail side icehouses for storage of beer barrels until artificial refrigerator units were produced in the 1880s. H.J. Heinz Company of Pittsburgh reorganized after the business panic of 1875 to become famous for its ketchup and five dozen other condiments. Now in the 1890s, Colgate's toothpaste was offered in a collapsible tube, B.J. Johnson Company of Milwaukee took on Procter & Gamble's *Ivory* soap with *Palmolive*, and Anheuser Busch reinforced its prominence with a super premium brand named *Michelob* to complement its *Budweiser* beer mainstay. Hundreds of other companies vied to make their brands popular with the public.

None was more successful than *Coca-Cola*. However, owner Candler made the mistake in 1899 of selling bottling rights to his product for only $1, thus siphoning off huge future profits to middlemen. Because in New Bern, North Carolina a pharmacist named Caleb Bradham concocted *Pepsi-Cola*, Candler suddenly had to contend with a potent challenger. Fortunately, the market for both grew to become enormous.

Genealogy of U.S. Household Products Industry, 1806-1940

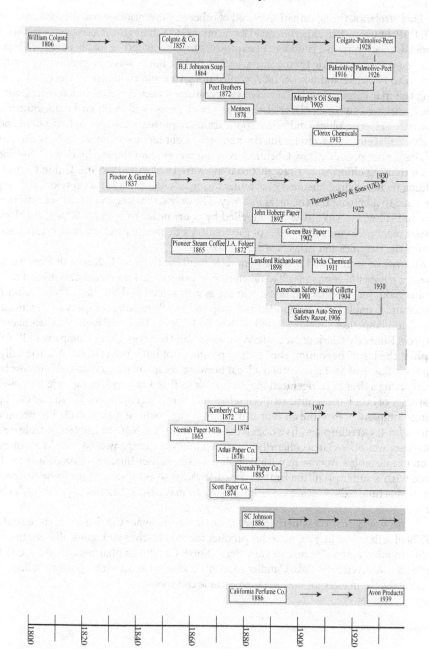

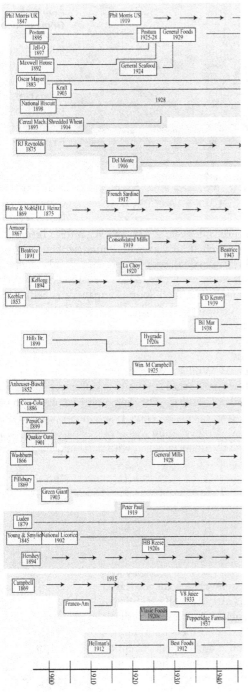

Genealogy of Food, Beverage, & Tobacco Industry, 1845-1945

Simultaneously, William K. Kellogg of Battle Creek, Michigan achieved notoriety for his corn flake cereal by accident when cooked wheat was exposed to the air for over a day then run through rollers, causing the flaking process. That success by the forerunner of Kellogg Company opened up an entirely new breakfast and snack food industry into which National Biscuit Company (later Nabisco) plunged by merging regional bakeries and bringing under one corporate roof the likes of Graham Crackers, Animal Crackers, and Oreo cookies. In 1903, James L. Kraft started a wholesale cheese operation in Chicago that would, after he began manufacturing his own cheese and other products in 1914, come to rival National Biscuit. Hellman's Blue Ribbon Mayonnaise, first product line in what would make Best Foods Corporation successful, was sold by German immigrant Richard Hellman in a New York City delicatessen.

171

Beech-Nut Gum packing room

Luck also played a part in the transformation of Joseph A. Campbell Preserve Company from a modest Camden, New Jersey producer of canned condiments, jellies, minced meat, soups, and vegetables into burgeoning success story. The general manager reluctantly gave his young nephew John T. Dorrance a job. But Dorrance was a chemist trained in Europe who stunned and delighted his uncle with a condensed soup to which water would be added by customers. By 1904, the company that would in 1921 be renamed Campbell Soup Company was selling 16 million cans of soup, mostly tomato, at ten cents a pop, one-third the price of competitor's heavier soup cans already containing water.

1909 cosmetics ad

Forethought helped William Wrigley Jr., a 29 year old soap salesman in Chicago, make the leap to successful entrepreneur. In 1891, he got the idea of offering chewing gum with each can of baking powder. Advent of his *Juicy Fruit* brand in 1893 insured the company's success. Wrigley's gum was so popular around the US that by 1910 he had the financial wherewithal to build a manufacturing plant in Canada.

Hershey Kiss

On the other hand, Milton Hershey, owner of the Lancaster Caramel Company in Pennsylvania, was already well established when in 1894 he began a Hershey Chocolate Company subsidiary. Sales were so promising that he sold the main business for $1 million in 1900 but retained the chocolate operation as an independent entity. Returning in 1903 to his birthplace near Harrisburg, he built up a town that bore his name. Mass production of milk chocolate in 1905, *Hershey Kisses* chocolates two year later, a devotion to his local com-

172

munity, and the increasing sweet tooth of the American public made the company the runaway industry leader in confectionary products.

Milton Hershey

Simultaneously, P&G added production facilities outside of Cincinnati, making it easier to reach the national market with new products, including in 1911 *Crisco* all-vegetable shortening. Colgate, Kimberly-Clark, and Scott also introduced new products. But the biggest new sensation was Gillette's American Safety Razor Company of Boston, demonstrating to American men that enclosing a disposable double-edged blade in a razor for self-shaving every morning was a better method than visiting the local barber's straight edge blade. After Gillette won the endorsement six years later of Major League baseball players, sales of his blades skyrocketed from an already impressive 17 million in 1910 to 35 million the next year and 70 million by 1915 as well as 450,000 razors. Gillette quickly became a million dollar sales company and more. The company controls a lion's share of the shaving products market to this day.

By and large, food products whether from local farmers or distributors were sold in local grocery stores. Aside from New Jersey based A&P, big operations did not exist until Barney Kroger of Cincinnati expanded the single store he opened in Cincinnati in 1893 to 40 by 1901 with $1.75 million of sales. Operating his own bakeries within the stores, he incorporated the next year as the Kroger Grocery and Baking Company. Wider distribution became possible throughout Ohio and neighboring states when in 1913 he began to replace delivery wagons and horses with *Model T* trucks. But at that moment, A&P revolutionized the industry and boosted profits from $30 million of annual sales by changing over to a cash and carry business. Previously, home delivery and charge accounts had been the norm.

Similarly, the reach of household and personal products was assisted by proliferation of five and dime stores. Founded in 1899, S.S. Kresge out of Pittsburgh expanded within a decade to 85 stores with $10.3 million of sales while James Cash Penney's Golden Rule chain out of Wyoming (1902) exceeded $1 million of sales from 22 stores. None could yet challenge Woolworth's, ringing up $100 million of sales from 1,000 stores by 1912. That company accounted for 5% of all chain stores, which reached a critical mass of 24,000 in 1914 and was only slowed from further expansion by advent of the First World War.

ROOTS OF THE ENTERTAINMENT INDUSTRY

The first public concert in colonial America was given December 23, 1731 in Boston. The first acting company was organized in Philadelphia by Thomas Kean and Walter Murray in 1749 to present Shakespearean plays in eastern cities. Only in 1766 was the first permanent theater, the *Southwark*, built in Philadelphia. The first professional dance performance was given the next year. Likewise, until the mid-eighteenth century there was no organized industry to print sheet music. Song-writing only achieved popularity after a British army surgeon named Dr. Richard Shuckburg wrote *Yankee Doodle* in 1754 as a parody of colonial soldiers in the French and Indian war, unintentionally given Americans another rallying cry for the impending Revolution.

Well after independence was achieved, organized entertainment continued to be haphazard. The Boston Philharmonic Society became the first regular performing orchestra in 1810 only to fold in 1824. However, a libelous newspaper editor from Bethel, Connecticut named Phineas Taylor (P.T.) Barnum suddenly achieved success with a low-brow form of fun. In 1842, he transformed the American Museum in New York from a respectable depository of stuffed animals and waxwork figures into a shameless but profitable exhibitor of beauty contests, over-dramatized plays, and so-called freaks of nature. In fact, the museum's most lucrative moment came during the Civil War when a 25-inch tall dwarf named Charles S. Stratton was billed by Barnum as *General Tom Thumb*. The brazen showman parlayed Stratton's notoriety and the 20 million tickets he sold into a visit with President Lincoln, an overseas tour, and an audience with Queen Victoria of England.

Buffalo Bill Show advertisement
Earlier in 1850, Barnum risked everything to bring over from Europe the *Swedish Nightingale* Jenny Lind, whom he had never seen or heard, for a national tour. The largest audience was a hall-filling 5,000 persons in New York City. After the Civil War, he went for even larger crowds by organizing in 1871 the *Greatest Show on Earth*, a circus in Brooklyn. After merging operations with James A. Bailey, the Barnum & Bailey Circus traveled between cities, attracting enthusiastic throngs to see Jumbo the elephant, purchased in 1881 from the Royal Zoological Society at London. Thereafter, competitors such as Buffalo Bill's *Wild West Show*, which opened in Omaha, Nebraska on May 17, 1883, caught the increasingly affluent public's fancy. After its owner and former army scout William S. Cody brought the rodeo back East and even crossed the Atlantic in 1889 to have sharpshooter Annie Oakley shoot a cigar out of the mouth of Kaiser William in Berlin, the world became fascinated by the American West.

New York Hippodrome
What entertainment lacked was an invention to preserve shows the way Eastman's camera recorded pictures. A further constraint on revenues was inability to

174

exhibit live performances for larger audiences than could be crammed into a theater, music hall, or stadium. Successful concert tours such as Barnum's success with Jenny Lind raked in profits but carried high travel, lodging, marketing, and other expenses. Few promoters could risk so much; few performers were paid so well.

Vitascope

All that began to change two years after Barnum's death. In 1893, Edison produced at final development cost of $24,188 ($490,000 in 2004 dollars) a *kinetoscope* that used a continuous roll of film to show "moving pictures." On April 14 the next year, *kinetoscopes* installed in a building on West Orange Street in New York City earned vendors 50 cents every time a customer watched a "peepshow." In 1896, the famous inventor acquired the *vitascope* of Thomas Armat of Washington D.C. to screen on April 23 a *kinetoscope* film at Koster and Bial's music hall in New York for a paying audience. That was the moment at which the motion picture industry took hold. Although Edison in 1904 invented a camera-phone to make the first sound motion picture and six years later improved the device, talking motion picture tech-nology was not sufficiently well advanced to inspire film makers to bear the expense and trouble of switching over from silent picture presentations until the late 1920s.

Audion receiver

On the other hand, technological advances in broadcasting sound were vital to the telephone industry and efforts to develop wireless communi-cations. In 1901, the Italian physicist Guglielmo Marconi broadcast *Morse* code. Building on that achievement as well as breakthroughs of other sound pioneers, a Yale Ph.D. from Council Bluffs, Iowa named Lee De Forest who had worked as a researcher in Chicago for the Western Electric Company and Armour Institute of Technology improved detection of wireless signals in 1906 with a 3-element vacuum tube (triode amplifier) called an *Audion*. Although efforts to build up a successful company around the device crumbled under the weight of financial and legal quarrels, in 1910 he did broadcast live from the Metropolitan Opera in New York the concert of the great Italian tenor Enrico Caruso. Two years later, he made wireless radio broadcasts of speech and music from a microphone pragmatic over long distances by improving the amplifier. His method for maximizing amplification was to send high-frequency radio signals through a series of tubes rather than just one as well as feeding back part of the output through a tube's grid. However, he sold the patent rights to AT&T for a modest price. In a career that extended through the Second World War, De Forest filed 300 patents, including in the early 1920s a phono-film method of sound recording and glow-light recording of sound films that became models for systems ultimately used by the motion picture industry, without making a large personal fortune.

Deforest's Audion

Business revenues from motion pictures and radio would, as with Ford's success with automobiles, be sufficient to reward more liberally employees of those industries. Unlike the rank and file of automobile companies who remained unknown cogs in a great wheel of production, actors and actresses would become stars of the Silver Screen. The most popular would emerge as the first Americans who did not own businesses or inherit property to become wealthy. That material success in a profession historically scorned by high society would add another facet to the dominant American ethic of Horatio Alger rags-to-riches success.

HARD CLIMB OF THE LABOR MOVEMENT CONTINUES

By contrast, the possibility of wage earners making a fortune was to say the least remote. Unrelenting immigration from southern and eastern Europe, maintaining a surfeit of labor, permitted business men to treat working men and women like any other saleable commodity governed by the law of supply and demand. Further, the corrupting influence of trusts and monopolies was not in 1890 matched by a government willingness and capability to correct abuses. Unions were far too weak to act as a effective counterweight.

The era began badly for labor with the depression of 1892-94. A series of bitter strikes over wage cuts was highlighted by a revolt against the Carnegie Steel Company's Homestead, Pennsylvania works near Pittsburgh. On July 6, 1892, workers set fire to two barges coming up the Monongahela River with 300 Pinkerton detectives called in by Henry C. Frick, the company president, in an unsuccessful attempt to quell the uprising. Seven people were killed. That provoked the governor to send in state militia six days later to rout the strikers and recapture the plant. The strike was so thoroughly broken by November 20 by using replacement workers willing to accept low wages that no successful steel union could again be organized in the country until the 1930s.

Because economic conditions continued to deteriorate over the next two years, labor demands became more radical not less. Proposing a public works relief program of road construction and local improvements paid for by the government and financed by $500 million of US legal tender notes, a Massillon, Ohio businessman named Jacob S. Coxey led 100 unemployed men, building to 100,000 from many locales, on a march to Washington D.C. in spring 1894. However, only Coxey and 400 supporters reached the goal. They were arrested for trespassing on the Capitol lawn.

Another serious challenge to authority, order, and the economy erupted on June 21, 1894 with a strike against the Pullman Porter Company. Eugene V. Debs and the American Railway Union cooperated by instituting a boycott against the nation's railway system. For several days in the Midwest, he and his supporters kept the trains from running. Finally, Attorney General Richard Olney sent in 3,400 special deputies to replace railroad engineers and President Cleveland dispatched US Army units to protect the mail and interstate commerce. Debs was eventually jailed on December 14 for ignoring a federal court injunction of July 2 to end the strike. Thereafter, federal injunctions were the government's preferred method to break transportation strikes.

Eugene V. Debs

Taking the offensive in 1895, businessmen organized the National Association of Manufacturers as an entity to fight unionism. However, as in the past, as the economy recovered and demand for skilled labor increased, the AFL was able to stabilize its membership at 1.7 million, 81% of the country's total union workforce. Rather than outlaw strikes, the Pullman debacle and its deleterious consequences persuaded Congress to pass on June 1, 1898 the Erdman Act setting up voluntary mediation of railroad strikes by the chairman of the ICC and commissioner of Bureau of Labor. In a blow to railroad management, it prohibited "yellow dog contracts" requiring workers, as a condition of employment, not to join a union. Public sentiment was not so much anti-union as anti-violence and chaos. Most Americans realized that were the nation's 2 million transportation and public utility workers to be provoked by business leaders into coordinating labor stoppages to gridlock the railroads and roads that kept the produce of 10.9 million farmers and the production of 6.25 million manufacturing workers from reaching domestic and foreign markets, the economy would grind to a halt.

Sensing an historic mood swing, the AFL proposed in 1900 a sweeping program that would benefit not just skilled labor such as the garment workers forming that year the International Ladies Garment Workers Union (ILGWU) but all the nation's 29 million workers, including 5.1 million women age 14 and up and the 1.42 million unemployed. The union wanted no less than "job ownership" wherein workers could not be fired, immigration controls to prevent employers from glutting the labor market with newcomers, relief from unemployment caused by the advance of technology, and collaboration with employers such as through the National Civic Federation to promote mediation of labor disputes. Not even La Follette could or would go that far nor was Roosevelt interested in causing radical economic upheaval. However, in 1902, Maryland did become the first state to enact workman's compensation for injuries sustained on the job. Employers were compelled to contribute to a fund to cover future expenses. Gradually over time, other states took the same step, with Mississippi in 1948 becoming last of the hold-outs to pass the necessary legislation.

Outraged in the first decade of the twentieth century that the government not only refused to curb immigration from Europe but permitted 8.2 million persons to cross the Atlantic, labor returned to strikes to force change. A startling success was achieved by the United Mine Workers of America (UMW), led by John Mitchell, with a work stoppage May 12, 1902 against anthracite mine owners. When the owners refused to arbitrate, Roosevelt on October 16 used the Erdman Act to appoint a commission to mediate, causing the strike to end five days later. On May 22, 1903, the commission ruled that the

Homestead Steel Works

industry was making sufficient profit to grant miners a 10% wage increase. Previously, they had earned about $300 a year. Now, their pay would be approximately $1.30 per day, equal to an annual income in 2004 money of $6,800.

Miners with compressed air drill
Encouraged not only by the UMW victory but booming economic times that dropped unemployment to 1 million persons or 3.1% of the workforce, in June 1905 William D. (Big Bill) Haywood and others organized the International Workers of the World (IWW or Wobblies) by merging the Western Federation of Miners (1893) and American Labor Union (1898). Its program called for an end to the wage system so that workers could share in profits, unionism of all industries, and organization of unskilled and migratory workers West and East who handled lumber, shipping, fruit picking, and textiles. Such ambitious plans had never panned out before for labor, but hunting for votes for the election of 1906, Roosevelt ratcheted up his increasingly strident anti-monopoly rhetoric. Railroad workers were encouraged to initiate a new series of railroad strikes that over the next seven years required 26 Erdman Act mediations.

Just when it seemed that organized labor would achieve the clout and respectability needed to boost the standard of living of working families and possibly even with Roosevelt's acquiescence claim a share of real economic and political power, the panic of 1907 struck. The President had to pull back from attacks on business abuses and kowtow to Morgan and the financial community. The next year, the Supreme Court further disappointed labor with a decision in *Adair v. US* that the Erdman Act provision banning yellow dog contracts was an unreasonable violation of freedom of contract and property rights guaranteed by the 5th Amendment. It tacked on a ruling in *Loewe v. Lawler* that a national as well as local boycott in 1902 against the D.E. Loewe & Company by the Danbury, Connecticut chapter of the United Hatters of North America was a conspiracy in restraint of trade per the Sherman Act. However, some consolation was provided by the persuasive brief of legal counsel for Oregon, Louis D. Brandeis (a future supreme court justice) in *Muller v. Oregon*, using statistical and other data to support the state's contention that Oregon's law limiting the maximum working hours for women did not impair liberty of making contracts as guaranteed by the 14th Amendment. That did nothing for manufacturing workers whose average wage in 1909 was only $0.19 an hour, at 10 hours a day equal to an annual income in 2004 money of over $11,000.

Tradesmen and men hired to work for Ford were substantially better off, of course, unless they had the temerity to strike. In 1912, he shut down a Buffalo plant to break a strike and shipped its equipment to Detroit. That sort of preemptive action, as well as the move to assembly line production, made it difficult for the skilled union labor force to account for little more than 7% of 38 million gainfully employed persons in a population of 92 million at the end of the first decade of the twentieth century. Most men earning Ford's minimum wage of $1,250 for 2,000 hours of annual work, equal to $23,850 in 2004 dollars, counted themselves as fortunate indeed.

Women in the bindery, National Cash Register Company

Almost none of the 7.9 million women age 14 and up in the workforce were so privileged. The plight of immigrant women working as seamstresses in the New York garment industry was so appalling that muckraking articles elicited widespread sympathy and calls for reform. However, it took a horrendous fire at the Triangle Waist Company factory on March 25, 1911 that killed 146 young women, many of whom jumped to their deaths, for the New York legislature to revise labor laws and building codes to improve sweatshop conditions. Brandeis formalized an arbitration agreement made the year before between Sidney Hillman of the United Garment Workers and the firm of Hart, Schaffner, & Marx to accelerate changes. The next year, an IWW-inspired strike by textile workers in Lawrence, Massachusetts provoked the Massachusetts legislature to pass a minimum wage law for women and minors, first in the country. In 1913, Congress saw fit to set up a Department of Labor.

Washington's policy was still to permit virtually open immigration so that 5.2 million more people passed through the Ellis Island clearing center near New York City between 1910 and 1914. Because less than 9% of the adult US population were high school graduates, native-born citizens who did not make a living as farmers or tradesmen had little beyond language and cultural familiarity to give them an edge over newcomers for the mass of unskilled jobs that dominated work opportunities. Moreover, there was no longer a westward outlet for the disgruntled and unemployed. A population boom in rural areas actually cut average farm size in the first decade of the twentieth century from 146 acres to 137 acres, leaving even less room for westward migration.

AGRICULTURE'S DEPENDENCE ON OVERSEAS TRADE

The growing efficiency and prevalence of farm machinery made large numbers of would-be farm laborers superfluous. On the centennial anniversary of Whitney's cotton gin, the first gas-powered tractor was produced. At turn of the century, $750 million of farm equipment was distributed over 5.7 million farms, an average of $130 per farm. That figure advanced in ten years to $1.27 billion of machinery on 6.4 million farms, for a $200 average. Wheat acreage expanded from 7 million to 8 million, cotton went up from 10 million bales to 16 million, and corn, tobacco, and citrus fruits also enjoyed substantial increases. Those farm families that had survived the downturn of the 1890s enjoyed one of the most prosperous agricultural upswings in the nation's history. On the other hand, an absence of major wars overseas and increases in foreign production cut beef exports between 1897 and 1914 by 80% to 194 million pounds and bacon three times as much. Adverse though the influx of immigrants was for wages and working conditions, the extra population boosted domestic demand for commodities.

Ellis Island

Overall on the eve of the First World War, farmers and ranchers could view with satisfaction herds amounting to 60 million head of cattle valued at $25 a head, 50 million hogs worth $9 a head, and a similar number of sheep priced in the market at $3.40 each. Adding chickens and other animals, the country's livestock was worth in the range of $2.5 billion. On the other hand, the cost of farm machinery, including by 1910 about 1 million tractors had put farmers on average $3,200 in debt, equal in 2004 money to over $600,000. Were commodity prices to fall and that burden grow proportionately larger, equity in farms might descend below 50% and signal a new rural crisis.

That was why, even with the rapidly expanding domestic market, exporting commodities continued to be so important to US agriculture. In 1890, $858 million exports exceeded imports by enough to provide 46% of the nation's favorable $150 million balance of payments. Over $80 million originated from financial inflows from investments abroad in excess of financial outflows from foreign investments in the United States. When Congress passed the Wilson-Gorman Tariff of August 27, 1894 to lower duties to an average of 39.9% and place on the free list raw materials then in high demand by US industry such as wool, copper, and lumber, the intent was to encourage bilateral commercial treaties such as made with Japan on November 22 and stimulate even greater exports.

Harvesting wheat in North Dakota

However, US trade policy was no more consistent than in the past. After the economy recovered, Congress passed the Dingley Tariff of July 7, 1897 to protect American farmers and manufacturers from foreign competition. The general tariff rate was raised to 57%, including raw and manufactured wool and hides.

Sugar from non-Hawaiian foreign sources, put back on the duty list in 1894, continued to be taxed at a prohibitive rate to protect southern producers. But then the imperial surge forwarded by Mahan caused the republic the next year to take over Puerto Rico and Hawaii. Sugar from the former as well as the latter could now be imported duty free. Over the next three decades, American investors spent $120 million developing Puerto Rican sugar plantations, in the process putting native farmers out of business. Sugar production from that future American commonwealth (1952) increased 16 times, much to the disgruntlement of domestic sources.

Despite that long-term success, Puerto Ricans, Hawaiians, Cubans, and Filipinos were far too poor to afford US manufactured goods or to provide a large, captive market for future exports. Rather, US exports mainly to traditional European markets overawed imports $1.4 billion to $850 million by 1900. Although baled cotton still led the way at $240 million, its 17.4% share was far diminished from the 60% share claimed in 1860. Meat exports at $175 million, grain and grain products at $160 million, as well as petroleum products at $84 million and machinery at $78 million demonstrated a healthy and growing diversity.

As for imports, Europe's share, composed of both manufactured and lower value commodities, fell to a 53% share. What the republic required more of now was raw materials and foodstuffs from whatever source to feed hungry industry and people.

Panama Canal

Critical for expansion of US trade was construction of the Panama Canal between 1907 and 1914. At cost of $352 million ($6.7 billion in 2004 dollars), it halved sailing time between New York and San Francisco. However, export growth slowed to an annual average rate of 2.25% in the first decade of the twentieth century while imports jumped despite the high tariffs at an annual average of 6.24%. Realizing that better relations with trading partners were needed to facilitate shipments overseas, Congress lowered tariffs. The 38% rate of the Payne Aldridge Tariff passed on April 9, 1909 became the 30% of the Underwood-Simmons Tariff on October 3, 1913. The duty free list was expanded to include iron, steel, and raw wool.

Newport News Shipbuilding

New President Wilson and his advisors judged correctly that US industry was now strong enough to compete in its home market without protection from imported manufactured goods. The best way to encourage foreign governments to open markets to American products and commodities was to demonstrate Washington's commitment to Free Trade. Wilson believed that a permanent lowering of trade barriers would tend to reduce international tensions. It was further expected that freer trade and adoption of liberalized business practices would translate into free governments and societies around the world. Then the possibility of war would diminish because countries with similar democratic political and economic systems would be less likely to find reasons to fight. Before the theory had a fair chance to be tested, Europe's mixture of constitutional democracies, republics, and absolute monarchies came to blows in the First World War.

To cover the loss of customs revenues from lowering tariffs and to reduce the nation's public debt of $12 billion, Congress proposed on July 12, 1909 — and the states by February 25, 1913 approved — the 16th Amendment to the Constitution authorizing itself "to lay and collect taxes on incomes, from whatever source derived, without apportionment among the several States, and without regard to any census or enumeration." Included with the Underwood-Simmons Tariff, the Senate and House imposed a graduated income tax of 1-6% with the first $3,000 exempted and the top rate applying to incomes over $500,000. That provision generated immediate business for small public accounting partnerships, including Alwin and Theodore Ernst of Cleveland and Scottish immigrants Arthur and Stanley Young of Chicago. Also enjoying an increase in fortune were the Philadelphia firm of Lybrand, Ross Brothers & Montgomery, later part of PriceWaterhouse-Cooper, as well as Marwick Mitchell & Co. of New York City, destined to unite with British accounting interests in Peat Marwick, then merge with a Dutch and German company into today's KPMG.

US Customs House, Charleston, South Carolina

More important for the country, for the first time in American history the government had the revenue and, through the Federal Reserve System and Progressive regulatory legislation of the past 25 years, the tools to prop up a faltering economy as well as confront business to protect the public good. Federal receipts that had grown from $99.7 million in 1890 to nearly $675 million in 1910 because of the surging economy and customs duties were poised to jump yet again. Although a political intention still did not exist even under Wilson for massive government intervention in the economy, the potential now existed for a considerable step up in the level of regulation. The First World War would provide a stage for the Wilson administration to exercise greater authority over Big Business than any nineteenth century adherent of Adam Smith ever thought possible.

Chapter VII. A Roaring but Inflated Good Time: 1914-1929

War is a catalyst for change. The longer and more intense is a conflict, the greater are the consequences for societies, economies, and political establishments. During the 19 months the US participated in the First World War (1914-18, but the US entered in April 1917), a further alteration in the relationship of the federal government to American business strengthened the power and prerogatives of the former. Because the war ended abruptly before Washington could fully mobilize the economy, and because Wilson's foreign policy and health problems undermined his standing with the public, much of the progress to some, abuse to others was rolled back. The Progressive era itself was finished off by return of a pro-business, hands-off Republican administration to office. However, the "return to normalcy," as Warren G. Harding's campaign of 1920 called it, obscured the fact that a precedent had been established for strong government intervention in the economy in emergency situations.

In the 1920s, a great and spontaneous shift in behavior on the part of millions of Americans indicated to most that good times had come for good. Citizens of the upper, middle, and even working class began to borrow against future income for present prosperity. Spurred on by clever advertising campaigns and installment financing plans, they purchased cars, radios, electric washers and driers, refrigerators, and other consumer durables with reckless abandon. As the decade roared on, they were enticed to invest in business stocks, increasingly by putting down a part of the price to obtain the whole (i.e., buying on margin). The fact that over-speculation and business panics had always in the past caused share prices to fall, wiping out investments, was ignored. In their enthusiasm for risk-taking and making money, persons of all stripes tried to vault ahead of where they would otherwise have been on the socio-economic plane.

Some experts got so carried away with the surging economy as to suggest that the natural business cycle would no longer apply. The idea of predictable up and down movements in the economy had evolved out of the research of French physician Clement Juglar who had asserted in 1860 that nine or ten year cycles were normal occurrences. Eventually it was understood in the US that the business cycle begins with new investment in transportation networks, production facilities, and other infrastructure. That investment generates further (or multiplied) spending by persons receiving payment who want and/or need housing, consumer durables, and other items. To meet accelerating demand, even more factories and infrastructure are built. If demand still exceeds supply, prices rise.

In theory, the process goes on until all available capital is invested and all unemployed workers are signed up. When production at maximum levels finally builds up inventories of goods beyond what consumers can or will purchase, producers cut prices to stimulate demand. If that does not work, they shut down factories and lay off workers to salvage at very least their original investment. The business cycle comes back to the point from which it began.

In point of fact, American prosperity in the 1920s rested on a more precarious base than was recognized. Not only was GDP, tripling between 1914 and 1929 (but lifting only 179% when accounting for inflation), too dependent upon a few major industries, but on the eve of the Great Depression 70 million non-working adults and children relied upon the livelihoods of about 50 million working people ages 14 and up. Therefore, when the stock market did burst the speculative bubble that had puffed up prices far beyond what business earnings could support, the loss of wealth on paper provoked millions of consumers to cut back spending, then businesses to slash production and jobs. Catastrophic loss of national income undercut the ability of business to gin up demand, even with huge price cuts, for its over-inventoried products.

Americans with knowledge of economic history should have seen the implosion coming. Somehow they convinced themselves that the usual principles of business behavior no longer applied. Too, they had been seduced by brief success during the First World War with borrowing against future income for present necessity to believe that a key to unlock the door of perpetual growth had been discovered. Never before had the government permitted public debt to rise so swiftly or so high.

FIRST WORLD WAR AND THE ECONOMY

Goodyear blimp factory, Akron, Ohio

Washington had been running a mild annual deficit off and on since 1903. In 1915, the federal government paid out $62 million more than it took in. After the declaration of war in April 1917, total federal debt climbed in 28 months from $1.3 billion to $26 billion or from 2.36% of GDP to about a third. Congress raised the money first through the Liberty Loan Act of April 24, 1917 that authorized selling bonds to the public, next through taxes. Although proceeds from the former were earmarked for Britain, France, Belgium, and Italy to buy US food and war supplies, only $9 billion of $20.5 billion was so allocated. The rest was diverted to fund the US war effort.

The purchasing agent in the US for London and Paris was John P. Morgan, Jr., son of the late, great financier. Additionally, he organized a consortium of 2,000 banks to underwrite $1.5 billion in allied bonds, and then at war's end placed $10 billion in loans for European war reconstruction purposes. J.P. Morgan and Company thus further entrenched itself as the dominant entity in US financial circles. However, the firm's hegemony would be challenged after the war by Chase National Bank, depositor of Rockefeller family funds, and other institutions that initiated a series of mergers in the 1920s.

On October 3, 1917, the President signed into law the War Revenue Act, which raised another $660 million by lifting the minimum graduated income tax rate to 4% on individual incomes over $1,000 climbing up to the maximum rate of 77% on incomes over $1 million. Although the corporate rate was only 6%, a graduated excess profits tax of 20-60% on corporations enjoying war profit windfalls yielded $2 billion. Increased postal rates (that facilitated the success of the two companies that in 1920 combined into Pitney Bowes Postage Meter Company, selling stamping machines to businesses) as well as excise taxes on alcoholic beverages, amusements, luxuries, tobacco, and transportation topped out the federal revenue take. Tax proceeds provided 25% of the $35.5 billion spent by the federal government during the war.

Right from the start of hostilities in Europe, the government opportunistically encouraged exports of food and war munitions to Britain, France, and other allied powers as well initially to the Axis powers of Germany, Austria, and Turkey. US shipments of goods increased three fold to $8 billion in 1917 and remained on that lofty plateau for another three years. The long-suffering US Merchant Marine received a boost from establishment of a US Shipping Board on September 7, 1916 and chartering of the Emergency Fleet Corporation, capitalized at $50 million, to build, purchase, lease, or requisition ships. Not only did the government seize 600,000 tons of German shipping, but US shipyards constructed by war's end 700 new ships (400 steel), lifting annual shipbuilding tonnage from $211 million in 1914 to $775 million by 1918.

At first, vessels carried traditional agricultural exports. Baled cotton worth $610 million, or 24.4% of total exports, crossed the Atlantic the first year of the war to supply British and French factories turning out uniforms for millions of men. After Congress on July 17, 1916 passed the Federal Farm Loan Act to set up 12 district Farm Loan Banks, each capitalized at $750,000, in which cooperative farm loan associations held membership, five to 40 year loans were granted to farmers at rates 5-6% lower than offered by commercial banks to double farm production. Eager wheat farmers expanded into arid regions of the Great Plains to harvest an average annual 870 million bushels and feed overseas armies and civilian populations. Further encouragement for the agricultural sector came from the August 10, 1917 Food and Fuel Control Act that permitted the President to fix wheat prices, which he did at not less than $2 per bushel with a guaranteed price of $2.20. A prominent mining engineer named Herbert C. Hoover, who had chaired the American Relief Commission in London, was named US Food Administrator.

Likewise, Congress bucked up farmers by passing the Stock-Raising Homestead Act of December 29, 1916. That legislation increased the maximum size of homesteads to 640 acres for grazing or forage land not suitable for irrigation and farming, excepting that land with mines and coal deposits were excluded. Livestock and US meat exports to Europe hit record levels, as a consequence. Afterward in 1920, the country boasted 70.4 million cattle worth $52.64 a head, 60.1 million hogs selling for $20.00 a head, and 37.3 million sheep worth $10.59 each while total US livestock carried a market value around $6 billion, twice the level as before the war.

The other component of US trade with Europe that caused exports to explode was manufactured goods, including weapons, supplies, and ammunition for war. The steel industry, in particular, made monster gains, climbing from 23.5 million long tons of steel ingots and castings to 45 million in 1917. In addition to steel for ships, trucks, and other vehicles, foods for American soldiers were sealed and preserved in tin-plate steel cans. There was such great demand for steel, including an average 1,500 pounds per automobile produced, that not only US Steel prospered but rising companies Bethlehem Steel and Jones and Laughlin Steel. Producing armor, guns, munitions, and ships, the former in eastern Pennsylvania quadrupled capacity to 4 million tons while doubling employment to 30,000. The latter became the largest steel producer in the Pittsburgh area with a 10,000 strong workforce at the Aliquippa Works on the Ohio River.

Moreover, electrically produced steel overtook crucible steel, making machine tools stronger, sharper, and more precise. As electric power nearly doubled to provide 32% of primary power in manufacturing establishments, research and development of metal alloys, including aluminum with steel forged at higher temperatures in electric furnaces, caused aluminum production to rise from 27,000 tons in 1914 to 512,000 four years later. All was controlled by Alcoa, selling its output predominately to car companies for auto bodies and castings even though the cost per ton was greater than for steel. The Pittsburgh concern branched out in the 1920s into aluminum cookware.

Once the US entered the war, domestic car production yielded to the US government's need for trucks and other vehicles. Charles F. Nash, former head of GM, became the leading producer of four-wheel drive *Quad* trucks while Ford's mass production techniques won contracts for gun carriages and *Liberty* motors. Spicer Manufacturing, now headed by New York lawyer and investor Charles Dana, also profited from making standardized parts for the one million Liberty trucks produced during hostilities. Other companies that enjoyed booming orders were the nation's largest truck manufacturer Republic Motor Truck Company, its Torbenson Gear and Axle Company subsidiary, making 33,000 truck axles in 1917 alone, the Teetor-Hartley Motor Company of Indiana that made pistons, cylinders, and piston rings, and the Harley-Davidson Motor Company, producing and selling most of the 20,000 motorcycles used by the US Army and eclipsing the prewar leader, the Indian Motorcycle Company.

Domestic motor vehicle transportation received an important boost when Congress passed the Federal Aid Highway Act of 1916. Henceforth, the federal government would match state spending on new highways dollar for dollar. Initial funding of $5 million rose to $75 million by 1922. The road construction boom was delayed by the war.

Meanwhile, annoyed by suppliers who could not keep up with his demand for wheels, upholstery, and other accessories and anxious to coordinate production to avoid delays and stoppages and so reduce the amount of capital tied up in inventory, Henry Ford decided to produce these items in his own factories. His expansion helped double total US construction to $6.7 billion annually by war's end. Then to insure timely access to raw materials, Ford bought 16 coal mines, 700,000 acres of timberland, a sawmill, railroad lines, and a fleet of Great Lakes freighters to transport iron ore from his Lake Superior mines. He acquired a glass works to complete the process of vertically integrating his business with every necessary component of the production process.

The acquisitiveness of Ford and other industry titans posed a problem for smaller manufacturers. To reduce potential conflicts, the government on July 28, 1917 set up the War Industries Board (WIB). Foraging in uncharted territories, the WIB had difficulty coordinating the distribution of materials around the country. On December 26, 1917, the US Railroad Administration had to take control of 397,000 miles of railroad track operated by 2,905 companies. As for production of munitions, not only DuPont but the Hercules and Atlas Powder Companies, split off from DuPont by court order in 1912, produced black powder for cartridges and shells as well as dynamite. Pistols, rifles, and artillery were turned out by Colt, Remington Rand, and other munitions makers. Still, the American Expeditionary Force in France was so short of weapons that French equipment had to be purchased. Not until Bernard M. Baruch became head of the WIB in March 1918 were myriad problems of assigning national production priorities, converting existing facilities to war production, assisting industry to purchase supplies, and fixing materials prices to prevent profiteering and hoarding substantially sorted out.

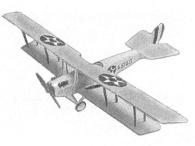

Curtiss Jenny

Overall, GDP surged 204% from 1914 to 1918 and another 63% through 1921. Although after accounting for inflation the jump over nine years was only 151% and the *per capita* increase only 139%, prosperity filtered down to working people, especially those fortunate enough to draw paychecks from vibrant industries. For example, Curtiss employed 18,000 people in Buffalo and another 3,000 in a factory in Hammondsport, New York while Wright-Martin required 15,000 people from Dayton to Long Island. They were part of a national workforce of 40 million people with only 1.4% unemployed, down from 9.7% unemployed three years earlier.

Liberty Bond

New labor laws, including the Adamson Eight-Hour Act of September 3, 1916 which set an eight hour work day for railroads engaged in interstate commerce (upheld by the Supreme Court in *Wilson v. New* because in an emergency Congress had power to set a temporary standard), also boosted the prospects of working men, women, and children. To preserve labor peace during the war, the Wilson administration set up a Mediation Commission. On April 8, 1918, Congress formalized a National War Labor Board (NWLB) as a court of last resort in labor disputes. Government insistence that corporations receiving federal contracts recognize the right of workers to organize and bargain collectively for wages and working conditions kept strikes in 1918 from involving more than 3% of all workers.

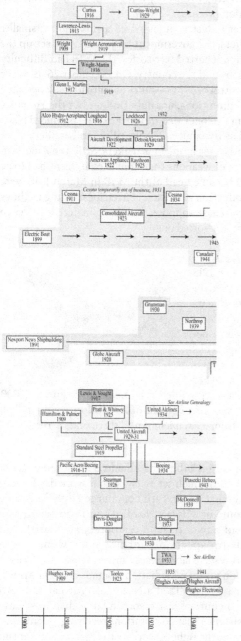

Genealogy of the Aerospace-Defense Industry, 1891-1945

Another reason that war production picked up was that on April 5, 1918, Congress established the War Finance Corporation. An initial capitalization of $500 million was authorized to back $3 billion in bonds and make loans to financial institutions that covered commercial credits extended to war industries, including new ventures. One such entrepreneur was Glenn H. Curtiss, who founded the Curtiss Aerospace and Motor Company in 1916 to build war planes for the allies. Once Washington came calling, ample private financing permitted Curtiss' production to shoot up to 10,000 planes for 1917-18, 62.5% of the national total. Wright-Martin, a company that combined the legacy of the Wright Brothers with the active energies of Glenn L. Martin, supplied the same number of aircraft engines. While the war lasted, the company generated annual revenues of $50 million.

REACTION AGAINST PROGRESSIVISM

While war production lasted, the NWLB wanted not only the 8 hour day to be standard practice but time and a half for overtime. That pleased unions, particularly the AFL which maintained its 80% share of 5 million union workers. If not respectable to most Americans, unionism was at least defensible. Had not a Red Scare, stemming from the establishment in Russia by Vladimir Ilych Ulyanov, a.k.a. Lenin, and his Bolshevik Party of a Communist "workers' paradise," swept over postwar Europe and crossed the Atlantic bringing fear to most, hope to a few that world revolution was in the offing, organized labor might have preserved more of its gains. But in autumn 1919, Attorney General Alexander Mitchell Palmer cracked down on

IWW labor and radical political leaders with raids and mass arrests. Business leaders like Judge Elbert H. Gary, chairman of the board of US Steel, were encouraged to take a hard line against unions. Strikes nevertheless proliferated, with 4.2 million workers demanding higher wages, collective bargaining rights, union recognition, permanent abolition of the old 12 hour work day, and an end to attempts to undermine unions with company-sponsored labor organizations.

Ford Motor night production

Failure on January 9, 1920 of a 110 day strike against US Steel was a signal that the tide had definitely turned in favor of companies getting control of labor forces and costs. The averaging manufacturing wage had now risen to $0.48 an hour or about Ford's minimum of $5 a day. Considering the fact that 8.43 million women (1.92 million married) composing a fifth of the total workforce and paid much less than men held down the average, a man of prime working age employed by a major industrial company might draw pay substantially higher. His annual earnings of, say, $2,000, would on paper be sufficient to sustain a comfortable life style. However, high inflation during the war years, partially encouraged by a change that permitted Federal Reserve Banks to issue notes "on the basis of gold as well as discounted paper" which despite the raising of gold reserves from $600 million to about $1.3 billion greatly increased the money supply, actually doubled the cost of living. A $2,000 per annum income translated into only $18,870 in 2004 purchasing power or $4,700 less than the effective purchasing power a $5 day wage carried in 1914.

One area organized labor counted on for progress was regulated industries. Although the Transportation or Esch-Cummins Act of February 28, 1920 returned the railroads to private control, it established a Railroad Labor Board (RLB) of nine members drawn three each from companies, employees, and prominent citizens in the general public. The board's purpose was to propose, cajole, and offer but not order labor arbitration to adjust wage disputes. Later on May 20, 1926, the RLB was replaced with a Board of Mediation composed of five presidential appointees.

The Transportation Act also charged the ICC with responsibility for concocting a plan to consolidate railroad companies from 186 major and over 1,000 total entities into about 20 competing groups exempt from anti-trust laws. The railroads had to agree that the ICC would establish valuation of assets, maximum and minimum rates, and fair return to shareholders as well as regulate service and traffic and new issues of railroad securities. The commission also would approve or disapprove new railroad construction. Companies had to turn over half of all net earnings in excess of 6% (the recapture clause) to build up a revolving fund to rescue railroads that did not make money.

Interurban electric railroad, Ohio

Although the ICC had no actual authority to force the industry to agree to its consolidation plan, commissioners could institute anti-trust proceedings to force companies to divest redundant lines and subsidiaries. However, when they procrastinated for the entire decade, railroad owners and executives took matters into their own hands. Alfred H. Smith of the New York Central persuaded Cleveland real estate developers Oris P. and Mantis J. Van Sweringen to cobble together a fourth major railroad system in the East from the Nickel Plate, Erie, C&O, and Pere Marquette railways without materially injuring his company's material hauling, merchandise shipment, and passenger businesses. With loans from J.P. Morgan and other banks, the brothers Van Sweringen went on to assemble by 1930 a loosely confederated system covering over 29,000 miles and accounting for 11% of the nation's rail lines, including the Missouri Pacific Railroad and other properties west of the Mississippi. In the process, they used an innovative holding company structure that maximized their

Cleveland Union Terminal Tower

control while minimizing the amount of their own money at risk. Their highly leveraged business empire, topped by the Terminal Tower Complex in Cleveland, amounted at its peak to $3 billion of assets anchored by only $20 million of their own equity. So long as the economy continued to surge and the industry hauled over four-fifths of the nation's freight, a business underpinned by blue smoke and mirrors was possible. If fundamentals deteriorated, such a rickety financial structure would collapse as surely as a decrepit railroad bridge strained to the breaking point by an overloaded train.

Quite a reverse policy was adopted by the government toward the US shipping industry. Although the Merchant Marine (Jones) Act of June 5, 1920 extended the power of the US Shipping Board to propose shipping routes, promote mail and trade service, and operate shipping service, the latter was eventually given over to private hands. The law also authorized the sale of 1,100 government-built ships to private owners and used proceeds up to $25 million for loans to same to build new ships. To insure that the Merchant Marine did not suffer unduly from foreign competition, it mandated that coastwise commerce and mail where practicable be carried in US vessels. From a high of 18 million in 1923, US shipping tonnage slipped to 16 million in 1928. Therefore on May 22 that year, Congress further supported the Merchant Marine with the Jones-White Act, doubling a $125 million ship construction loan fund from which builders could borrow three-quarters the cost of new or reconditioned ships.

Greater certainty about the transportation industry encouraged insurers to cover its risks. INA solicited business not only from railroads but shipping and trucking companies. Brightening prospects and available financing in the latter industry not only permitted Torbenson to regain its independence in Cleveland in 1922 under the name Eaton Axle and Spring Company but expand with the purchase of Cox Brothers of Boston, maker of truck bumpers. A new company called Navistar started making heavy duty trucks, then truck engines, to become by the later 1930s the top producer of medium and heavy trucks in the country. More vehicles of whatever kind was good news for Teetor-Hartley after changing its name to Perfect Circle in 1924 in acknowledgement that its *Perfect Circle* piston ring was by far and away its most important product. Foundation of the National Automotive Parts Association (NAPA) in 1925 followed by the Genuine Parts Company three years later to distribute automotive replacement parts facilitated sales of Spicer's universal joint and other products as well. The company hit $10 million of sales by 1928 and moved operations to Toledo. The next year, it purchased Brown-Lipe, a leading maker of auto transmissions.

Other important sectors of the economy earmarked for regulation by the Wilson

Power house on Mississippi River, Iowa

administration in its dying days were water and power. The genesis was construction by the government in 1918 of a hydroelectric plant costing $145 million to power two munitions factories at Muscle Shoals on the Tennessee River in Alabama. After the war, an attempt to sell the now unnecessary establishments to private interests for the manufacture of fertilizer failed. That state of affairs not only left open the door to what Lenin would call government ownership of the means of production but encouraged Congress to establish a legal basis for doing so. On June 20, 1920, the Senate and House passed the Water Power Act setting up a Federal Power Commission (FPC) composed of the secretaries of War, Interior, and Agriculture with control over water power reserves on public lands (except reservations), navigable streams, falls, rapids, and shallows. The FPC issued licenses for a maximum 50 years for construction of power houses, dams, reservoirs, and transmission lines. The goal was to improve water navigation and regulate water and power rates. At end of leases, the government had the right if desired to take ownership of these properties.

As TR's unexpected rise to the Presidency began the Progressive era, Wilson's precipitous political collapse over failure to push the Versailles Treaty through the Senate and the overwhelming defeat of Democrat James M. Cox, governor of Ohio, in the 1920 election officially ended it. Business leaders now had full support from a Republican-controlled White House and Congress to bully workers into company unions. Reaching a membership of 1.4 million in 1921, or 3% of the workforce, they still posed a mortal threat to the AFL, whose membership was stuck at 4 million. A recession that year sent unemployment surging to 5 million people, 11.9% of the workforce, brought wages down sharply, and caused 20,000 business failures, including of the Maxwell Motor Company. Because only one in six adults had a high school education and a new surge of immigrants had fled war-ravaged Europe for the New World, the labor glut seemed likely to return working men and women to the uncertain existence of the pre-war era. A change in government policy inspired in part by the Red Scare that swung Washington around in the 1920s to strict curbs on newcomers removed that threat. In fact, not until refugees abandoned Europe during and after the Second World War did the country again experience what could be called a flood of immigrants. Still, the American working man and woman did not yet prosper.

Strip coal mining in Kentucky
Organized labor had one last nominal victory before being marginalized by national euphoria over the Roaring 20s and company paternalism. A strike in 1922 by 600,000 bituminous coal workers led by John L. Lewis's

194

United Mine Workers (UMW) forced mine owners to revoke cuts in the $7.50 per day wage rate agreed to three years earlier. Unfortunately, both coal and textile workers split sharply into mainstreamers who wanted to concentrate on wages and working conditions and radicals, inspired if not in some cases taking orders from Moscow, who wanted to use a general strike of all US workers to install a Communist regime. Without unity of purpose, unions struggled even in prosperous times when business profits were peaking to attract new members. Thus by 1929, AFL membership declined to only 2.9 million, 84% of all US workers, while the UMW alone plunged to 80,000 members. Average hourly wage that momentous year was 56.6 cents. Assuming a ten hour work day, average annual wage was $1,415. In 2004 money, the amount would be just $15,550.

Farmall tractor

Meanwhile, the rare episode of prosperity and maximum production enjoyed by farmers during and immediately after the war created an opportunity for a company with deep pockets to muscle in on the farm equipment industry. In 1918, Ford came out with its *Fordson* tractor, producing 34,000 that year to undercut the competition with a price of only $350, as opposed to McCormick-Deering's $1,000 plus price. Also diversifying, Deere acquired the Waterloo Boy Company and its annual production of 5,600 tractors but was promptly blindsided by labor trouble in 1919 over union recognition that caused debilitating strikes. A recession that started in rural areas late the next year eviscerated demand for *Waterloo Boy* tractors so that production fell to only 79 machines in 1921. That forced Deere to slash wages and cut the workforce despite continuing labor protests. By contrast, financial clout permitted Ford to keep prices rock bottom, double sales to 67,000 tractors generating $23.5 million in 1922, and continue to pay healthy wages.

Reasons for the farm recession were twofold, the overexpansion of the war years and the postwar recovery of European agriculture. Once the overall economy slumped, GDP plummeted from $91.4 billion to $77.2 billion. As prices collapsed 40-50%, many of the nation's 6.5 million farms, averaging 146.7 acres and $550 of farm equipment, became highly vulnerable. Swollen already by mortgages on the additional acres added during the war, farm debt climbed 37% by 1923 to $10.8 billion. Exports were further undermined when on May 27, 1921 the new Republican administration and Congress passed an emergency tariff to raise government revenue and reduce the federal deficit. The permanent Fordney-McCumber Tariff of September 21 engendered foreign retaliation by raising duties as high as 53% on manufactured goods, boosting tariffs a lesser amount on farm products, and granting the President only limited authority to adjust individual tariff rates up or down by no more than 50% after recommendation by a Tariff Commission (set up in 1916).

Furthermore, institution of a so-called "American selling system" of establishing duties on chemical products not based on foreign market value but on the selling price of US domestic output made them higher still. That was bad for purchasers of chemicals but good for the Allied Chemical and Dye Corporation, formed in 1920 from a merger of five US companies as a reaction against First World War shortages caused by Germany's traditional domination of the world chemical industry. Allied subsequently built a plant in Hopewell, Virginia to produce and take the global lead in ammonia. DuPont also benefited from protection against foreign chemical imports.

A growing industry much better positioned to weather the vicissitudes of nature and import competition was lumber. Having profited during the war building wooden planes, ships, and army barracks, afterward Weyerhaeuser exploited the Panama Canal to transport Douglas fir from its northwest operations to the east coast on surplus merchant ships. That was the beginning of Weyerhaeuser Steamship Company, the forerunner to Westwood Shipping Lines. The company not only standardized lumber grades, cuts, and sizes with its *4-Square* program but went on during the 1920s to use shavings, scraps, and other leftovers from the milling process to produce *Balsam-Wood* as a fluffy building insulation, *Nu-wood* as composite insulation board, and other new products. Neither did the International Paper Company stand still. Responding to the challenge from Canadian imports, the New York based company bought forest tracts and newsprint mills in Quebec province, then diversified into Southern kraft paper, used for grocery bags, cardboard cases, and other products. Business was so good that company leaders began an employee benefits program including stock options, company housing, life insurance and disability, and nurses and aid stations at mills. Its progressivism created an expectation by employees that munificence would continue indefinitely.

Since a majority in Congress had grown up on farms or in rural areas, senators and representatives could not bear to let market forces alone sort out the agricultural mess. On February 18, 1922, they passed the Cooperative Marketing or Capper-Volstead Act which exempted agricultural producers, cooperatives, and associations from antitrust laws, then the next year the Intermediate Credit Act to facilitate loans for crop financing. The intent was to encourage economies of scale and aggregation of farm financial power, but only massive government support could have rescued farmers producing on marginal lands brought under the plough during the war. At attempt with the McNary-Haugen Act to have Washington purchase the annual surplus in specified commodities for warehousing until prices rose for sale abroad at world prices was defeated. Critics argued that such purchase combined with improved farm machinery, most importantly the *Farmall* tractor of International Harvester (IH, formerly McCormick-Deering), would have encouraged the planting of even more acres, forcing down commodity prices to rock bottom levels. The *Farmall* used a so-called tricycle configuration of front wheels close together and rear wide apart to cultivate row crops, and thus dispense with the need for horses. The model was so successful that IH captured 60% of the tractor market by end of the decade, inducing Ford to give up the American market until 1939 and move production of the Fordson to England. In addition to Deere's 1929 introduction of the *General Purpose* or *GP* tractor, able with a tricycle configuration to fit front wheels between two rows and straddle both with very wide rear wheels, IH's most significant competition came from tracked tractor maker Caterpillar Company, formed by the 1925 merger of Holt Manufacturing Company and C.L. Best Tractor Company.

Despite these technological improvements, agriculture went into a period of stagnation in which numbers of farms and acres per farm remained about the same and government policy failed to alleviate distress. Still, Congress tried with the August 24, 1924 Agricultural Credits Act that loaned dealers and cooperatives $304 million through 1932 to buy and hold farm goods for domestic and foreign trade and so prevent dumping at low prices and farm bankruptcies. Growth in acres of soybean crops encouraged, as Carver had hoped, construction of southern mills to extract oil. A mechanical device by John and Mack Rust in 1927 increased efficiency of cotton-picking but could not, even in combination with other innovations, spark a general recovery. That was the reason, Aetna Insurance Company, with over $30 million annual revenue but much of its assets tied up in farm mortgages, had to take possession of so many bankrupt properties. After effecting repairs and making improvements, the firm leased them to tenants in the hope of selling them back to farmers when prices rose again, but with the coming depression, this was not possible until after the Second World War.

The woes of farmers were a large reason that foreign trade fell about 55% from a 1920 peak to only $3.8 million exports against $2.5 million imports the next year. On the other hand, the balance of trade and more importantly balance of payments which includes financial transactions remained favorable. In addition to the $9 billion loaned by Washington to the allies, US investors had purchased $2.3 billion of allied bonds, which generated interest payments from across the Atlantic. By 1920, total US investment overseas was at $7.9 billion over twice the foreign investment remaining in the United States. Thus, for the first time in American history, the republic changed from a debtor to a creditor nation. With subsequent loans, principally to alleviate crises revolving around stalled German reparations payments to the victorious allies, total foreign liabilities held by the US government and citizens mounted by 1929 to $15 billion. Trade, too, despite the higher tariff of 1921 picked up after the recession. By end of the decade, the US sent $5.2 billion worth of goods overseas and took back $4.4 billion.

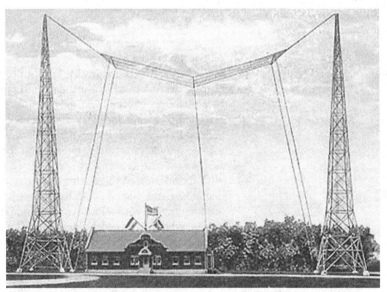

Radio broadcasting from Zion, Illinois

To a policy of protection for industry and labor markets was added a repugnance of foreign ideas. Legislation culminating with the Radio Act of February 3, 1927 capped direct foreign ownership of US radio airwaves at 20%. Indirect ownership through minority stakes in US companies was held to 25%. The FTC had the right to make exceptions but almost never did.

As for regulation beyond what had already been left in place by the Wilson administration, the entire thrust of the "return to normalcy" approach was to reverse or at least cap government intervention in the economy. Rather Washington concentrated on putting its own fiscal house in order. Taxes on individual incomes, now accounting for nearly 47% of revenue, were so severely cut on the advice of Secretary of the Treasury Andrew Mellon to a top marginal rate in 1925 of 25% on incomes over $100,000 that even with a flat corporate tax rate fluctuating between 13.5% and 11% the federal government had only $70 million to spend. Assigning three dollars of every ten to interest payments on the national debt steadily reduced the public burden to $16 billion by 1930. The only other major expenses considered the legitimate province of government were federal administration, military costs, and veterans' benefits. Once the Army was reduced to about 220,000 men, the Navy forced by the Washington Naval Treaties of 1921-22 to scrap 845,000 tons of shipping, and an isolationist policy focused on defense of the Western Hemisphere, national defense cost the government little more than $15 million a year. Naturally, then, Washington had neither the wherewithal nor inclination to stick its nose into private business matters beyond what was required by legislation on the books. With the recovery of 1923-24, revelation of widespread graft and corruption in the Harding administration, and election of "Silent" Calvin Coolidge as permanent replacement for Harding, who died of an embolism in August 2, 1923, federal activism virtually disappeared.

MASS COMMUNICATIONS AND ENTERTAINMENT

Simon Smith Kuznets

Heretofore, government statistics about the economy had been haphazard and imprecise. Many of the figures included in this book in previous chapters were derived from estimates after the fact. Establishment of regulatory agencies necessarily required to gather industry data as well as the Federal Reserve System began to build up a more reliable system for gathering information about the economy. A further step forward occurred in 1926 with foundation of the National Bureau of Economic Research. Simon Smith Kuznets, a Russian-born immigrant with a Ph.D. from Columbia University, who came up with a definition of national income as the sum of earnings from wages, profits, interest, and rents, was employed in that office. Eventually in the 1930s, a calculation of GNP as the total market value of final goods and services produced during a calendar or fiscal year was made more exact. GDP differs from GNP in that the former does not include income earned from investment abroad paid to Americans nor income earned from investments domestically that is then paid to foreigners abroad. In 1941, Kuznets published *National Income and Its Composition, 1910 to 1938*, for which thirty years later he won the Noble Prize for Economics.

Because of the efforts of Kuznets and other economists, it was ascertained that old industries in coal, textiles, lumber, flour milling, and of course agriculture were no longer enjoying the robust growth rates of the previous century. Even steel came down from the First World War peak, though Bethlehem Steel grew swiftly to 8.5 million tons of capacity and 60,000 employees by 1925 through acquisitions and contracts to build the USS *Lexington*, the nation's first aircraft carrier, as well as steel for famous landmarks the Golden Gate Bridge in San Francisco, Rockefeller Plaza in New York City, the Supreme Court building in Washington D.C., and other structures in major cities. Rising industries included chemicals, especially dyes, synthetic fibers in particular rayon, automobiles, radios, and other consumer durables. The one that really caught the temper of the times, however, was entertainment.

Back in March 1915, the epic silent film *The Birth of a Nation* film by David Llewelyn Wark (D.W.) Griffith opened in New York City to rave reviews and titanic box office. Costing $100,000 (or about $1.9 million in 2004 money), it ultimately over the years earned $48 million. After the war, the motion picture industry capitalized on the larger-than-life, very bankable images projected onto over 10,000 movie theater screens to double annual ticket sales above the pre-war level of 5 million. Italian-born *great lover* Rudolf Valentino, British-born *little hobo* Charlie Chaplin, America's Canadian-born *sweetheart* Mary Pickford, and the *dashing* Douglas Fairbanks (from Denver) all became huge public idols. With Griffith, the latter three formed the United Artists studio in 1920 to distribute their independently made films. Chaplin and Pickford each made at their peak $350,000 a picture.

Mary Pickford

Competing companies, including Metro-Goldwyn-Mayer (MGM), Warner Brothers, Paramount, and 20th Century Fox fostered a "studio system" in which major stars under contract for salary up to $10,000 a week not only were featured in *A* films but promising actors churned out enough *B* pictures to satisfy the entertainment and movie-hungry public. Technological improvements such as the *Technicolor* process of Herbert T. Kalmus in 1922 and De Forest's phonofilms the next year transcribing sound waves into electric impulses, which were then photographed on celluloid and passed around a photo-electric cell in a projector, sold even more tickets. Improvements in motion picture quality were essential because competition for the entertainment dollar grew fiercer as the decade progressed. Especially during the recession, Americans needed an outlet that did not consume a major part of their paychecks.

Unwisely from an economic perspective, the country had through the 18th amendment of 1919 to the Constitution banned "the manufacture, sale, or transportation of intoxicating liquors within, the importation thereof into, or the exportation thereof from the United States and all territory subject to the jurisdiction thereof for beverage purposes." Congress then passed the National Prohibition Enforcement (Volstead) Act of

October 28, defining intoxicating liquor as any beverage containing more than 0.5% alcohol, with a starting date for the Prohibition era of January 16, 1920. The net effect of this legislation was to force Anheuser Busch and other heretofore legitimate producers of beer and alcohol to diversify into ginger ale, ice cream, root beer, and other products they would otherwise have ignored and added illegal booze to the enticements of gambling and prostitution proffered by crime organizations, in particular the Italian *La Cosa Nostra* or Mafia, to the public in speak-easy night clubs. The most notorious and murderous Mafioso of the time, Al Capone of Chicago, quickly aggregated an annual income for his syndicate of $60 million. Although Capone was finally in 1931 convicted of tax evasion and sent to prison, the tentacles of the Mafia gradually wrapped around the construction industry, labor unions, and loan sharking. Even after Prohibition was repealed in 1933, its financial clout was enormous. Although exact figures for crime syndicate revenue are impossible to estimate, an idea of the financial rewards for catering to human vice can be obtained from present day earnings. Legal gambling activities alone in 2004 brought in over $25 billion.

For those citizens who desired a vicarious thrill that carried no risk of arrest and conviction, the *New York Daily News* of the McCormick-Patterson chain rode sensationalist stories about crime and sex to a circulation of 1.75 million. After 1922, newspapers included photographs sent over telephone wires, after 1925 from across the Atlantic. They were assisted by AT&T's decision to complete universal service to all parts of the country. To concentrate resources on the effort, Ma Bell not only spun off at mid-decade what became the Graybar Corporation, distributor of non-telephone electrical devices made by other manufacturers, but sold its international operations to newly formed International Telephone and Telegraph Company.

Man O'War

A more cultured look at the world was found in articles in *Time Magazine*, founded March 3, 1923 by Henry R. Luce, son of a missionary in China. Luce steadily built up a publishing empire that included *Fortune* (1930), *Life* (1936), *House and Home* (1952), and *Sports Illustrated* (1954). Too, more popular novels appeared, including Harry Sinclair Lewis' 1926 best seller *Elmer Gantry*. Hawking books in 1920 to the country's population of 106 million people (rising even without large-scale immigration to over 121 million by 1929), of whom 29% now had a high school education, could bring large profits.

Another entertainment phenomenon that exploded before the public's eyes was spectator sports. Construction of racetracks and stadiums seating tens of thousands of people permitted crowds of fanatical supporters (hence the derivative "fans") to watch the racehorse Man O' War pile up $250,000 in winnings in 1919-20, the *Galloping Ghost* Red Grange dodge tacklers for the University of Illinois and the Chicago Bears, and slugger Babe Ruth of the New York Yankees hit 60 home runs while receiving a huge salary that would peak three years later at $80,000, the equivalent of $880,000 in 2004 money. Touring Vaudeville acts in small towns, Broadway shows by George M. Cohan and other playwrights, magic acts performed by the great Harry Houdini as well as plays and symphonies were also considered healthier

entertainment than frequenting speak-easies, betting on the outcome of events, and boosting the wherewithal of organized crime to corrupt with bribes city officials, police officers, and judges. Even during the Depression, public need for diversion pushed numbers attending live sporting events and performances to new heights. Present day revenues for the former are about $20 billion, for the latter $10 billion. The pay of most athletes and entertainers, however, lagged for decades.

As movies and sports captured the rapt attention of Americans of all ages, music filled them increasingly with joy. In 1919, they purchased 25 million 78 revolutions per minute (rpm) records playing on Victor, Columbia, OKeh, and other phonographs, generating $150 million in revenue for the industry. In addition to classical music, marches, speeches, and novelties, they listened to a more spirited Dixieland sound that had its origin with the compositions of Scott Joplin and other black Americans. Ragtime music, begun in 1911 with Irving Berlin's *Alexander's Ragtime Band*, reached a peak of popularity with Nick La Rocca's *Tiger Rag*. Joplin, who died in 1917, did not receive public credit for his musical innovation until decades later when popularized by the 1973 movie *The Sting*. The first American recognized as a great and prolific composer was Russian-born George Gershwin, whose *Rhapsody in Blue*, launched a career in which he wrote hundreds of songs and persuaded hundreds of thousands of his countrymen to buy sheet music for pennies a page from Harm, Inc., Jerome H. Remick and Company, and other firms. Electrical recording techniques and the advent in the mid-1920s of less expensive electric phonographs with higher volume also pleased the public. Columbia and the Music Corporation of America (MCA) became the leading music producing companies by signing up Mamie Smith, Louis Armstrong, and other singers and musicians.

Itching to get a piece of the growing music pie, GE had its general counsel Owen D. Young round up AT&T, the United Fruit Company, and Westinghouse to take over the assets of the Marconi Wireless Company. Pooling applicable patents, they established the Radio Corporation of America (RCA) on August 20, 1920 and appointed chairman Russian-born David Sarnoff, who had worked as a wireless operator for Marconi and come to prominence by staying doggedly at his station for 72 hours in 1912 to receive distress signals from the doomed ocean-liner Titanic. As Westinghouse established the radio station WWJ in Detroit to play classical music intermixed with radio dramas and news and AT&T founded WEAF in New York City, RCA as well as many small companies including portable radio innovator Zenith Corporation manufactured and sold radio sets to the public. The number of receivers not only picking up popular music but broadcasts of local independent stations owned by churches, colleges, newspapers, and even city governments grew from a scant 5,000 in 1920 to 2.5 million four years later.

Radiola

In 1925, refrigerator manufacturer American Appliance Company came up with a gaseous rectifier or tube to permit radios to be plugged into wall sockets instead of using batteries. Within a year, the *Raytheon* brand radio tube raked in over $1 million for the firm, renamed the Raytheon Manufacturing Corporation. As standardization of electrical outlets and plugs required by national electric and housing codes as well as high-capacity wiring and multiple wall outlets in new houses proceeded, radio sales exploded. *Radiolas* and other radio equipment generated $46 million in sales for RCA alone in 1925. But in 1928, the Philadelphia Storage Battery Company, already in the business of making radio batteries, not only started making home sets but radios for installation in cars. Philco, as the company came to be known, hit the jackpot in summer 1930 with its Model 20 *Cathedral* home radio set.

Hot on its heels was the Galvin Manufacturing Corporation of Chicago. Founded in 1928 by Paul V. Galvin to make battery eliminators so radios could feed directly from house current, it developed *Motorola* brand radios for car installation that cost as little as $110. However, subsequent improvements by Philco, including high fidelity and wireless remote control, made that company and not Galvin the industry leader throughout the 1930s. By decade's end, four out of five American homes had a radio, and radio advertising revenue exceeded magazine ad sales.

The hodgepodge of radio stations began to be organized into networks with the founding in 1926 of the National Broadcasting Company (NBC). A subsidiary of RCA but minority owned by GE (30%) and Westinghouse (20%), NBC bought WEAF in New York City from AT&T as its anchor, and then expanded swiftly to include 25 other stations nationwide. Recognizing that order must be brought to what quickly could have become sound wave chaos, on February 23, 1927 Congress passed the Radio Act to claim ownership of the heretofore unappraised airwaves. A five man Radio Commission assigned licenses.

Furthermore, the government encouraged the United Independent Broadcasters to establish the next year the Columbia Broadcasting System (CBS), headed by William S. Paley, a Chicago cigar manufacturer who early on recognized the value of radio advertising, as a rival radio network. Licensees had to agree to serve the public interest by providing equal time for political candidates and persons with different political points of view and keep speech and material considered obscene off the air. Worried that the RCA network was becoming too powerful, the government in 1931 put pressure on RCA to split into Red and Blue networks and GE and Westinghouse the next year to give up their stakes. Later, the Radio Act of June 19, 1934 expanded the Radio Commission to seven persons and added jurisdiction over telephones, thus encouraging AT&T to cut long-distance rates, including trans-Atlantic and trans-Pacific calls at $75 for the first three minutes to nearly half.

Walt Disney

Radio put pressure on the movie industry to liven up films. Previously, the only music possible for silent pictures was provided by pianists playing mood scores in theaters. That technique worked best for action pieces and a new innovation called cartoons. In 1923, Walter E. Disney moved from Chicago to Hollywood, California to have graphic artists draw and colorize over the next three years the animated film *Alice in Cartoonland*. *Oswald the Rabbit*, combining animation with live action, followed. Disney and graphic artist Ubbe Iwerks made a breakthrough in 1928 by making *Plane Crazy* starring the cartoon character that became an American icon Mickey Mouse.

Another 1928 Mickey Mouse vehicle *Steamboat Willie* was the first cartoon that included a talking sound track. That innovation became possible after Warner Brothers bought the *Vitaphone* system in 1926 and began working on pictures with music and sound effects, the first being *Don Juan* starring John Barrymore. But it was *The Jazz Singer*, released October 6, 1927 and featuring Al Jolson singing, that forced every other studio to give up silent productions. 20th Century Fox developed the *Movietone* system to make sound newsreels for theaters and encourage the large investment needed to install sound equipment in the nation's theaters.

BIG INDUSTRY GETS BIGGER

In the 1920s, entertainment was still considered ancillary to the country's economic fortunes. Revenue, profits, and jobs depended overwhelmingly on industries with manufacturing operations and new innovations and inventions to make them more cost-efficient. However exciting and pleasing the emergence of talking pictures, the discovery in 1928 that tungsten carbide, then tantalum carbide, could be used to make "super-speed" cutting tools on materials formerly uncuttable was more fundamental to national progress. The expectation on the part of captains of industry that American know-how would always provide new business opportunities and expansion was high.

Fortunately, electric power for manufacturing was growing. As well as new generating plants being built in cities, J.P. Morgan Company saw wisdom in following the pattern of Pennsylvania Power & Light (PPL) in consolidating control of many companies in the industry. Thus, the New York firm financed holding companies, most particularly GE's Electric Bond and Share Company (EBASCO) which came to control other holding companies in a multi-tier arrangement that, for example, owned PPL four levels down. Edison's former associate and president of Chicago Edison Samuel Insull formed the Middle West Utilities holding company. Additionally, American Gas and Electric Company acquired a network of utilities from Virginia to Michigan, Western Power Corporation as well as Pacific Gas and Electric accumulated concerns in California, Southeastern Power & Light and Commonwealth & Southern did the same in Dixie, and the Public Service Corporation, forerunner of today's Public Service Enterprise Group, gobbled up power companies in the East, Central and South. After Frank Jay Gould's Virginia Railway and Power Company bought up Engineers Public Service in 1925 and other consolidations took place, by decade's end 16 holding companies possessed 85% of the nation's utilities while the top three alone controlled 42%. In fact, with wildcat drillers in Texas and Oklahoma growing into mammoth oil companies in a short time, seemingly the only possibility for a small entity to survive in energy was in out-of-the-way corners of the country. The El Paso Corporation got its start that way in 1928, finding natural gas near the west Texas city that looks across the Mexican border at Ciudad Juarez.

During and after the First World War, there arose a new kind of business leader presiding over more complex corporate organizations. The first was Thomas J. Watson, Sr., a National Cash Register executive signed away in 1914 to serve as general manager, then president of the Computing Tabulating Corporation of New York City. The company sold mechanical key and hand-operated gang punch machines as well as vertical sorters and tabulators to chemical and life insurance companies, railroads, and utilities. It needed Watson's innovations of sales incentives, excellent service, and team spirit for over 3,000 employees to double revenues by 1918 to $9 million with net profits of over $1 million. New products, including the first electric accounting machine in 1920, as well as acquisitions of other businesses selling similar or related products doubled revenue and employees again over the next ten years but boosted profits seven fold. Watson renamed the company International Business Machines or IBM in 1924.

**Genealogy of Business Machine
Companies, 1886-1945**

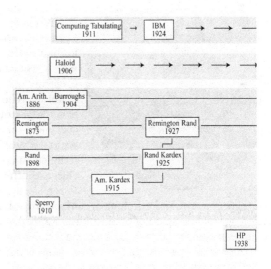

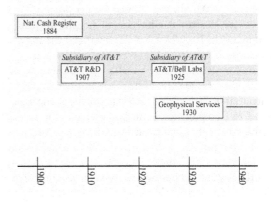

205

Alfred P. Sloan, Jr.

Another role-model for would-be corporate leaders was Alfred P. Sloan, Jr., owner of the Hyatt Roller Bearing Company. In May 1916, he sold out for $5 million to Durant's United Motors Corporation, which also combined Durant's Chevrolet Motor Company and Kettering's Dayton Engineering Laboratories. When Durant used the financial backing of GM's Chairman of the Board Pierre S. DuPont to accumulate enough GM stock to oust Nash, Sloan went to work for Durant at GM. Durant's retirement in 1919, then DuPont's in 1923 made him chief executive officer (CEO).

What Sloan brought to the job was a genius for strategic concept and efficient organization. After establishing overall objectives, including building up major product lines to appeal to different segments of the market ("a car for every purse and purpose"), he permitted division executives substantial autonomy carrying out the plan. In 1924, he ordered GM's first overseas assembly plant in Copenhagen, Denmark. His success with a low-end to high-end approach, spearheaded by the middle-of-the-road Chevrolet division, persuaded Ford in 1925 to buy the struggling Lincoln Motor Company and its luxury V-8 car from former Cadillac and GM executive Leland for $8 million. That was too little, too late to prevent GM, beginning to make Pontiac cars in its Oakland division in 1926, from tripling market share to 40% and surging past Ford for industry leadership. Ford was compelled to shut down *Model T* production, retool to make an improved *Model A*, and come back to 34% market share of 4.45 million cars produced in 1929.

Ford Model A

Another competitor that survived a consolidation in the automobile market from 108 producers in 1920 to 44 in 1929 was former Buick/GM executive Walter P. Chrysler's Chrysler Motor Company. In 1921-22, Chrysler arranged the purchase of the bankrupt Maxwell Motor Company's assets for $10.8 million as well as the Chalmers Motor Company assets for $2 million. Although the 32,000 cars he made in 1925 were few by comparison to Ford's and GM's output, in 1928 he bought Dodge Brothers, Inc. from the New York banking firm Dillon, Read, & Company for a whopping $170 million. Adding a Plymouth low-end and DeSota high-end line, he soon turned out over one hundred thousand cars and trucks a year. Five other still notable entities — Hudson, Willys-Overland, Nash (formerly Jeffrey's), Packard, and Studebaker — with aggregate production of 700,000 cars and trucks, filled out the roster of important motor vehicle companies providing over the years employment directly or indirectly through tire, engine, and other suppliers for millions of Americans.

In 1918, the DuPont Company's invested $25 million in GM. The chemical producer also sold *Fabrikoid* artificial leather for convertible tops and seat covers to car manufacturers. Then in 1923, DuPont came out with *Duco*, a long-wearing, fast-drying finish for GM's Oakland line that cut that part of the manufacturing process from 14 days to two. *Duco* subsequently improved the appearance and durability of appliances, hardware, and toys. Likewise, innovation from the Minnesota Mining and Manufacturing Company (3M), founded and failing in 1902 to mine corundum to make sandpaper and grinding wheels only to succeed by purchasing a waterproof sandpaper for auto finishing work from a Philadelphia company, advanced the fit and finish of cars. The company's big moment came when masking tape for auto part painting developed into the more consumer oriented *Scotch Tape* brand.

Another company that scored a breakthrough eventually useful in car dashboards and paneling was B.F. Goodrich. In 1926, Dr. Waldo Semon concocted polyvinyl chloride, a resin which when mixed with rubber could be used to make phonograph records. Though the company could not rival Goodyear's sales that year of $230 million, share of world production of rubber products equal to about 15%, and tire sales exceeding 20 million by end of the decade, it did gain the wherewithal like Firestone, world leader in truck tire production, to shape the industry. Buying up smaller companies eventually made US Rubber a fourth major player and consolidated the industry from 134 companies during the First World War to a few dozen.

The growing size and complexity of GM and other corporate giants at a time when government was turning its back on labor permitted Sloan and other CEOs to rule as Carnegie and others had the last century with an iron hand. However, because tremendous profits could be won by keeping production lines open while the economy boomed, they adopted what has been called Welfare Capitalism. In essence, this was a program of reform instituted from above in which businesses voluntarily went to shorter work weeks, offered marginal wage increases, and built new factories with better lay out and equipment. Business leaders pointed to a low 4% unemployment rate at mid-decade or 1.8 million out of 45 million as evidence that paternalism would improve working conditions, efficiency, and modernity better than confrontation. Believing the changes permanent, employees saw less reason to organize into independent unions and implement strikes. William Green of the UMW, head of the AFL after Gompers' death in 1924, had to contend with 400 company unions across the country.

Upgrading plants required substantial financing. Accepted corporate policy evolved from paying out a substantial portion of profits in dividends to using a higher percentage of cash for capital investment. Increased emphasis on reducing accounts outstanding and limiting inventories with more rapid turnover of materials and supplies also freed capital for factory construction and other improvements. Annual construction spending nearly doubled from $6.7 billion in 1919 to $12.1 billion seven years later before slowing gradually to $10.8 billion in 1929.

But it was the automobile and truck industry that led the way in lifting the US economy to $103.7 billion of GDP on the eve of the Great Depression. By 1929, annual production of cars and other motor vehicles exceeded 5.3 million. Not only the major vehicle producers but parts manufacturers such as the Parker Appliance Company of Cleveland (later Parker-Hannafin) that made pneumatic braking systems for trucks and buses as well as planes reached an apogee. Gasoline production rose to 48% of all refined products.

Oil tank farm in Oklahoma

More paved roads out of cities permitted construction of housing in what became the first large suburbs. In addition to residential construction companies, sub-contractors provided electrical wiring, heating, and plumbing systems. Although builders remained local entities, a broader national market did become possible for makers of radiators, sinks, and toilets. The most notable firms to emerge were the American Radiator Company (1872) and the Standard Sanitary Company (1875) which merged in 1929 to claim a 50% share of the market for their American-Standard brand products in both the US and Europe.

The one industry most adversely affected by the motor vehicle boom was of course railroads. Not only cars and trucks but airplane transport caused track in use to decline nearly 140,000 miles by 1929 to 260,000 miles and the passenger component of operating revenue to fall from $105 million in 1923, or 25%, to $86 million, less than 20%. The ability of trucks, in particular, to delivery to residence doors gave a boost to Sears Roebuck, Montgomery Ward, and other mail order houses. Although trains still carried 450 billion ton-miles of freight, their 90% share of the total would steadily erode over ensuing decades.

Immediately after the First World War, air transport won a high profile coup. The government let contracts for airmail service, first in 1918 between New York City and Washington D.C., then across the continent two years later, finally in October 1920 with the Western Hemisphere Company for international delivery. Night flights began with a Chicago to Cheyenne, Wyoming run in 1923. The Kelly Act of 1925 made the system more orderly and cost-effective by requiring private bidding to win airmail contracts. The Air Commerce Act of 1926 provided direct government assistance to civil aviation and navigation by building airports, thus encouraging INA to begin insuring aircraft and Connecticut General to insure airline passengers as well as provide group insurance for aircraft manufacturing company employees. Air passenger service stood poised to expand beyond its small footprint of 8,252 miles of domestic air routes carrying 5,782 paying passengers.

What popularized the industry was the May 20-21, 1927 success of former army pilot and air-mail flyer Charles A. Lindbergh, Jr. making the first nonstop flight across the Atlantic from New York to Paris on the *Spirit of St. Louis* and winning a $25,000 prize. When on September 1 the American Railway Express Agency and the airlines made a pact to facilitate air express mail and package delivery, the industry took firm root. Having won a contract for the Chicago to San Francisco route, Boeing Air Transport delivered 220,000 pounds of air mail and express cargo. Its move into passenger transport also helped it become an industry leader, employing 800 people by 1929.

Planes, trucks, buses, and cars required fuel. The unrestrained expansion of the automobile industry would not have been possible without all-out effort to make more gasoline, including operations by newly founded Signal Gasoline Company in California to turn natural gas into that product. However, abundance did not come until discovery of more huge crude oil fields in East Texas, Oklahoma, and California jacked up production to 443 million 42-gallon barrels worth $3.07 at the well head, or just over $57 billion. A maturing system of oil pipelines, refineries, and tanker trucks brought this precious resource to consumers. Concomitantly, oil company efforts, such as Richfield Oil Company giving Fluor Construction Company its big break to build a 10,000 gallon a day natural gas plant, increased supplies of that more abundant, cheaper, cleaner burning, and heat efficient energy source for home heating. Technological advances in longer distance transport through pipelines of natural gas created another prodigious coast-to-coast energy industry for the republic.

INNOVATION OF CONSUMER SPENDING FUNDED WITH DEBT

Ford's *Model T* followed by GM's Buick and Pontiac cars and Chrysler's Plymouth brought the most prestigious consumer durable within the financial wherewithal of the middle and best paid working class. What helped the motor vehicle industry to surpass all others in revenue was development of a more sophisticated credit industry that permitted consumers to buy big ticket items on installment plans. In actual fact, the Studebaker Motor Company had been first in 1911 to permit purchase on a deferred payment plan, but GM was more successful eight years later with its General Motors Acceptance Corporation. The extended period of prosperity that bathed the country in a glow of excess after 1923 encouraged not only installment plans but charge accounts with stores and single-payment loans. Soon, the principle of borrowing against future income for present prosperity was so aggressively applied that even persons of marginal income obtained credit. The consumer credit industry ballooned to $7.1 billion or 9.2% of personal consumption by 1929, half installment plans and half other debt as well as interest payments. Unwittingly, Congress helped increase the attractiveness of indebtedness with the Revenue Acts of February 26, 1926 and May 29, 1928 that lowered personal income and inheritance taxes. Each dollar cut from government coffers and returned to citizen pockets could be leveraged for purchases, causing consumer durable spending to surge.

Thus, annual sales of heavy household appliances such as Westinghouse's first fully automatic electric range priced at $325, refrigerators made by GM's subsidiary Frigidaire Corporation falling in price from $600 to $290 by end of the decade, and washing machines from the Maytag Company, begun in 1893 as a maker of farm threshing machine feeders, rose from $109 million to $268 million. Portable electric devices, including a phonograph put out by RCA in 1927, advanced from $71 million to $106 million. More fantastic gains were made by the technological wonder of the era, radios, to 13.75 million sets owned by Americans in 1930. Annual revenue from radios and related equipment vaulted 1,400% to $843 million. In fact, on the eve of the Great Depression, Americans owned consumer goods of all kinds worth $34 billion. That was seven times the figure for 1914.

Consumer durables are categorized as fixed assets. Unlike houses and other buildings which in theory maintain value, cars, radios, washing machines, vacuum cleaners, and

Genealogy of US Oil Companies, 1859-1948

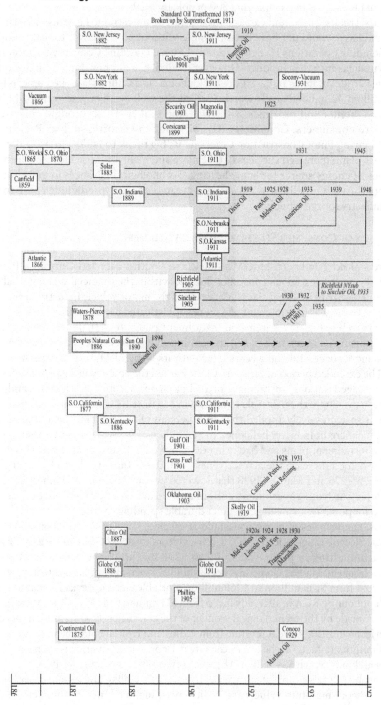

other such possessions depreciate over time until they break down, rust out, or diminish in value to a small residual amount. On the other hand, non-durable consumer items including food and even clothes are quickly used up and lose value for accounting purposes. Whatever residual value they have is typically not included in household net worth calculations.

Cigarette ad

Nevertheless, it became the purpose of the advertising industry, amounting annually to around $3 billion of revenue, to convince Americans that products of convenience and luxury including cosmetics, disposable razors, shampoo, soap, and toothpaste were not only advantageous to enhance personal appearance and sexual attractiveness but essential for the mental, emotional, and physical well-being of human beings. Using billboards, signs, magazine and catalogue ads, and increasingly radio spots, advertising agencies hawked a growing volume of non-durable products including San Francisco-based Clorox Chemical Company's liquid bleach, DuPont's sensation cellophane, providing transparent packaging of foods and other products as well as moisture-proof sanitation, Kimberly-Clark's *Kleenex* facial tissue, and P&G's *Camay* beauty soap. By strengthening brand name foods, they increased the incentive for National Biscuit to buy Shredded Wheat (cereal and *Triscuit* wafers) in 1928 to gain the clout to compete with Kellogg, adding *Rice Krispies* the same year, and Postum, making *Maxwell House* coffee, *Jell-O* gelatin, and *Kraft* cheese in addition to cereal. A government naturalist from New York City named Clarence Birdseye, who had worked in Labrador as a fur trader, was encouraged enough by the trend to start the General Seafood Company and develop a *Birdseye* line of frozen packaged fish, fruits, and vegetables, which Postum purchased in 1929 before changing its name to General Foods Corporation. Meanwhile, a merger in the household and personal goods industry put Colgate together with Palmolive-Peet in 1928. Gillette took over Gaisman's AutoStrap Safety Razor Company two years later.

The most influential consumer non-durable products maker in the country and Canada remained Procter & Gamble. Alarmed because surges and slumps in orders from wholesalers caused instability in production and difficulties managing inventory, company executives in 1919 decided to cut out the middleman and sell directly to retailers. Emulated by other household, personal, and food producers, that decision then freed groceries and drug stores from the grip of wholesalers. Benefiting from the fact that urban dwellers now outnumbered rural, Kroger's, Skaggs, Safeway, and others kept more profit and emerged as major companies, albeit not nearly the size of A&P, surging toward $437 million of sales in 1925 and over $1 billion five years later from over 15,700 stores. Among drug store chains, Walgreens of Chicago experienced the most spectacular rise from 20 stores in the Chicago area in 1919 to 525 in 1929. Wider aisles and Ivar "Pop" Coulson's 1922 innovation of a 20

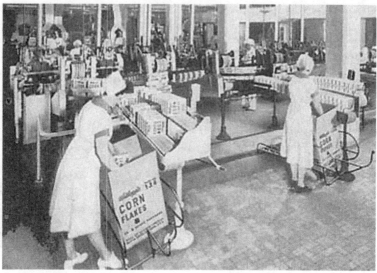

Packing Kellogg's Corn Flakes, Battle Creek, Michigan

cent milk shake mixed with Walgreen's extra rich vanilla ice cream scoop pulled in customers.

In point of fact, virtually every drug store in the country had a soda fountain. Frank Mars and son Forrest walked into one in Tacoma, Washington and suddenly had a good idea to produce a chocolate malted milk product that customers could put in their pockets for later consumption. The result in 1923 was the *Milky Way* bar. Later additions to the product line in the 1930s of *Snickers* and *Mars Almond* bars as well as *M&Ms* put the Mars Company of Minneapolis and eventually McLean, Virginia on solid footing.

The other major product at soda fountains was soft drinks. They became all the more pervasive and popular after Pfizer in 1919 discovered a way to mass produce citric acid by mold fermentation of sugar, obviating the necessity of citrus concentrate imports from Europe, and caused the price of a pound of citric acid to fall from $1.25 to only 20 cents in 1939. Another supplier of soft drink additives was Monsanto Chemical Works of St. Louis. Originally founded in 1901 to make saccharin for Coca-Cola, it had expanded into caffeine and vanilla to reach $1 million of sales in 1915. However, government allegations in 1917, not beaten back until 1925, that saccharin was unsafe for people to ingest, caused a strategic shift. The company became the nation's largest producer of aspirin.

Ironically in the 1920s, Bristol-Myers abandoned the pharmaceutical business altogether to concentrate on its main products *Sal Hepatica* laxative, *Ipana* toothpaste, and other toiletries, antiseptics, and cough syrups. By 1924, profits from sales in 26 countries exceeded $1 million. That success inspired Johnson & Johnson, a company founded in 1885 in New Brunswick, New Jersey to make antiseptic surgical dressings, to strike commercial gold with its *Band Aid* brand bandages, Johnson's *Baby Cream*, and other commercial products. Plough Company, started in 1908 by 16 year old Abe Plough with $125 borrowed from his father to sell homemade remedies out of a horse-drawn wagon to rural folk around Memphis, Tennessee, became incorporated in 1922 to produce popular consumer products, ultimately including *Dr. Scholl's* foot powder, *St. Joseph's* aspirin for children, and

Postum Cereal plant, Battle Creek, Michigan

Maybelline cosmetics. More focused on pure pharmaceuticals, Eli Lilly saved many lives by introducing in 1923 *Iletin*, the first commercial insulin product for diabetes, then a fatal disease. American Home Products, founded in 1926 by William H. Kirn and others to purchase Deshell Laboratories of California, a maker of prescription laxative *Petrolagar*, mixed medicinal lines with consumer products by buying *Old English* floor wax and going overseas in 1929 with *Kolynos* brand toothpaste.

The continuing trend toward urbanization helped Sears as well as Woolworth's, now selling everything from Newell curtain rods to Hoover vacuum cleaners, make the Dow Jones Industrial Average of the nation's top 20 industrial stocks by 1924. Penney's establishments doubled to 626 in 1926, doing $91 million of sales, then doubled again to 1,252 stores with about $180 million sales in 1929. No wonder that Sears and Montgomery Ward at mid-decade supplemented their mail order businesses with retail stores. Within four years, the former had 319 stores, the latter 531. Meanwhile, Skaggs and Safeway combined their 750 grocery stores under the former's control but the latter's name. New companies such as A&W Root Beer, started in Lodi, California in 1918, opened fast-food stands. In fact by 1929, 150,000 chain stores accounted for 20% of all retail sales, up from 4% in 1919. Kroger alone had a whopping 5,575 stores. Only specialized businesses like W.W. Grainger, founded in Chicago in 1927, to sell electric motors through a catalog called the *Motorbook*, escaped for the moment the movement toward retail. Nevertheless in the 1930s, that company was forced to add branches in two dozen cities serviced by territory sales representatives.

Immune for the most part to downward price influence of discounters, big department stores found it necessary to merge into larger operations and standardize merchandise to compete against each other as well as Sears and Montgomery Ward's higher end goods selling at lower prices such as Upton Machine Company washing machines. In 1928, the Hahn Department Stores holding company combined previously independent operations. Promptly the next year, a Federated Department Stores based in Columbus, Ohio merged the operations of Abraham & Strauss, Lazarus (including subsidiary Shillito's of Cincinnati), Filene's in Boston, and Bloomingdale's. Its first year combined sales were $112 million. Overall retail spending topped $48 billion. Consumer purchases now composed nearly 50% of GDP.

Drake Hotel, Chicago

The surge in consumer durable purchases was made possible by major retail stores and chains offering installment purchases. Customers took possession of goods, and then paid over time with a level monthly amount that included principle and interest on principle. This was an extension of the practice that had been applied by banks to house payments since before the turn of the century. Although several institutions, including Chicago-based Associate Financial Corporation in 1925, stuck with real estate loans to rise up in the industry, high rates on installment purchases tempted banks to find ways and means to become part of the riskier but more lucrative business of financing cars and large appliances.

In 1921, National City Bank of New York obtained even more means than the $1 billion asset base achieved in the year following the end of the First World War by offering compound interest on savings accounts. The next year, Bank of New York also achieved enhanced ability to assume risk by linking up with the New York Life and Trust Company, inspiring Wells Fargo the next year to combine with the Union Trust and other mergers to take place. Washington Mutual took a different tack by advertising a school savings program for children that attracted 17,000 little depositors the first day. In 1924, State Street became the nation's first custodian of a mutual fund. At mid-decade, Household was first of banks specializing in consumer finance to go public, acquiring through stock sale more financial clout. National City was first of the majors to offer unsecured personal loans in 1928.

The previous year, however, purchases of homes, cars, and consumer durables slowed down. That caused corporate revenues and profits to flatten out. Particularly vulnerable was the rising industrial equipment industry, including *AC* motors made by *GE* and Reliance Electric of Cleveland with its adjustable-voltage, multi-motor controlled *Corey* motor for the paper and textile industries that in the mid-1920s challenged *DC* motors. If annual sales of industrial equipment, which had seen an increase from $46 million in 1920 to nearly $1 billion in 1929 or just under 1% of the American economy faltered, tens of thousands of workers with good paying jobs would have to be laid off. Oblivious to the larger trend, citizens suddenly accelerated another spending kick, investing in the stock market.

As electricity and radio stocks continued to attract dollars beyond what their profits should have supported, the Dow Jones soared during the decade 500%.

The potential disaster was aggravated by margin buying by persons of so little net worth that the meager savings of many non-skilled working men, shop girls, and store clerks were fully invested. Any fall in share prices would leave them vulnerable to a margin call to put in more money. For example, brokers might stipulate that an investor maintain 50% equity in a stock. If he borrowed half the cost of a stock in the first instance, say $50 out of $100, and the price fell to $80, he would have to put in another $10 of his own money to reduce his debt to $40, half the new price and no higher. If the stock fell again, say to a price of $60, he would have to contribute another $10 to reduce his debt to $30, again half the new price. This process could go on until the stock rose in price or the investor could not meet the margin call, in which case he defaulted and lost all his remaining equity in the stock.

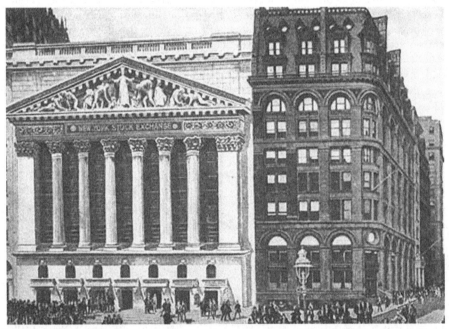

New York Stock Exchange

Seeking to prick the stock bubble before it was too late and thus effect a gradual reduction of the margin buying hysteria rather than a total collapse in stock prices, Federal Reserve officials decided in 1928 to start raising interest rates. Debt became steadily more expensive, reining in consumer purchases, too quickly in the opinion of some. Thus, a brief panic on Wall Street on May 16 undercut the price of stocks, but they quickly shot back up to $67.5 billion of value by end of the year. Smart money investment insiders such as Joseph P. Kennedy of Boston, father of the future President John F. Kennedy and investor in the film company that would become RKO Pictures, pulled out of the market. They realized that with consumers cutting back purchases, companies with at least $1 million in sales that controlled 70% of US production would necessarily slash production to reduce inventory. Small businesses in the $15-20,000 sales range would suffer a sudden and rapid decline in demand. Although "mom-and-pop" entities provided little more than 1% of national production, the number of jobs and family incomes dependent upon their fortunes was disproportionately higher. Many sole proprietors too had invested their savings in and indebted their businesses gambling on the stock market.

In 1929, farmers, laborers, and others echoed the call from three decades in the past for a policy of loose money and free coinage of silver. They wanted to increase circulating currency from the stable level of just over $8 billion maintained throughout the decade to a higher plane, thus making repayment of debt easier. US monetary authorities not only held firm but reaffirmed commitment to the gold standard. The wherewithal of individuals to put more money into stocks was finally constrained. However the stock market climbed higher, buoyed by electricity and radio equities, to reach a peak value on August 31, 1929 of $89.7 billion. Although over the next two months the market inched down a bit, its value in excess of $80 billion seemed to the ill-informed to be in line with GDP.

The country's wealth was not entirely intangible. For the decade, investment in residential fixed assets rose nearly 25% to $118.4 billion while consumer durables ended the decade tripled at $36.5 billion. Business investment kept pace with an 8% increase in nonresidential buildings value and a 52% jump in equipment. Only the government's fixed asset investment remained conservative, at $40.6 billion of value only 2.3% higher than in 1920.

State Capital Building Hartford, Connecticut

Although federal, state, and local property was not at risk, the assets of individuals and businesses were funded with far too much debt. Should stock market investments collapse, bank deposits, life insurance policies, and other financial instruments would come under pressure. The result might not only be implosion in financial markets but sale of fixed assets to cover the losses. Once the law of supply and demand took over, with an excess of the former and a dearth of the latter, the result might be free fall of valuations. Overall, what had ballooned so grandly in the decade of the 1920s might just as spectacularly contract. The downward stroke of the delayed business cycle might crush the dreams of material prosperity of tens of millions of people.

CHAPTER VIII. GOVERNMENT AND WAR RESCUE THE ECONOMY: 1929-1945

To state the problem with the American economy of 1929 simply, both stock market values and GDP were greatly inflated by debt. When on October 29, Black Friday, panic set in that American prosperity was illusory and share prices plummeted, the effect was like a rippling earthquake. Investors rich and poor who had bought on margin without the wherewithal to answer calls for more capital were wiped out. Brokers on the floor of the New York Stock Exchange were overwhelmed by orders to trade 16.4 million shares, virtually all to be sold. By November 13, 40% of the market value of stocks had been lost. Although opportunists pushed prices back up toward $65 billion by end of the year, bad economic news over the winter drove them down even more calamitously.

Decades after the fact, Italian-born economist Franco Modigliani, American Merton H. Miller, and others provided the hypothetical underpinning to explain why the crash was so steep and severe. The value of any investment is equal to the cash flow it produces discounted back using a rate equal to the weighted average of a) the interest rate an investor must pay on funds borrowed to make the investment and (b) the rate he wants and expects to earn on his own money. The higher the risk of the investment, the higher the rate he should earn. Although companies usually paid out part of the positive cash flow from operations directly to investors as dividends, which were then taxed by the government, the entire amount including what was used to make capital investments in plant and equipment as well as a residual value that also needed to be discounted back determined the value of the business. The residual value might be calculated, variously, as the net worth (assets less liabilities) remaining on the books, a break-up value of operating divisions when sold, or some theoretical number equal to a multiple of annual cash flow. Because valuation is dependent upon future estimates of business operations, a range of values based upon low, medium, and high estimates is normally calculated to guide investors when trading shares.

Unfortunately in the 1920s, very few Americans even among savvy businessmen had a clear appreciation of how to make these calculations. As in every other period of business boom, stock prices were governed as much or more by the law of supply and demand than

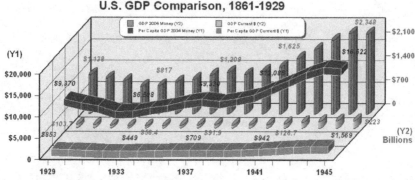

U.S. GDP Comparison, 1861-1929

sober assessment of cash flow. As enthusiasm to get rich quick waxed, prices and valuations were bid up to extreme levels. A herd instinct overrode hard information about declining business conditions.

Exacerbating the problem was failure of government officials to learn from past mistakes. At precisely the wrong time, Congress passed and President Hoover signed the protectionist Smoot-Hawley Tariff of 1930, collapsing any possibility of stimulating growth by trade with the world. Nor were Hoover and the Republicans able, despite the examples of Progressive era regulation and First World War controls, to think beyond the old Adam Smith, *laissez-faire* way of doing things. They would not use governmental power, even in so grave an emergency, to intervene on the scale required.

Franklin D. Roosevelt
Neither initially did successor Franklin D. Roosevelt (FDR). However, Roosevelt's failure stemmed from ignorance at how to go about effective government intervention rather than unwillingness to do so. The New Deal program of his first administration was a trial-and-error affair that did much for millions of people without pulling the country all the way out of its slump. A sharp recession in 1937 in the midst of the Depression provoked him to more radical ideas. For he latched on to the theory of British economist John Maynard Keynes that pump-priming the economy with temporary but substantial government spending beyond federal revenues would provide the stimulus needed to spur business investment and consumer purchases. As measured on a *per capita* basis in 2004 dollars, the economy in 1939 finally returned to the level of 1929.

A more dramatic resort to government borrowing against future income for present need came because of the ramp up for the Second World War. Hitler's aggression in Europe followed by the Japanese attack on Pearl Harbor motivated Roosevelt and the Congress to adopt the traditional strategy of billions for defense, not one cent for tribute. Ultimately, the United States borrowed $201 billion, a figure twice as great as 1940 GDP, to gear up the American war machine and conduct military operations around the globe.

Mobilization of industry for war and the full employment that resulted caused the economy to soar by end of 1945 to $223 billion. In the process of fighting the Depression and the war, the federal government secured a powerful and permanent position both as a contributor to US GDP and as a manager of economic growth. It was a role that Washington never again fully relinquished.

INITIAL GOVERNMENT RESPONSES TO CALAMITY

When the stock market crashed, Hoover was only eight months into his term of office. He had three full years remaining before the election of 1932 in which to alleviate national distress, reverse the business panic, and propose solutions to the fundamental flaws in the US economic and financial system. Because the country had gone through severe recessions and depressions before and bounced back, he did not at first recognize the need for massive government intervention. But the news kept getting worse and worse.

Between 1929 and 1933, the annual income of individual Americans fell from $81 billion to half. Principally, this was a consequence of businesses laying off workers, boosting the unemployment rate from 4.5% to 25%, and slashing better paying union jobs to 2.9 million or 11.5% of non-farm jobs. The UMW alone lost 70% of its members. Wages dropped to an average 44.2 cents an hour or about $1,100 a year, in 2004 money about $15,900. Women ages 14 and up, numbering 10.7 million or 22% of the workforce, and more likely to work for very low wages and/or part-time, were worse off. The only silver lining to the employment crunch was that teenagers stayed in school, boosting the percentage of adults with high school educations to half by end of the decade.

Unofficially by 1932, one-third of the work force or 16 million people received no pay check. Since 100 million citizens had little or no net worth to start with, when breadwinners lost jobs, families lost homes. The situation was aggravated by the fact that mortgages typically ran in those days 5-10 years, compared to 15-30 years in present times. The monthly payment burden relative to income was high. No wonder that 40% of all mortgages ultimately went into default. Millions of people wound up living in "Hooverville" shacks on the edge of cities or roaming around the country looking for work.

As citizens emptied savings to keep themselves afloat, the rate of disposable personal income put aside plunged from 4.7% in 1929 to -1.5% four years later. Bank withdrawals not only caused deposits to fall 50% to about $40 billion in 1933 but shut the doors of 5,000 banks, one-sixth the national total. A surfeit of houses — including foreclosed mortgages — caused annual investment in residential buildings to fall from $3.9 billion in 1929 to $616 million. The value of residential buildings and equipment plummeted from $118.5 billion to $86.3 billion at its nadir.

Although well-to-do Americans could still afford big ticket items, annual purchase of consumer durables fell 56% to only $4.1 billion in 1933 while retail sales were halved to $24.5 billion. Individuals consequently owned only $26.5 billion of consumer durables, $9 billion less than in 1929. With reduced demand, businesses had first to slash production, next close whole factories. They cut prices 24% over four years and struggled to pay principle and interest on debt taken on in the boom years. New investment in plant and equipment, except in select cases where great risk was taken and not always rewarded, shut down. Private investment in nonresidential fixed assets dropped annually from $10.4 billion to $2.3 billion by 1933. Even the federal, state, and local government, because tax receipts fell from $5 billion in 1929 to less than $2.1 billion for 1933, had to slash investment. Adding government's $5 billion loss in tangible asset value to the total, the country as a whole saw its holdings of fixed assets drop 22.6% to only $256 billion by 1933.

Light and power plant, Galena, Illinois

As for stocks, a paucity of demand sent them free-falling in winter 1932-33 to just less than $10 billion of value. One of the industries most savaged was public utilities, high-lighted by the collapse of Insull's Middle West Utilities, in which many Americans of limited income had invested all their savings. The fall-out caused Insull, originally a British subject, to flee the country for southern Europe only to be brought back for trial. Ulti-mately acquitted of all charges, he died nearly broke in Paris of a heart attack.

Because the 1,300 or so companies on the NYSE were on a discounted cash flow basis worth more, their share prices came back up to a more natural bottom of about $33 billion by end of 1933, an average price of between $25-26 a share. Thereafter, they rose or fell with the economy's fortunes rather than with what current Federal Reserve Chairman Alan Greenspan calls "irrational exuberance." They did not again reach a market value equal to the pre-crash level until 1950. The lure of stock speculation was discredited for decades more after that.

Consequently, it was nearly impossible for corporations to raise money by offering new shares. The republic's ability to generate income and wealth and pull itself out of eco-nomic depression was hamstrung. GDP collapsed by nearly half to $56.4 billion in 1933; as measured on an average *per capita* basis in 2004 dollars, Americans were back to the standard of living of 1911. Mal-distribution of income, with the bottom 80% of Americans earning only 46% of all income and the bottom 40% receiving only 12.5%, made the situ-ation far worse and far more dangerous politically.

For example, farmers in the Midwest and plains states saw prices for agricultural commodities tumble. Hoover hoped that the Agricultural Marketing Act, passed before the crash on June 15, 1929 and authorizing the federal government to pay farmers an export bounty equal to one half the duties on commodities they were charged overseas, thus bridging the difference between US and world prices, would improve conditions, but it backfired. A Federal Farm Board established under the law to administer a revolving fund of $500 million for low-interest loans to farmers for orderly purchasing, handling, and selling of surpluses of cotton, grain, livestock, and other commodities only encouraged farmers to plant the maximum number of acres possible. Inundated with even larger surpluses, Cotton, Grain, Wool and other Stabilization Corporations set up by the board in 1930 failed to prop up prices.

Next, Congress tried to protect farmers from foreign competition by passing the Smoot-Hawley Tariff of June 17, 1930. That law jacked up duties on agricultural products from 38% to 49%. However, as other nations retaliated, US exports fell 25% in 1930 to $4.4 billion against nearly as much in imports. Only because by 1933 foreigners pulled out over half the $8.4 billion formerly invested in the US while US investments overseas remained substantial at the $14 billion level did the overall balance of payments not turn negative.

Caterpillar tractor factory, Peoria, Illinois

The agricultural collapse devastated farm equipment manufacturers. Consolidation of the industry left only Deere and IH as major competitors. Among smaller fry trying to hang on until government efforts to rescue American agriculture stimulated demand to double the number of tractors to 1.6 million by decade's end and proliferate other machines as well, Caterpillar continued to dominate the tracked tractor niche with its 1931 *Diesel Sixty* built on a new assembly line in East Peoria, Illinois. Deere reached a nadir of only $8.7 million in sales in 1933 before taking the industry lead with its Models A and B wheeled tractors that increased revenue 11.5 times in only four years.

Caterpillar wheeled tractor

Having watched Democrats win control of the House in November 1930 and take eight more seats in the Senate, Hoover decided he must act in what he considered unprecedented fashion. His recovery plan included up to $150 million in federal spending for construction of roads and public buildings, development of airways, and flood control. Because the Treasury had accumulated an annual surplus in 1929 of $1.6 billion, the budget remained balanced. To keep it so, Republicans in Congress talked up a federal sales tax that Democrats charged would add to the crushing burden of less affluent Americans. When the Federal Reserve decided in 1931 to tighten interest rates still further to fight what turned out to be a nonexistent danger of inflation, by autumn record numbers of banks collapsed, wiping out the savings of millions more Americans. Hoover persuaded bankers to form a $500 million pool of reserves to rescue weaker institutions, but over $3.4 billion in deposits was lost.

As a last desperate attempt to revive the economy and his political fortunes, Hoover backed legislation approved in Congress on February 2, 1932 for a Reconstruction Finance Corporation (RFC) within the Treasury Department with initial capitalization of $500 million financed by tax-exempt bonds and authorization to borrow $2.5 billion more. The RFC made loans to banks, savings & loans, railroads, and farm mortgage associations to stave off bankruptcies. Headed by the well respected Charles G. Dawes, first head of the Bureau of the Budget in 1921 and co-author of the Dawes Plan of 1924 that had loaned money to Germany to make reparations payments to Britain, France, and other countries to repay loans from the US, the RFC reached the limit by July 21. That day, Congress passed the Relief and Construction Act, boosting the RFC's limit to $3 billion and authorizing a further $1.5 billion in loans for state and local public works that paid for themselves with tolls and fees as well as $300 million to states unable to pay for public relief for individuals. The next day, the Federal Home Loan Bank Act set up a five man board and eight to 12 discount banks with authority to make long-term loans to building and loan associations, savings banks, and insurance companies. The maximum capital of $125 million was woefully inadequate to accomplish the goal of reducing foreclosures on unpaid mortgages, boosting home construction and construction jobs, and increasing home ownership.

Because Republicans who wanted to keep the budget in balance yielded to Democrat insistence that individual income and inheritance taxes as well as taxes on stock transfers be raised instead of a federal sales tax installed, Americans had even less money to make purchases. That ended any chance that consumer spending would be the vehicle for economic recovery. The party of Jefferson and Wilson further flexed its political muscle by pushing through Congress on March 23 the Norris-La Guardia Anti-Injunction Act forbidding court injunctions to sustain anti-union employment contracts or prevent strikes, boycotts, and picketing. They were stopped short in June from authorizing $2.4 billion to pay in a lump sum adjustment compensation certificates issued years earlier to veterans of the First World War by Republican control of the Senate. Infuriated at the callousness of politicians, 17,000 ex-soldiers formed into a "Bonus Expeditionary Force" to march on Washington. Hoover ordered out the army under Chief of Staff General Douglas MacArthur to evict from shacks and empty government buildings 2,000 men who refused an inducement to go home with money provided by the government.

Never before or since has a sitting President had less chance of being reelected than Hoover. Economic conditions were so bad that the press ignored or hid the fact that his opponent FDR, governor of New York, had been stricken a dozen years earlier by an attack of infantile paralysis that cost him the use of his legs. Nor did the Democrat's "New Deal" program of preserving a balanced budget, providing further relief for farmers, and rehabilitating business amount to more than just a sketchy outline not substantially different that what Hoover already had attempted. The real change was in FDR's determination and will to try whatever was necessary to overcome adversity and a spirit of optimism and hope that rallied similar emotions in his countrymen.

Bold statements, including a promise to repeal Prohibition and return the production and income of that industry to public scrutiny, were enough on November 8, 1932 to sweep Roosevelt into the White House by a 22.8 million to 15.8 million vote victory and a 472 to 59 electoral advantage. The landslide permitted him to move with dispatch on inauguration day March 4, 1933 to restore confidence about the fiscal state of the economy. Declaration of a four day bank holiday was followed by the Emergency Banking Relief Act, giving the President wide power over credit, currency, gold, silver, foreign exchange, and penalties for gold-hoarding. The Thomas Amendment authorized him to fight price deflation by devaluing the gold content of the dollar and having the Treasury issue $3 billion more in US paper currency. To protect the gold reserve, he took the US off the gold standard on April 30. No longer required to convert dollars into gold by request of foreign governments and individuals, the Treasury also called in all gold and gold certificates from US citizens. Although for fear of igniting a ruinous inflation FDR never had the Treasury print billions of US dollars, he did take advantage of the Silver Purchase Act of June 19, 1934 to buy all silver in US at 50 cents per ounce except newly-mined silver which was bought at 64 cents per ounce with silver certificates. Not only was money infused into the economy and repayment of debts facilitated but the silver to gold ratio was set effectively at 54 to 1, much higher than the old 16 to 1 benchmark, because an ounce of gold sold at the time for $34.83. Conversely, the Economy Act of March 20, 1933 tended to tighten the money supply by requiring the administration to slash government salaries up to 15%, cut veteran pensions, and reorganize and consolidate government agencies. The fact that FDR signed the legislation was an indication he felt political pressure to fulfill his campaign promise to balance the budget.

Too, the President wanted to deflect Republican charges, stemming from all the programs pushed through Congress in his first 100 days and afterward, that he was going hog wild with irresponsible government spending. Far more generous to citizens than Hoover's recovery plan, the New Deal produced in its first year federal spending equal to 8.2% of GDP, compared to 3.8% in 1930, while the budget deficit hit $2.5 billion. In point of fact, New Deal legislation did help preserve the remaining wealth of the American people, in particular through the Home Owners Refinancing Act, passed June 13, 1933, to create a Home Owners Refinancing Corporation (HORC) with capitalization of $200 million and authority to loan $2 billion, subsequently raised to $3 billion. HORC lowered the rates and monthly payments of 1 million mortgages. A year later on June 28, the National Housing Act set up a Federal Housing Administration (FHA) to insure loans by banks and other institutions for new home construction and repairs. Its funds could also be used to modernize farms and small businesses. Within three years, residential fixed assets recovered the 54% of value lost since 1929. The remaining loss was made good by 1939.

Montana sheep

After four years of deflation, rising debt, and ruinous drought that from spring 1932 forward made a dust bowl of the Great Plains, the plight of farmers was now extreme. Not only had prices, such as for a bushel of wheat down to 32 cents, plunged to 1899 levels but farm revenue had collapsed one-third and a quarter of all farmers had lost their land. Farm debt for the remainder had soared to 60% of assets. The total value of cattle, hogs, and sheep had plunged from $4.6 billion to about $2 billion. The price of hogs fell so much, in fact, that it was more profitable slaughtering entire herds then fattening them up for market. By 1935, the number of hogs in the country had fallen 30% to 39 million while head of cattle had increased 13% to 68 million and sheep were about the same at 46 million.

What remained for farmers to build on was 320 million acres still under production with 920,000 tractors, 900,000 trucks, 61,000 combines, 50,000 corn pickers, and milking machines on 100,000 farms, altogether worth about $2 billion. To buck up prices and further increase farm income, Congress on May 12, 1933 passed the Agricultural Adjustment Act. That law planned to eliminate surplus crops through a cut in production induced by subsidies paid for by a tax on flour millers, meat packers, and other processors of farm goods. The Agricultural Adjustment Administration (AAA) established so-called parity prices based on the 1909-14 period for corn, cotton, wheat, rice, hogs, and dairy products and on the 1919-29 period for tobacco as a basis for the payments. Later on April 7, 1934 the Jones-Connally Farm Relief act added barley, flax, peanuts, grain sorghums, rye, beef and dairy cattle to the subsidy list while the May 9 Jones-Costgan Sugar Act added sugar cane and sugar beets. Maximum crop sizes were set and enforced by punitive action, such as in the Cotton Control (Bankhead) Act of April 21 and Tobacco Control Act of June 28, taxing excess acreage planted above stipulated quotas.

To prevent public land heretofore not brought under the plough from being farmed, the Taylor Grazing Act of June 28 set apart 8 million acres, later expanded to 142 million, for grazing. The next year, FDR withdrew from sale all remaining public land so that federal government ownership eventually stabilized at 455 million acres out of the national total of 1.9 billion or 23.9%. Included were 181.2 million acres of national forest land, 47.9 million acres of land reserved for minerals, water power, and oil production, and 20 million acres of land protected for irrigation purposes. After the war in 1946, the Bureau of Land Management took control of all surface and subsurface resources.

Tree farm in Ohio

Meanwhile, Weyerhaeuser took the private industry lead once again in cooperating with the preservationist thrust of government land policy. It was encouraged to do so by decision in 1931 to use its heretofore unexploited tracts of hemlock trees to compete in pulp and paper. Beginning in 1937, the company experimented with selective logging to leave smaller trees untouched and re-seed cut areas. It was first in 1941 to found a tree farm, beginning a process that increased such operations from 200,000 acres to 95 million by end of the century.

New techniques for re-growth of forests were all to the good for everyone, but International Paper was hard-pressed by Weyerhaeuser's move into pulp and paper during the depression to maintain sales and profitability. Layoffs only stiffened the resolve of labor leaders to organize loggers and mill workers into unions to fight for wage and other concessions. To get by without further erosion of business and financial strength, the company branched out into making a crude liquor turpentine in Arizona as well as manufacturing linerboard on a *Fourdrinier* machine for use in corrugated containers. In 1940, it bought Agar Manufacturing Corporation, its major customer for that latter product, which also gave it a base in bleached kraft paper for folding cartons, milk cartons, and the like.

The net effect of FDR's agricultural and land policy was to lift farming to a peak of 6.8 million farms averaging 154.7 acres. Annual cash receipts for farm products shot up by 1935 to $7.7 billion, a 60% increase. The Trade Agreements Act of June 12, 1934 authorizing the President to make bilateral pacts based on most favored nation status with other governments without specific congressional approval and to lower tariffs as much as 50% put those receipts over $8 billion annually for the next five years. Total exports recovered to over $4 billion by 1940 with imports at $2.6 billion and the overall balance of payments $1.4 billion in the black. Moreover, with the rise of Nazi Germany in Europe, foreigners saw the US as a safe harbor for money. As US investment overseas slipped to $12.3 billion by end of the decade, foreign investment in the US shot up to $13.5 billion.

Just as housing and farming legislation propped up the tangible wealth of citizens, landmark legislation of June 16, 1933 called the Banking or Glass-Steagall Act took a first step toward protecting intangible. A Federal Bank Deposit Insurance Corporation was inaugurated to guarantee individual bank deposits up to $5,000. While banks were permitted to establish branches in other cities, they had to divest themselves of all investment banking operations. The Federal Reserve received broader authority to oversee savings and industrial banks. The big winners were quite naturally large deposit banks led by Chase National Bank of New York City, combining $2.3 billion of assets with the Bank of Manhattan in 1935 to overtake J.P. Morgan and Company, which proceeded to expand into other regions of the country. J.P. Morgan, Jr. was forced to divest his firm of its investment banking arm, afterward known as Morgan Stanley and Company. In a short time, the nation's largest city came to control three quarters of investment banking activity. The metropolis strengthened its position as undisputed center of American finance.

If financial stability was the first thrust of FDR's New Deal program, the second was direct government intervention in heavy industry. The President had knowledge and experience of such practice from having served as Assistant Secretary of the Navy from 1913 to 1920. He shocked and outraged conservative Republicans by having Congress establish the Tennessee Valley Authority (TVA) as an independent public corporation headed by a board of three to build dams, hydro-electric plants, and inland waterways to stop flooding and soil erosion, produce fertilizer, and generate electric power. Eventually, nine big river dams and many smaller ones produced, distributed, and sold electric power and nitrogen fertilizers to people and companies of the Tennessee Valley region. As had Muscle Shoals in Alabama, the TVA also set up munitions and aluminum plants to sell explosives to the federal government. Alcoa was able to increase production to half a million tons by 1939, including of corrosive-resistant *Alclad* sheet alloys used in B-17, B-24, and DC-3 aircraft, and still knock the price of a pound of aluminum down to $0.20.

DC-3

TVA's electricity would help boost the share of that cheaper, more efficient energy source for manufacturing power to 60% during the Second World War and proved crucial for operation of the atomic bomb plant at Oak Ridge, Tennessee. Of more immediate assistance to industry in 1933 was the National Industrial Recovery Act of June 16, setting up the National Recovery Administration (NRA). Although business groups were supposed to write industry codes and regulate themselves, the NRA had authority to set maximum hours and minimum wages, scrutinize the accounting books of businesses, and enforce fair competition codes that dated from the First World War as well as crack down on unfair price-fixing with court injunctions. Not only were unions permitted to "organize and bargain collectively through representatives of their own choosing," but the NRA moved again as during the Progressive era to eliminate sweatshop and child labor abuses.

A second provision of the National Industrial Recovery Act was creation of a Public Works Administration (PWA) to build roads, public buildings, and other structures with a fund of $3.3 billion. Ultimately, the PWA spent $4.25 billion on 34,000 projects. However, the Supreme Court struck down the law as unconstitutional on May 27, 1935, cutting short that particular effort to boost consumer purchasing power by government-financed employment and pay checks. The NRA was further hampered by codes that

Indianapolis Municipal Airport

favored Big Business over small and price fixing that set prices too high and wages too low to build up a pool of purchasing power in the pockets of individuals.

Generating employment was the third thrust of FDR's efforts. Approved a year to the day after his election, the Civil Works Administration (CWA) supplemented the PWA as an emergency unemployment relief program by putting four million people, or a quarter of the unemployed, to work on federal, state, and local projects. Nearly 80% of the $933 million spent on 180,000 projects over five months was paid out in wages. After the CWA was subsumed in March 1934 in the Federal Emergency Relief Administration (FERA), originally set up to disperse half a million dollars to states, another 2.5 million people found temporary jobs. FERA itself was replaced by the Works Progress Administration (WPA), set up by the Emergency Relief Appropriation Act of April 8, 1935.

Under the direction of former New York social worker Harry L. Hopkins, the WPA employed 8.5 million people over eight years with a peak employment of 3.4 million in March 1936 and paid out 85% of $11 billion spent in wages. The unique aspect of the WPA was not that it built 850 airport landing strips, 124,000 bridges, 8,200 parks, 125,000 public buildings, and 650,000 miles of roads but that it provided employment for actors, artists, musicians, writers, and other creative Americans in their specialties. The intellectual boost to individuals and the economy paid off many times after the war in new ideas and inventions. Lastly, millions of young people ages 16 to 25 also found full and part-time employment in the Civilian Conservation Corps and National Youth Administration. Character and discipline-building activities turned out good human material for Second World War soldiers.

The fourth thrust of FDR's first term in the White House was to use the Great Depression to reinvigorate government regulation of the economy and provide a counterweight against business abuses in favor of employees, consumers, and farmers. The thicket of government agencies overseeing business was strengthened in June 1934 with the Securities & Exchange Commission (SEC) to regulate securities trading and prohibit price manipulations, the Corporate Bankruptcy Act to give one-third of a bankrupt business's creditors veto power over reorganizations, and the Communications Act to replace the Federal Radio Commission with a Federal Communications Commission (FCC) to regulate not only radio but take over telegraph and cable communications from the ICC. Odious to financiers but welcome to millions of individual Americans who felt oppressed by the power of monopolies, Congress passed the Public Utilities Holding Company Act of 1935 after Democrats swept the 1934 elections. The law not only permitted the government to bring suit to break up big holding companies but forced entities that resulted to register with the SEC, divest themselves of non-related properties, and submit to rate regulation by state agencies.

The *quid pro quo* was exclusivity in service areas. Companies such as American Gas and Electric (forerunner to American Electric Power) and United Gas Corporation, formed in 1930 from a merger of 40 small companies in Texas, Louisiana, and Mississippi, were permitted to retain an integrated system for power generation, long-haul transmission, and local distribution. In fact, the natural gas industry expanded rapidly in a continuing drive to replace manufactured gas in furnaces and heating. Pennsylvania Power & Light diversified into natural gas to complement steam electric generation stations burning annually over 1 million tons of anthracite coal, a finite source that would some day have to be replaced by less efficient bituminous coal.

Even better received by average citizens was the Social Security Act of August 14, 1935. The federal government would now tax employers with eight or more workers beginning at 1% of salaries and wages but rising to 3% by 1938 to build up a social security fund to pay retirement pensions ranging from $10 to $85 per month. Together with taxes for old-age and survivors' insurance as well as the Railroad Retirement Acts of 1935 and 1937, the Social Security program laid the foundation for the social-welfare system still in place today. Over time, it expanded to cover more people, tax at higher rates, and pay out larger retirement incomes.

Blue Cross and Blue Shield health insurance symbols
Heretofore, health insurance for Americans had been reserved for the well-to-do. Although Pacific Employers Insurance Company of Los Angeles added in 1923 to the patchy network of workers' compensation plans, a very low percentage of the nation's industrial workers were covered prior to the end of the decade. Most hospitals could certainly not afford to invest in new technologies such as Zimmer Manufacturing Company's aluminum splints and fracture beds to support patients while sheets were changed, stainless steel orthopedic implants, or intravenous solutions prepared by Dr. Don Baxter, founder of the company that became Baxter International. Sulfa to fight infection, introduced in 1932, as well as other drugs taken for granted today were slow to proliferate.

In 1929, also in Los Angeles, the Ross-Loo Company was founded to organize the first health maintenance organization (HMO) in the country. Although the nation's system of private hospitals and charities seemed sufficient for the needs of most Americans, the sudden plunge into economic chaos overwhelmed these institutions and revived interest in national socialized medicine, such as was found in Germany and other European countries. Rising automobile accidents and collapsing incomes in the early 1930s provoked new calls for government oversight and regulation. In 1932, non-profit Blue Cross associations formed to take up the challenge. That put pressure on associations of hospitals to concoct prepaid plans for Americans to build up a reserve to cover low-cost emergency care for the public as well as sustain institutions while a high percentage of beds were empty. The larger goal was to keep government out of health care.

Failing to stop passage of the Social Security Act, with its obvious implication as a minimum pension plan funded by business taxes for a similar experiment with health care, insurance companies such as Aetna and Connecticut General decided to offer companies new group health insurance plans. Blue Shield medical societies also were organized to pay doctors' fees for those who could not afford coverage. In piecemeal fashion, the skeletal framework of a revived private health care system evolved. It was enough, while Washington was concerned with broader economic issues, to stave off socialized medicine.

PARTIAL INDUSTRIAL RECOVERY

By 1935, FDR and his advisors thought the timing was right for starting the Social Security System because overall GDP climbed back to $73.3 billion with projection of another $10 billion increase the next year. The rebound had been made possible in the first instance by the firming up of US financial institutions, wherein over half the remaining asset value of the country resided. Larger banks with clout such as Chase, Manufacturers Trust, and Chemical become even more powerful by taking over failing institutions. Local leaders such as Washington Mutual became regionally important in the same way. In 1932, Giannini came out of retirement to put TransAmerican, the holding company he had formed in 1928 when taking over Bank of America of New York, on firmer footing. He renamed its California holdings Bank of America and returned to time-tested methods of personal banking. That was the tack taken by Household as well, assuming debts of unemployed customers and delaying repayment until they returned to work. Citigroup in 1935 offered monthly payment loans to small businesses with cash flow insufficient to make larger annual and quarterly payments and attracted supplementary funds the next year to support the program by accepting checking accounts with no minimum balance. Even MetLife, which in 1930 claimed 20% of the combined population of the US and Canada as covered by its

Empire State building

life insurance policies and loaned money to keep major building projects such as the Rockefeller Center project and Empire State Building going, agreed to pay out cash values to needy persons from policies that had lapsed due to non-payment of premium. After dispersing $1 billion in claims that year, Aetna forked out another $177 million over four years, equal to 17.2% of its assets, in loans against policy value.

Another innovation was the decision by Sears to found the Allstate Insurance Company for car insurance. Agents signed up droves of people in Sears' stores as well as at popular events like the 1933 Chicago World's Fair. Later in 1939, Allstate revolutionized the car insurance industry and generated $3.7 million in premium by adjusting rates based on age, mileage, and use of cars. The Progressive Mutual Insurance Company of Cleveland, founded in 1937, had already pleased drivers by permitting quarterly instead of annual payment of premium on car insurance and opened offices for drive-in claims.

That same year, full implementation of the Social Security program as well as higher taxes prompted some employers to inquire with life insurance companies about setting up retirement programs funded by premium payments that would grow cash value tax-free inside of policies and pay out tax-free death benefits to survivors. Marsh & McLennan specialized in pension consulting as did a new firm Putnam Investments. Government policy in forcing powerful deposit banks out of investment banking also played a role in convincing brokerage house Merrill Lynch to enter the business by taking over the investment banking division of Cassatt & Company, an old Philadelphia firm. Citibank reclaimed the title in 1939 not only of largest US but international bank by opening 100 offices in 23 major overseas cities.

Overall, the willingness and wherewithal of big banks and insurance companies to meet their obligations kept millions of Americans financially afloat during the depth of the Depression. Together with New Deal programs, they bought time for US industry to recover. And indeed, by mid decade, technological advances on factory floors, including synthetic abrasives, electric drive and control, hydraulic feed, and pneumatic accessory devices for the improvement of machine tools as well as electrical arc welding made a difference in efficiency and cost control. In the automobile industry, pressing, stamping, and punching replaced metal cutting, creating the possibility, later realized during the Second World War, of high production speeds in the manufacture not only of motor vehicles but aircraft and ships.

1935 Packard

Automobile production innovations came none too soon because the Great Depression put the industry in sorry shape. Annual US motor vehicle production dropped from 5.3 million in 1929 and sales accounting for perhaps 5% of GDP to 1.1 million three years later, compelling wage cuts of 35%. Not only did the 80% market contraction wipe out small producers including all motorcycle manufacturers, except Harley-Davidson and Hendee with its *Indian* brand, but prompted the majors to focus on basic cars. By 1935, Ford's *Model A*, Chrysler's Plymouth and Dodge, and GM's Pontiac models each reached 1 million cars sold. Coming along more modestly with nearly 80,000 produced in 1934, GM's Olds proved that a market still existed for mid-price cars offering amenities such as hydraulic brakes, independent front wheel suspension, and automatic safety transmission. Ford bridged the gap between low and high ends with its Mercury division in 1938. Ultimately, the Big Three secured 85% of the automobile market and emerged from the decade as potent forces able during the Second World War to gear up production of war materiel. In the postwar period, they recovered their status as industry powerhouses central to the fortune of the country and its people.

Golden Gate bridge
Recovery in the auto-mobile industry was doubly important for US Steel because orders for rails from the nation's rail-roads declined dramatically over the decade of the 1930s. Still by far the nation's largest pro-ducer, it developed cold-rolled and aluminum-killed steel for auto bodies. Bethlehem Steel, one of the so-called Little Steel seven, became the next largest competitor by acquiring in 1930 plants in Seattle, San Francisco, and Los Angeles and the next year taking over McClintic-Marshall Corporation, a fabricator and erector of bridges and buildings. Beth-lehem prospered with large construction projects, including the Golden Gate Bridge in San Francisco, Rockefeller Plaza and the Waldorf Astoria in New York, the Chicago Mer-chandize Mart in the nation's second largest city, and the US Supreme Court building in the capital.

For steel companies that could not compete in cars and construction, the end of Pro-hibition on December 5, 1933 opened a new market. Put together in 1927 by Cleveland fin-ancier Cyrus Eaton from companies in northeast Ohio, Republic Steel survived high transportation costs for coal and iron to produce beer cans and other light steel products. Another significant competitor National Steel arose from a merger in 1929 of Weirton Steel, Great Lakes Steel, and M.A. Hanna Company. In the Midwest, Inland Steel of Chicago gambled on $15 million of new plant structure in 1932 to produce roofing material, buckets, and other such products. In fact, by 1937, the steel industry employed 349,000 people in manufacturing and 83,000 in transportation of iron ore, coal, and limestone dug out by 81,000 miners, or about 1% of the nation's workforce. New innovations such as hot-rolled, seamless tubes for oil and natural gas pipelines, Panhandle Eastern's $25 million order for 24 inch pipe to provide Illinois and less distant locales with Texas natural gas, and Northwestern Steel and Wire's electric arc furnace (EAF) to produce carbon or stainless steel laid the foundation for recovery and expansion once business conditions turned around.

As well as government assistance, what the economy needed more than anything else was new growth industries. Old pillars of stability not only were shaken by the Depression, in many cases they were cut in half, never to regain their former greatness. For example, annual railroad revenues plunged over 50% to $206 million by 1933. Stock value of railroads collapsed 90%, in the case of Van Sweringen holdings 99%. The brothers' properties soon came under control of bankers, investors, and other creditors. Only the C&O, with its profitable bituminous coal-hauling business, emerged as a major player in the East. But overall, the share of freight carried by US railroads dropped by 1939 to three-fifths. Public works programs for the building and improvement of roads and highways made the trucking industry a mortal peril for railroads.

Genealogy of US Airlines, 1916-1945

One of the most promising new industries was aerospace, including airplane construction, air passenger service, and air mail delivery. Just before the Depression, Boeing bought several engine and propeller manufacturers as well as airlines, changed its name to the United Aircraft and Transportation Corporation, and came out with the all-metal *Monomail*, the first monoplane built to carry cargo and mail and thus render obsolete biplanes. That same year on July 5, 1929, Curtiss merged with Wright to accelerate research and development of more reliable, cost-effective passenger planes. Following the crash, in 1931 United Aircraft formed a United Airlines division by purchasing and merging National Air Transport and Varney Air Lines and holding company North American Aviation (NAA) combined its interests in Transcontinental and Western Airlines (later TWA) with Douglas Aircraft and Western Air Express. However, worries about monopoly abuses, including what turned out to be false charges of collusion with the Attorney General in 1930 bidding for airmail contracts, provoked Congress to pass the Air Mail Act of June 12, 1934 forbidding airframe manufacturers from owning mail-carrying airlines. Forced to spin off United Air Lines, United Aircraft split into an entity under the same name responsible for airframe and airplane parts manufacturing in the East and another called again Boeing to perform the same function in the West. Simultaneously, NAA cut loose all but its manufacturing division. The company later in 1967 merged into the company that became Rockwell International.

The new law also restored confidence by letting the ICC determine "fair and reasonable" airmail rates, including airmail postage that was reduced to 6 cents an ounce. Although the breakup of United Aircraft and NAA weakened the financial clout the avi-

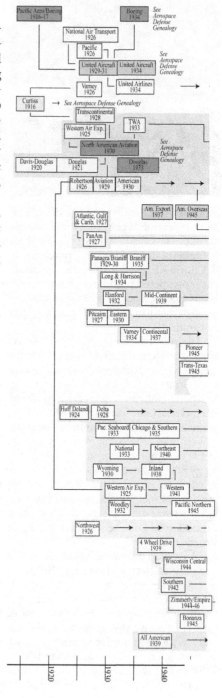

ation industry could mobilize for economies of scale in production, orders for Boeing from the US Army for a heavy bomber that became the B-17, from Canada and France for military aircraft, and from airline companies for a commercial version of the B-17 called the *Stratoliner*, the first pressurized airliner for higher altitude flight, as well as flying boats turned the company into one of the nation's leading airframe manufacturers. Its main competition in commercial aviation became the Douglas Aircraft Company, delivering in 1936 the legendary DC-3 using a Curtiss *Cyclone* engine. By 1939, domestic air travel on the Big Four airlines of United, American, TWA, and Eastern as well as smaller companies jumped to 1.4 million paying passengers over 35,500 miles of air routes and 2.2 million people. The next year, Pan American Airlines began flying regularly between San Francisco and Manila. Congress firmed up federal authority in 1938 by putting a Civil Aeronautics Authority (CAA) in charge of regulating air transport rates.

Oil refinery, Tulsa, Oklahoma

Air travel picked up part of the slack for the oil industry from cuts in automobile sales. The fact that Americans kept driving the millions of aging cars they already owned also pushed petroleum production to 1 billion barrels of annual production by 1935 and 1.4 billion by end of the decade, offsetting a 20% price drop to about $1.00 a barrel. Improvements in the catalytic cracking process, including Sun Oil's first large-scale plant in Marcus Hook, Pennsylvania, boosted the amount of gasoline derived from a barrel of oil to 40%. Reconsolidation of the oil industry, which had begun shortly after the 1911 breakup of Standard Oil, picked up pace when Standard Oil of New Jersey (a.k.a. Jersey Standard and later Exxon), Standard Oil of New York (called Socony and later Mobil), Standard Oil of Ohio (Sohio), Standard Oil of Indiana (later Amoco), Standard Oil of California (later Chevron) as well as Gulf Oil, Phillips Petroleum, and the Texas Oil Company bought up smaller competitors and carved out regional and international empires. Even after 1938 when Mexico nationalized $450 million of US and British oil company assets, wells in Texas and Oklahoma more than made up the loss. Other international acquisitions, such as Jersey Standard's expansion into Indonesia and Texas Oil's moves into South America and Arabia, boosted profits.

Hoover Dam

Meanwhile, electric power now composed over 50% of all primary power in manufacturing establishments. The government facilitated the industry's ascendancy not only with the TVA but the Boulder Canyon Project Act of December 21, 1928 to construct the massive Hoover Dam in Black Canyon of the Colorado River for hydro-electric power. The project was deemed so important to control floods such as covered the Imperial Valley of California with a lake from 1905 to 1910 that a contract made for $485 million with six companies including W.A. Bechtel Company of San Francisco, actually founded in Oklahoma in 1898 by Warren A. Bechtel to grade railroad beds with a mule-drawn scraper, survived the stock market crash. After completion in 1935, millions of acre feet of water were allocated between states, including 4.4 million for California, of which 3.1 million went to irrigate the Imperial Valley for agriculture. A second massive project, the Grand Coulee Dam on the Columbia River for similar purposes, was begun in 1933. By contrast, the Army Core of Engineers drew the assignment from the Flood Control Act of May 15, 1928 of constructing levees on the Mississippi River over ten years with a total appropriation of $325 million.

Cheaper electricity boosted the home appliance market. Adding to the machines and devices already available to the public, an electric dishwasher was marketed in 1932, an electric clothes drier three years later, and a hand-held vacuum cleaner in 1937. Determined to generate sales to keep open production lines, GE formed a GE Capital division to finance consumer purchases of GE appliances, albeit with more careful appraisal of individual's income and ability to make installment payments. Persistence paid off in a tripling of house refrigerator sales between 1929 and 1935 to 2.7 million units.

Too, the end of Prohibition and the need of commercial establishments to keep beer and other bottled and canned drinks chilled opened the door to foundation of the Amana Refrigeration Company in 1934 as a beverage cooler manufacturer. Two years later, Amana produced cold storage lockers for groceries and restaurants. Meanwhile, Trane Company, founded in 1913 in LaCrosse, Wisconsin to make low-pressure steam heating for homes and businesses, turned in 1931 to production of air conditioning systems for movie theaters. Over the decade, consumers and workers in department stores, factories, offices, shops, and restaurants became more comfortable.

The restaurant industry now included dining rooms in elegant hotels such as Conrad Hilton's establishment that bore his name in Dallas. His franchise, begun in 1919, was well established before more economical competitors Western Hotels, founded in Yakima,

Washington, sprang up in 1930 and Sheraton Hotels, centered on Boston, got its start in 1937. Simultaneously, the Howard Johnson restaurant chain drew in travelers along east coast highways with 28 flavors of ice cream using a secret formula. Founder Howard W. Johnson counted 107 restaurants generating $10.5 million in revenue by 1939.

Taking a contrary approach, John Willard Marriott turned his A&W root beer stand in Washington D.C., opened in 1927, into a Hot Shoppe serving hot food including Mexican dishes with curbside service for motorists. His business expanded in 1937 by opening an airline catering business for Capital, Eastern, and American Airlines at Hoover Field, the present site of the Pentagon. Thereafter in 1939, he won a food service contract with the Treasury Department. During the war, Hot Shoppes fed tens of thousands of defense workers in the District of Columbia.

Proliferation of refrigerators helped create a frozen foods industry led by Bird's Eye Foods. Especially after the tax processors of food paid to subsidize the elimination of surpluses was voided by the law's unconstitutionality (see below), an industry expansion began. Higher beef, chicken, and pork prices encouraged the foundation of Tyson Foods in Arkansas. That firm, started in 1936 by John Tyson to haul chickens to Chicago, Detroit, and other big cities, eventually became an international powerhouse with at present time 300 facilities in 32 states and 22 countries, employing 120,000 people, and sales of $23.4 billion.

The increasing availability of hydro-electric power could not prevent the textile market from contracting 16% through 1935. The pain would have been far worse had not production of rayon shot up four fold, boosting women's clothing sales 50% and compensating for a 50% cut in silk production and 22% drop in cotton. The invention in 1934 of nylon by Wallace H. Carothers, a DuPont researcher, led five years later to a nylon yarn for adornment of ladies' legs with stockings and hose. Carothers had already come up with a rubber-like polymer and neoprene synthetic rubber that DuPont used to make toothbrush bristles in 1938.

The other electric appliance that achieved major gains during the Great Depression was radios. By mid-decade, Americans owned 21.5 million; on the eve of the Second World War 33 million. Philco continued to lead in volume, but Galvin was the innovator. While adding table and console models to match its rivals, it also in 1936 came up with a police cruiser mobile radio preset to a single frequency that was subsequently developed into two-way radios and walkie-talkies for the US Army. The company's sales jumped during the decade from $287,000 to $10 million and profit of $470,000 while providing employment for 985 people. Galvin marketed first in Philadelphia in 1941 a two-way frequency modulation (FM) radio system and equipment much quieter than the amplitude modulation (AM) version.

Saturation of the country with receivers facilitated the entertainment careers of stars such as Eddie Cantor, Jack Benny, George Burns and Gracie Allen. In addition to comedy and variety hours, the NBC and CBS networks supplemented previous programming centered around dramas and symphony orchestra concerts with serials such as *The Goldbergs*, mystery and crime sagas including *The Shadow, Charlie Chan*, and *Sherlock Holmes*, and quizzes and game shows. A new FM system of static-free radio, developed over two decades by Edwin H. Armstrong, an Army signal corps officer, was not ready to challenge the old AM system until 1940. The crackling timber of Orson Welles' voice coming over the CBS network on March 30, 1938 added to the drama and hysteria attending his *War of the Worlds* program that spooked millions into believing a bogus invasion of earth by beings from another planet was actually taking place.

Genealogy of Motion Picture Industry, 1882-1945

The 1930s were remembered as a golden era for motion pictures, but the reality was a time of financial and legal trouble. As with other industries, hard times put some studios out of business and forced consolidation of the rest. After 20th Century merged with Fox Films in 1935, that studio and four other majors — MGM, Paramount, RKO, and Warner Brothers — held a captive audience at theater chains they owned. Columbia, United Artists, and Universal as well as eight significant independent film companies and many smaller entities without such control were at a competitive disadvantage. However, success or failure usually boiled down to star power, including child actress Shirley Temple making a string of light hearted comedies at Universal, the team of Fred Astaire and Ginger Rogers dancing up a storm of musicals for RKO, and Errol Flynn swashbuckling at Warner. Profitability was further secured through low-cost B films such as Universal's *Dracula*, *Mummy*, and *Frankenstein* horror pictures as well as shorts, in particular Columbia's *Three Stooges* comedies. The Holy Grail for all studios was winning academy awards. Columbia earned greater respectability than could be provided by Larry, Moe, and Curly, no matter how hilarious, after *It Happened One Night* starring Clark Gable and Claudette Colbert won 1935 Oscar awards for best picture, director, actor, actress, and screenplay. MGM's stable of big names made it the biggest studio and justified to Loew's Corporation overseers the $1 million salary eventually paid to Louis B. Mayer.

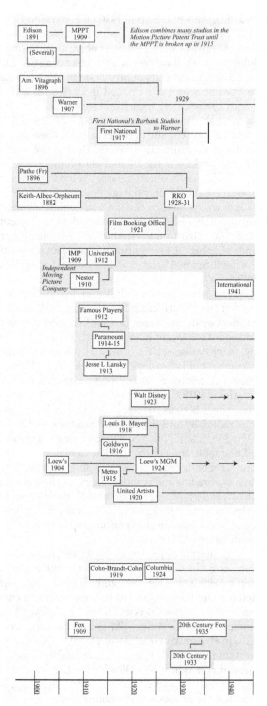

Clark Gable

Unfortunately, major studio practice of forcing theater owners to accept blocks of *A* and *B* films regardless of quality and box office potential caused the Justice Department to file suit in 1938 to stop the practice. Legal maneuvers and negotiation delayed a resolution until after the war when in 1948 the Supreme Court banned block booking and forced the majors to divest themselves of their theater chains. In the interim, the industry enjoyed a burst of creative and box office success with Disney's *Snow White and the Seven Dwarfs*, earning $8 million in 1938, David O. Seltznick's *Gone With The Wind* raking in $10 million the next year as well as many academy awards, MGM's classic *Wizard of Oz*, and Disney making eyes and ears pop open again with 1940 *Fantasia*'s stereo sound. Movie theater attendance kept up during the war years with war films and real footage from overseas.

Two important technological advances that arrived in the 1930s but were not ready for exploitation until after the Second World War were in photography and television. In 1932, Edwin H. Land, a Harvard University dropout who failed at inventing an affordable, non-glare car headlight, succeeded with *Polaroid* sunglasses and five years later *Polaroid* glass for *Kodak* cameras made by his Polaroid Company of Boston. Although Land's breakthrough made it possible in theory to make a positive print without taking a negative out of the camera, mass production took some doing. A somewhat heavy, one-step instant camera and film was not marketed until 1949 at a price of $89.75.

By contrast, the first television image, of Secretary of Commerce Hoover talking into a telephone, had already been broadcast by AT&T from Whippany, New Jersey to New York City on April 7, 1927. Television technology and even local station broadcasts within a few big cities were offered in the same metropolis by NBC and CBS in 1930, but FCC licenses for ten commercial stations were delayed until further technological advances and better economic conditions in 1941. Pearl Harbor and national urgency to overcome the Axis Powers then intervened. Not until 1946 did AT&T develop a coaxial cable to transmit a TV signal from New York City to Washington DC; microwave technology for long distance transmission based on repeater stations every 25 miles swiftly followed.

Perhaps the saving grace of American industry was the large domestic market, rising to 128 million people by mid-decade for food, drink, clothing, shoes, and household products. Companies with the financial wherewithal to survive falling demand, lower prices, and depressed sales and profits positioned themselves to gear up production once the bottom of the economic abyss had been reached. For example, Sears continued to expand to 400 retail stores by 1933 doing around $200 million of sales while Penney's survived a 10% revenue decline to about three-quarters that amount to rebound with double that volume by end of the decade. The Allied, Federated, and May department store groupings were able to offer "pay when you can" credit to many customers. With wartime prosperity in the early 1940s, big retailers would return to high profitability. Sears sales would reach $1 billion in 1945.

Likewise, big consumer products companies found ways to position themselves for better times. Colgate-Palmolive increased economies of scale and revenue to $100 million by further expansion overseas while P&G followed suit by crossing the Atlantic for the first time to England. The latter also introduced a flurry of new products, including *Oxydol* soap powder, *Dreft* synthetic detergent, *Drene* detergent-based shampoo, then tailored a separate marketing strategy for each. P&G's sales surpassed $230 million in 1937.

Companies in the pharmaceutical industry continued to expand into bigger businesses, all the while blurring the line between consumer products and medicines. Having in 1930 purchased the maker of *Anacin* aspirin and the next year John Wyeth & Brothers from Harvard University for $2.9 million, American Home Products at mid-decade adopted a concerted strategy of acquisitions under the leadership of CEO Alvin G. Brush, a certified public accountant by training. Brush oversaw nearly three dozen in the next 15 years, including S.M.A. Corporation, maker of infant formulas and Chef Boy-Ar-Dee packaged foods. Size, diversity, and financial strength was increasingly necessary in the pharmaceutical industry, now challenged by the entry of bulk chemical producer Merck & Company, still under the chairmanship after 40 years of George W. Merck but now determined to acquire the expertise from academia to invent and market innovative medicines.

Monopoly board game

Meanwhile, with lesser financial resources but equal grit, IBM purchased Electromatic Typewriters, Inc. in 1933 and produced its first electric typewriter two years later. CEO Watson judged that corporations in pursuit of higher productivity and lower labor costs would purchase many such devices to permit one secretary to do the work of several. Big Blue, as IBM later came to be called, was rewarded for its gamble in 1936 when the Social Security Administration required punch card equipment for its operations. That contract not only doubled IBM's revenue to $38 million in 1939 but justified Watson's decision to put all employees on salary and offer benefits that expanded from a group life insurance plan to holiday and vacation pay in 1937. More government contracts during the Second World War, including for bomb sites, rifles, engine parts, and other war-related equipment, tripled revenue to nearly $140 million in 1945. IBM came to employ 18,250 people.

Despite anti-monopoly breakups in airlines and finance, the Great Depression and the need for economies of scale undermined Progressive Era successes at trust-busting and promoting diverse industry competition. Aside from automobile industry concentration, DuPont, Dow, and Union Carbide took a similar share in chemicals, six companies, of which R.J. Reynolds was the largest and Philip Morris the smallest, owned over 90% of tobacco assets, and Alcoa continued to possess all the virgin aluminum production in the country. Moreover, the top 30 US corporations each had assets in excess of $1 billion, or about 8.5% of all private assets. Of the top ten, six headed by MetLife with $4.2 billion were insurance companies or banks, two were the Pennsylvania and New York Central Railroads (with $2.9 billion and $2.4 billion of assets respectively), and the others were

AT&T with $4 billion and Standard Oil of New Jersey with $1.9 billion. It was all this merging and consolidating that inspired the Parker Brothers of Salem, Massachusetts to buy the rights in 1935 to Charles B. Darrow's *Monopoly*. Over years and decades, it became the world's best selling board game and Darrow became the first millionaire game designer.

THE RISE OF ORGANIZED LABOR AND MORE RADICAL PROPOSALS

Organized labor wanted a bigger piece of the pie, in particular through further wage increases to boost pay, in 1935 averaging about 60 cents an hour or $1,500 a year, about $20,500 in 2004 money. Leaders could not, did not want to count on the benevolence of the Fords and IBMs. Although unemployment of 10.6 million people or one in five workers frightened 2.5 million into taking safe harbor inside company unions, independent union membership was up to 4.5 million, of which the AFL had 70%. The goal was to extend to all workers the right established for railroad employees by the Railway Labor Act of June 27, 1934 and a National Railroad Adjustment Board in Chicago to organize and bargain collectively through representatives of their own choosing. Fire-side chats on the radio in which FDR assured Americans that they had "nothing to fear but fear itself" convinced working class people that the patrician in the White House identified their best interests and a sound economy as one and the same. The main-streaming of Labor was further guaranteed by the National Labor Relations or Wagner-Connery Act of July 5, 1935 that established a National Labor Relations Board (NLRB) to determine appropriate collective bargaining units, certify unions, and stop unfair labor practices. In November, the AFL organized within its ranks a Committee for Industrial Organization (CIO) to unionize the automobile and steel industries. It was ready to challenge the power of Big Business.

New York Central train station, Utica, New York

Thus, strikes proliferated and were often marked by violent confrontation between picketers and police. Taking an even more confrontational approach, Lewis of the UMW and Sidney Hillman of the Amalgamated Clothing Workers broke with the AFL and set up a rival Congress of Industrial Organizations, also with the moniker CIO, to make demands for radical social, political, and economic change. They were encouraged by the populist, some said socialist, "Share Our Wealth" program of Senator Huey Long of Louisiana who promised a homestead allowance of $6,000 and a minimum annual income of $2,500 to every US family. The King Fish, as he was known in his home state, announced that if elected to the White House he would pay for this federal munificence by limiting individual fortunes to about $4 million and taking the rest in taxes.

Huey Long

Although Long was shot in Baton Rouge on September 8, 1935 by a man whose wife, daughter of a political opponent, Long had alleged had partial African-American ancestry, FDR co-opted part of his plan and much of his political appeal with a program of his own to redistribute income and wealth. Democrats announced this intention with the Revenue or Wealth Tax Act of August 30, 1935. That legislation placed a surtax on incomes over $50,000 and estates and gifts over $40,000. Incomes over $1 million got hit with a graduated tax that peaked at a whopping 75% on income over $5 million. By contrast, small corporations had their income tax lowered from 13.25% to 12.5%. Larger corporations with income over $50,000 were taxes at 15% with an additional graduated tax climbing from 6% on profits in excess of 10% of revenue to 12% on profits over 15% of revenue. The next year on June 22, Congress punished corporations again with a graduated tax ranging from 7% to 27% on undistributed profits. That part of the Revenue Act soon backfired, however, by depriving businesses of capital needed for plant and equipment expansion as well as reserves needed to get past periods of slack demand.

Most frustrating for property owners, business leaders, and high earners subject to FDR's confiscatory tax program was the inability of the Republican Party, traditionally the champion of conservatism and stability, to slow the New Deal steamroller. Reduced to minority status in Congress and discredited by Hoover's failure with the American people, its leaders had to watch impotently as myriad New Deal programs ballooned the national debt from $20.9 billion when FDR took office to over $33 billion in 1936 with annual government spending up to 10% of GDP. Only the Republican-filled Supreme Court, headed by the redoubtable Charles Evans Hughes who had served on the court from 1910-16, narrowly lost the 1916 election to Woodrow Wilson, crafted foreign policy as secretary of state 1921-25, and returned to the court in 1928, after 1930 as Chief Justice, acted as a last bulwark of resistance. In 1935, the justices ruled unanimously in *Schechter Poultry Corporation v. US* that the NIRA, by permitting the executive branch to make industry codes, was an unconstitutional delegation of Congress' power to legislate. In subsequent cases the next year, they knocked down the Railroad Retirement Acts and AAA. Only the TVA survived a court challenge because the federal government had the power, the justices conceded, to control navigable streams and provide for the national defense.

Not two months after the AAA was ruled unconstitutional, Congress on Feb. 29, 1936 replaced it with the Conservation and Domestic Allotment Act. That law planned to achieve a similar purpose of restricting agricultural output through benefit payments to growers who practiced soil conservation. In essence, farmers received payments for lands leased to the government that would now not be planted with soil-depleting crops such as corn, cotton, tobacco, wheat, and oats. They were paid to switch to soil-conserving crops.

Picking lettuce in the Imperial Valley, California

However, without the ability to specify quotas for acres of crops needed by the country, Washington watched food shortages develop in some regions. Well-off farmers with larger operations were much better equipped to shift production to other crops than small farmers. For that reason, the number of farms declined by 1941 to 6.3 million while the number of acres under production remained about the same at 1.06 billion. To handle the larger average farm size of 168 acres, farmers invested in more equipment, boosting the number of tractors to 1.67 million, trucks to 1.1 million, combines to 225,000 combines, corn pickers to 120,000, and farms with milking machines to 210,000, all together worth over $3.3 billion.

Grain elevator, Buffalo, New York

Despite denunciation by critics that FDR had launched a class-warfare "soak-the-rich" campaign, the American people in November 1936 rewarded the President with another landslide victory. This time he swamped Alf Landon, Republican governor of Kansas, by a 27.8 to 16.7 million vote margin, gathering up all but eight electoral ballots and carrying into the Senate and House 80% Democratic majorities. Landon promised a balanced budget without neglecting the poor or raising taxes, but the public did not believe it possible. They wanted more of Roosevelt and the nearly 40% rise in *per capita* GDP experienced on his watch.

With three-fifths of his countrymen firmly in his corner, the President announced a Second New Deal to raised standards of living for the third of the nation who were "*ill-housed, ill-clad and ill-nourished. The test of our progress is not whether we add more to the abundance of those who have much, it is whether we provide enough for those who have too little.*" That type of rhetoric and a feeling that now was the time to bring about fundamental change encouraged even more aggressive tactics by labor leaders. So-called sit-down strikes in the automobile, oil-refining, rubber, ship-building, steel, and textile industries eventually totaled a half million workers. The highest profile action began December 31, 1936 when to the outrage of Sloan a few hundred workers seized GM plants in Flint, Michigan. Within days, 40,000 GM workers struck and another 110,000 workers in other firms were caused to be idle. After 44 days of confrontation, the company finally gave in to demands for recognition of the Steel Workers' Organizing Committee (SWOC) of the AFL's CIO as the workers' union representation. Wages were increased 10% to 50 cents an hour with time and a half for overtime while the regular work week was pared to 40 hours, so that assuming no overtime auto workers received annual earnings equal in 2004 money to $13,200.

Youngstown Sheet and Tube night production

Even more intransigent than Sloan was head of Republic Steel Tom M. Girdler. He and other Little Steel companies Bethlehem, Inland, National, Youngstown Sheet and Tube, and Jones & Laughlin had since 1933 fought back against labor leaders with the so-called Mohawk Valley formula reminiscent of tactics used by coal companies in the 1870s against the Molly Maguires. Not only did they compile blacklists of workers active in unionization efforts and hire private security forces to guard their establishments but spied on employees and used vigilantism to fight fire with fire. Republic Steel and Youngstown Sheet and Tube went so far as to accumulate private arsenals of weapons. After Girdler and the others challenged the constitutionality of the Wagner Act, on May 30, 1937, union demonstrators at a Republic plant in south Chicago frightened outnumbered police into firing into their midst and tossing tear gas canisters, killing 10 and wounding 84 in what newspapers called the Memorial Day Massacre. Although the Supreme Court ruled the next year in *Hague v. CIO* that sit-down strikes were illegal, its refusal to overturn the Wagner Act, as well as pressure by the Roosevelt administration, persuaded virtually all steel companies by 1941 to sign agreements with the CIO. US Steel led the way in 1937 by recognizing SWOC and agreeing to a one year contract for a $5 per day wage and 40 hour work week, in 2004 money equal to $16,400 annually. SWOC became the United Steelworkers of America in 1942 with membership of 170,000 workers.

An important reason the justices backed away from the obstructionism that had voided the AAA and NRA was FDR's astonishing proposal to increase the Supreme Court from nine to 15 with a mandatory retirement age of 70. He wanted, further, to add up to 50 more judges at other levels of the federal judiciary as well as make other reforms to expedite court hearings and increase executive branch influence on constitutional issues. Even after conservative Democrats in Congress joined hands with Republicans to prevent FDR from "packing" the Supreme Court, the intimidated justices let stand not only the Wagner Act but Social Security. As they now began to die off or retire, FDR replaced them with more liberal minds.

Thus, the way ahead to a social-welfare state in which government bullied business for the protection of workers, farmers, and consumers appeared clear. Another piece of the puzzle went into place on September 1, 1937 with the National Housing (Wagner-Steagall) Act setting up a US Housing Authority under the Secretary of the Interior to make low-interest 60 year loans to public agencies to fund low-rent public housing projects. The next year, Congress established the Federal National Mortgage Association (Fannie Mae) as part of the FHA to buy FHA-insured loans from banks to replenish the supply of money in their accounts to make new loans. However, four consecutive years of improving economic conditions abruptly came to an end with a severe recession in late summer 1937 that carried over into the next year and caused unemployment to jump back up to 10.4 million people.

Hard hit were farmers who suffered from another bout of overproduction and price declines. To stem the contraction in the farm population, on February 16, 1938 Congress passed another Agricultural Adjustment Act. This law used a parity price level slightly below the 1909-14 period to stabilize prices without conflicting with the constitution by having a Commodity Credit Corporation make loans to farmers based on the value of their surplus crops. The government then stored the crops with the intent of having farmers market the surpluses and repay the loans in years when crop failures caused commodity prices to equal or exceed the parity level. The system as well as the war in Europe in 1939 helped wheat prices rise to 90 cents a bushel, cattle prices to recover to over $40 a head, and number of hogs to increase to 61 million. During the Second World War, farmers enjoyed another boom period.

However, in 1938, agriculture generated less than 10% of GDP and provided only 15% of employment. To sustain the rest and prevent another plunge into economic catastrophe, FDR needed a way to stimulate consumer demand and/or business investment, as was now clear from Kuznets' research the key components of GDP. Therefore, he supported the Revenue Act of May 27, 1938, repealing the undistributed profits taxes on corporations and installing a level 19% tax on corporate income over $25,000, which was reduced by a flat 2.5% of dividends paid out. That law also reduced progressive taxes on capital gains.

The *quid pro quo* business had to pay was the Fair Labor Standards Act (Wages and Hours Law) of June 25, 1938. It codified for persons employed by companies engaged in interstate commerce a nationwide minimum wage of 40 cents an hour, up from 25 cents, a maximum regular work week of 40 hours with time and a half pay for overtime, and no child labor for anyone under 16. In 2004 purchasing power, eight hours of work per day

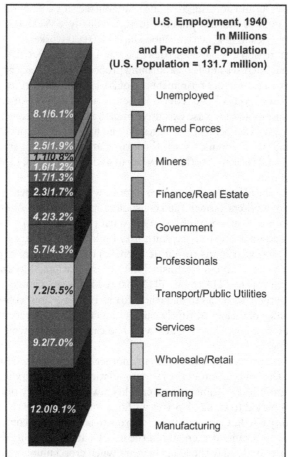

U.S. Employment, 1940
In Millions
and Percent of Population
(U.S. Population = 131.7 million)

- Unemployed
- Armed Forces
- Miners
- Finance/Real Estate
- Government
- Professionals
- Transport/Public Utilities
- Services
- Wholesale/Retail
- Farming
- Manufacturing

8.1/6.1%
2.5/1.9%
1.1/0.8%
1.6/1.2%
1.7/1.3%
2.3/1.7%
4.2/3.2%
5.7/4.3%
7.2/5.5%
9.2/7.0%
12.0/9.1%

five days a week for 50 weeks at 40 cents an hour amounted to annual earnings of $10,670, hardly a living wage but enough for the poor to scrape by. The minimum wage would be raised to 75 cents an hour in 1949 with periodic increases thereafter to the current level of $5.15, or at $10,300 for 2,000 hours in 2004 not quite the purchasing power as the original minimum.

Because FDR still mistrusted corporations and knew that business leaders prayed for the return to political dominance of Republican, he laid the groundwork for a further assault on business power. A Temporary National Economic Committee (TNEC) he appointed in April 1938 had a mandate to investigate monopolies and their effects on all aspects of the economy as well as propose corrective measures. If enacted, TNEC recommendations in a final report of March 31, 1941 would have greatly strengthened government anti-trust power to prevent mergers, promote competition, and defeat a further concentration of economic and financial power. Because at that point FDR needed business cooperation to gear up the "arsenal of democracy" for the Second World War, the sweeping reforms were never implemented.

John M. Keynes

Rather, with a mixture perhaps of desperation to keep political enemies at bay and determination to get the economy rolling again, the President turned to the theory of British economist John Maynard Keynes. Keynes argued that the US economy required a large-scale but temporary "pump-priming," in other words deficit spending beyond what had already been tried, to put large quantities of money into the pockets of consumers and provoke businesses, out of self interest, to invest capital for plant expansion. Accordingly on April 14, 1938, FDR asked for appropriations to double the employment rolls of the WPA to 3 million people, provide $3 billion backed by gold sitting idle in the Treasury reserve in recovery and relief payments to the poor, and offer stimulus loans through the RFC. The Emergency Relief Appropriation Act of June 21 made it so; further, the President pushed a loose money policy on the Federal Reserve.

Lastly, FDR satisfied concerns in Congress about protecting the homeland and Western Hemisphere from Europe's and Asia's woes by backing a Naval Expansion Act (May 17, 1938) worth $1.1 billion over several years to build up a powerful carrier-based, two-ocean navy. When the next year international tensions built toward war, he and Congress raised total defense spending to over $1.8 billion. The Selective Training and Service Act of September 16, 1940 put two million men temporarily in uniform over 12 months and greatly reduced unemployment. Because Pearl Harbor occurred before enlistments were up, the country did not require another major civilian jobs program.

Overall, pump-priming added another $10 billion to the public debt, or $325 *per capita*. That was but a tiny percentage of the funds, paid for by bonds and taxes, which the US would ultimately spend to win the Second World War and boost the American economy.

On the whole, FDR's New Deal programs were successful by 1939 at lifting the country out of the economic Depression. Although GDP did not come up to the level of 1929 until the next year, *per capita* GDP as measured in 2004 money reached $9,465, $100 more than the year of the stock market crash. Moreover, income had been redistributed in favor of the less affluent. By 1940, the income share of the top 5% earners fell to 24%, the top fifth dropped to 48.8%, the second fifth jumped to 22.3%, the third fifth lifted to 15.3%, and the rest improved to 13.6%. Likewise, the share of wealth held by the top 1% was cut from 44% in 1930 to 36.3% a decade later. The tangible wealth of the country recovered to $330 billion in fixed assets ($67 billion held by government), $32 billion of consumer durables, and about $440 billion in financial assets.

IMPACT OF SECOND WORLD WAR SPENDING

Keynesian economics became by necessity the centerpiece of American economic policy during the Second World War. To put over 12 million men and women in uniform, meet production goals that called for 50,000 planes a year, 90 aircraft carriers and hundreds of other combat ships, 2.6 million tanks, 660,000 jeeps, tens of thousands of artillery pieces and other heavy equipment, tens of millions of rifles, pistols, machine guns, artillery rounds, bullets, grenades, boots, knapsacks, other paraphernalia of war, and transport for millions of tons of food, water, oil, lubricants, and parts required the expenditure of nearly $150 billion dollars. From 1940 through 1945, Washington paid out for all purposes a grand total of $370 billion, of which $169 billion was covered by taxes. The public debt rose to an astronomical $258 billion, which was equal in 2004 dollars to $2.72 trillion or about $19,150 per person. The fact that GDP skyrocketed as well to $223 billion while consumer spending hit $120 billion (of which $78 billion was retail purchases) made the burden more tolerable. The economy climbed to an impressive if precarious peak from which it might easily fall should Keynes' theory not prove sustainable.

Sherman tank

FDR really got the ball rolling on June 25, 1940 when he authorized the RFC to make loans for acquiring, producing, and/or stockpiling strategic raw materials and for constructing, expanding, and operating plants. Subsequently on March 26, 1942, he issued an Executive Order permitting the government to guarantee or participate in loans made by banks to finance war production. Federal Reserve Banks ultimately made 8,000 agreements, 80% for loans of $1 million or above, which totaled nearly $10 billion for extension of credit. Through the Defense Plant Corporation, the government financed five-sixths of the $160 million invested in new plant construction. In fact, Washington came to own 90% of synthetic rubber, aircraft, magnesium, and shipbuilding plants and facilities. Half of machine tool plants, 70% of aluminum capacity, and 3,800 miles of pipes in the 24 inch diameter "Big Inch" (Longview, Texas to Linden, New Jersey) and 20 inch diameter "Little Inch" (Beaumont, Texas to Linden) systems to transport petroleum to the East Coast were carried on the government's books.

Army Walkie Talkie

Critical for coordination of the ramp-up of war production was creation on December 20, 1940 of an Office of Production Management (OPM) headed by Danish-born, former Ford and GM executive William S. Knudsen. The OPM was also charged with accelerating material aid "short of war" to Great Britain and other potential allies. London was the major beneficiary of the Lend-Lease Act of March 11, 1941 that ultimately transferred overseas a net $42 billion in military equipment and supplies. After the US officially entered the war, the OPM was replaced on January 13, 1942 by the War Production Board (WPB) under Donald M. Nelson, a Sears executive. To conserve materials, Nelson halted all non-essential residential and highway construction on April 8. Six days later, FDR designated Vice President Henry A. Wallace head of a Board of Economic  Warfare to take control of the US stockpile of critical war materials, particularly rubber and synthetic rubber, petroleum, coal and other solid fuels as well as some food, tires, cars, and shoes. The WPB's successor on July 15, 1943 was the Office of Economic Warfare

(OEW). Together with other agencies, OEW so successfully prevented black markets for springing up for commodities, especially gasoline, that a limited re-conversion to civilian production was possible by August 1944.

Meanwhile, the President took steps to prevent hoarding and shortages from igniting inflation, which had been running less than 1% in 1940. Twenty days after Pearl Harbor, he instituted rationing of automobile tires to conserve rubber. Early the next year, the government issued ration books to civilians with coupons for sugar, coffee, gas, and fuel oil. In 1943, a point system went into effect to ration meat, fats, oils, butter, cheese, processed foods, and shoes. Too, FDR used the Emergency Price Control Act of January 30, 1942 to create an Office of Price Administration to fix ceiling prices on all commodities except farm products as well as control rents in designated defense areas. Farmers enjoyed another boom time with 25% more cattle increasing 65% in price and slightly fewer hogs selling for nearly triple 1940 levels. Thus, cash receipts for farmers rose during hostilities from $9.1 billion to $22.3 billion. The value of the nation's livestock doubled.

The windfall for farmers and others would have been far greater had not the government instituted a program of heavy taxation to help pay for the war and the President on April 8 issued a "hold-the-line" order freezing prices, wages, and salaries. Individual income taxes climbed until the top marginal rate for high income earners peaked in 1944 at 94%. The standard personal exemption fell to $500 per person. The top corporate rate jumped from 19% to 40% while excess corporate profits were hit with a flat 90% tax in 1942, and then 95% the next year. The effect of all these actions was to keep inflation at a 5% average while the war lasted. Limited in what they could buy and how much they could spend, citizens saved 24% of disposable income, causing household financial assets to surge to $563 billion by end of 1945, half the country's intangible total.

Consolidated Aircraft plant, San Diego, California

There were still inadequacies and inefficiencies in the US economic effort until FDR agreed on May 28, 1943 to centralize power in the Office of War Mobilization (OWM). In charge of allocating resources between the armed forces, war industries, the allies, and the American civilian population, he placed former Supreme Court Justice and Senator from South Carolina James F. Byrnes. While shipping $60 billion in supplies to the British, $16 billion to the Soviet Union, and $4 billion to other allies, the OWM effected an amazing surge in war production to meet and exceed goals. Expenditure on military production facilities and equipment jumped from only $1.84 billion or 2% of GDP in 1939 to $87.9 billion or 40% in 1944. The next year, government spent $126.5 billion on structures and

$103.5 billion on equipment, of which only $4 billion was state and local, for a 13 fold increase over 1940 spending. The Manhattan Project alone cost $2 billion for development of the atomic bomb.

P-51 Mustang

In point of fact, the US spent much more converting existing facilities from domestic to war production than constructing new factories and industrial equipment. In addition to the motor vehicle companies and other capital goods manufacturers switching over to production of war equipment and munitions, the greatest beneficiaries were airframe and ship builders who began a transition that would in the postwar period turn them into major aerospace and defense contractors commanding billions of dollars in government contracts. Most prominent among the former that were already well-known were Curtiss-Wright, making 30,000 planes during the war and in particular the *P-40 War Hawk* and Navy *Hellfire* diver, Boeing turning out thousands of *B-17 Flying Fortress* bombers, NAA buttressing the *B-17* in Europe with 14,500 *P-51 Mustang* fighters, United Aircraft producing 150 Sikorsky helicopters, half a million Hamilton Standard propellers, and 300,000 Pratt & Whitney aircraft engines, and Douglas employing 160,000 people in several factories to build *C-47* and *C-54* transports and other planes. Smaller or new aviation companies that vaulted into the big time with military orders included the Glenn L. Martin Company producing the *B-26 Marauder* bomber, then the *B-29 Liberator* that carried the atomic bombs, Lockheed Aircraft Company making *P-38* fighters but working in secret in its "Skunk Works" on the *XP-80 Shooting Star* jet fighter, McDonnell Aircraft Corporation providing seven million pounds of airplane parts for other companies, Northrop Aircraft working on sub-assemblies for Consolidated Aircraft's *PBY* reconnaissance planes, Grumman Aircraft Engineering Corporation employing 22,100 people on Long Island, New York to produce 12,275 *F6F Hellcat* fighters, and another Long Island firm Vought Corporation making as many *F4U Corsairs* for the Navy.

Liberty Ship

Meanwhile, the quirky Howard Hughes, Jr., who had inherited his father's Toolco machine tool company in 1923 and in the 1930s expanded aviation holdings from a four employee Hughes Aircraft Company building racing planes to take over majority share in TWA, went in a different production direction. Although his idea for a huge wooden seaplane called the *H-4 Hercules*, derided as the *Spruce Goose*, intended to be a *Liberty* ship in the air, cost the government $18 million and flew only briefly in 1947, Hughes Electronics as a subdivision of Hughes Aircraft employed 80,000 people to supply weapons systems to the Army Air Corps and Navy. After the war, he became a billionaire combining radar and computers to help US pilots locate and attack enemy planes day or night in all weather conditions. His fortune, legend, and reclusiveness grew until he went mad.

Likewise, the Raytheon Manufacturing Company scored with radar, a British invention using magnetron tubes to transmit microwaves to reflect off German bombing formations and permit the Royal Air Force to direct fighters to intercept. Although initially AT&T's Western Electric division got the big contract from London, improvements to the manufacturing process of magnetron tubes made by Raytheon engineer Percy L. Spencer permitted the company to leapfrog competitors by end of the war. Raytheon shipboard radar on PT boats combined with Raytheon radios coordinated the hunt for U-boats in the Atlantic Ocean.

As for shipbuilders, Newport News traded on its history of battleship construction to win contracts for its 31,000 employees to lay the keels not only for that largest of capital ships but aircraft carriers, cruisers, and ship designer Henry J. Kaiser's *Liberty* merchantmen. The Electric Boat Company continued as the nation's primary submarine producer with 74 boats as well as 398 PT boats. Bethlehem Steel established itself as the largest shipbuilder in the world with 180,000 of its 300,000 workers so employed in 15 shipyards turning out over 1,100 ships. Overall, US vessel tons tripled to 775 million, including annual production in 1945 of 61.5 million.

As shipbuilding claimed 20% of all steel production, up from just 1% before the war, production of long tons of steel peaked at 80 million in 1944, of which 94% was by the Open Hearth method. During all war years, the industry produced 427 million tons of finished steel, two-thirds the world production. Similarly, the US oil industry drove the allied military machine, exceeding 1.7 billion barrels in 1945 with a well head value at $1.22 per barrel. With spending by civilians on consumer products curtailed, heavy industry had by necessity to carry the economy.

However, American know-how, supplemented in some cases by expatriate brains, developed advanced technologies for military purposes that had important long-term domestic economic benefits. For example, when the Japanese overran Southeast Asia in early 1942 and cut off 600,000 tons of US imports of rubber from Dutch Indonesia, Goodyear and B.F. Goodrich geared up production of a synthetic substitute first concocted in 1937. From only 2,000 tons in 1939, 930,000 tons of synthetic rubber were produced by 1945. Rubber companies turned out billions of dollars of tires, rafts, flotation devices, and other war-required products.

Lumber yard and saw mill in Michigan
Too, while steel factories in the Three Rivers area of Pittsburgh, in Gary, Indiana, and elsewhere ran night and

day, advanced aircraft design emphasizing an optimum combination of speed, strength, flexibility, and heat-resistance required increasing amounts of aluminum, magnesium, and other alloys and light metals. Shortages necessitated incorporation of more plastics into planes, vehicles, and equipment. Thus plastic production jumped up from 170,000 tons in 1939 to 1.5 million in 1945, or half of aluminum production, which itself rose six fold in that time. A decade after the war, plastics would have myriad applications in consumer and industrial products, pushing by 2004 toward 50 million tons of annual production.

Companies that were transformed by war orders from bit players to significant companies included Rohm & Haas, originally a German company making leather bate but separated from its American division during the First World War. In the second great conflict of the twentieth century, the company's *Plexiglas* acrylic sheet breakthrough, made in 1936, translated into a 900% increase in sales for military aircraft purposes. Likewise, tiny Georgia Hardwood Lumber, with only five sawmills in 1938, became a leading supplier of lumber to the US armed forces. Although its sales slumped to $24 million after the war, it was positioned to grow into the powerful Georgia-Pacific Company of today.

Several entirely new fields of scientific and economic endeavor resulted from the war. Not only had the atomic genie of nuclear weapons, power, and propulsion flashed into existence but the bio-tech, computer, space, and modern pharmaceutical industries. Building on the 1928 discovery of British doctor Alexander Fleming of the antibiotic qualities of penicillin, Washington contracted with the American pharmaceutical industry to mass produce the substance. Pfizer, using a deep tank fermentation technique, Abbott Laboratories, also leading the way in radiopharmaceuticals for immunodiagnostics, Bristol-Myers, coming back into the industry in 1943 by buying Cheplin Laboratories of Syracuse and its acidophilus milk product, Squibb with the biggest penicillin plant in New Brunswick, American Home Products' Wyeth division, also producing artificial blood plasma, typhus vaccine, quinine, and atabrine tablets for malaria, and Eli Lilly all had a hand in the effort. Sulfa drugs also improved treatment and recovery from battlefield wounds with benefit to civilian populations. In 1944, Canadian-born Oswald T. Avery of the Rockefeller Institute in New York City discovered that the basic genetic material of cells was deoxyribonucleic acid (DNA). Not until 1953 was the exact double-helix structure of DNA established and research begun over four decades deciphering the human genetic code.

ENIAC

In December, 1940, Drs. John Presper Eckert, Jr. and John Mauchly of Moore School of Electrical Engineering at the University of Pennsylvania put together the first automatic electronic computer called the Electronic Numerical Integrator and Computer (ENIAC). Weighing 30 tons, occupying 1,500 square feet, and utilizing 18,000 thermionic valves or vacuum tubes that tended to over-heat, ENIAC was capable of making 5,000 additions or subtractions per second. Although the behemoth accomplished little during the war, afterward the Eckert-Mauchly Corporation they formed was absorbed by Remington Rand, which built the Universal Automatic Computer (UNIVAC) for the Bureau of the Census. Not until radio tubes were replaced in the late 1950s by transistors would miniaturization reduce computers to box-like sizes and make possible rapid advances in computing speed, memory, and functions.

An even longer development period had been required for rockets. The first patent was awarded in 1914 to Robert H. Goddard, Clark University professor of physics and inventor during the First World War of a solid-propellant projectile that became the bazooka used so effectively by US soldiers during the Second World War. But the first true rocket flight was only achieved by Goddard in 1926. Unfortunately, it was Nazi Germany that mass produced *V-2* rockets to bomb Britain, not the US to attack its enemies. On the other hand, capture in 1945 of Werner von Braun and many other German scientists vaulted the US into a postwar ballistic missile and space competition with the Soviets. Great commercial benefit from satellite communications put into orbit by rockets followed.

Oak Ridge atomic bomb plant

Until the forces of the universe were successfully marshaled to crush the enemies of the republic, mass mobilization of flesh and blood had to suffice. Between 1942 and 1945, the military accepted into its ranks 15 million persons, mostly men. The booming economy absorbed 7 million others previously unemployed as well as 7 million new workers. So many women emulated the "Rosie the Riveter" campaign pushed by the government that the allegedly gentler sex came by 1945 to compose 35% of employed persons or 19.3 million. Too, a great migration of blacks took place from the south, both to work in northern factories and escape segregation. Overall unemployment bottomed out at only 670,000, 1.2% of available workers, and most of these were seasonally unemployed.

The favorable consequence for the AFL was membership leaping up to 9 million by 1943, 13 million by early the next year and 14.8 million by 1945, or 36% of non-farm workers and 27% of all civilian workers. The average wage rose to $1.02 an hour, equal in 2004 money to an annual income of $22,200, assuming no overtime. For patriotic reasons and to insure continued production of tanks as well as cars, the United Auto Workers (UAW) pledged no strikes while the war lasted. As during the First World War, the government took control of all railroads. As for the nation's communication system, aside from an October 12, 1943 order by the FCC compelling NBC to sell off its "Blue Network," thus resulting in the founding of the American Broadcasting Corporation (ABC), Washington meddled very little. Hollywood moguls, network executives, and newspaper publishers were more than happy to jump on the patriotic bandwagon, in the process entrenching their control of entertainment and information industries and insuring the continued flow of revenues and profits.

Anthracite coal operation

Not all labor leaders were so cooperative, however. On May 1, 1943, Lewis led 450,000 soft-coal miners and 80,000 anthracite miners, or about two-thirds of all the nation's miners, into a coordinated strike. At once, FDR demonstrated his determination not to permit chaos to undermine the war effort by ordering Secretary of the Interior Harold L. Ickes to take over all coal mines in the eastern US. Thinking better of giving up hard-won gains of the past several years, the UMW encouraged miners to return the next day. But AFL leaders judged that once the war ended, it would have strength enough, including the majority of 15.5 million manufacturing and 3.9 million transportation workers, to push for a more ambitious agenda than just wage increases, shorter hours, and better working con-ditions. Labor leaders wanted a more equitable distribution of the fruits of the American economy.

By 1945, these were so impressive as to make the Great Depression seem like a bad but distant memory. On top of $691 billion in tangible assets, business, government and indi-viduals owned over $1 trillion in financial assets, including $151 billion in bank deposits and $48 billion in currency and coin, of which $27 billion was circulating. Purchases of consumer durables brought the total net value held by citizens to $48 billion. Although investment overseas of $16 billion was exceeded $1 billion by panicked foreign investment in the US, the huge excess of $14.3 billion of exports over $3.9 billion of imports put the balance of payments $12.5 billion in the black.

Those figures might have excited the envy of the poor but for the fact that share of national income taken by the top 5% earners had fallen to an historic low of 20.7% and the top fifth to 45.8% while the bottom three-fifths now received 32%, trends Democrats intended to continue. Individual income taxes, falling heavily on the rich, now accounted for 40% of federal revenue while another 33.5% came from corporation income and excess profits taxes. Once the war ended and national defense no longer claimed 82.5% of budget expenditures ($92.7 billion in 1945), other priorities could ascend. The debate would center on whether to continue to use the power of the federal government to dominate the economy or disassemble the agencies and taxing authority built up since 1933 to return the republic to a *laissez-faire* business environment and what once in the economic, society, and politics had been considered normal.

Likewise, national leaders would have to choose between 1920s-style isolationism or active involvement in world affairs. Although few people were aware of it, the issue had already more or less been decided. For to avoid a second fiasco such as Wilson's failure appending the US to the League of Nation's, FDR promoted early on a movement for a United Nations (U.N.) of more potency and permanence than its predecessor. In July 1944, the US hosted 1,300 specialists from 44 nations at the Bretton Woods resort in New Hampshire for a Monetary and Financial Conference. The attendees agreed to establish an International Monetary Fund, capitalized initially at $8.8 billion, to stabilize currencies and facilitate international payments. A World Bank, capitalized at $9.1 billion, was sanctioned to make loans to nations for postwar economic reconstruction and development. Still dominated by Democrats, Congress approved membership to the U.N. in July 1945. Even key Republicans conceded that the US could never again withdraw into a tortoise shell of hemispheric defense without great risk to its strategic and economic interests.

Thus was put in place with little political strain the infrastructure that was to foster with varying results international order and free market ideology over the next several decades. A world system of democratically elected governments, capitalist-based economies, and lowering tariffs would be inhibited by the Cold War competition between the

US and Soviet bloc, European and Japanese rebuilding and recovery, and regional conflicts. However, the network of alliances forged by Washington protected the burgeoning economic environment and eventually became a juggernaut for growth. No nation benefited as much as the American republic.

PART 3. BROADENING OUT OF ECONOMIC POSSIBILITIES: 1946-1989

Strong-arming of the American economy by Washington with high taxes, New Deal programs, and government regulation of private industry could only work so long the rest of the world was on its back. Particularly as the US geared up to fight the Cold War with Moscow and limited wars in Korea and Vietnam, both domestic production and foreign trade were required to prevent a relapse into depression. After an extended *per capita* recession, pent up demand for housing, cars, and consumer durables stoked a belated postwar boom. American leadership of the Free World fulfilled the expectation of 1890s theorists that overseas markets could soak up excess US production and mute social tensions.

The country had a precious two decades to build up a stronger economic base and larger financial reserves before global competitors recovered. In the interim, government insistence that Big Business negotiate in good faith with unions brought prosperity for working class Americans in established industries. As the mass market for consumer goods and services broadened to more households, additional economic growth was stimulated. Although Republicans rested content to husband the nation's resources for the seemingly endless standoff with Communism, Democrats aspired to a government-directed Capitalism beneficial to all. Hence, they cut taxes to spur a 1960s economic boom. Hence, they committed a greater share of Washington's largesse to fund Great Society programs.

No one counted on having to pay for an excess of guns and butter simultaneously, however. By the time in 1973 when the US was blindsided by the first OPEC oil embargo, the Vietnam War quagmire, foreign import competition, government red tape, and an increasingly adversarial relationship between corporations and unions made the American economy as sluggish to respond as a punch-drunk fighter. Just as the republic was confronted in the economic theater of operations by European and Japanese allies, the Soviet Union finally achieved nuclear parity. Although Moscow's challenge turned out to be less devastating to the American world position than political and social fall-out from Vietnam, the consequence for the US of more nimble economic rivals was erosion of

State Capital building, Jefferson, Missouri

middle and working class living standards and the worst *per capita* recession since the post-war adjustment period.

Fortunately, another technological revolution saved the day. Inspired by Second World War and Cold War R&D on munitions, missiles, electronics, and computers, it spilled over into applications for the domestic economy. Although the Japanese were swifter in the short run to take advantage of automation and transistors, in the long run the digital age belonged to the US. English-language software made the hardware work. Too, it was Americans who were most imaginative and successful with entertainment and information. The size of the American mass market permitted retail, wholesale, and other service industries to take full advantage of gigantic economies of scale.

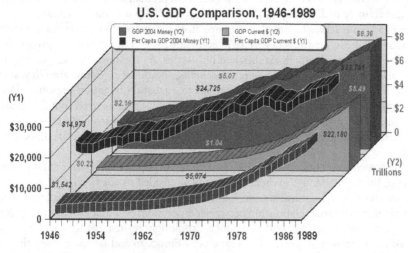

Thus, when Ronald Reagan led Republicans back into power to loosen Washington's grip on the economy and permit Free Market forces to work, American businesses big and small were ready to take advantage. New technologies expanded the horizon of economic

256

opportunity so swiftly that government could not re-regulate industries without risk of throwing the country again into recession. Nor did politicians want to corral the bucking bronco of growth. State and local government as well as federal agencies continued to allocate abundant tax dollars to the infrastructure and services that citizens demanded, in the process providing a living for a fifth of the workforce.

Nevertheless, the gap between economic haves and have-nots widened abruptly. As old industries with good-paying jobs struggled to retrench against foreign competition, employment opportunity shifted to the service sector. These included professional positions in finance and health care but were more plentiful in fast food, hotel, retail, and other lower-paying jobs. The stratification of society based upon extremes of wealth and income that had existed before the New Deal resumed.

Chapter IX. A Relatively Golden Era of Economic Growth: 1946-1960

An understandable focus by historians on the origins of the Cold War and the subsequent tense stand-off between the United States and Soviet Union has obscured the extent to which the economic vitality of the American republic was also imperiled after the Second World War by internal factors. The great mountain of debt accumulated by Washington to climb out of the Great Depression and overcome German and Japanese aggression weighed down the material prospects of the country. However, a unique set of circumstances not only spared citizens a return to major distress but fueled a boom. In a few short years, the United States reached a critical mass of economic vitality.

The first factor buttressing the nation's postwar fortunes was that contrary to present day, in 1945 nearly half of all debt (equal to $332 billion) was held by federal, state, local, and government-sponsored agencies. Possessing unchallenged taxing power, flexible borrowing power, financial assets of $187 billion, and tangible assets, including hundreds of millions of acres of undervalued real estate, listed on the books at $108 billion, Washington in particular could more easily bear the burden of liabilities 1.5 times as great as GDP than could private institutions and citizens. Since federal debt was heavily composed of US Savings Bonds and other long-term instruments rather than short-term borrowings, Washington had time aplenty to pay off obligations. Even demobilization and re-conversion problems that required massive shifts of manpower and resources and temporarily put the country into a recession were not a cause for undue alarm.

Equally as encouraging as the nation's debt burden falling on the party most able to manage its affairs, wartime rationing and saving had created both a backlog of demand for consumer durables as well as the wherewithal to pay for them. Household assets of $762 billion, 74% financial, were only encumbered by $30 billion of liabilities. Making citizens feel more secure about returning to a more affluent but by no means 1920s-style profligacy, home equity of $112 billion was over 85% of home value. In a pinch and once secondary mortgage lending markets were developed, homeowners could borrow against the value of real estate to tide them over. Further, New Deal programs, progressive taxation instituted during FDR's second term, and full employment during the war had improved the distribution of both income and wealth, permitting a higher percentage of citizens to shop for houses, cars, large household appliances, and the necessities of life. Although the wealth gap between rich and poor would widen again in the 1950s, income equalization would advance into the early 1970s.

To motivate Americans to open their wallets, industry was primed to offer a wider variety of desirable products and services. Chief among these were television sets receiving free broadcasts that surpassed the lure of radio with both pictures and sound. In fact, TV invaded homes so swiftly that 80% of all households or 60 million had at least one set in 1960. The small screen surpassed motion pictures shown in theaters, sporting events staged in auditoriums and stadiums, and participatory recreation as the nation's top leisure activity. That did not mean that radio was dead. With improved car models as well as record players and small, portable transistor radios giving a boost to the music industry, entertainment provided a mobile spectrum of possibilities. Additionally, the fact that 41% of the adult public possessed a high school education by 1960 while the percent of people 25 years old and up with a college degree moved up to 7.7% advanced the prospects of book, magazine, and newspaper publishing and retailing. Together, these disparate elements of media and entertainment began to fuse into an important sector of the economy.

A third reason the United States did not suffer a relapse into recession or even depression was continued federal spending on aerospace-defense needs. Potential confrontation with the Communist bloc dictated that a substantial military establishment be maintained even as overall spending was brought down and an attempt made to balance the budget. Particularly during the Eisenhower administration, acquisition of both conventional and nuclear weapons systems substituted for keeping millions of men in uniform and permitted their reassignment to civilian employment. Ramp-up for the Korean War provided a further spending jolt to smooth out the business cycle. However, federal largesse did not come close to the kind of pump-priming FDR employed in peace and war to stimulate industry and employment. It was the expanding domestic economy that carried more and more of the burden.

How was this accomplished? In part, this was a consequence of more cautious resort to the strategy of borrowing against future income for present prosperity. As the percentage of debt to assets held by households as well as businesses again began to thicken, an additional stimulus to production was provided. Had not taxes remained relatively high and the government demanded incrementally more for the Social Security fund, a better time might have been had by all. However, the chances of a boomerang into depression would have been greater.

With the desire of state and local officials to have resources to improve services, build and improve roads and bridges, and generally expand the scope of their authority, the citizenry had to fund an average 7.5% annual growth in state and local government fixed assets. These rose from only $69 billion in 1945 to $205 billion in 1960. By contrast, the federal government's fixed assets, despite Korean War and early Space Race acquisitions, ascended at a much slower average annual pace of 5.5%. They did not return to the 1945 level of $117 billion until early 1952.

A problem coming down the pike was that although the economy was still overwhelmingly geared toward domestic commerce, foreign competition might begin to make inroads into US markets. Overseas sales were counted on to soak up excess production from agriculture, manufacturing, and financial services. Rapidly rebuilt with Marshall Plan aid, Military Assistance Programs, other sources of American funding, as well as indig-enous reserves, economies in Britain, France, Germany, Japan, and Italy eventually put into operation more modern factories and equipment with which to compete, while their work forces accepted far lower wages than Americans. US share of world production began to fall from the artificial high achieved in 1945 of 50% to more normal levels.

Oil refinery, Illinois

It helped that raw material prices, including for oil as Persian Gulf fields were exploited, remained low. Surging beyond an annual growth rate of 2.8%, business produc-tivity permitted corporate executives to yield on higher wages rates and thus higher standard of livings for working men and women so long as the American public main-tained a patriotic preference for US goods over foreign imports. It was only a matter of time, however, until the cost benefit calculation most consumers do in their heads when weighing the price of an item relative to its quality and value began to turn against American household appliances and cars. European and Japanese products, lower on price, sometimes superior on design, began to take a share of key consumer durable markets.

Washington might have reacted with a high tariff policy such as tried without much success in the past. Aside from the overriding objective of keeping the goodwill of allied nations for the fight against Communism, it was decided by successive administrations that freer trade was the swelling tide that would lift all boats. Surely the US economy, rising to $294 billion of GDP by 1950 and $527 billion by 1960 was capable of absorbing a certain yet undefined percentage of foreign goods without harming American industry. Proof of the assertion came with a near doubling in the period of *per capita* GDP from $1,542 to $2,919. The more accurate measurement for increase in standard of living given by *per capita* GDP as calculated in 2004 dollars showed a less remarkable but still steady 2.1% average annual increase from $14,157 in 1947 to $18,555 in 1960. Household liabilities, advancing in a decade and a half from 4% of household assets in 1945 to 10.7%, demon-strated that a restrained measure of debt was not an imprudent idea.

For the Baby Boom generation, the economic vitality of the country seemed to promise a bright future. All the modern conveniences of the late nineteenth and twentieth centuries were now readily available from telephones to electric light and power to stylish automobiles to consumer durables and brand name household, personal, and food products. More and better items were coming all the time from well-known corporations as well as small businesses destined for bigger things. As memory of Great Depression and great world conflict dimmed, most Americans enjoyed what in retrospect seems an economic golden era.

POSTWAR ADJUSTMENT AND GOVERNMENT POLICY

Inheriting FDR's legacy, Truman moved with dispatch in September 1945 to demobilize while attempting to consolidate the economic gains of the war years. His Fair Deal recovery plan aimed for continued full employment, protection for workers against unfair termination by a Fair Employment Practices Act, increase in the minimum wage from 40 to 65 cents an hour, a public housing program that would finance 1 to 1.5 million homes a year, and a comprehensive government health insurance plan based on prepayment of medical costs. To help businesses shift to domestic production, Congress repealed the excess profits tax and cut the top corporate rate to 38%. All individual income tax rates were cut 5% to put more money into the pockets of consumers.

Still wedded to New Deal thinking, the President proposed to keep development of atomic energy under government control rather than private enterprise through the agency of an Atomic Energy Commission. Reaffirming and expanding FDR's decision to reserve and protect remaining public land and mineral assets, his administration claimed government ownership of the continental shelf out to a three mile limit. That was an important decision because it set a precedent, later upheld by the courts, for claim under the May 22, 1953 Continental Shelf Act to the outer continental shelf. In the subsoil and seabed of an even broader area existed an estimated 10 to 50 billion barrels of crude oil and 40 to 80 trillion cubic feet of natural gas. Later on July 31, 1947, the Materials Act permitted the Secretary of the Interior to sell rights to clay, gravel, sand, stone, timber, and other related resources on public lands to private interests without transferring title. To insure that, contrary to policy in the nineteenth century, the government would maximize revenue, competitive bidding had to be used when resources worth more than $1,000 were at stake.

The German and Japanese people had been so thoroughly defeated and cowed that it was possible before year's end 1945 to ship back to the states US soldiers, sailors, Marines, and airmen eventually numbering 10 million. In addition to mustering-out pay of $20 a week for 52 weeks, veterans were rewarded through the G.I. Bill of 1944 with educational benefits of up to $500 a year for four years for college tuition and fees. Other legislation provided home-loan guarantees and advantages in starting businesses. Total government benefits granted in this manner to US veterans over the next three decades amounted to $70 billion. For those who wanted to go back to work, factories made room for this mostly white male influx by dismissing female and black workers, who in the former case mostly returned to traditional homemaking, in the latter were reduced to lower paying jobs or unemployment. However, as government contracts with defense industries dried up, some relatively high-paying factory and assembly work was completely lost.

B-373 Stratocruiser

For example, Douglas had such a big glut of military transport aircraft while switching over to production of the DC-6 commercial knockoff of the Army Air Corps' C-54 that it laid off 99,000 persons in six months. Boeing, too, found that building and selling *Stratocruisers* instead of *C-97*s for national cross-country flights was not so easy because rail- roads, trucks, and even cars had replaced domestic air transport during hostilities. Regional airlines such as Alaska Air were content for the moment to use surplus military transports rather than invest in new airliners. Even after Douglas came out with the DC-7, the fact that propeller planes still took many hours to carry passengers between cities restrained the industry.

Adding to the burden of business executives trying to gear up domestic production, labor unions moved in the winter of 1945-46 to push for greater wage and benefit conces- sions. Because of severe labor shortages during the war, big companies had been forced to offer health care insurance for employees. Now the AFL proposed not only to entrench that concession but add pension benefits, job security, and cost of living wage increases that would kick in every year to match inflation. Believing that demand for automobiles would rapidly increase as factories were converted from tank to car production and petroleum formerly reserved for the military was released for domestic gas, motor, and lubricating oil refining, its affiliate the UAW led 320,000 workers in a strike for a 30% or 33 cents an hour increase from GM to maintain the overall pay level, including overtime pay, received during the war.

Harry S. Truman

The Truman administration was not unsympa- thetic to the aspirations of organized labor. The last day of 1945, a Wage Stabilization Board replaced the NLRB. On February 20, 1946, Con- gress even passed and the President signed an Employment Act declaring US policy to be maximum employment, production, and pur- chasing power and setting up a three person Council of Economic Advisors to help the Pres- ident oversee the effort. Not set down in ink but understood by all concerned was the fact that Democrats would continue to use deficit spending and unbalanced budgets to support the economy and the American people.

With shortages and labor disturbances proliferating, including against farm equipment makers like Deere, prices on the basket of food and other basic commodities and services making up the general inflation rate surged to a 11% annual rate. To prevent worse inflation, an Office of Economic Stabilization was established on February 21 to phase out maximums except on rents, sugar, and rice. Hoping strikes would end as did the UAW's in March with a compromise 18.5 cents an hour increase not only from GM but Ford and Chrysler, bringing auto worker basic annual pay to $2,600, worth $25,240 in 2004 money, Truman only intervened in labor's tussle with business after Lewis of the UMW marched 400,000 bituminous coal workers onto the picket lines on April 1 and 1.1 million railroad workers threatened to shut down the nation's still vital rail system. On May 25, he placed the nation's railroads under government control.

John L. Lewis

Recession took hold. Truman sent federal mediators to negotiate a compromise and get the coal miners back into the mines. However, a hard line by mine owners in refusing to sign the contract paid off later in the year when a frustrated Lewis ignored a federal injunction to end a second walkout on November 21 and was jailed and fined $10,000 while the union was forced to ante up $3.5 million (later reduced to $70,000). Unable to stand up to extreme financial pressure, Lewis capitulated on December 7, the anniversary of Pearl Harbor.

Now at last, Truman's recovery program had a chance to work. A cut in federal taxes of $6 billion was intended to stimulate consumer spending and replace government spending as the main stimulus for the economy, but income tax rates, 35% on personal incomes over $5,000 for single filers and $10,000 for joint, and 38% on corporate incomes over $50,000, were still extraordinarily high compared to rates before the Second World War. Riding that issue, Republicans won back control of Congress for the first time since 1930. They not only pushed for lower taxes and lower government spending but wanted to reverse the entire Democratic agenda for government intervention in business and the economy.

Most vital in this respect was the Taft-Hartley Act of June 23, 1947 passed over Truman's veto. Bolstered in part by international developments, a rise in anti-Communist feeling, and fear that Communist sympathizers were infiltrating the American labor movement, it made the closed shop in which only union workers could be hired illegal. The law also permitted states to pass "right to work" laws prohibiting union shops wherein employees had to join a union after being hired. Not letting business leaders have it all their own way, it established a Federal Mediation and Conciliation Service that required employers to give 60 day notices of termination of labor contracts and put injunction power into the hands of the President to impose an 80 day cooling off period in which strikes and factory closings were suspended if national security or public health issues would be affected. Unions got the sharp end of the stick, however, in provisions that compelled them to make public financial statements, prohibited their direct (so-called "hard money") contribution to political campaigns, and deprived them of the check-off system in which employers deducted union dues from worker paychecks. By making union leaders file affidavits disclaiming any connection to Communism, Taft-Hartley tainted them with a suspicion of disloyalty and anti-Americanism. Although an October 22, 1951 amendment permitted union shop contracts without first polling employees as to their opinions, one long-term effect of this legislation was to make it infinitely more difficult for unions to get started in industries not previously organized. In the South, traditionally conservative, rural, and agricultural, there was precious little union success.

U.S. Employment by Sector, 1950-1960
In Millions

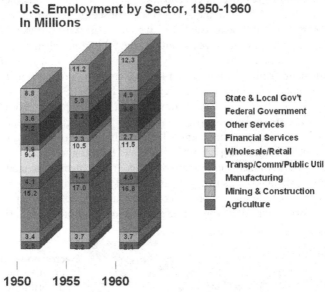

1950   1955   1960

Nevertheless, American wage-earners as a whole had never had it so good. Although union contracts such as forged with the steel industry in 1949 kept wage increases under control by refusing automatic cost of living increases, compensation came in the form of higher retiree benefits, including medical coverage and life insurance. Weyerhaeuser and other companies were earning enough to start employee pension plans. The generation of young white males that came home from Europe and Asia in 1945 and went to work in the factories of major corporations finally achieved the working man's version of the material American dream.

By 1950, in fact, out of 45 million gainfully employed Americans, a third worked for manufacturing companies while another 4 million held jobs in transportation and public utilities and 2.3 million were in construction. These were all industries that could afford to pay a living wage twice the minimum that year of 75 cents an hour, in other words a basic annual income equal in 2004 money to $24,440. Nearly 9.4 million people working in wholesale but especially retail were less well off while over 12 million civilian employees of government agencies generally had it better than 5.4 million still in the armed forces. In the relatively lucrative fields of finance, insurance, and real estate, only 1.9 million were employed. Then there were the 2.5 million still working in agriculture. The old rural way of life was about to come under pressure again from mechanization, consolidation, and the variability of weather and harvests.

As for women, many returned to the home, but 18.4 million or 28.8% of the total still took home a pay check. That included 33.9% of women of working age, only slightly less than in 1945 and debunking the notion that all Rosie the Riveters had babies soon after hostilities ceased. As late as 1955, 20.6 million women worked outside the home, composing 30.2% of the labor force and 35.7% of women of working age. Since men had returned to manufacturing, job opportunities for women were less attractive and their pay, no matter the industry, was generally half to two-thirds what men received.

The Communist takeover of Czechoslovakia in March 1947 and other hostile acts and pressures against nations rimming Soviet power caused the locus of government attention to swing increasingly overseas. The US answered in part with the Marshall Plan of June 5 in which the republic over four years doubled the $11 billion in loans, grants, shipments of food and other supplies already dispatched to Europe since VE day. Building on the effort that began at Bretton Woods in July 1944, a General Agreement on Tariffs and Trade (GATT) was completed in Geneva on October 30, 1947 by 28 nations to work toward free trade. On January 20, 1949, Truman announced a *Point IV* program of US technical and capital assistance to underdeveloped areas of world. Although the Congress on September 27 provided only $26.9 million in annual appropriation for that effort, the Marshall Plan proved as much a boon for export of US goods and farm commodities as for Europe. As the overall economy stabilized and started to expand, rising incomes generated taxes that not only produced small federal surpluses but justified a provision in the Anti-Inflation Act of August 16, 1948 to tax business profits considered excessive. Immediately, that legislation discouraged price hikes that would have resulted in excess profits. Inflation plummeted to 2.6%, then 1.3% in 1950.

Electric power plant, New York
In point of fact, the New Deal assumption by government and the public that Big Business was not to be trusted was very much alive. Reinvigorating anti-trust activity, the government immediately forced Alcoa to spin off significant aluminum production for the creation of competitors Reynolds Metals and Permanente Metals (later Kaiser Aluminum). Dissolution of public utility holding companies, per the 1935 act, was belatedly completed by 1949. GE's EBASCO was completely broken up. On the other hand, because electricity use would double with the coming housing and appliance boom to 900 billion kilowatt hours, regional electric utility companies that survived would become multimillion, then multi-billion dollar enterprises. Among utilities so blessed would be Detroit Edison (later DTE), Florida Power and Light, benefiting from a surge in state tourism and population that would quadruple demand for power in the 1950s, and Middle South Utilities (forerunner

of Entergy), which was a re-congregated collection of electric and natural gas companies in Louisiana, Arkansas, and Mississippi put together originally from 1913 onward by Harvey Couch of Arkansas until subsumed in 1925 into EBASCO.

Equally as lucrative for the energy industry, the government decided to sell the Big Inch and Little Inch pipelines. Construction firm Brown & Root bought and converted them in 1947 to transport natural gas for their Houston-based subsidiary Texas Eastern Corporation (later part of the El Paso Company) to New York City and other places in the Northeast. In fact, new commercial construction projects amounted to nearly $26 billion by 1948. After so much war-related activity in the first half of the decade, government investment in fixed assets plunged to only $7 billion.

First Postwar Economic Boom

Far less lucrative to the construction industry through 1947 was home-building. New residential construction was held back by labor shortages as well as high construction and material costs. Weyerhaeuser might have kept up with surging lumber demand but for shifting resources into mills that churned out grocery sacks, multi-wall bags used for pet foods as well as lawn and garden seed, bleached paperboard, plywood, ply-veneer plants, particleboard, containerboard, and hard board. The company also diversified into a bark-processing plant that provided products for asphalt roofing, flooring, fertilizer, chemicals, and landscape materials. Eventually, use of power chain saws and logging trucks began to make up the difference as did expansion outside the US to buy virgin forests in Canada and South America as well as International Paper emulating Weyerhaeuser with a super tree program to selectively breed superior pine trees to replenish domestic forests. Production of lumber rose to 33 billion board feet by 1960.

At last in 1948, the movement of middle class families out of city centers that had begun in the 1920s and stalled during the depression and war was revived. Annual investment in residential fixed assets jumped from $11.5 billion in 1947 to $15.9 billion the next year. Among the firms that prospered by raising up 13 million new homes over the next dozen years were start-up builders Centex out of Dallas, Pulte Homes from Detroit, and after 1957 KB Homes in the Los Angeles area. Other companies made their reputations by supplying fixtures that went inside.

One such was the Minneapolis-Honeywell Regulator Company, founded in the 1880s from companies that manufactured furnace regulators, alarms, and dampers to let in air to make fires burn hotter. In 1953, the firm offered the *T-86* round thermostat that not only went into new homes but gradually replaced rectangular thermostats in old ones. Already a leader in industrial controls and indicators such as pyrometers to measure extremely high temperatures in foundries and kilns, the firm grew with acquisitions such as a 1957 move into fire detection and alarms. "Protected by Honeywell" signs appeared in windows throughout the US and Canada.

Likewise, Masco Screw Products Company of Michigan, founded in 1929 to sell parts to the Hudson Motor Car Company, innovated with the single-handed *Delta* faucet that controlled both hot and cold water. That product alone produced $1 million in sales by 1958 and began Masco's transformation from an industrial products company into a producer of household fixtures and furniture.

Postwar Suburbia

Supplying materials for residential construction turned out to be a gold mine for Georgia Pacific. Buying up 1 million acres of timberland in Dixie and the Northwest to supply 54 saw mills acquired during the war years, the company began to manufacture plywood from southern pine instead of California Douglas fir. A rival innovation was Goodyear's introduction in 1948 of vinyl flooring for kitchens and other rooms where rugs and carpeting over hardwood floors would not do. A complement to wood construction technique was research and development by DuPont on its *Tyvek* non-woven building wrap.

While these and other companies grew over the next half century into multi-billion dollar enterprises, they carried along to prosperity thousands of local subcontractors in hundreds of communities providing electrical wiring, heating systems, and plumbing. By 1950, the annual value of new construction in the country, residential and otherwise, climbed to $33.6 billion, and then more than doubled to $69.5 billion a decade later. Of this total, residential at $29.3 billion surpassed nonresidential for the first time. The total value of US fixed assets stood at $1.7 trillion, of which two-thirds, even excluding consumer durables, was privately owned.

Genealogy of US Household Appliance Companies, 1848-1960

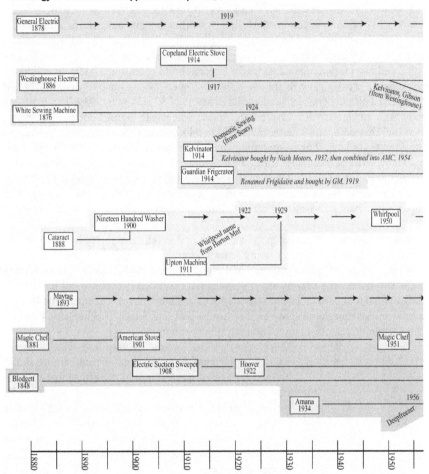

All those houses had to be filled up with couches, chairs, tables, beds, bureaus, cabinets, and other furniture and fixtures. Into kitchens and laundry rooms went ranges, refrigerators, automatic washers and dryers, and air conditioners. Full line producers of consumer durables GE and Westinghouse geared up production but so also did washer and dryer maker Maytag, which found an untapped market in coin-operated machines for commercial laundries. Amana distinguished itself first with upright freezers for homes, then side-by-side refrigerator-freezers, and finally after a 1956 acquisition of the Deepfreezer Company with central air conditioning units to compete with Carrier.

Altogether in 1948, households spent $21.5 billion on consumer durables. That was the reason that even as US share of world GNP descended, the republic's two-third domination of world manufacturing remained. In fact, over a three year period to mid-1950, domestic production met demand for 5 million cars, 6 million refrigerators, 7 million TV sets, over 14 million radios, and even more telephones (by Western Electric). Annual investment in consumer durables doubled by 1960 to $42 billion while the value of same held by households reached $176 billion.

It was both the surge in home and property-owning as well as increase in driving miles from 249 billion per year to 370 billion, resulting in many more traffic accidents, that focused minds on the need for insurance. Blue Cross and Blue Shield organizations, including the Indiana companies that merged into Anthem, evolved into non-profit, multi-hospital and association organizations for larger spheres of coverage. MetLife, billing itself as the world's wealthiest private company, followed its customers into suburbia with decentralized offices. Travelers accumulated assets of $2 billion by 1949. The 1950 slogan "You're in Good Hands with Allstate" and special interest in high school drivers education helped fuel that company's meteoric rise from $45.3 million of premium in 1949 to $439 million ten years later. The burgeoning American market persuaded American International Underwriters, originally started by C.V. Starr as a marine and fire insurance agency in Shanghai in 1919, to follow the troops home. In 1952, the firm bought the Globe & Rutgers Fire Insurance Company, including its subsidiary American Home Assurance Company. Its financial advantage was retaining and expanding operations in Europe and Asia.

Other insurance companies got bigger with new products. Liberty Mutual and Aetna innovated with corporate benefits in the form of major medical plans. St. Paul's growth depended upon insuring hospitals and real estate and packaging various types of policies. INA did the same with a homeowner's policy that bundled fire, theft, and liability. Still leading in reinsurance west of the Mississippi, Lincoln bought the Reliance Life Insurance Company of Pittsburgh in 1951 to break into the East and South. It penetrated Canada by buying Dominion Life Assurance Company of Ontario in 1957.

Much more so than manufacturing and retail companies with the problems of bulk transport and foreign tariffs, financial concerns were able to go international to achieve size and strength. Likewise, pharmaceutical makers realized early on that their industry was suited to overseas ventures. Already in 1943, AHP got a jump on the competition by acquiring Canada's Ayerst, McKenna and Harrison, a maker of *Premarin* conjugated estrogens product, and thus a leader in the field of hormones. In 1946, it bought Gilliland Laboratories and Reichel Laboratories to branch into vaccines. On the other hand, Squibb marketed its products in South American, then Europe. Merck in 1952 merged with Sharp & Dohme to create a fully integrated, international producer and distributor of pharmaceutical products.

Tupperware

As for other non-durable goods, a great sensation was made by Earl Tupper's plastic food containers. Although retail sales lagged, he hit on the innovation of sending sales reps door-to-door to stage *Tupperware Home Parties*. That tactic was so successful that after 1950, all the company's sales came through home visitation. *Tupperware* led the surge of the plastics industry through the ensuing decade. Too, Avon Products, begun in 1886 as a New York City perfume company and maker of talcum powder, make-up, and hundreds of other products, mostly for women, found that face-to-face selling was the right formula for success. Over 3,000 representatives ringing doorbells increased sales from $16 million in 1946 to $55 million eight years later.

The postwar recession behind them, American consumers had so much ready cash to spend that even after splurging on homes and cars, home appliances, utility costs, and other necessities, enough was left over for toys and games. Because the profession of the majority of American women was once again home-making and child-rearing, demand exploded. *Candy Land*, a board game by Milton Bradley, *Tonka* trucks from the Mount Metal Company, wax crayons and paint sets from Hassenfeld Brothers (later Hasbro), and *Playskool* kits were all big sellers. The first baker's dozen Baby Boom years saw the nation's population climb from 146 million at the start of 1948 to 181 million at the close of 1960.

Fortunately, farmers were well prepared to feed more mouths. Wider use of machines, fertilizers, better seed, and irrigation and drainage continued to shrink the number of farms to 6 million by 1950 but increase their size, efficiency, and crop yield. In 1945, aspirin maker Monsanto signaled its interest in capitalizing on the growing market for defeating infestations, disease, and weeds by building a plant to make insecticides and herbicides at Nitro, West Virginia. Despite a disaster at Texas City, Texas in 1947 when a ship loaded with ammonium nitrate fertilizer caught fire and exploded, leveling much of the town and killing 500, the company's move into agriculture-related and other chemicals was irreversible.

Meanwhile, improved feed and breeding stock combined with escalating demand at home and abroad for meat products brought head of cattle in 1950 to a pre-Korean War peak of 76.7 million worth

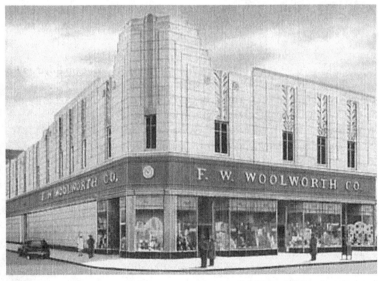

$119 each and hogs to 58.9 million priced on average at $27. Although the nation's sheep herd had been slashed over 40% since 1935 to 26.1 million, the price per head of $17.80 made it more valuable. During the Korean War, 88.6 million cattle sold on average for a whopping $179 a head while 62.1 million hogs went for $29.90 each and nearly 28 million sheep were each worth $28.80. Adding a couple hundred million chickens, the value of the nation's edible livestock hit $11.5 billion in 1950, then $19 billion in 1952, which in 2004 money was worth $136 billion.

In the immediate postwar years, the primary place most Americans went to buy food was still small groceries. However, pressure to compete with big chains forced the amalgamation of more local stores. Winn & Lovett of Florida bought out 31 Steiden Stores in Kentucky, and then 46 Margaret Ann Stores to force Publix in the central part of the state to shift from a strategy of buying up small groceries to constructing big supermarkets. Meijer in Michigan, H.E. Butt in San Antonio, and Albertson's in the Northwest all did the same. That meant just enough business to keep local middlemen, including C&S Wholesale Grocers of Worcester, Massachusetts, in business. The Consolidated Grocers Corporation of Chicago, put together from 1939 onward by Nathan Cummings, did better by moving from food processing, packaging, and distribution into retail food with the purchase of the Kitchens of Sara Lee.

In addition to brand name foods including Mars Company's *Uncle Ben's* long rice, supermarkets were now selling more brand name household and personal items. In 1946, Procter & Gamble brought out *Tide* detergent and *Prell* shampoo. That compelled Colgate-Palmolive to counter with *Fab* detergent as well as its *Ajax* cleaner. *Tide* nevertheless swamped all other laundry detergents by 1950. Big chains were big winners as well. Kroger's sales surged toward $1 billion in 1952, putting it in the same big league park as A&P.

William Boyd as Hopalong Cassidy

Likewise, revival of consumer purchases, composing by 1950 nearly two-thirds of GDP, pumped up the volume at major retail chains but not all. While Sears moved at once into newly constructed suburban malls, Montgomery Ward's held back for fear of cheapening its image. Thus, J.C. Penney became Sears' major competition with $1 billion of sales in 1951. Kresge's went into malls too and got an early cost edge by converting stores to checkout operations requiring fewer sales people. But now the availability of higher tag consumer durables and upscale clothing and other products at what previously had been regarded as discount chains put pressure on department stores to find greater efficiencies. May Company used a strategy of acquisitions, beginning with Kaufmann's of Pittsburgh and moving on to Hecht's in the Washington D.C. and Baltimore area, to gain the size to cut costs while still keeping prices and margins high.

An image of quality was critical to department stores when competing with discounters and discount chains. The advantage of brand names in general was reinforced in the public's collective consciousness by advertisements on TV shows, usually sponsored by big companies. Although only 8,000 families had sets in 1946, four years later when the

Colgate Variety Hour starring the comedy team of Dean Martin and Jerry Lewis debuted 3.9 million owned at least one. In 1952, the number of households with what critics called "the boob tube" was 22 million. In point of fact, Americans tuned in to watch many types of shows but especially children's' entertainment, including *Howdy-Doody* and Disney's the *Mickey Mouse Club*. *Hopalong Cassidy*, played in the movies since 1935 by actor William Boyd, was not only the smash TV hit of 1950 but generated $100 million in merchandising sales, everything from lunch pails to tricycles.

The first impact of the TV craze was to undercut the profitability of movies. Particularly after Aetna's *Playhouse 90* and other such dramas and features appeared, the comfort of living rooms began to outweigh the excitement of movie theaters. From a peak of 90 million tickets a week in 1948 at 25 cents a ticket, box office plunged to only 40 million by 1960, though higher ticket prices produced more revenue. The industry was further disrupted by a 1948 Supreme Court order forcing studios to divest themselves of theater chains. To survive a few more years, RKO was forced to sell its pre-1948 movies to TV stations as well as MGM. Even innovations such as panoramic screens, vivid *Technicolor*, and better sound systems could not reverse the trend.

1951 Zenith TV

TV also savaged radio stations and radio maker Philco, crippled until its acquisition by Ford in 1961. Galvin, on the other hand, got on the bandwagon early in 1947 and sold over 100,000 *Golden View* TVs for under $200. Changing its name to Motorola, it rang up $177 million of sales by 1950 while employing 9,325 people. The company remained a major player in car radios with contracts for factory installation from Ford and Chrysler. Programming with color broadcasts and sets by RCA would have generated even more ad revenue and sales of TV sets had not the FCC frozen licenses for TV stations at 108. The Korean War caused the commission to suspend plans for general transmission of color signals.

IMPACT OF THE KOREAN WAR

In late June 1950, President Truman's judgment that the US would not stand idly by while Communism overran South Korea mandated a new military buildup. Because federal revenues at $39.4 billion in 1950 were already $3.12 billion short of expenditures, it was necessary either to raise taxes, borrow money, or do a combination of both. Since progress had already been made cutting the federal debt as a percentage of GDP from 120% in 1945 to 80% five years later, the President and his advisors felt confident that even larger deficit spending would not impair prosperity, signified by *per capita* GDP for 150.7 million Americans of $1,953, 40% higher than a decade earlier. In addition to boosting the top marginal rate on individuals and corporations to 91% and 57% respectively, and tacking on new excise taxes on alcohol, tobacco, gasoline, and cars, they persuaded Congress to finance the war with more borrowing. Thus, the annual deficit jumped to $9.4 billion by the last year of the conflict in 1953. It turned out that as during the Second World War, military-related pump-priming gave a new jolt to the economy, increased capital spending, and cut unemployment but with the added benefit of actually reducing the federal debt as a percentage of GDP to two-thirds.

The government raised taxes of another kind. On August 28, 1950, Congress passed amendments to the Social Security law that fattened the wage base on which Social Security taxes were levied to $3,600 and raised the rate to 3%. The additional revenue helped pay for a 70% increase in benefits to recipients to boost the income of those without any other subsistence above the poverty line of about $2,000 annual family income, or about $15,625 in 2004 money, eased eligibility for the aged, and extended the system to 9.2 million self-employed, domestic, agricultural, and state and local workers, who were all required to contribute to the fund. In 1952, benefits were increased again but only slightly.

Although it seemed for a brief time that MacArthur's Inchon landing behind enemy lines in September 1950 and drive toward the Yalu River border with China would swiftly end the war, the administration moved through the Defense Production Act of September 8 to obtain broader powers for the President to stabilize prices and wages. After the Chinese army counterattacked and drove MacArthur back down the peninsula to a tenuous defensive position ultimately straddling the 38th Parallel, Congress on January 26, 1951 created a new Office of Economic Stabilization. As the war became a stalemate but defense spending escalated, the Federal Reserve facilitated Washington's borrowing by letting US government bonds sell below par for the first time in a decade, pushing up interest rates earned by creditors. Required by the Fed to have larger reserves, banks gradually raised rates on business loans, causing short-term rates to rise from 2.7% in 1950 toward a peak of 5% in 1959, the highest level since 1931.

That was all right with depositors. Already possessed of $164 billion in accounts, they poured in more at an average annual rate fluctuating between 7-11% of disposable personal income for the next 44 years. All that capital accumulation provided more funds for loans to individuals to buy homes and to businesses for expansion. To insure that corporate executives did not misuse borrowed money as well as large profits reaped from the booming economy, Congress in the Celler-Kefauver Act of December 29, 1950 amended Section 7 of the old Clayton Anti-Trust law to prohibit acquisitions where the effect might be substantially to lessen competition. The intent of course was to head off monopolies before they could be formed. So long as American companies were competing in a fairly closed national marketplace without a potent challenge from foreign cartels, now reforming within national boundaries in Europe, the change would not redound to the disfavor of domestic industry.

C-130 Hercules

No sector of the economy was more vibrant and exciting to businessmen than aerospace and defense. At the expense of domestic industries — for example, annual automobile

production was cut two-thirds by 1952 while 40% fewer radios and TVs were marketed — military equipment and gear of all kind enjoyed a feast of government orders. The most lucrative contracts were for better warplanes ranging from Boeing's *B-52* long-range bomber to Lockheed's *C-130 Hercules* transport to NAA's *F-86 Sabre* and *F-100 Supersabre*, Northop's *F-89 Scorpion*, McDonnell's *F-1 Phantom*, and Douglas's *F3D Skynight* and *F4D Skyray* fighters. NAA also got the nod to develop the *Redstone* rocket while Northrop did the first R&D on the *N-69 Snark* guided missile.

With a lower public profile but increasingly vital role to play in high-tech weaponry, Raytheon became expert at missile guidance systems. That led to contracts for the *Sparrow* air-to-air and *Hawk* ground-to-air missiles. Weapons systems specialists Simon Ramo and Deal Woolridge, working for Hughes, developed a combined radar and computer package that made their reputations as cutting edge innovators. They then started their own company, Ramo-Wooldrige (later TRW), and secured a contract to oversee the coming US ICBM program.

US Steel plant, Duluth, Minnesota

Electric Boat also looked across the horizon of the future with government money to build the *USS Nautilus*, the first nuclear powered submarine. To signify a corporate decision to diversify beyond naval products, the company in 1952 changed its name to General Dynamics (GD), and then acquired Convair. That company had in 1948 produced the first US jet-propelled commercial plane, the *Consolidated Vultee Convair*. GD now had a foothold in industries — airlines and making planes for airlines — destined to record growth later in the decade. By contrast, venerable Curtiss-Wright no longer made whole planes. It supplied reciprocating engines, propellers, and flight simulators to other companies with a foreboding that the jet age would collapse a great part of its business.

As might be expected, the steel industry was not pleased to see automobile and big ticket consumer durable production decline. Oil pipeline and military equipment requirements kept annual steel production around the 100 million ton level so that larger more cost effective blast furnaces using "turbo-hearth" techniques could be built. Reasoning that profits had suffered very little, the USW demanded again in 1952 despite the war and government restrictions on raising the price of steel that wages go up. Although a federal Wage Mediation Board agreed on March 20, the steel companies balked. That provoked a strike followed by Truman's decision to seize the nation's steel plants on April 8 under emergency wartime powers he believed he still possessed to prevent injury to national security. In that contentious election year, with public sentiment turning against the administration for mounting casualties in Korea, the Supreme Court on April 29 issued a preliminary injunction ordering him to release the factories to employer control. A final ruling on June 2 in *Youngstown Sheet and Tube v. Sawyer* declared that the President's action had been unconstitutional. Swiftly, the USW called another strike.

But the President, though weakened politically by not running for reelection, still occupied what Teddy Roosevelt had called the "bully pulpit." On July 24, he brokered an agreement between steel companies and the union increasing wages by 16 cents an hour to a $2.00 per hour level and promising more retiree benefits. The *quid pro quo* was the government permitting an increase in the price of steel by $5.20 per ton to pay for those increases as well as the USW agreeing to modify union shop agreements to give employers more flexibility in hiring non-union workers. The precedent set in 1949 to deflect part of labor demands for present wage improvement into future benefits was reinforced.

Interior of Hydro-electric plant on the Mississippi River

Consequently, the distribution of national income that had been adjusted in favor of the least affluent members of society during the Great Depression and Second World War began to turn back toward increasing inequality. In 1950, the share claimed by the top fifth climbed above 46% while the bottom three-fifths fell to below 32%. Determined to prevent retrogression, Congress on July 16, 1952 passed a Korean G.I. Bill of Rights, emulating the favorable treatment given to Second World War veterans with mustering-out pay, educational benefits, and housing, business, and home-loan guarantees. The latter were in particular an important stimulus to keep the economy humming once Eisenhower came into office to end the Korean conflict with a threat to use atomic weapons but an intention to force a truce agreement, which occurred in July 1953.

EISENHOWER ECONOMICS AND BIG BUSINESS

An important part of the new President's strategy for winning the Cold War was renewed concern for advancing the economy. Eisenhower wanted private industry, rather than government direction, to lead the charge and in the process provide Washington with the wherewithal to contain Communism around the world. Central to his philosophy was limitation of federal debt. He was willing to keep taxes where they were to pay for what in a traditional Republican view was considered the legitimate province of government — national defense, administration, and foreign affairs — and even leave untouched Social Security and other popular vestiges of the New Deal but refused to consider extension of Washington's interference and control unrelated to national security. Because his defense strategy required a) maintenance of a still potent conventional military establishment to buttress NATO and other regional alliances, b) buildup of a huge nuclear arsenal to threaten Massive Retaliation for any major Communist aggression, and c) Mutual Defense Assistance Agreements such as the pact with Spain on September 26, 1953 in which the US obtained naval and air bases in exchange for military and economic assistance amounting over the next 24 years to $1.6 billion, he was unable to balance the budget through two terms in office. He did reduce annual federal outlays to $64.5 billion in 1955 before permitting a steady rise to $80.6 billion in 1959 when the annual deficit was $12.4 billion and the statutory federal debt limit was pushed up to $286.2 billion. As a percentage of GDP, however, federal spending continued to fall. When Eisenhower left office in January 1961, federal debt was about 55% of GDP.

Shippenport Nuclear plant

Red ink precluded a major income tax cut. Congress provided on August 16, 1954 some stimulus through Internal Revenue Code changes that provided for accelerated depreciation for business capital expenditures as well as dividend credits and exclusions. Deductions for medical expenses, an increase in the maximum charitable deduction, as well as a retirement income credit helped families and individuals. However, the House and Senate gaveth with one hand and tooketh away with another by September 1, 1954 amendments to Social Security that added 7.5 million workers, mostly self-employed farmers, to the system while boosting the wage base on which Social Security taxes were levied to $4,500 (and to $4,800 in 1958) and raising the rate by 1960 to 6%. Two years later, the minimum age for Social Security benefits for women was lowered to 62 while disability insurance was provided for persons 50-64 years old if permanently disabled. In 1960, a minimum age for disability coverage was eliminated.

Relying on Big Business to lead the way in boosting GDP to $415.2 billion by mid-decade meant an end to most government regulation. Backed by the Republican-controlled House and Senate, the President ended all price controls on March 17, four months before the end of the Korean War. Much to New Dealers' displeasure, he championed provisions in the Atomic Energy Act of 1954 that permitted private power companies to own nuclear reactors for electric power production, nuclear materials feeding the reactors, and five year patents on nuclear plant design innovation. The first went to Enrico Fermi and Leo Szilard for reactor work accomplished for the Manhattan Project. However, Westing-house Corporation not only won the contract to build a nuclear reactor for the *Nautilus* but opened the first US commercial nuclear power plant at Shippingport, Pennsylvania in 1957. Confident that the new nuclear industry would come to dominate electric power production in decades to come, many utility companies made plans to build plants. For example, Duke Power put together and acquired a 34% interest in Carolinas-Virginia Nuclear Reactor Associates, which built the Parr, South Carolina nuclear station in 1960. Other companies moved with more deliberation to license, build, and operate the new technology.

In point of fact, the growing economy did require ever increasing voltages of electricity. Demand pushed local power companies, still watched by state regulatory agencies, to apply for licenses to build more non-nuclear plants. It was in these years that firms with greater regional and financial strength developed. The federal government and states sometimes cooperated to encourage that trend. The Niagara Power Act of August 21, 1957 authorized the New York State Power Authority to build a $532 million hydro-electric project at Niagara Falls. Completed in 1961, it was second only to the Grand Coulee Dam on the Columbia River in hydro-electric power production.

Eisenhower's drive for privatization ran into political trouble when a scandal erupted over the Dixon-Yates contract. That was an AEC plan to authorize private companies to build generating plants to feed power into the TVA system to supply Memphis as well as help Alcoa, Kaiser, and Reynolds boost aluminum production to alleviate shortages of that material in the aerospace and other industries. Democrats rallied public outrage and congressional votes to block the plan after it was discovered that a government consultant who drafted the plan would benefit financially. Nevertheless, the TVA system managed to quadruple capacity to 11.3 kilowatts by 1960, which was more than the electricity industry average of 250% growth.

Likewise, the Supreme Court checked a possible deregulation of the natural gas industry with a 1954 decision confirming Washington's power to use provisions of the Natural Gas Act of 1938 to control the price of natural gas at wellheads. Transmission and sale of natural gas, the justices ruled, was interstate commerce and thus within Congress' constitutional power to regulate. Companies such as Panhandle Eastern, which in 1950 had bought the Trunkline Gas Supply Company and its 740 mile pipeline from the Gulf of Mexico to Illinois, found themselves with assets less valuable than previously assumed. The long-term impact of the decision was to discourage investment in the search for new natural gas fields, restrain supplies, and limit profits. When in 1958, Texas Eastern attempted to get around federal regulation by leasing rather than buying Louisiana Gas Corporation oil and gas properties near Opelousas, Louisiana for $134.4 million, Eisenhower's Federal Power Commission looked the other way. However, in the 1960s under Democratic administration, the FPC reopened the case.

As previously stated, Eisenhower was not averse to using federal government power to advance the national security interest. The most important legislation affecting the economy in this respect was the Highway Act of June 29, 1956 that authorized $32 billion over 13 years for 90% of the cost of a 41,000 mile interstate system, the balance to be contributed by the states. The law also approved federal aid to highways on a one-to-one

Cement trucks

dollar basis with states. Revenue in a Highway Trust Fund would initially be provided from a 1 cent per gallon tax on gasoline and 3 cents per pound tax on tires. Ultimately by 1972, $76.3 billion was spent on a 42,500 mile Eisenhower Interstate Highway System, 80% complete. Its construction was a primary reason that the trucking industry, handling 285 billion ton-miles by 1960 equal to 21.5% of all domestic freight, boomed to even greater heights.

Consolidation among truck manufacturers, competing in a market that increased to 1.25 million trucks and buses sold in 1960, had already begun. Pacific Car & Foundry (later Paccar), founded in 1905 to produce railway and logging equipment and later in 1930s power winches, entered the heavy-duty truck market in 1945 by purchasing Kenworth Motor Truck Company of Seattle. Later in 1958, the company acquired Peterbilt Motors in the same niche. It also took over the Dart Truck Company, a producer of vehicles used in mining operations.

One of Pacific's most important suppliers was Cummins Engine of Columbus, Indiana. Founded in 1919, that company had struggled until a diesel engine it produced in 1929 for the Packard Motor's limousine proved a success. In 1954, it introduced a pressure-time fuel injection system that revolutionized the market for more powerful engines. By 1958, it took the lead in making diesel engines for heavy trucks with $100 million of sales.

Meanwhile Spicer, which was renamed Dana Corporation in 1946, bought Auburn Clutch of Indiana. Its sales marched upward from the $100 million level as well. Overall, however, the US share of the world truck manufacturing market declined from 80% in 1950 toward half that by the late 1960s due to recovery from the Second World War by foreign competitors. When the recession of 1957-58 cut US sales of vehicle parts by a fourth, Dana decided to expand overseas by taking a 30% stake in Albarus of Brazil. Too, the economic downturn persuaded Eaton, still the leading maker of truck axles, to absorb Fuller Manufacturing Company, known for its *Roadranger* truck transmissions. The transmission-axle combination completed the company's ascent into the top ranks of truck part makers.

Heretofore, the truck carrier industry had been fragmented among small and medium size companies. That began to change even before the interstate system was contemplated when in 1952 a small firm called Ryder took over Great Southern Trucking, became publicly traded three years later, and began a steady rise in the truck leasing and rental businesses while branching out into auto transport, insurance, school buses, and even public transportation. The decade also witnessed the rise of Portland-based Consolidated Freightways, specializing in shorter, lighter trucks with cab-over-engine and aluminum

alloy design, and Arkansas-Best Freight, formed by merger in 1957. A narrower niche was carved out by United Parcel System (UPS), founded 1907 in Seattle as a messenger company but evolving over decades into contract deliverer for retail stores. When wartime fuel and rubber shortages caused retail stores to convince customers to take packages home themselves, UPS decided to gamble everything on competing directly with the US Postal Service as a "common carrier" delivering packages between customers, private and commercial, in states where such competition was not forbidden by ICC and state commerce commission regulations. It fought a two decade court battle, ultimately successful, in key state California and elsewhere to obtain its common carrier certification.

Expansion in trucking and oil pipelines as well as autos and airplane transport, discussed below, pummeled the profitability of railroads. Despite a switch to more efficient diesel engines as well as other modernization projects including development of special cars, the Pennsylvania Railroad but especially the B&O suffered loss of business and revenue. The latter company began the decade of the 1950s with 2,050 locomotives, of which 150 were diesel and 9 were electric, but finished with only 1,129, all diesels. It was taken over in 1961 by the C&O, which dominated transport of coal, made its operations more efficient with a large computer system, and diversified by merging with the old Pere Marquette Railway of Michigan and Ontario to carry raw materials to the auto industry as well as transport finished autos around country. Likewise, 14 railroads operating along the Gulf coast merged into the Missouri Pacific in 1956, Norfolk and Western took over Virginia Railway three years later, the Union Pacific proposed a hostile take over of Chicago, Rock Island & Pacific, ultimately unsuccessful, and the Southern Pacific and Santa Fe besieged the Western Pacific. Consolidation could not prevent shrinkage of the nation's railroad network to 230,170 miles carrying 675 billion ton-miles of freight, about 45% of all freight but only about $400 million in passenger revenue, with employment a third less at 790,000. By contrast, trucks and other motor vehicles carried slightly more than one-fifth of all ton-miles of freight, oil pipelines slightly more than one-sixth, barges and other water vessels about one-sixth, and airplanes the last 0.6%. However, the $1.5 billion of annual passenger revenue for air carriers was already nearly four times as high as flowing to railroads.

Western Electric telephone

Other Eisenhower-era legislation intruding into economic matters were few and relatively minor. Ten days after the Highway Act, Congress passed an amendment to the Water Pollution Control Act of June 30, 1948 authorizing $500 million of federal grants over 10 years for sewage treatment works. Reaffirming AT&T's old corporate strategy of spinning off non-telephone equipment production, the Justice Department obtained Ma Bell's consent to limit the great monopoly's Western Electric subsidiary to producing equipment for the Bell System and contract work for the government. That entity was forced to sell its own small non-telephone subsidiary Westrex to Litton Industries and the public. The communications giant still retained a 96% share of the US telephone system, generating by the mid-1950s $3.8 billion of local service annual operating revenue and another $3.2 billion of toll service. Each year the stream increased on average 4%.

Putting it to monopolies was popular because Americans, even during Eisenhower's pro-business administration, had not shaken their inherent distrust of big business. After so many years of New Deal paternalism, they still appreciated the benefit of government regulation. Too, they liked government spending programs if well focused and explained. The National Defense Education Act of September 2, 1958 fell into that category. On the eve of mid-term elections, Congress authorized $295 million for a fund that would make $1,000 loans to college students at 3% rate of interest with a 10 year repayment period, excepting that payments would be reduced 50% if the graduate later taught elementary or secondary school for five years. The people's representatives and senators further allocated $280 million in grants to state schools to construct facilities for the teaching of science or modern foreign language, matching grants by the states. Another $28 million was provided for language study in higher institutions with $18 million allocated for the educational use of TV, radio, motion pictures, and related media. The government paid for 5,500 fellowships for graduate students planning to teach in colleges or universities.

New Roosevelt High School Des Moines, Iowa

As state governments subsequently realized, any kind of aid to education was wildly popular with Baby Boom parents already worried about feeding and housing the 40 million children born in the 1950s. Also thought to be a good idea was the Housing Act of

August 2, 1954 that financed construction over one year of 35,000 houses for families dis-placed by urban redevelopment, slum clearance, and urban renewal programs. By reducing down payments for these units, lengthening payment periods, and increasing the maximum mortgage permitted, the law made home-ownership more affordable. Four sub-sequent acts through 1959 with Eisenhower's grudging approval added another 45,000 houses, raised mortgage amounts, cut down payments, lowered monthly payments, boosted funds available for home mortgages toward $1.5 billion, and provided $650 million for slum clearance and urban renewal. Overall by 1960, the construction industry was building 1.1 million new homes a year and 220,000 rental and other multifamily units. The contribution to GDP was nearly $57 billion, or about 10.8% of the total.

Most Americans interested in purchasing a new or existing home had no recourse to government assistance, of course. They had to go to savings and loans (S&Ls) as well as banks for financing. Fortunately, the number of institutions with the wherewithal to meet this demand was steadily growing. A government-ordered breakup of TransAmerica into several independent entities including Bank of America was the exception rather than the rule. Rather, the Supreme Court in 1954 approved the use of the word "savings" by Franklin National Bank of Inwood, New Jersey for interest-bearing accounts, thus opening the door for other banks to impinge on the marketing realm of S&Ls. Chase promptly the next year expanded its financial clout to take in deposits and make loans by buying Bank of The Manhattan Company and forming Chase Manhattan. However, on May 9, 1956, the Bank Holding Company Act made it illegal for such combinations to acquire bank stocks without prior sanction by the Federal Reserve System. In most cases, bank holding com-panies had to divest themselves of positions in non-banking organizations. On the other hand, regulators two years later permitted creation of First Union National of North Carolina from a number of entities. Authorities decided that creation of regional banking powers in various parts of the country would not be too great a threat to fair competition. That forbearance helped concentrate savings-bank deposits amounting to over $100 billion by end of the decade. The overall monetary base rose to $250 billion of deposits and $53 billion of currency.

INNOVATION IN FINANCIAL SERVICES, INSURANCE, AND PHARMACEUTICALS

Prior to 1946, the only major competitors for banks and S&Ls accepting cash deposits were brokerages that invested in stocks for long-term capital gain but did not provide interest. That began to change when Edward C. Johnson II founded Fidelity Investments in Boston and his Puritan Fund the next year to derive income from stocks. In the 1950s, he offered an array of funds to suit the financial needs of clients. His success convinced Dean Witter to buy up other brokerages and compete in the same market.

By 1960, there were 2.5 million shareholders with stakes in mutual funds. The share of financial assets held by non-bank intermediaries increased from 30% when Fidelity began to half. Meanwhile Morgan Stanley continued to succeed in the securities business by placing a large World Bank bond offering of $14 billion in 1952. Merrill Lynch and six other firms pooled resources in 1956 to handle a huge $600 million Ford Motor Company public stock offering and put the company over $1 billion of underwriting business for the year.

Size and financial strength were also key to the insurance industry. Although life insurance in force in 1953 amounted to about $270 billion, other products lagged. That began to change in 1954 when state law changes permitted companies to offer multiple line insurance products. Packaging two or more together helped cut premiums, make insurance more affordable for new home and car owners, and increase the pool of insured, which again made possible more affordable rates. Continental was most aggressive with this strategy, offering fire and casualty in combination and selling $225 million worth of the product in 1956. After it bought two-thirds of National Fire Insurance that same year, combined revenue of $415 million made it the third largest multiple line insurer in the country.

MetLife headquarters
New York City

Twice as large with $1 billion of new premium in 1960 was Travelers. It seized on the fact that life expectancy for women now topped 70 while men lived on average five years less to offer lower rates for the former. Hartford bought Columbia National Life of Boston in 1959 to complement its fire as well as property and casualty lines with a life insurance component, now in the country exceeding $500 billion in force and $12 billion of annual premium. The company's diversification guarded against cyclical downturns in revenue and pushed its rank to third overall behind MetLife and Travelers.

To survive in such a competitive environment, innovation in methodology and product was key. In 1953, the General Insurance Company of America, founded thirty years earlier in Seattle, used computer-based automation to establish a Selective Auto and Fire Insurance Company of America (later in 1968 SAFECO). In short order, Aetna, CGA, INA, and others bought computers to refine the risk of offering coverage. For auto insurance, they examined type of car, repair cost, and likelihood of accidents in various locales, for fire whether businesses and homeowners installed the latest sprinkling and other safety systems, and for life age and health problems.

In 1957, Continental became the first insurance company to offer professional liability for architects and engineers as well as comprehensive group dental insurance, generating an extra $28.6 million premium. Marsh & McLennan continued to excel with a strategy of combining insurance with other activities by buying Cosgrove & Company brokerage, largest such firm on the west coast, then two years later acquiring the employee benefit consultant William M. Mercer of Canada (now as Mercer Human Resources Consulting the largest human resources consulting entity in the world). That same year, INA agreed to insure the Shippenport nuclear plant. Smaller companies too distinguished themselves by assuming risk, including Progressive Insurance of Cleveland which made its fortune by writing insurance for high risk drivers. Meanwhile, American Family Life Insurance Company of Columbus, Georgia offered a cancer care policy in 1958, three years after its founding. The fact that non-life insurance products proved substantially more profitable brought the share of $142.2 billion in industry assets held by companies offering such products in 1960 to 18.6% from only 12.5% in 1945.

In health insurance, multi-state operations permitted Aetna and other insurers to undercut prices the Blues, restricted to intrastate business by their non-profit status, could offer on comprehensive medical expense plans. Annual premium rose by 1960 to $7.5 billion worth of annual premium, including $2.8 billion through Blue Cross, Blue Shield, and other such non-profit organizations. Potentially more lucrative, the federal government instituted the Federal Employees Health Benefits Program. Government workers would now have a broad choice of health insurance plans with varying premiums, deductibles, co-payments negotiated by Washington with individual companies. That handed the health insurance industry a new pool of 8.4 million people (as well as 7.4 million in the military) who would build up annual premiums to $12.1 billion by 1965 and overall spending by consumers on health care to nearly $25 billion, up from $19.5 billion or about 3.7% of GDP in 1960. Health care spending of all kinds would become an increasing component of the economy.

Both life and medical insurance companies were vitally concerned with the health of individuals, of course. Profits depended upon longevity and absence of accidents and illness. Naturally, comprehensive medical insurance plans covered hospitalization, drugs, and treatment, including cutting edge techniques in kidney dialysis pioneered by Dutchman Dr. Willem Kolff. His 1956 breakthrough helped Baxter International, a small Chicago area firm emerging from the war with $1.5 million of sales, achieve and maintain a 20% compound annual growth rate for the next quarter century.

Because prescription drugs purchased at drug stores, regulated and approved by the FDA after passage on June 25, 1938 of the Food, Drug, and Cosmetic Act, were increasingly covered, it was in the interest of pharmaceutical makers to persuade doctors to prescribe their products. Additionally, they increased research and development of new drugs that might combat known scourges. Along these lines, Abbott in 1952 concocted the *erythrocin* antibiotic to attack gram-positive bacteria, while two years later, Pfizer discovered the broad spectrum antibiotic *terramycin*. Eli Lilly's entry into the field was *erythromicin* for those persons allergic to penicillin as well as the powerful antibiotic *vancomycin* to fight hospital infections associated with resistant bacteria. Meanwhile, Merck initiated a strategy of cooperating with foreign firms that might benefit from Merck's drugs and substances and vice-versa by entering into a joint venture with Banyu of Japan. Five years later, Johnson & Johnson got into the industry of prescription pharmaceuticals by buying McNeil Laboratories. As a wholesaler, McKesson benefited from the successes of 100 drug companies nationwide. Even a single successful prescription drug could rake in tens of millions of dollars.

Recognizing that fact, American Home Products (AHP) developed drugs to combat alcoholism, high blood pressure, convulsions, angina, and sleeplessness. Accounting eventually for 50% of sales and 67% of profits, these and other pharmaceutical lines were so lucrative that AHP like other pharmaceutical companies was able to fulfill the aspiration of Dr. Jonas Salk, inventor of the polio vaccine, to distribute the product at very low cost.

But AHP did not abandon the non-prescription, over-the-counter pharmaceutical business. Its *Dristan* tablets to combat nasal drip brought relief to millions as well as black ink to the bottom line. Also interested in commercial success with non-prescription products, Pfizer in 1953 bought J.B. Roerig and Company, a nutritional supplement maker. Four years later, Bristol-Myers acquired the highly popular *Clairol* hair coloring business.

THE CONGLOMERATE CONCEPT

In 1955, Monsanto continued its diversification out of pharmaceuticals by buying Lion Oil. In addition to securing petrochemical materials for its fertilizer business, it moved into plastics, synthetic resins, and surface coatings, which within two years provided 30% of sales and justified acquisition of the Plax Corporation and its plastic bottling operation. The company's strategic shift into fertilizers and chemicals pointed out the fact that although farming in the strict sense of the word was a declining component of US GDP, food processing, packaging, transportation, and other related, value-added operations were still of major importance.

Wheat storage elevators in Kansas

Cargill Company, for example, began its march toward becoming the largest privately held company in the US by diversifying into soybean processing, developing feeds for livestock and poultry, operating barges on the Great Lakes and Mississippi River, bringing rock salt up from Louisiana, and sending bulk corn down to Brazil. Additionally, as the number of farms declined to 5.1 million on 1.16 billion acres in 1955, then only 4 million on 2 billion acres in 1960, the market for new farm equipment expanded. Deere took the lead in 1953 with its first-of-a-kind *Model 70* diesel row-crop tractor followed by six-row planters and cultivators four years later. Capacity in corn and cotton areas was thereby boosted 50%.

A major cause for agricultural sector prosperity was changes in farm and commodity export law. The Farm Bill of August 28, 1954 replaced the old parity system with a new one. Instead of a rigid 90% of parity for wheat, cotton, rice, and peanuts and 75% for dairy, farmers would receive 82.5-90% for the former and 75-90% for the latter. The Department of Agriculture had authority to barter surplus crops to foreign nations for strategic goods.

Genealogy of US Farm Equipment Industry, 1837-1960

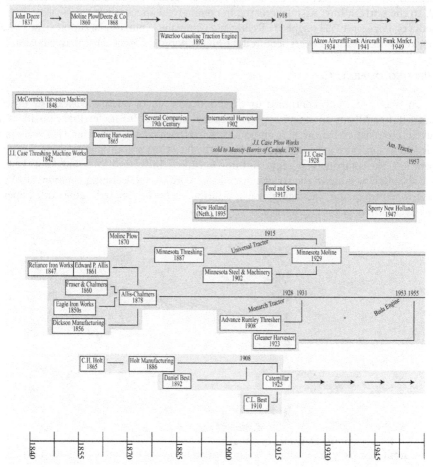

Moreover, governments buying US crops received easier credit terms. Food aid to poor nations quickly escalated to account for half of US wheat exports.

Four years later, the 1958 Agriculture Act gave farmers a choice between modified price supports and increase of crop allotments. Dairy farms, contracting from 3.65 million with nearly 22 million cows to 2 million with only 17 million cows, albeit producing at 8,500 pounds of milk per cow over twice as much as in 1940, received another increase in price support on August 31, 1960. Thus, at the end of the Eisenhower era, gross farm income on 4 million farms averaging just less than 300 acres per farm was up to $38.1 billion, including $702 million of federal subsidies. The nation boasted 4.7 million tractors, 2.8 million farm-used trucks, 1 million combines, 792,000 corn pickers, and 660,000 farms with milking machines.

That was small potatoes in comparison to what was happening in other sectors of the economy. In 1952, 59 US companies possessed over $1 billion in assets. Although most were confined to banking, finance, manufacturing, and utilities, a significant number were gravitating toward the new model already achieved in a *de facto* sense by GE, Monsanto, and others. Because the old ideas of vertical integration pioneered by Rockefeller in Oil and horizontal integration demonstrated by Carnegie in steel were outlawed, the only possibility for achieving unusual growth appeared to be through conglomerations that gathered unrelated or thinly related lines of business under a single corporate roof. Added benefits would include removing cyclical fluctuations in revenues and profits, cutting headquarters costs, creating operating synergies, and achieving greater overall size and financial strength not possible in a single industry. Even small companies could follow this path to business glory. For example, textile manufacturer Textron generated only $67.8 million of sales in 1949. After a series of small acquisitions culminating in 1960 in the purchase of Bell Aerospace, revenues rose to $383 million, predominately from non-textile operations.

1958 Ford Thunderbird

GM headquarters, Detroit, Michigan

Conglomeration was still rare in the Eisenhower era, however. Many of the most successful companies remained single industry entities, increasingly going public to acquire more capital for expansion. With much fanfare, Ford took that path in 1956. As well as acquiring 300,000 shareholders, it obtained financing to pump up its Thunderbird model for the automobile mid-market as well as battle in the low end. Both markets were surging as over 35 million American households, 73.5% of the total, owned a car by mid-decade. The old bromide of a chicken in every pot became not one but two cars in every garage. As for the high end, GM's Cadillac models claimed four-fifths of the market, with Ford's Lincoln and Chrysler's Imperial taking the rest. Number of premium cars sold was in the quarter million range.

Although Chrysler jacked up annual production to over 500,000 Plymouths, in 1955, that was only 6.3% of the nation's production of passenger cars. GM's Chevrolet division still dominated, reaching an amazing 50 million of that model produced in aggregate, and helping the nation's car industry leader reach annual production of 3 million, or roughly half what was sold by end of the decade. Desperate to hang on against the Big Three, Nash-Kelvinator and Hudson merged in 1954 under the name American Motors Corporation (AMC). Because a planned merger of Studebaker and Packard as a precursor to joining AMC never took place, those companies eventually went out of business.

An old market for auto makers that was growing was rental companies. The first was founded by Walter L. Jacobs in 1918 in Chicago to rent Ford *Model T*s but was purchased five years later by John Hertz, head of Yellow Truck, then by GM when the auto maker bought Yellow Truck. Still run by Jacobs though called Hertz Rental Car, the company was bought from GM in 1953 by Omnibus Corporation. Divested of all bus operations the next year, Omnibus renamed itself Hertz. That same year, Boston financier Richard S. Robie purchased a rental operation begun in 1946 at Detroit's Willow Run Airport by Warren Avis with $85,000. As the rental car industry steadily expanded, the purchase price of $8 million for what would become the second largest rental car company turned out in retrospect to be a bargain.

One advantage auto rental companies had was that their service, spreading across the country mainly at large airports, did not have to worry about foreign competition. In an ominous development for Detroit car executives, international imports sold 614,000 cars in 1959. Although US companies still made nearly half the world's cars, rejuvenated overseas producers would cut that figure to one quarter in ten years. They would salivate over an $18.8 billion American market (including car parts) already possessed in 1960 of 61.7 million passenger cars and 12.2 million trucks and buses.

**Firestone factory
Akron, Ohio**
Concomitant with the rise in automobiles and trucks was tire production. Goodyear topped 500 million tires in aggregate in 1951 and $1 billion in annual sales. New technology for oil-extended, synthetic rubber expanded the company's capacity 25%. Cost savings and higher profits from the innovation put pressure on competitors to acquire greater size and operating efficiency. While Firestone bought Dayton Tire and Rubber in 1960 to achieve economies of scale, Goodrich began to realize that its long-term interest might not be served by standing permanently in Goodyear's shadow.

Innovation was key to survival in the steel industry as well. Although companies did not yet have to worry about foreign imports, it gave executives cause for concern that a ton of steel produced in the US in 1955 required $2.72 of labor while the same quantity in Japan required only 43 cents. That discrepancy would tend to grow as the USW pressed for more concessions. Fortunately, the new basic oxygen furnace (BOF) which used a technique of injecting oxygen from the top into a vessel filled with molten iron and scrap steel cut the Open Hearth standard of 9-10 hours down to 45 minutes. Additionally, a continuous casting process that produced billets, blooms, and slabs directly from molten steel rather than in a series of time-consuming steps was adopted by smaller, more aggressive companies. Having difficulty mastering the process, US Steel, Bethlehem, and the other majors improved quality with quenched and tempered steel, tin-free steel, and coated steel sheets, and quantity with bigger blast furnaces. Overall, because of the automobile industry expansion, home appliance boom, and resurgence in naval shipbuilding, production of steel surged in 1960 to 148.5 million tons. Although down from its 35 million ton production peak in 1953, US Steel had about a fifth of the market, Bethlehem 17%, and mini-mills less than 1%, while employment in the industry hovered around 575,000.

1953 Corvette

If serious foreign competition in steel was some years away, substitution of other materials for steel was an immediate, albeit still minor threat. For example, Rohm & Haas manufactured *Plexiglas* for auto tail-lights while Monsanto's maleic anhydride chemical enabled PPG to supply GM with a reinforced fiberglass to build its 1953 Corvette sports car. *Plexiglas* was also used in skylights, room dividers, and safety glazing. Rohm & Haas diversified into latex paints and waterborne acrylic polymers under the *Rhoplex* name, including inks, floor polishes, and roof adhesives.

B-707

General prosperity in the 1950s, the increasing size and market reach of more companies, and the need of business and account executives to travel finally created sufficient demand to fulfill the promise of air passenger service. On July 15, 1954, a *B-707* using a Pratt & Whitney jet engine flew out of Seattle. All the major airlines — United, American, TWA, and Eastern — committed to buy jet and phase out propeller planes. The most desirable routes were between New York and Los Angeles, New York and various southern cities including Miami, and overseas, particularly to Europe. On the other hand, Northwest prospered with flights from Chicago, the Twin Cities, and Milwaukee to Florida as well as to Alaska, Hong Kong, and Tokyo. Its long distance plane of choice was the Douglas *DC-8*.

In 1955, Delta combined with Chicago and Southern Airlines. Using a hub-and-spoke system out of Atlanta that proved more efficient and cost effective, it moved in on Eastern's business with a flight to New York. By end of the decade, its *Convair 880* jets with radar in the nose flew coast to coast in less than four hours. *Convair 880*s, as well as CAB approval for Boston and New York to Miami and Tampa routes, also revived Northeast Airlines, whose safety record never measured up to Eastern's and Delta's. Overall, the number of domestic paying passengers soared by 1960 to 38 million. Domestic ton-miles of mail flown amounted to 87 million and domestic ton-miles of non-mail reached 228 million.

After production of civilian airliners, the second major revenue stream for the aerospace and defense industry continued to be federal government spending, at mid-decade accounting for over 10.4% of GDP. While Boeing was turning out commercial and military jets, it also won contracts in 1957 for the *Bomarc* missile and afterward *Minuteman* ICBMs. Douglas also profited from missiles, including the *Nike* anti-missile missile, the *Honest John* theater missiles for the Army, and the *Thor* IRBM for deployment in Britain. It was Martin's *Vanguard* rocket that launched the *Explorer I* satellite in 1958 and its *Pershing* IRBM and *Titan* ICBM that first put an immediate fear of God into the Soviets. Until a solid fuel was perfected in the 1960s, all these missiles required tons of liquid oxygen and nitrogen. Air Products, founded in 1940 in Detroit, became a chief supplier, which also paved the way for leadership in commercial industrial gases in both the US and Europe.

More mundanely, Northrop made money with the reliable *T-38* trainer jet, Hughes Aircraft competed with Sikorsky in the market for light military helicopters while turning out a civilian model for TV crews, police, and other purposes, and Curtiss-Wright consolidated a niche in flight simulators. Behind the scenes, NAA's *Hound Dog* missile gave greater nuclear punch to *B-52s*, Ford Aerospace produced a missile guidance control system and GE Aerospace made radar to track Soviet missiles. Texas Instruments (TI), founded in 1930 as the Geophysical Service for seismographic exploration of oil fields, built on its airborne radar system work for the Air Force to research and develop terrain-following radar. Some of the 18,000 people working for AT&T's Western Electric subsidiary were allocated to perfect guided missiles and military communications, including the computer-assisted air defense system called the Distant Early Warning Line built from 1954 to 1961. However, the parent company was compelled by a consent decree signed with the government to divest itself in 1956 of Western Electric. That company was itself forced to spin off Northern Electric of Canada, which now as part of Nortel Networks is the third largest world producer of telecom equipment.

The "sexiest" government contracts were for satellites and space exploration. TI's lead in transistors, discussed below, won a contract to provide same for the Explorer. But McDonnell got the big plumb of constructing the *Mercury* spacecraft for the first US astronauts. IBM's computers guided those flights as well later as the *Gemini, Apollo, Skylab,* and *Space Shuttle* programs. Meanwhile on the high seas — rather beneath the waves — General Dynamics built the USS *George Washington*, the first *Polaris* submarine, then 41 others. Lockheed was equally favored by being chosen to put *Polaris* missiles on the subs, and then later *Poseidon* and *Trident* missiles on the next generation sub.

Polaris subs were nuclear-powered. The new generation of jet planes required *AVJET* fuels from the Texas Oil Company, after 1959 Texaco. However, gasolines with higher octane ratings as well as motor and lubricating oils for automobiles, trucks, other vehicles, lawn motors, snow blowers, and the like were the products that carried the oil industry to enormous financial return. In 1950, the 2.3 million barrels pumped at domestic well heads resold for many times the 6.2 cent price per gallon at gas stations. Much lower costs of less than $1.00 a barrel were possible in Saudi Arabia, where the Texas Oil Company made an agreement to transfer Persian Gulf oil from the kingdom of Saudi Arabia to Sidon in Lebanon over a 1,000 mile Trans-Arabian Pipeline constructed by Bechtel. In 1957, Sun Oil explored Venezuela's Lake Maracaibo area, and thus found cheaper oil fields producing much higher profits.

In 1953, because domestic production was flattening out at about 2.6 million barrels annually, the US needed to import oil for the first time. To protect domestic producers from petroleum and petroleum products shipped in by both US and foreign companies to the tune of $1.6 billion by end of the Eisenhower Era, the government in March 1959 slapped on quotas. US production of oil in 1960, including from Phillips off-shore rigs in the Gulf of Mexico, 40 miles out, was as a consequence only slightly lower than in 1955. Well head price was only slightly higher.

Price stability was good news for owners of regional gas station chains. Unocal's 76 logo now proliferated in California while Clark Refining Holdings establishments spread across the upper Midwest, supplied by their own refineries. Further, Unocal's *Triton* motor oil dominated in the West while in the East and South, Penn Oil Company's *Pennzoil* competed with Phillips' all season motor oil. Phillips also distinguished itself with a process for producing high-density polyethylene plastics (polypropylene) used in containers, electrical insulation, and packaging. Other oil companies exploring the plastics market were Jersey Standard and Socony-Vacuum. Texaco developed a new market by making high-purity hydrogen from synthetic gas, oil, coal, and other hydrocarbons to make fertilizers overseas for countries formerly dependent upon hydrogen imports.

In the early years of the Cold War, the Congress had so little fear that foreign competition would negatively impact the economy that the decline of the basic US tariff rate to only 15% from the 53% peak of 1930-33 was not a significant political issue. On the contrary, because annual exports of $15.5 billion by 1955 exceeded imports by $4.2 billion, and total US investment overseas of nearly $45 billion overawed foreign investment in the US by 50%, the balance of payments was every year several billion dollars in favor of the republic. What was coming in was two-thirds industrial raw materials and food products, including meat, fish, and commodities from Latin America such as coffee, cocoa, and bananas, one-third manufactured goods. What was going out was large quantities of non-electrical machinery, transportation equipment, metals, manufactured metal products, grains, and prepared foods.

Bananas imported through New Orleans

Further, the government continued to move aggressively to promote trade for both small producers and big companies. The Trade Agreements Act was extended another three years on June 21, 1955. That legislation granted the President authority to reduce tariffs 5% a year in return for foreign concessions, and on duties in excess of 50% make the concession unilaterally. Another four year extension was passed on August 20, 1958. By then, however, the surplus of exports over imports was beginning to shrink, causing Congress to tack on a provision authorizing the President to increase rates 50% above those in place as of July 1, 1934. In addition to quotas on oil the next year, quotas at 80% of the average imports for the preceding five years were instituted on lead and zinc.

These provisions failed to halt a diminishment in the gold reserve to $18 billion by 1960 from $25 billion in 1949. That contraction inhibited the Treasury from increasing circulating currency, limited by law to four times the gold reserve, above the $53 billion level. Heavy US tourism overseas, which was encouraged by the high value of the dollar in relation to foreign currencies, also tended to reduce the government's holdings of the precious metal because foreign governments could trade dollars for gold. The other major factors causing a negative $3.9 billion balance of payments in 1960 were increasing foreign investment in the US, resulting in an outflow of interest payments, and annual military aid to foreign governments of about $4.5 billion.

Overall, however, the combination of favorable business conditions and rising but still moderate labor costs, discussed below, offset the balance of payment problem to generate $50 billion of US corporate profits by 1960. While manufacture both of durable and non-durable goods generated 30% of national income, the wholesale and retail trade chipped in another 15.5% while government was next in importance at 12.7%. Coming swiftly were finance and services, together providing slightly more than a fifth of income. Never before did Americans have so much to spend.

Consumer Purchases Drive the Economy

One mistake US political leaders did not want to make was to swing back toward protectionism and in the process drive up the cost of raw materials, make US goods more expensive, and choke off consumer spending. In 1954, retail spending alone amounted to $170 billion or 43% of GDP. Five years later it rose to $215.4 billion. Because of heavy government purchases and business capital expenditures, its share of GDP was down slightly to 41.5%, while all consumer spending composed over three-fifths of the economy.

Resumption in particular of purchase of all manner of home appliances as well as furniture and fixtures amounting to $16.6 billion in 1955 and swelling to over $19 billion by 1960 brought greater prominence and profits to a raft of companies. For example, Whirlpool, formerly the Nineteen Hundred Washer Company of Binghamton, New York, offered automatic washing machines with options for various garments, water levels, and temperatures. Its expansion to a full line of products including dryers and refrigerators challenged Westinghouse, which impressed the public with a frost-free refrigerator. That company added a credit subsidiary to finance purchase of its appliances. Emerson Electric grew by acquisitions and diversification but increasingly made components for other companies, not end products. That strategy eventually by 1973 generated over $1 billion in revenue. As for entirely new appliances, Raytheon licensee Tappan Stove Company was first out with a microwave oven, which because of its high price tag of $1,300 only did modest business. A greater long-term threat to Westinghouse, GE, and other companies that boosted profits with finance divisions was introduction in 1958 of the *American Express Card* and *Bank Americard*. For the moment, only the well-heeled could obtain such portable credit. The average citizen still financed major household purchases through consumer durable makers and sellers.

Coca-Cola truck

Meanwhile, competition among brand name makers of food products, household and personal items accounting for nearly $125 billion of nondurable goods spending in 1955 and advancing above $150 billion by 1960 intensified. Companies with the wherewithal to launch major advertising campaigns often captured the public's fancy. For example, Kellogg persuaded a generation of mothers and children that its *Frosted Flakes* breakfast cereal was as cartoon pitch character Tony the Tiger roared "Grrreat!" C.A. Swanson & Sons' ready to heat and eat frozen TV dinners caught on so quickly with families that Campbell bought the company in 1955, and then supplemented its soup line with acquisition five years later of Pepperidge Farms snacks. Arguably, there existed products of equal or better taste, but marketing power and shelf space in grocery stores counted for as much as quality. The costs of attracting customers to new products and building up distribution channels to sizeable markets, affordable even at $80 million of advertising for P&G in 1957, were formidable for lesser companies.

Pabst beer factory, Milwaukee, Wisconsin

Although there was mounting evidence that cigarette smoking enhanced the danger of emphysema, lung cancer, and other ills, R.J. Reynolds surpassed all rivals with its *Salem* brand menthol filter-tipped cigarettes. While Anheuser-Busch dominated the beer market with *Budweiser*, *Michelob*, and after 1953 *Busch* beer, Coors of Colorado established a footprint west of the Mississippi by marketing beer in all-aluminum cans. Still, its production in 1959 of 1 million barrels was only about one-eighth of Anheuser-Busch's production. Individual tastes in various regions and locales let dozens of brand name beers exist.

There was less room in household and personal items for small players. Particularly for plastics-based products, volume production was critical. Thus DuPont continued to churn out cellophane until improved *Mylar* was ready to replace it. The company came out as well with *Dacron* polyester for clothes. To please homemakers who wanted to rewrap food for freshness once it was opened, Dow Chemical introduced *Saran Wrap*. Plastic products, including containers in competition with *Tupperware*, provided over 20% of its revenue in the 1950s and continued to rise so that by 1963 its production of plastics exceeded 1 billion pounds and its overall sales topped $1 billion the next year. Too, International Paper bounced up to that magic revenue figure by 1959 in part because of a plastic coated milk container for dairies and home delivery. Because in 1956 the FTC contested its acquisition of Long-Bell Lumber Corporation as anti-competitive and thus discouraged IP from further acquisitions, its growth rate slowed for a decade and a half.

Not so Gillette, which in 1953 expanded its main product line with *Foamy* aerosol shaving cream, then seven years later *Right Guard* aerosol deodorant. In 1955, it scored a coup by buying the PaperMate Company for only $15 million then raking in profits from the $1.95 *Capri* ballpoint pen brought out the next year to eclipse fountain pens. Also in 1955, Scott broke a taboo by advertising bathroom tissue on TV. That success provoked P&G to buy Charmin Paper Mills two years later, a maker of that previously unmentionable product as well as paper towels, and napkins. Another competitor Kimberly-Clark chose the next year to tout rather its *Kleenex* facial tissue by co-sponsoring the *Perry Como Show*. Forty million Americans were educated in the cosmetic and sanitary benefits of using a disposable product rather than washable cotton cloths.

Kodak Brownie Starmatic II

Another big seller was Kodak's *Brownie Starmatic* cameras. Between 1957 and 1961, the company sold 10 million. Making photography for the masses pay off even better, consumers bought *Ektachrome* color film for development at local kiosks and camera and drug stores. With employment of 75,000 persons, Kodak was on its way to $1 billion of sales by 1962.

Sears, J.C. Penneys, department store chains, including Allied which bought Stern Brothers of New Jersey and Federated which acquired J. Burdines, and other general merchandising stores doing $24 billion of sales annually by 1960 were the main outlets for sales of major household appliances. Supermarket chains, led by A&P with 10% of grocery sales from over 4,200 stores, began to trump both local groceries in the $53 billion market for food products as well as drug stores ringing up $7.5 billion in sales of household and personal items. In 1955, Winn & Lovett bought the 117 store Dixie Home Stores chain, then chains in North Carolina, Louisiana, Mississippi, and Georgia to become Winn-Dixie Stores, Inc. Competition came from Consolidated Foods, which bought 34 Piggly Wiggly supermarkets. Both were supplied in part by SuperValu, which began a strategy of buying up regional food wholesalers in the Southeast, Midwest, and Northwest. Another good customer in the latter region was Albertson's, which innovated in 1957 by incorporating drug stores into its supermarkets.

Of course in the 1950s, most food was still purchased in stores for preparation and consumption at home rather than consumption in restaurants, but the increase in disposable income as well as the spreading road network out from cities into suburbs created an opportunity for more fast food franchises. Destined to be the most successful of all was Ray Kroc, who at age 52 in 1954 mortgaged his home and life savings to move to California and become exclusive distributor of a milk shake maker called *Multimixer*. It so happened that the *Multimixer* milk shake was the big draw for the McDonald Brothers' chain of hamburger stands. After Kroc opened a McDonald's restaurant the next year, he became successful enough by 1961 to buy out the chain for $2.7 million. Likewise, the increasingly rushed public appreciated the convenience of Kentucky Fried Chicken restaurants, begun by Colonel Harlan Sanders in 1939 in Corbin, Kentucky. The first Pizza Hut restaurant, started in 1958 in Wichita, Kansas, founded a successful chain despite stiff and persistent competition from local pizzerias around the country.

Although limitations on driving during the Second World War nearly ruined the Howard Johnson restaurant chain in the Northeast, renewed growth in the 1950s along national and state highways revived the company's fortunes. A new innovation, the Howard  Johnson Motor Lodge, pushed sales up from $115 million in 1951 toward $1 billion by end of the decade and an initial public offering of stock to obtain even greater financing in 1961. Marriott had already gone that route in 1953 to add more Hot Shoppes along the New Jersey turnpike. The first Marriott hotel was constructed in Arlington, Virginia. The next year, the Ramada Inns chain began in Flagstaff, Arizona, entering a market that would grow beyond $4 billion by 1960. The Interstate Highway Act, a national mania for family vacation travel by car, and cheap, stable gas prices insured business mounting to $16.1 billion in 1960 for all eating and drinking establishments.

The food grocery business was also challenged by an innovation by Mars Company, still privately held. The firm began installing electronic vending machines in malls and other public places. Instead of just a candy and chocolate bar maker, Mars became the nation's leader in vending machines. By siphoning off pennies, nickels, and dimes from every sale of other companies' products, it vaulted from tens of millions of dollars in sales to $300 million by 1972. Competition west of the Mississippi arose from the Automatic Retailers of America (later Aramark). During the Second World War, the company had arisen from nothing by providing food service and vending machines to Douglas Aircraft plants in California.

A TIME OF TRANSITION IN ENTERTAINMENT, LEISURE, AND THE ARTS

In 1952, the FCC removed a four year freeze on TV licenses, causing the number of stations across the country to increase rapidly to 1,809 commercial and 242 educational stations. Most used the very high frequency (VHF) band of 13 channels. Ultra high frequency (UHF), another 71 channels, was opened as well but new TV sets were not required to receive all UHF signals until April 30, 1964. In the interim, the major networks ABC, CBS, and NBC captured the nation's attention with a proliferation of dramas, quiz shows, westerns, movies on TV, and variety hours, headlined by Milton Berle, Sid Caesar, and other versatile stars. By 1955, nearly 31 million families had TVs; by end of the decade 60 million, 85% of all households. The medium easily shrugged off a 1958 scandal when it was discovered that quiz shows *Twenty-One* and *The $64,000 Question* were rigged for certain contestants to win.

Elvis A. Presley

Meanwhile, a new kind of music called Rock 'n' Roll caught the nation's attention in the 1950s because of car radios, sock hop balls, and a rebellious streak in teenagers. The craze started with *Rock Around The Clock* by Bill Haley and the Comets and went into high gear with the September 9, 1956 appearance of Elvis A. Presley on the *Ed Sullivan Show*. The King, as he was later styled, sang for 54 million people and boosted his income to $100,000 a month from record sales. His earnings temporarily plunged the next year to $83.20 a month when he was willingly inducted into the US Army.

Presley's polite demeanor impressed the older generation and relieved anxiety that Rock 'n' Roll was at best an assault upon ear drums, at worst a Communist plot to undermine American society and the Capitalist system. Middle age adults and more mature listeners still preferred the big band sound of the war years as well as Frank Sinatra, Rosemary Clooney, and other more easily understood singers. While mainstream music was sold typically on long playing albums, teenagers preferred affordable 45-rpm records brought out by RCA in 1949 with hit singles on one side and a second song on the reverse. Transistor radios, first introduced in 1952 by the Japanese company Sony and in the US in 1954 by Texas Instruments, not only made music portable to the beach, shopping mall, and other locations but helped radio stations stage a comeback. For that reason, CBS founded Epic Records in 1953, two years later British music company EMI bought Capital Records, and Warner Brothers in 1958 founded Warner Brothers Records. Helped by the innovation of stereophonic sound, US record sales soared from $277 million in 1955 to $600 million by 1960.

Music but especially TV put extreme pressure on motion picture companies to innovate to slow the erosion in theater attendance. They came out with wide screen pictures shown in Technicolor and better stereo sound. Walt Disney decided to diversify, however, and began building its Disney Land amusement park in the Los Angeles area. The

Disney's Magic Kingdom for American leisure time

company was counting on tourism to supplement revenue from animated films as well as the *Mickey Mouse Club* TV show. Financially strapped in 1954 and needing an infusion of cash to finish construction of the park, founder Walt Disney accepted a $500,000 investment from ABC in exchange for a 35% stake in the park. The decision proved sound when 1 million customers, including hundreds of thousands of children, passed through the turnstiles in the first six months of operation. In fact, revenues climbed so swiftly that Disney bought out ABC's stake six years later for $7.5 million and paid off all other outstanding loans. Disney was off and running to become not merely a motion picture producer but an entertainment conglomerate that would generate billions of dollars of revenue through films, movie theaters, TV shows, music, theme parks, and merchandising.

Other motion picture companies were not so fortunate in the TV age. In fact, TV westerns put Republic's film westerns out of business altogether. Universal, despite a 1946 merger with International Pictures, was purchased six years later by British company Decca Records, then in 1962 MCA. Its business in horror, comedy, action, and teenager movies had been undercut by American International Pictures, founded as a small budget producer in 1954. Also falling on hard times was RKO, which went first to General Tire and Rubber then ultimately in 1959 Desilu, the production company of TV stars Lucille Ball and Desi Arnez. Chaplin and Pickford sold off their combined half interest in United Artists at mid-decade for only $4.1 million.

Francis A. Sinatra

On the other hand, Columbia got into TV in 1951 by founding Screen Gems. A successful series of big film hits, including 1953's *From Here to Eternity* which won an academy award for Sinatra for best supporting actor, gave the company the wherewithal to remain independent. Warner Brothers, anticipating a downward turn in the movie business, sold off much of its film library in 1948 to MGM. Paramount remained independent until it was purchased in 1966 by Gulf+Western, which later renamed itself Paramount Communications and became a formidable media and entertainment company. As for MGM, despite its big 1959 blockbuster *Ben Hur*, cost overruns and box office debacle for the epic *Cleopatra* in the early 1960s devastated profitability. The legendary film-making company became financial vulnerable to stronger entities.

In 1950, about 80% of the assets of non-financial businesses were classified as tangible — that is property, plant, and equipment. Because of the building success of entertainment and information companies, that share diminished to 78% in 1955. Print media, including newspapers with daily circulation in 1950 above 50 million, magazines at 75 million copies, and even comic books at 30 million contributed to the rise of assets that contained a large intangible component. The maxim that "beauty is in the eye of the beholder" meant that the valuation of companies whose assets included, say, a successful TV show, the contract of a popular recording artist, or even fine art could reach enormous heights. In 1957, for example, French painter Gauguin's *Still Life with Apples* sold in Paris for $255,000, marking the beginning of soaring value for works of art. However, another truism that "what goes up, must come down," warned that the fickle tastes of the public as well as changing conditions might undermine the value of intangible assets as quickly as they were inflated.

NEW TECHNOLOGY IN BUSINESS MACHINES

Another threat to the revenues and profitability of successful media companies was innovation and technology. Just as automobiles, trucks, airplanes, and pipelines had ravaged the business of railroads, so too could more innocuous inventions turn the entertainment and information industries upside down. In 1953, GE produced *Lexan*, a resistant, clear plastic that would later be used to manufacture CDs and DVDs. The days of long-playing record albums and 45-rpm vinyl discs were numbered already in their infancy.

1956 GE transistor radio

More positively, an entirely new industry was about to spring up because of R&D spending by private business that reached $3.5 billion in 1953. Many companies were eager to exploit the breakthrough made six years earlier by William B. Shockley, John Bardeen, and Walter H. Brattain of Bell Laboratories who in 1956 won the Noble Prize for Physics for coming up with the transistor, a solid-state electronic amplifier, switch, or semiconductor, 0.5% the size of a vacuum tube, that became the key component for computers and other electronic equipment. A year after IBM in 1951 delivered the first large-scale, general purpose computer using vacuum tubes to the Census Bureau, Texas Instruments licensed the right to manufacture semiconductors. After company scientist Jack Kirby invented the first integrated circuit in 1958 and TI merged the next year with Metals & Controls Corporation, a US company with operations on four continents, revenue of $233 million, and 16,900 employees was created.

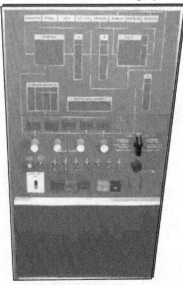

IBM 1401 computer

Now under the direction of Thomas J. Watson, Jr., IBM announced its first electronic calculating machine for businesses on May 24, 1954. Big Blue then forged ahead with a series of innovations, including random access computer disc storage systems, the FORTRAN computer programming language, and in 1959 putting transistors into its IBM model 7090, used to run the USAF Ballistic Missile Early Warning System. As revenues climbed to $1.6 billion, net earnings exceeded 11%. Employment hit 95,000.

Another major player moving into semiconductors in 1955 was Motorola. The company concentrated on mass producing transistors for radios. Its first Motorola portable transistor radio appeared in 1959. Revenues jumped to $300 million the next year with employment of 14,740.

By end of the decade, the US boasted 6,000 computers and annual computer industry revenues of $1 billion. Since even minicomputers, such as the *PDP-1* brought out by Digital Electronic Equipment, founded in 1957, were priced in the $100,000 range, the future looked rosy. Any company with a connection to business machines might decide to enter the market. National Cash Register did so after a 1952 purchase of Computer Research Corporation of Hawthorne California, a maker of digital computers for aviation applications. For the moment, the software that ran computers was included with machines. Different computers running different programs could not cooperate.

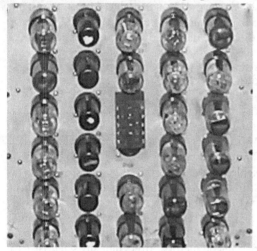

Old technology: vacuum tubes
Thus, for large-scale operations involving many calculations, IBM and other mainframe makers had an advantage. Companies such as Automatic Data Processing (ADP), founded in 1949 by Henry Taub in Paterson, New Jersey to prepare payroll information, were obvious customers. Semiconductors would have even wider reach, for example in postage meters by Pitney-Bowes, which generated tens and hundreds of millions of dollars of revenue for the company. An electronics revolution would transform American consumer appliances and business office machines.

In 1959, another important breakthrough in the latter field was achieved by the Haloid-Xerox company, originally founded in Rochester in the first decade of the century to make photographic supplies for cameras. The technology stemmed from the 1938 process of Chester F. Carlson for dry-copying or herography, which produced an image by heat-fusing powder particles in electrically charged areas of sensitized paper. Carlson's 1940 patent won no financial backing until Battelle Memorial Institute made the first *Xerox* copies in 1944. Only after Haloid acquired a license for commercial development in 1947 and produced the first xerographic copier two years later was an industry born. But it took another decade for the company to introduce the *Xerox 914*, the first automatic, plain-paper office copier. Xerox machines were so successful that the company dropped Haloid from its name in 1961.

BALANCE BETWEEN WAGE-EARNERS AND WEALTHY

Business machines increased productivity but tended to require fewer workers than before. The jump in GDP from improved technology boosted overall white collar employment, however. The real consequence of mechanization was permanent reduction in blue collar factory employment. Another threat to labor, unrelated to self-inflicted wounds, was increased mechanization. As early as 1948, Norbert Wiener, a child prodigy who had in 1913 obtained a Ph.D. from Harvard, came up with a concept called *Cybernetics: On Control and Communication in Animal and the Machine*. What he was touting was making automatic information-processing machines operate like the human nervous system. The end product would be machines or robots that could replace workers on assembly lines.

For business and industry, the result would be lower labor costs, higher capital expenditures, and an overall net improvement in efficiency, production, and the bottom line. Unions unwittingly opened the door to automation by trading relaxation of work rules and introduction of labor-saving devices for wage and benefit increases. Such a pact with the Pacific Maritime Association was agreed to by the International Longshoremen's and Warehousemen's Union (ILWU) in 1960. Although employers agreed to reimburse existing workers for wages lost because of automation from a $27.5 million automation fund, the 100,000 strong labor force was steadily shrunk by retirement and attrition to 11,000 by the turn of the century.

Nevertheless, the Eisenhower Era can be seen as the first leg of a two decade march by unionized workers to a satisfactory standard of living and other wage-earners to a stable existence. With the economy growing and immigration, at 2.5 million for the 1950-59 period, 60% from Europe, hardly as a percentage of total population overwhelming, increase in wage rates was possible. The average manufacturing wage by mid-decade hit $2.00 an hour, equal in 2004 money to annual earnings of $28,170, while minimum wage as of March 1, 1956 was half that. With family incomes up, the US middle class had much more discretionary cash to spend. Too, another 1.5 million blacks moved north from Dixie, looking with the unemployment rate down to 4% for higher-paying work than tenant farming. The general absence of competition from foreign producers in US markets until the later 1950s also tended to keep economic indicators for labor positive.

On the other hand, the contentious relationship between business and union leaders continued. After the AFL on Sept. 22, 1954 kicked out the International Longshoreman's Association for racketeering, then merged on December 5 with the CIO, the new AFL-CIO with George Meaney as president was well positioned to make demands on industry. A 52 day strike by the United Rubber Workers against Goodyear resulted in meager 6 cent an hour raise to $2.15, equivalent in 2004 money to annual earnings of $30,280, but better wage advances in subsequent years. Two years later, the USW used the same tactic to pressure steel companies into a 50 cent an hour wage rate phased in through 1958 that caused higher prices. Worse from organized labor's point of view, a special Senate committee chaired by John L. McClellan (D., Arkansas) convened in December 1957 to take testimony about racketeering and crime in labor-management relations. The Teamsters Union was severely tainted when its head Dave Beck was convicted on embezzlement charges in Seattle state court, and then his successor James R. Hoffa subsequently was linked to organized crime.

The USW finally overplayed its hand in 1959. A strike over 116 days starting on July 15 by 540,000 workers complaining about companies arbitrarily changing work conditions and eliminating past practices halted 88% of US domestic steel production. The prolonged confrontation opened the door for the first time to imports of steel surpassing annual exports. Because of lower labor costs and newer, more efficient plants and equipment, foreign companies realized that a substantial chunk of the 150 million ton market was theirs for the taking. As for the strike itself, a federal injunction on November 7 for an 80 day cooling off period under the Taft-Hartley Act sent the workers back to their jobs pending negotiation of a 41 cents per hour wage increase. Although it was phased in over 30 months to an average rate of $3.06 an hour, the steel strike was a catalyst for the recession of 1960-61 that hurt cars and appliances orders and lowered demand for steel by 40% below capacity.

Johns Hopkins hospital, Baltimore, Maryland

Overall, 60 million American workers in 1960 made an average wage of $2.26 per hour, equal in 2004 dollars to an annual income of $28,790. About 28% were employed in manufacturing, 6.7% in transportation and public utilities, and another 4.8% in construction, most paying wages better than the average. It might have given pause to some that only 2.1 million people worked now in the agricultural sector, that 11.5 million were in wholesale and retail occupations, and that too many of the 23.3 million women in the work force earned the latter's average wage of $1.63 an hour, equal in 2004 dollars to about $20,760 in annual income. The hope of many of the 39.8 million Americans, or 22.2% of the total, designated as impoverished and wishing to move into the middle class was that the youthful and energetic John F. Kennedy, about to enter the White House, would oversee another period of booming prosperity.

In point of fact, the United States was measurably better off from a national income and wealth standpoint than in 1945. Not only did the country boast an increasing number of high earners, including actors such as Humphrey Bogart and Bette Davis who made several times the President's salary of $100,000, but the middle class was twice the size in 1955 as ten years earlier. A continuation of that trend over the next five years caused income distribution to improve slightly, with the top 5% of earners receiving 20% of all income, the top fifth taking in 45.5% and the lowest three-fifths holding remaining about level at 31.9%. Very low inflation averaging 1.2% made the country's $410 billion in personal income count for more.

Nor were citizens excessively taxed. They handed over only about 12.5% of income to government. That was enough to provide nearly 55% of federal revenues. The budget, including $45.9 billion for defense, $18.7 billion for social and other income security, $8.2 billion interest payment on the national debt of $287 billion, $5.4 billion for veterans' benefits, $4.8 billion for commerce and transportation, $3.3 billion for agricultural subsidies and rural development, and $3.0 billion for international affairs and finance, was only $300,000 in deficit.

In 1954, the Dow Jones Industrial Index finally regained the 1929 peak. Even as the monetary base swelled, the stock market continued to advance steadily in accord with company earnings because new margin requirements compelled most trading to disdain debt for cash. That measure of confidence and stability convinced Fidelity and other mutual funds, trusts, pension funds, insurance portfolios, and foundations like Ford's, which in the 1950s gave grants of $1 billion to colleges, universities, and hospitals, to take large positions in the market. Cumulatively, they came by end of the Eisenhower Era to control $70.5 billion of stock, 20% of the total for traded issues of $352.5 billion, equal in 2004 money to $2.25 trillion. In fact, since 1949, the value of publicly held stock had risen $275 billion. Had not interest rates been so low and many privately held corporations preferred private debt financing through investment banks to the scrutiny that came with public stock issuance, the figure might have been much higher.

CHAPTER X. PROLIFERATING THE MATERIAL AMERICAN DREAM: 1961-1972

The way most Democrats of progressive and liberal persuasion saw it, Eisenhower had done well holding the Communist world at bay but had ignored many pressing needs at home. Most urgent was Civil Rights for blacks, alleviation of the poverty that afflicted more than one-fifth of the population of 180 million Americans, and other socio-economic inequalities. That gave pause to some that the republic might be headed for another period of domestic dislocation and disturbance. Although John F. Kennedy (JFK) saw merit in bridging differences between whites and blacks, rich and poor, employers and working class, in his inaugural address on January 20, 1961 he did not promise an upheaval in economics. Rather, he told citizens, "ask not what your country can do for you — ask what you can do for your country." He took office without an intention of interfering directly in the conduct of Big Business. What he might have hoped to accomplish on socio-economic policy was rendered impossible by entrenched conservatism in Congress as well as two years of crises over Berlin, Cuba, and Southeast Asia. Aside from cuts in taxes and tariffs — not to be underestimated in providing new stimulus to the economy — he won few political battles.

His assassination on November 22, 1963 left it to Lyndon B. Johnson (LBJ), another hard-line, anti-Communist Democrat but with rural and agricultural roots in Texas, to envision a war on poverty to spread prosperity to every nook and cranny in the land. Tax changes, regulation, and legislative fiat would be the tools that lifted Washington's role in the economy to a higher plain than had ever been attempted except during the Great Depression. As with FDR's supporters, Johnson Era Democrats intended the restructuring of the government-business relationship to be permanent. Not only would they use levies on corporations, as well as individuals drawing remuneration from corporations, to fund the shift in power but would manipulate business institutions themselves to be the levers of change. What gave liberal economists confidence that they could intrude so recklessly in the *laissez-faire* environment that still prevailed in many industries without wrecking all was a renewed surge in production that seemed to presage a period of perpetual prosperity. Once again, a few heady optimists speculated that business cycle dips would no longer plague the republic.

By mid-decade, key statistics for the economic boom provided grist for the mill of confidence. Chief among these was overall GDP growth from $526 billion in 1960 to $719 billion in 1965, a 6.5% annual clip. Because inflation remained quiescent at 1.2%, four-fifths of the gain was real. Even with the Baby Boom generation propelling the republic's population over 192 million, 40% under age 20, *per capita* GDP jumped 4.7% to $3,745, equal in 2004 money to $22,425. Though the share of wealth possessed by the top 1% of families rose incrementally to around one-third, or about $840 billion, share of income for the bottom three-fifths also inched up to a level above 32%. Prosperity for the second fifth of families, climbing to 23.5% of national income by mid-decade, broadened out the middle class. Many of the bread-winners in these latter households were office workers in middle management earning between $7,000 and $15,000. Only 7.6% of families had income of $15,000 or higher, equal to at least $89,820 in 2004 money. The median family income, by contrast, was $6,880. The median income for white families was 4% higher than that.

If FDR's New Deal has used government programs to rescue millions of previously prosperous families from poverty and Eisenhower had permitted Big Business to craft less linear means of solidifying and improving the lot of that group, LBJ now wanted to raise up the bottom fifth of families, receiving income below $3,500 or about $20,960 in 2004 money, into an affluent working class. The difficulty with this concept lay in convincing Americans that the kind of government effort launched during emergency times in the Great Depression was needed now that the economy was expanding and businesses such as Deere and Inland Steel, Consolidated Foods and PepsiCo, Dow Chemical and Federated Department Stores were joining the $1 billion revenue club. Republicans continued to believe that a hands-off approach, rather than government meddling, was the ticket that would transport citizens to the promised land of material well-being. In the election of 1964, they put up Senator Barry M. Goldwater of Arizona to rally voters to the cause. But the country wanted change as much for non-economic reasons as to spread the wealth. LBJ rode public sentiment to a landslide victory. Surviving conservatives in the House and Senate, Democrat as well as Republican, could not then significantly obstruct implementation of a full and ambitious Great Society agenda. Ambitious legislation not only brought political and social rights for blacks as well as education and environmental reform but helped cut the number of Americans in poverty by 1972 to about 25 million, or 12% of the population.

Because Johnson refused to raise taxes to pay for this largesse, nor even to fund defense spending claiming over half the federal budget, added expenditure had to be covered by new debt. On the other hand, state and local governments did raise taxes to pay for operating expenses but especially highway and bridges, buildings and other fixed assets that surged by 1972 to $602 billion, a 9.4% annual increase for the entire period. The federal government's fixed asset growth, by contrast, was only 5.4% annually, this despite the simultaneous burden of the Vietnam War and Great Society. By 1970, non-government liabilities to assets had increased to about the same level as government liabilities to assets — 60%. All US debt to assets again approached the 40% top reached in 1945. That meant that households and businesses were picking up more of the tab.

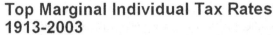

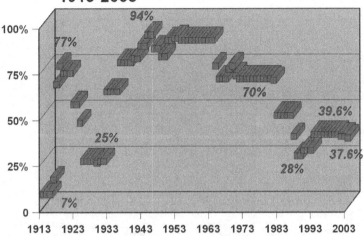

The additional burden on private parties made consumers more vulnerable to an economic downturn and businesses more inclined to rein in purchases at any sign of trouble. Though few storm clouds appeared over the horizon prior to 1972, the potential for contraction increased as the business cycle completed a decade long rotation. Worrisome was the fact that inflation, stoked by federal deficits, higher material costs and shortages, and wage increases, jumped between 1966 and 1972 to an annual average of 4.4%. Although the economy expanded at an 8.1% annual rate to $1.24 trillion of GDP, the real rate of increase was less than the preceding five year period. Thus, the likelihood of continued progress on the path to prosperity for the vast majority of Americans was called into question. Government attempts to hasten the process with impositions on Big Business that favored consumers, unions, and the environment wove a web of what came to be called "red tape." In a closed market where all competitors would be so afflicted and have time to adjust, the impact might not have been so economically harmful. With foreign competition gathering strength to invade both overseas and domestic markets, Washington's political and bureaucratic intrusiveness hampered the ability of corporate executives and entrepreneurs to respond.

What American business needed to beat back the challenge from outside was more economies of scale and automation to cut production costs. Although the average US wage rate was hardly excessive, unions in steel, rubber, automobiles, and other heavy industry had won, and would win in the 1960s, enough concessions to put US producers at a sizeable disadvantage vis-a-vis European and Japanese competitors. The Kennedy Administration's commitment to free trade and low tariffs proved a double edge sword, aiding agriculture and industries such as machine tools wherein the republic retained an export advantage but inviting an attack on the market share of US auto, home appliance, and other domestic companies. Tokyo with its Ministry for International Trade and Industry proved particularly adept at targeting consumer durable niches, including cars, TVs, and other electronic products, and directing Japanese companies to the assault. All this economic warfare took place while Washington marshaled resources and alliances to contain the Soviet and Chinese geo-political challenge. While the US fought a Cold War against Communism, its allies plotted to undermine American business.

US Post Office, Atlanta, Georgia

Fortunately, the US economy was much more diversified than in the 1920s. Important sectors that had not previously existed or been adequately developed included commercial airlines, aerospace-defense industries, pharmaceuticals and related chemicals, radio and television, and business services. Domestic construction of residences, business properties, and large public projects was still an all American endeavor. Textile producers had yet to be undermined by Third World imports. Equally as important, the financial institutions and reserves of the republic were by far the greatest in the world. Assets of $4.3 trillion at the beginning of the period, 55% financial, became in excess of $11 trillion, 60% financial, at the end. Overall net worth of the country approached $7 trillion, of which households held nearly two-thirds. The ratio of net worth to GDP was twice the level of 1929.

KENNEDY ECONOMICS AND THE GROWTH OF US FINANCIAL ASSETS

US personal income tax rates ranging from 20% to 91% were still enormously high in 1961. A legacy of the confiscatory policy of the New Deal and Second World War as well as a continuing necessity for funding Cold War defense budgets, they absorbed income that otherwise might have been directed to an even greater splurge on houses, consumer durables, and non-durables than occurred under Eisenhower. Enough disposable income remained to jack up consumer spending to 62% of GDP but not to pump up stock market values. Although the composite index of the NYSE had increased by an annual average rate of 11% since the end of the Korean War, most shares were held by businesses, pension funds, and other large institutional investors.

Those individuals who did take the plunge were the sort who could also afford the minimum $100,000 required for negotiable certificates of deposit (CDs), invented by First National City Bank in 1961. When brokerage houses such as Merrill Lynch and Morgan Stanley wanted to attract extra customers, instead of wasting time on middle income Americans, they expanded into fixed income securities for institutions or ventured overseas to Japan and Europe to market stock and real estate investment advice to wealthy  foreigners. Resources came to include computer models to predict trends and turns in the market; trades involved large blocks of shares. Only in 1963 did Fidelity begin to tap into latent demand from a broader cross-spectrum of Americans for equity investments by offering a mutual fund later renamed *Magellan* that in three years accumulated $2.7 billion of assets.

What had occurred to free up more disposable income for investments? In October 1962, the Kennedy administration and Congress granted corporations a 7% investment tax credit to fund $1 billion in plant modernization. The next year, the President proposed that taxes on individuals be lowered 30%. The tax savings would be $7 billion for calendar year 1964, or about 7.75% of what government revenue otherwise would have been, and $4 billion thereafter. After most of the cut was agreed to after JFK's death, additional disposable income flowed into stocks. The NYSE composite index averaged 10% growth for the next five years.

Meanwhile, more government help was given to the poor. Increasingly, persons in the lowest income group were concentrated in big metropolitan areas such as the New York City area with 11 million people, or 6% of the national total, Los Angeles-Long Beach with 7 million and Chicago with 6.5 million. The 100,000 additional public housing units authorized by the Housing Act of June 30, 1961 demonstrated a commitment by Congress to social welfare. Grants and fund increases equal to $136 million for urban planning, urban renewal, mass transportation, and acquiring land for permanent open space also made an attempt, however inadequate, at solving endemic problems. Senators and representatives showed more enthusiasm for an $11.5 billion appropriation to finish the interstate highway system by 1972. The political advantage of that vote was that it benefited each and every state.

Right from the start, JFK was as concerned with international economic developments and trade as he was with domestic. Seven weeks after taking office, he announced an Alliance for Progress for Latin America, which was chartered on August 17 in Punta del Este, Uruguay, to pool $100 billion over 10 years for Organization of America States (OAS) countries, of which $20 billion would be contributed by the US The lofty goal was to achieve annual GNP increases of 2.5%, more equitable income distributions, an increase in agricultural production and thus food self-sufficiency, industrial growth, price stability, tax reform, land reform, improved education, better public health and medical services, and more low-cost housing. Because other OAS governments did not have the wherewithal to meet the ambitious commitment, the plan quickly morphed into a typical US foreign aid program with direct bilateral negotiations between Washington and individual countries.

Since the President wanted to pump up exports, stop the erosion of the gold supply, and firm up balance of payments, new commercial treaties with Latin American governments was not a bad idea. The Trade Expansion Act of October 11 gave authority to cut tariffs up to 50% below the current level or raise them up to 50% above the 1934 level within the next five years as an instrument to persuade or coerce foreign trading partners to lower their tariffs. Congress also granted the chief executive power to remove tariffs entirely on products in which the US and Western Europe accounted for 80% of free world trade, on select agricultural commodities where such action would increase US exports, on tropical agricultural and forestry products not produced in US if the European Economic Community (EEC) did the same, and on articles where the *ad valorem* (variable depending on value) rate was 5% or less. If an industry, a company, or a workforce were seriously hurt economically by tariff concessions and/or increased imports, the injured party could obtain compensation in the form of loans, tax relief, technical assistance, unemployment allowances, retraining, and/or relocation of workers.

After Kennedy's assassination, his commitment to free trade was honored by naming four years of talks in Geneva between 50 countries accounting for 80% of world trade the Kennedy Round. Ultimately, the participants effected a 50% tariff reduction on certain industrial products to bring the average cut to 35% while tariffs on other products were cut 30% to 50%.

It turned out that the gold deficit that had worried both Eisenhower and Kennedy was eased by new discoveries of that precious metal. Established in 1921 to wildcat oil in Texas and Louisiana, the Newmont Mining Company suddenly uncovered the largest deposit ever found in North America in the twentieth century at Carlin, Nevada. With a dozen such mines on the continent as well as operations in South Africa, the company became an industry leader. By 1971, it was using a heap leach method to extract gold from sub-mill grade ores.

To protect US gold reserves, Congress on September 2, 1964 passed an Interest Equalization Tax to discourage US investment abroad. When the next year, President Charles De Gaulle of France exchanged $200 million in US dollars held by the French treasury for gold, LBJ encouraged US citizens to take vacations at home rather than in Europe. Voluntary curbs by banks and corporations on foreign investment became mandatory limitations on January 1, 1968. The Federal Reserve raised its rediscount rate, the rate charged banks on short-term loans, from 3.5% to 4.5% to keep excess capital at home.

THE GREAT SOCIETY AND CONSEQUENCES FOR THE ECONOMY

Naturally, tariff and trade policy was designed to advance the prospects of American business and the economy. So too was the Tax Reduction Act of February 26, 1964 intended to put more money into the pockets of individuals to spend and invest. Personal income tax brackets were dropped to a range of 14-70% over a two year period. The top corporate rate was also knocked down from 52% to 48%. The next year, Congress tacked on an Excise Tax Reduction Act, phased in through 1969, that cut another $4.6 billion annually, or about 42% of the 1965 excise tax take, from government revenue. The price Americans paid for alcohol, beer, tobacco, gasoline, telephones, and other ordinary items was restrained or fell.

Lyndon B. Johnson

Conservatives in Congress approved prudent stimulation packages. They had less enthusiasm for proposals to expand government's role outside of national defense, which absorbed $46.2 billion or 54% of the projected budget for the fiscal year ending June 30, 1965, as well as interest on the public debt, which consumed another $11.4 billion. A host of programs that might today be grouped under the classification social welfare amounted individually to no more than 6% of expenditures. The fear was that increasing the amount of money to which certain classifications of people would become entitled would dangerously balloon the budget deficit of $3.5 billion without an ability subsequently to bring the munificence under restraint. Nevertheless, because it was an election year and LBJ was arguably the most effective arm-twister of the century, he muscled through the House and Senate on July 9 the Urban Mass Transportation Act. That bill provided $375 million in aid to cities to build bus and rail systems to reduce traffic congestion and pollution as well as provide an economic stimulus and employment in city centers. Consistent with the republic's tradition of funding roads, canals, railroads, and interstate highways, it was a departure in that the objective was not chiefly to promote interstate commerce, the constitutional prerogative of Congress. The House and Senate later on October 5, 1970 brought the concept to full flowering with the Urban Mass Transit Act, authorizing grants and loans up to $3.1 billion, to be administered by a Department of Transportation that began operations April 1, 1967.

Senators, representatives, and the country also approved passage of the Economic Opportunity Act of August 30, 1964. Under the law, Congress authorized $948 million for ten separate programs supervised by the Office of Economic Opportunity, including the Job Corps, Volunteers in Service to America or VISTA, work-training programs, work-study programs, and small-business

311

incentives. The general idea was to attack causes of poverty, illiteracy, unemployment, and inadequate public services by helping people help themselves. It served the same purpose, on a smaller scale, as FDR's jobs programs of the 1930s of boosting incomes and self esteem while reducing chronic unemployment.

Dallas Expressway's parallel highways

For the moment, that was all the additional direct government assistance to the needy LBJ could obtain. However, when on November 3 he gathered up 61% of the voters and electoral votes from all but six states to rout Goldwater and strengthen Democratic control of Congress, the floodgates of change were flung wide open. Even before inauguration day, he announced on January 4, 1965 the goal of a Great Society to address a wide range of social problems and ills. In addition to civil rights for blacks, these included alleviation of disease, cleaning up pollution and other environmental problems, improving basic education, and addressing the overall health and medical needs of older, needy, and disabled citizens. Although in the first fiscal year ending June 30, only $1.5 billion of additional spending authority was requested, raising the budget to $97.7 billion (at 13.6% of GDP the lowest federal expenditure in 15 years), larger program outlays in later years would ratchet up a projected deficit of $5.3 billion to many times that size. No one really knew how much the ultimate cost of creating a Great Society would be.

Nevertheless, Congress plunged ahead with the Elementary and Secondary School Act of April 11, 1965 authorizing $1 billion over three years for a first ever large-scale aid to such schools. Funds would be distributed on the basis of need and would include payments, under public school supervision, to parochial and private school pupils. In October, the Higher Education Act provided federal funded scholarships up to $1,000 a year for needy college students. The law also authorized federal guarantees of private loans to same. By 1967, federal grants to education totaled $12.2 billion, up from $5.4 billion in 1963. That was 7.9% of all US education spending, traditionally a state and local affair.

Additional spending by Washington, as well as the continuing Baby Boom, boosted the fortunes of school and textbook publishers. One of the most successful was McGraw-Hill, founded in 1909 and prospering enough to buy F.W. Dodge Corporation, publisher of construction industry information, in 1961. As revenues climbed into the tens, then hundreds of millions, the company further diversified into business publishing with the acquisition in 1966 of Standard & Poors. Purchase in 1970 of Canada's 142 year old Ryerson Press persuaded British publishing magnate Robert Maxwell that he might want to take over McGraw-Hill. Although the company's competitors Harper & Brothers and Row, Peterson, & Company merged in 1962, Random House succumbed to RCA four years later, and Little Brown & Company came under Time, Inc. in 1968, McGraw-Hill executives cleverly in 1972 bought television stations in four cities to stave off Maxwell's hostile bid. FCC rules still forbade foreign majority ownership of American TV and radio stations.

Because Standard & Poors now had more resources to compete with Dun & Bradstreet, that famous business publishing firm obtained greater size and strength itself by buying Rueben H. Donnelley Corporation. The company thus became parent for Moody's, publisher of the Manual of Industrial and Corporation Securities, and the *Official Airlines Guide*, and ten other trade magazines. In 1971, it started a new revenue stream with *Harris InfoSource*, providing a state database directory. It later spun off R.R. Donnelly as a separate company.

Increased spending on educational books and business directories helped triple publishing revenues from $1 billion in 1960 to over $3 billion by the early 1970s. The industry turned out between 26,000 and 29,000 new titles a year. However, the federal gravy train would finally come to an end in the 1970s with a decision for budgetary reasons to thrust more of the cost back onto states. The pressure on publishing companies to link up with other media and entertainment entities would increase.

On the other hand, Washington's commitment to health care never subsided. It became a significant budget item on July 30, 1965 with the Social Security Amendments Act which not only increased Social Security benefits 7% and extended them to widows age 62 and over but set up a Medicare insurance plan covering hospital and post-hospital treatment for persons age 65 and over. Funding came from an increase in the Social Security tax on individual salaries and wages to 3.85%, matched by employers, with a taxable wage base maximum of $6,600 as well as a new Medicare tax component beginning at 0.7%. In 1967, the combined taxes and base were raised respectively to 4.4% and $7,800 with further tax rate increases in subsequent years; in 1968, benefits were raised another 13%. That year, Congress created Medicaid, in essence a Medicare plan for needy and disabled persons not covered by Medicare for which states and the federal government split the cost. By June 1968, 19.7 million persons in 30 states were covered.

Although health insurers such as Aetna had benefited from the Federal Employee Health Benefits Act of 1960, they had opposed Medicare and Medicaid for fear that a full-fledged, national socialized medical system would follow. Even non-profit Blue Cross and Blue Shield organizations had prospered in the early 1960s by standardizing plans to keep up with for-profit companies. But Congress structured Medicare to give private insurers a piece of the pie and put some of their fears to rest. Ample opportunity still existed to sell comprehensive medical plans to the swelling middle class. Health care as part of business benefit packages was a growing market as well. From 1964, Connecticut General even had a dental insurance plan for a minimum 35 employees. In 1969, the company organized a Health Maintenance Organization (HMO) in Columbia, Maryland with an object of encouraging regular check-ups, preventive health problems before they occurred, and lowering long-term costs.

One important barrier to an HMO-preventive medicine concept for the country was legal limitations on the construction of new medical facilities. *Certificates of Need* were required of regulators in many states to prove that new brick and mortar was necessary to fill existing and/or projected demand for medical services. The idea was to prevent unnecessary construction that raised the cost of health care. Interference with the judgment of hospital administrators tended to entrench conservative practices and ideas.

A company called Humana found a way around restrictions by building up a system of non-conventional medical care facilities. Founded in Louisville, Kentucky with $2,000, it opened the Heritage House nursing home, and then expanded by 1968 to a chain of seven Extendicare facilities. After an initial public offering, the company bought the Medical Center Hospital of Huntsville, Alabama, then under construction. A flurry of acquisitions brought Humana's holdings to nine such facilities by 1970. As a holding company for hospitals, it was better positioned to push a managed care approach than single entities. The Hospital Corporation of America, founded in Nashville by family doctors, also assembled a collection of 51 hospitals by 1973.

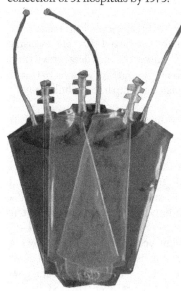

IV Bag

Hospital holding companies not only had more leverage to deal with insurance companies but could afford the latest medical products technology, such as produced by Baxter International. Specializing in blood therapy, it was so successful in 1966 with its *Factor VIII* concentrate to treat hemophilia and four years later with *Viaflex* plastic IV container that revenue topped $200 million. Another innovator was tiny Stryker Corporation of Kalamazoo, Michigan. The firm became notable for orthopedic devices and implants. Its success gave competition to Zimmer Holdings, now doing $30 million of sales of splints, braces, stainless steel hip prosthesis, and knee replacements. Medi-Tech (later Boston Scientific) achieved a breakthrough in 1969 with steerable catheters to make procedures in the body less invasive.

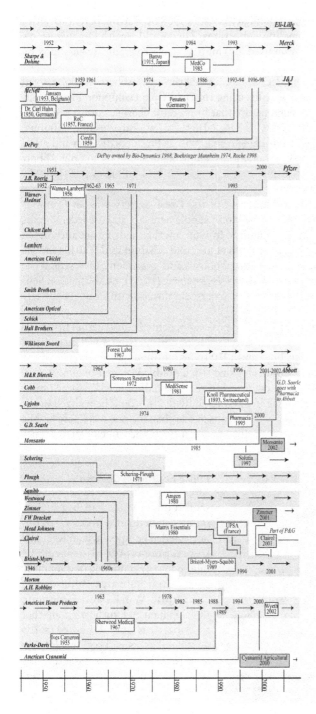

Genealogy of US Pharmaceutical Industry, 1946-2004

Meanwhile, pharmaceutical research and development broadened out the range of products available by prescription. Because the R&D investment required for even a single drug was large, newcomers had less opportunity to succeed than with medical instruments. Seventeen year patent protection and the FDA approval process also constructed formidable barriers to entry against smaller fry. Huge potential rewards for even a single successful drug kept big players doggedly in the industry. As well as concocting anti-cancer drugs derived from rosy periwinkle plants, for instance, Eli Lilly worked for a decade on oral and injectable antibiotics of the *cephalosporin* class. Its *Ceclor* product was not ready until the 1970s, however.

In 1963, a more modest company Upjohn appeared to have a very lucrative market opening. Clinical trials of its *Depo-Provera* injectable contraceptive, effective for three months, got under way. But when four years later the product was ready for distribution as *DMPA*, it was blocked by the FDA for fear of dangerous side-effects. Because it remained in regulatory limbo until 1992, AHP's oral contraceptive *Ovral* became the leading product of its kind. AHP got a publicity boost in 1968 by waiving patent royalties on its new bifurcated needle for smallpox injections. The World Health Organization's Global Smallpox Eradication Program used 200 million a year to eradicate smallpox by 1979.

Rather than wait years or even decades for a breakthrough, Abbott in 1962 copied Merck's strategy of overseas alliances by licensing the right from Dainippon Pharmaceutical Company of Osaka, Japan to manufacture that firm's radiopharmaceutical products. Two years later, the company merged with M&R Dietetic Laboratories of Columbus, maker of *Similac* infant formula, which became Abbott's Ross Products division and originator in 1973 of the *Ensure* adult medical nutritional supplement. That product put Abbott into competition with Pfizer's nutritional supplements. With $1 billion of sales by 1972, Pfizer was still a formidable opponent.

After health care, the next major initiative of the Great Society was an Omnibus Housing Act on August 10, 1965 to provide new rent supplements to, and use federal funds to buy, private housing for low-income families. In 1968, another housing act authorized $5.3 billion over three years for 1.7 million units of new and rehabilitated housing for the same group as well as to subsidize the rental of houses and apartment. Overseeing the effort was a Department of Housing and Urban Development (HUD), established on September 9, 1965. That agency consolidated 13,600 federal employees with a budget of $4.35 billion.

Federally financed and sponsored building projects benefited construction firms and contractors as well as the poor. The fixed asset value of non-housing, residential fixed assets more than doubled between 1960 and 1970 to $8.6 billion, of which 60% of the increase came after Johnson's legislation. Housing stock doubled as well to almost $170 billion, of which 75% of the increase occurred in the last half of the decade. Similar impressive gains, funded by government and private individuals, would be realized in the early 1970s. Less desirable but necessary for persons of marginal income were new mobile homes, amounting to nearly 2 million from 1969 through 1972. The value of all new construction that year reached $123.8 billion.

Public housing in Chicago
Although public housing projects were concentrated in big cities, impoverished rural areas were not neglected. The Appalachian Regional Development Act allocated $1.1 billion for the economic development of an eleven state area. Additionally, the Public Works and Economic Development Act authorized another $3.3 billion over five years for depressed areas and regions. Having seen rural poverty growing up, this was a particular interest of the President's.

For the other end of the social spectrum, Congress passed a law on September 29 creating a National Foundation of the Arts and Humanities (NFAH). Although financial assistance was directed to talented but struggling painters, actors, dancers, and musicians, the beneficiaries were perceived to include anyone who appreciated aesthetic beauty. Wealthy individuals increasingly fancied themselves connoisseurs of good artistic taste. They bid up the price of paintings such as Rembrandt's *Aristotle Contemplating the Bust of Homer*, which sold for over $2.2 million in 1961, and Velasquez's *Juan de Parcja*, that brought in $5 million in 1970. Such liberality not only brought attention to the art world, but higher attendance at art exhibits and business rationale to spend money on the construction of more museums. The public only began to question the wisdom of directing tax dollars to the NFAH after religious and conservative groups began to complain that some modern works of art were not only in bad taste but without real intrinsic value.

Blue skies over the Arizona desert

Lastly, the Great Society emphasized the environment as no administration had since Teddy Roosevelt. Water quality and clean air acts set standards for interstate rivers and lakes and car emissions. States were required to enforce the standards, as was the Department of Health, Education, and Welfare (HEW) if states proved recalcitrant. Several billion dollars were provided to match state spending on sewage treatment plants. The culmination of the clean air and water drive actually came during Richard M. Nixon's first administration with passage in 1969 of the National Environmental Policy Act and establishment the next year of the Environmental Protection Agency (EPA). While the former required all federal agencies to file an *Impact Statement* detailing the effect on the environment of all major projects, the latter consolidated various government departments with a renewed aim of combating pollution and environmental accidents such as an oil spill off the coast of Santa Barbara, California in 1969 that prompted legislation to force offenders to pay up to $14 million to repair damage.

The consequence over time of environmental legislation was to improve air and water quality, add to the expense of production, and create new industry niches. Particularly after the Clean Air Act of December 31, 1970 required cars to emit 90% less carbon monoxides and hydrocarbons by 1975 and 90% less nitrogen oxides by the next year, development of catalytic converters for exhaust systems by Delphi Automotive Systems became an urgent matter. Manufacturers who polluted rivers, streams, and other bodies of water came under the gun with the October 18, 1972 Federal Water Pollution Control Act Amendments. Three weeks before the fall Presidential election, Congress limited and made illegal without a permit effluent discharge, thus giving a boost to makers such as Crane Company of factory pollution control devices.

That final piece of legislation was remarkable for one other reason. It provided a whopping $24.7 billion for waste treatment plant construction, including $18 billion in federal grants to states. That was going too far for President Richard M. Nixon, who vetoed the bill only to be overridden by the House and Senate. The President had become alarmed that a $25 billion annual deficit for fiscal year 1968 inherited from Johnson, although turned briefly into a surplus for 1969 by Nixon's decision to reduce forces in Vietnam and make other defense cuts, had helped push the national debt up to $382.6 billion on June 30, 1972. Worse from a budgetary point of view, Great Society programs quickly spawned special interest groups whose lobbyists, like advocates for the aerospace and defense contracting industry, gave campaign contributions and applied other inducements and pressures on members of Congress with a goal of continuing said programs in perpetuity. Because so-called "entitlements" of Social Security, Medicare, and Medicaid as well as interest on the national debt continued to grow, from a structural point of view the budget eventually contained a dollar majority of non-discretionary items.

Abundant harvests in the American heartland

LBJ and the Congress got around to pleasing the other vital constituency under the Democrats' big tent — farmers — on November 5, 1965. The Omnibus Farm Bill provided cash payments as incentives not to plant wheat, cotton, and other crops where surpluses pushed down prices and farm income. The idea was to save small and tenant farmers, but because of mechanization and economies of scale the long term trend was contrary. The national catalogue of farm machinery now included 4.6 million tractors, 3 million trucks used in farming, 790,000 combines, and 635,000 corn pickers, actually less than in 1960 but with far greater capacity per machine.

That was good news for Deere, which passed IH as the number one farm equipment producer in 1963. However, the company boosted revenues above $1 billion three years later only by moving aggressively into lawn and garden tractors. In 1968, those products came with color options. Non-farm equipment became so popular that sales composed half Deere's revenue of over $2 billion by 1972.

Overall in 1970, rural America boasted 2.9 million farms and 9.7 million farmers on 1.12 billion acres. Over 1,580 farms had annual sales of at least $1 million. Monsanto's revolutionary *Lasso* herbicide, introduced in 1969, helped produce bumper crops of 4.1 million bushels of corn, 1.38 million bushels of wheat, 1.14 million bushels of soybeans, and 909,000 bushels of oats as well as growth for the company beyond the $1 billion of sales achieved in 1962. Nixon negotiated farm sales to Moscow to ship out much of the surplus. However, the Soviet Union's bumper crop two years later undermined exports and farm income that had grown to nearly $58 billion. The Agriculture Act of November 30, 1970, providing over $3.7 billion of annual subsidies, helped make up for shortfalls.

Meanwhile, the nation's 112 million cattle and 57 million hogs, increasingly fattened up by corn-enriched feed developed by ADM, and 20 million sheep had a total value of about $22.5 billion. Some farmers diversified into chickens and turkeys, boosting the former to 440 million and the latter to 7.5 million. A prime beneficiary was Cargill, expanding into broiler-chickens and feed-eggs-poultry as well as overseas to supplement the company's basic corn and flour milling operations. The company paid $1.20 for each chicken and $5.30 for each turkey, while cattle, by contrast, sold for $180 a head.

Under the Omnibus Farm law, land spared from the plough was supposed to be diverted to other purposes or permitted to go back to nature. This goal was consistent with the Kennedy administration's Retention and Multiple Use land policy, itself a continuation of FDR's conservation thrust, which did not permit further homesteading on valuable lands. Already on September 3, 1964, the National Wilderness Preservation System had designated 9.1 million acres of national forest as wild, wilderness, or canoe, in effect safeguarding that land permanently, subject to existing rights, against commercial use as well as road and building construction. The only exceptions were mining claims and mineral leases through December 31, 1983. However, restrictions angered western cattle-grazing, lumbering, and mining interests and led to fierce opposition to designation of a further 1.9 million acres in 1973. Total federal ownership of public land, now up to 755 million acres, seemed at one-third of the total excessive.

California redwood

Ironically, only Native Americans, who had possessed all land before the coming of Europeans, were able to whittle down Washington's holding. By the Alaska Native Land Claims Act of December 18, 1971, 53,000 Eskimos, Native Americans, and Aleuts received 40 million acres of federal land plus $962.5 million to divide amongst villages and regional corporations as compensation for past confiscations. Later Indian law suits for hundreds of millions of additional acres, including the Chippewa claim to half of Wisconsin's harvestable natural resources, were impractical. The Sioux did win an award in 1990 from the Supreme Court of $107 million for the 1877 seizure of the Black Hills in South Dakota.

One industry that opposed a strict conservation policy was Big Lumber. Although Weyerhaeuser added 1.8 million acres to its holdings by buying Dierks Forest in Arkansas and Oklahoma, the company subsequently in 1962 lost billions of board feet in the northwest to Typhoon Frieda. A major salvaging operation and shipment of softwood lumber to Japan saved the day economically. Purchase of the Hamilton Paper Company of Pennsylvania as well as an initial public offering in 1963 kept growing the business.

Competition came from Georgia-Pacific (G-P), which bought the Crossett Lumber Company in 1962 to increase its forested acres by 565,000. Throughout the decade, the company continued to buy up land, pulp and paper mills, pine plywood production plants, and chemical facilities. When sales reached $1 billion in 1968, the FTC took a look at G-P's dominance in the Southeast and did not like what it saw. In 1972, the commission forced the company to spin off the Louisiana-Pacific Corporation, with assets of $305 million. Even so, G-P kept expanding by purchasing redwood forests and saw mills in California. The next year, sales surpassed $2.2 billion.

The emergence in the lumber and paper industry of Boise Cascade in Idaho, Mead of Dayton, and Westvaco of Sidney, New York put pressure on IP. The company diversified into real estate and manufacturing of medical products. However, heavy debt and interest payments hurt profits and made IP vulnerable to takeover attempts. To survive, the company was forced to sell off non-core businesses.

THE RESURGENCE OF AMERICAN FINANCIAL INSTITUTIONS

Meanwhile, the innovation of the American Express card signaled to banks and other financial institutions that the time might be right to resume a strategy of helping Americans borrow more aggressively against future income for present prosperity. Success with such a program would help fend off the challenge of non-bank intermediaries such as Fidelity with its mutual funds which threatened to siphon off savings to the stock market and other investments. A prerequisite, however, was achieving larger size, financial reserves, and confidence to provide unsecured credit. Because of legal and regulatory restrictions, the 42 US bank holding companies in existence at beginning of 1961 controlled only 1,463 commercial bank offices, or 6% of the total, as well as only 8% of all deposits. High profile mergers such as Manufacturers Hanover were permissible if in one locale. Such also was Boston's State Street Bank and Trust Company absorbing rivals Rockland-Atlas National Bank and Second Bank.

Some banks got bigger by building branch offices in city neighborhoods and the suburbs. By 1966, 70% of all bank resources were held in such locales. Typical was California Federal in the greater Los Angeles area. In 1970 and prior to expanding in the direction of San Diego, the firm attained a size of $2 billion of assets.

On the other hand, mergers of insurance companies proceeded without much concern by federal regulators about financial strength and geographic reach. That neglect can be explained by the fact that many firms acquired entities with complementary, rather than overlapping, product lines. For example in 1962, Connecticut General took over the Aetna Insurance Company (not Aetna Life) to obtain a property and casualty division. Lincoln National bought American States Insurance Company of Indianapolis to become a "one stop shop" for customers and by 1967 the 10th largest insurance company in the US and the largest life re-insurer in the world.

Genealogy of US Financial Industry (Non-Insurance), 1946-2005

In 1963, Continental obtained the American Casualty Company of Reading, Pennsylvania, which was the third largest fire and casualty company, to reach combined premium of $600 million and assets of $1 billion. That was still only a quarter of Travelers' size before that company bought Phoenix Insurance in 1966. INA got a presence on the west coast and a foot in workers compensation by gobbling up Pacific Employers Group. The insurance industry was so lucrative that in 1970 conglomerate ITT bought the Hartford for $1.4 billion. Back in the banking industry, an amendment in 1966 to the Bank Holding Act of 1956, followed by a second amendment four years later, caused a huge consolidation. For example, Bank of New York took over Empire Trust Company, expanded its presence in the Manhattan area, and then moved out beyond New York City into the suburbs. By end of 1972, 1,607 bank holding companies owned 2,720 banks with 13,441 branches controlling 61.5% of total commercial bank deposits and 63.2% of total commercial bank assets. Now the time was ripe for a move into full-service banking.

First and foremost, that meant getting on the credit card bandwagon and enjoying the boost in revenue and profits that flowed from annual fees equal to two or three percent off every consumer credit card purchase as well as interest on rolled over balances. Purchase of computers, albeit at first refrigerator size like the *IBM 1401* with only 4 kilobytes of memory and able to handle only basic calculations, provided a potential capability for processing thousands, but later millions of credit card transactions. First National City Bank got into the business as early as 1965, then came out with its own *Everything* card two years later. The more important long-term development was Wells Fargo helping Master Charge (later in 1979 MasterCard) introduce a credit card that could be licensed through any bank. After First National City switched over in 1969, Master Charge was on its way to industry leadership. Because American Express required customers to pay off balances each month, the company swiftly fell behind.

The financial clout of US banks to reassert themselves against competitors came none too soon. Paral-

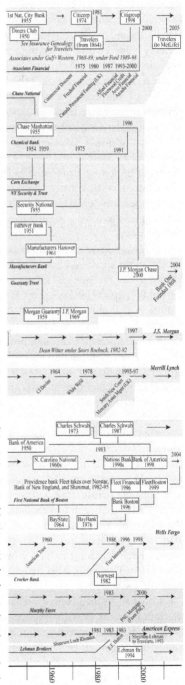

leling the resurrection of international cartels in industry, European banking consortia were pooling assets to advance national and Old World economic interests. In 1968, Fannie Mae became a private company to buy mortgages beyond traditional government loan limits and reach a broader segment of the national housing market. That development actually helped banks by letting them sell old mortgages and obtain capital to make new ones, in the process earning closing costs and other fees. Two years later, Congress doubled the fun by chartering the Federal Home Loan Mortgage Corporation, popularly known as Freddie Mac, as a "stockholder-owned corporation to create a continuous flow of funds to mortgage lenders supporting home ownership and rental housing." Mortgages bought from lending institutions were then packaged as securities and resold to investors.

What was not favorable for banks was foundation two years later by American Express of an asset management group to attract the funds of institutional investors. All the major brokerage firms such as Dean Witter already had departments targeting banks' best customers. Investment banking firms led by Morgan Stanley got a leg up with corporate clients by creating specialized merger and acquisition divisions. A natural progression was to offer a combination of services, including investment advice and money management.

Likewise, insurance companies leveraged their relationships with wealthy individuals to offer other services. The rise of Marsh & McLennan from a company in 1962 with only $52 million of revenue and net income of $5 million was due to decisions to offer shares to the public, expand brokerage operations in Europe, and then use waxing financial might to acquire Putnam Investments in 1970 and build up assets under management to $2 billion. Another fast comer was American Insurance Union, which restructured in 1962 to sell commercial insurance through brokers, offer personal accident insurance through a subsidiary, make acquisitions to build up a Domestic Brokerage Group, and construct a property-casualty network. In 1967, all these operations were consolidated under the name American Insurance Group (AIG).

Formidable and even more flexible was Allstate. The company had to be open to change because the car insurance industry ran afoul of prevailing state "fault" systems wherein guilty parties were liable for the expenses of victims but more often than not contested and dragged out court proceedings. The problem was that insurance policies could not be canceled during the duration of their terms. Even tougher underwriting standards and higher premiums did not compensate for all the claims paid out. Thus, while remaining in car insurance and championing auto safety measures including seat belts and airbags, Allstate began to supplement revenue and profits by founding in 1961 the *Allstate Motor Club*, offering auto, boat, and recreational vehicle financing, and buying savings and loan, mortgage-banking, and mutual fund companies. Its life insurance division hit $1 billion of policy in force in 1963, while property premium ballooned six years later to nearly $1.5 billion. That year, Allstate had 11.4 million policies in force. The company employed 30,000 persons.

Other insurance concerns that got into mutual funds included Travelers and Connecticut General. Equally important for success was diversification of product lines. In 1965, Continental introduced long-term care insurance, then doubled its value by going public three years later. To distinguish itself, American Finance Life Insurance Company changed one word of its name to *Assurance*, and hence coined the acronym AFLAC while changing its strategy to concentrate on "cluster selling" to groups rather than individuals.

Yachts in St. Petersburg, Florida

However, life insurance remained the bread and butter of the industry. Companies and divisions specializing in that product had $240 billion of assets by 1972, covering life insurance in force of $1.63 trillion.

ECONOMICS AS AN EXTENSION OF POLITICS

The Tet offensive by Communist forces in Vietnam of January 1968 as well as other international uncertainties caused speculative buying of gold in world markets. As the price was bid up, the danger was renewed that foreigners would demand gold for dollars. To surmount the crisis, the Johnson administration agreed with Western European nations to establish an official $35 an ounce price for gold, forbid sale of gold by monetary authorities on the free market, and yet permit the free market price to continue to fluc-tuate. Only when Congress removed the legal requirement of a gold reserve equal to 25% of US currency was $10.4 billion in the precious metal freed to satisfy temporarily interna-tional demand.

Next on June 28, Congress finally passed a one year, 10% surcharge on personal and corporate income to cover the rising cost of the Vietnam War and Great Society programs. Since LBJ had decided not to run for reelection, it was Vice President Hubert H. Hum-phrey of Minnesota who narrowly lost to Nixon. More interested in economics as an extension of politics rather than as a means in itself to achieve a more prosperous nation, the new President made legislative concessions, as detailed above, to the Democratic con-trolled Congress not merely to preserve but extend the social-welfare state. He also went along with a Treasury proposal, subsequently accepted by the House and Senate, to install a minimum tax, effective in 1970, that would compel Americans with high incomes to pay an additional 10% tax on the amount to which their reductions of tax liability exceeded $30,000. This fairly simple flat tax was later in 1976 increased to 15% on a larger taxable base. Two years later, Congress adopted an Alternative Minimum Tax (AMT) law that taxed capital gains less an exempted amount of $20,000 at 20%, and then in the 1980s was computed on ordinary income, less an exempted amount for various classes of taxpayers (married, single, etc.) that failed to keep up with inflation at rates that eventually rose to a maximum of 28%.

By 1970, export of all goods and services expanded to $57 billion. Most important were non-electrical machinery, transportation equipment, electrical machinery, and metals and manufacturing. Because of Canadian imports, first in rank since 1945, as well as $9 billion of Japanese cars, machines, and other products crossing the Pacific in double the proportion as US exports went the other way, the same categories dominated $55.8 billion of imports. Only LBJ's insistence on "voluntary quotas" on import of Japanese steel and textiles, continuation of the 1959 quota on petroleum imports, and other limitations on sugar, meat, and dairy products held the US balance of payments level.

However in 1971, yet another surge of foreign demand for gold in exchange for US dollars drained over $3 billion from the Treasury reserve, including $1.2 billion in August alone. Nixon responded by suspending the convertibility of dollars into gold, imposing a 10% surcharge on imports, and reducing foreign aid by 10%. He also proposed to stimulate the economy by repealing the 7% excise tax on automobiles, reinstating the 7% tax credit on business investment, and increasing the minimum standard deduction for individuals to $1,300. These proposals were accepted by Congress in the Revenue Act of December 10. Additionally, the House and Senate tacked on a provision permitting US exporters to send goods through Domestic International Sales Corporation (DISC), which were later renamed Foreign Sales Corporations (FSC). Taxes on 50% of DISC income would be deferred indefinitely if 95% of DISC receipts and assets were export-related. Little noticed at time by foreign competitors, the law became a major point of contention between the US and Europe a quarter century later. For the moment, Europeans focused on the 10% surcharge on imports.

Realizing action must be taken to revamp the old Bretton Woods system and assure Washington that Paris would no longer follow de Gaulle's policy of exchanging American tourist dollars for gold, new French president Georges Pompidou agreed that the so-called Group of Ten powers — the United States, France, Britain, Germany, Japan, Canada, Italy, and the Benelux countries — would set new currency exchange rates at their meeting of December 17-18, 1971 at the Smithsonian in the capital. After the heads of government re-pegged the value of the dollar to gold at $38 an ounce (approved by Congress March 31, 1972), Nixon removed the surtax on imports. As for the tax cuts and other stimulative measures in the Revenue Act, they did contribute to a 9.9% increase in GDP. A $6 billion increase in federal receipts for the fiscal year to $208.6 billion was nearly offset by a $4.2 billion rise in expenditures to $231.9 billion.

Just to make certain that the country remembered its commitment to society's disad-vantaged while stepping into polling booths, both houses of Congress passed on October 17, 1972 and the President signed amendments to the Social Security Act. Not only was the wage base boosted to $9,000, with regular annual increases compensating for inflation thereafter, but the combined tax rate that included the component for Medicare was pro-jected to increase from 5.2% to 5.85%, still matched by employers. A Supplemental Security Income program for the aged, blind, and disabled was created to replace joint federal-state programs as of January 1, 1974. The overall burden of non-income taxes on wage-earners rose steadily.

Although state and local governments already received $39 billion in federal assis-tance, three days later the House and Senate agreed to Nixon's idea for a Revenue Sharing

Act to distribute $30.2 billion of federal tax revenues over five years to state and local governments to supplement annual revenues that for the 50 states alone had grown to $98.6 billion and all local governments to approximately $102 billion. Much to the joy of governors, mayors, and state and local legislators, there were no strings attached. However, had they thought more carefully about the action, they might have realized that the rising expenditures to which they had committed and would commit themselves on education, highways, public welfare, health and hospitals, police and fire protection, as well as other obligations would put them at increasing risk should federal largesse be curtailed. In the final analysis, generosity from Washington depended on the continued growth of the American economy and businesses.

In the 1960s, corporate profits rose from $50 billion to $86 billion, a steady 5.5% annual increase. Despite a cut in rates, taxes on corporate income mounted at an average 5.9% pace to $38.3 billion. Though it may have been in the government's fiscal interest to accommodate further mergers and acquisitions to maximize business profits, the Sherman and Clayton Anti-Trust laws were still on the books. The Supreme Court interpreted those and other laws in 1966-68 to block Pabst Brewing Company's purchase of Blatz, void a franchise program by the Brown Shoe Company, a 90 year old St. Louis area company that became famous for its *Buster Brown* shoes, rule that Borden Company's marketing of milk under its own as well as private brand names was price discrimination that lessened competition, and defeat once and for all P&G's 1957 bid to take over Clorox as a monopolistic attack.

The justices did on January 15, 1968 permit the merger of the Pennsylvania and New York Central railroads, however. Although the ICC rejected Southern Pacific-Acheson Topeka Santa Fe's bid to take over the Western Pacific two years earlier, the clear trend was to permit regional powerhouses for greater cost and operating efficiency. Thus, the Union Pacific and Southern Railway came to dominate west of the Mississippi, Norfolk and Western built strength in the Midwest, and the Chessie System, combining in 1973 the C&O, B&O, and Western Maryland, prospered in the east. Without these mergers, the railroad industry would have succumbed completely to competition from other modes of transportation. On the other hand, the decision in 1967 by the US Postal Service to remove most first class and storage mail business from the railroads was a blow from which Penn Central, even after Congress voted on February 5, 1970 to provide loans totaling $6.4 billion to modernize and revitalize the nation's railway system of 220,000 miles carrying 800 billion ton-miles of freight, about 39% of the total, could not recover. Railroads generated only $260 million of passenger revenue.

When Penn Central filed a bankruptcy petition of June 22, 1970, Congress immediately stepped in. Senators and representatives agreed to provide $125 million of specific federal loan guarantees for the company. However, they then passed the Rail Passenger Service Act of 1970, effective May 1, 1970, to consolidate most intercity passenger operations within a new system called AMTRAK. The profitable Washington to New York City *Metroliner* helped boost AMTRAK's demand by 11% in 1973.

Trauma in railroads seemed to validate the wisdom of corporate leaders not putting all financial eggs in one industry basket. The 1960s saw the peak of the merger boom for conglomerates. Mergers and acquisitions by such entities of manufacturing and mining companies exceeded 2,400 in 1968 alone. Among the polyglot giants created were LTV in electronics, airplanes, and steel, Litton Industries in typewriters, ships, and other non-related businesses, and ITT taking over Sheraton hotels, Hartford Fire Insurance, Levitt & Sons home construction, and Avis Rental Cars, though the latter two were subsequently divested and Avis, purchased for $51 million by ITT, became far more significant after introducing its Wizard real-time information management and reservation system in 1972. Among industry titans that grew larger by expanding multinational operations were GM, Standard Oil of New Jersey, Ford, and IBM. By 1970, mergers and acquisitions specialists were doing 5,000 deals annually worth on average $2 million.

There was still room in some regulated industries for small players to surge into prominence. For example, Tom Fatjo started American Refuse Systems in 1967 to collect garbage in his own neighborhood in Houston, Texas because the previous garbage collector was unreliable. When two years later, he had the size and strength to buy Browning-Ferris Machinery Company and rename the combined entity Browning Ferris Industries, his solid waste services businesses was booming. By 1972, he had $100 million in revenue, 4,200 employees, and operations in 26 states, Puerto Rico, and Canada.

Aside from public utilities, the other industry that was still dominated by regulated monopolies was telephone and telegraph communications. Unlike the railroads with their dispersed strength, AT&T kept right on growing with the population, more so as pay phone connections accelerated, until annual revenue from local and long distance telephone service reached $100 billion in 1972 or about 8.5% of the economy. Western Electric turned out units like hotcakes while Ma Bell expanded its phone switching network and lines. A trans-Pacific telephone cable in 1964, complementing one laid across the Atlantic eight years earlier, brought the cost of international calls down to $12 for the first 3 minutes. In fact, the monolith's only competition in wired communication was several small telephone companies accounting for only 4% of the market. These included GTE, United Utilities, later to gain fame as Sprint, the Century Telephone and Electronics Company, the Citizens Utilities Company, and Allied Telephone of Arkansas.

Meanwhile, however, Western Union built on its intercity facsimile microwave system to introduce in 1964 an intercontinental microwave signals system to replace wired lines altogether. Bell Labs responded with a network of radio transmitters in hexagonal "cells" using multiple radio frequencies to create the possibility of wireless cell phones connecting citizens in moving vehicles as they had New York City police in 1924 and St. Louis cops since 1946.

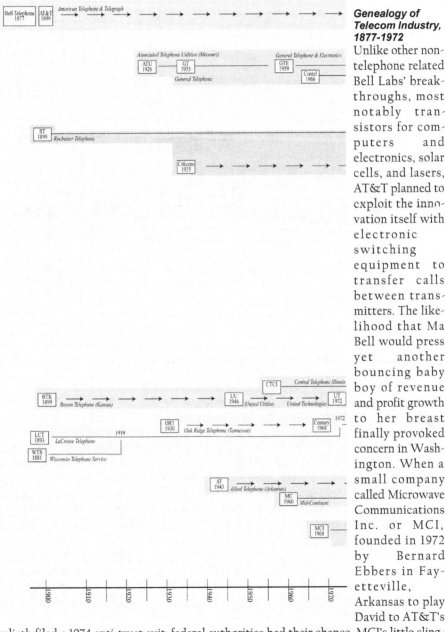

Genealogy of Telecom Industry, 1877-1972

Unlike other non-telephone related Bell Labs' breakthroughs, most notably transistors for computers and electronics, solar cells, and lasers, AT&T planned to exploit the innovation itself with electronic switching equipment to transfer calls between transmitters. The likelihood that Ma Bell would press yet another bouncing baby boy of revenue and profit growth to her breast finally provoked concern in Washington. When a small company called Microwave Communications Inc. or MCI, founded in 1972 by Bernard Ebbers in Fayetteville, Arkansas to play David to AT&T's goliath filed a 1974 anti-trust suit, federal authorities had their chance. MCI's little slingshot would within a decade splinter apart the greatest monopoly in US business history.

HIGH TIDE FOR US MANUFACTURING

In 1960, the US made nearly half the world's automobiles. Detroit also turned out millions of trucks and buses, both increasingly important as the former took domestic freight market share from railroads and the latter transported 366 million passengers on Greyhound Corporation, with over $300 million of annual revenues, and other inter-city bus lines. Although airline travel would chop long-distance bus transport nearly 8% over the next two decades, intra-city bus traffic exploded with Washington's interest in mass transit. Larger vehicle production helped offset a relative decline in US auto production share to 28% by 1970.

Ford Mustang
In absolute figures, however, the US auto industry was still humming. In 1964, Ford captured the imagination of young men with its *Mustang* model, and then cooperated with Motorola and RCA to install the first eight-track tape players in its cars. When GM's Olds division introduced a front-wheel drive model in 1966, it surged past 100 million cars sold in aggregate. Chrysler was still the third player in the industry but highly profitable. AMC, too, prospered when its *Rambler* climbed to third place in model year sales. Lesser companies, including Studebaker, diminished to insignificance or died off.

To compete with Avis rental cars, a company sprang up called Executive Leasing. It had been founded in St. Louis in 1957 by a US Navy veteran Jack Taylor who had served in the Second World War on the aircraft carrier *USS Enterprise*. As increasing airline passenger service created greater demand for rental cars at airports, Taylor in 1969 renamed his company Enterprise Rent-A-Car and expanded to Atlanta. His fleet of cars grew to 5,000, providing a small but promising new market for Detroit's vehicles.

That was more business for car part makers as well. Motorola carved out another niche with silicon rectifiers for auto alternators to replace less durable generators. Dana enhanced its position by buying Perfect Circle as well as companies that supplied *Atlas* forgings, connecting rods, and cam shafts. It got into the $4.5 billion replacement parts market by purchasing Victor Manufacturing & Gasket in 1966. The company's sales topped $500 million the next year. Cash flow funded investments in British and European companies from 1972 onward.

Radial tire

As for Goodyear, demand for tires boosted sales to $2 billion by 1964, and then $4 billion by 1972. To keep up, Firestone acquired Dayco (formerly Dayton Tire), clung tight to its relationship with Ford, and came out with non-skid tread and the first US radial tire with cord angles of 90 degrees and a belt over-wrap under the tread surface for less distortion under load. Cooper Tire & Rubber Company, an Akron based entity, claimed a smaller share of the market. Cooper secured a long-term cost advantage by building non-unionized plants in Arkansas, Atlanta, and Los Angeles.

At 2,500 pounds of steel per car, demand from auto makers averaged 15-20 million tons of steel during the 1960s. As well as making continuous casting standard industry practice, US Steel and other companies built hot-strip mills to service Detroit. To pay for capital investment, in April 1962 they acted in concert to boost prices $6 per ton, but fearing an inflationary effect Kennedy bullied them into canceling the move. Thereafter, the industry was unable to institute coordinated across-the-board increases.

Exposed financially by decisions to build an integrated steel plant in Burns Harbor, Indiana to produce up to 5.3 millions tons annually of sheet and plate steel as well as a BOF plant in Lackawanna, Pennsylvania, Bethlehem Steel made out by supplying big construction projects, including Madison Square Garden in New York City and the Delaware Memorial Bridge. By 1973, the company was producing 23.7 million tons of raw steel, going into 16.3 million tons of finished steel, with net income of $207 million. On the other hand, lesser steel makers decided to stop producing beverage cans. Aluminum, which was much lighter and more cost competitive, took the market. Steel companies did continue to make tin-plated food cans, however, keeping the beverage can loss to a few million tons of steel annually. There was enough demand around to lift even medium-size players like Inland of Chicago to $1 billion of revenue by 1966.

One reason that traditional steel-makers passed through the decade in reasonable shape was that so-called mini-mills using electric furnaces that melted scrap like old steel cans produced only 250,000 tons a year, about 0.2% of the market. However, after adding continuous casters and small bar mills to produce reinforced rods, small diameter bars, and angles less expensively, they became an increasing threat. An example was Nuclear Corporation, a maker of nuclear instruments and electronics, which in 1967 took over Vulcraft, founded in 1946 to make chain link fences, steel building supplies, and other such products. Building a steel bar mini-mill in Darlington, South Carolina to take advantage of non-union labor, the company prospered by producing steel joists for non-residential building construction such as shopping centers, schools, and office buildings. Most of its business was in Texas, Alabama, and the South. It changed its name in 1972 to Nucor and began a steady rise.

A more immediate threat to big steel makers was foreign imports. The share claimed by overseas competitors climbed from 5.4 million tons in 1963 to 10 million tons two years later to 18 million tons in 1968, or 14% share of the US market. To halt the erosion, which halved profits and hampered modernization efforts, LBJ strong-armed restraints on imports from Japan and Europe. Federal and local subsidies for steel companies failed to reverse the trend.

Off-shore oil platform, (courtesy Phillips Petroleum)

Meanwhile, the quota on petroleum and petroleum products remained in effect until May 1973. Restrained supply of crude limited oil refinery capacity and hurt profitability, which as always relied upon economies of scale. The fundamentals of the game for domestic producers in the 1960s became exploration at home and overseas to secure new reserves of oil, expansion of refining and pipeline capacity to fill every year hundreds of thousands more gas tanks, and increasing brand competition to impress an impressionable public. The government tried to strike a balance between upholding antitrust laws to promote competition and permitting business consolidations to improve the financial health and efficiency of the industry.

One big find of natural gas or oil could turn a small company into a major player. Occidental Petroleum, for example, discovered the former in 1961 by deep drilling in the Sacramento basin, and then four years later tapped its first billion barrel field of the latter in

Libya in North Africa. Meanwhile, Texas Eastern, after buying Pyrofax, a propane retailing company, from Union Carbide for $30 million and extending the Big Inch pipeline into New England to provide liquefied petroleum gases to that region, joined Amoco in 1963 in a hunt for oil and gas in the North Sea. Phillips too struck black gold under that body of water six years later. But the biggest find of the decade was Prudhoe Bay in north Alaska in 1968 by Arco, Sohio, and British Petroleum. Insufficient financial resources to exploit its share caused Sohio to merge into British Petroleum the next year.

Wherever the discovery, companies that provided oil well services profited. Founded in 1919 as the New Method Oil Well Cementing Company in Oklahoma, Halliburton finally came to prominence in 1962 by buying Brown & Root. That was an engineering and construction company that had built the first off-shore oil platform fifteen years earlier. Halliburton began winning energy related building projects around the world.

Another merger compelled by the financial demands of energy exploration and development was Union Oil's takeover of Pure Oil Company of Illinois in 1965. With a presence in 37 states, Union Oil was now in position to explore and drill in southern Alaska, the Gulf of Mexico, Indonesia, the North Sea, and the gulf of Thailand, where it found natural gas. Arco itself was formed in 1966 after Atlantic merged with Richfield, which had merged with Sinclair Oil two years earlier. Pennzoil in 1970 was taken over by United Gas Corporation, which then spun off its gas distribution unit into a company later called Entex.

Despite all these moves, annual US domestic oil production peaked in 1970 at 3.5 billion barrels of oil, or about 9.6 million per day. Despite construction of the Alaskan Oil Pipeline, the industry began a long slow decline to under 6 million barrels a day by 2002. Exotic projects, such as Sun Oil's 1967 investment in a subsidiary called Great Canadian Oil Sands Limited to process Athabasca tar sands, estimated to contain 300 billion barrels of recoverable oil but yielding only 45,000 barrels a day, had little effect. Extraction of oil from shale deposits in the Rocky Mountains that held twice the tar sand total was far more costly than traditional methods of pumping oil from underground deposits. Falling natural gas reserves, state laws restricting the burning of coal with high-sulfur content, such as the bituminous deposits PPL had to use as its anthracite reserves diminished, and the unavailability in most areas of large hydro-electric plants inhibited a switch to practical energy alternatives. Nevertheless, between 1960 and 1972, the nation's overall production of energy rose from 41.7 quadrillion British Thermal Units (BTU) to 72.2 quadrillion BTU. The share contributed by petroleum jumped from 36% to 42% while coal plunged from 27% to 17%. Natural gas rose incrementally from 33% toward 36%

Nuclear power, which for a brief time had appeared to be the ultimate answer to US and world energy needs, was by 1972 beset by mounting technical and political obstacles and limited in the country to only three dozen plants producing only 576 trillion BTU or 0.8% of the country's total energy output. Hydro-electric generators produced over 5 times as much, by comparison. Americans began to have doubts about the wisdom of building more nuclear installations in densely populated areas, such as the Cook Nuclear Plant of American Electric Power (AEP) in the Chicago area on the shores of Lake Michigan. It was only a matter of time, some believed, until the intrinsic danger of the technology resulted in a catastrophic accident.

Thus, it became advisable to drop the quota on imported petroleum and petroleum products, worth about $2.8 billion in 1970. As oil became a commodity whose price fluctuated globally depending upon world supply and demand, a surer method of securing a steady flow of revenue in the industry was by control of refining facilities and pipelines. Coming to that conclusion in 1969, Koch, a small, privately held oil business out of Wichita, Kansas, bought Pine Bend Refineries of Minnesota. The company branched out into natural gas, petroleum coke, coal mines, and asphalt to produce revenue of $1 billion by 1972.

Another comer was Amerada-Hess. The Amerada part had started in 1919 as a British company looking for oil in North America using geophysicist methods while Leon Hess had founded a successful business in the 1930s transporting by truck the "resid" or thick refining leftovers from the refining process for resale as heating fuel to hotels. Over decades, he had expanded into refining itself, and then purchased pipelines and gas stations. Williams Brothers also stepped into the big time in 1966 by buying the Great Lakes Pipe Line Company for $287 million.

Meanwhile, the various corporations that had been spawned by the break-up of Rockefeller's Standard Oil found that similarity of title was a marketing draw-back. They moved to distinguish themselves by adopting new brand names. Thus, Sohio, Amoco, Exxon, Mobil, and Chevron eventually appeared. The latter was originally the logo like a corporal's stripes fashioned by Standard Oil of California. Other competitors also refined their marketing approaches. The Ohio Company was renamed Marathon with a tag line "Best in the long run," Texaco advised Americans to "Trust your car to the man who wears the star," and Gulf attracted customers with an orange disc sign. Although many drivers were loyal to a brand, others did not care so long as gas remained affordable. In 1972, a typical price was 32.9 cents a gallon, falling another four cents whenever there was a "gas war."

Pratt & Whitney JT8D engine
Low fuel costs were essential for the airline industry, coming fully into its own in the 1960s. *B-727s*, using Pratt & Whitney JT8D engines, and *DC-9s* were the main-stays that steadily phased-out propeller aircraft and made flying times shorter and air travel more comfortable. Adoption of IBM's Semi-Automated Business Research Environment (SABRE) for computer booking within the US as well as to Canada and Mexico created the second largest real-time data processing system after the government's Semi-Automatic Ground Environment or SAGE system that integrated radar and computers for national air defense. IBM also collaborated with Sperry-Rand and Lockheed to assemble a computerized air traffic control system. By mid-decade, US airlines were carrying annually 92 million domestic paying passengers, 943 million domestic ton-miles of non-mail cargo, and 226 million domestic ton-miles of mail. In the 1960s, annual revenue advanced over 700% to $11.2 billion.

After buying Capital Airlines in June 1961, United Airlines became the world's largest air carrier. The company spent the rest of the decade consolidating its position only to suffer a sharp reversal in 1969 when the Civil Aeronautics Board delayed its application for Asian and other international routes. That decision undercut the profitable of its US mainland to Hawaii flights and helped turned a $45 million profit into a $46 million loss.

Another part of the downturn was due to premature purchase of *B-747 Jumbo* jets that carried a maximum 500 tourist-class passengers but high operating costs not compensated for by purely domestic routes.

B-747

Rather it was PanAm which did well in 1970 with *B-747s* crossing from New York to London and Frankfurt. That company's main competition was TWA, using the same plane as well as *DC-10s* and Lockheed 10s and 11s with 400 passenger capacities. Because PanAm owned no connecting US domestic routes, TWA soon overtook its rival as the top transatlantic airline. In short order, PanAm fell on hard times.

Not so Northwest, which in 1969 began a San Francisco or Los Angeles to Honolulu to Tokyo service. Tie-ins from Minneapolis-St.Paul to the west coast as well as Chicago to Hawaii proved so popular that the airline led the industry in percent profitability. Likewise, Continental Airlines improved its position by transporting US military personnel to Vietnam during the war, competing with Northwest on west coast to Hawaii service, and forming Air Micronesia to connect Honolulu with Saipan. Spun off by LTV in 1972, Braniff also flew *B-747s* to Hawaii and then smaller planes into the South Pacific.

Braniff's other business was flying business passengers and tourists to Latin America on *DC-8s*. Its main competition came from Delta, connecting California with the Caribbean, Eastern, flying to the Bahamas, and Trans Caribbean Airways, purchased by American Airlines in 1970. The former hit the jackpot after Nixon approved on May 19, 1972 its bid to take over struggling Northeast. That airline's direct flights from New York and Boston to Florida made Delta a major player.

As for regional carriers, Alaska Airlines was carving out a nice business in the nation's 50th state, Southwest sprang up with cheap fares between Dallas, Houston, and San Antonio, and Allegheny Airways built up a base by acquiring Lake Central Airlines in 1968 and Mohawk Airlines four years later. Its territory ranged from the east coast as far west as St. Louis.

As the airline industry reached maturity, however, it seemed almost passé. The reason was that President Kennedy had told the nation in 1961 "we choose to go to the moon" and thrust the space program run by the National Aeronautics and Space Administration (NASA) into high gear. That dramatic decision, on top of increasing jet passenger airplane orders and Vietnam War spending, meant big pay days for virtually all aerospace and defense contractors. Between 1961 and 1972, the federal government spent $775 billion on national defense programs, of which 27% was paid for procurement of military hardware.

However, the government did not pay in advance, so that some companies had to combine resources to afford development costs. In 1961, LTV was formed from the merger of Ling-Temco, a Dallas-based company specializing in electrical engineering and construction as well as missile electronics, with Vought as was Martin-Marietta from the link up of Martin with building and road construction firm American-Marietta. Thereafter, Martin-Marietta built the *Titan* missile that carried McDonnell's *Gemini VII* spacecraft that docked with Lockheed's *Agena* spacecraft in 1965. Lockheed continued working on *Polaris* missiles even while developing the top secret *SR-71 Blackbird* spy plane. McDonnell, too, was overburdened handling the *Gemini* program, the vertical take-off and lift (VTOL) or *AV-8b Harrier* jump-jet, the *F-15 Eagle* replacement for its *F-4* fighter, the Navy's *Talos* missile to fight MiGs in Vietnam, and the *Tomahawk* cruise missile program. It merged with Douglas in 1967, which helped that company afford the *DC-10* airliner. Additionally, NAA saw gold over the horizon if it could just win a contract to build a *B-1* bomber to replace its *B-52.* Company executives decided to merge into Rockwell Standard Corporation, which was doing well in the automobile, electronic, industrial products markets, to insure their future.

F-16

Boeing, however, was mighty enough on its own to provide systems integration on *Apollo* missions and build *Lunar Orbiters* even while turning out *B-727*s and *B-747*s. Another powerful contractor General Dynamics, riding high with *Polaris* submarine business for its Electric Boat division, which would be followed by an even more lucrative contract to build the ultimate naval weapons systems, *Trident* submarines, teamed with Grumman to build the *F-111.* That plane was the disappointing (from a military aviation point of view) consummation of Secretary of Defense and former Ford executive Robert S. McNamara's decision to demand an aircraft capable of filling both fighter and bomber functions. Though the *F-111* turned out to be proficient at neither in Vietnam, it did make several hundred million dollars for General Dynamics. More effective was the company's *F-16* lightweight fighter, beating out Northrop's *F-17* prototype in 1972. Including overseas sales, the *F-16* production line eventually by 2001 turned out over 4,000 planes, generating $80 billion in revenue.

AH64 Apache helicopter

The exigencies of war also feathered the nest of Howard Hughes, Jr., eventually so paranoid that he died a total recluse in 1976. Although an underbid by Hughes Aircraft to win a contract as sole supplier to the US Army of 1,434 *Oh-6 Cayuse* observation helicopters resulted in millions of dollars of losses between 1965 and 1970, expertise gained in the production as well as a subsequent absence of competition won the very lucrative contract in 1981 to build the *AH-64 Apache* helicopter. No fewer than 807 of the *A* model were produced by 1994, generating over $11 billion in revenue.

Military helicopters, *F-16* fighters, as well as *DC-10* and *B-747* passenger jets translated into revenue for Alcoa. Its aluminum alloys were essential for integral casting of blades, vanes for small gas turbine engines, jet engines, and even missiles. Production of the latter redounded to the benefit of Texas Instruments as well. Its integrated circuits helped provide guidance for *Shrike* missiles and *Minuteman I* and II ICBMs.

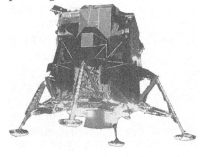

Apollo Lunar Orbiter

The culmination of the *Apollo* program was the landing on the moon on July 24, 1969 by astronauts Neil A. Armstrong and Edwin E. (Buzz) Aldrin, Jr. Dating back to 1956, the civilian space program had cost the taxpayers $24.6 billion, a large chunk of which had gone to aerospace and defense contractors. Included among the companies that profited was Motorola with a radio transponder on the *Apollo 11* lunar module. Westinghouse made the cameras that recorded Armstrong's first moon walk. After the excitement of involvement in the space race and other business making nuclear generators, the company found consumer durables boring and profits thin. It sold its electric house wares division in 1972 and its major appliances division two years later.

The Wide World of Entertainment

Walter Cronkite

Nevertheless, developments coming out of the defense and space race, including electronic guidance, control, and communication, miniaturization of instrumentation, lightweight metal alloys containing beryllium, titanium, molybdenum, refractory metals not damaged by exposure to high temperatures, and fuel cells that converted energy from hydrogen and oxygen into electricity all had commercial applications. Already on July 10, 1962, the first communications satellite *Telstar I* was launched into orbit at cost of $50 million to broadcast AT&T signals from Europe to America. The next year on May 7, *Telstar II* conveyed public TV pictures to the public. It was the *Syncom III* satellite that on October 10, 1964 let NBC broadcast live the opening ceremonies of the 1964 Summer Olympic games from Tokyo, Japan. That same year, the *Ranger VII* probe sent back the first TV pictures from the moon. News on TV delivered by NBC anchors Chet Huntley and David Brinkley and on CBS by Walter Cronkite became the chief source of information for Americans.

To generate more ad revenue, both networks began in 1963 to broadcast news in color. That year, Motorola stole a march on the competition with a color TV set with a rectangular picture tube. Its technological lead widened four years later after introduction of its *Quasar* all transistor model. To cut production and distribution costs, it opened manufacturing plants in different locations around the world. In fact, by 1968, color TVs from

Motorola as well as RCA, Zenith, and foreign importers such as Sony of Japan outsold black and white models. A record 97% of American households possessed at least one set.

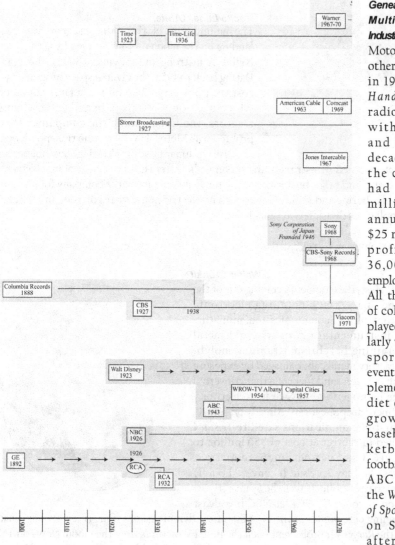

Genealogy of US Multi-Media Industry, 1888-1972
Motorola's other big seller in 1969 was a *Handi-Talkie* radio popular with adults and kids. By decade's end, the company had $800 million in annual sales, $25 million in profits, and 36,000 employees. All that splash of color on TV played particularly well with sporting events. To supplement a rich diet of home-grown baseball, basketball, and football games, ABC offered the *Wide World of Sports* show on Saturday afternoons. Americans voraciously consumed not only track and field but figure skating, downhill skiing, and other winter activities. Advertising revenue from commercials on news, sports, and popular TV series pushed combined profits for the three major networks and 619 affiliate stations to $2.3 billion in 1967.

TV signals over the public air waves were free. However, a different business model with a revenue stream not wholly dependent upon advertising arose in 1963 when a company that later became Comcast Corporation began a cable TV system for 1,200 subscribers in Tupelo, Mississippi. Cable made sense in communities which experienced diffi-culties receiving clear, static-free reception from satellite broadcasts. Comcast proved so successful in its niche that the company was incorporated in Pennsylvania. Rather than a listing on the New York Stock Exchange, shares were traded on the National Association of Securities Dealers Automated Quotations (NASDAQ). That exchange specialized in new, high-tech companies, many of whom turned out to be the fastest growers of later decades.

Quite naturally, the major networks looked upon cable TV as a long term threat to its business. CBS hedged its bet by getting into cable itself. However, in 1971, the FCC forced the company for anti-trust reasons to spin off that operation into an entity that would become Viacom. Another cable competitor that soon emerged was Cablevision.

What the major networks had that cable carriers lacked was a steady supply of new and original programming as well as live news and sports. While Viacom had been given some of CBS program-syndication operations, others had to rely on whatever old shows they could purchase. In many cases, licenses to air vintage TV series were bought by local UHF stations that had sprung up in big cities after the FCC removed its freeze on new licenses in 1952. Robert Edward ('Ted') Turner III came to own just such a one, WTBS in Atlanta, in 1970. An arrangement whereby UHF stations were carried by cable networks for a fee worked to the benefit of both, since a regional or even national audience translated into amplified advertising revenues. Recognizing that cable might turn out to be a major industry, magazine publisher Time started its Home Box Office (HBO) channel to show old movies in 1972.

Elizabeth Taylor as Cleopatra

Meanwhile, the motion picture industry viewed movies on UHF stations and cable net-works as a mixed blessing. TV still posed a poten-tially crippling obstacle to profitability, particularly as production costs, including salaries for big stars, rose and MGM's *Cleopatra* fiasco frightened studios away from blockbuster films. Rather, some of the most successful films were pro-duced by independent companies that raised financing on their own and made arrangements for the majors to assist with distribution to theaters. Such a gem was the 1969 sleeper *Easy Rider*, which cost $500,000 but grossed $25 million while advancing the career of actor Dennis Hopper. His contemporary Jack Nicholson also started on the road to mega-stardom and Academy Awards in smaller pictures. Critics applauded the fact that independent films had an edge and realism lacking in big screen productions.

That was not to suggest that major motion pictures with a popular theme and pol-ished look could not still attract tens of millions of Americans, as well as overseas theater-goers, and make money. Columbia Pictures proved the viability of traditional methods with the 1962 epic *Lawrence of Arabia* and 1968 best picture *Oliver!* Disney embarked on a string of successful comedies and musicals, including 1965 Oscar winner *Mary Poppins*, while Warner Brothers made *My Fair Lady* the same year and later in 1967 came out with

Camelot, both previously Broadway hits. The fact that each of these films starred in the main British actors and actresses was irrelevant to the ultimate address of gross receipts.

Suddenly, sole surviving Warner brother Jack sold out to Seven Arts for $95 million. Warner-Seven Arts then bought Atlantic Records to supplement Warner Brothers Records. In short order, Kinney National Services, publisher of *DC Comics* and *Mad Magazine*, gobbled up Warner-Seven Arts only to change its name in 1969 to Warner Communications. The company then strengthened its presence in music by taking over Elektra Records.

A strategic move into music was wise because US record sales were shooting "with a bullet," as it was called, toward $2 billion of revenue by 1973, a 9% annual growth rate. Introduction in 1963 of audio tape cassettes, and then cartridge audio tapes two years later that could be played in cars came at just the right time to advance the popularity of American musical stars. These included Presley, Bobby Vinton singing for the Epic Records label, and Sinatra on Reprise Records. The arrival in 1964 of John, Paul, George, and Ringo — the Beatles — in New York City and on the *Ed Sullivan Show* was just the beginning of a "British Invasion" that brought music popularity to a peak. CBS capitalized by setting up a branch of its Columbia Records in Britain, then founding a Columbia House direct mail order club, whose sales ascended steadily to $1.2 billion by 1978. The company formed a joint venture with Sony to market CBS products alongside Japanese products in the Far East. Sony had already in 1967 caused the entertainment industry to sit up and take notice with a *U-Matic* device to play prerecorded movies on a videotape cassette recorder (VCR) for home use. Other Japanese firms also moved aggressively to invade and conquer the US home electronics industry.

Rock 'n' Roll's popularity offset TV competition and permitted AM radio stations not only to survive but prosper. FM stations gravitated toward other audience niches, including R&B, Country, Easy Listening, and Classical music. An innovation that caught the public fancy was Talk Radio, begun in Boston in 1970 to fill dead spots between musical interludes and commercials. Excitement about sports teams naturally created an opportunity to gab and take phone calls, while political issues inspired anger and passion and inevitably increased listeners as well as ad revenue. After the forerunner of Clear Channel Communications purchased a station in San Antonio, Texas for $125,000, radio stations began to link up. Radio company executives began to realize that they could maximize revenues and profits by targeting a broader audience with more popular music and talk, hiring the most exciting radio "personalities," and building up radio networks to generate operating synergies and cut costs.

Economies of scale were also the be-all and end-all of publishing. Under attack by TV, movies, music, and radio, newspaper readership fell off, causing an industry consolidation that by 1969 left New York, Philadelphia, and Washington with only three major dailies, Los Angeles, Detroit, and St. Louis with only two, and San Francisco and other major cities with but one. To cut materials costs and secure supplies, the New York Times Company bought a 49% stake in Gaspesia Pulp & Paper Company of Quebec, Canada and 35% stake in Malbaie Paper Company, also of Canada. The firm obtained greater financial strength in 1967 by offering shares to the public. Thereafter, its corporate executives got into sports publishing by buying the *Golf Digest* magazine, *UK Golf World*, and *Tennis Magazine*. They created operating synergies by taking over regional newspapers, especially in Florida. Full diversity in information, entertainment, and media came after the remaining 49% of Arno

Press was purchased in 1971 and Cowles Communication was bought for $67 million. Control of that company brought ownership of *Family Circle* and *Look* magazines, the Cambridge Book Company, more regional newspapers, and a Memphis TV station.

Two other important newspapers also branched out beyond local areas. In 1961, the Washington Post Company bought *Newsweek* magazine. Out in Los Angeles the next year, the Times Mirror Company, publisher of the *Los Angeles Times*, suffered a reverse when its *Los Angeles Mirror* newspaper ceased publication. However, pumped up by ad revenue that topped 100 million lines of print by 1965, the company came back strong by setting up a joint Los Angeles Times-Washington Post News Service, buying General Features Corporation five years later, taking over the *Dallas Times Herald* in 1969 as well as broadcasting interests in Texas for $91.5 million in 1969, and absorbing *Newsday* magazine the next year.

As for other high-profile magazines, the *Saturday Evening Post* failed after 148 years of continuous operation before coming back as a quarterly. Increasing postal rates and competition for advertising dollars from TV closed the doors of *Life* and *Look*. The latter trend was accelerated by the increasing clout of advertising agencies, especially Interpublic Group (IG), a holding company for McCann-Erickson, which had combined entities dating from 1902 and 1911. IG offered shares to the public in 1971.

Older newspaper chains were not inactive. While Hearst bought up more papers, Gannett went public in 1967, built up its *Today* magazine, and then merged in 1971 with the Federated Publications chain. Meanwhile Knight Newspapers, founded in 1933 when John Knight inherited the *Beacon Journal* in Akron, Ohio and then later gained control of the *Miami Herald*, the *Detroit Free Press*, the *Chicago Daily News* (subsequently sold in 1959), and two Charlotte papers, scored a coup in 1969 by buying both the *Philadelphia Inquirer* and *Philadelphia Daily News* from Walter Annenberg. The company then sold shares to the public, as did Ridder Publications, a chain dating from 1892.

Newspaper companies could distribute their product directly to the public, of course. News stands on street corners and in coffee and donut shops pushed magazines. Increasingly, however, all manner of print products were carried by bookstore chains, most notably Walden Books, arising from a Bridgeport, Connecticut bookstore founded in 1933. Competing for mall space was B. Dalton Bookseller, founded as a Minnesota subsidiary of the Dayton-Hudson Company (later Target) in 1966. Meanwhile, New York based Barnes & Noble, holding court on Fifth Avenue, struggled until being taken over in 1971 by Leonard Riggio's Student Book Exchange chain of six college-based stores. Future competitor in big box bookstores Borders was started modestly that same year as a local establishment in Ann Arbor, Michigan. Print material was also found in grocery stores and supermarkets. The trend toward bigger retail operations demanded that purveyors of newspapers, magazines, and other non-durable goods win space in establishments where most Americans shopped on a daily basis.

CORNUCOPIA OF CONSUMER GOODS

The nation's largest supermarket chain A&P was suddenly challenged by a trend toward cost cutting. While it struggled to adjust, Kroger invested in computers to handle inventory and pricing for higher volumes that pushed annual revenue to $2 billion by 1963, and then $3 billion six years later. In 1970, a major modernization program added deli bakeries and other specialty shops for selling flowers, cheese, and the like. Check out lines, from 1972 switching over to a system that scanned bar codes on products to read prices and speed the process, encouraged impulse buying of everything from candy bars to tabloid newspapers, razor blades to soft drinks.

Simultaneously in the 1960s, H.E. Butt in Texas built up to $250 million of annual sales and Winn-Dixie expanded to 715 mostly smaller stores throughout the South. Publix in Florida reached $500 million of annual sales and then $1 billion by 1974 by concentrating on supermarket construction. Consolidated Foods rose from that plateau despite selling its Eagle and Piggly Wiggly supermarket chains in 1967. The company subsequently branched out into women's intimate apparel and *Isotoner* gloves as well as acquiring more food operations. In the northwest, Albertson's generated $420 million of revenue from 200 stores in nine states staffed by 8,500 employees. After purchasing a wholesale company in Boise and taking control of its own distribution system, sales jumped to $1 billion annually by 1975.

Grocery industry concentration, as well as proliferation of existing and new fast food chains such as Taco Bell in 1962 and Long John Silver six years later that competed with grocery sales, made it absolutely essential for food products companies to claim shelf space with supermarkets. Major players sought to protect overall market share by introducing new brands or making acquisitions. Thus, Hershey bought H.B. Reese Company and its *Reese's Pieces* peanut-butter and chocolate product for $23.5 million. After buying StarKist with its popular *Charlie the Tuna* figure in 1963 and Ore-Ida potatoes two years later, Heinz built up to $1 billion of annual sales by 1972.

Meanwhile, Coca-Cola's proliferating product line, now including *Sprite*, *Tab*, and *Fresca*, forced the company that made *Mountain Dew*, a high carbohydrate drink popular with kids and teenagers, to sell out to PepsiCo. Although purchase at mid-decade of snack food company Frito-Lay and its new *Doritos* brand tortilla chips, eventually the most popular snack in the US, was more important in the short term for PepsiCo by 1970 to exceed $1 billion of annual revenue, a belated decision to put resources behind *Mountain Dew*, including in 2 liter plastic bottles, advanced that soft drink into the top 10. Company sales doubled to over $2 billion four years later. The workforce rose to 49,000.

In prepared foods, competition from General Mills and Pillsbury forced Consolidated Mills Company to sell its *Duncan Hines* mixes to Procter and Gamble. The firm, which later changed its name to ConAgra, then implemented a strategic shift into the poultry growing and processing industry in the South. P&G continued to diversify by introducing *Pampers* diapers as a replacement for cloth diapers, buying Folgers Coffee in 1963, and supplementing its *Downy* brand liquid fabric softener with *Bounce* anti-static sheets. Its principal competitor Colgate-Palmolive pushed beyond $1 billion of annual sales, achieved in 1967, by introducing *Colgate* toothpaste with the *MFP Fluoride* additive, *UltraBrite* toothpaste, *Palmolive* dishwashing liquid, and *Irish Spring* soap.

Diversification of product line also helped Clorox Company remain independent and grow. In addition to coming out with *Clorox 2* dry, non-chlorine bleach, the company bought Liquid-Plumr and plotted out an acquisition strategy that eventually brought in-house *Glad* bags, *STP* auto additives, *Pine-Sol* cleaner, *Black Flag* insecticides, and other well-known products. In 1967, Gillette pushed toward $1 billion of annual sales, achieved six years later, by buying Braun, a German maker of electric shavers. Avon Products door-to-door approach got three-quarters of the way to that goal by 1970.

Despite a Surgeon General's mandated warning on cigarette packages that smoking was harmful to health, smoking on screen by Hollywood stars, the addictive quality of nicotine, and powerful advertising images overrode common sense. Most successful were *Marlboro Man* ads evoking the country's western history with a rugged but handsome actor (who later in 1992 died of lung cancer) for Philip Morris. The company rose from smallest of the country's six major tobacco companies to largest by 1983. R.J. Reynolds countered in 1969 with its *Doral* brand. To reduce exposure to potential lawsuits over the adverse effect of smoking, corporate executives started to diversify into other businesses. R.J. Reynolds aspired to be a full-line food products company.

Meanwhile, the 1960s witnessed another big surge in plastics products. Dow Chemical reached over $1 billion of sales in 1964 in part by producing plastic plates, glasses, containers, and other products. Overseas sales of plastic-based items swelled to a half million dollars seven years later and provided one quarter of company revenues. The product line ranged from epoxy resins that helped fabricate the heat shield for *Apollo* capsules to *Ziploc* food bags.

In fact, it was the seemingly limitless applications for plastics that caused Air Products to get into the plasticizing industry. The company began manufacturing chemicals to convert petrol refinery by-products into oxo-alcohols. That move led to a further shift into chemicals by buying the Houdry Process Company, maker of organic chemicals and catalysts. Later in 1969, the firm took over Escambia Chemical Corporation of Pensacola, Florida, producing industrial chemicals and fertilizers.

In 1962, DuPont introduced *Lycra* elastic fiber to mix with cotton, wool, silk, and nylon. That polyurethane additive gave clothes a better fit and feel and over time brought in huge revenue. By supplementing its acetate fiber tow product with a polyester fiber line, Kodak's Eastman Chemical division more than doubled sales to $558 million in 1970. The parent company used plastic in its 1963 *Instamatic* camera to keep costs down and lift annual revenue to $4 billion by 1966.

Barbie Doll

Plastic was indispensable to an entire range of consumer products. Mattel, founded by Ruth Handler and her husband, used it to mass produce the dolls named *Barbie* and *Ken*, achieve sales of $100 million by 1965, and fund development of its *Hot Wheels* toy car racers. Hassenfeld Brothers needed it for *G.I. Joe* and later *Mr. Potato Head*. Even Milton Bradley's *Twister* game that sold 3 million in 1966 after late night talk show host and comedian Johnny Carson played it on his *Tonight Show*, was basically just a vinyl mat with colored circles.

Sam Walton

The spread of cheaper, plastic goods and toys, although not a threat to main-line retailers, did indicate a growing predilection of consumers to buy what they could afford. Installment plan credit was available from GE Capital and other financial units of household appliance makers, but the vast majority of families still did not qualify for American Express or bank credit cards. While Whirlpool did enough business by 1968 to generate $1 billion of annual revenue, Amana, now owned by Raytheon, produced the first countertop microwave for home use, in the process eliminating the necessity in many apartment residences of owning convection ovens.

In 1969, the company also began making microwave ovens and furnaces for commercial operations.

One of the most far-sighted businessmen to realize that Americans would flock to discount stores in increasing numbers for household and personal product purchases as well as food, clothes, and even consumer durables was Sam Walton. A long-time employee of J.C. Penney, he was ready in 1962 to open his own store in Rogers, Arkansas. Precisely at the moment when J.C. Penney was shifting strategy to open full-line department stores in major cities that offered not only merchandise like big-ticket appliances, sporting goods, and gardening products but services, including restaurants, beauty salons, portrait studios, and auto repair, Walton emulated J.C. Penney's original strategy of targeting under-served rural areas with lower priced goods. Throughout the decade, he built up a three dozen Wal-Mart discount store chain in Arkansas, Kansas, Missouri, Oklahoma, and Louisiana. In 1970, he put in place a spoke and wheel distribution system that greatly cut costs and every day sent some of his 1,500 employees to scrutinize competitors' pricing. Sales that year amounted to $44.2 million.

That was a far cry from J.C. Penney's $2 billion of sales in 1965, supplemented by an in-store catalog business created by the purchase three years earlier of the General Merchandise Company. J.C. Penney retained a foothold in off-price goods by hanging on to the acquired firm's Treasury Discount store chain. Like Sears executives, J.C. Penney officials believed that the greatest long-term threat arose from Kresge, opening its first K-mart discount store in a Detroit suburb in 1962, and then rapidly building 161 more in four years, out of 915 stores overall, to double sales to over $1 billion. Dayton Company founded the Target discount chain the same year to cut into the same market. By 1971, after Dayton merged with the J.L. Hudson department store company, its annual revenue also exceeded $1 billion. Two years later, J.C. Penney did that amount in December alone from over 2,000 stores, including 300 full-line operations, while ringing up annual sales of $6 billion.

In the 1960s, older department store chains lost significant business to Sears and J.C. Penney and the new discounters. Although Federated topped $1.2 billion of annual sales by 1964 and both Allied and the May Company hit $1 billion three years later, all had to absorb other stores and expand the size of new ones in a vain attempt to hold market share. However, as Walton proved with the Wal-Mart chain, some areas of the country, including medium size cities, were underserved. Nordstrom department stores began as a Seattle-based shoe store chain that expanded to clothing, went public in 1971, and topped $100 million of sales two years later. Tiny Dillards, founded in Nashville, Arkansas back in 1938, shot to prominence and publicly traded stock after opening a department store in an Austin, Texas shopping mall in 1964 and then following a strategy of aggressive mall expansion over the next five years. Interstate Department Stores bulked up by buying out Charles Lazarus' four Toys'R'Us stores and assembling a 60 store chain by 1972. Even so, the discounters might have overwhelmed these and larger operations had not department stores begun to accept bank credit cards verified by computers at point-of-sale cash registers. Quick credit approval not only pleased and reinforced the loyalty of customers, but automation greatly facilitated inventory control.

General merchandising appeared to be a prerequisite for success in the retail industry. However, several operations arose in the 1960s to indicate that a more specialized approach could also succeed. For example, a North Wilkesboro, North Carolina hardware store called Lowe's went public in 1961. It was first of those companies that eventually formed the home improvement retail industry. Likewise, Charles Tandy and his Tandy Corporation, originally a maker of leather parts and tools, bought in 1963 the bankrupt RadioShack chain of nine retail stores, which sold electronic parts and do-it-yourself kits. For a price of only $300,000, Tandy gained a small foothold in the consumer electronics industry. Then there was the first Limited store in Columbus, Ohio. By selling bright, trendy clothes to teenagers, college students, and young adults, the Limited Brands Company was able to go public in 1969.

Overall, retail sales quickened to $448 billion by 1972. Wholesale operations that were not, like Wal-Mart's suppliers self-contained, jumped to 311,000, including 52,000 in machinery, equipment, and supplies, 40,000 grocery related, 34,000 in petroleum and petroleum products, and 31,000 in motor vehicles and auto equipment. In aggregate, consumer purchases accounted for 65% of GDP. In addition to basic necessities, durable goods, and luxury items, American industry was turning to more exciting products.

ON THE VERGE OF A HIGH-TECH REVOLUTION

In the 1960s, solid-state transistors steadily replaced vacuum tubes in radios, TVs, computers, and other electronic devices. The quest for semiconductor makers was to shrink the size of computer chips, condense the circuits, and cut the time it took for electronic impulses to carry the codes of zeros and ones that translated into "digital" commands. Because as speed and utilization on chips increased, heat built up to damage and burn out circuits, methods had to be developed to contain and/or disperse that heat. Motorola at mid-decade produced plastic-encapsulated transistors for that very purpose.

Wang electronic calculator
The next year, Hewlett-Packard, an entity that had begun operation in 1938 as a maker of electronic instruments to test sound equipment, produced its first computer. The *Model 2116A*, a programmable test and measurement computer linked to standardized lab instruments that was priced as low as $25,000, was sold to Woods Hole Oceanographic Center. Two years later, HP, as the company came to be called, produced its first desktop scientific calculator. This device proved so popular with experts and students alike that in 1968 annual revenue hit $326 million revenue, nearly seven times higher than at the start of the decade. Too, HP's operations supported 15,840 employees, proving that IBM, with $7.19 billion of revenue, $934 million of net income, and over a quarter million employees in 1969, would not remain without new and formidable competitors. In 1972, HP challenged Big Blue with a dynamic random-access memory (DRAM) minicomputer that was powerful enough to convince some companies to move away from IBM System 360 mainframes and future models.

Texas Instruments Datamath

HP also took on Texas Instruments in the field of mobile computing by bringing out a hand-held scientific calculator. TI had started the ball rolling in 1967 with a simpler hand-held machine without scientific functions. That move helped boost revenue in 1970 to $827 million and employees to 44,750, but the company was not satisfied. Introduction the next year of a single-chip microcomputer and the first portable data terminal followed by the *Datamath* model hand-held calculator to replace slide-rules in 1972 and 4 kilobyte DRAM chip in 1973 made TI a broader-based competitor in the computer industry.

Minicomputers for process and industrial controls became the fastest growing segment of the industry. With $100 million of sales in 1968, Johnson Service Company gained the wherewithal after buying Penn Controls, a maker of refrigeration and gas heating controls, to produce by 1972 the *JC80*, the first minicomputer to control building systems. IBM contributed unwittingly to the progress of a new software niche by "unbundling" computer hardware from its command language. AT&T's Bell Labs was then able to develop its *UNIX* operating system as a time-share software system designed to run on computers of all sizes.

IBM System 360

But if it was going to be possible for independent developers without AT&T's resources to write language for computers, there needed to be a better method of storing and accessing that software on machines. Intel, founded in 1968 to make RAM chips, solved the problem three years later by inventing the first central processing unit (CPU) or microprocessor for computers. Now a race began to produce software programs to replicate business office functions, including secretarial and accounting work. An intermediate step in 1971 was Wang's *Model 1200* word processor that gradually doomed manual and even electronic typewriters. Overall by 1973,

125,000 general and special-purpose computers were being purchased and installed. Though software for the former was sparse, private business was allocating a small but increasing portion of the $19.2 billion spent annually on R&D to bring the country into a new technological era.

Aside from speeding up and making more cost-efficient business office operations, entrepreneurs were anxious for more computing power to expand business services. For example, payroll company ADP increased revenue fifty-fold between 1962 and 1971 to $50 million by opening new data centers in Florida and Connecticut. H&R Block, founded in Kansas City in 1954 as a bookkeeping firm, moved to tax preparation after local IRS offices became too busy to provide that service free of charge to citizens. With demand soaring in New York and other big cities from wealthy Americans anxious to be relieved of the increasingly difficult, time-consuming, and disagreeable task of filling out tax forms, what was needed was a spreadsheet on a computer program to greatly accelerate productivity. For the moment, however, paper, pen, and ink had to suffice. At least after 1966, the product of H&R Block accountants could be tele-copied almost instantaneously to clients and IRS agents by Xerox's new facsimile or fax machine.

MAINSTREAM FOR BIG LABOR; MORNING AGAIN FOR WEALTH

Automation to replace workers was a hot topic but not a practical reality until the 1970s. In the 1960s, the push on the part of government was to increase minimum wages to eliminate poverty, on the part of unions in manufacturing industries encouraged by successive Democratic administration to secure both wage increases linked to annual jumps in the cost of living and a full panoply of benefits ranging from pension to health to disability to vacation pay. The tactic of choice in the first instance was, of course, legislation. On May 5, 1961, Congress amended the Fair Labor Standards Act to raise the minimum wage to $1.25 per hour with coverage for an additional 3.6 million workers. Nearly six years later, the minimum wage was bumped up to $1.40 per hour, and then the next year to $1.60, except that migrant farm workers had to make do with $1.30. In 2004 money, the lowest of the low full-time workers received annual income little more than $14,000. And although the war on poverty showed broad statistical progress, persistent pockets of unemployment persisted in a civilian workforce approaching 80 million. At the peak of prosperity in 1968, teenage unemployment was over 15% and black unemployment nearly 9%.

The main cudgel of Big Labor remained strikes. Where industries such as newspaper publishing were consolidating, job actions could backfire in layoffs and closings. Where industries were expanding, however, real and significant gains were achieved. A 2.5% average annual wage increase that prevailed in manufacturing between 1960 and 1965 was doubled from 1966 to 1972. In the latter period, even public service workers such as in the New York City transit and school systems stayed away until concessions were granted. Strikes eventually hurt business productivity and contributed to higher inflation.

On the other hand, unions were generally able to secure wage packages that exceeding cost of living increases. In 1964, the Teamsters used their clout to push through a National Master Freight Agreement covering 400,000 drivers. Under the leadership of Jimmy Hoffa, the union was flying high until his 1967 conviction and jailing for jury tampering. In 1971, with evidence abounding that the Teamster hierarchy was controlled by the Mafia, the AFL-CIO not only kicked out the Teamsters but the Bakery Workers and Laundry Workers unions. Shrugging off the rebuff, new Teamster boss Frank Fitzsimmons as well as various hard-hat construction unions gained a measure of political influence by endorsing Nixon for reelection in 1972. Labor solidarity was splintered on the eve of more difficult economic times.

However, for the moment, annual income without overtime in manufacturing averaged a healthy $7,620, which translated into $34,480 in 2004 money. The high was

Collecting hay in Illinois

$11,940 for oil and gas workers while the low was $5,200 for textile employees. Much of the advance was due to the heavy program of strikes advanced by unions, including 1970 walk-outs by the UAW and UMW that pushed man-days lost to a peak of 66.4 million. Mine workers, in particularly, made up for the meager rewards of past eras with a 30% wage and fringe benefit increase over three years that raised annual pay to about $8,000.

Another favorable factor was moderate legal immigration for the decade of 3.3 million that might have kept supply and demand for labor in rough approximation and unemployment under 5%. However, Great Society changes as well as contraction in farm employment brought a migration of more Americans from rural areas to cities. Now the surge was supplemented by Hispanic Americans as well as Mexican and other illegal immigrants. By 1970, four-fifths of 12 million Hispanics were urban-dwellers.

Cesar Chavez

Although most illegal aliens were seasonal workers picking produce in fields in California and other places, they built rapidly toward 4 million by end of the period. The AFL-CIO empowered Cesar Chavez and his United Farm Organizing Committee to form a union of grape pickers. This was part of a larger drive to unionize other farm employees, southern workers, Kentucky coal miners, and service trades, including government workers and even college professors. Because workers in the retail trade, hotels, tourism, and other such industries averaged only $4,480 of annual income, or $21,850 in 2004 money, it was believed that the service industry in particular was ready for exploitation. But with the rise of big discounters K-mart, Target, and later Wal-Mart, the trend in retailing was price competition, thin margins, and restrained wages. The percent of gainfully employed, non-farm workers who were union members peaked at about 20 million, or 28% of the total workforce, and begin to fall.

In an ominous development for white males who formed the core both of white collar office workers and blue collar factory hands, competition for better paying jobs began to come from women. Rising incrementally from 34% of the work force in 1965 to 36.7% by 1970, including 43.4% of women working age, they were spearheaded by a determined group of middle class women fired by the feminist movement to carve out independent economic existences. Men of all creeds and color who served in the military still had the advantage of veterans' benefits, however. Congress enhanced their prospects in 1966 by adding new education payments to vets who had served at least 180 days on active service after 1955. The country could afford such largesse because corporate profits mounted in 1968 to $87.6 billion, divided after taxes 54.5% for business, 45.5% for federal, state, and local government. Times appeared so good for some companies that they gave employees a piece of real wealth.

For example, auto parts maker Dana Corporation instituted a stock purchase plan in 1969. It proved so beneficial in building a nest egg for the future that four-fifths of the company's workforce eventually signed on. That kind of development was just what LBJ had hoped for to add a prosperous blue collar element to the middle class. By end of the period, the second fifth of families possessed a quarter of national income while the bottom 60% shared a little more than 32%, but as a group, the bottom four-fifths of families still shared less than 20% of household net worth.

Meanwhile, the top 5% of earners now received only 16.5% of national income, well down from its 21.4% share in 1950. These included the President himself, whose salary was raised in 1969 to $200,000, supplemented by a non-taxable travel allowance of $40,000 and a taxable allowance of $50,000. Retirement pay, first authorized in 1958 to take care of Truman, was increased from $25,000 to $60,000. A surviving spouse of a deceased President would in 1970 receive $20,000, a 100% increase.

Nixon was first beneficiary of the change. Although his annual income in 2004 money now exceeded $1.2 million, GDP in 1970 of just over $1 trillion, $4.9 trillion in 2004 money, appeared to warrant remuneration for the nation's chief executive comparable to corporate CEOs. Total fixed asset value of $3.25 trillion, of which three-quarters was in private hands, $675 billion of equity value in the NYSE, a half a trillion dollars in bank deposits, and pension funds topping $100 billion also caused the public to pass over the fact that the nation's highest public servant would become a rich man on the government's payroll. In addition to foreign policy successes, Nixon kept Washington's nearly $200 billion annual budget not too far out of balance. Given the fact that social and other income security programs had ballooned to 28% of expenditures while national defense at about a third still totaled $66 billion to fight the Vietnam War and hold Soviet Communism at bay, this was a solid achievement. The American people without much complaint handed over almost a quarter of national income of $800 billion in taxes.

At the end of Nixon's first term in office in 1972, the republic wound up not with a Great Society, perhaps, but with an even more formidable economy than before and the promise of further material gains. Now, however, revived foreign competition and an emphasis on overseas trade exposed more American businesses to the uncertainties of international economics outside the control of the US government. Companies large and small needed to react more swiftly to changing conditions, but the chief concern of business leaders continued to be the parasitic power of Washington to drain away profits. That myopia was a major reason they were soon blind-sided by the oil embargo of 1973. But changes that had been filtering into the economy for over a decade were more fundamental to the distress that then gripped the nation. The country had to decide whether to place trust in government to solve economic problems or turn back toward free enterprise.

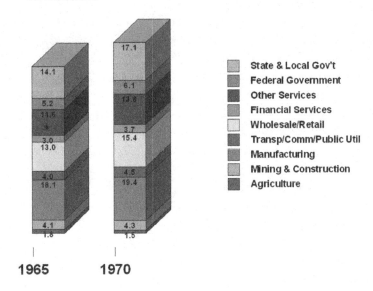

U.S. Employment by Sector, 1965-1970 In Millions

	State & Local Gov't
	Federal Government
	Other Services
	Financial Services
	Wholesale/Retail
	Transp/Comm/Public Util
	Manufacturing
	Mining & Construction
	Agriculture

1965   1970

Chapter XI. Economic Complexities Beyond the Control of Government: 1973-1980

Within the boundaries of the United States, Ricardo's principle of Comparative Advantage, wherein regions specialize in what they do best and force less efficient producers to turn to other economic activity, had long applied. With the right and ability to move east to west, south to north, and to all parts of the compass within the country, American working men and women had always managed over time to adjust. After the Second World War, however, international commerce proved a double-edged sword. Trade agreements opened new markets to US businesses, but let in small but increasing volumes of foreign imports.

While government quotas, restraints, and subsidies held off a greater deluge for two decades, the trend toward closer economic relations between the US and its political allies foreshadowed a day of reckoning. That moment came sooner rather than later after the Organization of Petroleum Exporting Countries (OPEC), dominated by Saudi Arabia and other Middle East nations, reacted to American support of Israel in the *Yom Kippur* war against Egypt and Syria by imposing in October 1973 an oil embargo on the US and Western Europe. In the inflationary and recession-prone period that followed, weakness in many US industries vis-a-vis foreign competitors was exposed. The consequence was rising prices for goods and services averaging 7.9% between 1973 and 1982, interest rates ballooning into double digits, and unemployment cresting over 7%.

Unionized sectors with higher labor costs and less flexibility to "restructure" suffered most. Corporations with foreign operations or the wherewithal to shift production overseas, including in agri-business, household and food products, and pharmaceuticals, not only survived but prospered. Although in some cities factories closed and good jobs were lost, consumers continued to gravitate toward lower cost products to sustain standards of living. The business community went through a period of self-doubt and self-analysis that brought under critical examination basic assumptions. These ranged from the prevailing autocratic management style, learned by exposure to military service, to a focus on short-term results demanded by public trading of stock, to an ethic of engineering for planned obsolescence, which forced consumers to make purchases at regular intervals to keep business revenues and profits flowing. Inflexible work rules, seniority protection for aging, less nimble workers, and sloppy workmanship contributed to a decline in the quality of American manufactures. Trying to cope, US businesses accelerated methods previously employed to obtain more financial and operating efficiencies. In addition to mergers to create greater economies of scale, mechanization was accelerated to slash labor costs. The principle of comparative advantage was utilized to move factory production from the Northeast and Midwest to the South and West. In Dixie where unions were almost non-existent, a much lower wage scale was installed.

The problem from a national perspective of paying workers less was that such economies undercut the trend begun by Henry Ford of providing employees a living wage that permitted sufficient disposable income to buy the goods they produced. The next logical step for businesses was exporting production and jobs to the lowest cost regions of the world. In the process, the less affluent half of the US population, only lately introduced to the pleasures of the material American dream, would lose the means to buy cars, heavy household appliances, and other pricey consumer goods that kept the economy humming. Old socio-economic and political ills would return.

To maintain standards of living, families adjusted by having wives and even older children go to work. Although a sizeable percentage of women from less affluent households had always held down jobs, now their employment tended to be full time rather than part time. Too, economic necessity as much as feminist philosophy compelled more middle-class women to seek professional, technical, and managerial employment. Labor competition intensified.

After a second oil embargo in 1979, the country was hit by a period of stagflation. As prices for housing soared to nearly double the level of 1973, increased cost of health care, food, and other necessities combined with low productivity and government red tape in businesses sent the country into recession. Interest rates peaking over 20% added to the "misery index" of average Americans, especially debtors and the 13% of citizens classified as under the poverty line. Economic insecurity was rife.

To be sure, a mass market for lower priced goods remained within the wherewithal of almost all citizens. Because of the size of the population, rising by 1980 to 228 million persons, sufficient demand for higher cost consumer durables and capital goods sustained a weakening manufacturing sector, by 1980 providing only 22.6% of GDP. Inflated to $2.8 trillion, GDP relied less heavily than in the past on primary economic activities — agriculture and mining — as well as manufacturing, construction, public utilities, transportation, and communication. Tertiary activities such as the retail and wholesale sectors that facilitated $1.8 trillion of annual consumer spending but also financial services, government purchases, and trade now generated over 58% of national production.

Something had to be done to stop the erosion in heavy industry. Resisting business and labor appeals to turn to protectionism, applied so disastrously at the start of the Great Depression, Washington instead pressured the Japanese and other foreign producers to build factories, particularly automobile plants, in the US Although profits from such installations flowed overseas, worsening the nation's balance of payments situation, the bulk of material purchases, labor payments, and taxes remained in the country. A minimum level, never definitively defined, was imagined below which automobiles and steel, industrial products and other basic manufacturing establishments could not go without undermining permanently the ability of the US to control its own economic destiny.

On the other hand, some economists wanted to let the forces of free trade and comparative advantage play themselves out without any government interference at all. Except for industries critical to national security, recognized even by Adam Smith, they thought the US would be better off in the long run cutting away declining businesses the way a physician amputates a gangrened limb. By repealing laws and regulations that inhibited US business leaders from exercising independent judgment, government would unleash the age-old American entrepreneurial spirit. The growing knowledge and brain power of Americans, indicated by the fact that 16.2% of persons 25 and over came by 1980 to hold a college degree, would facilitate discovery of new inventions and innovation that would gin up entirely new industries.

Even restrictions against monopoly power had proved disadvantageous in the face of powerful foreign cartels subsidized by foreign governments, free traders believed. What was required to level the global playing field was deregulation of industries. That idea gained momentum in the latter half of the 1970s for political as well as economic reasons. President Jimmy Carter and Democrats in control of Congress realized that Republican attacks on government red tape were resonating with the electorate as much as public disgruntlement with high energy costs, bullying unions, and other maladies. Thus, out of adversity came a sea change in thinking that swung the pendulum back toward *laissez-faire* economics. While the era of big government making decisions that affected the material prospects of households and businesses never really came to an end, the direct influence of Washington definitely did begin to decline.

OIL EMBARGO AND ITS IMPACT

Alaska Oil Pipeline

It is quite possible that Nixon, having won a mandate in the 1972 election to withdraw US forces from Vietnam, could in his second term have assembled sufficient political strength to move toward less government intervention in the economy. However, the Watergate scandal that ultimately forced his resignation in August 1974 limited his options. Early calendar year 1973 was dominated by news from Southeast Asia as well as the President's decision to further

devalue the dollar to $42.22 an ounce of gold. That action precipitated a free fall in the dollar's traded price to $127 an ounce by July. Although a decision in November by the US and its principle Western European allies in the wake of the oil embargo, discussed below, to permit monetary authorities to sell gold on the Free Market drove the price down temporarily, more uncertainties caused a dramatic escalation to $307.50 in 1979. The inflated peak of over $800 came in 1980 before the price fell to a more stable $400 the next year.

In September 1973, Nixon went to Tokyo for the seventh round of trade talks under the GATT regime intending to persuade and cajole a further opening of European and Japanese markets for US exports. The entire web of policies and relationships he had spun for five years to drive a wider wedge between Moscow and Peking, firm up the containment of Soviet ambition in Third World regions, and improve American capability to carry on the Cold War even as the nuclear balance tilted toward parity came undone the next month. On October 6, the Egyptians and Syrians launched a surprise attack on Israel as payback for Tel Aviv's preemptive strike in the Six Days War in 1967. Outraged that Nixon, despite close and intimate ties between the Arab world and US oil companies, would rally unquestionably to Israel's side, Saudi Arabia led OPEC oil ministers in announcing an embargo on shipments to the West on October 17. The kingdom also nationalized 25% of the Arab-American Oil Company (ARAMCO). Riyadh absorbed the rest seven years later.

At once the price of oil jumped. From $3.27 per barrel, it climbed to $8.57 by 1977. With the Watergate investigation hanging over his head, Nixon responded along predictable lines. A speech on November 7 emphasized energy conservation measures such as implementing Daylight Savings Time, construction of more nuclear power plants, utilization of coal in preference to oil, increased production from oil reserves held by the US Navy in Elk Hills, California, and more energy research to make the US self-sufficient by 1980. Nine days later, he signed the Alaskan Pipeline Act authorizing construction from the state's North Slope through Alaskan wildlife areas to the ice-free port of Valdez on the Gulf of Alaska of a 799 mile, four foot diameter pipeline that would bring 2.1 million barrels of oil daily to tankers waiting to transport the crude to the lower 48 states. The states got on the bandwagon by lowering speed limits to conserve gasoline and reduce long lines at gas stations.

Santa Fe Six-Pack

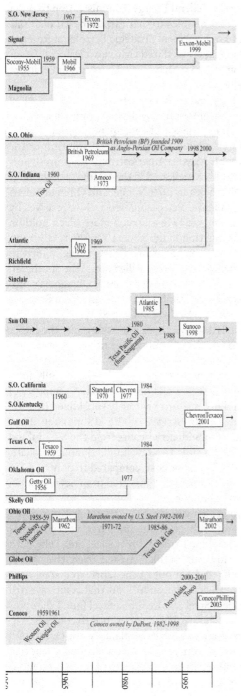

Genealogy of US Oil Industry, 1949-2004

In the Federal Aid Highway Act of 1974, Congress permitted the Highway Trust Fund to be used for mass transit projects. The next year, the House and Senate authorized $11.9 billion for new construction, capital improvements, and daily operation of same. If Washington wanted mass transit to cut city driving, government officials counted on railroads to reduce gasoline consumption in cars and trucks between cities. The Rail Reorganization Act of January 2, 1974 provided up to $1.5 billion in guaranteed loans to design a new rail system. A further $2.1 billion from the 1971 authorization was used, per the Railroad Revitalization and Regulatory Reform (4R) Act of 1976, to fund a federal subsidized corporation out of the salvageable remains of Penn Central and six other bankrupt companies in the Northeast and Midwest. Called the Consolidated Rail Corporation or CONRAIL, that entity was created by Congress on November 10, 1975. Another $1.85 billion was loaned to improve the vital Northeast Corridor rail service connecting Washington, New York, Boston, and other major metropolises along the way. About a third as much was allocated to build an electrified, high-speed rail service in the same area. Where private railroad companies were concerned, however, initiative was lacking. Only the Atchison, Topeka, and Santa Fe Railway, with the first *Six-Pack* articulated inter-modal railcar with a skeleton design for lighter weight, lower center of gravity, and reduced fuel consumption as well as other innovations, strove mightily to arrest the industry decline. Older railroad engines were still powered by coal. Since the country was producing about 750 million metric tons annually from reserves that would last many centuries longer, Congress on December 22, 1975 passed the

Energy Policy Conservation Act to empower the Federal Energy Administration to order major power plants to switch from other energy sources to that carbon-based material. Additionally, the law authorized a 1 billion barrel National Strategic Petroleum Reserve, equal to one-third of US domestic production, and mandated that new car fuel mileage increase from an average of 18 miles per gallon to 27.5 mph by 1985. Construction of lower cost nuclear power plants was also encouraged.

However, the American public and industry had such a structural dependence on oil that petroleum's nearly 50% share of energy consumption only declined over time to 41% by 1991. The US continued to consume a quarter of the world's energy production. Rather than government fiat, the old law of supply and demand proved the solution to the problem. As the price of oil doubled and doubled again, American and other producers went out looking for more. For example, Hunt Oil participated in the discovery of the huge Beatrice Field in an unexplored area of the North Sea in 1976. While Gulf Oil made seven major finds in the Gulf of Mexico alone, Occidental Petroleum boosted its reserves by drilling in Africa, Asia, and South America, Amerada Hess struck more black gold on Alaska's north slope, and Getty increased production in Oklahoma. On the retail front, Amoco abandoned gas stations in the South Central and Southwest parts of the country to concentrate on keeping its Midwest base profitable. Arco, too, pulled out of the Southeast.

In 1977, Getty bought out Skelly Oil to claim an even greater share of Oklahoma's production. Three years later, Sun Oil purchased Texas Pacific Oil Company from Seagram Company Limited of Britain for $2.3 billion as well as Viking Oil Limited, which had a 20% stake in some North Sea Oil fields. Mobil tried to take over Marathon, but the latter company went looking for a "white knight" to take its independence but not its pride. In a big surprise, US Steel eventually came to the rescue.

Why? Diversification was seen as an important strategic move by the 20 fully integrated steel companies operating nearly 50 full-scale mills because by 1977, imports of foreign steel, boasting cheaper labor costs and not-so-surreptitiously subsidized by their governments, were up to 21 million tons or about 15% of the US market. That encroachment had whittled down American steel industry profits from the $2.5 billion achieved in the fiscal year that included the oil embargo to a few hundred million dollars. Because a ton of steel in the US contained $9.08 of labor cost, compared to only $4.19 in Japan, bleaker days appeared to be ahead. Even cheaper steel imported from new plants in less developed countries was not too far over the horizon.

The steel industry was also beset by strong competition from aluminum in aerospace applications, plastic in appliances, and composite substitutes in cars. To secure economies of scale and make larger profits, LTV in 1977 combined Youngstown Sheet and Tube with Jones and Laughlin in a LTV Steel division. However, Bethlehem Steel executives pared excess steel-making capacity in Pennsylvania and got out of the fabricated steel construction market altogether. When the next recession came in 1979-80, that company tried to wring profits from $7 billion in sales. National Steel and Republic Steel found that production sliding to 50% of capacity made success impossible. They too had to contract.

Another long-term problem for the industry was that as plants were closed and workers laid off, the ratio of current workers to retirees narrowed. Promises made to employees for continuing health, pension, and life insurance benefits loomed as a monstrous liability, overawing the market value of shares. Over the next two decades, restructuring resulted in a ratio of one active to six retirees, at Bethlehem an incredible 1 to 10 ratio. Astute observers knew that to survive, sometime in the distant future the industry would have to renege on a substantial portion of its commitment.

Meanwhile, the first energy shock of 1973 also wounded businesses dependent upon the American love affair with cars and driving. Howard Johnson's, operating 1,000 restaurants and 500 motor lodges along highways and interstates, lost business to lower-price, more conveniently placed, fast-food restaurants, in particular McDonald's that in 1979 seduced parents and children with *Happy Meals* for kids. The success of the *Golden Arches* was a boon for Huntsman, founded in 1970 to make plastic packaging and other containers, including a clamshell food container familiar to anyone who frequented McDonald's. Another chain that reached no fewer than 2,000 establishments by 1980 and cut into the business of middle-of-the-road restaurants was Wendy's Old Fashioned Hamburgers, founded eleven years earlier in Columbus, Ohio.

Howard Johnson's also suffered competition from discount lodgings. Super 8 Motels out of Aberdeen, South Dakota did so well that Imperial Group of Britain made a successful offer for its five year old business in 1979. On the other hand, the 100 hotel Marriott chain remained immune and obtained $1 billion of sales by focusing on the tourist trade, by 1981 including Hawaii and Europe, and diversifying into two *Great America* theme parks. Carnival Cruise Lines, founded in 1972, and a future component called Princess Cruises, then owned by a British company, also achieved success providing sea vacations for Americans with a small fleet of huge ships.

Cruise ship

US tourism outside the country prior to the oil shock was a big reason governments in Europe and Japan found themselves holding $6 billion in US currency. Although the falling dollar might have made US goods more competitive overseas, devaluation of foreign currencies cut the advantage. To stimulate more trade, Congress passed the Trade Act of January 3, 1975, authorizing Nixon's successor Gerald R. Ford to make trade agreements eliminating tariffs on goods with duties of 5% or less and reducing tariffs otherwise up to 60%. Should foreign governments prove resistance to friendly persuasion, he might increase tariffs up to 20% of 1973 rates or 150% of 1934 rates, whichever was lower. Further, he could apply easier criteria for industries to obtain relief for losses from import competition and for workers if displaced. Generally speaking, Congress empowered the President to take action without explicit resort to the House and Senate against "unjustifiable" or "unreasonable" import restrictions by other governments.

Harvested field in the Midwest

The new emphasis on trade coincided with a policy of detente, originated by Nixon and pursued by Ford, to reduce Cold War tensions with Moscow. On October 25, 1975, Ford and counterpart Leonid Brezhnev signed a grain agreement in which the Soviets pledged to buy up to 8 million metric tons of grain each year beginning October 1, 1976. Together with a November 11, 1976 deal with East Germany, approved by Brezhnev, for annual shipments up to 2 million tons through 1980, the pacts helped alleviate supply and demand imbalances and therefore price surges for US farmers. The government made out better from a budgetary standpoint as well because with the Agriculture Act of August 10, 1973, Congress had ended the old fixed priced support farm subsidy system and replaced it with target prices for wheat, feed, grain, and cotton. Under the new system, farmers were paid the difference between those targets and market prices. Although, after inflation became a concern, Democrats and Republicans in farm states wanted subsequently to raise the targets, Ford held the line with a veto of an emergency farm bill.

Deere lawn tractor

Even when Carter, a former peanut farmer, did raise the targets, the contraction in the number of family farms was slowed but not stopped. By 1980, only 1.6 million remained, while 700,000 corporate operations raised average farm size to 455 acres on agricultural land now worth at $737 per acre over $770 billion. Larger businesses bought bigger equipment, such as the four row cotton picker brought out by Deere to boost productivity 90%. The company also sold under its name smaller tractors that were actually made by Yanmar of Japan to achieve $5 billion of sales and earnings of $310 million in 1979. In fact, the corporate farm model was a primary reason that grain production built to 325 million metric tons in 1980, milk production 60 million, vegetable production 27 million, and fruit production 25 million. Livestock herds stabilized at 111 million head of cattle, 67 million hogs, nearly 11 million sheep, and 400 million chickens, including hens turning out 4.1 million tons of eggs. That was about the same quantity by weight as fish caught in marine areas. The government in 1976 moved to secure permanent control of valuable fisheries by extending its Exclusive Fishing Zone from 12 to 200 miles out from coastlines and giving through the Coastal Zone Management Act $1.2

billion to coastal states to deal with the effects of offshore oil and natural gas developments.

Buttressing farm and thus food prices was not applauded by consumers. As family incomes were squeezed by rising energy inflation, more Americans wanted relief from price increases that began to filter into everything from housing to education, health care to cars. The economic slowdown following the oil embargo knocked down *per capita* GDP by 2.5% through 1975 but 4.5% when accounting for inflation. After Nixon's resignation, Ford convened a "domestic summit" of business, consumer, and labor leaders as well as economists on September 27, 1974 to discuss ways and means of bringing inflation and interest rates down from 12%, reversing a trend that would drive unemployment between May and December up from 5% to 7.2%, and cause the stock market to fall 28% by year's end. Although no consensus was reached, the President settled on a *Whip Inflation Now* or *WIN* program that included tax and spending aid for hard-pressed industries, a 5% tax surcharge on incomes, reduced federal spending to balance the federal budget, a voluntary energy conservation plan, and an even tighter monetary policy. When the situation only worsened, Congress on March 29, 1975, changed tack with a Tax Reduction Act that cut $18.1 billion from government revenues through a 10% rebate on 1974 taxes (capped at $200). Other provisions, including a unified rate schedule and identical $175,000 exemption for estate and gift taxes, an increase in the investment tax credit to 10% as well as cut in tax rates on small businesses that was projected to amount to $4.8 billion of relief, and $1.9 billion in "countercyclical" spending, in the form of Social Security bonus payments and an additional 13 weeks of emergency unemployment benefits to jobless in nine hard-pressed states, also had a stimulative effect that helped bring the economy out of its *per capita* recession by 1976. Senator Russell B. Long, Democrat of Louisiana and son of the legendary Huey Long, sponsored an Earned Income Tax Credit to make work more attractive than welfare for low income families with children.

Ford's problem politically was that the up-tick in the economy came too late to overcome the big lead in the polls held by Democratic nominee Carter in the 1976 election. He lost the November vote narrowly because pocket-book issues dominated citizens' judgments. One of the chief anxieties of Americans was the cost of health care, surging 96% between 1970 and 1978, whereas the previous two decades it had risen 47% and 52% respectively. Leading the way were doublings in physician and dentist fees and a jump in hospital stay charges by 153%. In addition to higher labor costs and doctors salaries, hospital administrators had to take into account rising medical malpractice insurance rates and construction costs for new facilities that outpaced the general rate of inflation. Desirable for those wanting to provide the finest medical care but not mandated by law were more and better medical devices and treatments.

For example, Baxter International, now headquartered in Deerfield, Illinois, generated over $1 billion in sales, in part by coming up with a continuous ambulatory peritoneal dialysis (CAPD) treatment as an alternative to hemodialysis and marketing the first automated blood-cell separator. Zimmer's revenue increased as well because of a metal-plastic knee prosthesis and adapting computer aided design and manufacturing (CAD/CAM) techniques to speed and improve R&D of products. Tiny competitors with big futures included Stryker, Boston Scientific Corporation, and Biomet, founded in 1977 to make orthopedic products. For-profit hospital chain projected big profits by catering to the need and vanity of richer clients.

By decade's end, the country was spending a total $212 billion on health care, which at $943 per person was 8.3% of GDP, double the rate as 30 years earlier. The federal government's bill was $91.3 billion or 43% of the total. No wonder that as early as 1973 Congress had in the Health Maintenance Organization Act backed the HMO movement to control rising costs. The next year, it required states to have *Certificate of Need* laws to regulate new medical facility construction. By 1980, the country boasted 6,900 hospitals, of which 87.6% were general, full-service facilities and half were non-profit. Federal, state, and local governments owned slightly more than a third, while private corporations owned 925, many of these specialized clinics. As for health care providers, 430,000 physicians and 126,000 dentists were supplemented by 1.16 million nurses. Numbers of installations and employees would grow only larger as the population aged and health care became a larger share of GDP.

Nevertheless, as concern picked up that Washington would not be able to maintain its commitment to Medicare, the United HealthCare Corporation was founded in 1977 to buy Charter Med Incorporation to create the first network-based health plan for seniors. INA capitalized on fear that medical benefits would eventually bankrupt many companies that had promised health care to employees even after retirement to set up an HMO in Dallas. The company bought the Ross-Loos Medical Group, the country's oldest HMO. In 1982, it merged with Connecticut General to form CIGNA.

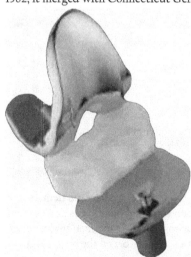

Zimmer knee prosthesis

One field of health care in which costs were still reasonably under control was pharmaceuticals. Prices for prescription drugs only went up about 40% for the decade. A big reason was consolidation of wholesalers, including AmeriSource Health Corporation, begun in Cleveland in 1977 as Alco Standard to buy The Drug House. Two years later, Cardinal Foods got into drug wholesaling by buying Bailey Drug Company and renaming itself Cardinal Distribution. With larger size, these and other companies had leverage to buy prescription drugs from pharmaceutical makers, including Squibb with its new *Capoten* anti-hypertensive agent (an ACE inhibitor) to treat high blood pressure. After the landmark *Roe v. Wade* Supreme Court case of 1973 voided state abortion laws as violating the right to privacy, AHP marketed *Lo/Ovral*, a low-dose contraceptive. Meanwhile, McNeil Consumer Products, a division of J&J, came up with *Tylenol* brand pain-reliever and cold and flu medicines. In

1980, Pfizer scored big with its *Feldene* prescription anti-inflammatory medication, the first product to reach $1 billion of annual sales in the US Too, growth in pharmaceuticals boosted the fortunes of drug store chains. Based in Lowell, Massachusetts, CVS quadrupled sales to $414 million by 1980 with an expectation of improving dramatically on its rank as 15th largest pharmacy in country in the next decade.

The pharmaceuticals sector was destined to become an even larger and more important part of the economy as more wonder drugs were developed. These would include substances that were "bio-engineered." Already by 1975, 100 genes that composed the "code" for the make-up of human beings had been mapped out. The appetite of researchers was whetted to understand the full array of some 30,000 genes in human DNA. Thus, the next year a venture capitalist and a bio-chemistry professor from the University of California at San Francisco founded Genentech to work on a synthetic gene to produce human insulin and growth factor. The basic technique was to insert human genes into bacteria and other cells for rapid reproduction and growth. However, it took another three and a half years to produce *Interferon*, a naturally occurring virus-fighting agent. The drug eventually rang up $2 billion in global annual sales. Also in 1980, venture capitalists saw such long-term potential in bio-tech engineering that they financed Applied Molecular Genetics (Amgen) in Thousand Oaks, California. Amgen would make a splash three years later with its *EPO* drug that eliminated the need for blood transfusions in kidney-dialysis patients.

Advances in medicine and drug-therapy provoked admiration and excitement in Americans, whether benefited directly themselves or not. The naive assumption prevailed that the most up-to-date treatment would be provided to most citizens at modest cost. For the moment, household income, averaging $21,063, in 2004 money equal to $48,300, gave assurance that a sizeable portion of the population would indeed enjoy the best fruits of bio and other technology. After putting out a quarter of household budgets for food and clothing, slightly more than a fifth for mortgage or rental payments, another 15% for energy, about the same for transportation, 8% for furniture and appliances, 6% for health care, and 1.8% for education, about 7.5% was left over for recreation and personal effects.

Similar to health care, education spending would climb as Americans wanted more, and more advanced, schooling. Despite an Elementary and Secondary School Act on August 21, 1974 that pumped another $25.8 billion of federal spending into the system over the next four years, tuition, book, and other costs for the nation's 30 million students continued to rise. By end of the decade, the average cost of private college doubled from 1970 to $5,900. The average cost of four years of public college went up almost as rapidly to $2,500. By itself, inflation in health care, or education, or other components of what comprised not only the standards of living of Americans in an economic sense but also quality of life was bothersome but not severe. In combination, and with the likelihood that even greater price increases and periodic recessions would afflict household budgets in the future, the accelerating rise in all components of inflation threatened to contract the middle class and destroy the well-off working class.

CARTER ECONOMICS FRUSTRATES THE COUNTRY

The major reason for run-away inflation was that higher energy costs were rippling through the economy. As soon as Carter took office, he moved aggressively, but not necessarily effectively or consistently, to get control of the situation. The Emergency Natural Gas Act of February 2, 1977 granted the President authority to order transfers of interstate natural gas to areas hit hard by severe winter. Five months later, the House and Senate tacked on authority to approve gas sales to interstate buyers at unregulated prices. To import gas and boost national inventories, Newport News Shipbuilding invested in three huge liquid natural gas (LNG) carriers, each over 390,000 deadweight tons. Company revenues climbed to over $1 billion by 1981. Also profiting from LNG importation as well as helium was Air Products. That firm developed processes and giant heat exchangers for better liquefaction of gases. Meanwhile, Allied Chemical saw such potential in oil and natural gas exploration that it sold off other less profitable business lines. Its Union Texas Natural Gas subsidiary, bought back in 1962, came to provide four-fifths of income.

Air Products liquid natural gas tanks

More comprehensive than the natural gas legislation was a national energy program proposed by Carter on April 18 but not fully implemented by Congress until November 9, 1978. Republicans protested in vain that it was more evidence that Democrats preferred a policy of "tax and spend" as well as regulation that stifled incentives for energy producers to find and bring to market new sources of oil and natural gas, rising to 1.48 billion cubic feet consumed by 1980, compared to 328 billion cubic feet of manufactured gas. Although the President and Congress actually relaxed controls on the price of domestic oil and ended price controls on gasoline, they placed a new tax on domestic crude oil at the wellhead (rebated to some needy consumers), continued the excise tax of 5.3 to 18.4 cents a gallon paid by refiners of gasoline (though gas blended with 10% ethanol from corn was exempted), imposed new controls over interstate transfer of gasoline, tied the price of new natural gas to the price of domestic crude oil (albeit with a provision permitting a 10% price rise per year until 1985), and penalized with a tax owners of cars failing to meet existing federal mileage standards. They taxed as well the industrial use of oil and natural gas and mandated that new industrial and utility plants had to use coal or a fuel other than oil and gasoline while existing utilities had to switch over by 1990.

Catalytic converter for trucks

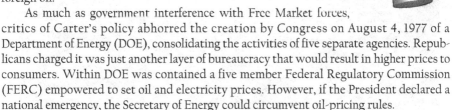

Industry leaders were subsequently frustrated, environmentalists pleased, that strict enforcement of clean air standards for factories crimped efforts to switch over to coal burning plants. Supporters of the legislation pointed to funding and tax credits for specific conservation efforts, such as $900 million for schools and hospitals to install energy-saving equipment, as a major force reducing annual US oil consumption from 18.8 billion barrels in 1978 to 16.9 billion in 1980. Also intended to enforce conservation was re-imposition of a federal tax on gasoline, rising ten fold to 50 cents per gallon. Increasing volume through the Trans-Alaska Oil Pipeline, which opened on June 20, 1977, also helped reduce temporarily the country's dependence on foreign oil.

As much as government interference with Free Market forces, critics of Carter's policy abhorred the creation by Congress on August 4, 1977 of a Department of Energy (DOE), consolidating the activities of five separate agencies. Republicans charged it was just another layer of bureaucracy that would result in higher prices to consumers. Within DOE was contained a five member Federal Regulatory Commission (FERC) empowered to set oil and electricity prices. However, if the President declared a national emergency, the Secretary of Energy could circumvent oil-pricing rules.

Playing up traditional Democratic concern for the working class and have-not Americans was a big reason that Carter defeated Ford for the White House in November 1976. A few months later on May 13, 1977, he approved passage of an Emergency Public Works program costing $4 billion. To firm up the retirement system, Congress raised Social Security taxes to 5.85% (matched by employers) on up to $16,500 of wages or salary. Since the Social Security system benefited nearly 35 million people, including the disabled, even Republicans could not vote against raising average monthly benefits for retired workers to $293 and for disabled workers to $321. In 2004 money, that was equal to annual payments of $10,950 and $12,000 respectively. Subsequent increases in Social Security taxes, in 1981 to 6.65% on $29,700 of income and in 1987 to 7.15% on $42,600, helped benefits keep pace with inflation.

Contrarily, a need to get the economy moving again persuaded the executive and legislative branches to agree to a tax cut on May 23. Reinforced by a Revenue Act the next year, it let citizens keep another $34.2 billion of their own money. The method was lifting the standard deduction, for example for joint filers to $3,400, widening and reducing the number of tax brackets, and dropping the top corporate rate another 2% to 46%. Under Carter, the government tooketh away and gaveth almost in the same instant.

Unfortunately, all these moves failed to curb inflation, rising to an 8% annual rate early in 1978. Despite restraints on defense spending, permitted by the peak of detente with the Soviets, the projected federal budget tilted by fiscal year 1980 $73 billion out of balance. In response, Carter in April limited wage increases for federal government employees, postponed the income tax cut, and approved a provision in the Revenue Act repealing the non-business deduction for state and local taxes on gasoline. In October, he pushed a voluntary annual wage increase cap of 7% by private industry and a voluntary price increase cap of 5.75%. When business leaders did not comply, inflation climbed to 9%. Citizens in California were so angry at the cumulative tax bite they were forced to pay by federal, state, and local governments that they voted in November for Proposition 13, to cut local property taxes by more than 50% and force the state government to slash expenditures and services. California Governor Ronald W. Reagan wanted to see a nationwide move to reduce the size of government. He told voters that the salaries of 16.4 million workers, other operating expenses, and capital expenditures and improvements that increased fixed assets during the decade an average of 8.5% (but only 0.6% after inflation) for Washington and 11.7% (but only 3.6% after inflation) for state and local authorities, should all be restrained.

Blue skies over a Rocky Mountain forest

In November, 1978, Congress passed and Carter signed the Public Utility Regulatory Policies Act (PURPA). The law was intended to encourage more efficient use of oil and natural gas through co-generation, or simultaneous production of steam and electricity by companies who produced steam for their manufacturing operations and could also generate the latter for private sale. Electric utilities were required to buy the electricity thus produced. The consequence of this legislation was to foster the rise of independent power utilities not connected to regulated utilities. Separate companies specializing in transmission and distribution increased competition and opened the possibility of an industry for buying and selling of energy. For example in 1980, the Public Service Electric and Gas Company sold its transportation system to the State of New Jersey. That year, the nation's production of electricity rose to 2.2 quadrillion kilowatt hours; of that amount, 13.5% originated from hydro-electric plants and 12.3% from nuclear reactors. More construction of the latter was counted on, with coal, to ease the demand for oil.

In point of fact, considerable nuclear plant building was underway. The share of electricity production claimed by nuclear facilities would as a consequence rise to 20% by year 2000. Projects included Rockwell's Clinch River breeder reactor in Tennessee that produced more nuclear material than it consumed. Breeder reactors were seen as a more cost-effective way of supplying nuclear fuel to other, more traditional nuclear plants. However, on March 28, 1979, an accident at the Three Mile Island nuclear facility in Pennsylvania that caused a partial melt-down of the core, released radioactive steam into the air, compelled an evacuation of pregnant women and children within five miles of the site, and ultimately cost up to $2 billion to repair and clean up changed public opinion about the dangers and acceptability of nuclear power plants. Not only was construction of 125 new plants halted, but the expense of operating 72 existing reactors with stepped up security measures was greatly increased. Public utility companies took on higher costing debt to cover losses as well as liability for accidents, later capped by Congress at $560 million per incident. Most of the expense was eventually passed on to consumers.

Electric coal loading machine

As news of Three Mile Island roiled the stock market, inflation soared again into double digits. Realizing belatedly that permitting the forces of supply and demand to work unfettered might solve the country's economic ills more swiftly than government meddling, worried that Republican political attacks on Carter's failure to turn the corner on energy might destroy their party's majority in the House and Senate, Democrats in Congress joined hands with Free Market advocates to pass the Oil Price Decontrol Act on April 5, 1979. As of June 1, oil prices would rise or fall with supply and demand. However, Congress could not resist tacking on a windfall profits tax ranging from 30% to 70% on oil company profits, effective April 5, 1980. Senators and representatives also on June 30 funded a leap into the future with $20 billion over 13 years in a US Synthetic Fuels Corporation to produce 500,000 barrels annually of synthetic fuels by 1992. The main thrust of the country's synthetic fuels effort turned toward extracting oil from shale in the Rocky Mountains. That legislation also encouraged Southern California Edison to explore renewable and alternative energy sources. Most promising in the Great Plains and other vacant areas was wind power.

However, energy exploitation in the West ran counter to conservation efforts. The trend of public policy continued to be to protect unspoiled natural resources. On October

25, 1978, the Public Grazing Rangelands Improvement Act established a fee system for ranchers' livestock feeding on federal land. A program was funded to reduce the wild horse and burro population that was eating and trampling vegetation. Two weeks later on November 10, the National Parks and Recreation Act provided $1.2 billion for expanding national parks in 44 states. The Alaska National Interest Lands Conservation Act two years later on December 2 also expanded the park and wildlife preserve by withdrawing 56.4 million acres in that northern most state from sale or mineral leasing and restricted mining and timbering operations on another 49 million acres. Ironically, all these measures fueled a revolt by westerners against federal control of state land. Indignation at Washington's high-handedness helped Reagan sweep the region in the election of 1980.

Oil price decontrol was just one part of a general push toward deregulation that encompassed the airline, trucking, and railroad industries, discussed below. Because of the January 1979 ouster of the Shah of oil-rich Iran by the Ayatollah Khomeini and his Islamic fundamentalist supporters, leading to the taking of hostages at the American embassy in Teheran, the price of oil doubled by early 1981 to $31.77 a barrel. That translated into $1.25 per gallon at the pump and two to three times that price in Europe. When Carter proved unwilling to use decisive force, the oil crisis continued to dominate headlines.

The President poured fuel on the fire on July 15, 1979 by convening a ten day summit of 134 leaders at the Camp David Presidential retreat in the Maryland mountains. He concluded the meeting with a TV speech to the nation in which he spoke of a "crisis of confidence" and "malaise" in the land and need for the "moral equivalent of war" to solve the crisis. His solution was a decade-long, $140 billion national energy program. He only confirmed for a majority of citizens the political attack of Reagan that "tax and spend" was all Democrats knew how to do.

New construction with Tyvek home wrap

Economic news was all bad by autumn 1979. Inflation shot up to an annual rate of 13.3%, provoking Fed chairman Paul Volker to raise the Federal Reserve discount rate to an unprecedented 12% and require higher reserve requirements for bank deposits. Banks responded by raising the prime rate charged to their best corporate customers from 14.5% to 15.75%. Since the interest rates that S&Ls as well as banks had to charge new home buyers to make a profit went in some cases above state usury limits, home mortgages became legally impossible in some areas. The consequence was that home-ownership stalled at 60% of dwellings while the monthly cost of owning a home was three-fifths higher than in 1973. Renters now routinely paid landlords over a quarter of their income.

The Iran hostage crisis, a Soviet invasion of Afghanistan and a rising misery index in 1980's first quarter of 18.2% annualized inflation, 22.5% prime interest rate, and 7.4% unemployment brought Carter's government to near paralysis. Desperate to rally his political fortunes, he proposed on March 14 yet another anti-inflation package of reduced government expenditures, wage and price targets for private industry, and higher taxes on imported oil. The latter provision was intended not only to increase government revenue but reduce demand for oil, increase supply, and force down prices. While domestic production was pumping over 3.1 billion barrels annually in 1980 with a value at the wellhead of $39 billion, imports were in fact down to less than $2.5 billion barrels, 27.8% from the Middle East. On the contrary, the problem was not excessive demand but a severe bottleneck in the refining industry, where 189 companies owned 324 refineries with capacity to refine no more than 15.5 million barrels per day, just barely enough to cover consumption, that came in by tanker or from domestic fields through 167,000 miles of pipeline. It was a six-fold increase in the decade of the 1970s to $6 billion of revenue that provided Koch Industries with the wherewithal to start buying up rivals and help consolidate and improve capacity in the industry. For the moment, however, members of Congress were desperate to do anything to appear to be easing long lines at gas stations and bringing down prices. Over Carter's veto on June 6, 1980, the House and Senate eliminated the fee on imported oil that was adding 10 cents a gallon to the price of gasoline.

DEREGULATION AND FREE TRADE

Perhaps it was inevitable that Americans, dispirited by the economic, foreign policy, and social disturbances of the later 1960s and 1970s and disillusioned with government's fecklessness to find permanent solutions to problems, would turn back toward Free Market choices. Already, many politicians had come to understand that one vital component of economic growth was new investment in plant and equipment, hence cuts in corporate tax rates and beefing up of investment tax credits. The overall burden on individual tax payers through income, Social Security, and excise taxes had never been so high, amounting to a staggering 83.6% of Washington's $517 billion of receipts. Because of the need to fund $590 billion of expenditures in fiscal year 1980, including 53% for items that can be classified as social welfare programs, Democrats in Congress were afraid to bring down the burden on private citizens. They could, however, provide further indirect help to the 74 million Americans who relied on private business for their livelihoods by untangling the red tape that choked entrepreneurship and corporate decisions. For political reasons — to counter Republican charges that the party of Jefferson and FDR, Truman and Kennedy was degenerating into Socialism — they were inclined to compromise.

One industry ripe for more freedom was air transportation. Even with FTC restraints in the 1970s, airline revenue increases justified capital expenditures to expand air assets seven-fold to $57 billion by 1980 as well as passenger-pleasing innovations like American Airlines' one-stop automated check-in and Super Saver fare discounts, first for New York to California routes, then all others routes including flights to Mexico and Canada.

Genealogy of US Airline Industry, 1946-2004.

Southwest Airlines in Texas, Alaska Airways along the west coast, and Allegheny, which became US Air, were just waiting for permission to go national and provide more competition to the majors. Delta and Northwest wanted to cover all major US cities and cross the Atlantic besides.

The momentum for deregulation was so powerful in early 1978 that former astronaut and head of Eastern Airlines Frank Borman decided to go ahead with a purchase of 23 Airbus A-300 jets, the first acquisition of passenger planes from a non-American company by a US airliner. Boeing was not pleased, but neither were Eastern share-

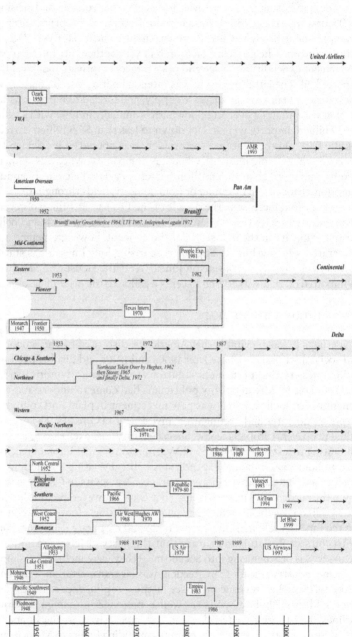

holders when Borman's clumsy management eventually brought down the company.

Airline deregulation to promote competition did finally come on October 24, 1978 by congressional fiat. Federal price and market-entry controls were phased out and the CAB abolished over seven years, except that air service was in theory guaranteed for small communities. As hoped, many start-up air carriers were founded, boosting capacity and resulting in price wars beneficial to passengers. By 1980, the nation's 820 airports hosted planes carrying 300 million domestic passengers flying 250 billion passenger miles. However, price competition also provoked an industry consolidation that began in 1979 with Republic Airlines forming out of the merger of North Central Airlines and Southern Airways, and then paying $38.5 million to add Hughes Air West the next year. In addition to Eastern, Braniff ran into immediate trouble trying to expand too fast, incurred heavy debt and losses, and swiftly by 1982 collapsed. In the overall scheme of things, bankruptcies for weak sisters did not immediately impair the industry. Deregulation prepared the way for profits once fuel prices came down in the 1980s.

Similarly, the federal government moved to reduce or eliminate the burden of regulations on other transportation industries, increase competition, and cut costs. Already in 1975, UPS received permission from the ICC to begin interstate service to Montana and Utah, complete service in Arizona, Idaho, and Nevada, and connect west coast facilities to new ones on the east coast. Although it was not contemplated that the monopoly possessed by the US Postal Service for delivery of mail, by 1980 totaling 90 billion pieces through 30,000 post offices, would be challenged, its more lucrative package delivery business started to come under pressure. Consumer choices increased again after Federal Express, founded in 1971 in Little Rock, Arkansas, installed *FedEx Drop Boxes* in key locations and in 1979 purchased a *COSMOS* computer system to manage packages, people, packages, routes, vehicles, and even the weather.

The nation's 35 million trucks carried in 1980 a quarter of the 2.3 trillion ton-miles of freight hauled each year. These now included thousands of Ryder vehicles for leasing and rental as well as auto transport that brought annual company revenues to $1 billion in 1978. After Congress passed the Motor Carrier Act on October 15, 1980 wiping out 45 year old regulations in the trucking industry, Consolidated Freightways was able to service all parts of the country from its 300 terminals. Household moving companies merged, reducing the cost to consumers of relocating to other cities and regions.

Because Ford and General Motors produced light trucks in addition to cars, they benefited in theory from truck deregulation. However, Chrysler with 9.1% of the US auto market was pummeled by high labor costs and falling sales. Because the company had lost $700 million over 1978-79, Congress decided to step in to save the tenth largest US corporation with $1.5 billion of loan guarantees. Federal backing permitted new company president Lido (Lee) A. Iacocca wrangle concessions from creditors, negotiate lower interest rate on new debt, and persuade the UAW to give back temporary wage concessions.

Because European but particularly Japanese car imports were smaller, more fuel efficient, generally better constructed, and less costly, they began to seize and hold a significant chunk of the US market. Constrained by the rising cost of living, Americans tended to hang on longer to older cars. That was a boon for Dana, whose sales of car parts after several acquisitions and strengthening of an overseas distribution network peaked in 1979 at $2.8 billion. The next year's travails cut $300 million from that figure, though employment held firm at 30,000. A problem for both vehicle makers and parts suppliers trying to preserve market share was that the annual population growth rate was slowing to less than 1%. The nation's fleet of 123.5 million cars would grow haphazardly and include more foreign models.

An expansion in trucking meant a further contraction in railroads. On September 29, 1979, Congress voted to cut the AMTRAK system 10% or 4,000 miles to eliminate unprofitable routes. An industry wide solution to the woes of high operating costs, antiquated equipment, and heavy debt only came the next year on October 14 when the House and Senate, simultaneous with the Motor Carriers Act, passed the Staggers Rail Act to permit railroad companies more leeway in setting prices while removing some immunity from anti-trust laws, that had been the fairly worthless *quid pro quo* for decades of regulation. At once, the Union Pacific, Missouri Pacific, and Western Pacific filed to merge their companies, which action was approved by the ICC in 1982 after Chicago, Rock Island & Pacific lines were sold off.

In the east, C&O was formed by the merger of the Chessie System with the Seaboard Coast Line Railroad. The latter's earliest roots had been put down in 1836 by the Richmond and Petersburg Railway, but by 1980 it included all major railroads in the Southeast. Another major player, Burlington Northern, strengthened its position by acquiring the St. Louis-San Francisco Railway, known as the Frisco. Altogether, the country still boasted 216,000 miles of RR track carrying 11 billion passenger miles and 919 billion short ton-miles of cargo.

If Carter and the Democrats came around to Republican thinking on deregulating transportation industries, they remained far apart on tariffs, even while agreeing in principle that the republic and its allies should move even further toward Free Trade. The crux of the problem was that foreign companies often received subsidies from their governments to "dump" goods in the US at prices below real production costs. The purpose was two-fold, to gain market share at the expense of US companies not so favored by Washington and preserve industry and employment at home. No industry was more affected by this practice than steel. Because US companies in 1980 produced about 110 million tons of steel and employed 750,000 people at wages that averaged $11.00 an hour, in 2004 money equal to annual income of $50,460, Carter moved to protect them by setting a minimum price for steel imports. That decision helped slow but not reverse the rate at which foreign competitors encroached on the business of US Steel, Bethlehem Steel, and the rest.

What many Republicans and a growing number of Democrats preferred to protectionism was innovation and flexibility such as demonstrated by Nucor and other mini-mills. The most committed to Free Market principles unadulterated by any political consideration contemplated the ruthless replacement of aged, crippled, and decrepit companies by new, nimble, and innovative entities. Only then, they believed, would export of goods and services, by 1980 running $15 billion behind the $294 billion of imports, surge. The country would no longer have to rely on interest income from overseas investment, valued at $936 billion while foreign investment in the US was only $544 billion, to keep the annual balance of payments $15 billion in the black. One great and growing cause for concern was that the goods imbalance alone, because of heavy Japanese and European manufactured imports, was $50 billion in the red. The President attempted to boost the prospects of food, machinery, and other important exports and help bring down inflation by negotiating a 1979 Multilateral Trade Pact. The treaty lowered the average US industrial tariff rate from 8.3% to 5.7%, making foreign imports cheaper and keeping pressure on auto companies and other producers of big ticket consumer durables not to raise prices as high as the rate of inflation. Countervailing duties against the value of foreign export subsidies were permitted, and *vice-versa*, if US industry was harmed.

F/A-18

The one manufacturing sector that was largely immune to foreign imports was aerospace/defense. Despite pulling out of Vietnam, the federal government had to ratchet back up spending on military hardware and equipment, first to force the Soviets to negotiate strategic arms limitations, next to modernize US nuclear and conventional forces to maintain powerful deterrent forces. That meant a new contract for McDonnell-Douglas to produce *F/A-18 Hornet* jets, eventually numbering 1,200. Alcoa supplied a high-strength alloy for the plane as well as the *A6 Intruder* and cruise missiles, destined to be deployed by the thousands and capable of carrying nuclear or conventional warheads. In 1977, Boeing produced the first *Airborne Warning and Control System* (*AWACS*) plane based on the *B-707* frame. IBM was paid billions to develop after 1978 a ground control computer system for a *Global Positioning System*. The next year, Martin Marietta began work on the *Pershing II*

IRBM for deployment in NATO countries. General Dynamic's Electric Boat Division launched the USS *Ohio*, the first of 18 *Trident* subs. For the fiscal year beginning October 1 1980, Washington was spending $160 billion annually on national defense, equal to 7.2% of GDP. Another $6.4 billion went to science, space, and technology. Although the space race to the moon had been won, follow-on *Apollo* flights, including a detente-driven link-up of an *Apollo* capsule with a Russian *Soyuz* spacecraft, brought in revenue for Rockwell and many sub-contractors to the program. A new generation of defense and telecom satellites being readied for orbit as well as a shift from long-distance, manned rocket launches toward the *Space Shuttle* concept meant that NASA would continue to spread lucrative contracts around to aerospace companies.

Trident submarine

Travelers insured the *Apollo-Soyuz* link up in 1975. The wherewithal of MetLife and other big players, overseeing by 1980 over $4 trillion of life insurance in force as well as other policies permitting companies in the industry to assembly $650 billion of financial assets, meant that even the riskiest government project could be covered. However, six times as much came to be concentrated in the hands of banks. Aside from household savings, investments, and other holdings, amounting by 1980 to $6.63 trillion or 42% of the nation's total, major accumulations of money were held by non-financial businesses ($1.6 trillion), government and quasi-government agencies ($1 trillion), and pension funds ($710 billion). Although by comparison, other managed funds at $146 billion seemed overshadowed, they had nearly tripled since 1975 and would increase ten-fold in the decade of the 1980s. That meant a huge windfall for Fidelity, innovating with check-writing on mutual funds and tax-exempt mutual funds.

Because interest rates were sky-high, even safe mutual fund investments in government bonds proved very lucrative. Banks and S&Ls demanded of the government regulatory changes to make them more competitive with brokerages, in 1974 including Charles Schwab, a discount operation taking advantage of the deregulation of commissions. In the Depository Institutions Deregulation and Control Act of 1980, Congress phased out interest rate ceilings on savings accounts, permitted the paying of interest on checking accounts, overrode state usury limits on mortgage rates, let S&Ls make real estate loans the same as national banks, and made uniform reserve requirements for all depository institutions. The size of deposits insured by the FDIC was raised from $40,000 per account to $100,000. An unforeseen problem that developed over time because of this latter decision was that to attract investors who would raise their holdings in an account to the maximum, S&Ls started to offer interest rates that left them too little profit to cover loans to individuals and companies with too much risk. They increased their exposure so quickly with riskier loans that what previously had been a relatively safe and uncomplicated industry was undermined.

Rather, the future belonged to bigger financial institutions such as Citibank, formerly First National City Bank, catering to customers with 24 hour automated teller machines (ATMs) and progressively freed from government-imposed restraints on expansion. Wells Fargo moved aggressively into ATMs as well and became the first company to process both *MasterCard* charge cards and its fast-rising challenger *Visa*. There was still room for late-comers such as Conseco, a diversified financial company founded in suburban Indianapolis in 1979, to deal in insurance and investments. But that company struggled half a dozen years and had to survive Chapter 11 bankruptcy before taking firm root, going public, and proving its acumen in a booming market.

DIVERSIFICATION AND SPECIALIZATION IN DIFFICULT TIMES

Rough economic seas confirmed for some top executives that the conglomerate model for large corporations was preferable to a narrow industry focus. Although the energy crisis added to the variability of sales and profits accounted for by the cyclicality of businesses, other sectors with counter-cyclicality might smooth returns on investment. Such was the experience of 3M Corporation, rising to $5 billion of revenue in 1980. A slowdown of sales of automotive fasteners was partially alleviated by an upswing in fasteners for diapers. Efforts to build up a backup security business for computers were funded by profits from dental filling materials. Revenue from insulated clothing and other products contributed to the bottom line.

Because US manufacturing as a share of GDP slowly declined in the period toward 21%, diversification into business services was wise. From food vending, Aramark expanded into environmental, health, child care, and uniform services. Avery Adhesives, founded in 1935 to make self-adhesive labels, took advantage of government regulations to branch out into environmentally safe coatings. Competing with 3M, the corporation's self-adhesives for diapers (such as Kimberly-Clark's sensation *Huggies* with elastic at the legs and an hourglass shape, *Kotex* feminine pads, and *Depend* incontinence product for adults) helped lift sales to nearly $1 billion by 1980.

In absolute terms, the manufacturing base of the country was still formidable. In addition to $81.5 billion worth of food, beverage, and tobacco products as well as $47.3 billion of textiles, apparel, and leather, US factories produced $153.6 billion of primary and fabricated metals and process minerals, $216.5 billion of non-electrical

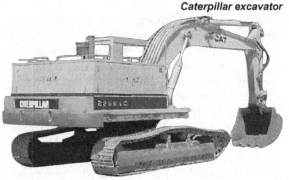

Caterpillar excavator

machinery and transport equipment, and $73.2 billion of electrical and electronic machinery. The largest component of all became chemicals and related goods at $224.5 billion. Illinois Tool Works contributed to the sector with a line of epoxies and sealants.

Also doing well were firms that turned out construction equipment. These ranged from Snap-On's wrenches, ringing up $373 million of sales by 1979, to Caterpillar's big excavators, tracked and wheeled earth movers, and other heavy vehicles. With improvements to homes accounting by 1980 for 17% of the $3.5 trillion value in 87 million dwelling units, construction of houses, apartment buildings, and condominiums was steady. Georgia Pacific built plywood plants in Dixie and a roofing manufacturing plant in Franklin, Ohio to provide wood materials and, after buying Hudson Pulp and Paper Corporation of Palatka, Florida in 1979 to acquire another 550,000 acres of timberland, topped $5 billion of sales. The next year on May 18, Weyerhaeuser lost 68,000 acres of trees when an exploding volcano in Mount St. Helens in Washington State destroyed $2.7 billion worth of property. An emergency salvage operation put enough wood on the market to build 85,000 homes. Meanwhile, Masco Corporation made acquisitions in the US and overseas to get into the ventilating equipment industry, where a surge in central heating units to 69% of dwellings was followed by a rush into central air conditioning. Because 99% of residences enjoyed indoor plumbing, the company expanded its line of faucets, showering products, and water pumps.

Indispensable and ubiquitous were televisions and radios. Nine of ten US homes had at least one of the former by 1980, including 71 million color sets and 79 million black and white, while 79 million was also the number of radios in homes. However, as radios in cars became a commodity of slight profitability, Ford sold its Philco division to GTE-Sylvania. Although radio tubes still bore the *Philco* name, they were made in Japan.

Ted Koppel

The popularity of TV continued to increase with the size of screens as well as proliferation of programming. After a decision by the Supreme Court in 1974, supplemented by a copyright law two years later, resolved concern by cable TV companies over liability for picking up programming, that branch of the industry surged to 4,350 cable systems with 18.5 million subscribers, a 400% increase in a decade to coverage of 20% of homes. Most aggressive was Turner, reaching a national audience in 1976 by broadcasting WTBS signals by satellite to cable providers. His Turner Broadcasting System came to true prominence after he launched the 24 hour Cable News Network (CNN) in 1979. Specifically, the *Nightline* program, airing at 11:30 p.m. and anchored by Ted Koppel, gripped the nation's attention by playing up the Iran hostage crisis. Turner also increased the value of his newly purchased Atlanta Braves baseball and Atlanta Hawks basketball teams by putting games on national broadcasts. In fact, the TV success of Major League Baseball and the National Basketball Association (NBA) proved to National Football League (NFL) owners and other purveyors of big-time sports, including the Olympic Games, boxing matches, and golf and tennis tournaments that sporting events, by 1980 selling 84 million tickets in 3,700 facilities, the largest of which seated 100,000 persons, could be sold to the major networks for tens and hundreds of millions of dollars.

Once players and their agents realized the kind of profits new TV contracts were bringing owners, demands for higher salaries, eventually up to and exceeding 50% of league revenues, became vocal, persistent, and backed by threat of strikes.

By comparison, 1,650 museums attracted 175 million visitors but could never be as profitable because stationary attractions, no matter how exquisite and rare, had far less appeal on TV. The fact that 160 million tickets were sold to performing arts shows indicated that a TV market for Broadway type show entertainment might be more practical. However, in order for that type of spectacle and sound to be properly appreciated, a theater setting was necessary. From time to time, a hit show such as the 1978 musical *Grease*, the highest grossing film of that genre of all time, did translate well from the Great White Way to the silver screen.

Additional proof that motion picture entertainment was big business even in difficult economic times was the success of adventure and fantasy movies. New director Steven Spielberg made *Jaws*, *E.T. the Extra Terrestrial*, and *Close Encounters of the Third Kind* into huge blockbuster successes for Universal and Columbia with the definite possibility of lucrative sequels. The innovation of multiplex cinemas made it possible for theater owners to show several pictures at once, pleasing discriminating viewers and spreading the risk. In 1980, 1 billion tickets were sold in 15,000 cinemas for 225 feature pictures and lesser-budget films.

Spin-off revenue from movie-related merchandising and music increased. The largest US record company and first in 1978 over the $1 billion sales mark worldwide was CBS Records. Two years later, the first compact discs (CDs) and CD players came out. Consumers with stacks of vinyl records and cassette tapes had to decide whether to purchase songs they already possessed as well as new offerings in the more durable, clear-as-a-bell CD format or wait for devices that would somehow let them "burn" a blank CD with the old recordings.

Government regulation still inhibited media companies from gobbling up entities in other niches willy-nilly. Limited penetration was permitted, however, so long as competition and choices were maintained for consumers. Thus, after Knight Newspapers and Ridder Publications merged in 1974, Knight-Ridder bought VHF TV stations in Providence, Rhode Island, Albany, New York, and Flint, Michigan. When Gannet merged with Combined Communications five years later, the company possessed 78 daily and 21 weekly newspapers, a national news service, and seven TV and 14 radio stations. The New York Times Company slipped into broadcasting as well by buying up local stations in Arkansas and Alabama. However, the New York Post came under the thumb of Australian magnate and owner of *The Times* (of London) Robert Murdoch and his growing international News Corp organization.

The New York Times signaled concern about the future of book and magazine publishing by divesting itself of Cambridge Book Company and *Us* magazine. RCA, which had bought Ballantine Books in 1973, sold Random House to Advance in 1980. In addition to newspaper publishing, consolidating to 1,700 newspapers with circulation of 62 million, the best place to be in print was textbooks. McGraw-Hill proved that assertion by topping $1 billion of revenue and escaping a take-over attempt by American Express.

No matter the waxing of intellectual and intangible property values, sales of consumer goods continued to carry most of the economy. Enjoying a 250% surge in revenue from cameras and film, copier-duplicators, microfilm machines, and plastics for beverage machines, Kodak reached $10 billion of sales in 1981. Whirlpool's household appliances generated a fifth as much. Amana's success with microwaves insured that 65% of house-holds had at least one. Overall, US consumer durable assets held by Americans swelled to $930 billion by 1980. That was an average of $10,700 per household, in 2004 money equal to over $24,540, and more than a fifth of all tangible household asset value.

The popularity of microwaves translated into a big rebound for Tupperware, now making microwave safe containers. Marketing a rival line as well as myriad other plastic products, Dow Chemical grew revenues to the $10 billion level a year before Kodak. In 1980, P&G reached double-digits as well by branching out from household and personal products into pharmaceuticals with its *Didronel* drug treatment for Paget's disease. Avon Products was 30% as large by putting over 1 million representatives into the field globally to sell women's cosmetics. Competition in that area as well as clothes and accessories came from Jones Apparel of New York, spun off from W.R. Grace in 1975. Liz Claiborne the next year was a fashionable new competitor. But to obtain better brand names, shoppers had to go into higher end department stores such as the May Company, coming up slowly but steadily to $3 billion of sales by 1981. Its success stimulated Federated to buy Rich's of Atlanta for more economies of scale.

Nike's Zoom Waffle Trainer

Even with the Baby Boom giving way to a Baby Bust generation held down by economic uncer-tainties and more women working full time, com-panies that catered to children could still succeed by selling fun products. Although Mattel stumbled in 1977 trying to branch out prematurely into electronic games, Kenner Products cut into Mattel's doll market by making a *Star Wars* line of action figures only 3 3/4 inches tall. For adults who were still young at heart, or who wanted to remain so by joining a nationwide fitness movement advanced by President Carter's commitment to jogging, *Waffle Trainer* running shoes by Nike were the cool product. Founded in 1964, monikered after the winged goddess of victory, the company made itself a household name by providing the *Tail Wind* model with an air sole cushioning system worn by British champion Steve Ovett to win the 1500 meters in 1980 Olympics in Moscow. Nike's strategy of sports star endorsements, including by brash tennis champion John McEnroe, as well as wide distri-bution through Woolworth Company's Foot Locker stores in malls such as Simon Property Group's huge North Riverside Park Mall, west of Chicago, made possible an initial public offering of stock and surging sales. Even after Reebok, a company founded far back in the 1890s, and German import Adidas as well as other companies sprang up to challenge, Nike dominated the field.

When makers of brand name clothes and sports shoes realized how anxious Amer-icans were to be "with it," they raised prices. Profits were further increased by having some textiles made in Central America, the Caribbean, South Asia, and other Third World regions. Under the Multi-Fiber Arrangement of 1974, four dozen countries were awarded set quota shares of the US and European markets to avoid an unregulated flood of cheap clothing, damaging to domestic industry. In return, the US and European nations got better protection for intellectual property rights and overseas investments. As with ticket price escalations at sporting events and live theater, the force of inflation eroded the ability of tens of millions of lower middle and working class Americans to afford such goods and entertainment. To stretch a dollar, more value-conscious consumers gravitated to discount chains for household and personal products. The decade of the 1970s brought Wal-Mart into Tennessee, Kentucky, Mississippi, and Texas with sales jumping to $340 million from 125 stores by 1975, and then after buying Mohr-Value stores in Michigan and Illinois, the Hutcheson Shoe Company, and adding pharmacies, auto service centers, and jewelry divisions, $1.25 billion from 276 stores and 21,000 employees by 1979. Discount store success also inspired Kresge to rename itself K-mart in 1978 and Dayton-Hudson to take greater pride in its Target subsidiary, the next year contributing a majority of company revenues surging toward $5 billion. A year after clothing retailer The Gap, founded in 1969, went public in 1976, rival T.J. Maxx was founded in Massachusetts.

But the company destined by 2000 to become the nation's second largest retailer after Wal-Mart was not founded until 1979. Operating in Atlanta, Home Depot rang up $22 million of sales the next year. Its revenues from selling products to do-it-your-selfers in the home improvement market would grow over 2,000% in the next two decades. It would reach $50 billion of sales faster than any other company.

The rise of the new discounters, including a company called the Price Club, founded in San Diego in 1976 that later became Costco Wholesale and reached the $1 billion sales plateau within eight years, posed a mortal threat to the old discounters. Although J.C. Penney approached $11 billion of sales by 1978 and generated $1 billion from catalogue sales alone the next year by accepting both MasterCard and Visa credit cards, its infrastructure as a full-line merchandiser carrying heavy inventory of furniture, household appliances, and consumer electronics as well as the burden of operating costs inflated by a veteran workforce of tens of thousands of employees expecting to earn living wages put it at a long-term cost disadvantage. Like the nation's largest retailer Sears with its middle-of-the-road brands, the company retained the loyalty of millions of consumers, but the price discrepancies with the Wal-Marts in clothing and lesser durables drew away less affluent shoppers. Specialized companies such as the entity founded as a TV store in Richmond, Virginia in 1949 that 25 years later became Circuit City with 32,000 square foot store offering consumer electronics and major appliances also were destined to undermine revenues and profits.

What made the challenge from Wal-Mart so imposing was that founder Sam Walton and other company executives saw no reason to limit the chain to general merchandise. They came to understand that a conglomerate concept of goods and services offered within increasingly huge warehouse-size stores would produce the financial wherewithal to overawe even the most powerful retailers in other areas. Centered within the scope of their ambition were big grocery chains, competing to sell food but also small personal products, such as Gillette's innovations *Cricket* disposable lighters and *Good News* twin blade razors that boosted revenues to $2 billion by 1980. Canned goods like *Bumble-Bee* tuna fish, bottled sports drink *Gatorade*, and *Planter's* nuts could be sold just as easily from a Wal-Mart shelf as a Kroger's or Albertson's or Publix's. And from the point of view of big agri-businesses led by Cargill, importing Brazilian frozen concentrated orange juice and coffee, buying up food processing plants around the world, exporting grain, and competing with Archer Daniels Midland in corn wet milling to make products as diverse as high fructose corn syrup and fuel ethanol, the end destination of its products did not matter. Cobb, purchased by UpJohn, and Tyson Foods, competing and cooperating with Cobb in the burgeoning chicken processing business, would be just as pleased to sell to a sprawling discount as a grocery chain. That was why food retailers varying from Kroger, with nearly ten-fold Wal-Mart's sales in 1980, Publix and Albertson's with almost twice as much, and H.E. Butt opening a milk plant and bakery in Texas to control more of its supplies worried about the new discounters. They all began building supermarkets with check-out scanners and credit card terminals and innovating in goods and services anyway possible.

Critical to the success of any food retailer was offering the most popular brand names. Simultaneously, major companies protected their dominance of the food products market by seeking to acquire brands in new niches. Jumping on the fitness craze, General Mills bought Yoplait Yogurt in 1977 while Heinz the next year obtained Weight Watchers International, designer of a weight loss program, to compete with *Slim-Fast* products. After Heinz then ventured overseas with its line of nutrition and wellness products, Kellogg was persuaded in 1981 to offer *Nutri-grain* cereal bars. However, Hershey stuck with its strategy of catering to the public's sweet tooth by buying Y&S Candies, a Canadian maker of *Twizzlers* licorice. Coors introduced *Coors Light* beer to take sales to young men out on the town or at sporting events away from Anheuser Busch.

Meanwhile, condensed soup sales began to give way to ready-to-serve products from Progresso of New York, a company with roots in Italy, New Orleans, and New Jersey. Campbell not only shifted some production itself to ready-to-serve but diversified by purchasing Vlasic Foods, a maker of pickles and other condiments. With the growing popularity of frozen foods and premixed products, Pillsbury obtained Green Giant and its line of frozen vegetables. Consolidated Foods took over Chef Pierre's frozen prepared desserts. However, in a major strategic shift, the latter corporation bought Hanes of North Carolina to get into women's hosiery, swimwear, men's underwear, and cosmetics. Other acquisitions brought its 1980 sales to $5 billion.

Another entry to the $5 billion club was PepsiCo. The company reached that plateau by 1979, as well as 110,000 employees, after purchasing Pizza Hut's 3,200 restaurants and Taco Bell's 1,000 establishments. Equally as lucrative as selling soft drinks was the plastic bottles in which they were contained. Although Monsanto stole a march in 1976 with its *Cycle-Safe* soft drink bottle, the FDA banned the product the next year as a cancer risk. That opened the door for Goodyear with a polyester resin shatterproof soft drink bottle to take market share, supplement business from its new *Tiempo* all-season radial tire, and reach $8.4 billion of sales by 1980. Eastman Chemical's *Kodapak* polyester (PET) product was the other major competitor in soft drink bottles, helping the company climb to over $2 billion of sales by end of the period.

MAN VERSUS MACHINE

One hot field for research and development in the 1970s was without question computers and software. Texas Instruments, Motorola, and others focused on developing microprocessors able to handle more and faster calculations. The former built steadily to $4.1 billion of revenue in 1980 and nearly 90,000 employees by coming out in 1973 with a 4 thousand bit (4K) DRAM chip, and the next year the first single-chip microcomputer. The company continued to compete with HP, rising to $2.4 billion of revenue and 52,000 employees, by selling electronic calculators not only to businesses but home and school users. But Motorola jumped ahead with the first 8K-bit microprocessor containing 4,000 transistors for automotive, desktop computing, and video game applications. By 1979, Motorola had a 16K-bit microprocessor capable of 2 million calculations per second.

Bill Gates

By contrast, Xerox in 1973 produced the *Alto*, the first personal computer (PC) prototype with a mouse, a graphical user interface, and bit-mapped display. This innovation was a first step in a strategy of getting out of the mainframe competition with IBM. However, the cost of developing PCs was so small relative to mainframes and supercomputers, including the first *Cray-1* turned out a few years later by Cray Research, that many small players, such as MITS Corporation of Albuquerque, New Mexico could easily enter the market. The most important barrier to overcome was not hardware but software. Enter Bill Gates, Paul Allen, and Steve Ballmer with their start-up Microsoft Corporation. *BASIC* language software written for MITS' shoebox-size *Altair* computer generated $1 million of sales for Microsoft by 1978.

Apple II System

The problem with the *Altair* was that without a keyboard it was not "user-friendly." Rather, the *Apple I* introduced April 1, 1976 by the Apple Company of Steve Jobs and Steve Wozniak achieved the first real personal computer success. Featuring a black and white video monitor, 8K of dynamic RAM, a keyboard, and a 6502 processor designed by Rockwell and produced by MOS Technologies that cost only $25, the machine generated $133,000 of revenue. Only the fact that each of the 200 *Apple I* computers sold had to be assembled by hand limited its business potential. Thus it was RadioShack, billing itself as "biggest name in little computers," that raked in revenue with the first mass-produced computer, the *TRS-80*, including a 5.25 inch floppy disc drive for easier software loading. The *Trash-80*, as some called it, sold 10,000 in one month in 1977, and then 200,000 cumulatively by 1981 through RadioShack's own stores.

In response, Jobs and Wozniak came out in 1978 with the *Apple II*. The machine added a color monitor and audio cassette drive for storage that was later replaced by a floppy disk drive. In fact, it was the *Apple II*'s easy-to-understand graphical interface, running on Microsoft's *BASIC* language source code, that convinced many schools to enter the computer age. Once Visicalc's spreadsheet software became available for the *Apple II*, sales to businesses also exploded. Despite the fact that at $1,298 the machine cost twice as much as the *Apple I* and 63% more than its principal competitor, Commodore Company's *PET*, cumulative sales mounted to an incredible 750,000 by 1980. As the *Apple III* was coming out that year, Jobs took the company and its 1,000 excited employees public.

However, the big gorilla of the industry with $22.9 billion of revenue by 1979, $3 billion of net earnings, and 337,000 employees was still IBM. Big Blue's executives recognized the potential of PCs and decided to enter the market. They were fortunate that Intel sprang up in the Silicon Valley south of San Francisco, California in 1978 to provide an *8086* microprocessor followed by an *8088* chip, and Seagate also of the Golden State arose the next year to make hard drives on which operating system software for IBM's planned personal computer would be loaded. When ready in 1981, it was called the *PC* and thus knock-offs by other companies were referred to as *PC* clones. However, because IBM's collective corporate intelligence did not realize that software revenues and profits would in the long run come to rival and exceed hardware, they signed a contract with Microsoft to provide a disc operating system (DOS) for the machine, rather than write and own such software themselves. Microsoft actually bought its *DOS-1* software and the future of PC computing from a small Seattle software company for $50,000.

In point of fact, software already by 1975 accounted for 42% of the computer industry's $22.1 billion of net fixed assets. Although that share would decline over the next decade to less than 40%, albeit of a more than quintupled pie, the foundation was being laid for a tremendous software explosion in the later 1980s. Applications from start-up companies already ranged from Compuware's *Abend-Aid* to detect errors and suggest corrective actions in corporate mainframe systems to Oracle's relational software for databases to Wordstar's word processing software to Lotus Corporation's *1-2-3* spreadsheet.

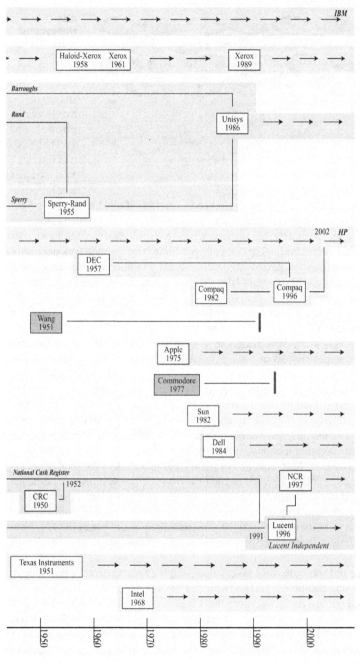

Genealogy of US Computer Hardware Industry, 1946-2004

Ross Perot's EDS grew revenues from $90 million in 1972 toward $500 million by end of the period by offering a *Life Management System II* for large life insurance companies, airline ticket processing software to big air carriers, and administrative software for the federal and state government, including processing health insurance claims. But it would be the rise of IBM *PCs* and *PC* clones running on Microsoft *DOS* software that would lift computers from the 1 million in use in the US in 1980 to many times that number. The value of operating and application software would eventually by turn of the century exceed hardware by 250% and come in aggregate with hardware to match the fixed asset value of communications equipment.

IBM Honeycomb mass storage system

In the interim, however, phones and switching networks and other such com-
munications devices came by end of the period to claim 48% of all the country's $251 billion in information processing equipment and software fixed assets. One reason was that in 1975, AT&T began computerizing its network with digital electronic toll switches each capable of handling a maximum 350,000 calls per hour. The upgrade was necessary because annually Americans were placing 220 billion local, 18 billion long-distance, and 500 million international calls. Two years later, Ma Bell opened a Network Operations Center in Bedminster, New Jersey to manage the entire long-distance network. Addi-tionally, Bell Labs installed and tested the first fiber-optic light wave communications system under the streets of Chicago in 1977 as a precursor to the first long-distance fiber-optic system connecting Boston, New York, and Washington D.C. That was a necessary advance to stave off competition from smaller but still substantial companies such as United Utilities (later Sprint) with 1976 revenues of $1 billion, who were also looking into fiber-optic cable and digital switch technology. AT&T went them all one better by using the windy city as testing ground for a cellular system that by 1980 used digital signal pro-cessors for better sound, greater channel capacity, and lower cost than analog processors. The nearly century old behemoth based in New York City was determined to continue its domination of American communications.

Already in 1973, however, Motorola had designed its *Dynamic Adaptive Total Area Coverage* or *DynaTac* portable radio telephone as the first true cellular system prototype for public. It was installed in the Washington-Baltimore area four years later. Focusing for better profitability on wireless systems and semiconductor production, the company sold its *Quasar* TV business to Matsushita Electric Industrial Company of Japan in 1974. Revenues soared nevertheless from $3.1 billion net to $186 million by period's end, and employment to 71,500.

Just as computer and software fixed asset value composed one quarter of the value of all information processing equipment and software in 1980, the latter accounted for nearly one quarter of the $1.1 trillion fixed assets of all US business equipment and software. A small but high-profile niche was photocopying machines, rising from over 1 million in use in 1973 with a value of $8.5 billion to about triple those figures in 1980. Because of a 1975 anti-trust settlement with the FTC, Xerox was forced to license its xerographic patents to other companies. To generate new revenue, the company two years later brought out the *Xerox 9700*, the first laser printer. TI's *OMNI 800 Model* series provided prompt competition, but the biggest threat in the long run would arise from HP, belatedly entering the field in 1980.

Computers and communication were high-profile, high-tech fields. Behind the scenes, the American economy also benefited from a proliferation of new petrochemical products that included weed and brush killers, insecticides, fungicides, soil conditioners, mold inhibitors, fertilizers, synthetic hormones for animals, acrylic and polyester fibers, durable press garments, and detergents and solvents for cleaning. Additional innovations in heavy-duty construction materials, higher-octane gas, insulation materials, lubricants, man-made industrial diamonds, nylon-tire cord, paints and pigments, polyethylene packaging materials, synthetic carpets, synthetic rubber compounds, and tools and equipment transformed many businesses and industries. Automation, such as electronic knitting machines and electronic signals driving needles that could change a pattern in minutes rather than the previous standard of eight hours, boosted textile production but obviated the necessity of maintaining on the payroll so many workers. Sophisticated household appliances such as self-cleaning ovens made daily living easier even as other technological innovation undermined the wherewithal of millions to afford them. For those who maintained economic viability in the modern age, the world of science and technology produced limitless vistas; for those whose skills could be improved upon by machines, innovation and invention proved a curse.

No labor sector was harder hit than manufacturing. In the 1970s, employment in companies that made consumer, commercial, and industrial products fell below 20% of all employment for the first time since the nineteenth century. Within manufacturing companies, production workers as a percent of all workers fell five percentage points to 65% while production payroll share dropped to 55%. Average annual wages for production workers came down incrementally toward 62% of what salaried employees earned.

Oil freighter in drydock
Toledo, Ohio

But the most notable ratio change was the increase of capital expenditures as a percent of production payroll. Having already climbed from 18.2% in 1960 to 24.2% in 1970, by 1980 they hit one third. That helped overall annual investment in nonresidential fixed assets balloon in the decade of the 1970s by 275% to $352 billion. The figure was 20% higher than in 1970 when measured in 2004 money.

Meanwhile, successful union negotiations for higher wages and benefits were the straw that broke the camel's back as far as business leaders were concerned. Two out of five union contracts contained "automatic escalator" clauses providing annual cost-of-living wage increases. For example, the USW deal by president Iorworth W. Abel with major steel companies in March 1973 guaranteed a minimum 3% annual wage boost after the current contract expired. Other major provisions were a no-strike pledge by the union, a no-lockout pledge by companies, and resort to binding arbitration in the event that subsequent talks became deadlocked. When the next year, the union concluded a so-called *Experimental Negotiating Agreement* with the companies, workers not only received the 3% annual wage increase but cost of living adjustments based on the rate of inflation. Through 1982, as a consequence, wages in the steel industry soared 179% to an average without overtime of $11.55 per hour, equal in 2004 money to annual income of $45,200.

The problem, of course, was that imported steel and steel substitutes were buffeting the industry. Profits in good times that might have been reinvested in new plant and equipment to make companies more efficient were siphoned off in part to pay higher labor costs. As productivity — the amount produced per worker — fell not only in steel but all US manufacturing by half to an annual average increase through 1995 of only 1.4%, the tendency was to slash employment to free up funds for capital investment. USW membership, peaking in 1973 at 1.5 million persons, was steadily cut to less than half over the same time frame. Yet unions, as energy and other inflation spiked toward double digits, kept pushing for higher wages to preserve the hard-won standard of living of the heavy industry working class. To keep labor peace and steady production to fend off foreign competition, corporation executives countered in part with lucrative benefit packages that promised secure pensions as well as full medical benefits after retirement. They knew full well that continuing downward trends in revenues and profits might leave them unable in the future to make good a substantial part of the commitment. They counted in the last resort on the government to do for the steel industry what Congress did in 1974 for the railroad industry when it bailed out the railroad retirement system with $285 million annually until 2000.

Among the most militant unions was the UMW. In 1977, despite the fact that coal miners' average wage of $8.44 produced annual income equal in 2004 money to $52,585, the union called a strike for higher wages. Finally after 110 days, Carter invoked the Taft-Hartley cooling off provision and sent in federal mediators to assist negotiations. Miners wound up with annual wage increases that boosted wages 17% the next year. But despite further increases to $13.05 per hour by 1982, rampaging inflation actually cut miners' purchasing power to the level of the mid 1970s. All American workers, no matter what their income level, were simultaneously affected.

As previously discussed, the second oil shock of 1979 sent inflation through the political roof and helped destroy Carter's presidency. Many business leaders in manufacturing concluded that the only way to survive roughening economic seas and beat back foreign competition was to restructure to cut labor costs permanently. One method was to

Strip mining in the West

move production from unionized factories in the Northeast and Midwest to the West as well as the South. Because in the latter region unions had never taken root, companies could take advantage of a much cheaper labor force, including 53% of the nation's African Americans. Through 1979, the West gained 28 million people and the South 25 million. Although a substantial portion of the increase was caused by natural population growth, millions, including a net change of 80,000 blacks into Dixie, relocated to find work.

An even cheaper labor force than African Americans were the 4.5 million immigrants who entered the country in the 1970s. In addition to the 1.6 million Asians, including from South Vietnam after the Communist victory there, flocking mainly to California and other Western states, 637,000 Mexicans crossed the border legally into the West and South while many more illegal immigrants came to do seasonal agricultural work. Although these persons were not generally a threat to take mainstream manufacturing jobs from white males, American women in all parts of the country increasingly were. By 1980, nearly 48% of all workers were female. Granted, their primary entry into the job market was as retail and other service workers, but newcomers of any kind were inclined to accept lower wages and shy from union membership for fear of alienating employers. Attempts by unions to organize service industries faltered as a result.

Lastly, and perhaps most ominously for the labor movement, more companies saw wisdom in moving production entirely out of the United States. By opening factories in Third World regions, they accessed dirt-cheap work forces whose wages would be far less than the cost of transporting goods back into the country on a Merchant Marine fleet of 29 million dead weight tons capable of carrying 320 million metric tons of cargo, supplemented by foreign merchant carriers. Already since the Second World War, a few American manufacturers had tested out the concept in Puerto Rico. Industrial production in that US Commonwealth state passed agricultural output of such staples as sugar, tobacco, and rum as far back as 1956. By the 1970s, Puerto Ricans not only turned out textiles, apparel, and leather goods but higher-value electrical and electronic equipment and chemicals. That flow contributed to annual imports of $130 billion of manufactured goods brought into the country, particularly from Europe and Japan. Moreover, despite a vibrant tourism industry that welcomed after 1968 more than 1 million visitors a year, Puerto Rico's unemployment rate never fell below 13%. Employers could offer very low wages under $1 per hour to workers and still by 1972 lift average annual income on the island to $1,713, highest in Latin America.

By contrast, the minimum wage on the US mainland was raised to $2 per hour on May 1, 1974, and then $2.10 per hour eight months later, and finally $2.30 per hour a year after that, except that the minimum wage for farm workers did not reach that figure until January 1, 1978. A full-time employee making the minimum wage that year took home annual income equal in 2004 money to $13,333. Although Congress tried to mandate that 7 million more workers, including state and local government employees, receive the minimum, the Supreme Court ruled in 1976 that the federal government could not constitutionally determine state wages. The House and Senate did have authority that year to extend unemployment compensation payments to 8 million more workers of all kinds.

WEALTH AND WORRY

The American middle class, defined broadly by the US government as those persons enjoying income above the poverty line but below what was considered wealthy, peaked in 1973 at 60% of all households. Widespread affluence manifested itself in annual investment of residential fixed assets of $74 billion topped by annual purchase of $118 billion of consumer durables. With household net worth exceeding $5 trillion and over 30% of families invested either individually or through pension or mutual funds in stocks, Johnson's vision of a Great Society with material abundance seemed realized. In 2004 money, household net worth of over $21.2 trillion had increased 280% since 1945.

However, after the OPEC oil embargo exposed weaknesses in the economy, the next several years turned into a rollercoaster ride for the middle class. An immediate drop in the stock market drove out a third of investors and wiped out a quarter trillion dollars of value. By 1980, although annual investment in residential fixed assets was up to $123 billion and consumer durable purchases $207 billion, inflation actually cut the figures as measured in 2004 money by 11.5% and 5.5% respectively. On a *per capita* basis the shortfall was even sharper.

That was the reason that household net worth dipped sharply when measured in 2004 money to $18.3 trillion by 1975 before coming back up to $21.9 trillion in 1980. On a *per capita* basis in 2004 money, perhaps the best average indicator of distress, household net worth plunged 15% to a nadir of $84,715 in 1975 before recovering to $96,280 in 1980. On the other hand, the wealthy continued to be extravagant even as want was all around them. In 1976, founder of Getty Oil John Paul Getty made a bequest of over $1 billion in company stock to found the Getty Museum in the Los Angeles area. Because he stipulated that the museum spend tens of millions each year to increase the institution's collection, the values of paintings, statuary, and other kinds of works of art were bid up. Despite the fact that the share of all national income claimed by the top 5% of earners declined by 1980 to 15.8%, because the share of wealth claimed by the top 1% of 82 million households had risen to over one-third of $9.6 trillion of household net worth, rich people could afford to pay premium prices for beauty.

By contrast, the second fifth of earners enjoyed more income but less real wealth. The bottom three-fifths experienced less of both. In fact, the so-called 80-20 rule that the bottom 80% of households should in a progressive capitalist economy have at least 20% of wealth suffered a blow. The share of wealth claimed by the vast majority slipped to only 18.8% with a continuing downward trend. Overall, *per capita* GDP rose from $6,550 in 1973 to $12,280. Because of inflation, the rise in *per capita* GDP in 2004 money was barely discernible, from $27,830 to $28,100.

Getty Museum

Higher unemployment and reduced incomes caused the city of New York nearly to go into bankruptcy in 1975. The local government had to be bailed out by $2.3 billion of federal loans and another $1.65 billion in federal loan guarantees two years later. Congress passed a law on April 8, 1976 permitting cities to file for bankruptcy without approval of creditors while continuing to borrow to maintain services. This was a reason that federal, state, and

local government in aggregate were able to double annual government investment in fixed assets between 1973 and 1980 to $99 billion and Washington was able to continue revenue sharing with states. Government debt as a percentage of government assets was simultaneously reduced below 59% or nearly half the level as 1945. Federal government liabilities as a percentage of GDP, meanwhile, bottomed out at 31%.

These figures gave credence to Reagan's assertion that Democrats in control of Congress and state governments could not break the taxing and spending habit. Rather than grant significant tax relief beyond Washington's moves to cut top marginal tax rates to stimulate investment, the people's representatives voted themselves a 27.8% pay raise in 1977 to $57,000, albeit while restricting earnings from *honoraria* and forcing disclosure of outside income and gifts. Abuse of such gifts, including from private industry and lobbyists, got several high ranking politicians into hot water. Culmination of congressional wrongdoing in the ABSCAM bribery and conspiracy scandal resulted in conviction of the first member of the House of Representatives since 1861.

Meanwhile, Congress did pass legislation on October 6, 1978 to ease the conditions for individuals declaring personal bankruptcy. An immediate consequence was an 82% increase in the annual number of such declarations. Because bankruptcy protection from creditors could now be obtained so readily, profligate individuals were encouraged to use credit card and installment debt more liberally. By 1980, consumers owed $70 billion of the former and $300 billion of the latter. That was a major reason that the ratio of household liabilities to assets rose from 10.3% in 1970 to 13.2% by 1980. Inflated values of homes kept the burden from appearing even larger.

All things considered, American taxpayers emerged from the 1970s bloodied but still determined to pursue the dream of widespread material prosperity and security so elusively close a few years before. A division, reinforced by high interest rates, between those who had substantial assets and net worth and those who had little, would grow wider as the US economy continued its shift away from manufacturing might toward services, away from good-paying production jobs toward lower-paying service sector work. Government policies were therefore even more critical to the survival of have-nots than before. In an act of defiance both at economic reality and political probability, Democrats in control of Congress passed the Full Employment and Balanced Growth or Humphrey-Hawkins Act on October 27, 1980. That law insisted that national policy be no less than to promote full employment, increase real income, balance the federal budget, boost productivity, improve the balance of trade, and foster price stability. The only problem was that no specific program or proposals were set forth or enacted to achieve these lofty goals. Seven days later, Reagan swamped Carter 43.9 million to 35.5 million votes and 489 to 49 electoral votes to claim the White House and the right to redefine national priorities. After his inauguration in January, government intervention in the economy took a back seat to Free Market forces.

Chapter XII. Pendulum Swing Back Toward a Freer Economy: 1981-1989

The "Reagan Revolution," as it was styled, had several components but two major themes. The new President wanted to make Free Market forces once again the principle determinant of economic direction as well as adopt a tough anti-Communist stance to buttress the Free World against Soviet expansionism. The success of the former would generate tax dollars to pay for a military build-up to accomplish the latter. Defense spending as well as other Washington largesse, preserving but reducing a still generous social welfare network, would complement a massive tax cut to stimulate domestic production. Operating under the *Supply Side* economic theory of California economist Arthur Laffer, he maintained that the end result of accelerated growth and diminished tax rates would be higher federal tax revenues, not lower, in fact more than enough to offset the initial loss in resources caused by the tax cut. Washington would eventually be able to liquidate the public debt.

Ronald W. Reagan

Challenging Congress to live within its means, the President proposed a *Balance Budget Amendment* to the Constitution. The greatest obstacle arose from the huge increase in annual defense spending insisted upon by the White House from $180.5 billion for fiscal year 1981 to $279 billion four years later. Aggregated with social welfare spending and payment of interest on the burgeoning federal debt, military outlays outpaced the additional tax revenues resulting from economic growth. Following a deep recession in 1981-82 that drove the unemployment rate toward one in ten workers and wages down in purchasing power to 1961 levels, the 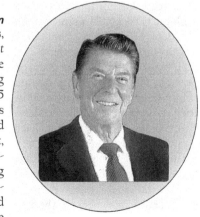 annual federal deficit soared over $200 billion to 5.9% of GDP. Thus, total federal liabilities of $1 trillion in 1981 tripled by 1990 to over 51% of GDP. Equally distressing to fiscal conservatives, state and local debt as a percentage of GDP matched the federal burden in 1985 and exceeded it by end of the period. Overall liabilities for all US government entities reached 106% of GDP, the highest level since 1949. Although Reagan did succeed in lowering income tax rates, the overall percent of income paid by Americans to government entities did not, because of higher Social Security, state and local taxes, property, and other taxes, fall as much as desired.

To pay for purchases of homes and consumer durables, families took on more debt. Although the risk was covered in aggregate by a huge swelling of household financial holdings from $6.6 billion in 1980 to $14.8 billion a decade later, the windfall was concentrated as before in the most affluent fifth of the population. Claiming by end of the period 83.5% of all household wealth, their investments in stocks and bonds as well as mutual funds boosted the share of household assets claimed by financial instruments to three-fifths. A 350% increase in household pension holdings to $3.4 trillion exceeded for the first time both household bank deposits at $3.3 trillion and the value of private businesses, sole proprietorships, and professional practices at $3.2 trillion.

Naturally, Wall Street firms celebrated. Fees from catering to 37 million households in the top two-fifths receiving 70% of national income boosted profits into the tens and hundreds of millions of dollars. By making liberal use of puts and options, derivatives, hedge funds, swaps, and other esoteric financial tools, brokerages spread risk and maximized revenue. Computerization of operations quickened reactions to market ups and downs.

Investment banking companies also made vast sums by facilitating the consolidation and deregulation of industry. In the process, old-line businesses with substantial assets but faltering operations became the target of leveraged buyouts (LBOs). The basic method was to raise capital from investors by selling high risk, unsecured "junk bonds" bearing high interest rates, and then using the proceeds to acquire companies. Instead of carrying the debt directly on their own books, buyers saddled takeover targets with that burden, forcing divestitures of entire divisions and subsidiaries to reduce principle and interest payments. Although junk bond king Michael Milken and other financial "masters of the universe" claimed that winnowing out the weak from the strong made American business leaner, more efficient, and more able to fight foreign competition, the fact that they themselves reaped exorbitant fees called into question their motives. Covert illegal means employed to accomplish some of these deals were exposed.

More distressing to American workers than corruption and greed was the fact that their livelihoods became the play things of financiers. Those adversely affected now included hundreds of thousands of white collar office workers and middle managers ousted by highly leveraged companies cutting operating costs. Politicians whose constituents went from middle class comfort to straightened circumstances cried foul. Because by firing striking air traffic controllers early on in his administration and weakening anti-trust enforcement Reagan signaled antipathy to unions, business and corporate leaders resisted pressure from Congress and state legislatures to soften the blow of downsizing and automation. Thus, as manufacturing jobs and production plants were exported to non-union areas of the country and then to locations outside the US, the blue collar work force was ravaged. Union membership declined at a precipitous rate.

Overall employment, on the other hand, jumped by 10 million new jobs through 1985, due in large part to creation of eight million more, mostly lower-paying service jobs. More computer industry, finance, and marketing positions gave hope that a new technology-based economy would be an improvement on the old industrial one. By end of the period, even manufacturing employment rebounded by 1.3 million workers to the level of 1966. Construction and transportation work also firmed up.

Still, the labor supply for higher-paying, blue collar jobs exceeded demand, restraining wage increases. Workers of all kinds in all industries discovered, despite the lower inflation of the 1980s, that purchasing power was stagnating or falling. Although big corporations continued to pay a living wage to heads of family, a growing percentage of wage-earners in households in the bottom three-fifths of income required all adult persons and older children to work to  maintain standards of living. Because the US workforce was becoming part of a global job market, economists considered a 5% unemployment rate "full employment."

Where producers of food products, household and personal items, and other consumer goods were concerned, preserving and increasing a share in a US market growing by 1990 to 250 million people translated into higher annual revenues and profits. By consolidating companies and industries and forcing bigger production and operating economies of scale, they could also keep prices low. Foreign imports in cars, steel, machinery, textiles, and home electronics served further to restrain the cost of living. The deregulation of the oil industry boosted supplies and reduced the amount of household budgets allocated to energy.

While in absolute numbers more households had sufficient income to pay for higher priced goods and luxury items, a lesser percentage of the total could do so without falling more heavily into debt. Ballooning mortgage and rental costs caused by rising real estate values also made the American Dream of material prosperity more tenuous for tens of millions. Of crucial importance for persons of marginal resources was that fact that tax law still permitted deduction of interest payments on mortgage debt. Falling interest rates, including a decade long plunge in the prime rate from 18.87% in 1980 to 6.25% in 1990, and more lenient bank policy that required smaller down payments for home loans also contributed to an increase in home ownership to 65% of households. But it was a renewed emphasis on consumer debt through credit card use, installment purchases, and other unsecured sources amounting to $525 billion by mid-decade that permitted middle and working class Americans to pay for what they wanted while covering the rising cost of what they needed. The latter category included health care, now a major burden on family budgets but an important component of GDP.

Ironically, the apparent savior of the American worker and his bane were one and the same — new technology. The personal computer industry exploded as no sector had since automobiles in the early decades of the century, even as heavy industry resorted to automation to boost the number of industrial robots from 6,000 in 1981 to many times that number by end of the period and cut its workforce. Because Washington's mantra was now deregulation, the market for computer hardware and software could truly be described as free. High salaries for computer equipment and software designers proved that not all new job creation would be in lower-paying retail, hotel, telemarketing, and other service sector work. Moreover, personal computers, laser and ink jet printers, Xerox copiers, fax machines, and other business office devices boosted the productivity of the American worker. More productive businesses generated higher profits and paid better salaries and wages.

The larger question for the economy and country was whether high tech industry in all its manifestations, including advances in bio-technology, medical instruments, pharmaceuticals, and telecommunications, would be sufficient to compensate for slowdowns and reverses in older industries. Although a nominal annual growth rate of 7.6% produced by 1990 GDP of $5.8 trillion, after accounting for inflation the rate was only 3%. More to the point, the *per capita* GDP growth rate in 2004 dollars came in at an unimpressive 2%. Because increases in productivity accounted for much of that growth, high tech businesses needed and wanted fewer workers.

Thus, despite Reagan's determination to thrust responsibility for the economy back on the private sector, government policy continued to be critical to the material wellbeing of Americans, including 18.4 million citizens employed by federal, state, and local agencies by 1990. Not only was direct spending by Washington and other government entities indispensable for sustaining vital sectors of the economy, in particular construction, communication, transportation, and aerospace-defense, but federal government authority and intercession created the conditions wherein new industries could flourish. Specifically, the "information superhighway" of the Internet would not have been poised to provide the next great boost to the economy had not universal standards been required. As the Cold War came to an end and relations between the US and other Great Powers moved toward economic cooperation and competition rather than geopolitical confrontation, what emerged was an environment of autonomous markets within a broad framework of government direction and control, as opposed to a truly Free Market model.

REAGAN DEREGULATION POLICY AND IMPACT

On January 28, 1981, Reagan jumped with both feet into the pool of Free Market possibilities by dropping all oil price controls for the first since 1971. In the tax cut legislation that followed in August, he slashed the windfall profits tax on "new" oil discovered after January 1, 1979 to 15%, half the previous figure, over a five year period. The welcome consequence for American consumers was a decade of falling oil prices prompted by rising supplies. To prop up profits, players in the oil and petrochemical industry embarked on a new round of mergers and acquisitions.

Batting first, Dupont announced the takeover of Conoco. The attraction for the chemical company was a secure supply of petroleum for fiber and plastics manufacturing operations. By 1986, company scientists created a new and lucrative market niche with a *Teflon* spray application called *Stainmaster* to make nylon carpets more stain-resistant. Announcement that chlorofluorocarbons (CFCs) such as Dupont's *Freon* refrigerant were damaging the earth's ozone layer by as much as 10% provoked new innovation with non-CFC refrigerant propellants. After Congress on July 1, 1989 ratified the *Montreal Protocol* to cut production of ozone-destroying chemicals by one-half, Dupont made a decision to phase out CFCs altogether by 1996, four years earlier than required. Its *Suva* and *Dymel* non-CFCs were ready the next year.

ConocoPhillips refinery in Texas (courtesy ConocoPhillips)

In another aggressive deal, Apex Oil bought Clark. Because company strategists wanted to shift out of retail to supplying and trading oil, the number of Clark stations contracted throughout the decade until they were purchased by Horsham Corporation, a Toronto investment company. By contrast, Sun Oil decided to focus on retail gasoline with its new *ULTRA 94* octane, highest offered in the US. After selling its shipping division and spinning off in 1988 its Sun Exploration and Production subsidiary, the company used proceeds from these deals to purchase Atlantic Petroleum, consisting of one refinery and a network of eastern service stations and pipelines spun off from ARCO three years earlier.

Following US Steel's rescue of Marathon in 1982, the next big acquisitions in the oil industry were the 1984 takeovers of Gulf Oil by Chevron for $13.3 billion and Getty Oil by Texaco for $9.9 billion. The latter deal was consummated at the last minute after Getty had agreed to be taken over by Pennzoil. Unable to consolidate all the assets of Gulf, at the time the fifth largest US oil company, Chevron sold off Gulf's Northeast operations to Cumberland Farms, a company that operated convenience stores at Gulf stations. Gulf's operations in the Southeast were purchased by BP America. By contrast, Texaco had no intention of parting with any of Getty's assets, including 1.9 billion barrels of proven domestic and overseas reserves, until Pennzoil sued. A whopping $11 billion judgment for Texaco's alienation of corporate affection put the huge oil company in a worse financial position than would otherwise have been the case had it not obtained Getty.

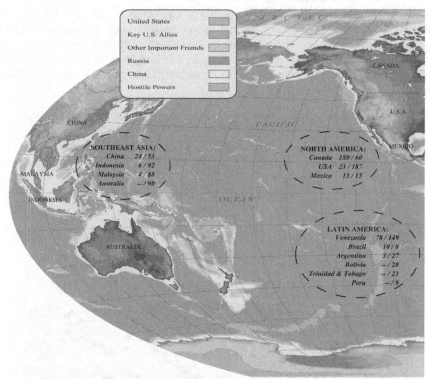

Falling oil prices undermined the feasibility of extracting oil from shale in the Rocky Mountains; thus, the Reagan administration persuaded Congress to cancel funding for synthetic fuels. Because oil companies were relieved of government regulation and inter-ference, and because new technology such as Phillips Petroleum's method of injecting polymers — substances with large molecules that combine simpler chemical units — into wells to boost production increased the percentage of recoverable crude from deposits, wildcatters still made small fortunes drilling in the US. Included in the national geography was the continental shelf, where a floating platform secured by Texaco to the sea floor per-mitted drilling to 1,800 foot depths. The exploration equipment business looked profitable enough for PACCAR to buy Trico Industries, a maker of oil field pumps and accessories.

In long run, however, the cost of exploration, discovery, and exploitation made rarer the kind of project Hunt Oil initiated in 1984. After making a major find in Yemen that eventually generated 150,000 barrels of crude a day, or 55 million barrels a year, the company built a 260 mile pipeline over mountains to the Red Sea. Henceforth, new oil dis-coveries needed to be in the 1 billion barrel range to offer sufficient profit. It helped whenever natural gas, such as the 10 trillion cubic feet found by Hunt with the Yemeni oil, could also be turned into LNG for shipment back to the US.

Acceleration of domestic and global oil and petrochemical operations carried more than just the usual development costs. Union Carbide got into severe difficulty because of air pollution and toxic spills in the US that provoked class action lawsuits and fines in the early 1980s amounting to $1 billion. More catastrophically on December 2-3, 1984, a

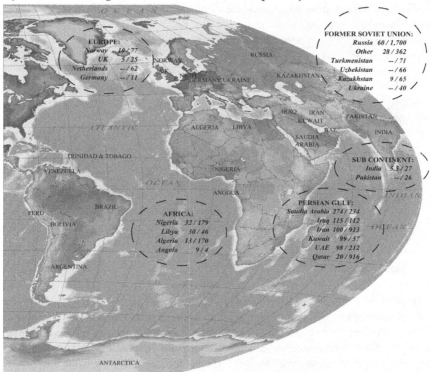

company plant in Bhopal, India released gas resulting in environmental damage and human casualties that ultimately cost the firm a $470 million judgment in an Indian court. After suffering many times that loss in stock price plunge and other economic impact, Union Carbide was forced in 1986 to sell its battery operations to Ralston Purina for $1.4 billion.

Closer to home, Exxon's oil tanker the Exxon-Valdez ran aground in Prince William Sound off the south Alaska coast on March 24, 1989. The 11 million gallons of crude that spilled out washed over 1,000 miles of shoreline, killing 250,000 birds as well as seals, otters, whales, and other species and scarring the landscape. Ultimately, Exxon spent $2.5 billion to clean up the mess. Its financial strength, oil reserves, and operations were so huge, however, that unlike Union Carbide the company continued to climb toward industry leadership. Also on the cutting edge but with a much lower public profile, Koch purchased John Zink Company of Tulsa from Lone Star Technologies to compete in the market for pollution control devices in petrochemical plants and operations. The privately held company moved toward $20 billion of revenue.

Elsewhere in energy, companies anticipated a deregulation of the natural gas industry. In 1982, Williams bought Northwest Energy Company and began patching together a nationwide interstate gas pipeline system. Morgan Stanley then took the lead in forming the Natural Gas Clearinghouse. That distribution company, later known as Dynegy, began operations in 1984 with six natural gas pipelines. While Eastman Chemical of Tennessee helped pump up sales to over $3 billion by building a coal gasification plant, Air Products entered into a joint venture with Browning-Ferris Industries and bought GSF Energy to recover natural gas from landfills.

In 1985, the Federal Regulatory Commission finally issued FERC's *Order 436* for open access transportation, permitting companies to use natural gas pipelines of competitors. Because of the high cost of bringing in LNG supplies from Algeria as well as natural gas through pipelines from Canada, Panhandle Eastern and Trunkline — without sufficient indigenous supply and now forced to handle the natural gas of rivals — were hurt. By contrast, Texas Eastern boasted substantial domestic reserves. After that company bought Algonquin Energy in 1988, Panhandle Eastern was forced to pay a premium for Texas Eastern the next year to retain its position as an industry leader. However, the $3.22 billion purchase price necessitated selling off North Sea oil reserves and other non-natural gas assets. The door was opened for other competitors to enter the market.

For example, Houston Natural Gas merged with InterNorth of Omaha to form Enron, in possession of a 37,000 mile pipeline system. The company continued to expand rapidly, buying into electric power in Britain before beginning to trade natural gas like a commodity in 1989 through GasBank. That was an entity launched in North America and Europe to permit producers and wholesale buyers to buy gas supplies and hedge their price risk on the spot market. Among distributors compelled to open up their systems to accommodate producers was Florida Gas Transmission, which used fees it was paid to expand its pipeline throughout the state.

Falling natural gas prices, accelerated by deregulation of 70% of natural gas sales on January 1, 1985, and still high oil prices created incentive for electric power companies to switch over to natural gas burning plants from oil-fired plants. Florida Power and Light did so while adding nuclear and coal-fired plants to reduce oil-burning plants to one fourth its total generating capacity. But continuing political fall-out from the Three Mile Island nuclear accident as well as a 5.5% drop off in electric power production to 2.24 trillion kilowatt hours during the recession year of 1982 motivated some companies, including Duke Power, to cancel nuclear plant construction and eat hundreds of millions of dollars of construction costs. Although the South Texas Project (STP) by Houston Light & Power and Central Light & Power in association with the city governments of San Antonio and Austin was not halted, the latter metropolis sold its 16% interest while the lead engineering firm was changed from Brown & Root to Bechtel Power with Ebasco Services becoming prime contractor to complete the project. A decision by Congress in August 1988 to raise nuclear accident liability to $7.1 billion further undercut the nuclear power industry. However, the US Supreme Court relieved some anxiety by sorting out costs related to Middle South Utilities' shutting down of its nuclear plant construction. The company was permitted to resume dividend payments and change its name to Entergy. Although planned proliferation of nuclear power sites could not, because of political and public opposition, resume in the next decade, the share of US electric power produced by existing nuclear installations steadily increased to one-fifth by end of the century.

Reacting to the recession in the Midwest, DTE, PPL, and other companies launched development efforts to bring new business and economic activity to Detroit, Pittsburgh, and other big cities. However, Westinghouse sold off its lamp business in 1982 and four years later its Medium AC Motor Division to Reliance Electric. Reliance became the largest US industrial motor manufacturer, even as competitor Lincoln Electric was so hard hit by higher electric energy costs that its annual sales dropped temporarily by 40%. On the other hand, W.W. Grainger, a Chicago maker of electric motors, attained $1 billion of sales in 1984 because its *Motorbook* catalogue was such a powerful marketing and sales tool. Profitability was enhanced by an automated storage and retrieval system as well as construction of decentralized regional distribution centers, beginning in Kansas City. Other equipment manufacturers who went the way of massive plant modernization exceeding $1 billion in automation included Caterpillar and Cummins.

Trying to help the energy industry adjust to changing times, the FCC permitted the Southern Company to branch out beyond domestic electric power. Its Southern Energy subsidiary built and operated power plants on four continents. Overall, however, electric companies did not really bounce back until end of the period when production reached 2.8 trillion kilowatt hours. As US oil production declined below 2.7 billion barrels, foreign imports surged. Although natural gas production bottomed out at mid decade before recovering, the real winner in the energy field was the coal industry. Annual production soared by 1990 to 940 million metric tons, a 65% increase since 1978. Mine owners were able to increase wages 70% in the same period to $16.80 an hour, equal in 2004 money to annual earnings of $48,550.

DEVELOPMENTS IN TRANSPORTATION AND HEAVY INDUSTRY

Another sector that Reagan wanted to see fully deregulated was transportation. Under the Northeast Rail Service Act of 1981, the government was authorized to sell Conrail to the private sector once it turned an annual profit. However, Congress voted on

May 13 to hand over Conrail's commuter operations to public agencies as of January 1, 1983. The largest so transferred became Metro-North, a unit of the New York State Transportation Authority. As for the remainder of the company, although the government held a bidding contest won in 1985 by Norfolk Southern, dissatisfaction with the purchase price prompted Congress to order instead an initial public offering (IPO). In 1987, the Conrail IPO yielded $1.76 billion, largest to that time. Likewise, the House and Senate interfered to spare AMTRAK from Reagan's attempt to cut off the railroad's public subsidy. The President did succeed in halving that largesse from the peak of $1.2 billion granted in 1980.

Consolidation continued in the railroad industry. After the Union Pacific, Missouri Pacific, and Western Pacific merger was approved by the ICC in 1982, six years later the enlarged Union Pacific bought up the Missouri-Kansas-Texas Railroad (the Katy), and then the next year took a 25% stake in the Chicago & North Western. In 1986, B&O merged into C&O, which then was renamed CSX. In 1988, the ICC approved the $1 billion sale of the Southern Pacific by Santa Fe Industries to Rio Grande Industries, which then put its Denver & Rio Grande Western Railroad and as well the St. Louis to Chicago line from the bankrupt Chicago, Missouri & Western Railroad under Southern Pacific's control. But the Santa Fe Railroad shocked everyone by concluding an inter-modal partnership with the J. B. Hunt trucking firm. Conceding most passenger and package business to motor vehicles and airplanes, railroads settled down to become primarily carriers of bulk cargo.

Highway overpasses

Meanwhile, on August 12, 1983, Congress passed the Surface Transportation Assistance Act. Weakened politically by the recession, from which the country had not yet recovered, the President was unable to muster enough political support to prevent a 5 cent a gallon increase in the federal tax on gasoline. Some Republicans admitted that the idea of passing the new revenue along to the states for highway rebuilding and repair, including completion of the Eisenhower Interstate Highway System, was not altogether a bad idea. The nation's existing 40,752 miles of interstate highways were critical for car and truck transport. Later on April 2, 1987, Democrats in Congress, buoyed by Reagan's Iran-Contra scandal and their own victory in the 1986 mid-term election, passed a Highway and Mass Transit Act over the President's veto. They voted to authorize $87.5 billion in spending on the nation's road and mass transit transportation system over five years as well as permit states to raise the speed limit in rural interstate areas from 55 mph to 65.

Highway construction and improvement was good news for trucking concerns of all kinds, now becoming large businesses. After ABF bought East Texas Motor Freight in 1982 to expand geographic coverage, the company advanced toward $800 million of revenue by end of period. CNF too grew its long-haul cargo business by starting up Con-Way Carrier as a regional next-day shipper. The company purchased Emery Air Freight Corporation in 1989 to transport heavy air cargo in North America and overseas.

As for package delivery, FedEx in 1983 became the first US company to achieve $1 billion of revenue without a merger or acquisition. After improving efficiency with a *Super-Tracker* hand-held, bar code scanner in 1986, revenues from overseas operations were boosted again by takeover of Flying Tigers. But UPS, already providing next day air service and international delivery to Europe, won an FAA decision in 1988 to permit operation of its own planes. Within a decade, UPS Airlines cracked the top ten US air carriers in terms of revenue.

Moreover, UPS soon achieved 10 million packages and documents delivered a day by switching over to a *COMPASS* computerized system that cost $1.5 billion over six years and helped restrain the growth of labor costs. By contrast, a decision by the US Postal Service in 1988 to set an automation target of 70% of all letter mail sorting, up from one quarter, to permit a workforce reduction of 20,000 persons, generated controversy that spilled over into congressional debates. The government-owned mail deliverer continued to slip behind the technology curve, lose money, and alienate citizens with frequent increases in basic postage cost from 25 cents for a first class letter to 37 cents by the new century. Delivery of unwanted, third class "junk" mail came to compose a third of all mail volume and 40% of USPS revenue.

Back on the ground, proliferating truck carrier business was good news for truck and parts makers such as Eaton which sold its materials handling businesses and entered into a joint venture with Sumitomo Heavy Industries of Japan to make hydraulic motors and transmissions. Although International Harvester, after merging with Case in 1982, spun off its truck division as Navistar in 1986 to concentrate on farm equipment manufacturing, the new company developed in partnership with Dana a 9-speed heavy truck transmission. Potential customers included PACCAR, which had bought Foden Trucks of Britain a few years earlier. However, that firm moved to specialize in the aftermarket for auto parts distribution and retailing by obtaining auto supply businesses in Washington and California. PACCAR executives reasoned that the automobile parts market would continue to expand as Americans, with tight budgets, held on to cars longer. Although the US share of the world new car market had dropped below 21% in 1980 and would fall below one-fifth by mid-decade, the Big Three turned out a record 16.3 million motor vehicles of all kinds in 1986.

These models now incorporated innovations such as flexible, rust-resistant body panels, front fenders formed from two resins reinforced with milled fiberglass, and fenders painted with flexible acrylic enamel, all used on GM's 1981 *Olds Sport Omega*. Although Detroit continued to excel in big cars and a new innovation, minivans, smaller foreign models with better gas mileage took on Ford's *Taurus* sedan sensation and claimed a growing market share. Hammered by Japanese imports such as Toyota's *Corolla* model with base sticker price of $5,400, new federal safety requirements, in particular air bags that added $800 to the price of cars, and tighter environmental standards to reduce air pollutants, AMC was sold by Renault to Chrysler in 1987. Because the US market still contained three big auto makers to battle overseas imports, claiming 24% of the market by mid decade, renewed tariff protection was ruled out. By contrast, motorcycle manufacturer Harley-Davidson appealed in 1983 for tariff relief against Japanese companies dumping unsold motorcycles into inventory in the US. Washington agreed to five years of protection.

Ford Taurus
As the percent of households that owned cars moved toward 85% by 1990, an important growth market for cars and car parts became rental car agencies. The 1980s saw the rise of Enterprise Rent-A-Car from 5,000 cars to 75,000 by concentrating on big markets and airports. That put the company in direct competition with Hertz, which was peddled by RCA to United Airlines in 1985, and then two years later by United to Park Ridge Corporation, a subsidiary of Ford. While Hertz was proclaiming its *#1 Club Gold Service* for fast service a big success, Avis was number two and "trying harder" by installing its *Wizard* system in Europe to link reservation systems in 2,000 locations and prepare for similar efficiency in the US.

Goodyear plant in Alabama
Annual production of 180 million tires was not as lucrative for Goodyear and Firestone because of competition from Bridgestone of Japan, Michelin of France, and other foreign firms. Home-grown challenger Cooper Tire & Rubber reached $500 million of sales in 1985, double that in 1991, by expanding its non-union operations across the South and into Mexico. After Firestone lost its independence to Bridgestone for $2.8 billion in 1988, creating the world's largest tire and rubber company, the Akron headquarters was shuttered and staff moved to Nashville. Declining profitability forced Dayco to sell off its hose and belt business to Armstrong Rubber, rename itself Day International, and sell its remaining printing and textile lines to M.A. Hanna of Cleveland.

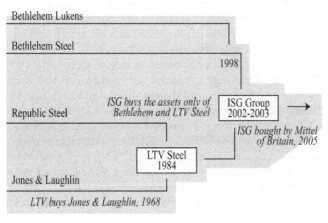

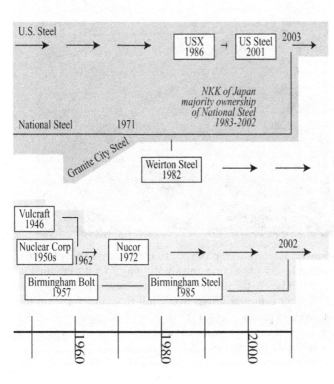

Genealogy of US Steel Industry, 1960-2005 Too big and important to the American economy to suffer the same fate, GM still worried that more of the US new car market would be lost to foreign competitors. These now included Honda of Japan, which in 1982 opened the first foreign-owned car plant in the US at Marysville, Ohio. Detroit executives watched in anxiety and awe as Honda's assembly line, using a "no cripple" rule of fixing cars on the spot, got moving on November 1. Over the next two decades, 16 more Japanese, German, and finally Korean owned plants employing 60,000 US workers challenged the predominance of GM, Ford, and Chrysler. No wonder that GM tried to improve competitiveness and cut costs in 1984 with plastic-bodied cars. The company outsourced more parts, such as automotive seating to Hoover Universal, a maker of plastics machinery purchased the next year by Johnson Controls to vault sales to the $5 billion level. The transition to non-metallic components, while favorable to industries dealing in alternatives materials, hurt US steel companies. Although Big Steel benefited from new orders for oil pipeline and other tubular products, mini-mills cut into other business to claim an 18% market share. During the recession of 1981-82, US production of crude steel plunged 42% to less than 67 million metric tons. Annual foreign import of steel surged toward 25 million tons.

Capital investment and fewer workers was the response of National Steel in 1983 after it became 53.4% owned by NKK, the second largest Japanese steel maker. The next year, National spun off Weirton Steel to its employees, and then initiated a $2 billion plan to buy more modern plant and equipment. That year, Bethlehem and the USWA filed a *201 Petition* under US trade laws. In part because it was an election year, the Reagan Administration forsook Free Market principles to impose "voluntary restraints" on foreign imports. In reality, that policy amounted to a quota system for the world's big steel producing nations, including Brazil, Argentina, and Turkey, limiting their share of the US market to 18.5%. The arrangement was ultimately amended by President George H. Bush in 1989 to include Russia while Washington badgered foreign governments to cut subsidies to their steel companies.

Nucor plant

Despite a recovery to 95 million tons of steel produced in 1984, over-capacity forced a consolidation of the US steel industry to 14 companies with only 23 mills employing 225,000 people, one-third less than before the recession. USX (the new name of US Steel after taking over Marathon Oil) alone contracted from 46,000 full-time employees turning out 11.3 million tons to 18,000 workers producing two-thirds as much. Capacity was maintained by committing to a strategy of capital investment and subcontracting. The move away from steel continued in 1986 with purchase of Texas Oil & Gas.

Government protectionism fooled some steel executives into believing that a more permanent US steel industry comeback was in the offing. That was the reason that LTV bought Republic Steel to combine with its J&L properties into a behemoth producing 24 million tons. But LTV Steel's antiquated mills and overcapacity caused it to go bankrupt in 1986. The company steadily contracted to only 10 million tons of annual production a decade later. By contrast, Bethlehem benefited from large construction and ship-building industry orders to achieve a record $426 million profit in 1988. US steel companies in aggregate recovered to an annual production level of nearly 100 million tons, now accounting for about 13% of the world total.

Rather, the future belonged to mini-mills that installed computer control centers and made steel from scrap instead of original raw materials. Nucor opened a plant in Craw-fordsville, Indiana in 1989 to produce two-inch, thin-slab bars, one-quarter the usual diameter. The process combined continuous casting with direct hot-charging to turn out a finished product in as little as three hours. Productivity soared to 1 ton per man-hour.

Inherently better off than cars and steel were the airlines. The deregulation of the late 1970s combined with US law forbidding foreign carriers from operating within the country made up for the Reagan administration dropping as politically impossible an idea to barter entry into major overseas markets, especially Western Europe, for reciprocal entry into the United States. True, big airlines needed flights to and from international cities to boost revenue and keep a leg up on smaller competitors, but local carriers could still prosper by keeping labor costs low and targeting profitable routes. When locals pulled out of small markets to concentrate on longer, more lucrative routes, six dozen little cities lost air service.

In 1983, America West Airlines sprang up out of Phoenix. Despite competition from Southwest, enticing the public with cut-rate *Fun Fares* to St. Louis, Missouri, and Chicago's Midway Airport, the revenue of both regional carriers surpassed $1 billion by 1990. A third competitor in the region, Pacific Southwest Airlines of San Diego, was gobbled up in 1987 by US Air Group. That company then purchased Piedmont Airlines to obtain hubs at Charlotte and Baltimore while closing down others in Dayton and Syracuse.

Locked in to higher wage union contracts, American, Delta, Northwest, and United fought back against the regionals by phasing out fuel-guzzling *B-707s* and purchasing more cost-efficient *B-767s, B-757s,* and *B-747-400s.* Other viable alternatives were McDonnell-

Douglas' *MD-80* and Airbus' *A320*, using Pratt & Whitney's *V2500* engines. However, even with lower fuel costs, Braniff, Eastern, PanAm, and TWA could not survive the highly competitive environment and fell by the way-side. Continental, which despite merging with Frank Lorenzo's Texas International in 1982 filed Chapter 11 the next year, emerged from bankruptcy to become a fifth major by starting nonstop flights to Europe. Lorenzo then gobbled up Eastern's assets for only $615 million, laid off that airline's workers, and cobbled together a bigger Continental that as the third largest US carrier not only controlled Texas but People's Express, Frontier Airlines, and New York Air. Despite a 1988 global alliance with Scandinavian Airline Systems, Continental had to file for bankruptcy again in 1989 to fend off creditors.

To maintain the loyalty of corporate customers, the majors instituted frequent flier programs. In 1981, American also began copying Delta's hub and spoke system. United finally flew beyond US borders two years later with a Seattle to Tokyo route. In 1985, the company bought PanAm's Pacific division.

Delta and Northwest decided in 1984 that within the US it was not in their best interests to fight the regionals on every route. Instead, they cut joint marketing deals, with Republic and Western respectively, to feed passengers into their systems. Two years later, Northwest bought Republic for $884 million to double its employees to 33,000 and lock up control of Detroit, the Twin Cities, Memphis, and Milwaukee. Delta merged with Western the next year to obtain trans-Pacific routes and become the fourth largest US airline, fifth largest in the world. Northwest, too, increased its financial and operating resources by coming under control of Wings Holdings, an investment group out of New York city that already held a majority share in KLM Royal Dutch Airlines. Northwest's flights to the Far East and Europe made it highly profitable.

American, by contrast, tried to drive the regionals out of business by offering *Super Saver* fares with up to 70% discount. Its *SABRE* system was used by 10,000 travel agency offices. Too, the company took on FedEx and UPS with American Eagle, a regional service offering second day freight delivery and by 1988 same day service. In addition to a big chunk of the 454 million paying passengers flying annually within the US, the airline saw profit in claiming a share of the 10.3 million ton-miles of non-mail packages and 1.9 million ton-miles of mail flown by 1989.

Another way to measure the relative growth in the airline industry was by assets. Although the communications industry with $295 billion in communication equipment and motor vehicle industry with $245 billion in cars, trucks, and buses had more, the airline industry, confined to a few thousand locations, could by 1990 boast $108 billion in airplane assets. That was a 100% increase in just a decade. Airline employment also reached a peak of 550,000 people.

TAX CUTS SPUR THE FINANCIAL INDUSTRY

Although deregulation was important for the economy, the centerpiece of Reagan's policy was still the Economic Recovery Tax Act of August 4, 1981 and budget changes approved July 31, 1982. The President used his popularity with the American people, as well as Republican control of the Senate, not only to push through promised tax cuts but a $695 billion budget that boosted defense spending $12.3 billion while cutting $35.2 billion from social welfare and cultural programs. Laffer's philosophy, later described as "voodoo economics" prevailed in legislation that slashed personal income taxes 25% across the board over 33 months, including a lowering of the top marginal rate from 70% to 50% within five months and an indexing to inflation by 1985 of all tax rates, personal exemptions, and standard deductions. The top capital gains rate was dropped retroactively from 28% to 20%. Moreover, the estate/gift tax exclusion was raised by 1987 from $175,000 to $600,000. Individual Retirement Accounts (IRAs), in which maximum annual contributions per individual of $2,000 and twice that for married couples were tax-deductible and annual earnings built tax-free until retirement, were created for participants in employer-sponsored plans.

Increasing the percentage of income Americans could keep proved a boon for the stock market. Once the recession ended in 1982, small investors returned to equity investing in record numbers, helping double the value of stock held by households to $1.8 trillion by 1990. That development convinced Sears executives to buy the Dean Witter brokerage to combine with their Allstate insurance and Coldwell Banker Realty subsidiaries. The addition of Discover Card International in 1986 gave the company a powerful financial group.

Likewise, Bank of America bought Charles Schwab for $57 million in 1983, in time to profit from record trading days on the NYSE, including $236 million of shares bought and sold on August 3, 1984. Three years later and six months before the stock market suffered a sharp but temporary crash on October 19 that caused the annual value of stock and option sales to plunge 32% to $1.7 trillion in 1988, the company cashed in its investment by selling the firm back to Schwab's management for $280 million. Meanwhile, Bear Stearns distinguished itself with an "asset management" strategy and emerging markets investments. Founded in New York City in 1920 as an investment banking firm, the company finally went public in 1985 with a portfolio of high-yield bonds, public finance, government securities, mortgage-backed securities, and financial institutions services.

The stock market kept booming even after publicly traded companies cut average dividend yields to 4.3% in the early 1980s, and then lowered payouts to shareholders again after the 1986 Tax Reform Act, discussed below, ended the $400 dividend income exemption. Japanese banks and speculators arrived flush with cash to pump up foreign investment in the US to $2 trillion by end of the period. While conservative shoppers bought up what they believed were safe, high profile real estate properties, the more adventurous took the plunge with high-yield junk bonds. Milken and Drexel Burnham Lambert, the New York firm run by Frederick H. Joseph that paid him tens of millions of dollars to fuel an LBO boom from Beverly Hills, California offices, seduced many investors with the prospect of taking over and breaking up for profit the biggest American corporations. Concerned that deal-makers would feather their own nests at the expense of average investors, Congress passed in 1984 the Insider Trading Sanctions Act to force violators not only to give up ill-gotten gains but pay treble penalties. In *CTS Corporation v. Dynamic Corporation of America*, the Supreme Court in 1986 ruled that an Indiana law discouraging hostile takeovers was constitutional.

Michael Milken

Not particularly worried about legal and political impediments, Milken continued to organize LBOs. The industry peak of 383, about 15% of all US mergers and acquisitions, was achieved in 1988 with total value of $200 billion. The June 2, 1985 acquisition of food company Nabisco Brands by tobacco firm R.J. Reynolds alone was valued at $4.9 billion. That merger was overshadowed three years later by Philip Morris acquiring Kraft for $13.1 billion and investment firm Kohlberg Kravis Roberts & Company claiming RJR Nabisco for $25 billion.

However, in the interim Milken, Ivan Boesky, and others of Milken's associates flaunted the law with such brazenness that charges of insider trading leveled against them in November 1986 rocked Wall Street. Milken was eventually convicted, jailed for ten years, and forced to pay fines totaling $600 million dollars. Boesky too went to prison for three years and paid $80 million. Drexel Burnham Lambert kicked in another $650 million to the government and defrauded parties and went out of business. Angry that Joseph and other CEOs escaped responsibility by asserting a lack of knowledge about all the wheeling and dealing, Congress in 1988 passed an amendment to the Insider Trading Sanctions Act authorizing fines and other sanctions against corporate supervisors who neglected to keep control of subordinates. All penalties from the 1984 act were doubled.

Although the number of LBOs declined to 254 in 1990, other kinds of mergers and acquisitions continued to break records. The financial rewards of deal-making were just too extreme to ignore. For example, in March 1989, Time and Warner Communications merged in a $15.2 billion deal. The TV industry alone witnessed 2,000 deals valued at $50 billion.

A more agreeable development for American financial markets was an enormous increase in mutual fund investments. Fidelity's *Magellan Fund* rose from $1 billion of assets in 1983 to $13 billion by 1990. Overall, the company's assets under management topped $50 billion in 1987 and ballooned toward $100 billion by end of the period. In addition to offering IRA management, adding a trust division for employee benefit funds, and instituting computerized trading in 1984, its *Spartan Funds* provided a low cost, long term alternative for high asset investors.

In fact, by 1990, Fidelity claimed about 9% of the market for managed funds, which had exploded from $146 billion of assets at the beginning of the period to $1.15 trillion at the end. Because revenue increased more than proportionately, other competitors were anxious to increase their share. For example, Bankers Life, a firm founded in 1879 that later became the Principal Financial Group, suddenly in 1983 offered mutual funds in the investment fields of real estate, total return fixed income, and international equity. When in 1990, the company brought out small-cap and mid-cap equity funds, its assets under management reached $25 billion. Another player was Commercial Credit of Baltimore which purchased Primerica, took that company's name, and moved its headquarters to New York. Among Primerica's assets was the Smith Barney brokerage.

The growing power of mutual fund and brokerage firms was a source of major concern for banks and S&Ls. Like State Street of Boston, the leading custodian of pension and investment assets amounting by 1991 to $1 trillion as well as assets under management approaching $100 billion, they needed a lion's share of customer financial activities to offset lower profits in retail banking. Citibank expanded its credit card fees and interest revenue in 1981 by acquiring the *Diners Club*, membership in which permitted New Yorkers and others in big Eastern cities to eat at restaurants without carrying cash. By decade's end, the company led in securitized credit card receivables. Equally important, Citibank got around still stubborn restrictions against expanding retail banking operations by taking over S&Ls in California, Florida, Illinois, and Washington D.C. and becoming the nation's largest bank holding company. In 1985, it preceded Wells Fargo's movement into on-line banking services such as check statements, transferring money between accounts, and paying bills electronically from PCs by linking its offices with customers' home computers.

To assist home-grown institutions to compete with Citibank, Chase, and other Big Apple entities, states led by Pennsylvania changed laws to permit statewide and then interstate banking. Taking advantage of the liberalization, Pittsburgh National Bank and Provident National Bank of Philadelphia merged in 1982 into PNC Financial, the largest such bank combination in US history. When PNC continued gobbling up lesser state institutions and even between 1986 and 1989 took over banks in Louisville and Cincinnati as well as Bank of Delaware, dating to 1795, Mellon Bank of Pittsburgh began a similar buying binge. But Mellon had to sell off $1 billion of lower-yielding assets to prepare for further strategic expansion.

One of the fastest growing regional banks of the decade was Fifth Third Bancorp. Originally founded in 1858 as the Bank of the Ohio Valley, it was well positioned geographically to penetrate the tri-state area of Ohio, Kentucky, and Indiana. Meanwhile in Georgia, SunBanks and the Trust Company of Georgia combined into Sun Trust Banks, which the next year added Third National, second largest bank holding company in Tennessee. Its capital management subsidiary reached $5 billion of assets by end of the period.

In the wake of Citibank's move into savings and loans, California Federal became the first S&L to cross state lines by making acquisitions in Florida, Georgia, and Nevada. Permitted by federal regulators to innovate with adjustable rate mortgages (ARMs), interest on checking accounts, and more consumer and commercial lending, the company eventually transformed itself into California Federal Bank with assets by 1989 of $26.2 billion. Likewise, Washington Mutual became a capital stock savings bank after buying the Murphey Favre securities brokerage firm. In 1986, Ford's subsidiary First Nationwide Financial Corporation, parent of First Nationwide Savings with operations in California, Florida, and New York, began an aggressive expansion in the Midwest and East.

Genealogy of US Insurance Industry, 1946-2005

On the other hand, World Savings, a subsidiary of Trans-World Financial of California, remained an S&L while buying rivals in Colorado, Texas, and three other states and expanding lending operations to a dozen others. Its size of $19.5 billion of assets helped it survive a national S&L crisis, discussed below, that caused the S&L industry to implode. Countrywide Financial also reached substantial size by obtaining a listing on the NYSE and benefiting from a housing boom. Its computerized mortgage lending system as well as sales of mortgages to Fannie Mae and Freddie Mac caused a tripling of business to $3.1 billion in 1987 alone.Banks got a big leg up on S&Ls on April 29, 1987 when the government began easing Depression-era banking limits imposed by the Glass-Steagall Act of 1933. They were now permitted to lower loan standards to companies in order to win fees for placing public offerings of stocks and bonds. The rationale was that knowledgeable investors, more sophisticated rating agencies, and a stronger SEC would put "outside checks" on bad decisions. The consequence was increased competition for investment banking firms including Merrill Lynch, which topped the US and global debt and equity underwriting business with annual placements worth $2.25 billion. Among the first to take advantage of the change was J.P. Morgan, which won Federal Reserve permission in 1989 to underwrite and deal in corporate debt, and then the next year stocks. Total US bank assets rose to $5.4 trillion by 1990.

Meanwhile, after Reagan was reelected in November 1984 by a huge landslide over former Vice President Walter F. Mondale, his hand was strengthened to carry through further fiscal and economic reform. However, citizen and Democratic opposition to cuts in popular federal pro-

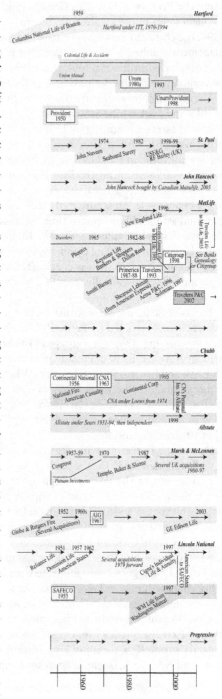

408

grams was so tenacious that a Balanced Budget Law known as the Gramm-Rudman-Hollings Act was not passed until December 12, 1985. Cuts were made in non-entitlement programs, however Social Security and Medicare still accounted for nearly 28% of the 1986 federal budget of $973.7 billion while interest on the national debt of $1.4 trillion consumed another 14.6%. Since defense spending was peaking at $285 billion, barely more than a fifth of federal funds were allocated to other social welfare programs. Nor was a balanced budget in the offing any time soon. A fiscal year deficit of $221 billion would only shrink to the $150 billion range by the last three fiscal years of the decade.

A far more substantial restructuring was accomplished by the Income Tax Reform Act of October 22, 1986. On the eve of mid-term elections that would overturn Republican control of the Senate, the President finally succeeded in convincing Congress to condense 14 personal income brackets down to two at 15% and 28% and cut the top corporate tax rate from 46% to 34%. The *quid pro quo* demanded by Democrats was that the AMT remain on the books, many tax deductions and shelters be eliminated, corporate tax credits and depreciation be restricted, and henceforth capital gains be treated like ordinary income. Because of increase in the standard deduction and personal exemption as well as changes in tax bracket amounts, millions of low-income citizens were dropped altogether from the tax rolls. The federal budget was still financed 43% by personal income taxes, 11.5% by corporate income taxes, and 36.5% by Social Security and other such taxes. In the last few years of the Cold War, top federal spending priorities were national defense at 27%, Social Security at 21%, other income security at 12%, and Medicare at 7.5%.

Naturally, the financial sector received another shot in the arm from taxpayers being able to keep more of their own money. After retirement holdings, bank deposits, and the value of private businesses, sole proprietorships, and professional practices, the major items in the portfolio of household financial assets were US bonds and other securities, trusts, mutual funds, and life insurance in that order. By 1990, the aggregate value of these other investment categories approached $2 trillion. Although life insurance at $392 billion was only 2.6% of household financial assets, the face value of policies topped $7 trillion.

One reason for the renewed popularity of life insurance policies was an innovation called universal life insurance. That product contained both a term insurance component as well as an increasing cash value investment like whole life. After buying First Penn-Pacific Life Insurance of Oakbrook Terrace, Illinois, Lincoln National became a national player and reached $100 billion of life insurance in force with $10 billion of assets under management. Further acquisitions brought diversification into property & casualty, investment management, group health, security placements, and third-party administration.

1987, Progressive attained $1 billion of annual premium in its niche of high-risk auto insurance and won a listing on the NYSE. Marsh & MacLennan also got into the seven figure club after becoming a Lloyd's broker, opening a Tokyo office, and embarking on an acquisition strategy for growth. Because by 1990 MetLife, Travelers, and other huge insurance companies claimed the lion's share of the $1.9 trillion of financial assets held by US insurance companies of all kinds, newcomers such as AON, founded in 1982 with the merger of Ryan Insurance Group and Combined International Corporation, had a better chance to succeed in the global insurance business, including insurance for cargo ships and as a reinsurance broker.

Already powerful overseas with $3 billion of foreign premium receipts, AIG launched new international ventures in Europe and China. In the US the company offered a corporate risk management service for aviation, provided mortgage guaranties, and diversified into managed health care. Its multifarious domestic and foreign interests made it better positioned to survive claims from natural catastrophes. For example, Hurricane Hugo struck Charleston with 138 mph winds in September 1989, resulting in $7 billion of property damage and costing the industry $4.2 billion in claims.

Exposure to such risk helped motivate Sears to spin off AllState's property and casualty business with its nearly 56,000 employees to new shareholders. The company's move was contrary to the trend of capital goods, consumer durables, and other large businesses acquiring and profiting from financial services subsidiaries. Caterpillar, Deere, and Xerox all bought such concerns to finance equipment purchases and leases by customers of their equipment. Dana got into finance in 1981 by taking over General Ohio Savings and Loan, renaming it Diamonds S&L, and boosting sales to $4.8 billion. In 1989, Ford bought The Associates from Paramount for $3.35 billion because receivables from US and Japanese operations, including a $200 million revolving loan from The Associates to Chrysler that helped keep the rival auto maker afloat, had tripled during the decade to $13.6 billion. However, Westinghouse Credit suddenly ran into trouble by investing billions in commercial real estate and LBOs just at the moment real estate values were at their peak, the insider trading scandal was breaking, and the S&L crisis undermined mortgage values.

In actuality, trouble had been brewing in the S&L industry for years. A loosening of federal and state regulation had permitted unwise practices to proliferate. Rising real estate values, pushed up to a peak by a record net private foreign capital invested in the US of $130 billion at mid-decade, convinced S&L executives to finance real estate purchases not supportable by the underlying economic value of properties. Even Japanese investors, thought to be shrewd businessmen, bought prime US properties, including 80% of Rockefeller Center in New York City for $1.4 billion and the Pebble Beach golf resort in California, at a super premium.

Banks and S&Ls now demanded on average a 10% down payment from first-time home buyers, half the previous standard. Falling interest rates and the ability of bigger institutions to take less profit on individual mortgages but make greater profit overall wounded smaller entities. The number of S&L failures rose from 11 in 1980 to 48 three years later to 221 in 1988. The next year, California Savings & Loan Association failed and had to be bailed out by Washington at cost to tax-payers of $2 billion. But a scandal alleging that Senator Allan Cranston (D., California) and four of his colleagues had used influence in return for benefits of various kinds to help that and other S&Ls brought a full-fledged political crisis. By August 1989, real estate values were crashing in various regions and the financial situation was worsened by defaults on loans made to developing countries and losses from LBO loans. Thus Congress voted to dissolve the Federal Savings and

Pebble Beach

Loan Corporation, place S&Ls under the FDIC, create a Resolution Trust Corporation capitalized at $50 billion to buy and sell off 500 failing S&Ls and increase capital require-ments on S&Ls that survived to avoid a reoccurrence of the debacle. Ultimately, the gov-ernment ponied up $166 billion to save the industry.

All this financial turmoil turned out to be good business for accounting firms. Joining in the merger and acquisition trend, Peat Marwick International combined with Klynveld Main Goerdeler of Europe in 1987 to become KPMG, while Ernst & Whinney linked up with Arthur Young two years later to produce Ernst & Young. Increasingly, accountants who specialized in auditing the books of major corporations began to offer financial and tax consulting services as well. As methods of accounting for revenues and expenses became more inventive to minimize tax payments to federal, state, and local governments, the ties between accounting firms and their clients became closer and more corrupting.

BOOM TIMES FOR AEROSPACE- DEFENSE AND TELECOMMUNICATIONS

As odious as it was for Democrats in the 1980s to see "the rich get richer and the poor get poorer," it was equally wounding to have social welfare and cultural programs reduced at a time when defense spending was going up and corporate tax rates on incomes up to $25,000, intended to help the nation's 10.8 million small businesses and entrepreneurs, were going down. Not only were cuts, or cuts in planned increases, made in environ-mental, health, housing, and urban aid programs, food stamps, and federal subsidies for school meals as well as the National Endowments for the Arts and Humanities and the Corporation for Public Broadcasting, but the number of education programs was shrunk from four dozen to 30. Only Social Security and Medicare/Medicaid funding increased because those entitlements were mandated by law. Payroll taxes to cover the cost were increased. Moreover, although government officials spoke of Social Security and Medicare/

Medicaid as if they were segregated for revenue and expense purposes from other items in the budget, in actual fact surpluses building up from payroll taxes were aggregated with deficits elsewhere to calculate the overall government surplus or deficit. Annual federal budget deficits, climbing to the $200 billion figure and beyond, would have been deeper in the red without including the entitlement accounts.

Space Shuttle

Supply side economics did not work precisely as advertised in part because of the recession that did not let up until December 1982. A second and perhaps more fundamental difficulty was that budget cuts in social welfare programs were overwhelmed by budget increases for securing the Free World's defenses against Communism. Critics complained that expenditure for military hardware and equipment as well as personnel and other operational expenses did not have the same stimulative effect as new investment in private industry plant and equipment. They were further outraged that Reagan and his administration did not scrutinize defense and aerospace spending as much as they should have to eliminate cost-ineffective programs such as the *B-1B* bomber built by Rockwell that failed to meet performance expectations. Media reports of bogus and excessive charges by defense contractors, including for mundane items such as wrenches, toilet seats, and fasteners, infuriated the public. Even the *Space Shuttle*, one of the highest profile and most acclaimed programs of the decade, never proved that its $10 billion R&D price tag was a wiser economic investment for the country than unmanned rockets.

The first test flight of the *Columbia* shuttle took place on April 14, 1981. The vehicle employed Martin Marietta external fuel tanks, which were reusable after recovery, Lockheed heat-resistant tiles, Hamilton Standard electric power fuel cells, space suits, and environmental control systems, B.F. Goodrich wheels and brakes, and parts and systems from many other contractors. Eventually a fleet of five shuttles was constructed for missions that ranged from scientific experimentation to military spying. NASA's goal was a flight every two weeks to sustain profitable commercial enterprises, such as taking advantage of weightless conditions in space to perform specialized manufacturing operations. However, the *Challenger* blew up on January 28, 1986 because of a leak through an O-ring on the *Centaur* liquid-fueled, upper stage made by General Dynamics that failed to seal, killing seven astronauts 74 seconds after liftoff. A debacle four years later with the $1.5 billion *Hubble* telescope mission because of faulty mirrors again highlighted the improbability of making a profit from operations in outer space. On the other hand, the innovation of satellite dishes on earth to receive TV and other electronic signals from satellites proved that telecommunications space operations could succeed. By 1989, the US had 2.4 million dishes in use.

B-2 Spirit

Not all aerospace and defense programs proved a technological disappointment. While Lockheed was secretly turning out the *F-117A* stealth fighter, Northrop won a contract to produce the *B-2 Spirit* stealth bomber and *ADM-136A Tacit Rainbow* anti-radiation missile to destroy active radars, and Rockwell worked on *Hellfire* missiles and launchers. Unfortunately, a $4.8 billion contract by the US Navy for McDonnell-Douglas and General Dynamics to build the *A-12* stealth attack-bomber for aircraft carriers ran into technical trouble and was eventually cancelled. GD got back into the Navy's good graces after its Electric Boat division began constructing *Seawolf* attack submarines. Likewise, Newport News Shipbuilding went beyond $1 billion of annual revenue with contracts to build *Nimitz* nuclear aircraft carriers and *Los Angeles* class nuclear attack subs. These were all part of a powerful 600 capital ship navy that Reagan proposed to build but which peaked at about 540 ships, far more than enough, it turned out, to overawe what the Soviets could put at sea.

Also climbing to $1 billion of revenue by end of the period was Science Applications International. The company won contracts to work on Strategic Force modernization, including the Strategic Defense Initiative announced by Reagan in March 1983 that was derided by critics as "Star Wars." Equally as lucrative but less controversial was computer software work performed by EDS for the US Army to build information systems for human resource activities and for the Navy to perform inventory control. In addition to contracts with health care and commercial insurance companies, this business pushed company revenue over $650 million in 1983. In fact, GM was so impressed with EDS' growth that the Detroit auto maker purchased the company for $2.5 billion, and then provided the capital to expand overseas operations. By 1989, revenue climbed to $5 billion and employment more than doubled to 30,000.

Despite Washington's splurge on aerospace and defense hardware, equipment, and information systems, the bulk of industrial companies still generated revenues from non-military contracts. Although Allied Chemical bought the Bendix Corporation in 1983 to enter the aerospace industry, the acquisition brought an automotive parts business as well. Then after taking over Signal Companies that same year, the company boasted a

strong engineered materials line of products. At mid-decade, the newly named Allied-Signal sold off half its holding in Union Texas Natural Gas, and then spun off 35 non-core businesses as The Henley Group.

Another conglomerate making a move to prominence was Tyco. Achieving $500 million of revenue by 1982 from four principal business lines — electrical and electronic components, healthcare and specialty products, fire and security systems, and flow control — company executives emphasized high-quality, low-cost production as well as reliability and customer service in whatever endeavor was attempted. Major cost savings were achieved by consolidating headquarters staff and computerizing financial reporting. In the last four years of the 1980s, Tyco broke into the $10 billion dollar revenue club by taking over Grinnell Corporation, a manufacturer and distributor of industrial and construction products, Allied Tube and Conduit, a maker of steep pipe and related tubular products, and Mueller Company, producing water and gas flow control devices. Meanwhile, Masco climbed from $1 billion of sales in 1984 to $5 billion eight years later by expanding its holdings in hardware, cabinet manufacturing, and specialty products. The company was well positioned to take advantage of growth in the nation's construction industry to $196 billion of revenue by 1990.

Textron, too, went on a buying binge — but to prevent a takeover by investment bankers. By using debt to acquire Avco Corporation in 1984, the company gained $2.9 billion in annual revenue and nearly doubled its size. After buying aerospace, defense, and automotive products maker Ex-Cell-O with $1.1 billion in annual sales in 1986, Textron was too heavily leveraged to be swallowed whole. Prudently, company strategists began selling off small units to obtain cash while concentrating on raising revenue from foreign operations to one-fifth of Textron's total. Also fearing a hostile takeover, American Standard achieved greater size and diversification by taking over Trane's heating and air conditioning business. Management then effected a leverage buyout in 1988 to go private.

More interested in high-tech developments than old industry, 3M looked outside Minnesota to build a research and administration complex in Austin, Texas to be near other high-tech electronics and telecom companies and accelerate revenues toward $10 billion by end of the period. The reason that so much excitement was building around the telecommunications industry was that on January 8, 1982, AT&T settled MCI's antitrust case by agreeing to spin off 22 Bell Telephone operating systems worth $80 billion and paying MCI $1.8 billion. But the FCC decided that Ma Bell's supremacy must end once and for all time and pushed for a division of the company into an AT&T that still provided long-distance service while seven so-called "Baby Bells" would handle local telephone service. Although the Baby Bells would continue to have a monopoly in different parts of the country, AT&T would have to contend in long distance with MCI, Sprint, and others. The break-up of AT&T was actually implemented in 1984. The parent company not only retained its long distance business but the Bell Labs and Western Electric subsidiaries. As compensation for losing 77% of its assets, 70% of its revenues, and 63% of its employees, AT&T was now permitted to go beyond development and manufacture of telecom equipment and residential telephones and equipment to information systems that integrated voice and data, network systems that made businesses more efficient, and computers and other non-telephone consumer products. AT&T also retained control of overseas switching and transmission systems with plans for new joint ventures in the Netherlands, Italy, Spain, Ireland, Denmark, Korea, Japan, and other countries.

Genealogy of US Telecom Industry, 1973-2005

As for the Baby Bells, the entities that emerged were named Bell Atlantic, NYNEX, Bell South, Ameritech, Southwestern Bell, Pacific Telesis, and US West. Some had aspirations to go beyond local telephone service. For example, Bell South with $21.5 billion of revenue and 96,000 employees bought Mobile Communications Corporation of America (MCCA) in 1988 to move into paging and answering services. By end of the period, the company owned 445,000 miles of fiber optics lines capable of transmitting calls via light waves on a single fiber to service 500,000 cellular customers.

Anticipating a strong challenge from competitors for long-distance business, the reduced AT&T immediately cut rates 6.4%. Company executives hoped it would take upstarts time to attract capital to take full advantage of technological breakthroughs. However, Sprint built a fully digital, fiber optic system in two years. MCI offered long-distance service at such low cost that revenues rapidly jumped into the billions of dollars. In response, Bell Labs continued to innovate, including with photon switches, to make the company's operations more efficient and less labor-intensive. In 1988, AT&T laid down the first fiber-optic trans-Atlantic cable, 3,148 miles long and capable of handling simultaneously 40,000 calls.

The Baby Bells were not the only companies to take advantage of an FCC decision to authorize cellular telephone service nationwide. Motorola activated its *DynaTAC* cellular system for businesses and started manufacturing a handheld phone weighing 28 ounces. After mobile phones appeared in cars in 1985, Allied and Mid-Continent merged into ALLTEL to get into the wireless phone service. Two years later, 1 million Americans communicated while driving. The prospect of a perpetually increasing market even induced cable TV provider Comcast to try cellular telecommunications. The company bought the American Cellular Network Corporation or AMCELL with its lucrative New Jersey to Washington D.C. territory. AT&T, having decided to stop making cell phones, conducted a survey that revealed that Americans believed the

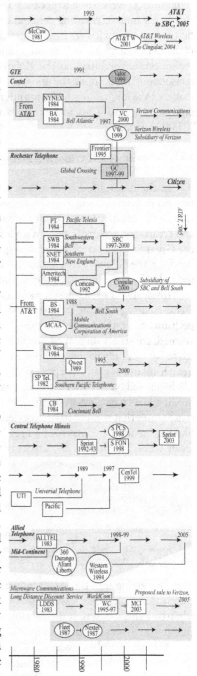

415

company was still the second largest maker of those devices. Since the "customer is always right," orders were given to get back into the market as a major force.

Badly underestimating demand for cellular phones, the FCC allocated only 40 megahertz of spectrum for wireless communications. That limitation put brakes on Motorola's plans to match a rapid expansion taking place in Europe. Therefore, the Finnish company Nokia established itself as the global leader in manufacturing handsets. Motorola took consolation in becoming the number one US supplier of cellular telephones. When in 1990 Robert W. Galvin, son of the founder, stepped down as chairman of the board, annual company revenues hit $10.9 billion and net profit $500 million. Motorola employed 105,000 people.

HEALTH CARE AS A NATIONAL ASSET — AND A HOUSEHOLD BURDEN

In the 1980s, life expectancy at birth climbed past 72 years for American males and beyond 78 years for females. The improvement over the average 45 year life expectancy at turn of the century was a result of dramatic advances in medical knowledge, technology, and treatment. Progress came with a not insubstantial price tag that accelerated during the Great Society attempt to bring quality health care to less affluent citizens. Overall, however, the bill for health insurance, hospital care, and prescription drugs had not gotten too radically out of line with the cost in other industrialized societies.

Ironically, a broad-based move on the part of Washington and many state governments to deregulate the industry by dropping *Certificate of Need* laws to generate more competition and restrain cost increases, had the opposite effect. As critics of deregulation had warned, construction of new hospitals and purchase of advanced medical equipment was passed on not only to those who used the health care system but all Americans who carried health insurance and corporations who picked up much of the tab. States such as Michigan and New York that kept strong *Certificate of Need* laws on the books succeeded in holding health care costs to one half to one third of the bill in Wisconsin, Indiana, and other states that weakened or repealed such statutes. Because hospital holding companies, like big insurance concerns, had regional and national operations, extravagance in one locale tended to force up costs to a greater or lesser degree everywhere.

In the 1980s, for example, Humana became the world's largest hospital company with 80 US and overseas institutions. The company focused on quality care, including a new emergency room design to have patients checked immediately by a health care professional rather than a clerk. An artificial heart research center in Louisville, its headquarters, became a leader in the field. By getting into the HMO industry in 1984 with its Humana Health Care Plans, the company signaled that it was pursuing a vertical integration strategy of insuring citizens, admitting them to hospitals, developing drugs and medical treatments to heal them, and charging high fees to maximize profits.

Another big player was HCA. Already in 1981, the company boasted $2.4 billion of revenue from 349 owned and managed hospitals of much smaller size than Humana's institutions. Although the corporation reached 49,000 beds in 463 hospitals six years later, 104 facilities were spun off to an employee-owned company called HealthTrust. In 1988, executives took the company private with a $5.1 billion LBO of its own stock. Next, they sold off their HCA Management Company as well as clinical labs and international operations. By end of the period, HCA controlled 77 acute care and 53 psychiatric hospitals, the most profitable segments of the lot. Since National Medical Enterprises (NME), founded in 1969 to build up a system of psychiatric and substance abuse hospitals in 30 states, had been accused of paying kickbacks and bribes to doctors, referral services, and others to refer patients to NME's institutions, as well as of fraudulently billing Medicare and Medicaid for those services, HCA's timing was excellent. NME eventually had to pay $214 million in private settlements to insurance companies, pay a fine of $379 million to the government, and change its name to Tenet in 1995 to get out from under the cloud of fraud and illegality.

Despite HCA's fragmentation and NME's trials and tribulations, the hospital system moved generally toward greater consolidation. In Dixie, for example, HealthSouth cobbled together 50 institutions by end of the period. To maintain leverage with hospital holding companies, insurance entities too were compelled to combine. Blue Cross and Blue Shield of Indianapolis launched an ambitious program of mergers and acquisitions to meld other such non-profit organizations within the state.

Meanwhile, a group of physicians and other health care professionals went public in 1984 with UnitedHealthCare Corporation to provide a health plan alternative to Medicare for seniors. Aetna did the same in a joint venture with Voluntary Hospitals of America called Partners National Health Plans. Partners then bought up a regional HMO network out of Minneapolis in 1986 called American MedCenters to top 1 million members. Aetna took 100% ownership of Partners by 1989, committing fully to managed care, including mental health plans. Equally determined to enter the field, CIGNA offered reinsurance for organ transplants to let small insurers and HMOs lay off the risk. The company bought Preferred Health Care, doing pre-paid dental plans in 1984. Three years later, CIGNA signed up 37,000 of Allied-Signal's employees, expanding to 110,000 workers and dependents by end of the period, in a managed health and dental care plan. The company added to its strength in managed health care and substance abuse programs across the country by taking over MCC Companies.

The increasing cost of hospitalization and insurance did not mean that Americans received no value for their health care dollars. Quite the contrary, dramatic advances in medical technology eased the physical infirmity and pain of hundreds of thousands. For example, by 1984 Boston Scientific's Medi-tech division led the world with a peripheral vascular angioplasty balloon to open up blocked arteries pumping blood to and from the heart. Pharmaceutical giant Pfizer bought Schneider Medintag AG of Switzerland to obtain ownership of the first *Monorail* balloon catheter. In 1986, Pfizer's subsidiary introduced a *Wallstent* endoprosthesis, eventually settling in at a price of about $1,000, for the first human coronary stent implant. Although heart and other diseases of the circulatory system remained by far the most frequent cause of death for Americans, the percentage had fallen from 42% in 1983 to under 37% by 1990.

Likewise, fantastic progress was made in reducing the invasiveness and destructiveness of surgery. In 1983, Bristol-Myers's Zimmer subsidiary sponsored the first arthroscopy tele-session with a live satellite feed from Chicago to instruct 1,000 surgeons in 27 cities about the advantages of this procedure. Arthroscopic surgery, utilizing a fiber-optic instrument to look inside a joint and transmit pictures to a miniature TV screen, was such an improvement on previous methods that professional athletes, particularly football players, who had previously suffered career-ending knee injuries with alarming regularity on artificial turf fields might now in some cases make full recoveries in weeks not months. That was enough to convince Stryker in 1986 to purchase Syn-Optics and quintuple annual revenues to $200 million by end of the period. Snap-On in 1987 diversified out of industrial products by establishing a medical products division for orthopedic tools. Zimmer climbed past $500 million of annual sales by coming up with a total knee modular system to replace arthritic knees as well as a modular hip replacement system.

Further competition in orthopedics came from Biomet. The company made acquisitions to obtain a direct sales force to expand distribution in the US and Europe of a broad line of internal fixation, electrical stimulation, and external fixation products as well as operating room supplies. Baxter also got into health care products distribution by purchasing American Hospital Supply. After selling off Foremost Dairies, McKesson invested in surgical supplies, bought up hospitals and pharmacies, and no longer defined itself as just a wholesaler of drugs.

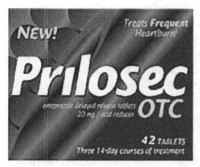

One reason for McKesson's change of strategic direction was that the field of drug wholesaling was consolidating. By taking over Ellicott Drug Company and Leader Drug Stores, with 17% coverage of the US population, Cardinal Distribution took a strong position in prescription drug distribution in the Midwest, and then divested itself of food distribution operations the next year. Simultaneously, Alco Health Services vaulted to third place in the wholesale drug distribution business. The company, which later became Amerisource Health Corporation, was spun off by Alco Standard as an independent company in an 1989 LBO. Other regional drug distributors were destined for success. Out in California, a company called Bergen Brunswig that was descended from firms founded in 1907 and 1947 came to prominence by gobbling up smaller companies.

Why was the field of pharmaceutical distribution becoming more competitive? Drugs filtering through the US health care network began to cost much more than before, and bring in more revenue. In 1981, Amgen started operations with a broad-based program in nephrology, hematology and oncology, bone and inflammation, neurology and endocrinology. Needing cash, the company was forced to sell marketing rights outside the US to its *EPO* drug to fight anemia-related fatigue in cancer patients to Johnson & Johnson. But J&J's move to market *EPO* inside the US as well led to a bitter decade and a half dispute. The various drugs Amgen produced to defeat anemia, arthritis, cancer, and other serious ailments nevertheless generated nearly $1 billion of annual revenue by end of the period.

Another bio-tech breakthrough was achieved by Eli Lilly in 1982 with a new diabetes treatment called *Humulin*. That was insulin produced with recombinant DNA technology identical to the substance generated by the human body. However, it was the company's *Prozac* anti-depressant drug, developed by more conventional means, which pushed the company toward $5 billion of revenue. To rise into the same financial stratosphere, Abbott came up with its *Depakote* treatment for epilepsy, the first diagnostic test for the Acquired Immune Deficiency Syndrome (AIDS), its *Hytrin* cardiovacular drug to treat hypertension, and its *IMx* diagnostic instrument for the immunoassay system.

Meanwhile, Monsanto executives proved once again in 1985, by acquiring G.D. Searle, a drug maker founded in Chicago in 1908, that they were interested in the best financial return for their investment dollars, rather than hunkering down in any one industry. In 1989, the company's *Cytotec* drug was the first anti-ulcer medication. The entry of other big players into pharmaceuticals, including P&G buying Norwich Eaton Pharmaceutical of New York, persuaded Bristol-Myers to merge with Squibb that year. The combined powerhouse was second in the industry.

Although prescription drugs offered potentially superior return on investment in comparison to over-the-counter drugs, the financial cost of development caused Merck to spread the risk with joint ventures. The industry leader combined with Astral for heartburn medication *Prilosec*, and turned out over-the-counter drugs as well in partnership with J&J. However, AHP's Whitehall division struck gold all on its own with non-prescription drug *Advil*, the first such pain-killing, ibuprofen pill offered in the US. Company executives were so pleased with this good fortune that in 1986 they divested all household product, food, and candy operations. The next two years, they claimed third place in animal health by acquiring a Bristol-Myers' division and the Parke-Davis Company. When AHP took over A.H. Robins, maker of *Robitussin*, *Chap Stick*, and *Dimetapp*, sales vaulted toward $10 billion.

FARMING BECOMES AGRI-BUSINESS

Even as the health care and pharmaceutical sectors were exploding, the decades long consolidation in agriculture came to a crescendo. The pace was accelerated by a farm recession, worsened by foreign competition in overseas markets, which slashed agricultural exports from $44 billion worth of commodities in 1981 to $26.3 billion five years later while cutting annual farm income to a low of $12.7 billion in 1983. Washington responded to building surpluses by expanding purchases for the Food Aid export program. Crops were then donated to non-governmental organizations (NGO) to sell to raise money for developmental and humanitarian activities in the Third World.

When even that effort proved insufficient to retain the favor and votes of farm belt inhabitants, Reagan and his party agreed just before Christmas 1985 to $52 billion of farm subsidies over three years, half front-loaded to 1986, as well as establishment of a Farm System Capital Corporation to assume bad agricultural loans. Because the surplus value of commodities in inventory had already been cut 80% by the farm recession to $5.5 billion, because Congress passed an anti-dumping law in 1987 designed in particular to protect US producers of citrus, beef, sugar and 200 other commodities, the agricultural sector began to recover. However, a drought in the Great Plains Corn Belt the next year caused $40 billion of economic losses. Buried under a cornucopia harvest in 1990 of 201 million tons of corn, 74 million tons of wheat, 67 million tons of milk, 52 million tons of soybeans, 50 million tons of sugar beats and sugarcane, trampled by herds of 98 million cattle, 54 million hogs, 11 million sheep, 2 million goats, and 1.5 billion poultry, all of which drove down prices and profits, the family farmer was an economic victim of his agricultural success.

California orange grove

By contrast, corporate farm operations and big agri-businesses not only survived but prospered. While Cargill used its world-wide contacts to branch out into coffee trading, cocoa processing and supplying, phosphate-fertilizing mining and manufacturing, and petroleum distributing, ADM completed the transition to corn sweeteners replacing sucrose in soft drinks. Although Deere's farm machinery sales were set back both by the continuing farm recession and a 1986 labor strike, a program of modernization with CAD/CAM and cellular manufacturing that organized production into individual units staffed by worker groups reduced rambunctious employees 40% to 37,500. As well as diversifying into a subsidiary called Heritage National Healthplan that came by end of the period to cover 400,000 employees of 700 companies, Deere reduced its risk and further integrated its business in a joint venture to assemble excavators for Hitachi of Japan and by purchasing Funk Manufacturing Company, a maker of power-train components.

The farm machinery company also moved toward a just-in-time inventory concept. That practice had previously been implemented, albeit to a limited degree, by Carnegie, Ford, and others in the late nineteenth and early twentieth centuries. If a business owned a raw materials and transportation network, it could manage its production flow more carefully than if resources had periodically to be ordered from third parties. Materials and parts need not be stockpiled well in advance of need.

The particular brand of just-in-time inventory practice attempted in the 1980s was copied from Japanese companies. Large corporations used size and financial clout to insist that independent suppliers respond promptly to orders as if captive subsidiaries and not separate business entities. While the end user of raw materials and parts could then minimize the amount of cash tied up in inventory and the interest lost thereon, as well as streamline operations and reduce costs, suppliers had to increase production and inventory to be ready to fill orders of varying quantity whenever demanded. Naturally, the financial and operational burden placed on smaller companies was extreme. Particularly in volatile economic times, such as recoveries from recessions, cautious executives sometimes waited too long to ratchet up production. Last-minute rush orders to take advantage of suddenly surging demand often caught suppliers short.

Fax machine

At a time when farm land values were plunging nearly 20% over a seven year period to $600 per acre, the value of forest land was actually increasing. One major reason was that the boom in office printers, copiers, and fax machines caused US businesses to expand from using 850 billion pages of paper in 1981 to 4 trillion in 1990. The number of fax machines alone increased nearly five-fold between 1986 and 1988 to 900,000 devices. Although the overall annual growth rate of the value of paper products consumed in the US, including more profitable bleach paper products and specialty products such as linerboard, newsprint, and kraft grades, was only 1%, a more torrid 3% growth rate in Europe convinced International Paper to spend $6 billion overhauling its mills. In 1986, IP bought HammerMill for $1.1 billion to obtain that company's line of paper products, nine pulp and paper mills, and advanced distribution network. After further acquisitions, including of Zanders Feinpapiere AG, the leading German producer of coated paper, which had been founded in 1829, and Aussedat Rey, a French manufacturer of office copying paper and specialty panels dating to the 18th century, IP introduced *Classic Pak* container for the burgeoning poultry industry. Company sales vaulted from $5 billion at mid-decade to $11.4 billion in 1989.

Hot on IP's heels was Georgia Pacific. Acquisitions brought more pulp and paper operations, container plants, sawmills, and 825,000 acres of timberlands. The last takeover, of Great Northern Nekoosa Corporation in 1988, swelled annual revenue from $9.5 billion to $12.7 billion two years later. Overall, the industry churned out 78.8 million tons of paper and paper products on top of 63 million tons of wood pulp.

Engineered wood product – I-Joists
The latter category now included engineered wood made by Weyerhaeuser from wood left-overs and trees not suitable for sawmills. The material was chipped, flaked, and compressed into structural and nonstructural panels for homes, doors, and furniture. America's first great lumber company also built a recycling plant in Charlotte to ride the swell of the environmental movement that among other successes persuaded Congress to pass a Clean Water Act over Reagan's veto on February 4, 1987 to spend $18 billion through 1994 for revolving loan funds and sewer construction grants as well as estuary and toxic "hot spots" cleanup and control of polluted water runoff. The precariousness of the nation's resource base and the need for development of recycling technology was demonstrated with sudden ferocity in a 1988 fire in Yellowstone National Park that destroyed one-third of the park's 1.8 million acres of forest.

King Consumer Spends Again

Lumber, furniture, and other wood products became a critical part of the growing home improvement market. Home Depot surged in the decade of the 1980s to $2.7 billion in sales, 118 nationwide stores, and 17,500 employees. In addition to Lowe's, competitors included Home Centers of America, which was purchased by Kmart in 1984 and renamed Builders Square. The attraction for do-it-your-selfers was huge, warehouse-size stores filled with all manner of materials, tools, and products at discounted prices that undercut the business of local hardware stores, including popular chains like Tru-Value.

Realizing that economies of scale in home improvement would work in other retail operations, the Price Club for businesses came up in 1983 with Costco Wholesale stores for the general public. The first in Seattle boosted the company to $1 billion of sales the next year. Meanwhile in Minneapolis, a company called Sound of Music changed its name to Best Buy and broadened out its product line to provide more home electronics products, including camcorders, satellite dish systems, and VCRs, appearing in 58% of households by 1988. Although Sony had been first out with its *Betamax* technology, US companies flooded the market with rival *VHS* tapes to doom the superior Japanese VCR standard to eventual oblivion.

Increasingly, however, the brand names Americans came to revere in home electronics were foreign — Panasonic, Hitachi, and Philips of the Netherlands, in addition to Sony. To compete, RCA and Zenith had to shift production out of the country to secure lower labor costs in Mexico and the Far East. Unrestricted by the Reagan administration, foreign imports not only cut into the market share of US companies in this industry but cars, textiles, and a wide range of machinery. Adding to the nation's bill for importing oil, natural gas, and related products, they caused the annual imbalance of trade to exceed $150 billion by 1987 before improving.

Fortunately, major US retailers did not have to beat back foreign competition. They did have to contend both with specialized retailers and giant discount chains. Having begun as the latter type of business, J.C. Penney decided to become "America's national department store" by spending $1 billion over five years to modernize its buildings and focus on apparel, leisure products, and home furnishings. Operations involving auto service, appliances, paint and hardware, lawn and garden, and fabrics were discontinued.

J.C. Penney's move compelled traditional department store chains to keep growing. May Company reached $7 billion of sales after taking over Foley's in Houston, Filene's in Boston, O'Neil's of Akron, and Associated Dry Goods Corporation, including Lord & Taylor in New York City. However, Allied Stores and Federated Department Stores were claimed by Campeau Corporation in LBOs. Although combined sales topped $10 billion, $8 billion of debt placed on their books by Campeau soon put both subsidiaries into bankruptcy. Their woes then created an opportunity for Dillard's to expand in the Midwest by buying 12 stores from R.H. Macy, 27 from Joske, and taking a half interest in 12 Higbees stores. A push into the south brought an additional 18 D.H. Holmes stores and 23 J.B. Ivey stores from North Carolina to Florida. By contrast, Nordstrom's only dipped its toe into eastern waters with a single store in Virginia. That company's big surge would come in the next decade.

Martha Stewart

Had mainline department stores been J.C. Penney's only competition, the company would have surged. However, the business of Best Buy and Circuit City grew so swiftly that company executives decided in 1987 to get out of home electronics entirely as well as hard sporting goods and photographic equipment. They hoped to grow sales beyond the $13.7 billion booked in 1985 by issuing their own *Visa* and *MasterCard* credit cards to supplement their J.C. Penney card. A *Best of Britain* clothes marketing campaign combined with new focus on national clothes brands such as *Haggar* shirts, *Vanity Fair* hosiery, and *Lee*, *Wrangler*, and *Rustler* jeans lost traction to Target's discount clothing, which helped that company's sales double between 1982 and 1987 to $10 billion. Kmart too got into less pricey sportswear, endorsed by T.V. star Jaclyn Smith. A line of clothing built up for the company by entertainment and lifestyle consultant Martha Stewart, who went on to assemble a Martha Stewart Omnimedia business empire, proved even more popular with the public.

Another major threat to department store chains arose from specialty clothing retailer Limited Brands. While the company's 1982 acquisition of 207 Lane Bryant stores and mail order business brought bigger headlines, purchase of Victoria' Secret for only $1 million proved a bargain in the long run with the surging popularity of women's intimate apparel. Three years later, Limited Brands spent $297 million to take over 798 Lerner stores. The clothier topped off the decade by creating an *Express Men*'s brand to sell in its 16 Express stores, which were later renamed Structure, buying out 25 Abercrombie and Fitch stores for $46 million, and adding a *Limited Too* brand for girls in its Limited stores.

Another niche player was the Gap. That retailer not only took over tiny Banana Republic's two-store chain to obtain a promising catalogue sales business but opened GapKids stores in 1986 and babyGap stores four years later. Meanwhile in Wisconsin, a company called Kohl's that had been founded in 1963 was purchased by investors from BATUS Retail Group, a British-American Tobacco Company subsidiary. After merging 26 Main Street Stores with its own 14 establishments, that company was poised by period's end for a decade of accelerated growth.

Air Jordan

Then there was Foot Locker, still owned by Wool-worth's. The subsidiary's mall stores profited selling Nike *Air Jordan* basketball shoes, endorsed by NBA star Michael Jordan of the Chicago Bulls. Nike's sales hit $1 billion in 1986 and $2 billion by end of period by pro-ducing *Air Max* running shoes and cross trainers. Foot Locker also carried Reebok's *Freestyle* aerobic dance shoe for women, its *Step Reebok* trainer, and shoes for football, baseball, soccer, track, and other sports that incorporated the breakthrough *Pump* air technology.

Beset by competitors large and small that cut into profitable business lines, J.C. Penney still managed to advance at a 4% pace through the rest of the decade. Its $16 billion in annual sales were half Sears' retail operations, a third when including Sears' financial business revenues. However, Wal-Mart topped $50 billion by opening Sam's Club ware-houses to compete with CostCo, changing over to bar-code scanners, building 16 regional distribution centers, and opening its first super center, combining supermarket products with general merchandise, in Missouri in 1988. Revenues and profits from rapid expansion more than tripled in the final four years of the decade.

In point of fact, Wal-Mart was growing so fast around the country with a *Made in America* campaign that it became a strategic threat to new retailers even as they achieved size and strength in their own niches. For example, the founding of Office Depot in Fort Lauderdale, Florida and Staples in Brighton, Massachusetts in 1986 provoked a consoli-dation in the office supply industry from about 20 competitors to half in just a few years. The former's *Copy and Print* centers inside stores and the latter's catalogue sales to small businesses pressured older, less efficient companies like Ames to takeover failing entities such as Zayre. Ames fell too into bankruptcy, even as Office Max out of Cleveland rose up to take market share in the Midwest. Since the products these chains offered, such as *Swingline* stapling machines and staples, *Wilson Jones* aluminum sheet holders, and *ACCO* paper-clips and binders, were ubiquitous, Wal-Mart could also buy and sell them in quantity. That was good news for Swingline's and Wilson Jones' owner American Brands (later Fortune Brands), which took over ACCO in 1987.

While brand familiarity and loyalty remained an important factor in buying habits, fidelity to retail establishments declined. Astonished by the variety of products and dis-count prices in warehouse-size establishments, wholesale clubs, and supermarkets, American consumers looked increasingly for the best deal. They flocked to shopping malls, outlet malls, discount stores, mega-discount stores even while placing mail-orders over the phone. The cable industry offered viewers TV showcasing of products.

In a separate category were operations like RadioShack's that offered state-of-the-art products such as stereo receivers with digital technology, high-performance satellite TV systems, and mobile cellular phones for do-it-yourself consumers through its own chain. Company executives were so pleased with prospects in the domestic market, that they spun off foreign operations in 1986 under the name InterTAN. Kodak, too, tried to acquire better control over its distribution by purchasing the Sterling Drug Store chain. In addition to disc photography (using a rotating disc of film inside cameras) and many other advances, the century-old firm diversified into flexible floppy disks for PCs, videotape cassettes, consumer batteries, color copiers, color printers, electronic image sensors, and even health care with a pharmaceutical division.

GE dishwasher pre-installed in condominium

By and large, however, consumer durable makers did not control their own destiny. When Maytag, Amana, and GE innovated with front-loading washers, stacked washer/dryers, quartz halogen cook-tops, built-in refrigerators, and 24 inch freestanding refrigerators, they counted on Sears, J.C. Penney, and other retailers to sell to end-users. They knew that consumers would pay more, sometimes substantially more, for quality name brand appliances. That was the reason that Maytag in 1989 bought Hoover Company, the famous maker of vacuum cleaners, despite proliferation of cheaper, less expensive alternatives.

Nevertheless, increasing sales at a pace that would boost profitability was becoming a problem for makers of brand-name appliances. As virtually all households came to have refrigerators and TVs and the vast majority washing machines, VCRs, and air conditioners, growth in volume began to slow down, prompting GE to severely contract its labor force from a peak of 400,000. Rather than muddy reputations for quality and accept slimmer profit margins by offering cheaper products, industry leaders preferred to expand overseas into markets where the affluent could afford, but had not yet decided, to purchase heavy household white goods. Whirlpool followed this strategy into Europe, Mexico, India, Canada, and Brazil to double annual revenues to $6 billion by 1989. Any increase in air conditioner and refrigerator sales was good news for producers of polystyrene, a chemical used to make housings for those appliances. Recognizing the continuing possibility of the industry, Huntsman began buying up polystyrene plants in Ohio, Virginia, Illinois, and Texas and then licensing the right to make the chemical, including overseas in Taiwan and Korea.

Cabbage Patch doll

Another consumer industry marked by strong brand name attraction was toys and other children's products. Hasbro brought back the legendary *G.I. Joe* in 1982 and then thrilled little girls the next year with *My Little Pony*, subsequently popularized in an animated TV series and feature films. Mattel countered with *He-Man* and *Masters of the Universe* dolls, but its aging *Barbie* doll line was temporarily eclipsed by the *Care Bears* from American Greetings. That greeting card maker rose to $1 billion of sales by 1986. Then there was the *Cabbage Patch* doll craze created by Coleco Industries that in 1983 distressed parents unable, despite shipment of 6 million dolls from Far East producers (who now made nearly a fifth of the toys sold in the US) to find them in stores for Christmas. Mattel had to sell off all non-toy products the next year and commit to a full *Barbie* make-over to regain the limelight.

To create economies of scale to deal with the whims and fancies of the children's marketplace, Hasbro bought out Milton Bradley for $360 million in 1984, which now included the Playskool Company of Chicago with large international sales. The company also had a huge hit with *Transformers* die-cast cars and planes, undercutting the business of Tonka Toys. The significance was not only that *Transformers* eclipsed Mattel's products for boys but sold for as much as $10 per robot. Company revenues expanded by end of the period toward $1 billion. Mattel tried to buttress its own position by obtaining the right from Walt Disney to bring out *Mickey Mouse*, *Pooh*, and other dolls for pre-school children. Overseas ventures, including purchase of Hong Kong based ARCO Industries, making plastic gun toys, outflanked the domestic competition. Meanwhile, surging toy and doll sales proved a bonanza for Toys'R'Us. In the 1980s, the company nearly quintupled stores to 404 and became the world's largest toy retail seller.

Tapping into the global marketplace was also a winning strategy for giant household products maker P&G. Not only did the company buy Richardson-Vicks of North Carolina, dating from 1905, to obtain the *Vicks* respiratory care and *Oil of Olay* product lines as well as *Blendax* toothpaste and other products in Europe but was first in the industry to negotiate joint ventures in the potentially huge, one billion person China market. The Cincinnati concern then marched toward $20 billion of sales by introducing new brand names *Always* and *Whisper* feminine protection products, *Liquid Tide* laundry detergent, *Pert Plus* and *Rejoice* shampoos, *Ultra Pampers* throw-away diapers, and *Luvs Super Baby Pants*. Its purchase in 1989 of Noxell brought control of *Cover Girl*, *Noxzema*, and *Clarion* make-up and skin care product lines.

The financial and marketing clout P&G put behind Noxell and other women's toiletries might have doomed competitor Avon had not the door-to-door seller belatedly come up with *Bio-Advance* skin care and *Avon Color* hair-coloring products. Kimberly-Clark too had to react to P&G's moves by introducing *Pull-Ups* training pants for toddlers. Meanwhile, Gillette passed $1 billion of annual revenue in 1982 by offering its *Right Guard* solid antiperspirant and taking the lead in selling writing instruments. After the company only narrowly beat back a hostile $4.1 billion takeover bid by the Revlon Group of New York, a multi-billion dollar cosmetics company dating from 1932, by selling off smaller lines, P&G took dead aim at *Right Guard* by purchasing *Old Spice* products from Shulton of New Jersey. More secure but still in P&G's shadow was Colgate Palmolive, solidifying its lead in soap by buying and combining the products of Minnetonka Corporation into a Softsoap Enterprises subsidiary. In other niche areas where P&G competed but was not dominant, rubber product maker Newell bought Anchor Hocking Corporation, an Ohio glassware company founded in 1905, while Monsanto purchased Greensweep's lawn and garden products.

Monsanto was first to modify genetically plant cells. The company then moved more deeply into the field of growing plants with genetically engineered traits by buying Dekalb's wheat research program and in 1983 Jacob Hartz Seed Company, working to bio-engineer soybeans to make them more weather and insect resistant. For the time being, the public was generally unaware that the food chain was evolving. Americans trusted that the brand names they purchased were not only inspected by the FDA but true to claims by marketers that they provided specific benefits when consumed.

For example, Anheuser-Busch introduced its *Bud Light* beer in 1982 with the tag line "less filling, tastes great." Because men and now women too agreed, the company surged toward 1 billion barrels of beer produced in its history by 1986. That success and the financial muscle arising from profitable beer sales gave the St. Louis company the wherewithal to buy up *SeaWorld* amusement parks three years later. In combination with its *Busch Gardens* parks in Tampa and Williamsburg, Anheuser-Busch became a major player and competitor to Disney in theme parks.

Taking control of retail distribution was a strategy favored by PepsiCo as well. After divesting itself of North American Van Lines and Wilson Sporting Goods in 1985, the company bought up KFC's 6,600 restaurants and 7-Up International. "Choice of a New Generation" TV ads starring pop singing star Michael Jackson as well as introduction of *Pepsi Free* and *Diet Pepsi Free* caffeine-free colas caused revenues to more than double in the last half of the 1980s to $15.4 billion. Persons employed by the company, including around the world, topped 300,000. Not only PepsiCo's success but Coca-Cola's fiasco in changing its nearly century old *Coke* formula to counter *Pepsi*'s popularity with younger consumers caused industry leadership to change hands. The Atlanta soft drink giant recouped the situation by bringing back the tried-and-true recipe under the name *Classic Coke* while retaining *New Coke* for those who preferred a sweeter taste.

Confection and indulgence continued to be the road to riches for several other food companies. In 1983 Pillsbury, also in possession of Burger King fast food restaurants, bought Haagen-Dazs, maker of premium ice cream. Two years later, the company came out with *Pop Secret* microwave popcorn, which eventually outpaced *Orville Redenbacher* and other competitors. That success only made it more attractive to gin and scotch maker Grand Metropolitan of Britain, which bought Pillsbury, and then merged with Guinness, another British liquor company, to form Diageo. Meanwhile, Monsanto obtained *NutraSweet* sweetener by taking over G.D. Searle. The next year in 1986, Hershey Foods bought up Ludents, maker of *Ludents* cough drops and *5th Avenue* chocolate bars. Hershey then acquired Peter Paul-Cadbury's. The former entity had been founded in 1919 to make *Almond Joy* and *Mounds* bars while the latter was known for *Cadbury's* fine chocolates and *York* peppermint patties.

Big food companies generally avoided competing in candies with Hershey and Mars. Although Nabisco did in 1981 gobble up *Lifesavers*, a product dating from 1913, the company received more notoriety for taking over Standard Brands and its popular *Planters* nuts products. That same year, General Foods strengthened its position in meats with acquisition of Oscar Mayer. The company then marketed its *Tang* powdered beverage and *Maxwell House* coffee brands in China. Also profiting overseas, Philip Morris, now the world's largest cigarette company, bought up General Foods in 1985. That move prompted RJ Reynolds to acquire Nabisco Brands, and then subsume its *Del Monte* canned goods, *Grey Poupon* mustard, dating to 1877, and *A.1.* steak sauce, tracing its lineage all the way back to the 1820s, into the new subsidiary. Trying to remain independent, Consolidated Foods built up a powerful presence in meats with acquisition of Standard Meat Company in 1982, Jimmy Dean Meats two years later, Bill Mar Foods, maker of turkey products, three years after that, and Hygrade Food Products, known for its *Ball Park* hot dogs, in 1989. Along the way at mid-decade, the company changed its name to Sara Lee Corporation, diversified into hosiery and athletic wear clothes, and pushed revenues over the $10 billion mark.

Also determined to carve out a chunk of the meat market, ConAgra bought Armour Food Company, a processor of hot dogs, sausage, bacon, ham, lunchmeats and owner of *Dinner Classics* frozen dinners. After picking up *Swift* brand pork, beef, and lamp products, the company took over Monfort Meat Company of Colorado in 1987. Monfort combined slaughterhouse, meatpacking, and distribution operations to provide hotels, restaurants, and supermarkets with its products. ConAgra thus became by end of the period a full-line food products company.

Substantial consolidation in the food industry was completed in the second half of the 1980s. Investment firm Kohlberg, Kravis, Roberts & Company paid $6.2 billion for Beatrice Corporation, maker of *Hunt's* tomato paste, *Wesson* oil, and *Butterball* turkey. The next year, Philip Morris bought Kraft to exceed RJR Nabisco briefly as the largest consumer products company in world. Kohlberg, Kravis, Roberts & Company then spent $25 billion in 1988 to claim RJR Nabisco. .

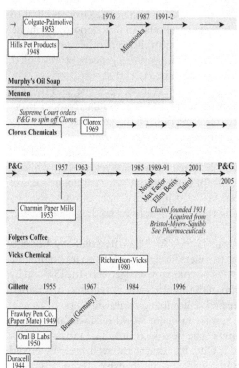

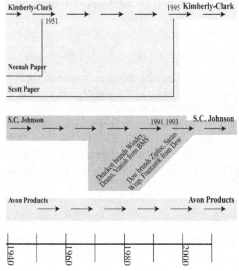

Genealogy of US Household Products Industry, 1941-2005

Including H.J. Heinz in condiments, Kellogg in cereal, Campbell in soups, most of the big names in food, beverage, and tobacco were now in place and would remain so through the end of the century. The industry was generating annually by 1990 about $150 billion in annual revenues, or about $600 per American, equal in 2004 money to $867.

The bulk of these sales was still rung up in supermarkets and grocery stores. While offering brand name products, Kroger boosted profitability by producing its own *Cost Cutter* brands. Acquisition by mid-decade of Dillon Companies convenience stores of Kansas and the Great Plains, 86 Tom Thumb Food Stores out of Dallas the next year, and 11 M&M Super Markets of Savannah in 1985 kept the chain neck & neck with A&P, also going on a buying binge, but were not enough to discourage hostile takeover attempts, though none was successful. So long as Wal-Mart, CostCo, and other huge discount operations, now including Meijer drug stores morphing into a supermarket chain of four dozen stores by adding Bulk Food departments and staying open 24 hours a day, kept eating into the food business, profit margins would remain thin and stock price low enough to tempt scavengers.

Fighting back, all the grocery store chains built bigger stores to achieve yet greater economies of scale, emulate Kroger's with check-out scanning, and move toward a system of distribution centers as large as 500,000 square feet. Publix in Florida was so successful with processing plants for its own foods that revenue jumped to $5.4 billion by end of the period from 367 stores employing 64,000 employees. Meanwhile, Supervalue squeezed out more profit by continuing its strategy of buying up regional food wholesalers in the Midwest, Northwest, and Southeast. In the Northeast, C&S Wholesale Grocers climbed toward $1 billion of sales by relocating to a bigger warehouse in Brattleboro, Vermont, winning the A&P supermarket account, and attracting the attention of other grocery store chains in the region. During the decade, corner and family-owned grocery stores failed. Specialized delicatessens and food stores, however, continued to thrive.

Food and drug retailing was nearly as large a sector as food, beverage, and tobacco products. However, growth was being restrained by the surging popularity, once prosperity returned and national income recovered, of eating out. All the large fast food chains benefited, including Wendy's International, doubling to 4,000 restaurants by 1992. Olive Garden, a newcomer out of Minneapolis founded by General Mills in 1982, began a belated expansion in 1986 that generated $500 million of annual sales in six years. Meanwhile in Seattle, Starbucks combined the coffee bar concept from Europe with catalogue sales of coffee beans to expand into many states. Even Marriott jumped deeper into fast food by purchasing Gino's of Philadelphia and changing the chain over to its holdings named after cowboy movie and singing star Roy Rogers.

But Marriott's principle business was still hotels. In 1983, the company began a Courtyard Hotels chain to appeal to business travelers, and then added to its holding by purchasing the Residence Inn Company in 1987. The company wedged into the low end by starting up a Fairfield Inn chain. Its portfolio of 500 worldwide hotels was diversified further the next year with vacation time-share and senior living establishments.

To build and operate luxury hotels and resorts in major world business and tourist capitals, Hilton Hotels founded Conrad Hotels. The next year in 1983, Embassy Suites Hotels opened its first all suites hotel in Kansas City. Pleasing to the well-heeled who did not wanted to be pestered by detail, Westin installed a comprehensive credit card reservation and check-out system. Las Vegas in the West and Atlantic City in the East combined five-star hotels with gambling tables, gambling machines such as the *Megabucks* progressive slot machine system from International Game Technology, and live entertainment to bring in the high rollers.

THE NEW TECHNOLOGY ECONOMY

On October 1, 1980, Bill Gates and tiny Microsoft signed a contract to provide operating software for the prototype personal computer IBM was developing to perform word processing and spreadsheet functions. The price per machine was $1. In point of fact, not until seven months later did Microsoft actually have the software. Instead of developing and writing the program themselves, Gates and his associates purchased software called *Q-DOS* software from Seattle Computer Products for $50,000. Renamed *MS-DOS*, the product became the foundation for turning Microsoft from a fly-by-night startup into a computer industry giant with market value of over $200 billion.

Along the way, Gates adopted business practices which critics charged at best were aggressive,
at worst piratical. Most famously (or infamously),
Microsoft emulated the graphical icon system
Apple was designing for its *Macintosh* system.
AT&T and Sun Microsystems were three years too
late in 1988 with their *UNIX* operating software to
prevent Microsoft's *Windows* from becoming the PC
industry's not altogether satisfactory standard.
Although compatibility problems between *Windows*
and application software programs caused com-

puters to "crash," *Windows* did permit users to run multiple application programs simultaneously and perform other tasks such as organizing, copying, and deleting files and
communicating with peripheral devices, in particular printers. As for IBM, although the
company profited handsomely from its *DOS*-run PC introduced in 1981 and subsequent
advances that increased PC computing speed toward 20 megahertz, RAM memory to 1
megabyte, and color monitor resolution to 640 by 480 pixel sharpness and 256 colors, Big
Blue executives came to the slow realization that failing to keep ownership of operating
software was a major strategic blunder. They consoled themselves with annual revenues
that surged toward $63 billion by 1989, profits that climbed beyond $6 billion, and
employment that peaked at 400,000.

The computer industry might have been radically different had IBM emulated Apple's
example of proprietary control of both hardware and software. In the early 1980s, the
company founded by Steven Jobs commanded a premium from schools, scientific institutions, and businesses for its *Apple II* and *Apple III* systems, priced respectively at $1,395 and
$2,995. The company eventually sold 2 million *Apple IIs*, bringing in over $2.5 billion in
revenue to itself and retailers. The *Macintosh* system, with a mouse device to point and click
on graphical icons instead of text commands typed on a keyboard, sold 500,000 units in
two years after being introduced to the nation through innovative TV advertising during
the NFL's Super Bowl championship game in January 1984. However, because PCs running
DOS and then *Windows* sold for substantially less than the Mac's hefty price tag of $9,995,
Apple's brief ascendancy vanished. Jobs was suddenly and unceremoniously ousted from
the company's leadership while 1,200 employees were laid off.

As much as IBM's PC, it was PC clones that eclipsed Apple. Founded in Houston in
1982, Compaq Computer rang up $111 million of annual sales the next year. Many other
companies big and small, including AT&T, DEC, and Xerox, jumped into the clone
market, driving down prices and taking share in the US market. Total number of PCs
climbed from 15 million in 1984 to nearly twice that number in 1986. The only hiccup in
revenues and profitability occurred at mid-decade when overcapacity cut memory chip
prices 80% in one year and revenues fell 17% with PC sales down 2%. The advent of faster
microprocessor chips, simpler word-processing software, & desktop laser printers re-
infused Americans with enthusiasm for home, school, and business computing.

A leader in computer memory storage was EMC of Massachusetts. The company
advanced from 64-K memory boards in 1981 to 1 megabyte RAM chips four years later. A
contract with HP the next year to double memory on *HP 3000* minicomputers led to even

more lucrative deals with IBM to turn out split-capability controllers for midrange disc subsystems and advance storage subsystems for the *IBM System/38* and *AS/400* computers. The company also produced *Orion* solid-state mainframe storage systems.

Meanwhile, the battle was rejoined in microprocessors by Motorola and Texas Instruments. They vied to cram transistors onto 3/8 inch square chips. The former succeeded in 1984 in turning out a 32-K microprocessor with 200,000 transistors. The latter exported manufacturing facilities to Mexico, India, Japan, Taiwan, Italy, and Korea to maximize profits from $6.6 billion of annual revenues by 1987 supporting 70,000 employees. But it was Intel with its 386 processor for PCs followed by its 486 processor in 1989 that took the industry by storm. After lower-cost Japanese competitors crowded out the company and other US suppliers in the DRAM chip market, Intel focused on capturing upwards of 90% of the domestic market in microprocessors.

Two notable companies piggybacked onto the success of semiconductor designers by advancing the process of making chips. In 1982, Rohm & Haas bought the Shipley Company, a manufacturer of photo-resists used in etching chips and microcircuits for electronic products. Five years later, Applied Materials, founded in Santa Clara, California in 1967 to make systems for processing silicone wafers, came out with its *Precision 5000*, single-wafer, multi-chamber platform. That breakthrough pushed annual revenues to $1 billion by 1993 and won a spot in the Smithsonian Information Age technology collection.

An alternative for businesses unable to afford $20 million super computers, mainframes, or even minicomputers that wanted to run an integrated system arrived. These were desktop workstations with monitors, keyboards, and floppy disc ports but no central processing unit and hard drive memory like PCs that were linked through a network to a powerful computer server. Leader in the field was Sun Microsystems, founded in 1982 with $100 million raised from venture capitalists. The company reached $1 billion of annual revenue by 1988, in part by working with applications software companies to write programs compatible with its software. The *UNIX* operating software subsequently ran the servers that linked the workstations. Sun's business boomed after making arrangements in 1989 for Oracle and Sybase to run their database applications through Sun's *SPARCstation 1* system. However, a strategic threat to the workstation concept arose when Novell of Irvine, California shifted from making computers and disk operating systems to software and hardware for data networks. Its *NetWare* local area network software, linking PCs together without a central server, as well as later development of wide area network software for big corporations, eventually captured 70% of the computer networking market.

Oracle version 3 software, introduced in 1983, was the first database management system to run on mainframes, minicomputers, and PCs. Cooperation with Sun pushed revenues toward $1 billion by end of the period. In addition to Sybase of California, start-up Computer Associates International provided Oracle with competition in relational database management software. That company's *Unicenter* software was so successful that annual revenues surged past Oracle's to $1 billion in 1989. Another newcomer with a niche approach was PeopleSoft, founded in 1987. Its *Human Resources Management Systems* began to take significant market share in the next decade.

Other application software leaders included Intuit, founded in 1984 to market its *Quicken* personal finance software. Although users with knowledge of accounting could build more sophisticated spreadsheets in Lotus *1-2-3* or Microsoft's *Excel, Quicken* came

Genealogy of US Computer Software Industry, 1959-2005

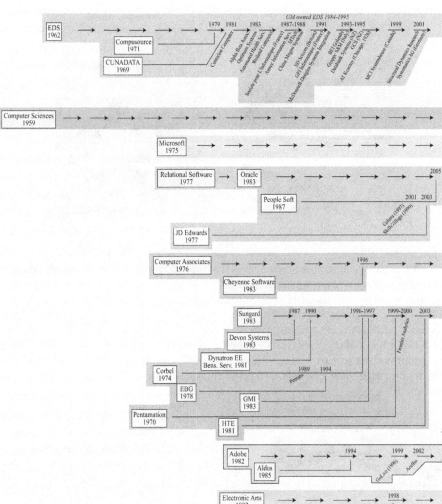

with pre-set models into which data could be imputed for quick calculation. The next year, Aldus brought out its *Pagemaker* desktop publishing software for Apple systems, followed by a PC version in 1987. The leader in graphics design software became Adobe, which marketed its *Illustrator* program in 1987 followed by *Photoshop* three years later to push annual revenue to $300 million. Pointing out the fact that in the software industry low labor costs and high operating margins pushed up profits and market values, Adobe employed only 1,300 persons. The downside of building a business around intellectual

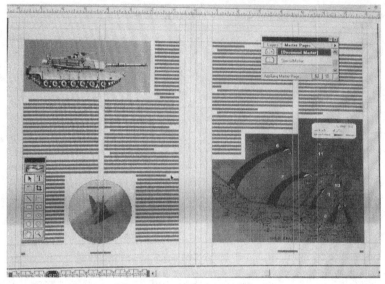

property, patents, and intangible assets was that new innovations could suddenly and cataclysmically collapse a company's position.

That was the reason that HP preferred to make computer hardware and peripherals. In 1984, the company innovated with inkjet printers that matched the 300 dpi of its laser jets. Four years later, mass production of *Deskjet* printers not only doomed dot-matrix printers but boosted revenues to $11.9 billion in 1989. The *HP Way* of selling printers for a nice profit but ink jet cartridges, without which printers were useless, for extortionate ransom supported the livelihoods of 95,000 employees.

HP Inkjet printer
By contrast, falling PC prices in the latter half of the 1980s forced a consolidation in the industry. While Sperry and Burroughs merged in 1986 into Unisys and turned increasingly toward software and consulting, Honeywell formed a joint venture with Compagnie des Machines Bull of France and NEC of Japan to make PC clones and try to keep up with IBM and Compaq, fighting it out for industry leadership. Outmaneuvered by these companies as well as Sun in the workstation market, Xerox gave up making computers altogether three years later and refocused on copiers. Although the company exceeded 2 million of those machines to date through 1988, the US possessed over 55 million computers of all kinds, half the world title, by end of the period.

About 90% of computers were PCs. These now included a couple million lap-top models that could be transported by students, business travelers, and others for plug-in use as well as battery operation. In fact, demand that peaked at 4.7 million in 1987 was so high that PC makers sometimes could not keep up. Companies like Solectron, founded in the Silicon Valley a decade earlier, Samnina of San Jose, California, and SCI of Huntsville, Alabama were hired by original equipment manufacturers (OEMs) to make printed circuit boards, backplane assemblies, and other parts. Over time, outsourcing permitted OEMs to concentrate on R&D, marketing, and sales. Because contract manufacturers invested heavily in industrial robots to maximize production and minimize cost, the system turned into a backdoor way for the industry to switch over to automation without getting into conflicts with organized labor.

Among companies that benefited from the proliferation of personal computers was ADP. As customers bought PCs to input and maintain payroll information, the ability of that firm to access, prepare, and expand its payroll services exploded. Acquisitions, including of stock information provider GTE Telent in 1983, also helped ADP reach $1 billion of revenue by mid-decade. The company then purchased Bunker Ramo's information system business to operate stock quote terminals at E.F. Hutton, Dean Witter, and Prudential-Bache. An even bigger coup was installing 38,000 workstations in Merrill Lynch's offices. Shearson-Lehman became a customer in 1988.

Competition for ADP in payroll services came from Paychex. By 1989, the company boasted of 100,000 clients, albeit much smaller companies with far fewer employees. However, Paychex also branched out into preparing tax returns. H&R Block countered by filing returns electronically with the IRS, thus reaching and exceeding $1 billion of annual revenue.

Even as the rise of PCs, workstations, and networking revolutionized business office operations, an even more ambitious idea emerged for creating a world-wide web for transmission of information. Already in 1969, the Advanced Research Projects Agency (ARPA) began organizing a network to connect US universities. Six years later, a company called Compuserve was founded in anticipation of the day when such an Internet accessible to both business and home customers would be created. In 1981, Western Union's First Data subsidiary linked the bank's ATM network through five orbiting satellites. But the true Internet with agreed language protocol operating on thousands of host computers took several more years to coalesce. In the interim, the race was on to found internet service providers (ISPs) to provide the software and hardware for a growing system of users to link up and log on to various networks.

An instant potential powerhouse appeared in 1984 when IBM, CBS, and Sears founded Prodigy. However, it was Quantum Computer Services, led by former P&G and Pizza Hut manager Steve Case, which the next year came up with the idea of delivering online information and other services to consumers via PCs and modem phone connections. When a global Internet was finally sorted out in 1989 by government decision and technological advance, Case changed the company's name to America Online (AOL). AOL's message service ("You've got mail") as well as games, special interest chat forums, and real time one-on-one conversations caught the nation's fancy. The company steadily outdistanced Compuserve, Prodigy, and other competitors.

Overall, the fixed asset value of computers and peripheral hardware held by businesses reached $91 billion while computer software approached $95 billion. That was 7.2% of total US equipment and software. More to the delight of the Reagan administration, the new technology economy came into being with very little interference by government. American ingenuity and creativity, backed by liberal amounts of investment capital, had made the US computer industry the envy of the world. Fears that the Japanese would succeed in developing what was called "artificial intelligence," in which computers would think for themselves and produce myriad scientific and technological advances helped prompt Congress in 1988 to fund an Advance Technology Program to preserve US leadership not only in computers but other key technologies. Ultimately, the Japanese initiative, like the Japanese economy, stalled.

THE WAXING VALUE OF INTANGIBLE ASSETS

Software is classified for accounting purposes as a tangible asset. In point of fact, the only material substance to it is the disc it is written on. Its primary value is a means for communicating with and between machines. Were every copy classified as intellectual property, as are original patents, the value of assets in non-financial US businesses, which shifted from 72% tangible in 1980 to only 53% by the turn of the century, would have been even more nebulous.

Wayne Huizenga

Nevertheless, the transformation toward intangible assets was dramatic. As the composition of the economy shifted away from agriculture, materials, and manufacturing toward computers, the financial sector, health care, and telecommunications, intellectual property rights and patents, innovative technology, and brand name reputation became indispensable commodities yielding incredible profits. In no sector was this more certain than in media, entertainment, and information. Although R&D and marketing costs for TV shows, major motion pictures, text books, and other such assets were often high, the payoff was substantial.

Media assets were also highly vulnerable to changes in viewer tastes and habits. This was demonstrated in the TV industry in the 1980s with the rise of cable broadcasts. Heretofore unassailable in capturing the attention of Americans, watching on average seven hours of TV programming per day, the major networks of NBC, CBS, and ABC suffered an erosion of their 80% market share that undercut advertising rates. The cable industry's model in which networks charged cable broadcast providers fees, passed along at a premium for profit to cable customers, for popular shows such as *CNN* in news, *ESPN* in sports, *HBO* in movies, and *MTV* in music created several major business powerhouses.

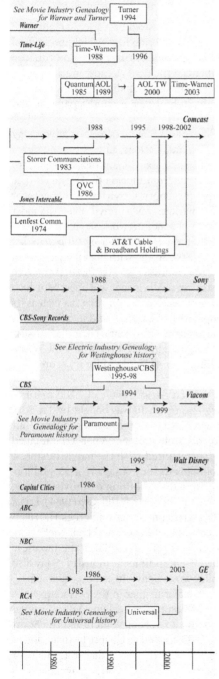

Genealogy of US Multi-Media Companies, 1973-2004

Initially, the cable industry was composed of thousands of small, family-operated companies. Rapid consolidation reduced that number ultimately by 2002 to three large networks controlling 65% of the industry. Along the way, thousands of merger and acquisition deals brought tens of billions of dollars to investment banking firms. For example, Westinghouse bought Teleprompter Corporation in 1981, the second largest cable TV operator in the world, and then four years later sold its Group W operations for $1.7 billion. In 1986, Comcast doubled to 1.2 million customers by taking a 26% stake in Group W. After founding the QVC home-shopping channel, that cable company nearly doubled its viewership and claimed fifth place in the industry by buying half of Storer Communications. Another major company that entered the fray was Knight-Ridder. The same year that Westinghouse made the plunge, the newspaper publisher entered into a joint venture called TKR Cable with Tele-Communications Incorporated (TCI). The company then added to its TV station holdings in several medium size cities but sold out of that industry in 1989 to refocus on its core business. AT&T jumped in to buy TCI.

NBC was already owned by RCA. In 1985, RCA sold NBC to GE for $6.3 billion. That deal as well as escalating production costs, competition from pay-per-view channels, but especially the challenge from cable, eventually in 1990 reaching 56% of American households, put pressure on the two other major networks to merge into companies with deeper financial pockets. In 1985, ABC capitulated to Capital Cities Communication for $3.5 billion. However, CBS with broader entertainment interests that included CBS Records, music videos, and a joint venture to help introduce Sony's CD to the public, hung on doggedly to independence. The company beat off a takeover

attempt by Turner and his cable empire by selling a 25% stake to Lawrence Tisch, president of Loew's. CBS executives knew that high-profile sporting events such as the 1984
Olympics in Los Angeles, NFL broadcasts, and the *March Madness* of National Collegiate
Athletic Association (NCAA) basketball playoffs could still bring in tens and hundreds of
millions in profits. However, after Tisch, who had previously turned around tobacco
company Lorillard in the late 1960s and CNA Financial the next decade, muscled in as
CBS's CEO in 1986, he began a severe cost-cutting campaign that alienated news anchor
Dan Rather and other key personnel and undermined the *Tiffany Network*'s panache and
industry leadership.

Still, TV claimed the lion's share of the $50 billion plus spent on broadcast advertising
annually. That was the reason that Clear Channel Communications, after obtaining rights
to radio broadcast NCAA sporting events over six FM and six AM stations, also got into
the visual medium with purchases of stations in cities from Florida to Arizona. Since
Americans paid out $90 billion for sports equipment, sport activities, and spectator
tickets, the gamble of diversifying into smaller TV markets was shrewd. Even the most
remote affiliate now benefited from satellite broadcast of major network signals.

A similar bet on industry growth where the film industry was concerned persuaded
Coca-Cola to buy Columbia Pictures in 1982 and revive the studio with liberal injections of
money. In a joint venture with CBS and HBO, Columbia founded Tri-Star Pictures to make
popular comedies such as *Ghostbusters* in 1984. Australian media magnate Rupert Murdoch
and his News Corp organization then took over venerable 20th Century Fox, as well as its
Metromedia broadcasting holdings. The rising popularity of VCRs, found in a fifth of US
households by mid-decade, resulted in the founding of many video rental chains. Most successful was Blockbuster, which Wayne Huizenga acquired in 1987 after selling off Waste
Management. Huizenga rapidly expanded by taking over 415 Video-Library stores and
reaching 1,500 establishments by 1990.

Meanwhile, Loew's sold MGM, as well the United Artist's vault of 1,200 pictures
MGM had acquired in 1981. Its 1,000 screen Loews Theater chain was bought by Tri-Star,
which helped parent Coca-Cola exclude sales of non-Coca Cola soft drink products. But
Turner then bought MGM's film library to show on his cable stations. When TriStar failed
to turn out any more big hits, Coca-Cola grew disenchanted with the movie business,
merged the subsidiary into Columbia, and sold Columbia to Sony of Japan for $3.4 billion.
The fact that Americans by 1989 were spending annually $5 billion on movie tickets,
including for blockbusters such as *Raiders of the Lost Ark* (1981), *Beverly Hills Cop* (1984), *Lethal
Weapon* (1987), *Die Hard* (1988) and *Batman* (1989), starring male action heroes Harrison
Ford, Eddie Murphy, Mel Gibson, Bruce Willis, and Michael Keaton and Jack Nicholson,
all of whom were paid millions of dollars for their star power, explains the Japanese
company's eagerness to claim a major stake in the US entertainment industry. Sony also
paid $2 billion for CBS Records Group, thereafter known as Sony Music Entertainment.

The motion picture industry witnessed one last major merger in the period. In 1989,
Time bought Warner Communications for $14.1 billion to create Time-Warner with
annual revenues topping $10 billion. The new media powerhouse included the Scott
Foresman publishing group, purchased by Time in 1985, as well as Chappel Music, added
to Warner's holdings for $275 million in 1987. Time-Warner then paid almost as much for
Lane Publishing, a west coast company with properties including *Sunset*, a magazine with
articles about gardening, food, recreation, and home design. Company executives believed

that operating and marketing synergies would dramatically increase revenues, profits, and shareholder value. As Americans spent by end of the period $7.1 billion annually on magazines, $11.4 billion on books and maps, and another $8 billion on music, Time-Warner's combined share of the film, publishing excluding newspapers, and music industries was just under 15%.

One media industry in trouble was independent city newspapers. Because of later commuting times for people returning home from work, evening paper circulation at 29.3 million daily in 1983 fell four million behind morning circulation. More disturbing, the insatiable appetite of Americans for TV viewing caused the percent of adults reading daily newspapers to drop below two-thirds. More of those who did read opted for a new offering from Gannett called *USA Today* that appeared around the country on September 15, 1982 with shorter articles and full-color pictures. For those who preferred in-depth analysis of political and social issues, foreign affairs, and economics, the *Wall Street Journal* and *New York Times* were also available nationwide. Daily circulation for the big three amounted to about 5 million. But forced to barter independence for financial backing, the Chicago Sun-Times sold out to Murdoch in 1983 for $90 million. Owner of the magazine *US News and World Report* Mort Zuckerman bought the *New York Daily News* for $38 million a decade later.

A DECADE OF WINNERS AND LOSERS

In addition to Gates and Milken as poster boys for the successes and excesses of the 1980s, Time CEO Steven J. Ross represented the best and worst of American corporate leadership. After overseeing negotiations combining Time and Warner, he pocketed a $100 million bonus on top of $34.1 million in salary for consolidating operations and boosting profitability, specifically by laying off 10,000 employees. Such cupidity at a moment when so many were sacrificed to the need for cost-reduction and efficiency brought down a firestorm of criticism on his head, and yet he was bewildered by the reaction. The next year when he succumbed to cancer, it seemed Divine retribution to some, cruel misfortune to his friends.

Small consolation was Ross' demise to union workers, who saw their ranks decline for the period from 14.9 million to 13.7 million. The percent of all workers who were unionized fell to 16.1% by 1990, the lowest in 50 years. Employment in the construction, industrial, and transportation sectors was of course the worst impacted. The only sectors in which unions picked up members were service industries and government agencies, including the US Postal Service. Prospects for a rebound in good-paying manufacturing jobs were made grimmer by NLRB policy permitting employers to shift production from union facilities in the Northeast and Midwest to non-union factories in the South and West. Even where union contracts precluded businesses from shifting work to non-union areas, bankruptcy voided all other legal commitments. And in fact, past union success in securing wage and benefit concessions for members began to backfire in the 1980s by driving companies into Chapter 11 or outright collapse. Recognizing the peril of old industry titans stumbling and being surpassed by foreign imports and new upstarts, union leaders resorted less and less to job actions to have their way.

The turning point actually came two months after the UAW in July 1981 rejoined the AFL-CIO after a 13 year separation. On August 3, 13,000 members of the Professional Air

Traffic Controllers or PATCO union struck. The complaint was over a demand for an across-the-board $10,000 pay raise to an average of $41,000, in 2004 money $85,240, but a maximum greater than congressional pay, simultaneous with a reduction in working hours from 40 per week to only 32 (four 8 hour days). Despite the government's refusal to countenance such a precedent-setting agreement, the legal problem lay in the fact that federal workers in such a nationally important profession did not have the right to strike. Infuriated, Reagan promptly fired 11,500 controllers who refused to return to work and permanently banned them from the profession. His use of military air traffic controllers until replacements were trained not only led to PATCO being decertified as official union for the remaining controllers but set the tone of his administration's tough and unyielding anti-union policy.

The recession of 1981-82 worsened the union position. With layoffs and business failures reducing employment prospects, union leaders such as Douglas Fraser, head of the UAW and a member of Chrysler's board of directors since 1980, decided to adopt a more moderate policy. The pact he negotiated with GM in 1984 provided for only 2.25% annual pay increases with cost of living adjustments deferred until more prosperous times. Although he could not prevent a partial shift of production and parts purchasing to other countries, he did win as compensation a $1 billion fund to retrain workers whose jobs were lost due to automation, plant consolidation and technological development.

Saturn plant

An even more significant compromise was an agreement specific to GM's new Saturn Division plant in Tennessee. Emulating Japanese practices, production was organized in six to 15 person teams, time clocks were eliminated in favor of personal responsibility to complete work, hourly wages were replaced by annual salaries, and union representatives sat on all plant and Saturn Company committees. While work slowdowns were banned, the union could strike to obtain concessions. GM committed to pay bonuses for rising profits and productivity.

At the bottom end of the labor scale, workers earning the minimum wage of $3.35 an hour in 1981, equal in 2004 money to annual earnings of $13,930, also suffered a reverse in the decade. Although the birthrate had fallen to a point insufficient to replenish the population, 7.3 million legal immigrants and 2 million illegal, including 2.8 million Asians and 1.65 million Mexicans, created an oversupply in the South and West in low-paying, seasonal, and temporary work. Nevertheless, returning prosperity after the recession finally drove down the unemployment rate to below 6% by 1988. Labor leaders had some hope that real wages for working class people would begin growing again. And in fact, wages in heavy industry bounced back after a sharp dip the year before. Making $16 per hour, equal in 2004 money to $51,120 in annual pay, coal miners were now on average paid 25% more than workers in primary metal and construction jobs.

The only truly silver cloud for the period had a dark lining — the fact that median salary for women rose 10% to $20,656 in 1990 while men's fell 8%. Although women came to hold 45% of all managerial and professional jobs, including a small but historically significant 6.6% of the executive level managerial positions, they still earned only 75 cents for every dollar earned by men.

Beneficial for the overall economy but another heavy blow to unions was the Free Trade Agreement with Canada concluded by the Reagan administration on January 21, 1988 but effective in 1989. The intent was to eliminate tariffs by 1999 as a first step toward a North American Free Trade Agreement that included Mexico and opened the door not only to the free flow of goods and services but accelerated relocation of factory work to *maquiladora* plants in Mexico. It was hoped that exporting jobs south of the border would have the effect of reducing the surge of illegal immigrants into the American Southwest. A lesser possibility was that companies like AT&T, which had built plants to manufacture consumer telephone equipment in Singapore and Thailand as well as switching equipment in the Netherlands, Taiwan, and South Korea, might see the economic benefit in opening factories closer to home. However, low oil prices put the Mexican economy in difficult straits. To pay foreign debts coming due, Washington loaned its neighbor $3.5 billion.

Virtually every member of Congress knew that Free Trade with Canada and Mexico as well as ongoing negotiations to create a World Trade Organization would hurt American manufacturing workers. To cushion the blow, the House and Senate passed on August 4, 1988 a Plant Closing Act requiring companies with 100 workers or more to give 60 days notice of shutdowns affecting 50 workers or one-third of a plant's workforce, whichever was smaller. Reagan neither signed the legislation nor vetoed it, hence it became law. Congress tacked on a Comprehensive Trade Bill 19 days later that reduced some tariffs 50% but protected industries hurt by imports if a company made what was termed "positive readjustments" to foreign competition.

Aside from retraining funds such as set up by GM, nothing was done by corporations or the government for employees replaced by automation. Plant modernization was a major reason that by 1990 US production workers drew only 51% of payroll from manufacturing companies. Further, their annual wages of $22,500, in 2004 money equal to $32,510, was down to 58% of salaried workers pay. Though capital expenditures of $105 billion were actually in 2004 money down from the inflation-adjusted 1980 figure, as a percent of production worker wages they had risen to 38.15%. Overall manufacturing employment now claimed only 15.6% of 123.4 million working Americans. Manufacturing's share of GDP had fallen to 18%.

No surprise given the Reagan era tax cuts and Wall Street surge that saw financial assets as a percent of all household assets climb to 61.7% in 1990, financial services contributed 17.5% of GDP, up from 15%. The problem from a labor point of view, the advantage from a profit perspective, was that the financial services sector was the most capital intensive by far. Even an October 20, 1987 stock market crash that wiped out 25% of shareholder value did not permanently dampen investor enthusiasm. Household wealth bounced back so swiftly that net worth topped $20 trillion by 1990, over $29 trillion when measured in 2004 dollars. *Per capita* net worth in 2004 money saw a 22% increase for the decade to $117,815. However, the top 1% of households claimed a fast growing 37.4% share.

Because household liabilities as a percent of assets had risen 50% in the decade, the nation's prosperity was mortgaged to a greater degree than ever before against future income. That did not matter so much to the top fifth of earners, enjoying a 46.6% share of national income, but the fall in the share of the bottom three-fifths to below 30% was ominous. Local developments, such as the bursting of a housing bubble in Boston in 1988 after a 73% up-tick in home prices while incomes only grew 42%, heightened the insecurity of the middle class. Los Angeles and other pricey metropolises containing tens of millions of Americans were also at risk.

However, just as the business cycle went round and recessionary pressures increased, the US won without firing a shot in anger the Cold War with Soviet Communism. The challenge for American foreign policy shifted toward putting down regional bullies, radical states, and terrorist organizations hostile to the US and its allies. Indispensable to forging a New World Order of peace, stability, and prosperity was expansion of the American economy globally by opening new markets and strengthening old ones for US multinational corporations and other exporters. Former adversaries like Russia and in particular China were to become valuable trading partners, but agreement to entrench the concept of Free Trade — or at least *Freer Trade* — had to be hammered out first. As in the march of the American Republic through other periods of economic growth and transformation, there would be as many winners as losers.

PART 4. OLD ECONOMY VERSUS NEW ECONOMY 1990-2004

By the last decade of the twentieth century, the American economy had come into schism. An Old Economy existed that revolved around three broad components: in the first instance primary activities of farming, husbandry, lumbering, mining, and drilling, in the second construction of buildings, homes, bridges, roads, and other structures as well as manufacturing of food products, clothing, paper and wood products, industrial and transportation equipment, consumer durables and non-durables, and chemicals, and in the third wholesaling and retailing. Traditional attributes of this Old Economy included an emphasis on tangible assets, large labor forces, operating economies of scale, and intense competition. Over decades the forces of automation, government regulation, and globalization had worked, respectively, to supplement and replace manpower, create and break up monopolies, and implement the Free Market advantages, and disadvantages, of a world economy. In spite of a belated swing in government policy toward deregulation and industry consolidation, Old Economy sectors typically exhibited lower profit margins. With notable exceptions, market values failed to match annual revenues.

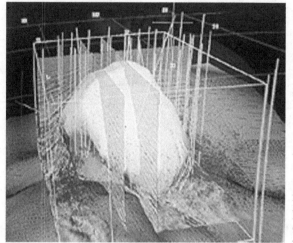

Computerized image of oil exploration (courtesy of ConocoPhillips)

By comparison, the New Economy had evolved in the main since the Second World War. Although the telecommunications industry went back to the nineteenth century, its fuller flowering in electronic, digital, and wireless form only occurred after twentieth century invention and innovation also permitted rapid development of computers, photo-copiers, printers, and other business machines. Software programs to let hardware function with a minimum of human direction developed into an economic sector that rivaled and surpassed industries built around plant and equipment. The coming of the Internet and web-based services proved the potency, and risk, of a business model built on the airy foundation of cyber-space rather than an iron and steel superstructure. In fact, the exchange of information between people and countries became more valuable than cars, planes, and home appliances. Technological inspiration, knowledge-based assets, and a spirit of daring, sometimes reckless entrepreneurism, produced soaring profits (and losses) for mere start-up companies. For most newcomers that survived the stock market crash in telecom and internet stocks in 2000, market values remained above annual revenue. Technology hardware and software as well as other leading New Economy fields such as bio-technology in food and drugs were seen as central to growth in the twenty-first century.

The intangible nature of financial services, the subjective delight taken by citizens in the content created by the media, entertainment, and sports industries, and cutting-edge pharmaceuticals and medical instruments places those centuries-old industries in a quasi-New Economy category. The inescapably labor-intensive nature of hospitals, hotels, restaurants, and tourism keeps those sectors quite properly in the Old. Above all else, the New Economy emphasizes automation to replace manual labor and global operations to create economies of scale without necessarily the same level of global competition as experienced in manufacturing sectors. A minimum of government regulation and interference has also opened the door to huge new monopolies able to carry over national preeminence to world domination.

Washington and state governments have become so eager to advance New Economy technologies to replace faltering Old Economy sectors that they have supplemented the hundreds of billions of dollars invested by banks, venture capitalists, foreign investors, and other private financial sources. Although the President and Congress rarely exercised their latent authority to regulate, tax, and otherwise interfere with New Economy businesses, when such pressure was exerted, for example over pharmaceutical and other health care costs, the impact on profits and valuations was dramatic. The response of businesses so impacted was to seek additional mergers and acquisitions for greater operating economies of scale. To restore revenues, profitability, and the tax base, government had to acquiesce.

Whenever possible, Old Economy sectors moved to incorporate New Economy attributes. Technological advances, for example in aerospace-defense as well as plastics and composite materials, improved existing and made possible new aviation and military systems. Had not the US government, as the primary customer for these products, controlled and limited contract prices, dramatically greater profits would have been the consequence. In the post-Cold War world, Washington not only permitted but encouraged consolidation in the industry.

In non-military manufacturing, automation on the factory floor slashed work forces. However, production continued to shift overseas to plants staffed by low-wage labor, still more cost-efficient than all but the most modern US industrial robots. Ironically, businesses engaged in the production and marketing of basic food and household products succeeded where heavy industry failed because brand name identification and advertising dollars stimulated demand to keep prices at comfortable levels. By and large, Washington refrained from preventing producers in these industries from combining into monster entities able to bring to the mass market staples and goods of high quality and sanitary condition at affordable prices. But only the greatest and most powerful could achieve margins and profitability sufficient to warrant superior market values, relative to industry competitors, not New Economy leaders. Whereas Procter & Gamble boasted a market value to annual revenues ratio (MC/AR) in 2004 of 2.5, Microsoft's revenues yielded over seven and a half times as much market value.

As a succinct summation of how to judge an industry's or a company's present and future prospects and profitability relative to others, the MC/AR is a key benchmark. Throughout Part IV chapters, graphs will refer repeatedly to the ratio. By contrast, stock analysts often look at earnings per share (EPS) to highlight relative improvement or decline. Because numbers of shares vary by company, however, EPS cannot be used as a comparative tool between companies and industries. Price-earnings (PE) ratio equal to market capitalization divided by annual earnings can but is thwarted by cyclical swings in profits. Also interesting is the level of employment required to support revenues; thus employment figures will be given repeatedly. Readers should pay attention to the relationship between relatively high MC/AR and relative low employment as well as size of revenue.

CHAPTER XIII. ROLLER COASTER RIDE FOR ENERGY AND TRANSPORTATION

Whether for Old Economy activities or new, the importance of world markets took center stage in the 1990s. An entangling trade relationship that had begun in colonial days with commerce to and from the mother country and its other colonies now burgeoned into a full-fledged business alliance with Europe, East Asia, Latin America, and other regions. True, overseas expansion by US car manufacturers, oil drillers, insurance firms, and other aggressive entities went back to the first half of the twentieth century, but never before had so many American companies of such diverse nature decided that present and future prosperity required global success. The new era in world relations occasioned by the fall of Communism in the Soviet Union and its satellites as well as accommodation with Capitalism on the part of China made the broader focus possible.

In point of fact, competition in the US among and between domestic and foreign companies, whose revenue derived solely from the sale of manufactured products aggregated to over $1.5 trillion by 2004, had saturated many markets. It became the opinion of most economists that carrying the principle of comparative advantage in production to its logical global conclusion was not only advisable for the republic's prosperity but essential. That belief was reinforced by government thinking that Free Trade between on the one hand the US and its principle allies and friends and on the other all other countries of the world was indispensable for the establishment of stable democracies and world harmony. Government and corporate thinking coalesced into a conviction that a new century of American ascendancy could only be maintained by securing a strong North American economic alliance with Canada and Mexico followed by negotiations to forge a World Trade Organization. In the process, tariffs and subsidies that inhibited the free flow of goods and services and stifled growth would be reduced and if possible eliminated. Each country would specialize it what it did best.

Putting the theory of unfettered Free Trade into practice was not simple. The greatest reservations were held by American labor leaders as to the place of unions and wage-earning people in the new economic world order. Nor was it certain that the New Economy of technology and service-based industries would provide the number of jobs and quality of living standards as had the best of the old in their heyday. Political restraints on permitting US auto, steel, and other production to dwindle translated into quotas, subsidies, and tariffs.

Leaders of less developed countries feared the impact on their own domestic production of US multinationals invading markets with size, financial clout, and innovative products and services. Anxiety increased in developed countries as the Japanese economy sank into a decade long period of recession and stagnation, European Union (EU) states with social welfare systems and chronic high unemployment struggled to match American economic performance in categories as diverse as efficiency of production and sales growth, job creation and technology usage. In the period, and despite recessions in 1991 and 2001, the US economy grew at an average annual pace of 5.2% — 2.3% after inflation — to GDP in 2004 of $11.7 trillion while *per capita* GDP for 296 million Americans moved ahead more slowly at 3.95% — 1.07% after inflation — to $39,600.

Even without precise understanding of the US economic juggernaut, some peoples around the world feared that Washington would use the republic's potent military forces to establish an unchallengeable hegemony. While attempting to convince nervous allies and trading partners that such was not their intention, US political leaders had still to make certain that American businesses and interests would emerge from the globalization movement in an advantageous position. It was almost fortunate, therefore, that the republic was given an opportunity to exercise leadership of a most righteous kind at the outset of the new era. On August 2, 1990, dictator of Iraq Saddam Hussein ordered his army to invade and occupy Kuwait.

CHEAP OIL FUELS THE ECONOMY

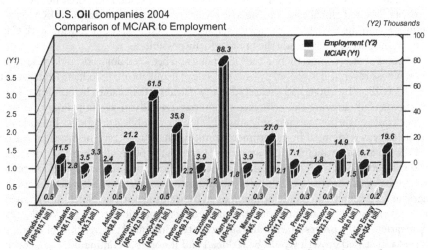

Within two months, oil prices doubled to $40 a barrel, inflation bumped up toward 4.2%, the US economy slipped into a mild recession, and unemployment lifted toward a peak of 7.4% (in 1992). President George W. Bush told the world that "this aggression will not stand," and then marshaled US and allied forces to make good the pledge. At cost of

$58 billion, but over four-fifths paid for by allies, coalition air power and a massive land assault overwhelmed Iraqi forces. Following the triumph, and once hundreds of oil well fires set by Hussein's retreating forces were extinguished, oil prices plunged progressively. Since oil still provided over two-fifths of the nation's energy needs, down from nearly half in 1977, the impact on the economy was immediate and positive. At its bottom in 1998, the price reached $10 a barrel before resuming a more normal trading range twice as high.

The Energy Policy Act of October 24, 1992, encouraging exploration for oil and gas by tax relief to independent drillers as well as improved methods to double the recover rate of oil from fields to 50%, helped stabilize US production by 1995 at just over 2.35 billion 42-gallon barrels. Canada and Mexico contributed annually another 1.1 billion barrels. Moreover, Chevron, Hunt, Occidental and other companies accelerated efforts through new discoveries in the North Sea, Venezuela, China, the Timor Sea between Australia and Indonesia, and other places to reduce dependence upon Middle East oil. OPEC nations from the Persian Gulf as well as Africa and Latin America still held a 46.7% share of the US import market, accounting for three-fifths of the 7.45 billion barrels consumed annually in 2004, about half going for gasoline. On the other hand, swift victory in the Iraq War persuaded Libya to surrender its nuclear weapons program to the US government and open the door to a return by the Oasis Group to their oil concessions. A re-development of Iraq's oil fields and infrastructure would, assuming political stability could be brought to that traumatized country, re-emphasize the importance of the Persian Gulf to the West.

Oil refinery in Texas

Late in the period, US production began to slide again toward 2 billion barrels while world oil production rested at 29 billion barrels annually. Because of depressed prices, US consumers saved about $500 billion in oil costs over a ten year period. Nor with a 600 million barrel reserve, half the world's stocks, releasable at 4 million barrels a day, was the republic as vulnerable to OPEC pressure as in the past. US oil spending fell to only 3% of GDP from nearly three times that level a quarter century before but still accounted for 38% of the nation's energy needs. Thus, when in 2004 a combination of factors, from the War on Terrorism to supply disruptions in a number of regions to increasing demand to tight US refining capacity, caused a surge toward $55 a barrel oil, prices at the pump did not spike proportionately. The higher plateau nevertheless helped big refining companies led by Valero Energy of San Antonio to jump revenues in one year by 44% to $54.6 billion in 2004, though employment for nearly 20,000 kept MC/AR down around 0.2.

Low wellhead prices at the beginning of the period also made it difficult for lesser oil companies that focused solely in exploration and production to stay profitable. Even though the Clean Air Act of 1990 required refiners to add either methyl tertiary butyl ether (MTBE), made from natural gas, or ethanol to gasoline to add oxygen and clean up emissions, some oil executives believed the better business model for the 1990s was value-added refining, marketing, and other petroleum-related activities. Thus, Sun Oil divested itself of all international oil and gas production as well as real estate holdings, renamed itself *Sunoco* in 1998 to highlight its best-selling gasoline brand, and three years later bought Aristech Chemical of Pittsburgh to double its chemical business and become a global player in that industry. Not far out of the stock market slump, failure to generate profit over 2% disappointed investors.

Prior to the stock market slump but while oil prices hit bottom, major oil companies won government acquiescence in a new round of mergers and acquisitions. In 1998, BP led off with a $62 billion takeover of Amoco to reach $84 billion of annual revenues and late in 2000 Los Angeles-based Arco for $32 billion to accumulate another $10 billion in sales. The FTC wrung a concession from the British company to sell over 1.5 billion barrels of proven reserves from Arco's Prudhoe Bay holdings in Alaska to Philips for $7 billion. A $285 billion revenue company, BP also put $8.1 billion into TNK of Russia in 2003 to boost proven oil reserves toward 20 billion barrels and unproven to 35 billion.

Exxon and Mobil followed the BP-Amoco deal with a 1998 merger of their own ultimately valued at $80 billion. ExxonMobil combined 21 billion barrels of proven reserves and sales of $200 billion, heading up toward $271 billion in 2004 as well as a work force heading down toward 88,300 employees, with market value 20% above annual revenues. The company's world-girdling clout permitted management to consider a risky investment of $15-20 billion in Yukos of Russia, good for a stake as large as 40%, which was promptly put on hold after the Russian government arrested Yukos' head on a variety of fraud and tax evasion charges. Total Russian proven oil and gas reserves topped 360 billion barrels, 100 billion more than Saudi Arabia, explaining why Moscow was determined to take back the subterranean treasure trove into its own hands.

Given the fact that the wholesale market price for oil in 2000 was around $25 barrel, the price Phillips paid for Arco's Prudhoe Bay holdings of $5 per barrel indicates the difficulty and expense of drilling for, extracting, and transporting crude through the Alaskan Pipeline to tankers in the Gulf of Valdez. Equal value was created in the refining and marketing process to transform crude into gas at the pump costing on average $1.25 per gallon (equal to $52.50 per barrel). In 2001, Phillips took a greater share of the retail market by purchasing Tosco Corporation (originally The Oil Shale Company), owner of the 76 and *Circle K* gas brands. That acquisition also carried the right to market ExxonMobil gas in Arizona, New England, and the Mid-Atlantic as well as the *Coastal* brand, reserved for Sunoco in the East, from Indiana to Wyoming and South Dakota to Oklahoma.

Value-added rationale explains Marathon's decision in 1992, while still part of USX, to conclude a deal with Ashland to control that company's downstream *SuperAmerica*, *Speedway*, and other stations. A decade later, after USX had spun off its steel operations and changed its name to Marathon Oil Corporation, management billed the company as an *American Company serving America*. Unimpressed, the Internal Revenue Service in 2004

balked at favorable treatment of Marathon's attempt to buy out Ashland's 38% in their joint venture. The $3 billion deal was put on hold.

Clark Refining Holdings, emerging as an independent company again with the name Premcor, also found slim profit pickings in the highly competitive market east of the Mississippi. To make money, the company combined gasoline stations with convenience or quick service stores and operated three refineries with 610,000 per day barrel capacity or about 1.33% of the republic's total refining capacity. As for Getty, the Oklahoma company with the famous name sold out in November 2000 to Lukoil of Russia, founded in 1991. That was the first time a Russian company had ever purchased an American company listed on the NYSE.

Although selling gasoline would not make oil companies highly profitable, marketing motor oil and other lubricants could. In 1998, Pennzoil merged with Quaker State to gain market share versus Ashland's *Valvoline* and Royal Dutch Shell's *Halvoline*. But Shell bought Pennzoil-Quaker State four years later for $1.8 billion. To avoid upsetting American nationalists too much, combined US operations of that Anglo-Dutch company were headquartered in Houston.

ExxonMobil's, BP's, and Shell's clout finally compelled Chevron and Texaco to get together in 2001 in the second largest US and fifth largest oil company in the world. Newly spun off by DuPont, Conoco linked up with Phillips that same year. The market liked the former's $143 billion of combined 2004 revenues and 61,500 employees more than the latter's $119 billion and 35,800 workers because of Conoco-Phillips nearly $19 billion of debt and off-balance sheet liabilities. But Conoco-Phillips began selling off non-core assets, including 1,600 *Circle K* convenience stores to Alimentation Couce-Tard of Canada, which combined *Circle K* with 3,000 other North American stores, including *Dairy Mart*, for fourth place in the convenience store industry.

Meanwhile, analysts were concerned that annual production from the republic's remaining 50 billion barrels of light medium oil, not to mention 40 billion of heavier oil not as suitable for refining into gasoline, would because of political and environmental objections to drilling in promising areas like the Alaska National Wildlife Reserve, estimated to contain as much as 16 billion barrels, begin again to diminish. By contrast, proven world reserves amounted to 1.2 trillion barrels of light oil and 540 billion of heavy. For the foreseeable future, the 30% of annual global production contributed by Middle East and the 10% chipped in each by Russia, Asian Pacific countries, and African countries would swell while North America's 18% share would decline. Not until better technology was developed to tap 626 billion barrels of oil recoverable from 1.7 trillion barrels trapped inside Rocky Mountain shale, or 57% of the world total, would the US have a possibility of becoming not merely self-sufficient in oil but a net exporter. Canada's tremendous tar sands deposits in Alberta, generating only 91 million barrels annually in 2002, also loomed as a potential source of major oil production. Once perfected by Shell and other countries, heating techniques, including pumping waste carbon dioxide from electric power plants powered by coal into the deposits, would release as much as 180 billion barrels annually at cost, albeit quite high, of $15 per barrel.

No matter the location of oil fields, US companies that provided drilling and other services were present. Halliburton's position in the market moved to number one in 1998 with acquisition of Dresser Industries, which had bought M.W. Kellogg a decade earlier. Halliburton's $20.5 billion revenues in 2004 included not only funds flowing in from oilfield services but engineering, construction, and providing support personnel for US military operations overseas. Because the company had to maintain 101,000 employees in 100 countries and was exposed to possible claims from asbestos-related lawsuits, its profitability was reduced. By contrast, principal competitors Schlumberger and Baker Hughes boosted stock prices by owning jointly WesternGeco, the world's largest surface seismic company, and branching out into more valuable activities, for example information technology networking and services to monitor and manage the exploration and production process.

Simultaneous with the push to broaden out the world's sources of petroleum, oil companies also re-emphasized natural gas discovery and production. From production of 22.7 trillion cubic feet in 1973, the US had fallen to just under 16 trillion in 1987. Principally, this was a consequence of American reserves being used up faster than new finds were made rather than a decline of world supply. However, prices that fell in 1992 to a bottom of $1 per thousand cubic feet before rising to $2.75 in expectation of winter encouraged resurgence in demand, and therefore a search for new supplies.

From the standpoint of gaining access to global reserves, the problem was twofold: first reaching agreement with natural gas rich countries, and second transporting a substance lighter than air from forbidding and exotic locales such as Russia's Sakhalin Island and the Persian Gulf to the US. Pipelines, of course, already carried natural gas from Canada's 50 trillion cubic meters of proven reserves. The republic's northern neighbor contributed just under a sixth of the 17.7 trillion cubic feet consumed in 1990, rising to 19.8 trillion five years later. However, Russia and the Persian Gulf each possessed a third of the world's 5 quadrillion cubic feet of reserves. Only by accessing those supplies would the US be able to meet and exceed demand by 2004 equal to the record set 30 years previously. Now because of the surge in coal, nuclear power, and alternative sources, natural gas accounted for less than a quarter of the country's energy needs.

LNG tanker Polar Eagle, property of ConocoPhillips
The solution to the first obstacle was money, of course. By offering to buy at a sufficiently high price, Russia, Saudi Arabia, Qatar, and other countries proved quite willing to sell. As for the second problem, technology came to the rescue. Although underwater pipelines such as built by Amerada Hess in 1993 from the North Sea to Britain were possible, for longer distances companies were able to freeze natural gas to minus 260 degrees Fahrenheit (minus 162 degrees Celsius) and turn it into liquid. Liquid natural gas (LNG) was then transported by huge tankers that cost initially $280 million per ship but as low as $150 million after a fleet of 140 was built. From only $10 billion cubic feet of LNG imports in 1995, the US brought in 240 billion by 2001, with an expectation of more than double that pace by 2004. The best aspect of the arrangement was that LNG could be purchased in the Persian Gulf for $1 per million BTU and sold in the US for about $4.25. Although that price was considerably higher than the traditional $3.00 paid by American consumers as well as companies that used natural gas to make chemicals, plastics, and fertilizers, it was lower than the inflated $6.00 caused late in the period by declining domestic production and rising demand. Therefore, ExxonMobil in October 2003 concluded a $10 billion deal with Qatar to produce LNG in that country and ship 15 million tons annually back to the US. Shell and other big oil companies were not far behind.

One of the chemical producers most exposed to natural gas price fluctuation was Dow Chemical. By 2002, the company used 700 million cubic feet per day in its plants, or

255 billion cubic feet per year, which was equal to 1.1% of the country's total consumption. Dow decided to experiment with moving some production overseas by making an agreement with Kuwait to open a plant adjacent to that country's natural gas fields. The company also intended to cut its costs by switching over as much as possible to cheaper LNG. Imports might come from distant foreign sources, but Philips also shipped LNG out of Kenai, Alaska. Its tankers not only descended to the lower 48 states but crossed the Pacific to Japan, where that energy-poor country had to pay a higher price.

CROSSED WIRES IN ELECTRICITY

Within the US, the Energy Policy Act as well as FERC *Order 636* separating the buying and selling of natural gas from its transportation encouraged, as with the oil industry, more mergers and acquisitions at all levels of the natural gas supply chain. At once in 1992, Koch bought United Gas Pipeline for $400 million to obtain a 9,600 mile system. Two years later, Panhandle Eastern merged with Associated Natural Gas of Denver to take third place among natural gas marketers, then changed its name to PanEnergy in 1996 and bought Mobil's natural gas operations. The next year, it was purchased by Duke Energy and then sold in 1998 along with Trunkline Gas, Duke's storage operations, and Trunkline LNG terminal to CMS Energy for $2.2 billion. Duke went on to buy Union Pacific Resources, a gatherer and marketer of natural gas, for $1.35 billion. Purchases of energy companies in Latin America as well in 2001 of Westcoast Energy of Canada for $8 billion were overshadowed by the negative consequences for the industry of the Enron debacle, discussed below; thus, Duke's market value fell temporarily to $12 billion, half its 2001 peak.

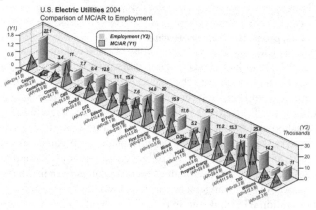

On the other hand, PanEnergy's rival Williams stayed independent and expanded its delivery system to the east coast by taking over Transco Energy Company. The company bought MAPCO, owner of natural gas reserves as well as a pipeline system for butane and propane, for $3.4 billion in 1998 and Barrett Resources three years later. A bigger competitor, in fact the nation's largest natural pipeline carrier, was El Paso Corporation. In addition to a 58,000 mile system, the company also developed deep drilling techniques to bring up natural gas royalty free from under land as well as the Gulf of Mexico's outer shelf. However, diversification into petroleum refining and telecommunications resulted during the recession of 2001 in $1.2 billion of losses and reduction in workforce below 12,000. A fine of the same amount imposed by California for manipulating gas prices during that state's energy crisis collapsed market value toward one quarter of $17.8 billion of revenue in 2003. To bring down $21 billion of debt, management began to sell off assets. A reorganization plan consolidated the number of operating units from five to two, leaving revenue in 2004 at only $6.1 billion but market cap above a one-to-one ratio with revenue. Future revenue projections were complicated by a $1 billion asset write-down, required by a one-third reduction in proven natural gas reserve. After all oil and natural gas companies were compelled by government mandate to scrutinize their reserves, many, including Royal Dutch Shell, had to admit to inflating proven reserve figures..

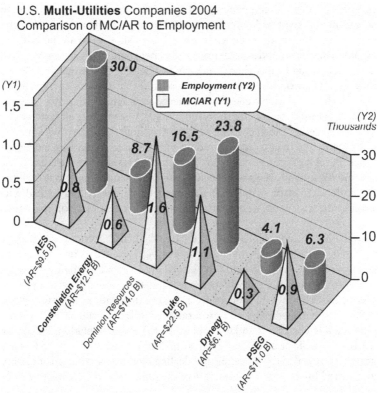

U.S. **Multi-Utilities** Companies 2004
Comparison of MC/AR to Employment

Two companies that made energy trading their lifeblood were Dynegy and Enron. The former began in 1995 as the Natural Gas Clearinghouse, an "energy store" that not only included natural gas supplies but petroleum (from Chevron), and electricity power generating companies. After FERC in 1996 issued *Order 888*, fulfilling the Energy Policy Act's requirement that electric utilities allow non-utilities open access to transmission lines, thus effectively permitting independent producers to enlarge their 10% share of the US electricity market composed by 2000 of 126 million customers, the company went on a buying binge. Purchase included 20 power plants from Destec Energy for $1.27 billion, the assets of Southern California Edison, and Illinova gas and electric for $2.8 billion. Even after high debts from these deals forced divestiture in 2000 of natural gas pipelines and processing plants contributing $300 million to annual revenue, Dynegy still reached $6.1 billion in 2004 revenues. The company expanded operations into the Hudson Valley of

New York and bought up natural gas storage facilities in Britain for $590 million. But high debt and low profitability prompted management to offer to sell Illinois Power for $2.2 billion. The company was in for a period of retrenchment.

Enron adopted an even more aggressive business model by trading natural gas and electric power as commodities in Britain in 1995, and then doing the same in Spain, Germany, and elsewhere in continental Europe. Its operations became far-flung after buying Portland General Electric for $3 billion in 1997, Wessex Water of Britain the next year, and building a Bolivia-to-Brazil natural gas pipeline. Wall Street really sat up and took notice in 2000 after the company signed a joint venture with IBM and AOL to form a New Power Company to provide energy to residential and small businesses in deregulated markets. From $40 billion of revenues in 1999, Enron shot up to an incredible peak of $100.8 billion the next year and a stock price of $83 per share.

Because accounting firm Arthur Andersen was helping company executives disguise revenue and profit shortfalls, no one as yet suspected that Enron's energy empire was a house of cards. That revelation came after an energy shortage in California, exaggerated by energy trading manipulations, began in June 2000. A year later, electricity as high as $12,500 per 50 megawatt block cost the state $100 billion. Rolling brown-outs were only alleviated by regulation to curb energy trading, shifting supply and demand back in favor of the former. Voter outrage eventually in October 2003 resulted in the recall of Governor Gray Davis and his unlikely replacement by Austrian immigrant and body-builder turned US citizen and movie actor Arnold Schwarzenegger. The state had to deal with a $38 billion budget deficit by spending cuts and a proposed $15 billion long-term bond issuance.

Meanwhile in autumn 2001, news leaked out that Enron's accounting practices included various shady practices, including asset swaps booked as revenue and hundreds of partnerships in the Cayman Islands and elsewhere to avoid paying US taxes. As Davis and the California legislature curbed energy trading, the company's stock price plunged from the $50 range to a low on January 10, 2002, the day trading was suspended on the NYSE, of $0.67. When Dynegy withdrew a takeover offer December 2001, the company sought protection in Chapter 11 and made plans to sell assets (including Portland General Electric to Texas Pacific at a $650 million loss in 2003). The fall-out was a Congressional investigation that revealed the wheeling and dealing by Enron's management's and Arthur Andersen followed by the severe contraction of the former and the complete dissolution of the latter.

The Enron debacle froze the drive to deregulate further the republic's electricity business. Expansion that had increased the capacity of power plants in the US by 24% since 1999 to 950,000 megawatts, creating with the recession a major glut, was halted. In 2002, about half the country was served by companies operating in a competitive retail power environment while the other half was served by companies that had effective monopoly power. Because in the Pacific Northwest and Southeast entities built plants only to meet demand, electricity rates in their markets were restrained. Overbuilding excesses and energy trading in states elsewhere continued to push rates higher than they would otherwise have been. For that reason, FERC wanted to standardized federal rules under a so-called *Standard Market Design*, which state authorities in regulated areas opposed.

Regardless of industry commotion and turmoil, a whole host of regional, hoping to become national and international, energy companies continued to deliver natural gas for home-heating and electricity to US customers. After the Clean Air Act of 1990 stiffened standards on power plant emissions, the new fuel of choice was low sulfur coal (for example, from deposits in the Powder River Basin of Wyoming and Montana) that came by end of the period to contribute over a quarter of annual US production of 1 billion metric tons. Overall, coal powered nearly three-fifths of electric power generation. By 2004, methane gas from coal also added nearly 1.8 trillion cubic feet to the nation's natural gas production, 40 times greater than in 1989.

In southern California, Sempra provided 1 trillion cubic feet of natural gas annually, almost 5% of the US total, to 18 million people. Electricity in that densely populated area was handled by Southern California Electric, whose parent Edison Electric also had extensive operations in Illinois and overseas in the U.K., Australia, and New Zealand. Despite the California energy crisis, Sempra's management had the foresight to divest the company of regulated electricity plants in the state in favor of gas production plants, including LNG conversion plants, elsewhere. They negotiated contracts with high fixed rates for future energy delivery. Failing to do so, PG&E of San Francisco had to file for Chapter 11 protection. Calpine of San Jose also struggled to secure profits from western operations using natural gas and geothermal steam to deliver 20,000 megawatts of electricity to people in California and 21 other states.

From the Rockies to the Mississippi Valley, the two largest entities were Xcel Energy and CenterPoint Energy. The former was created in 2002 by the merger of New Century Energies of Denver with Northern States Power of Minneapolis to sell both electricity and natural gas. However, Xcel's NRG Energy subsidiary carried $10 billion of debt and suffered $3.5 billion of losses. The entity had been formed in 1989 to invest in unregulated energy opportunities around the world.

One of CenterPoint's antecedents, Diversified Energies, competed with Xcel in the North Central region of the country through its Minnesota Gas (Minnegasco) subsidiary. In 1990, Diversified merged into Arkla, formerly the Arkansas Louisiana Gas Company, which then traded Minnegasco's South Dakota assets for Midwest Gas Company's Minnesota assets. Changing its name to NorAm Energy in 1994, the company marketed wholesale electric power until Houston Industries made a successful takeover bid of $3.8 billion two years later. Changing Houston Industries' name to Reliant Energy, company executives decided in 2000 to split the monolith into regulated and unregulated businesses. Reliant Resources became the moniker of the part offering unregulated electricity and energy services. CenterPoint Energy delivered natural gas to 3 million customers in six states as well as electricity from 12 power plants with over 14,000 megawatts in Texas to 2 million Houston residents.

By contrast, TXU supplemented core Texas operations generating 19,000 megawatts from a variety of fuel sources with energy investments in Australia. AES, a Virginia corporation with significant US assets but facilities in 28 countries on four continents accounting for two-thirds of the 44,000 megawatts of electricity generated annually by the company, made money until a write-down of assets caused a $2.6 billion loss.

Just east of the Mississippi, ComEd of Illinois combined with Peco, providing both gas and electricity in southern Pennsylvania, to create Exelon, a large utility in possession of 17 nuclear plants. With 14 nuclear reactors and 15,000 employees, Entergy of New

Orleans temporarily had an even better valuation premium over annual revenues. Up in Indiana, NiSource with revenue from both gas and electric operations competed with Cinergy, formed by the 1994 merger of Cincinnati Gas & Electric with PSI Energy of Indiana. Michigan belonged to DTE and CMS. However, the latter company built up such high debt buying the Panhandle interstate pipeline system, obtained a few years earlier from Duke, and trading energy wholesale that management had to sell Panhandle to Southern Union Company and AIG Highstar Capital, an investment group. The price was $1.8 billion, mostly assumed debt.

U.S. **Gas Utilities** 2004 Comparison of MC/AR to Employment

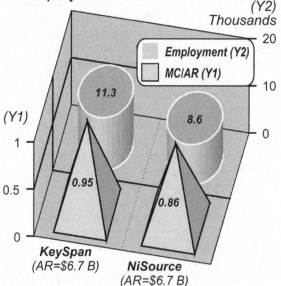

Straddling the Mississippi after merging with Central and South West Corporation of Dallas in 1997, AEP of Columbus, Ohio served 9 million customers. Dominion Resources of Ohio boasted a much better profitability because of natural gas and other non-electricity operations. Specifically, Dominion bought CNG of Pittsburgh in 2000 to get to 4 million customers, divested CNG's Virginia Natural Gas subsidiary while retaining its telecom business containing 400,000 miles of fiber optics through old gas pipelines. Management then bought Louis Dreyfus Natural Gas the next year for $2.3 billion to boost natural gas reserves 60% to 2.8 trillion cubic feet. By contrast, First Energy of Ohio had more revenue and employees but about half the market value because regulated operations were mainly concerned with providing 4.3 million customers with electricity. Profitability rose with attempts to diversify into supplying customers with natural gas as well as local phone service from Ohio to New Jersey, but the company's responsibility for starting the August 2003 power blackout in the eastern US and Canada highlighted failure to keep up plant and equipment.

Another company that decided to reorganize into still-connected regulated and unregulated divisions was Pennsylvania Power & Light. Eventually named PPL Corporation, the parent electricity provider bought Penn Fuel Gas in 1998 to sell natural gas and propane to 70,000 customers. Meanwhile, its PPL Global subsidiary bought stakes in Britain's South Western Electricity, Empresas of Chile, CEMAR of Brazil, and FuelCell Energy of the US for which it became a distributor. The company also took over Montana Power Company with 2,600 megawatts of generating capacity as well as Bangor Hydro-Electric in Maine.

PPL's entry into New England encroached on the territory of KeySpan, delivering gas in New Hampshire and Massachusetts as well as New York State. Nevertheless, that company maintained steady profitability. Further south, the Big Apple itself was dominated by Consolidated Edison, delivering gas and electricity to 8.3 million customers. Close by in New Jersey, PSEG suffered by comparison. Thus, in 2004 Exelon swooped in to buy PSEG for $12 billion in stock and $14.1 billion in assumed debt. Management was betting that public and government attitudes toward nuclear power generation were changing for the better.

Competing with Duke Energy in the Carolinas, Progress Energy also impressed observers in Florida by delivering electricity to 2.8 million customers and engaging in non-regulated activities including broadband internet service. By contrast, the Southern Company in 2001 spun off disconnected facilities from Florida to Oregon and New York to San Francisco as well as the Caribbean and the Philippines under the name Mirant to maximize shareholder value. What was retained was core electricity generating capacity in Deep South states Georgia, Alabama, Mississippi, and the panhandle of Florida where states did not allow unfettered competition. Investors applauded management for $1 billion plus annual profits. But Mirant, based in Atlanta, had to compete in many markets with many companies. Management sought shelter in Chapter 11.

Electric power lines

Except for Southern's position in Florida's panhandle and operations by Progress Energy, FPL dominated the rest of the Sunshine State. The company dabbled in wind power and purchased the distant Seabrook nuclear plant in New Hampshire to expand a foothold in New England. Seabrook had only come on line and started providing power to the patchwork national electricity grid on August 19, 1990 after a two decade delay occasioned by cost overruns. Countervailing environmental pressures, on the one hand to limit the danger to the public of nuclear plant accidents and accumulating nuclear waste, on the other to reduce industrial air pollution, already down as much as 40% in some metropolitan areas, by turning away from coal and oil as fuel sources, finally swung back in favor of the latter because of the national security imperative of reducing US dependence on foreign energy. Further, the energy industry was burdened by $40 billion in stranded costs, in large part from nuclear power plant construction and decommissioning that could only be recovered by charges to customers. By permitting delayed reactors like Seabrook to come on line and by expanding capacity at the republic's existing 104 plants, not quite a quarter of the world total, the nuclear industry could generate a fifth or more of US electricity needs.

However, political opposition to construction of entirely new nuclear facilities caused Westinghouse, the first US company to be licensed to build nuclear reactors, to sell its nuclear division in 1998 to a consortium headed by BNFL of Britain. Only GE remained in the field because of overseas contracts such as a $1.8 billion deal to build two boiling-water reactors for Taiwan Power. Although the great US conglomerate began the 1990s with $58.5 billion of annual revenue, only $6.4 billion came from production of power systems, nuclear and otherwise. Its main global competitors were Asea Brown Boveri (ABB) of Sweden with 53% of annual revenues of $30 billion derived from power systems, Siemens of Germany with 15% of its $49 billion annual revenue so obtained, and Alstom of Britain and France at $5.3 billion in annual revenue. Overall, GE's operations were far more diversified from both a business and global perspective and — after the work force was shrunk from 300,000 in 1990 to 221,000 five years later — leaner. By mid-decade, 38% of revenues came from overseas contracts and joint ventures with various foreign governments and companies.

Perry Nuclear Power plant in Ohio

Environmentalists who celebrated the twentieth anniversary of Earth Day on April 22, 2000 were not pleased that the nuclear power industry was enjoying a limited resurgence. Great opposition was rallied, unsuccessfully, to DOE's plan to transport by rail and truck all nuclear waste through populated areas to a specially constructed storage facility in Nevada. What activists clamored for was development of renewable energy sources, that is solar and wind power. Aside from solar panels on the roofs of buildings and homes, the former had struggled to emerge as a viable industry because inadequate technology prevented a high enough percent of the energy emanating from the sun's rays to be captured and stored for later use. By contrast, the latter had grown globally to supply 116,000 megawatts of energy, nearly one quarter in the US and Canada alone, or enough to generate 63 billion kilowatt-hours of electricity, and power 10.5 million homes. Although by 2003 only 3.3% of the world's electricity supply valued at $20 billion annually was attributable to wind power, expansion of its generation was growing at over 9% annually, compared to only 2.4% for fossil fuel sources. That trend would continue because the US price per kilowatt hour of wind power had fallen in two decades from 38 cents to a low of 3 cents, while the price of natural gas spiked upward to 6 cents in 2003. In Texas, some 50,000 wind turbines placed 25 acres apart already generated 1,100 megawatts to provide power to 300,000 homes.

Naturally, government was all in favor of any industry that would lessen US dependence on foreign energy. Although the share of world energy consumed by the republic with only 2% of the world's population fell from 27.7% in 1980 to just below a quarter by 1990, demand rose again because of the booming economy. For example, the US chemical industry, which accounted for 25% of world production, was heavily dependent upon oil and natural gas. Worth $400 billion annually by 1998, American chemical products jumped in value when prices of those two commodities rose dramatically in the next five years. The other major threat to the industry was environmental and political fall-out. Aside from deadly accidents such as Union Carbide's Bhopal, India fiasco, vociferous complaints were made about chemical pollutants and perils. Not liking the industry's fundamentals, Monsanto spun off its chemical operations as Solutia in 1997. By 2003, losses put Solutia into Chapter 11 and caused management to sue Monsanto for unfairly dumping retiree pension and chemical spill liabilities onto Solutia's books.

Other companies decided to remain in the chemical industry and adjust. For example, when Huntsman's business was undermined in part by McDonald's decision to bow to environmental pressure and phase out polystyrene-based hamburger boxes that did not bio-degrade in landfills, management embarked on an acquisition spree of other chemical businesses. In fact, Huntsman became the largest privately held chemical company in the world after purchasing Goodyear's film and flexible packaging business in 1992, Texaco's chemical operations two years later, Eastman Chemical's polypropylene business in Longview, Texas, Novacor Chemical's polypropylene operation, and ICI's polyurethanes and other petrochemical businesses in 1999. After the last acquisition doubled its size, Huntsman surged toward 2004 revenues of $10.5 billion and a work force of 11,600 employees.

Meanwhile, Kodak had already divested itself of Eastman Chemical in 1993. Despite reliable revenue from polyester fiber, acetate tow, and other products, rising energy prices that had persuaded Koch to get out of chemicals kept Eastman a low profitability, second tier chemical company that did not even rank in the top ten materials producers in the country.

Another alternative for maximizing shareholder value was to diversify into non-chemical operations. This Rohm and Haas did by purchasing Morton International's salt business in 1999, but the company still emphasized adhesives, specialty coatings, and electronic materials. Likewise, Air Products had an investment in a medical products division but focused on production of industrial gases and chemicals. Management exited the packaged gas and landfill gas recovery businesses.

In 1996, industry leaders and rivals DuPont and Dow decided that joining forces might boost profitability for both. They formed an Elastomers joint venture in which Dow's technological prowess created thermoset rubber polymers for the rubber industry and performance fluor-elastomers for the chemical processing and auto industries while DuPont contributed its neoprene products division and other assets. After concluding various joint ventures with foreign entities in Latin America, China, and South Africa, and then taking over Union Carbide in 1999 for $10 billion of stock, Dow's annual revenues vaulted to $40 billion while $500 million was wrung out of annual operating costs. Although the company's 2004 revenues actually exceeded DuPont's by $13 billion and work force was 47% smaller, profitability problems persisted. By comparison, DuPont's management decided late in 2003 to sell off the textile division to Koch for $4.4 billion. Although the company thus sacrificed $6.3 billion in annual revenue and 18,000 skilled employees, exposure to natural gas and oil price swings was reduced.

Two other powerhouses that in 2000 combined all chemical and plastic operations into a joint venture were Chevron and Philips. Even Koch, the largest privately held company in the world with 1994 revenue of $30 billion, producing annually 1 billion pounds of paraxylene for pop bottles, VCRs, computer tapes, and fibers for furniture and clothing, entered into a deal four years later with Mexico's Xtra to buy Hoechst' polyester division Trevira and create KOSA, the largest polyester producer in the world. Koch then purchased Xtra's stake in 2001, spun off Koch Chemical, Koch Pipeline, and Flint Hill Resources (petroleum) the next year, and wound up 2003 with estimated annual revenues of $40 billion. Because the company only employed 30,000 persons, its true worth was probably quite high.

GOVERNMENT INTERFERES WITH AND ASSISTS TRANSPORTATION

In the nineteenth century, construction of the national rail system had required massive government funding and land concessions. Regulation had belatedly been imposed to insure compatibility of operations, safety, and protection of the public interest, as defined by Congress and state legislatures, for example to combat monopoly power. From a business standpoint, however, excessive meddling by politicians undercut profits and the long-term capital investments needed to maintain infrastructure. When Washington and state capitals then bestowed their blessings upon roads and highways as well as airlines, the older child of the transportation revolution was suddenly passed over in favor of younger siblings.

Neglect changed to urgency to save railroad service in the Northeast. Conrail and Amtrak continued to struggle. With passage of a $151 billion Intermodal Surface Transportation Efficiency Act on December 18, 1991, $725 million was provided to build a magnetic levitation or MAGLEV train prototype. The Department of Transportation (DOT) pushed high-speed train service on five routes in the Northeast Corridor from Washington to Baltimore, Philadelphia, New York, and Boston to reduce road traffic congestion in that most heavily populated of all US metropolitan areas. However, the principal thrust of the bill was to spend almost $120 billion over six years to repair 265,000 miles of highways that were in bad condition, 642,000 of substandard, non-local roads, and 40% of the country's 564,000 bridges that were structurally deficient or functionally obsolete. Also funded was $31 billion for mass transit.

The only way to rescue the railroad industry in the final decades of the twentieth century without massive infusion of taxpayer money was to abandon the anti-monopoly bias of the past and sanction creation of regional powerhouses able to specialize in bulk cargo transport while supplementing truck and plane domination of freight service. Accordingly, federal regulators permitted the Union Pacific to buy the Chicago & Northwestern in 1995, merge with the Southern Pacific the next year and take over the Missouri Pacific in 1997. Similarly, Burlington Northern took over the Atcheson, Topeka, and Santa Fe in 1995. In the East, Norfolk Southern and CSX were permitted in 1998 to divide Conrail operations roughly three to two.

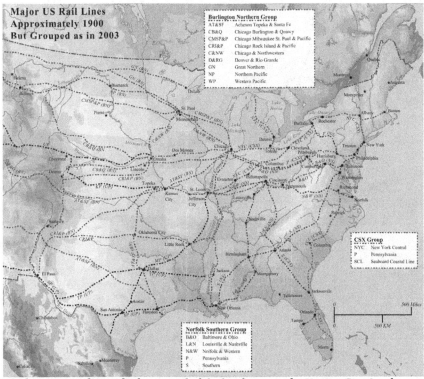

What remained outside the control of the big four was the Kansas City Southern, carrying coal and paper mill products from Missouri to the Gulf of Mexico and expanding its 39% stake in TFM of Mexico to full control. The railroad planned to rename itself Nafta Rail, hold employment around 2,700, and resume building up 2004 revenues of $640 million at the double-digit rates achieved in the five year period before the 2001 recession so that MC/AR of 1.9 would continue to rise. As for the Illinois Central, it was purchased by the Canadian National Railway for $2.4 billion in 1998 to connect Canada to Chicago and New Orleans. That foreign company's $4 billion of annual revenue thereby exceeded

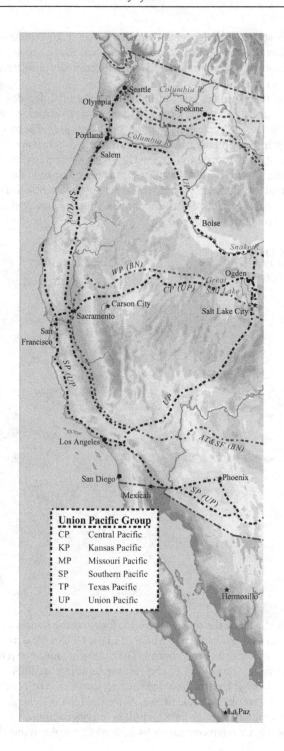

the $3 billion of the Canadian Pacific. But US passenger carrier Amtrak was still leaking red ink in massive quantities so that Congress, despite the Bush administration's desire to break up the railroad and sell off parts to the big four, had to maintain in fiscal year 2003 a $1.2 billion annual appropriation. The railroad's work force was cut another 12% to 22,000.

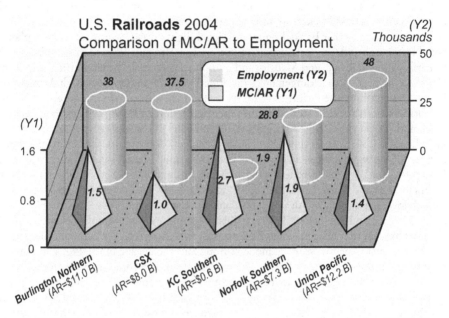

U.S. **Railroads** 2004
Comparison of MC/AR to Employment

By 2002, US railroads carried 2 billion tons of freight annually valued at $600 billion. Revenue equaled $36 billion, which was four-fifths of all railroad revenue generated in North America. Profitability was helped by the fact that total industry employment was down to 185,000 workers. Union representation lifted annual employee earnings to $57,000, $77,800 when including benefits. Coal was by far the most important cargo, accounting for 44% of ton weight carried, but contributing only 21% of all revenue, while chemicals were a distant second at 9% of ton weight followed by farm commodities at 7.8%, non-metallic minerals at 7.1%, and food at 5.8%. Inter-modal cooperation, in other words rail shipments transferred from road shipments and vice-versa, contributed a fifth of the $45 billion.

If the big four railroads were in relatively good shape, the airline industry was because of both national and international complications still in a state of less mature consolidation and flux. Congress tried to help on November 5, 1990 with a budget-reconciliation act that allowed airports to impose boarding fees to fund expansion, modernization, safety, and security. Further, the FAA imposed regulations to phase out excessive aircraft noise. But airline companies were on their own to maintain profitability during the Persian Gulf War gas price hike and afterward as the economy struggled to come out of recession.

Having in October 1990 ordered 128 wide body jets from Boeing for $22 billion to serve overseas routes to Europe and South America, United Airlines proceeded to take nearly $1 billion in losses through 1992. Management was forced to ground older planes more swiftly than planned, sell flight kitchens to cut $400 million of annual operating expense, and strike a deal with 54,000 employees to exchange part of salaries and benefits for United stock. In the process, the company became the largest employee-owned company in the world. Representatives of its machinist and pilot unions occupied seats on its board of directors. Belatedly in 1997, United forged a *Star Alliance* partnership with Air Canada, Lufthansa, SAS, Thai Airlines, and Varig of Brazil. Such arrangements as these permitted major US airlines to sell tickets for foreign partners and vice-versa.

Another carrier that banked on international flights was USAir. In the 1990s, planes out of Pittsburgh and Charlotte flew to Frankfurt, regular flights ensued from Philadelphia to Paris, Munich, Rome, and Madrid, and more business was planned in the Caribbean. However, as part of an arrangement sanctioned by DOT to permit British Airways to invest $300 million, the airline gave up its London Heathrow airport route, a decision executives came to regret later when they filed suit to force British Airways to sell USAir stock and return the Heathrow rights. After ordering 400 Airbus planes from Europe, including *A-330-300* wide bodies, the company changed its name without a thought about irony to US Airways. Management then bought the Trump Shuttle's daily round trips from Boston to New York LaGuardia Airport and LaGuardia to Washington National Airport flights in 1998, and started up a MetroJet single class, low fare airline using *B-737-200* jets up and down the east coast. Although the company then succumbed to United's blandishments for a $11.6 billion buyout, federal regulators and the airline's employees successfully objected to what they alleged would have been an anti-competitive, job-costing merger.

By contrast, Northwest made money throughout the decade of the 1990s, in part by following United's lead in giving up 37.5% of its stock and three seats on the board of directors in exchange for employee wage concessions amounting to $886 million over three years, in the main by soliciting DOT approval the next year of a 20% stake in Northwest by KLM of the Netherlands. Renamed Northwest Airlines Corporation, parent Wings Holding then approved flights out of Detroit, Seattle/Tacoma, and Minneapolis/St. Paul connecting to Japan, China, and Europe. By offering roomier *World Business Class* seating, the airline doubled profits from nearly $300 million in 1994 to $600 million four years later. That helped generate enough cash to increase the company's stake in Value Jet, founded in Atlanta in 1993 to emulate Southwest's cut-rate success, to 30% and take over Express Airlines I of Memphis, which was renamed Pinnacle Airlines in 2002. By becoming the first US airline to fly over Russian airspace in 1992, by forging relationships with Air China, Jet Airways of India, regional Norway carrier Braathens SAFE, Japan Air System, Malaysian Airlines, and by concluding a 1999 domestic code-sharing arrangement with Continental, the airline's global and national reach was second to none.

Meanwhile, an investment of $450 million by Air Partners/Air Canada permitted Continental to come out of Chapter 11 in spring 1993. Optimistically, the airline ordered 92 jets from Boeing. When profit of $640 million in 1997 was improved upon 20% the next year, Continental launched flights to Brazil. With Northwest, it joined United, American, and Delta as major US airlines.

Delta achieved that status after buying most of Pan Am's overseas routes and the Pan Am Shuttle in 1991. A competitive threat from Value Jet that might have undermined its business in the Southeast was temporarily defused by a Value Jet crash on May 11, 1996 in the Florida Everglades blamed on poor maintenance that killed 110 persons. Delta then tried to distinguish itself as a caring company by purchasing defibrillators for its planes. A *SkyTeam* global alliance with AeroMexico, Air France, and Korean Air as well as purchase of regional airlines in the Southeast encouraged management to order *B-777*s and 500 smaller jets for shorter routes to carry annually 120 million passengers.

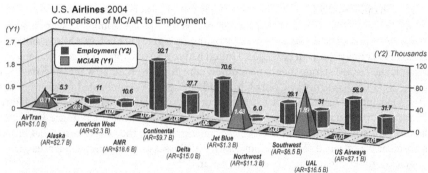

U.S. **Airlines** 2004
Comparison of MC/AR to Employment

Flying purely within the US, Southwest began to pose a major threat to the majors in 1993 by flying to the Baltimore/Washington area as well as other cities east of the Mississippi and finally Florida in 1996. Acquisition of smaller regional competitors in 1994 also incrementally boosted the airline's strength. However, the foundation of Southwest's prosperity was bare-bones operations with anywhere from one-fifth to three-fifths less operating cost structure than the majors. Purchase of fuel-efficient jets increased that advantage after jet fuel prices rose in the late 1990s.

Worst off relative to Southwest was United, but American Airlines was not much better positioned. Price competition early in the decade ruined a plan to distinguish the carrier by a *Value Plan* fare structure and agreement with Canadian Airlines to use parent AMR's *SABRE* computer system, which AMR then spun off in 1996. Its attempt to win over passengers with amenities such as defibrillators on every plane, more leg room, bigger overhead bins, and lounges in airports was effective only so long as the economy continued to grow and Americans could afford the company's stiffer fares. In the optimistic year prior to the stock market crash of March 2000, the company ordered more fuel-efficient *B-777* and *B-737-800* jets and bought TWA's assets cheap.

However, yet another discount airline rose up at that moment to challenge. Based in JFK Airport in New York, Jet Blue used an initial capitalization of $130 million to order 75 Airbus *A-320*s for $4 billion, and then in 2001 another 48 more for $2.5 billion. Already ValueJet had come back from the brink of liquidation by merging with AirTran. In response to the discounters, the majors turned to paperless e-tickets to cut down long lines at airports, more inter-airline cooperation to avoid destructive competition, and cuts in commissions paid to more than 15,000 travel agencies.

Whether the majors could have engineered a smooth transition to a more competitive cost structure and business model without damaging the value of their high-quality operations suddenly became a moot point on September 11, 2001. Fanatic Islamic terrorists who flew American and United planes into the Twin Towers of the World Trade Center in New York City not only caused billions of dollars of property damage but shook the airline industry to its core. In the wake of the attack, flights were cancelled, tens of thousands of employees were let go, and airline losses mounted toward $6.2 billion in 2001, $11.2 billion the next year, and $25 billion for the first four years of the twenty-first century. A federal government bailout in the Air Stabilization Act of September 21, 2001 of $4.5 billion in cash and $10 billion of loans as well as $7 billion pumped in by GE's Capital Aviation financing division was not enough to spare most remaining employees of major airlines an average 35% salary and wage cut, for example from $250,000 for senior pilots, $70,000 for senior mechanics, and $40,000 for senior flight attendants to lesser levels. Even United Airlines' surviving 80,000 employees, who owned 55% of the company, were asked to concede $7 billion over six years to win Washington's guarantee of another $2 billion in loans to avoid bankruptcy. In late 2002, United had to seek Chapter 11 protection anyway. Although the 13,000 strong mechanics union continued to balk at wage give-backs, in January 2003 US Bankruptcy Court Chief Judge Eugene Wedoff ruled in Chicago that United's machinists had to accept a 13% pay cut because without such concession United would suffer "irreparable damage." As it was, the company's revenue plunged from $19.3 billion in 2000 to $13.7 billion in 2003 before coming back up the next year to $16.4 billion. Employment was slashed to 58,900, but continuing losses and climbing fuel prices pushed management to terminate employee pension plans.

US Airways also had to resort to Chapter 11, not once but twice, to hang on. Although new routes to the Caribbean proved attractive to citizens concerned about terrorism, fierce competition in the East from majors and discounters alike caused continuing losses. As for AMR, the carrier avoided bankruptcy by asking for and securing permanent 25% wage cuts from the remaining 92,100 employees in its unions as well as non-unionized customer service agents and management and office personnel equal to $1.8 billion. Reduced flight operations at its St. Louis hub and other centers contracted revenues. Too, Delta permanently laid off 8,000 employees out of 78,000 and slashed half a billion in operating costs, which contributed to botched luggage handling and scheduling during the Christmas 2004 rush. Some analysts projected that the majors' 80% share of passenger fares might contract to 60% or less in the face of Jet Blue's, Southwest's, and AirTran's onslaught. Southwest kept the pressure on in the East by flying in and out of Philadelphia.

As for other regional carriers, Alaska Airline Group fell into the red as did American. Although investors liked the former's dominance in the Alaska and Pacific Northwest region much more than the latter's weak position in the shadow of not only the majors but Southwest, even later into 2003, Alaska was still losing money.

United's revenue dive accounted for one quarter the US airline industry's collapse from $135 billion of annual revenue in 2000 to under $100 billion four years later. Combined, US carriers carried $56 billion of debt, twice as much as in 1999. Even more alarming, the ratio of net debt (composed of balance sheet debt plus airport and aircraft lease commitments less unrestricted cash plus retiree liabilities) to annual revenue ranged from over 200% for United down to Delta's 140% with all the other majors between. Southwest, by comparison, was a low 29%. The future seemed to lie in larger global alliances, such as Air France buying KLM for $900 million in 2003 to combine $22 billion of revenues. *SkyTeam* associates Continental, Northwest, and Delta had nearly $30 billion of revenue while British Airways-American Airlines *One-World* alliance and United's and Lufthansa's *Star Alliance* were, without counting smaller partners, approximately at the same level.

Just about the only airlines not fundamentally affected by the September 11, 2001 terrorist attacks were the parcel carriers. FedEx controlled 45% of the overnight delivery market followed by UPS at 25%, Airborne of Seattle at 20%, the US Postal Service at 7% and DHL, almost half owned by Deutsche Post AG, itself controlled by the German government, only 3%. Internationally, however, DHL had two-fifths of the express delivery market while FedEx and UPS were under a fifth. An advantage the American carriers had for the long run was that US law continued to prohibit foreign ownership of US based airlines. For that reason, Deutsche Post had to divest itself of its stake in DHL's Airways unit, subsequently renamed Astar, and was only able to purchase the ground delivery unit of Airborne for $1.1 billion early in 2003. The overall $50 billion US market for parcel delivery was dominated 60% by UPS. Although the US Postal Service was second at a quarter share, twice as much as FedEx, the latter with 240,000 employees was bulking up ground delivery to please customers increasingly annoyed by high air delivery costs. Company executives fretted that 2004 profit margin of 4.75% was only half that of UPS. Moreover, UPS moved to cut labor costs and boost revenue with a *UPS Basic* delivery plan. As a "consolidator" of packaging, the company could actually have the US Postal Service make final delivery of parcels to out-of-the-way locations at discount prices less than the federal agency would otherwise charge itself.

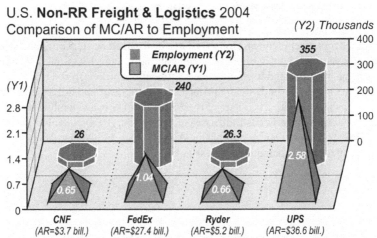

Heavier freight relied on ground transportation, of course. By 2004, the trucking industry carried 11.6 billion tons annually valued at $574 billion in a highly fragmented environment with 40,000 interstate trucking companies, 30,000 independent contractors, and 3 million truck drivers generating $165 billion of revenue. One of the largest freight companies was CNF. Privately held MBM of North Carolina generated about as much revenue distributing food products to restaurants. However the purchase of Roadway in July 2003 by Yellow Corporation for $1.1 billion created an even bigger entity, combining 18,700 truck tractors and 69,300 trailers with a 20% market share in the *less-than-truckload shipments from multiple customers* niche. ABF was far back. Part of the problem with the industry was that, rebelling against high shipping costs, customers sought alternative means of moving their freight. In the truck rental business, both Hertz, majority controlled by Ford, and Ryder were content to keep prices down and accept thin profit margins.

Garbage hauling in trucks to fill up company-owned landfills was another niche. Waste Management led the industry by 1995 with $9.2 billion of annual revenue. But accounting falsifications by Arthur Andersen to the tune of $3.5 billion resulted in shareholder lawsuits costing $464 million in penalties and fines.

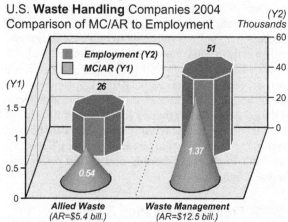

U.S. **Waste Handling** Companies 2004
Comparison of MC/AR to Employment

Three years later, upstart USA Waste of Oak Brook, Illinois with $2.6 billion in annual revenue took over its much larger rival in a deal valued at $13.5 billion in stock plus $7 billion in assumed debt. Come 2003, the company, which assumed Waste Management's name, had divested itself of waste treatment operations in the US, Mexico, and Hong Kong to ONYX, Vivendi's North American incinerator subsidiary. Management focused on consolidating its 23% share of the $50 billion US waste hauling market. Main competitor was Browning-Ferris Industries of Scottsdale, Arizona, which in 1999 emulated USA Waste's maneuver by purchasing Allied Waste Industries. Adopting Allied's name, management more than quintupled sales by 2004.

CHAPTER XIV. RETRENCHMENT OF US HEAVY INDUSTRY

The end of the Cold War occasioned talk of a peace dividend. The plan of the administration of the elder Bush was to cut defense spending from 25% of $1.2 trillion in federal expenditures to below 20% by steady reduction in military manpower from 2.1 million to 1.4 million and competitive bidding on acquisition contracts. In that manner, the annual budget deficit could be slashed well below $200 billion, interest on the public debt would be reduced, and red ink would eventually turn black. More dollars would be available for discretionary domestic spending beyond what was required by law for Social Security, Medicare/Medicaid, and other income security programs.

However, the Persian Gulf War and the recession delayed the peace dividend. By 1992, the public debt topped $4 trillion. Only as international tensions eased and the economy picked up was defense spending brought down to a low of about one-sixth of the 1999 federal budget of $1.7 trillion, compared with 48% for all income security programs. By then, the annual budget deficit had been wiped out and replaced by surpluses peaking in 2000 at $306 billion.

F/A-22 Raptor

Although the one-third cut in military personnel accounted for a large portion of the relative defense spending draw-down, ample dollars remained for acquisition of weapons systems. The President and Congress were especially anxious to continue improving the air power, missiles, electronics, tanks, helicopters, night vision equipment, and other hardware that had proved so overwhelming to the enemy in the short desert war. On the other hand, R&D of high-tech weaponry was yearly more expensive. The quantity of planes, tanks, ships, and munitions the Department of Defense could purchase had to be limited.

A different dynamic controlled the auto industry. Intense foreign import competition morphed into a critical mass of foreign owned motor vehicle plants on US soil. While a political issue was defused and that portion of the trade balance related to car imports improved, the Big Three had still to increase automation and outsourcing of parts to offset high union labor costs. As they continued to lose market share and struggle with profitability, pressure built for a major industry restructuring.

Also afflicted by foreign competition as well as substitute materials, the steel industry finally did undergo that kind of overhaul. As old companies went bankrupt and sold off assets, new investor driven entities took their place. The government then stepped in with new quotas and tariffs to protect big survivors. Freed of crushing legacy costs, steel companies looked again as solid and strong as, well, steel.

Dominated by multi-national corporations, the lumber industry yet received similar favorable treatment from Washington. As with steel, as many American companies were injured as helped. While mill and furniture workers had to fear for their jobs, the men and women who built the buildings and houses, roads and bridges for private companies and government generally did not. However even the construction industry, now with concern that panelization would introduce foreign import competition from Mexico by flat-bed truck and potentially from overseas by ship, had to fret that the increasing penchant of Americans to do it themselves would eat away at home improvement and repair profits.

CONSOLIDATING THE MILITARY INDUSTRIAL COMPLEX

After the Cold War ended and Persian Gulf War was won, it became necessary, both from a national security and business perspective, to encourage a new round of mergers and acquisitions in the aerospace/defense industry. Because oil price fluctuations and competition from Europe's Airbus, subsidiary of the European Aeronautic Defense & Space Company (EADS), had negatively impacted production and sale of commercial aircraft, the weakest of aircraft frame builders had to sacrifice their independence or fail altogether. The die was cast when a Lockheed-General Dynamics-Boeing team beat out a Northrop-McDonnell-Douglas partnership to develop and produce the *F/A-22* air superiority fighter as a replacement for the *F-15*. Plagued by aerodynamic design and engine performance problems that brought the company close to bankruptcy by 1994, McDonnell-Douglas cut its workforce by half and narrowed commercial air production to just *MD-80/90* planes and the *MD-11*, and an update of the *DC-10*.

In 1997, company management accepted a $16.3 billion takeover by Boeing that resulted in an entity with combined annual revenues of $48 billion and work force of 200,000. For the time being twice as popular as Airbus with an order backlog of 1,300 commercial planes as well as 10,000 planes of all kinds still flying, accounting for three-quarters of all airline seats in the world, Boeing enticed more sales at home and abroad with a new *B-777* twin-jet developed at cost of $12 billion and using Pratt & Whitney engines. President Clinton even intervened personally with the Saudi government to land a big order from Saudia, the Middle East country's airliner. After taking over Hughes Space and Communications and winning aerospace-defense contracts to produce the *Joint Direct Attack Munition, Unmanned Aerial Vehicles*, and still experimental ballistic missile defense system, Boeing's revenue lifted toward $54 billion.

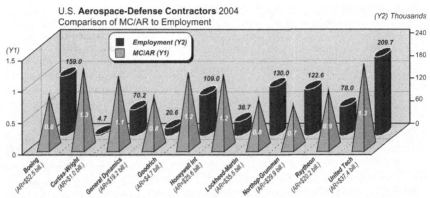

U.S. **Aerospace-Defense Contractors** 2004
Comparison of MC/AR to Employment

However, cost overruns, the premium paid for Hughes, and commercial jet order suspensions and cancellations stemming from the September 11, 2001 terrorist attack resulted in 30,000 layoffs and permitted Airbus to challenge for the lead in aircraft orders. By 2004, contracts with Washington, for example $14.9 billion for *Future Combat Systems* for the Army, $17 billion for leasing 100 air tankers based on the *B-767* frame, $9.7 billion for *C-17* cargo planes, and an $18.9 billion deal to develop next-generation sub-hunting jets accounted for 50% of all present and expected future revenue. Profitability sagged to only 4.3% of annual revenue. While shutting down production lines of the *B-757*, which had turned out 1,000 planes over a two decade period, the company announced that for the first time Boeing would bring out an entirely new plane, the fuel-efficient, 220 passenger *B-7E7*, designed for direct flight between cities rather than indirect through hubs, without advance orders by US carriers. Rather, promise of orders from two Japanese airlines was sufficient to make plans to produce a third of the plane's parts in Japan. US orders were expected once the economy fully recovered. Unfortunately, the tanker deal came under congressional fire as too lucrative for the company and Boeing officials misappropriated Lockheed documents, resulting in loss of $1 billion in rocket launch contracts. CEO Philip M. Condit was forced to resign.

To avoid tying its fortunes too closely to Boeing, engine-maker Pratt & Whitney produced the *PW6000* for Airbus' *A318* in 1999. That subsidiary of United Technologies also agreed with competitor GE for joint development of a more energy efficient, 76,000 pound engine for new US and European four-engine transports. Unable to compete in the big aircraft engine market against Pratt & Whitney's *PW4098* with 98,000 pounds of thrust, Britain's Rolls-Royce refocused on auto production and eventually was sold to a German company. While a quarter of GE's annual revenues came by 2004 from its aerospace/aircraft engine division, United Technology derived 40% of its $37.4 billion in annual revenues from similar operations, including its Sikorsky helicopter division. Fully half of United Technologies revenues and nearly as high a percentage of profits originated from its Otis subsidiary's stranglehold on the elevator and escalator market as well as *Carrier* air conditioning products, selling after a 2003 agreement exclusively at Sears.

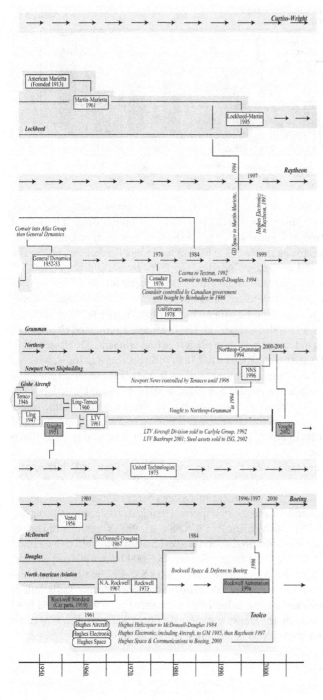

Genealogy of US Aerospace-Defense Industry, 1946-2004

Unlike McDonnell-Douglas, Northrop landed on its feet by purchasing Grumman in 1994 to diversify into defense electronics and radars, including *JSTARS*, fire control radar for *Apache Longbow* helicopter, and surveillance radar for *AWACS*. Although the defense contractor continued to make *B-2 Stealth* bombers, *A-6E Intruders*, *A-7 Corsairs*, *F-14 Super Tomcats*, and *A-10 Thunderbolt IIs*, it lost out by 1996 to Lockheed in a competition to make the *Joint Strike Fighter* for the Air Force, Navy, and Marines as well as the British Royal Navy. The company became attractive enough for Lockheed to attempt an $11.6 billion takeover in 1998 that the Justice Department blocked for fear of too great a consolidation in military aircraft. Nevertheless, Northrop-Grumman sub-contracted to make parts for the *Joint Strike Fighter*. When in 2001, Northrop-Grumman obtained Newport News, only lately in 1995 spun off from Tenneco, its combined ship-building operations generated $4 billion of revenue a year. After adding Litton Industries and TRW's Space & Electronics division that same year, the company won contracts to develop *Unmanned Combat Air Vehicles* for reconnaissance missions as well as *Hellfire* missiles for suppression of air defense systems and $4.5 billion over several years for a boost-phase missile interceptor. In the civil area, Northrop produced fuselage sections, tail sections, doors, and other parts for Boeing and Airbus as well as *Gulfstream* business jets.

Meanwhile, Lockheed's winning streak continued in 1994 with a $1.3 billion contract from Britain's RAF to build a replacement for 40 year old *C-130 Hercules* transport planes. The next year, the company engaged in a "merger of equals" with Martin Marietta to become the country's top aerospace-defense firm. As well as a high-prestige contract to run launch operations for the *Space Shuttle* fleet, Lockheed Martin was also signed up to build *Atlas V* expendable vehicles and the *X-33* reusable rocket plane. The latter was intended to replace the *Space Shuttle* in the second decade of the twenty-first century.

After Boeing, Lockheed Martin, and Northrop Grumman, the largest defense contractor was Raytheon. The company continued development of anti-missile technologies with the *Patriot II* system, which achieved great publicity but mixed success shooting down Iraqi *Scuds* during the Persian Gulf War. Later improvements made the *Patriot III* system highly desired by US allies such as South Korea and Taiwan facing hostile adversaries. After taking over Hughes Electronic's defense operations, Raytheon's annual revenue surged, but as with Northrop-Grumman, sub-contracting from primary contractors already pressed by Washington for lower prices did not in the post-Cold War defense environment lead to superior profits.

General Dynamics was somewhat better off than Raytheon in this respect. After its main stockholder died in 1992, the company restructured by selling its Cessna Aircraft Company, maker of light and medium-size commercial business jets, to Textron, its missile operations to GM-Hughes, its Fort Worth division producing fighter planes to Lockheed, and its space systems to Martin Marietta. What was left was shipbuilding, subbuilding, and marine systems in the Electric Boat division, land combat systems highlighted by the *M1A1* tank, military information systems and technologies, and *Gulfstream* business aviation and aircraft services. Like Honeywell, an even larger aerospace supplier, management intended to move plants to Mexico to lower labor costs by as much as 90% to a base wage of $2.50 per hour. FAA regulations still required, however, that all aircraft parts produced outside the US be inspected at a US site. Moreover, General Dynamics proposed to buy Veridian for $1.2 billion to diversify into high-tech intelligence systems useful for homeland security and other purposes.

Among other notable aerospace-defense contractors, Rockwell International had been subsumed into Boeing in 1996 for $3 billion. The parent had then spun off Rockwell's Allen-Bradley, Dodge transmission, Reliance Electric, and software divisions as Rockwell Automation. Although Vought had watched its *Army Tactical Missile System* fire surface to surface bolts at the enemy during the Persian Gulf War, when parent LTV came out of bankruptcy in 1992, the division was sold to Northrop and the Carlyle investment group of Washington D.C. Northrop bought out Carlyle's stake in 1994 only to sell the unit whole to Carlyle for $1.2 billion in 2000. Spun off two years later, Vought solicited business mainly as a subcontractor.

On the other hand, BF Goodrich in 1997 bought Rohr with sales of over $1 billion in complex integrated aircraft systems. Two years later, the company took over Coltec Industries, the largest maker of aircraft landing gear, for $2.2 billion. Management sold off their specialty chemicals operations and spun off its industrial products division as EnPro Industries. The cash was used to buy TRW's Aeronautical Systems.

By contrast, Eaton's belated effort to balance its truck transmission, hydraulics, fluid power, and electrical systems businesses with purchase of Aeroquip-Vickers for $1.7 billion to get into engineered components and systems for aerospace, automotive, and industrial markets was better rewarded. The company was selected by Lockheed Martin to provide fluid power systems for the *Joint Strike Fighter* for $1 billion. Meanwhile, ITT Industries did well drawing 30% of its revenue from defense and electronic services such as air traffic control, jamming devices against radar-guided weapons, digital combat radios, night vision devices, and satellite instruments. More of the company's employees were deployed in the world's largest industrial pump manufacturing operation, making devices for aerospace, industrial, and marine motion and flow control as well as specialty shock absorbers and brake friction.

Curtiss-Wright, the company that had started the US aerospace industry in the first place, was reduced to aircraft overhaul servicing for company transmissions as well as making actuators for wing-flap systems. Management bought Viall to do complete overhaul and repair of airliners. By diversifying into drives and suspensions for armored vehicles, the company could claim still to be a defense contractor. Tilting systems for high-speed railway cars were an operation that would not make a major contribution to annual revenue unless and until the US government got behind a national bullet train system with dollars and commitment.

With the reduction in military manpower, a significant business opportunity opened up for so-called primary military contractors to supply US forces deployed overseas with food and other necessities as well as perform logistic supply services, increasingly with lower-cost local labor. In 1992, Halliburton's Kellogg Brown & Root (KBR) unit won the Pentagon's Logistics Civil Augmentation Program (LOGCAP) contract. Although the take for supplying troops during the Somalia and Haiti operations 1992-94 was only about $240 million, the company hit the jackpot with US intervention in the Balkans. Between 1995 and 2002, Washington paid KBR $2.5 billion. And although KBR lost new LOGCAP revenue to Dyncorp after 1997, the contract was won back prior to the Iraq war. The subsidiary gathered in another $1 billion through summer 2003 for supplying US forces in the aftermath of that conflict to rise above $6 billion of annual revenue, or nearly half Halliburton's total revenue. Defense contracting business would only become more lucrative as the War on Terrorism accelerated. The Pentagon preferred a national security posture in which the government supplied the trigger-pullers and private industry supplied the logistics.

Overall, the republic's defense budget was jacked up to $1.2 trillion over three years following the September 11, 2001 terrorist attacks. The military spent $170 billion to fight the Afghan and Iraq wars with another $85 billion in occupation and reconstruction costs through fiscal year 2004. Despite plans by Europe's EADS to bid on Pentagon contracts and become a major player, congressional sentiment was either to formalize a buy American strategy or continue the informal arrangement whereby US aerospace and defense spending is the nearly exclusive domain of US contractors. Emphasis on tightening homeland security reinforces the bias not to undercut the US-owned national defense industry.

US MOTOR VEHICLE INDUSTRY UNDER SIEGE

Genealogy of US Auto Industry, 1946-2004

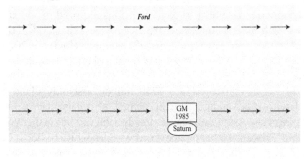

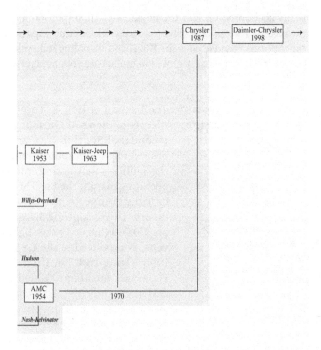

In the 1990s, US production of new cars, noncommercial light trucks, and associated parts accounted for 3.5% of GDP. The figure might have been considerably higher had Detroit been able to stave off foreign imports, claiming 26% of the new car and light truck market in 1993, over a third when only counting cars. Because the Japanese, South Koreans, and Europeans succumbed to pressure to shift vehicle assembly to the US, the continuing loss of market share to foreign producers ceased to be so extreme an economic and political issue. Yet, profits earned on transplants as well as imports together with the cost of imported materials and parts, hurt the balance of payments and trade. To reverse the trend, the Big Three auto makers needed to win back more of the one in seven households that bought a new car every year. Unfortunately, the numbers of cars and commercial vehicles they produced annually for domestic use as well as export did not again come near the 13 million plus figure achieved several times in the 1970s. After the decade-opening recession, the figures for 1993 were about 6 million cars and 4.8 million commercial vehicles. Despite an upsurge in rental company purchases, for example to triple the number of vehicles in Enterprise Rental's fleet to half a million by 1999 and lift 2004 sales to $7.4 billion, supporting 57,300 employees, as well as NAFTA's success in boosting car exports to Mexico ten-fold, economic and political considerations required producing vehicles sold in regions outside North America in those markets. From less than 20% of the Big Three total in 1990, overseas production leaped to a third of 16 million vehicles by 2000. Developments indicated that significant location of Big Three owned plant and equipment outside the US would continue.

For example, in 1995, GM began constructing a $750 million assembly plant in Thailand, a decision emulated later by Ford and its partially-owned subsidiary Mazda. The plan was to increase the 5% share of the Asian car market already achieved by smaller GM factories in India, Indonesia, and Taiwan. To keep pace, Ford was desperate to boost its 1.67% market share in the fast-rising 1.2 billion person China market. Some projections had the growing Chinese middle class buying over 4 million cars annually by 2006.

Back at home, Chrysler temporarily slipped behind Honda in US auto sales in 1991. Over 400,000 *Accords* sold annually accounted for half the Japanese company's total. But Toyota, in fifth place and spearheaded by its less expensive *Camry* model, built up capacity at a Kentucky plant to a quarter million. To raise cash for R&D and retooling, Chrysler dealt off its plastic operations to Textron, the largest global manufacturer of engineered fastening products.

U.S. **Car Makers** 2004
Comparison of MC/AR to Employment

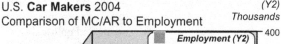

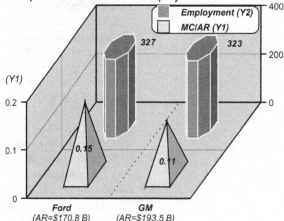

The location of Honda, Toyota, Mercedes-Benz of Germany, Hyundai of South Korea, and other foreign car production in the South severely undercut the operating margin the Big Three could achieve in northern plants. Toyota's profit margin on 900,000 cars and other light vehicles produced in the US in 1996, rising to 1.7 million in 2004, was pushing 10% while GM's was only 3%. Although average wages paid by trans-plants increased by 2003 to $25 per hour, full health and pension benefits for younger, non-union workers were much less than for Detroit's veteran work force. GM, Ford, and Chrysler had also to carry high legacy costs, in other words pension and health care benefits for retirees, which where GM was concerned equaled $3,000 for every car sold.

As a low-cost alternative to Japanese models priced between $8,000 and $12,000, GM developed its Saturn subsidiary. Unfortunately, bloat and inefficiency in the company's main corporate bureaucracy, highlighted in 1990 by the retirement of CEO Roger Smith with a $1 million annual pension, overshadowed the effort. After losing $4.5 billion the next year, the industry leader had to close 21 plants in the US and Canada. Market share for cars hovered just above one-third. Ford, by contrast, had a market share of about 22%. Its low-cost *Taurus* model accounted for one out of six of the 2 million cars it sold.

Goodyear tires on a Jeep Cherokee

What saved GM, Ford, and Chrysler from a worse drubbing by foreign competitors was their overwhelming lead in the non-car, light vehicle category as well as big cars. In fact, the best selling vehicles of all when the period began in the US were Ford F-series pickup trucks at 538,000 and Chevy C-K series pickups at 486,000. In 1992, Ford's *Explorer* sport utility vehicle (SUV) based on a truck chassis broke into the top-ten seller list at 275,000. To compete, GM cranked up production of its Chevy *Suburban* while Chrysler marketed the Jeep *Grand Cherokee*. Since SUVs and pickups returned a monstrous $10,000 profit per vehicle, the Big Three were determined to persuade the American public to buy more of these gas-guzzling vehicles and less of the fuel-efficient models desired by Washington regulators. Low gas prices through the end of the decade averaging $1.25 per gallon at the pump and larger *V-6* and *V-8* engines helped push SUVs, minivans, and pickups by 1998 to a 50% share of the nearly 16 million car and light vehicle US market. By contrast, the electric-powered *EV1* model GM developed through Saturn to satisfy the California Air Resources Board requirement that 10% of all new cars sold in the state by 2003 be electric, did minuscule business, and mainly to government agencies. Toyota and Honda both came in with electric and electric-gasoline hybrid competitors soon thereafter.

Because Washington imposed a 25% duty on foreign imports of trucks the Japanese and Koreans were initially limited in the light truck category. However, Toyota got around the problem in 1996 by building a plant in Indiana to produce annually 100,000 full-size pickups to take share in a market niche that grew to nearly $50 billion of sales by 2002. After Congress that same year voted to phase out over seven years a luxury tax of 10% on cars priced above $30,000, higher-end Mercedes-Benz and Lexus (subsidiary of Toyota) SUVs built on a car rather than a truck chassis, and therefore not subject to the truck import duty, found favor with upper-middle class consumers. The next step for all foreign SUV competitors was of course to build such vehicles in the United States.

Government preference for domestic motor vehicle production prevailed in foreign markets as well. In 1995, the Chinese government awarded Mercedes-Benz the right to build minivans for sale in China rather than Chrysler, and GM a license to produce its Buick *Regal* executive class passenger car rather than Ford. Although two years later Ford wrangled the right to build a truck version of its *Transit* van in China, Chrysler's compensation of a joint venture with the Peking government to make Jeep models was too little too late. Suffering from disappointing sales in the US and a slump in Mexico and Latin America, the company was persuaded in 1998 to accept a $36 billion takeover offer from Daimler of Germany, combining sales of $130 billion.

On the other hand, purchases by Ford and GM of car companies overseas increased Detroit's clout around the world. While GM acquired 50% SAAB of Sweden in 1989 and the rest in 2000, a 20% stake in Fiat of Italy for $2.4 billion, and two-thirds of bankrupt Daewoo of South Korea, and Ford boosted its ownership in Mazda of Japan from one quarter to one third while taking over Land Rover of Britain and Volvo of Sweden, their parts divisions achieved greater economies of scale for light bulbs, jacks, and radiator caps as well as engines and other higher value sub-assemblies. Although GM was able to close down its slumping Oldsmobile division in 2000 and its sinking Chevy *Camaro* and Pontiac *Firebird* models the next year while restyling *Cadillac* models with sports car features, political pressure to keep open the captive car companies of foreign countries tended again to reduce US production relative to overseas production. Of 323,000 global GM employees in 2004, only 46% were in the US while Ford's numbers were about the same.

A legacy burden of $32 billion in pension and health care benefits for retirees and dependents, health costs for current employees of $9 billion, and the fact that UAW contracts mandated 95% pay for workers when production lines were temporarily shut down were the reasons that the Big Three kept turning out vehicles at a 16 million annual clip during the recession of 2001, equal to 27% of world demand. They used rebate incentives and 0% interest rates over three years to keep market share in the United States. GM remained the world's largest auto maker at 9 million annually followed by Toyota (with annual revenues surging beyond $145 billion) at 7.5 million, Ford at 6.5 million, the VW Group of Germany at 4.8 million, and Daimler/Chrysler at 4.2 million. Aggressive plans by even lesser foreign competitors such as Hyundai and Nissan, controlled by Renault, to win sales in the US cut Detroit's profit per car to $400, compared with $1,500 forty years earlier. As Chrysler's market share of light vehicles dropped to 13.4% from 17%, the Daimler subsidiary lost several billion dollars. The global auto and light vehicle glut created a 30% overcapacity, equal to 20 million vehicles per year, 2.2 million in the US alone, which persuaded GM's and DaimlerChrysler's chief executives to agree on a joint venture to develop hybrid engine technology to compete with Toyota's.

Only because GM earned three times as much annually from financing car purchases as from car sales did the company wring 1.5% profit from 2004 revenues. Debt amounting to $300 billion was covered by only $57 billion of cash and marketable securities. Delphi, the parts division GM spun off in 1999, looked somewhat better with 40% of revenues from non-GM business. The company had an 18.3% share of the global $150 billion parts market.

Ford's ratio of debt to cash was worse at $173 billion and $23 billion. The second largest US car company's revenue came under pressure in the aftermath of problems with Firestone *Wilderness AT* tires on Ford's *Explorer* SUV that resulted in a $5.4 billion 2001 loss. Tread blow-outs killed 46 persons in accidents, prompting 50 lawsuits, and forced Ford to recall and replace 13 million tires. Bridgestone, parent of Firestone, shut down the subsidiary's Decatur, Illinois plant, making 10% of all company tires. Visteon, the parts supplier business with 77,000 employees Ford spun off in 2000 in emulation of GM's move, generated revenues from making integrated chassis, drivelines, electronics parts, audio systems, climate control systems, power trains, exteriors, and interiors. Because only a quarter of sales came from non-Ford business, the former parent company used its clout to keep down prices.

At the retail level, sales incentives and lower profit margins accelerated consolidation among car dealers. After selling off Waste Management, Huizenga put together a national chain called Autonation which by 2004 had 360 new vehicle franchises at 285 dealerships in 18 states. In fact, for every $1,000 of new car incentives offered by auto makers, used car values plummeted $850. Although trade-ins did not cost dealers as much, resale prices were proportionately lower. Largest used car dealer CarMax, founded in Richmond in 1993, managed nevertheless to sell annually by 2003 about 200,000 used cars and 10,000 new cars.

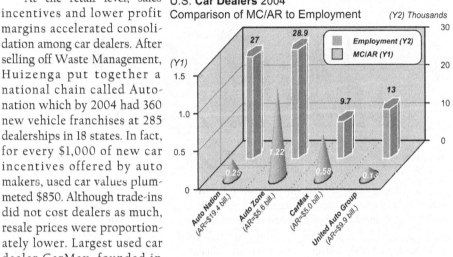

U.S. **Car Dealers** 2004
Comparison of MC/AR to Employment

By virtue of their connections to GM and Ford, Delphi and Visteon claimed leadership of the global new parts market. However, Johnson Controls actually came to exceed Visteon by purchasing Prince Automotive in 1996 to reach $10 billion of annual revenue. Acquisitions in Europe and Japan then doubled sales, albeit in part because of revenue from facilities management. The expense of employing over 123,000 employees in a down market after the stock market contraction and recession when the Big Three were pressuring suppliers for concessions held down profits. Spread across 33 countries and also specializing in auto interiors, Lear of Detroit was much worse off after taking on debt to buy Automotive Industries and Masland in 1996. With the advantage of selling replacement parts through 6,000 NAPA Auto Parts stores in the United States, Canada, and Mexico, Genuine Parts thrived.

Too, Dana prospered in the mid-1990s by making parts for SUVs, buying Reinz, a European firm founded in 1920 to make cylinder head gaskets for consolidation into its Victor subsidiary, and generating extra revenue from a credit division that bought big ticket items such as corporate headquarters and airplanes to lease back to sellers. After the turn of the century, however, smaller leasing and real estate deals and a move toward modular design of sub-assemblies and overseas production, including rolling chasses in Brazil for Chrysler, were not enough to offset stiff labor costs. Thus, ArvinMeritor of Troy, Michigan, created from a 2000 merger, made a hostile bid of $2.7 billion to takeover Dana. Because the aggressor's financial position was no improvement on Dana's figures, the target's management stoutly and successfully resisted.

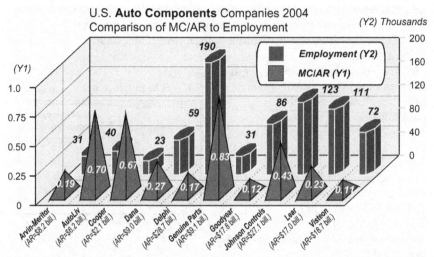

U.S. **Auto Components** Companies 2004
Comparison of MC/AR to Employment

Meanwhile, the US slowdown in auto production wounded companies that made materials for motor vehicle production as well. PPG Industries frowned as national glass production stagnated from 5.7 million metric tons in 1987 to 5.5 million a decade later. However, profit margins from making glass and fiber glass for cars as well as chemicals were much higher than from making car parts. Because of a similar calculation about auto paints and finishes, DuPont in 1998 bought the Herbert Group from Hoechst of Germany for $1.85 billion, while European firms Robert Bosch of Germany and Valeo of France improved their penetration of the American market with purchases respectively of Allied-Signal's Bendix brake business for $1.5 billion and ITT's auto electrical systems for $1.7 billion.

Continental of Germany bought ITT's brake and chassis line for $1.9 billion in 1999, bringing the fifth largest tire maker in the world additional revenue. Largest producer of tires was Michelin of France, which nine years earlier had passed Bridgestone of Japan and Goodyear by buying Uniroyal-Goodrich. Pirelli of Italy settled into fourth place and briefly considered a merger with Continental. Although the majors came to control nearly three-fifths of the global tire market, they all preferred some overseas production to cut down transportation and labor costs.

Moreover, Goodyear bought several tire plants in Eastern Europe after the fall of Communism. A $1 billion alliance with Sumitomo brought the right to market *Dunlop* tires, in a change of policy through Sears as well as company owned outlets and independent dealers. *Aquatred* wet-traction tires and the innovation of run-flat tires helped boost Goodyear's annual revenue. The large work force, including 19,000 UAW members earning $22 per hour, an agreement with the UAW to keep open all but one tire production plant in the US, $5 billion in debt, the auto industry slow-down, and competition from lower-cost producers held down profits.

Goodyear's 19.5% share of the US tire market was under pressure not only from imports and Firestone, fighting back from the Ford debacle to make the most of annual sales of $7.5 billion and 45,000 North American employees, but fast-riser Cooper Tire. By acquisition of Avon Tyre of Britain and Dean Tire & Rubber, hose and other automotive fluid handling component producers Southland and Seibe Automotive, and especially Standard Products Company, maker of automotive products, that company more than tripled revenues in the period. The fact that Cooper's employees were distributed over 55 plants in 13 countries and that main tire production was divided between Ohio and lower-labor costing Mississippi boosted profitability. Endorsement by golfing legend Arnold Palmer as well as diversification into non-tire operations helped counter cyclicality associated with new car sales.

Goodyear also tried to diversify in 2003 by entering into a joint venture with Treadco for 200 truck tire service stations and 77 re-treading plants. Since US trucks and buses combined passed 80 million in 1998, the thinking was sound. Likewise, PACCAR, preferring manufacture of trucks to the vicissitudes of the oil business, sold its Trico unit, manufacturing oil field pumps and other equipment, to EVI of Houston in 1997, just about at the bottom of oil prices. Two years later, the company sold its automotive lines to CSK Auto and refocused on a full line of light to heavy trucks.

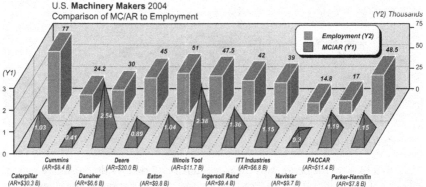

U.S. **Machinery Makers** 2004
Comparison of MC/AR to Employment

Rival Navistar not only made medium and heavy trucks but severe service vehicles for construction, waste collection, and military uses. Diesel engines, including for pickups, SUVs, and vans, did not have high enough margins to avoid losses during the new century economic slump. Engine manufacturer Cummins was no better off. The basic problem for both companies was that they stood in the shadow of mighty Caterpillar, leading the world in diesel engines after acquiring in 1997 Perkins Engines of Britain and MaK Motoren of Germany while manufacturing compact construction equipment and off-highway trucks.

A better plan than competing with Caterpillar was supplying parts. In 1997, Eaton and Dana jointly produced the *Roadranger* System of a complete commercial vehicle drive train, but Eaton then sold its axle and brake business to Dana for $287 million and used the proceeds to buy Dana's clutch business. Likewise, Parker Hannifin found relative prosperity developing motion and control technologies for trucks and other vehicles as well as planes. The company's applications also worked in refrigeration and soft drink dispensing systems.

Overall, the net fixed asset value of heavy trucks, buses, tractors, and construction equipment held by businesses more than doubled between 1990 and 2003 toward $600 billion. Because of the woes of the airline industry and unsuitability of railroads to handle and distribute cargoes other than bulk freight, the truck and construction vehicle and parts manufacturing industry was expected to continue to grow with a reviving economy. Moreover, importation of trucks from outside North America was rendered virtually impossible by tariff protection and transportation cost. Significant production capability was likely to remain in the republic for the foreseeable future.

EMBATTLED STEEL REORGANIZES TO FIGHT IMPORTS AND ALTERNATIVES

Likewise, the disappearance of the American steel industry was unthinkable both from an economic and political point of view. However, the 1990s did witness completion of a wrenching transition that reduced production and employment to a lower plateau. As before, the catalysts for change were foreign imports, advanced mini-mill technology, and competing alternative materials. Off-again, on-again quotas and tariffs failed to give corporate strategists a reliable environment for decision making.

ISG plant, Cleveland

The first blow of the period was the recession of 1991 that resulted in a 19% reduction to only 79 million tons of steel produced. When the administrations of the elder Bush and Clinton let the voluntary steel import quota limiting imports to 18.5% market share lapse, foreign companies nearly doubled annual shipments to the US to 30 million tons in 1994. Generally favorable economic conditions increased US production, nevertheless, to over 90 million tons. Big steel companies pumped $50 billion in capital improvements into their mills over a five year period to improve efficiency and try to compete with mini-mills' lower labor cost advantage.

However, unrestrained foreign imports peaked in 1998 at 40 million tons. Unable to compete in the glutted market that caused prices to tumble from, for example, $330 per ton for hot-rolled steel toward $200 per ton, many smaller US companies sold out to larger rivals or went bankrupt. Bethlehem took over Lukens in 1998 to become the largest US steel plate producer. The company had 11,000 employees producing steel for cars, construction, machinery, appliances, containers, service centers, and rails. Revenues from shipping 7.5 million tons of steel built to $3.5 billion annually. But falling prices forced Bethlehem into Chapter 11 in October 2001.

Already bankrupt the year before was LTV. Inland Steel of Chicago, the sixth largest US producer, was so hammered by labor and quality-control problems that the company was sold in 1999 to Ispat International of the Netherlands for $1.4 billion, pushing that firm up to 12.5 million tons and over $4.6 billion of annual revenue. But that was only good enough for eighth place among steel companies in the world. After Arbed of Luxemburg, Usinor of France, and Aceralia of Spain combined 46 million metric tons of production in a 2001 merger and Nippon turned out 28 million for second place, even the largest US producers were overshadowed.

National Steel, the republic's fourth largest with nearly 6 million tons of production in 2001 and 5,000 employees, could no longer bear up under the competition from importers, many now subsidized by home governments. After losing $650 million, the company, still a subsidiary of NKK of Japan, bowed to Chapter 11 the next year. That left only US Steel of Pittsburgh and Nucor of Charlotte as still profitable large operations. The latter increased its capacity from 11 million to 13 million tons by purchasing Birmingham Steel, another mini-mill with operations in Alabama, Illinois, Mississippi, and Washington, for $615 million.

As the total number of bankrupt companies escalated to 32 over five years, tariffs approved by the Clinton administration brought imports down to 30 million tons of steel products by 2001 and 25 million the next year. Of the total, 5 million tons came from EU countries, over 2 million from South Korea, 2 million from Russia, and 1.8 million from Japan. Although annual US steel production recovered to about 100 million tons, annual world production lifted from 750 million in 1995 to over 850 million. Because of NAFTA, the republic actually exported 8 million tons, or four times the level of the 1980s.

Despite the fact that the Chinese used all their 140 million tons themselves for building structural steel, railroads, bridges, and cars, the world still suffered from a 20% steel-making over-capacity. Actual consumption was about 100 million less than production. Therefore, prices plunged. In order for the US steel industry to pay for capital improvements and cover not only current operating costs from 160,000 employees but huge legacy costs for retirees and their dependents, they needed prices to recover as much as 50%.

For that reason, the US steel industry appealed to the administration of the younger Bush for tariff relief up to 40% on finished steel products accounting for more than a fifth of steel imports. He responded on March 5, 2002 with duties on slab steel for cars and many other products, flat rolled steel for cars and appliances, tin mill steel for food and beverage containers, and hot rolled-cold finished bar steel for furniture, farm equipment, and motor shafts of 30%, on rebar for highway and building construction, welded tubular steel for pipes, stainless steel rod for fasteners, and stainless steel bar for cars, airplanes, and other capital goods of half as much, and on stainless steel wire for medical goods, airplanes, and fasteners of 8%. The 30% and 15% tariffs would decline over two years to 18% and 9% respectively. Tariffs would be dropped after the third year. Moreover, a 5.4 million ton quota was imposed on slab steel, a quarter of which was reserved for Russia, but the Russians had the right under a 1999 anti-dumping deal with Washington to import up to 2 million tons if they so chose. The only steel not hit with a tariff was raw steel, accounting for 50% of EU, 75% of Japanese, and 85% of Australian imports, as well as tool steel for tools and dyes and stainless flange steel for pipe fittings.

Naturally, foreign importers were as displeased by the decision as big US steel producers were delighted. The EU not only protested to the WTO, in a process that would consume 18 months, that excess steel barred from the US would be dumped in their market but threaten $2.1 billion in retaliatory tariffs on various US products. Because of NAFTA, Canadian imports of 4.5 mill tons and Mexican of 1.65 million were not affected.

The US also left untouched imports from developing countries Argentina, South Africa, Thailand, and Brazil with combined production of 770,000 tons only accounting for 3% of the global total.

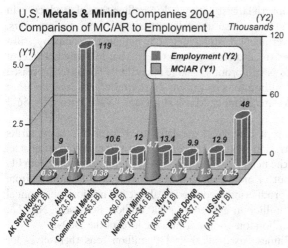

U.S. **Metals & Mining** Companies 2004
Comparison of MC/AR to Employment

Legend:
- Employment (Y2)
- MC/AR (Y1)

Also unhappy were some medium-size US companies operating blast furnace mills. These firms accepted up to 30% of all steel imports in the form of steel slab and billets because the price from foreign producers was a third less than the cost of purchasing iron ore from US mines or slab from US producers to make plate and sheet steel. Likewise, construction companies, buying steel mainly from west coast companies that imported steel slabs as well as cold and hot rolled steel by sea from Japan more cheaply than could be shipped at $50 a ton from the Great Lakes region, took a hit as hot-rolled steel jumped to $350 a ton and other steel products rose the intended 30-50%. The Big Three car makers, by contrast, had contracts of one year or longer duration for steel at a guaranteed price.

The steel tariffs had the beneficial impact to some, disastrous consequence for others of forcing a new consolidation of the industry. A group of investors centered on New York City billionaire Wilbur L. Ross formed the International Steel Group (ISG) to buy up LTV's assets for the bargain price of $325 million cash and $200 million of assumed debt. The holding company then made a deal with the USWA to limit wages to a range of $15 to $20.50 per hour, tie health and pension benefits for 3,000 workers, 60% of the pre-bankruptcy total, to company performance, and create a fund to pay limited health care benefits for LTV retirees. Freed of an excessive legacy burden, ISG then acquired the assets of Bethlehem Steel in February 2003 for $1 billion cash and $500 million assumed debt to create the second biggest American steel company with 18 million tons of annual production. Promptly the next year, Ross and his associates cashed in by selling ISG to Ispat of the U.K., which included American subsidiary Ispat Inland. Ispat also purchased LNM Holdings of the Netherlands to form Mittal Steel Group, boasting 70 million tons of annual steel-making capacity.

Bethlehem's $11 billion in present value legacy costs for 12,000 workers and 67,000 retirees and dependents did not, because of the asset purchase deal structure, have to be assumed. The government's Pension Benefit Guarantee Corporation stepped in to pick up retiree pension benefits but at an average 17% reduction to $1,400 per month.

US Steel once again emerged as the largest American company in the industry after acquiring National Steel from NKK and other shareholders for $750 million cash and $200 million assumed debt. The company added $1 billion in revenues and 5.9 million tons of annual production capacity to approach 26 million and claim a 30% market share of higher-quality steel products going on exposed auto, appliance, and construction surfaces compared to 25% for ISG. The deal was made economically viable by forcing 32,000 National Steel retirees to pick up a greater share of their health insurance costs as well as renegotiating the union contract for current employees to accept lower wages and a 20% reduction over time in the combined operations' work force.

Big steel producers argued that tariffs should be continued to stabilize industry fundamentals, including employment. However, critics pointed out that 12 million persons were employed in enterprises ranging from auto production to home appliances to construction that required steel at the lowest possible price. Ultimately, the WTO ruled that the tariffs violated world trade agreements. To avoid retaliatory steps by the EU, Japan, China, and other countries, Bush revoked the tariffs in December 2003.

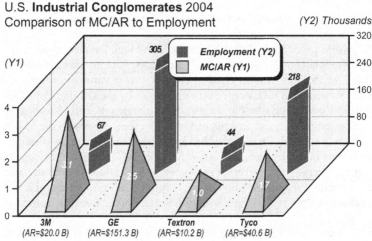

U.S. **Industrial Conglomerates** 2004
Comparison of MC/AR to Employment

One company that was pleased by the decision was conglomerate Tyco, which from 1986 forward bought up industrial and construction products firms such as Allied Tube and Conduit (1988) and American Pipe & Tube (1997). The latter company made steel pipe and related tubular products used in fire protection and fencing as well as steel studs and tresses for residential and commercial building. But Tyco continued to diversify into fire and security systems companies as well as manufacturers of electronics products, in particular by 1998 acquisition of AMP for $11.3 billion, a maker of electrical connectors. The company bought Lucent Power Systems, selling power systems in North America and products for telecom service providers and the computer industry globally. A bit more than 31% of revenues came from fire and security systems, a bit less than 30% from electronics, 23% from surgical supplies and other health care products, 13% from engineered products and services, and the rest from plastics and adhesives. Losses in 2002 from selling connectors, cables, and other electronic components, interest on debt of nearly $18 billion, and the fact that CEO L. Dennis Kozlowski allegedly misappropriated $600 million of company funds to pay for his lavish lifestyle, resulting in his resignation in June, kept market value below $30 billion. After plans to break up the conglomerate into four independent companies were scaled back to a $3.5 billion divestiture of a subsidiary running an undersea fiber optics network and a 3% cut in the workforce. The most profitable business was the health care division.

Getting back to the steel industry, by 2002 three-fifths of US production was being made in 40 huge blast furnaces, each with maximum capacity of 9,750 tons. A century earlier, blast furnace capacity had only been 500 tons. The size increase was critical because mini-mills had succeeded in reducing tap-to-tap times to one hour. In the 1990s, electric arc technology produced galvanized steel resistant to rust, fire, natural disasters, warping, and shrinking. That improvement permitted manufacturers of cars to give 10 year guarantees against rust. Greater durability of steel cooking ranges and other appliances was critical for the industry because cold-rolled and painted stainless steel yielded much higher margins and greater profitability.

Stainless steel's other desirable attribute was that it weighed less. New steel auto bodies and wrought steel drive train components also were marketed as ultra-light. With a price of 10 to 20 cents a pound compared to aluminum at 50 to 70 cents, steel by average weight of 1,500 pounds was over seven times more plentiful in cars. Aluminum was also hit after 2000 by higher electricity costs.

Even so, world production of aluminum rose from 15 million metric tons in 1995 to 19 million three years later to 21 million annually after 2000 with another 2 million recovered by recycling. About 20% was smelted in the US with a value of around $5 billion. However, the value-added total of products turned out by the US aluminum industry by 2002 was eight times as high, half for export. High margins permitted companies to pay 145,000 employees an average annual pay of $34,500, or the same cost as the $5 billion base value of aluminum smelted. On the other hand, the American market consumed 5.2 billion pounds for automobiles, airplanes, and other transportation products, 5 billion pounds for over 100 billion beverage cans and other packaging, and 3.2 billion pounds in construction, together exceeding 6.7 million tons. Imports of basic aluminum metal and finished products came in from Canada, the Caribbean, South America, Africa, Europe, and Australia.

Alcoa became the world's largest producer of aluminum after buying Alumax, the third largest US aluminum maker, in 1998 for $2.8 billion, merging with Reynolds Metals the next year, and getting into aerospace high-strength lockbolts and fasteners. Annual revenues jumped from $15 billion to a peak of $22.7 billion in 2000 before dipping and coming back up four years later to a new high with the economic slowdown and recovery. Although in 2003 Pechiney of France agreed to accept a $4.5 billion buy-out offer from Alcan of Canada to create a slightly larger but less profitable entity with $23.9 billion of annual revenues, Alcoa kept the lead in primary aluminum production with 13% of the world total to 12.5% for Alcan-Pechiney. The company was considering more overseas investments, including buying a half interest in Sual Holdings of Russia for $1 billion.

With operations in Australia, India, Brazil, China, and the Netherlands, Alcoa was able to diminish the impact on profitability of higher electricity prices. Prospects rose through 2004 as sky-high demand for aluminum in China drove prices back up beyond 90 cents per pound. The company also benefited from new alloys for airplane skins, strong brand names such as *Reynolds Wrap*, and an iron lock on the beverage can industry. The durability of aluminum, including 480 million metric tons out of 529 million produced since 1886 still in use, was far superior to steel.

The only other substance that could make as aggressive a boast was plastic. US production of plastic resin accelerated from 16 million metric tons in 1990 to 40 million by the new century, or about 27% of the world total. Even lighter than aluminum with excellent flexibility and fire-resistant qualities, plastic sold for $3.50 a pound. The US plastics industry employed over 1.3 million workers to turn out 28 billion pounds of soft polyethylene for sporting goods, shoes, handles, bottles, and films, half as much polyvinyl for floors and coverings, another 14 billion pounds of polypropylene for fenders, body panels, grilles, and under-the-hood parts, half that amount of polystyrene for gears, suspension bridge cables, and other structural members, 5 billion pounds of polyurethane for upholstery, carpets, clothing, and thermal insulation, and another 10 billion pounds for other purposes, including home appliances. And because makers of plastics goods ranged from chemical producers like DuPont and Dow to industrial firms such as Honeywell to consumer products company P&G to toy manufacturer Mattel, no dominant entity or entities came to control the market. World plastics consumption topped 100 million tons in 1993 and then surged toward 140 million, including an active global effort to recycle.

For that reason Newell paid an exorbitant $5.8 billion in stock for Rubbermaid in 1998. However, the resulting Newell Rubbermaid housing ware giant watched its stock valuation tumble from $12 billion to half that by 2004. The difficult lay in the fact that profits had never been high enough to warrant a superior market value, particularly after the new century recession came. Despite a 2000 purchase of *Paper Mate*, *Parker*, and *Waterman* pen products from Gillette to combine with its own *Sanford* writing instruments, future growth would be steady but not spectacular.

By comparison, production of advanced composites incorporating glass, carbon, boron, and even organic fibers was a much more specialized and promising business. Particularly because of demand for lighter but stronger, flexible, and heat resistant substances, production advanced toward 1.6 million metric tons by 1998. Uses ranged from aerospace applications to graphite tennis racquets to *Kevlar* helmets and body armor for military and police personnel. The high-value nature of advanced composite products permitted smaller companies to innovate and prosper.

Even less esoteric products, such as industrial tools, bearings, guides, and coatings could be made of composites. A company called Danaher that had risen from obscurity as a manager of real estate properties to diversify into industrial tools, fasteners, and pumps bought Easco Hand Tools in 1990 to gain control of the *Craftsman* line, marketed through Sears. After obtaining K-D Tools and several NAPA brands, management diversified again with purchase of electrical equipment and controls as well as motion controls and instruments businesses. A 1998 acquisition of Fluke Corporation, a maker of compact, professional electronic testing tools, for $735 million followed five years later by purchase of Radiometer of Denmark, making dental-imaging products and blood-gas analyzers, for $730 million, pushed annual revenues toward $7 billion in 2004.

Meanwhile in 1995, Sherwin-Williams bought Pratt & Lambert, which had acquired United Coatings the year before, to improve its position in architectural coatings and distribution. General industrial, powder, and aerospace coatings products were also thereby obtained. Because the main business remained four-fifths manufacture and sale of paint, profits and cash flow remained sluggish. Yet the company's dominant position in the industry foretold improvement once full-scale economic recovery took hold.

A BOOM IN CONSTRUCTION

In addition to the US supply of lumber, home-builders benefited from Canadian soft and hard wood, about one fifth the annual production as in the republic. However, in response to protests from IP, G-P, and other producers that Canadian timber imports were taking too much market share, the Clinton administration insisted in 1996 that the Canadians agree to limit soft lumber exports to the US to just under 40 million cubic meters. However, that pact caused lumber prices for US home builders to rise. Because Canadian imports, allegedly dumped below cost with Canadian government subsidy help, continued to afflict US competitors, Washington in 2001 slapped on duties.

Lumber at a home building site

Nevertheless, it continued to be the abiding aim of most Americans to own homes. Sales of new homes reached a record 909,000 in 2001 compared with 5.25 million existing homes sold. The wide discrepancy can be explained in part by the fact that the average price of a new home rose at an average annual clip of 4.9% between 1993 and 2001 to $225,400 while the average price of a used home was $35,000 less. Median prices for new and used were $170,200 and $151,400 respectively. Despite the premium required to buy a new home, falling 30 year mortgage rates to below 6.5% by November 2001 pushed home ownership to 68% of all households; however only 49% and 48% respectively of Hispanics and blacks owned homes. Of the 72.5 million homes inhabited by 2003, 3% had a value in excess of $500,000, double the figure for 1989.

New upscale suburban homes

Higher lumber prices did not prevent home-builders from starting construction on 1.5 million homes in 1996, rising to 1.7 million by 2002 at a cost of $230 billion, of which just over $200 billion was spent on single-unit homes. About as much money was going toward home additions and improvements. Centex of Dallas became the largest such company in the country. After merging with Del Webb, national leader in active-adult communities built around golf courses, fitness facilities, and other amenities and targeted at high net worth buyers, Pulte of Michigan claimed second spot with a strategy that included expansion into Mexico and an exclusive deal to have GE supply home appliances for Pulte homes. However, after going on an acquisition binge of companies with business in California and Illinois, Lennar of Miami almost equaled Pulte's sales and employment. Late comer D.R. Horton, founded in Dallas in 1979, was a close fourth. While KB Home of California was substantially further back, the company tried to solicit business in Lennar's home territory of south Florida. So long as one out of every 15 heads of households were in the market to buy a new home each year, there would be plenty of business for any well-managed, national firm. Given the fact that the aggregate sales of these top four companies amounted to less than 15% of the industry's new home market, the industry had room for three other builders with annual revenue above the Fortune 500 lower limit of approximately $3.2 billion and seven others who qualified as Fortune 1000 entities exceeding $1.2 billion of sales. Even regional companies still had the potential to expand and challenge in the three basic residential housing markets of first-time homes, move-up homes, and active-adult communities.

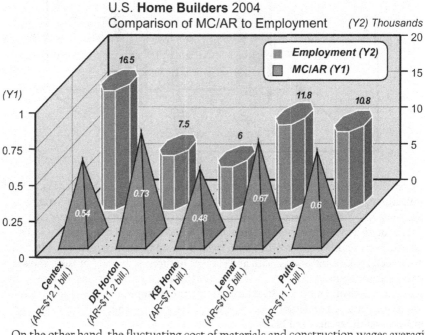

On the other hand, the fluctuating cost of materials and construction wages averaging $18 per hour increased the likelihood of consolidation. Only larger companies with economies of scale could push MC/ARs to 0.50 and beyond. Industry leaders tried to cut subcontracting costs by extending the pre-fabricated housing concept of the 1940s and 50s to "panelization." Entire walls, including studs, framing, and drywall preassembled in factories were pre-wired. A paucity of skilled local craftsmen necessitated in some areas panelization of concrete basements, exterior walls, structural beams, and even foundations. Home builders were not only able to squeeze out costs but raise houses faster.

At first, the 1990s house building boom, including an early recovery from the 1991 recession due to a need to replace homes destroyed the next year in Florida by Hurricane Andrew, shaped up as very good news for US furniture makers. Annual industry revenues climbed from $15 billion toward nearly $18 billion in 1994. Expectations were high that NAFTA would lead to growth of exports to Canada and Mexico. However, the northern neighbor cranked up its own production to match and exceed the contrary flow. Worse, the Chinese started making furniture with workers paid a tenth of US wages that topped $11 per hour by end of the decade. Although the US furniture market exploded from $20 billion in 1996 to $64 billion by 2002, a 40% share was claimed by imports. Industry employment tumbled to below half a million as a consequence. The economy of North Carolina, a center of furniture manufacture, was severely damaged.

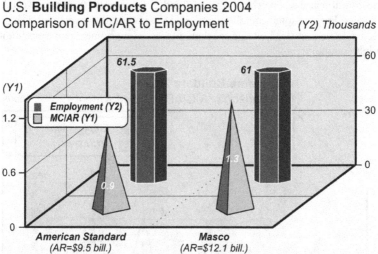

Too, the leadership of industry producers was undermined. Although Masco, the top manufacturer in 1993 with $1.5 billion of sales, rose to $2 billion three years later for a 10% share, company executives saw the writing on the wall and sold out. Management used proceeds for an acquisition spree to strengthen Masco's position domestically and abroad in home fixtures and hardware. By 2004, revenue from insulation, faucets, kitchen and bath cabinets, paints and stains, bath and shower fixtures, spas and hot tubs, shower and plumbing equipment, windows, lock sets, ventilating equipment and pumps jumped. Masco's competitor American Standard, with similar employment but a more limited product line centered on sinks, faucets, and toilets, survived a hostile takeover bid and returned to public trading in 1995.

Furniture Brands International, formerly Interco, stayed in the furniture business and advanced from $1 billion of sales in 1996 to $2.4 billion eight years later. Even more oppressed by cheap imports from China, including leather recliners selling for under $200 at Wal-Mart, was La-Z-Boy of Monroe, Michigan. Although company revenues more then tripled between 1993 and 2004 from vertically integrating operations to sell in manufacturer's galleries, single and multiple product specialty stores, as well as independently operated stores, profit margin fell into negative territory. Except for furniture makers that could distinguish themselves by making higher value products, delivering special orders quickly, or wringing more revenue out of still respected brand names, the industry was under extreme pressure.

Next in importance to home-building for the construction industry but using a variety of materials other than wood, including steel, brick, and concrete, was non-residential building. Fall-out from the recession of 2001 caused contract value of starts to decline slightly the next year from $165 billion. That brought to a temporary end a building boom that had witnessed a big expansion in commercial properties. Completion of the *Mall of America* in Bloomington, Minnesota back in 1992 at cost of $635 million to draw in retail revenue building to over $1 billion annually had sparked construction of dozens more regional malls and manufacturers' outlets.

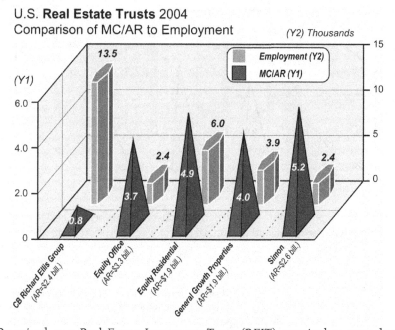

U.S. **Real Estate Trusts** 2004
Comparison of MC/AR to Employment

Organized as a Real Estate Investment Trust (REIT), required to pass down to investors at least 90% of revenue from tenant leases, the Simon Property Group of Indianapolis made its IPO in 1993. After taking over DeBartolo Realty of Youngstown in 1996, the company added 49 more malls to its inventory. A joint venture with Chelsea Property Group to develop upscale manufacturers' outlets put in place the Orlando Premium Outlets near amusement parks. Simon became the largest mall owner by a two-to-one margin with the buy-out of Corporate Property Investors in 1998. The mall business, charging an average of $300 per square foot for retail space but a peak of $900 for premium space such as under the World Trade Towers before their destruction, was highly profitable.

Equally attractive to landlords was office properties. In 1997, Chicago investor Sam Zell took Equity Office Properties Trust public. Within five years, the REIT bought out competitors, including Japanese investors burned when office occupancy hit a low of 81%

in 1991, and achieved monopoly control of 126 million square feet, over 90% of the country's total. Annual office rents on existing leases averaged over $25 per square foot, nearly six times industrial property rents, but little more than $22 per square foot for new leases because of the 2001 recession. Rental rates were about one-third the cost per square foot of buildings when sold. For office properties in the top 50 US markets, sale prices averaged $150 per square foot and as high as twice that in New York City. Operating costs from property valued at over $8.3 billion averaged only $11.20 per square foot with occupancy around 85%. Zell's Equity Residential, a separate REIT, enjoyed even better profitability from 1,000 apartment communities.

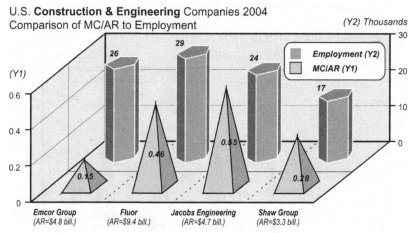

U.S. **Construction & Engineering** Companies 2004
Comparison of MC/AR to Employment

The third component of the construction industry was work on bridges, highways, roads, other paving projects, and mammoth public works projects topped by the $10.8 billion *Big Dig* in Boston to redirect interstate traffic underground, relieve congestion, and speed connection between parts of the city and the airport. Over $100 billion of such construction was begun in 2001. That helped the construction industry as a whole recover from a mid-decade dip of only $600 billion of annual contract starts to over $830 billion. Final share of GDP from construction of all kinds was 4.6%. Government spending on highways, hospitals, schools, urban public housing, and water treatment plants, the latter accelerated by the 1996 US Safe Drinking Water Act funding inspection and repair to the nation's 60,000 water treatment plants as well as a change from chlorine to an ozone disinfection process, contributed to the resurgence. Construction jobs, largely insulated from the world labor market, numbered 7 million, which was 5% of the employed civilian US workforce.

However, overall construction company business was more global than ever. Bechtel headed or participated in high-profile projects ranging from the *Space Launch Complex 3* in California to ExxonMobil's Singapore chemical complex to the *Channel Tunnel Rail Link* under the North Sea from Britain to France. Revenues by 2003 were around $16.3 billion and employees 44,000. Because the company was privately held, its profitability and valuation were not known. By contrast, Fluor with annual revenues of $9.4 billion and employment of 34,800 generated profit of 2%. MC/AR inched up toward 0.5.

Better results came from making equipment used in construction. Illinois Tool Works made over 100 acquisitions in the 1990s to consolidate companies that made metal fabrication, welding, and other equipment. By comparison, Ingersoll Rand focused on larger acquisitions. Management bought Clark Equipment, maker of *Bobcat* construction and farm equipment and *Steelcraft* steel doors and frames as well as Dresser-Rand, producing turbo machinery.

Meanwhile, the popularity of do-it-yourself home improvers knew no bounds. Millions of Americans purchased lumber, wood products, replacement plumbing equipment, paint, and other products as well as *Lenox, Black & Decker*, and *Stanley Works* power and hand tools. The two companies of the same name as the latter two product lines remained independent. *Lenox'* owner American Saw & Manufacturing Company succumbed to Newell Rubbermaid.

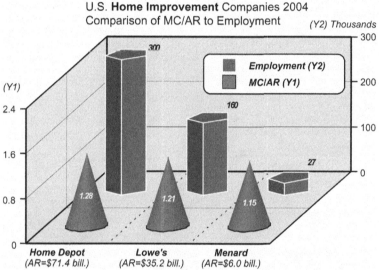

U.S. **Home Improvement** Companies 2004
Comparison of MC/AR to Employment

Much greater operating economies of scale were required from the purveyors of home improvement products. Retail giant Home Depot rode the crest of the do-it-yourself craze to a 15-fold increase in sales 1991-2004. Although most of the company's 1,800 stores were in the US, expansion into Canada, Mexico, and Chile was not insubstantial. By contrast, Lowe's $35.2 billion of annual revenues originated from 1,075 mostly newer stores in 48 states.

A distant third was Menard, founded in 1972 in Eau Claire, Wisconsin, with 200 stores from Indiana to North Dakota. That privately held company had an estimated $6 billion of sales by 2004 with 27,000 employees. Although Home Depot had the advantage of $40 million in annual revenue per store compared with $32.7 million for Lowe's and Menard's $30 million, the sales-per-employee advantage was less pronounced. Home Depot generated $238,000 to $220,000 for Lowe's and $222,000 for Menard's, indicating that were the smaller company to go public and profitability and cash flow scaled accordingly, its market value might land in the $7-8 billion range.

Chapter XV. Pressing a Global Advantage

By 1990, the US was exporting over $550 billion of goods and services annually while importing nearly $630 billion. Total US investments overseas amounted to just under $2.1 trillion compared with foreign investment in the US of $2.3 trillion. Because US investments earned a higher rate than what was paid out, the annual balance of payments was about the same as the trade gap. Political leaders realized that red ink from trade would only get worse unless the US found a way to boost exports. Because growth in exports was then accounting for 30% of the annual increase in GNP, negotiations to open foreign markets to US goods and services became doubly important. The GATT system, while generally satisfactory during the Cold War in fostering trade cooperation between the US and its allies and friends, had failed to break down formal and informal barriers that restricted, for example, US auto sales in Japan, agricultural shipments to both Japan and Europe and overall economic ties with China.

Nor could Washington continue an informal system of absolute quotas put in place over the last decade to limit individual countries to specific dollar amounts of imports of various kinds without risk of retaliation. In September 1990, the US switched to a tariff system that was swiftly undermined by the willingness of foreign competitors using cheaper labor to sell in the US at below production cost. The next year, in fact, one seventh of all world exports entered the US, while Germany took in a tenth, Japan and France a sixteenth each, and the U.K. even less. Because the American economy bounced back with a vengeance but the Japanese and continental European economies remained flat, the US share only increased over time.

Farmers and other US exporters of commodities benefited. Big American agri-businesses and other multi-national corporations pressed for unfettered free trade with all major economic areas of the world. Seeing political as well as economic benefit, successive administrations joined in negotiations that yielded progress toward a World Trade Organization (WTO). The growing economic might of the US relative to other major powers made success almost a foregone conclusion. On the other hand, neither the Europeans nor Japanese were willing to end all subsidies and tariffs for fear that vulnerable sectors of

McDonald's restaurant in Singapore

their economies would be overwhelmed, resulting in both economic and political upheaval. The US, too, had a great stake in protecting farmers and heavy industry.

The fact that two-thirds of the American economy was driven by consumer purchases drove Washington to persist. US companies ranging from big producers of consumer durables such as GE and Whirlpool to giant retailer Wal-Mart to household good power-house P&G to food products and cigarette purveyors Philip Morris and R.J. Reynolds to soft drink titans Coca-Cola and PepsiCo as well as many others depended heavily on overseas sales to supplement domestic operations. Global economies of scale redounded to the benefit of US consumers in lower prices. Afflicted by the high cost of education, health, and housing, American families of middle and lower income needed lower inflation on durables and non-durables to maintain standards of living.

Although in the process of moving toward Free Trade and more imports some American workers, particularly in manufacturing, lost jobs, it was assumed that an overall lift in the economy would create new employment opportunities in service industries and technology. Thinking globally meant focusing on the big picture without specific concern about the individual fate of citizens. And in fact, by end of the period, the panorama of progress in trade and the consumer economy was impressive. US multi-national companies entrenched themselves around the world to such a degree that returning to an economy confined in the main to national borders was not only unthinkable but impossible.

Political pressures did continue to influence government policy, however. The American Job Creation Act of 2004 offered a one year window for Pfizer, HP, Dell, Intel, and other corporations with huge troves of overseas profits, cumulatively topping $500 billion, to repatriate those earnings at a 5.25% in 2005, instead of the top marginal corporate rate of 35%. The name of the law indicated an expectation that re-investment of the profits would stimulate US job growth, preferably in manufacturing. Global forces beyond the control of even the powerful US government told against any effort to reverse the tide of economic history.

At the outset of the period, an aggressive response by the elder Bush arrested a movement toward protectionism by trade partners. When the European Community (EC) imposed restrictions on oilseed (cottonseed, rapeseed, and soybeans) imports used for high-protein meal and edible vegetable oils to protect their own producers, US retaliation against an equal dollar amount of EC exports to the US forced a stopgap agreement by the EC to pay their farmers to plant less oilseed. Likewise, the President flew to Tokyo in January 1992 with heads of the Big Three auto makers to (vomit by accident on the Japanese prime minister and) cajole the Japanese to double the purchase of US auto parts as well as open Japan to American computers, paper, and glass. Tokyo bowed to the pressure.

Nevertheless, feeling in the US was so hot against Japanese imports that had cost US auto and defense workers jobs that Los Angeles County Transport commissioners voted to cancel a $122 million order for railcars from Sumitomo. Car dealers, other retailers who sold goods made in the Far East, and most consumers who preferred lower costing, high quality Japanese autos, home electronics, and other products did not jump on a *Buy American* bandwagon, however. On the contrary, high tech railroad flat cars linked in mile-long trains now carried 50% of Asian imports from the west to east coasts in three days. *Land-bridging*, as it was called, made the trade more economical and efficient than the longer journey by ship through the Panama Canal to New York harbor.

Rio Grande River at Brownsville

A similar emphasis on pleasing consumers at the expense of blue collar workers caused the Bush administration to use authority from Congress to negotiate *Fast Track* trade agreements to shift into high gear on talks to create a North American Free Trade Association (NAFTA). Presidential election year politics dictated that bothersome disputes, such as the Mexican government reacting to a 10 year drought by reneging on a 1944 agreement to supply annually 350,000 acre feet (equal to 114 billion gallons) of water from the Rio Grande River to south Texas, costing the state an estimated $1 billion in economic activity and 30,000 jobs, be resolved. Anxious to secure permanent access to the US market, Canada and Mexico agreed to NAFTA on August 18, 1992. Because the economy did not recover before the November election, because labor groups were furious that elimination of tariffs, taxes, and regulations would undercut decades of progress in wages, benefits, and job security, and environmentalists complained about a similar negative effect on clean air, pure water, and protection of natural resources, Bush lost the White House to Governor William J. Clinton of Arkansas. Yet the new President promptly encouraged Congress to ratify NAFTA on November 20, 1993, thus creating on January 1, 1994 a Free Trade zone of 360 million people, generating annually $6 trillion of production of goods and services, about the same size as European Market countries. Supplemental agreements for the protection of US jobs, compensation for workers who lost jobs due to foreign imports, and environmental safeguards did not stand in the way of a surge of imports from both the southern and northern neighbors.

For that reason, a backlash against NAFTA provoked Congress to revoke Clinton's *Fast Track* authority. Because the leadership of the Republican and Democratic parties were irrevocably committed to NAFTA, US policy pushing global Free Trade did not change even after the GOP took back control of both houses of Congress in 1994, the first time in 50 years. Momentum for Free Trade carried through to final WTO negotiations in Marrakech, Morocco in April 1994. Beginning the next January, the WTO was empowered with authority to settle trade disputes, impose financial sanctions for violations, and work toward a truly global Free Trade system, including a move by the US and EU to phase out over a decade 20 year old quotas on clothing and textiles. Any nation could pull out after six months notice to escape interference with national sovereignty and economic decision-making. The benefits of Free Trade were expected to so out-weigh disadvantages that 146 nations eventually came to be included.

China at first was not. Centralized control of the economy, bureaucratic antipathy to the free flow of ideas and information, and violations of human rights, in particular vast prison camps turned into slave labor factories by the Chinese Army, offended sensibilities in the US and Europe. And yet *land-bridging* already included large quantity of toys, textiles, and other products made in China. American companies bought these goods to resell at a lower price and better profit than could be accomplished from production stateside. Because most consumers scarcely noticed labels that read *Made in China*, the influx did not at first cause a great stir. Chinese industrial products were no more objectionable than Japanese, German, and Italian. For example, machine tool imports exceeded $2 billion in 1991, twice US exports and two-thirds the total of US production. Japan and Germany dominated world machine tool production with over $20 billion of products.

Likewise, the fact that renewable but not permanent most favored nation (MFN) trading status conferred on China by President Carter and Congress on February 1, 1980 had permitted US corporations to pump $300 billion of investment into China initially escaped the public's notice. Although most joint ventures, including production of AMC's *Cherokee* jeep and McDonnell Douglas airplanes, could not surmount Chinese corruption, skimming, and other impediments to profitability, notable success stories with soft drinks, basketball shoes, shampoo, and other consumer items suggested that the vast China market of 1 billion plus persons was ready, particularly as the Communist Peking government grew accustomed to the post-Cold War world of less international tension, for Capitalist exploitation. Unfortunately, Chinese failure to sign a Missile Technology Control Regime (MTCR) treaty obliged Clinton in August 1993 to ban shipment of high-tech goods to China, costing exports worth $1 billion over two years. He nevertheless extended China's MFN status in 1994 to keep the door open to cooperation. Pressure on Peking to clean up human rights violations and stop infringement on US copyrights achieved little progress, but the Chinese did agree the next year to avoid 100% protective tariffs. As Chinese imports to the US climbed toward $50 billion, or over 6.5% of total US imports, leaders in Peking became increasingly anxious to protect that vital component of an economy approaching $1 billion of GDP by securing both permanent MFN status with the US and WTO membership.

Cargo containers piled high in the port of Singapore

In the interim, the US trade gap worsened. Although after mid-decade the growth in exports came to account for 40% of the growth in the economy and doubled to $1.1 trillion by 2000, imports outran exports annually by $160 billion, widening by 2004 to $618 billion as Chinese imports ballooned above $160 billion. More than half of goods imported into the US originated outside the Western Hemisphere. Because foreign direct investment in the US peaked in 2000 at nearly $250 billion, pushing up total foreign direct investment toward a 2002 figure over $1.5 trillion, or just over one-fifth of all foreign financial asset holdings in the US including credit market instruments as well as corporate equities and bonds, the total negative balance of payments topped out at $665.9 billion in 2004, just under 6% of GDP.

Also called the Current Account Deficit, it generated fear among some economists that purchase of foreign goods at cost of US domestic production and industry would undercut for all time American manufacturing. Should US inflation reignite and the value of the dollar versus other currencies be undermined, foreigners might withdraw investments in US stocks and bonds. On the other hand, US productivity growth and the success of large American companies in competing at home and abroad generated the best returns on investment in the world. The geopolitical position of the US as the only superpower meant that American equity and debt markets would continue to be the safest harbor for money.

Free Trade agreements or not, Japan and South Korea continued to restrict US auto sales while inundating the American market with imports. The Japanese were particularly determined to maintain the heavy flow of goods to the US because the booming economy of the 1980s was replaced by recession, stagnation, and an average of only 1% annual

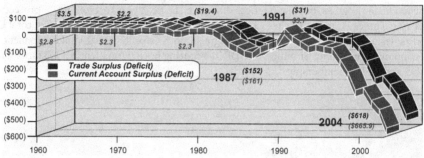

U.S. Trade and Current Account Balances
1960-2004, In Billions

growth 1990 to 2004. As previously discussed, the opening by Japanese car companies of more auto plants in the US diffused what might have been a show-down over trade between the two countries. Japanese productivity, weighed down by the fact that big companies accounted for only 10% of Japanese jobs and 17% of GDP with the remainder coming from smaller and less efficient entities, slumped to only two-thirds of the US figure. Although the number two economy in the world no longer seemed at less than 40% the US GDP such a threat, Japanese exports composed two-fifths of the $300 billion in ocean-bound trade that arrived at major US west coast ports in 2003. Railroad lines from the Los Angeles metropolitan area alone carried $100 billion of chemicals, apparel, electronics, toys, footwear, and other goods across the US, much from the land of the Rising Sun.

Meanwhile in 1995, South Korea shipped 200,000 cars across the Pacific while only taking in 2,000 US cars. Two years later, a financial crisis in Thailand caused by excessive government debt and inability to repay loans not only caused the Thai currency to collapse but spread over the next two years to Indonesia, South Korea, and to a lesser extent others of the seven *Tiger Economies* of the Far East. Ultimately, the IMF had to step in with loans of $17 billion for Thailand, $23 billion for Indonesia, and a whopping $58 billion for South Korea. The Seoul government pushed its people to buy domestic goods instead of foreign to improve business profits and Seoul's tax revenues. The strategy worked, but in the process the South Korean people ran up huge credit card debts, cash advances, and other loans that boosted household debt from $125 billion in 1999 to over $500 billion in 2001. Naturally, the *Buy South Korean* campaign further inhibited US exports at the moment when South Korean companies were shipping as many goods as possible to the US.

Failure to open the Japanese and South Korean markets as well as the Asian financial crisis left the US with three major alternatives for boosting exports and reducing the balance of trade and payments deficit. These were with the EU, first created as the Western European Union defense alliance in 1954, China, and the NAFTA neighbors. Building toward $600 billion, trade with the Old Continent appeared most promising because general European tariffs averaged by the new century only 3.9%, just below the US figure of 4%, Canada's 4.4%, and Japan's 5.1%. China, by contrast, came down toward but remained above 15% while general tariff rates for other developing countries ranged from 12.9% in Brazil to India's protectionist 30.9%. Yet the tightening of EU political ties gave European governments greater collective economic clout to encourage growth and resist US pressure. When Washington in 1998 complained about EU tariffs on US beef and bananas, the EU turned around and protested the old US Foreign Sales Corporation (FSC) device as an illegal subsidy. Investigation by a WTO panel resulted in a WTO "order" to modify US tax law. The EU in 2000 rejected a US proposal to resolve the FSC controversy by exempting all foreign-source income of US firms from tax, not just exports. Both the banana standoff and FSC dilemma dragged on into 2004. After the EU threatened $4 billion of tariff retaliation, Congress repealed the FSC but compensated corporations that exported with a $100 billion annual tax cut.

The rough and tumble of trade negotiations between the US and EU, including an EU ruling that bilateral open skies airline agreements between the US on the one hand and Sweden, Finland, Luxembourg, Denmark, Belgium, Austria, Germany, and the U.K. on the other which had facilitated global airline partnerships technically violated EU rules, gave no hope that the US trade deficit could be narrowed by increased exports to Europe. Another source of tension was Washington's refusal to agree to the Kyoto Treaty of December 1997 calling on industrial countries to reduce pollution, a growing problem in population dense Europe. Then the younger Bush decided to go to war with Iraq in spring 2003 over the objection of the French, Germans, and others. Although most trade between the US and Europe was never in serious peril, American anger at the French reduced French exports to the United States of wine and other products as well as diminished US tourism to Paris by as much as a fifth.

ConocoPhillips natural gas facility
Alberta, Canada (courtesy ConocoPhillips)

Unlike EU countries, China's economy grew for much of the 1990s at a double digit pace. Peking's willingness to subordinate political ideology to economic practicality attracted direct foreign investment equal to $300 billion, with $62 billion coming by 2004 alone. Although only about 60 million of the country's 1.3 billion people had disposable income to afford high value consumer durables, the mass market was broadened, for example to 5.2 million cars purchased in 2004, by resort to the old American strategy of borrowing against future income for present prosperity. The downside was that by the new century, China's banks had $500 billion of non-performing loans, equal to 40% of GDP. For that reason, and because 270 million people, including almost one-third of the country's 310 million city-dwellers, were unemployed, China's leaders were determined to join the world economy as a full and equal partner. After Clinton in summer 1998 flew to Peking to break the ice on permanent MFN status for China and entry into the WTO, subsequent negotiations secured those objectives in May 2000 and November 2001 respectively.

In exchange for Clinton's intervention, the US received recognition of and protection for US copyrights and patents of products as diverse as music, software, and telecom equipment as well as greater Chinese acceptance of US goods, both from transplants and imports. Among US companies doing profitable business in the world's most populous country were Eastman Kodak with $1.2 billion of capital investment, 8,000 photo stores, and 63% of the camera and film market, Motorola with $3.4 billion in two plants making mobile phones, cellular networks, and semiconductors, and 3M, pleased that its pioneering investment in China in 1984 was now paying off so well for itself and US businesses generally. Despite the fact that most Chinese could not afford big ticket items, they did frequent 800 KFC restaurants and 100 Pizza Huts, buy consumer soft drinks from 31 Coca-Cola bottling plants, and shop for food, personal care, household and other consumer products from five P&G plants. In the next several years, the value of US exports to China of airplanes, semiconductors, scrap and waste products (needed by the Chinese because of a lack of iron and pulp), soybeans, computers, and other products surged toward $25 billion annually.

Pepsi in Shanghai, China

The only problem from the point of view of some US politicians was that annual Chinese exports to the US of toys, sporting goods, office machines, computer chips and components, and other products came by 2004 to be worth $197 billion while only $35 billion went the other way. Big US companies such as Microsoft, Intel, HP, GE, and Dell that had built plants in the Far East to take advantage of labor costs as low as $5 per hour in Singapore, $2.50 next door in Malaysia, and under $2 in Indonesia now contracted with Flextronics and other producers to employ Chinese with wages as low as 50 cents per hour. Wal-Mart alone came to buy $15 billion worth of goods from Chinese factories while GE planned to take a third as much by 2005 and Ford wanted to increase purchases of auto parts ten-fold to $10 billion by 2010 to cut overall parts costs up to 40%. One-third of all Chinese exports to the US were made for US companies in Chinese factories.

Although American CEOs and economists who believed in the idea of comparative advantage were pleased that China's low wages complemented the US advantage in high-tech industries, the consequence for American manufacturing workers was devastating. Complaints caused Congress in the US–China Relations Act of 2000 to set a much lower standard for imposing sanctions on Chinese products than was typical in dumping cases. Because the Chinese feared a flood of US lawsuits over dumping, compromises had to be made. Peking agreed in 2002-2003 to buy $1.3 billion of car parts from GM, $800 million of telecom equipment from Lucent and Motorola, and more planes from Boeing. Thus hope did exist that the trade gap would narrow, particularly as Peking expanded orders of American commodities and electro-industrial machinery to fuel and power expansion. Nevertheless, in 2004 China moved into first place as an exporter and trade partner to the United States ahead of Japan.

Most important to Washington for the future in offsetting the growing trade deficit was Peking's fulfillment of its WTO commitment to open its market to US financial services and farm products. In the former, the expertise of American firms was needed not only to deal with the bad debt problem of four state-owned Chinese banks but make the most of $1 trillion of bank deposits and a Chinese stock market exceeding $500 billion in value, compared with $12 trillion in the US stock market and $2 trillion in Japan's. In October 2002, Peking finally did relax restrictions against foreign management of financial institutions to permit San Francisco based buyout-and-investment firm Newbridge Capital to take a 20% stake in and management control of Shenzhen Development Bank. Chinese officials pledged to complete the transition to a full market economy by 2010.

On the other hand, the Chinese proved as touchy about agricultural products as the Europeans and Japanese. In 2002, Peking alarmed the US by interfering with $1 billion a year shipments of bio-engineered soybeans, one-third US agricultural exports to China. Officials did so by imposing a 270 day waiting period on genetically modified crops. Fortunately the next year, a shortfall in Chinese crop production required large purchases of US commodities. The Chinese also moved to prevent foreigners from taking out of China teas, medicines, and other products with genetic value. They had been upset by the success of New Zealand companies in obtaining kiwi fruit samples, making genetic improvements, and shipping back products to best home-grown kiwi fruit.

B-777

Another source of leverage the US had over China was playing the Taiwan card. After taking back control of Hong Kong in 1997 after 100 years of British rule, the Chinese urgently desired to regain possession of the island formerly known as Formosa. But from the American perspective, a free Taiwan was a valuable economic, military, and political ally. Trade deals such as Taiwan's China Airlines agreeing in September 2002 to buy $3 billion worth of B-777 jets instead of Airbus A330s as well as 10 more B-747s at $200 million a piece on top of eight B-747s previously purchased guaranteed that the US would not countenance a Chinese takeover of Taiwan by force any time in the foreseeable future.

Avery Dennison shipping department, Singapore

The flow from South Korea, Taiwan, Singapore, Brazil, and other countries of products as diverse as consumer electronics and fabrics, semiconductors and coffee contributed tens of billions of dollars more to the trade deficit. Congress' weak response in 2000 was a Continued Dumping and Subsidy Offset Act which stipulated that any US manufacturer that successfully appealed for tariffs on imports that were being "dumped" at less than fair market value could keep proceeds of tariffs collected by the US Customs Service. In 2002, payments to US companies made on such items as sparklers, candles, and pineapple amounted to only $320 million. That would not compensate for ten days of the trade deficit with South Korea alone.

Thus, the last option for improving the import-export balance was the NAFTA partners. Great hope for additional US agricultural exports to Mexico arrived with the election in 2000 of Vincente Fox of Mexico's National Action party, breaking seven decades of monopolization of power by the Institutional Revolutionary party. In Republican George W. Bush, who defeated Vice President Al Gore, Jr. in a highly contentious and disputed election that same year, Fox appeared to have a willing partner to adopt a policy of more flexible treatment of migrant workers crossing the border to pick produce in US fields, permission for Mexican trucks to transport goods between Mexican and US cities, and a general uplift in trade that would boost the standard of living south of the border and permit democracy and Capitalism to flourish. However, the September 11, 2001 terrorist attacks caused a 180 degree shift toward closing border crossings and tightening up homeland security. Political pressure from millions of peasant farmers then hurt US exports of farm commodities. The Mexican congress imposed a 20% tax on US fructose corn syrup imports, albeit in response to complaints dating back to 1997 from Mexican farmers, reducing US exports by $600 million annually. Still under NAFTA, two-way trade with Mexico topped $265 billion in both 2003 and 2004. The only problem was that nearly two-thirds were Mexico exports of clothing, cars, plastics, and other products to the United States.

The trade deficit with Canada was even worse. Imports of $256 billion of paper products, plastics, cars, and other items were covered by only $190 billion of exports. In fact, that nation of 30 million people sent exports equal to 25% of its GDP to the US. Nearly two thirds of its manufacturing output was shipped south. Meanwhile, American manufactured goods accounted for over half of Canada's purchases. Almost one sixth of all US exports of goods and services wound up north of the border.

Pine trees—soft wood

Nor did NAFTA resolve all grievances with Ottawa. In the new century, America's largest trading partner had to endure a 27% tariff on shipments of soft-woods used in housing con-struction, a $6 billion market. Washington charged that 90% of Canadian timberland was publicly owned and leased by the government to private com-panies for cutting at very low rates. Had companies to pay a rate equal to what was charged by the US government or buy the land outright, they would

have had to increase prices 20%, it was alleged. Although US producers of southern yellow pine were pleased initially by the action of the Bush administration, US builders had to add about $1,500 to the cost of a new house. When Canadians jacked up lumber pro-duction to make a similar profit as before on greater volume, the tariff wound up causing an oversupply of lumber in the US that knocked down softwood prices to even lower levels than before.

The US and Canada tangled as well over shipments from 80,000 Canadian wheat farmers, accounting for 75% of all wheat imports but only 5% of US consumption. The fact that a Canadian subsidy of about $20 per ton was 28.7% of the American subsidy, made no difference to Washington. America's northern neighbor also got scant appreciation for providing one-twelfth of the beef US citizens consumed. Discovery in 2003 that one lone cow had somehow become infected with mad-cow disease caused a temporary halt in the $2.2 billion Canadian cattle trade with the US. Ironically, the identical misfortune then happened to the US from a dairy cow imported from Canada to Washington State. Canada, China, the EU, and Japan all rushed to ban US meat imports.

In the short run, imports and subsidies tended to raise the value of US assets because they could be sold for more. However, protectionism as a long-term policy amounted to a wealth transfer from consumers to owners of assets. Nevertheless, policy-makers recog-nized that the republic needed to maintain a minimum production capacity in key indus-tries such as farming, lumbering, steel, autos, airplanes, and even portions of the textile industry, including capital-intensive dying, finishing, and printing, imperiled by Caribbean imports, which were themselves threatened by the 2005 end of US and EU quota shares and an expected surge of shipments from China, India, and Pakistan. The overall 2004 trade imbalance of $618 billion and Current Account Deficit $30 billion more persuaded many politicians that further corrective measures must be taken.

First choice to level out the export-import playing field and give all countries a chance to compete fairly was negotiations through the WTO. However, talks that began in Seattle in 1999 and continued in Doha, Qatar in 2001 for a comprehensive agreement broke down in Cancun, Mexico two years later. A bloc led by Brazil, India, and South Africa insisted that industrialized country agricultural subsidies hurting their exports be immediately terminated. While the Bush administration agreed to cut agricultural tariffs to a world average of 25%, down from 62%, a complete cut was as politically impossible in the US as in Europe and Japan unless global trade in telecommunications, securities dealing, data processors, banks, express-delivery, oil drilling, software, and other such areas in which the US claimed an aggregate 37.5% share was boosted annually by $1.2 trillion by eliminating tariffs altogether. Washington proposed as well to phase down manufacturing tariffs to a world 8% average by 2010 while eliminating all tariffs currently at 5%. Because forsaking protectionism was too much for weaker Third World economies to stomach, the US would continue to be protected by a 20% average duty on imported textiles, footwear, and luggage accounting for 47% of all US tariff collections.

While preferring to revive WTO talks, the EU continued with plans to expand from 15 to 25 members with the addition of Cyprus, the Czech Republic, Slovakia, Estonia, Hungary, Latvia, Lithuania, Estonia, Malta, Poland, and Slovenia. The EU would thus encompass 444 million people with GDP of $8.4 trillion. By contrast, NAFTA had 387 million and GDP approaching $12.5 trillion. Instead of spending all efforts on further WTO negotiations, Washington intended to continue a side strategy of concluding bilateral trade agreements with willing nations around the globe.

For example, in June 2003, the Bush administration signed a trade treaty with Chile to permit duty-free shipment of 95% of Chilean goods into the US and 90% of US goods the other way. Chileans thus won the immediate right to export copper, fruit, jams, and other commodities while the US exported computers, mining machinery, and cars. Tariffs on US poultry, dairy, and other agricultural products would be eliminated over a dozen years, as would tariffs on remaining Chilean exports. The agreement would serve as a model for other treaties with Latin American countries.

Specifically, the Bush administration negotiated a Central Americas Free Trade Zone to boost exports to the countries of that region from $9 billion annually and imports up from $11 billion. An even larger ambition was to forge an Americas Free Trade Zone encompassing all countries except Cuba in the Western Hemisphere. Hanging over the heads of Central and South American as well as Caribbean countries relying on textile exports to the US was the fact that import quotas on Chinese textile imports expired end of 2004. Unless Argentina, Brazil, and other populous states reduced or eliminated tariffs averaging 15% but running as high as 50% on US manufactured goods, Washington would allow Chinese textiles to replace Latin American. To forestall that scenario, Latin American governments had to open markets for services, including by US banks, law firms, accounting firms, and express delivery companies. An Americas Free Trade Zone would permit US private companies to bid additionally on foreign government contracts and vice

World Trade Center, New York City

versa. But severe debt crises in Argentina, Brazil, and other countries had caused high inflation and recession that had reduced *per capita* income from an average of $4,200 in 1998 to only $3,200 four years later. Latin Americans simply could not afford even to match the $155 billion annually, accounting for 37% of US exports, taken in at their peak.

For that reason, the US was also pursuing bilateral trade agreements around the world. Because Congress on August 1, 2002 returned *Fast Track Authority* to the President, more successes such as the Chilean treaty and one made with Singapore were envisioned. Given the fact that US economic interests often ran counter to those of otherwise friendly countries, negotiations even with staunch allies were likely to prove complicated. While backing the US war in Iraq, for example, the Australian government was chagrined to discover that US occupation of that country had reopened the door for US wheat farmers to penetrate that country's $480 million annual grain market. Under a decade-long U.N. oil-for-food program, Australia had dominated the trade. Because GDP of $550 billion was only about 4.7% as large as the US economy, America's ally Down Under could ill afford an export loss of that size.

BATTLES ROYAL OVER AGRICULTURE AND FORESTRY

At first blush, it seems odd that trade in farm commodities would cause such a ruckus in the US. While farm cash receipts in 1990 were substantial at $170 billion, including about $40 billion each for cattle and corn and half as much for milk, farming as an industry had declined to only 1.9% of the economy and would slide even further to only 1.35% by end of the decade. The number of persons engaged in farming had plunged to less than 4.6 million, about 1.9% of the population, on 2.1 million farms covering 963 million acres. Only 1.3 million family farms remained.

On the other hand, consumers spent $440 billion in food stores. The food processing industry generated $125 billion of value-added revenue while employing over 1.5 million people. Eating and drinking establishments chipped in another $280 billion to final GDP while employing over 7.5 million workers. All businesses combined that used farm products and sold farm-related equipment accounted for nearly one-eighth of GDP and one-sixth of US jobs.

U.S. **Containers/Packaging** Companies 2004
Comparison of MC/AR to Employment

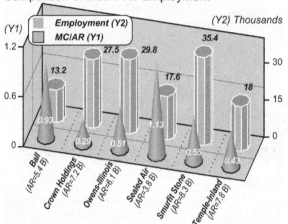

Likewise, the fact that US livestock and crop production as a percent of world totals had fallen and would diminish further was deceptive. By 1998, the republic possessed one-sixteenth of 1.5 billion head of cattle, down from 9.4% in 1990, a similar percent of 956 million hogs, and below 1% of sheep. Yet US share of world annual production of beef had increased slightly to 21.8% of the global total of 54 million metric tons. Ranching accounted for 20% of all farm income. Although US share of world annual production of chickens had fallen 5% since 1990, the republic still accounted for almost one quarter. All these figures did not take into account the fact that US agribusinesses owned livestock and food processing plants around the world.

No wonder that Congress in the Food, Agriculture, Conservation, and Trade Act of November 28, 1990 retained for another five years price supports for milk and sugar. Tariffs and guaranteed minimum prices were imposed on wheat, coarse grains (that is, corn, barley, and sorghum), soybeans, rice, and upland cotton for farmers who agreed to an area reduction program that kept up to 20% of fields unused, depending upon the size of national surpluses. On the other hand, farm price and income supports were frozen at current levels. A triple base-average plan was put in place in which 15% of farm land was ineligible for crop subsidies, though farmers could grow for market other crops than those qualifying for subsidies.

The law had the effect of cutting wheat production 28% to 54 million tons. However, still large surpluses combined with recession-induced lower demand caused the price per ton to fall 18% to $112. The only saving grace was export of 28 million tons accounting for nearly 30% of world wheat exports. A 5.8% drop in corn production to 190 million tons with similar low prices wounded farmers.

Political pressure to do something for Great Plains states with disproportionate share of US farm production, and two US senators per state, became intense. Following the election of 1992, the Clinton administration decided that a partial solution, beneficial also for the trade imbalance, the US Merchant Marine, and port system, was to accelerate food aid to poor countries. When famine afflicted millions in the East African states of Ethiopia and Somalia, the Agriculture Department drew down surplus grain stored by the government, and once those stockpiles were reduced bought commodities on the open market to ship overseas. In that manner, total US food aid to Ethiopia alone reached an annual $500 million while the US share of world wheat exports peaked in 1997 at over one-third.

However, after the Democrats lost the 1994 mid-term election, power to set agricultural policy fell into more conservative hands. Republicans decided to push for a Freedom to Farm Act to get Washington out of the business of acting as a buyer of last resort to support prices. When the law passed in 1996, it cut subsidies not to farm by $2 billion (except for sugar, peanuts, and tobacco), ended subsidies to farmers to store grain, and reduced funding for export programs to a lower level. The US government still maintained a 4 million ton grain reserve.

With farm prices up between 1993 and 1997, subsidies averaged $8.5 billion annually. However, despite the Freedom to Farm Act, they skyrocketed to an annual average of $20.6 billion from 1998 to 2002 because exports contracted in the wake of the Asian financial crisis, farm prices declined, and the law contained a direct payment component to compensate farm operators, rich or poor, corporate or family, for market prices that did not meet fixed guarantee prices. In a vain attempt to lift prices and alleviate the federal burden, the Clinton administration tripled food aid in 1999, including a donation of $250 million of wheat to Russia to defeat attempts by European and Australian competitors to win market share. Food aid peaking at $2.6 billion in 2002, out of a $10 billion total foreign aid package, was insufficient to prevent the US share of world wheat exports from plunging nearly to one-fifth.

In 2002, Congress again attempted to gain control of farm subsidies for 15 major crops, including corn, wheat, soybeans, and cotton by passing legislation to cap direct payments to farmers at $360,000, which the Bush administration proposed in 2005 to lower to $250,000. However, a loophole permitted direct payments up to 60 cents above guarantee prices regardless of the $360,000 limit. That opened the door to opportunists to expand acreage. If prices fell dramatically as a consequence, the government would be on the hook for considerably more than the projected tab of $124.6 billion over six years. In the final analysis, the program's overall effectiveness was contingent upon fluctuations in national and world supply and demand. As it turned out over the first three years of the program, only $37 billion was spent, $15 billion less than expected. The reason was soaring commodity prices.

For example, although the soybean guaranty price for annual production expected to come in around 2.5 billion bushels, equal to 75 million metric tons, was cut from $5.26 per bushel to $5.00, a sudden surge in Chinese demand absorbed surpluses. In 2004, prices were kicked up beyond $7 per bushel toward $10 per bushel, limiting the cumulative, three year subsidy to $4 billion. Corn, where the guarantee price for an expected bumper crop of 10.1 billion bushels was raised from $1.89 per bushel to $1.98 for 2003-2004, then reduced to $1.95 through 2007, was exceeded by a market price around $2.40 per bushel, projecting a subsidy of a couple billion dollars. Wheat, with guaranty price for an equally impressive 3.1 billion bushel harvest boosted from $2.58 per bushel to $2.80, then eased down to $2.75 in the same time schedule as corn, was well below the market price range hovering near $3.50.

Soybeans, in particular, had become an important crop for high-protein feeds, meals, and foods. The US supplied roughly half the world production in the 1990s. Complaining of genetically engineered strains, the Europeans took steps to inhibit US imports and favor their own soybean farmers. Shipments to Europe were cut in half over five years to only $1 billion in 2003 because of the EU stand, but fortunately Chinese demand skyrocketed. However, the Old World suddenly reversed course in 2004 out of fear of falling too far behind in bio-technology of food. Some US imports would be permitted.

Harvesting soybeans
(courtesy Pioneer, a DuPont company)

As for cotton, a tremendous global oversupply had driven prices down from a profitable $1.18 per pound in 1995 to as low as $0.30 in spring 2003 before coming back up to $0.75. Although the guaranty price for 20.3 million, 480 pound bales, or 9.75 billion pounds, was cut from $0.58 cents per pound to $0.50, Washington's liability was still substantial. With an added financial incentive to keep acreage under production in the form of $300,000 mechanical cotton pickers, US cotton producers with average net worth of $800,000 were certain to plant and harvest the maximum. Tens of millions of dirt-poor farmers from China, Pakistan, and Africa, too, needed to produce as much as possible to scratch out a living from prices as low on the latter land mass as 11 cents a pound.

Deere mechanical cotton picker
Out-of-control payments to farmers convinced the Bush administration that an international agreement must be forged to cut subsidies. Although the worst offender was the EU at $93 billion of annual farm subsidies in 2002, US federal and state governments paid out $50 billion, the Japanese handed over $47 billion, and all other industrialized countries combined contributed another $40 billion. Therefore, Washington proposed to cut farm tariffs in five years to a world-wide average of 15%. A limit would be set as well on EU export subsidies amounting to $2 billion annually to only $20 million for the United States. Since the farm sector was picking up again after a five year slump, the time seemed to be propitious for all parties to

come together. Even without a deal, value of US farm production hit $270 billion in 2004, a fifth from beef sales, while net farm income was a record $73.6 billion.

However, there was considerable doubt that the smaller and less efficient European and Japanese farm operations would be able and willing to take full patent advantage of innovations to improve production and competitiveness. Although the French had come up with the *sous vide* technique for vacuum packaging of raw or semi-cooked ingredients prior to cooking and pasteurizing processes, the EU was fundamentally conservative in its thinking about what went into the food chain. Specifically, the organization feared adverse health effects from US bio-engineered and irradiated foods. Americans suspected that a moratorium slapped on hormone treated beef was motivated more by political consider-ations than science and protested to the WTO for retaliatory fines. As in the US, the political leverage of Europe's and Japan's farmers far outweighed their direct economic importance. From both a national security and psychological perspective, no country wanted to be dependent upon outsiders for food.

And yet because of the global reach of US agri-busi-nesses many were. By far the largest US agri-business and still the biggest privately held company in the world was Cargill. In the second half of the 1990s, management purchased Vineyard, a maker of specialty food-corn hybrids used in corn chips, tacos, tortillas, and breakfast cereals, sold its broiler operations to Tyson while buying that company's pork operations in Missouri, took over Akzo Salt to become one of world's largest salt production and marketing companies, and acquired Continental Grain Company, a New York firm

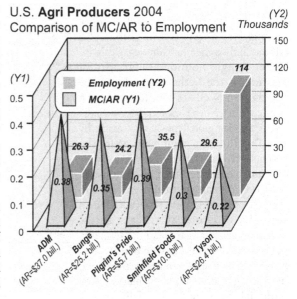

actually founded in Belgium in 1813 which stored, transported, exported, and traded grain not only in North America but Europe, Latin America, and Asia. The company's Nebraska subsidiary Cargill Dow Polymers produced corn-derived dextrose to make polymers for fibers, plastic packaging, and other products. Annual revenues surged toward $62.9 billion in 2004. Employment for 101,000 and other overhead expenses held profits to little more than 2.1% of that figure.

Before purchasing Cargill's chicken operations, Tyson bought Cobb's from Upjohn in 1994. Nine years later, the company processed over 2 billion chickens, 17 million hogs, and 10 million cattle. Next largest in chickens was Pilgrim's Pride of Texas, which in 2003 bought ConAgra's chicken division for $590 million to raise annual revenue to $3 billion. High expenses, including wages and salaries, restrained profitability for both companies.

Genealogy of Farm Equipment Makers, 1961-2004

Slightly larger than Tyson, ADM was also more successful. After expanding production of crystalline fructose, a sweetener that gives a sustained release of energy without a sugar crash, sorbitol, a low calorie additive for cough drops and candies that does not promote tooth decay, and maltodextrins, digestible carbohydrates made from corn starch, the company came by 2000 to use 550 million bushels of corn annually in the US, Europe, Asia, and Latin America. A $100 million fine was levied by the government in 1997 for price fixing lysene feed and citric acid flavor additives, but more serious was competition globally in oilseed and soybeans from vegetable oil leader Bunge. Founded originally in Amsterdam, the Netherlands in 1818, the company moved its headquarters to White Plains, New York in 1999.

A similar global push was made by John Deere in farm equipment. With the US market for tractors unlikely to increase very much over the 10.5 million in use in 1990, the company put time, energy, and resources into generating $3 billion annually of overseas tractor sales, including market share lead in Germany. Deere placed even greater priority on expanding its primacy in the fast-growing lawn and garden equipment market. Key acquisitions were SABO of Europe, a maker of lawn mowers, and Textron's Homelite division, specializing in handheld outdoor power equipment. After bringing out *Sabre* brand, mid-priced lawn tractors and walk-behind mowers to sell through national retailers, home centers, and John Deere dealerships, the company achieved $1 billion of profits in 1998. Although farm economy woes then slowed big equipment sales such as of

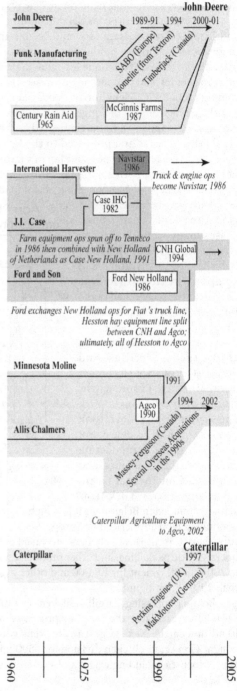

$110,000 combines, purchase in 2000 of Timberjack, producer of forestry equipment, advanced annual revenues.

Deere's move into forestry equipment was a bet that restrictions on lumbering operations on 192 million acres of federal lands, tightened substantially by the Clinton administration in the 1990s, would be eased by the younger Bush. Under an *Econo-System* management policy instituted by the Forest Service in 1993 and applauded by environmental groups, forest thinning to remove excess fire hazards had been abandoned. The consequence was a worsening fire situation that claimed, for example, 35,000 acres in northern California in 1995 increasing to 90,000 acres in 1999. The year 2000 witnessed a total of 8.4 million acres of forest destroyed by fire, costing $3 billion in control and recovery costs, the worst record since the 1950s. On his way out of office in January 2001, Clinton signed an executive order banning logging and road building on 58 million acres of national forest. Previous moves restricting other federal lands from development were a major reason that Clinton's would-be successor Gore lost all western states except California, Oregon, Washington, and New Mexico to Bush in the 2000 election.

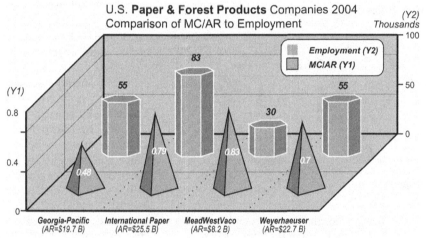

U.S. **Paper & Forest Products** Companies 2004
Comparison of MC/AR to Employment

In point of fact, much of the difficulty experienced by big lumber and paper companies was self-inflicted, rather than the responsibility of over-eager tree-lovers. They added capacity at a moment when the 1990-91 recession was about to strike. Thus as US lumber production surged toward 67 million cubic meters of soft wood and 33 million cubic meters of hard wood in 1997 and paper and pulp production hit 86.5 million tons, roughly 29% of world production, profitability plunged. Georgia-Pacific did not see black ink again for two years. In the interim the company exceeded $14 billion in sales by emulating Weyerhaeuser's development of engineered wood products. Once lumber prices shot up over a third at decade's end, G-P went on a buying binge that peaked with the 2000 takeover of Fort James Corporation, maker of *Brawny, Quilted Northern,* and *Dixie* cup products. Divestiture of commercial tissue, printing and imaging paper, and paper distribution operations combined with *Brawny's* decline toward 10% of the $3 billion US paper towel market, one-third dominated by P&G's *Bounty,* kept revenue growth restrained.

As the industry leader, and with better diversification, IP was much better positioned to impress investors. The company bounced back from the early decade recession to grow and buy its way from $15 billion of revenues in 1993 to $20 billion by 1996. Major acquisition was Carter Holt Harvey of New Zealand and Australia, a manufacturer of pulp, paper, tissue, container board, and wood products. That company also controlled 1 million acres of forest land. When paper sales stagnated, IP shifted production to specialty panels. A new buying binge brought Federal Paper Board for $3.4 billion in 1996, Union Camp for $5.9 billion in 1999, and Shorewood Packaging and Champion International for a combined $7.3 billion in 2002.

Weyerhaeuser followed IP into New Zealand in 1997. Management bought up 193,000 acres of forest land out of that island country's 43 million. Contrary to the situation in the US, environmentalists did not mind the American invasion because the tracts in question had been used decades earlier for sheep-farming, had been replanted with pines and firs, and did not constitute old growth forest in pristine condition. But back in the US, an $8 billion hostile takeover of Willamette Industries was so expensive that Weyerhaeuser had to close 32 mills and sell off 4% of company timberlands.

U.S. **Office Products Retailers** 2004
Comparison of MC/AR to Employment

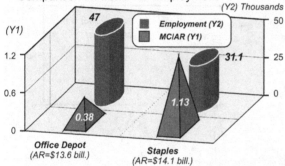

In 2002, Mead and Westvaco merged into a Stamford, Connecticut based company with higher-value coated and specialty papers as well as specialty chemicals operations added to the usual pulp and paper business. By contrast, Boise Cascade of Idaho derived revenue from office supplies and paper, packaging and building materials, and lumbering on 2.4 million acres in North America, Australia, and New Zealand. In 2003, the company bought OfficeMax and its 1,000 stores generating $4.3 billion in annual sales for $1.1 billion. Keeping the OfficeMax name, management then sold off the Boise Cascade timber and mill holdings to a private investor group for $3.7 billion.

The ups-and-downs of OfficeMax left Office Depot and Staples as the two largest independent office products stores still standing. The former tried to gain an industry advantage by launching its *Viking* brand of products in Europe and through Internet sales. However, Staples business model, including next day delivery of Internet and phone orders, proved superior. Although its attempt in 1996 to buy its chief rival for $3.5 billion was blocked by government anti-trust concerns and Office Depot succeeded in buying Guilbert of France, Staples had slightly more revenue.

An even better business than selling office products was producing them for sale. With headquarters economies of scale provided by a big conglomerate operation, 3M came up with innovative products such as *Post-it Notes* as "temporarily permanent" book markers as well as industrial capital goods to earn superior profits.

CHAPTER XVI. AS GOES CONSUMER SPENDING SO GOES THE ECONOMY

In the 1990s, household spending on consumer durables and non-durables, appliances and toys, clothing and sporting goods, household products and food, in other words tangible products excluding homes and other structures, came to account for over 38% of the economy. For that reason, business inventory on hand continued to rise from $950 billion in 1990 to $1.4 trillion a decade later. Venues to obtain goods ranged from department stores to specialty retailers to supermarkets to superstores to restaurants. Manufacturing establishments plus retail and wholesale operations employed over 55 million people.

Consumer durables were a bell-weather category because, like houses and motor vehicles, purchase of household appliances, electronics, computers, and other items transformed financial into tangible assets, albeit of a depreciating kind. After the recession of 1991, the sound of sales registers ringing up remained strong and clear for the rest of the decade with household assets of such products, including automobiles, climbing nearly 50% to $2.7 trillion. However, in 2001, durable goods purchases dropped 13% to $176 billion. An advance toward $3.6 trillion of household consumer durable assets by end of 2004 was only possible because of the fantastic incentives for car purchases.

More reliable for revenue and profit growth projections were products for children. The Baby Boom generation experienced its own baby boom to increase the mass market for toys, clothes, and school supplies toward 75 million boys and girls under age 18. As the overall population exceeded 295 million, household products and food sectors were all but immune to the new century economic slowdown. The number of successful companies in non-durables was quite large.

However, bigger producers and retailers of ubiquitous items obtained an ever increasing advantage over smaller players because of national and global economies of scale. Only the attraction and quality of brand name products as well as expertise in specialized niches prevented P&G, Coca-Cola, Altria's Kraft, and other powerful companies, possessed of their own leading brands, from crushing smaller, less diversified entities. In the long run, the largely unregulated environment for non-durables must lead to the kind of consolidation forced by the economics of consumer durable sectors. A trend did develop

in the 1990s for non-branded and discount products sold through Wal-Mart and other larger retailers and wholesalers to cut into the market share of brand name makers of household and food products.

COMPETITION NARROWS AND INTENSIFIES IN CONSUMER DURABLES

The market for large household appliances in the period was now controlled by a few large US producers challenged by medium-size companies with questionable prospects. Foreign competitors struggled at first with high transportation costs for bulkier items as well as distribution difficulties. GE with its conglomerate size was the strongest financial entity, of course, but Whirlpool had an equally popular brand name. Cutting costs with overseas production and belatedly a washing machine model priced as low as $150 for Brazil, China, and other developing countries, the latter company bought the second largest appliance maker in Mexico.

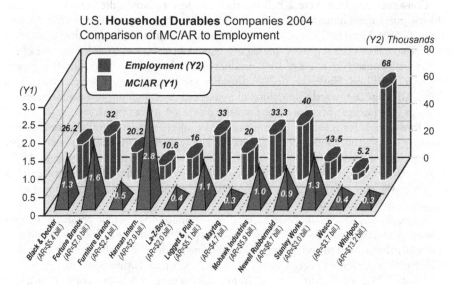

U.S. **Household Durables** Companies 2004
Comparison of MC/AR to Employment

Maytag, by comparison, stayed at home to acquire Blodgett in 1997 and Amana Appliance and Commercial Cooking from privately held Goodman Manufacturing of Houston four years later. Goodman had obtained Amana, including the air conditioning and heating units which it retained, in 1997. Despite moving toward a strategy of buying GE motors made in China and wiring in Mexico for final assembly in the US, Maytag was hurt by the challenge of cheaper appliances such as vacuum cleaners priced below $100 to undercut its *Hoover* premium line, produced by union labor in Ohio. The entry of Haier of China into the US market, for example to sell air conditioners in Best Buy for under $70 and negotiate to market larger appliances through Wal-Mart's and other mega-stores, also took a toll. Likewise, the position of Wesco International, owner of the *White-Westinghouse* full line of home appliances, with a value after a 1999 IPO of $1.1 billion, was precarious. Despite annual 2004 sales topping $3.7 billion, the company's economies of scale were insufficient to profit greater than 1.75% of sales in an increasingly competitive environment.

Whirlpool washer-drier
As for the $113 billion US market in 2004 for consumer electronics, LG Electronics of South Korea was an up-and-comer. By far the biggest foreign competitors, however, were Philips Electronics of the Netherlands and the Japanese companies Sony, Toshiba, Matsushita Electric Industrial, owner of the *Panasonic* brand, and Fuji. Whenever new consumer technology came along, these companies were in the forefront. They claimed, for example, the lion's share of 85 million digital video disc (DVD) players sold in the US between 1997 and 2004, 42 million in the final two years of that period alone. In fact, the DVD business was the fastest growing consumer technology. Prices for high-end, progressive scan DVD players with many features plunged below $200 while low-end models were obtainable by Christmas 2004 for less than $50. The average price of new movie DVDs fell from $29.95 to less than $20. Older movie discs could be obtained at Wal-Mart, Target, Kmart, and other discounters for less than $8. Thus, 2004 revenue of $15 billion from DVD sales and rentals exceeded movie theater revenue by 60%. Half of households with TVs regularly watched DVDs.

Computer makers tried to jump on the bandwagon by selling DVD players incorporated into personal computers. RadioShack was more successful selling DVDs separately. The company's strategy was to stay with brand leaders of whatever kind, including HP computers, and Sprint and Verizon wireless phones. One reason for that competitive retail environment was the power of Best Buy. With over 400 stores, management was on the

cutting edge of marketing technique by using electronic game software as well as CD and DVD discs to draw in customers.

U.S. **Home Electronics Retailers** 2004
Comparison of MC/AR to Employment

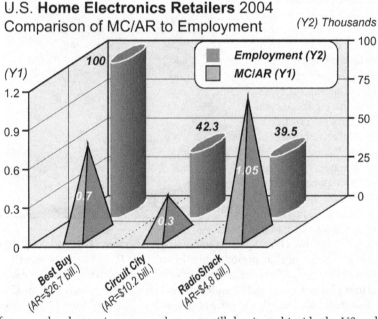

Of course, the electronic game market was still dominated inside the US and out by Japanese companies Nintendo and Sony. During the period, they switched over from 16-bit cartridges to CDs for game software such as Sony's *Mortal Combat*, which served as a metaphor for the industry battle. Fearing that Nintendo's *GameCube* and Sony's *PlayStation* might evolve into alternatives for Internet connection and playing movies and music, Microsoft ginned up an *XBox* priced below $150. By 2004, electronic game hardware was an $10 billion revenue business in the US while electronic game software on video game consoles, computers, and portable devices, discussed in the next chapter, accounted for an additional $7.3 billion.

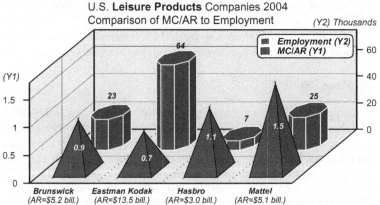

U.S. **Leisure Products** Companies 2004
Comparison of MC/AR to Employment

The toy market in the US, by contrast, grew to over $20 billion. Hasbro took the industry lead briefly after buying Tonka for $500 million in 1991. But Mattel surged back to first place with a $2.5 billion acquisition of Fischer-Price two years later, bringing in-house another $800 million in annual sales, four-fifths what the *Barbie* line did by itself in a single year. Other critical hits were *Hot Wheels* and Disney licensed merchandise. Particularly after the movie studio scored with the animated film *Lion King* in 1994 and *Pocahontas* the next year, Hasbro's licensing of *Star Wars* figures could not keep up. In 1995, Mattel even made a hostile offer of $5.2 billion for Hasbro that was rejected.

The fundamental difference between the business models of Mattel and Hasbro was that the former derived 85% of its revenues from just a few high-profile lines while the latter had no product line accounting for more than 5% of sales. However, excessive reliance by Mattel on *Barbie* and other mega-brands made diversification of revenues wise. For the Christmas season of 1996, the company won the right to distribute 700,000 *Cabbage Patch Kids Snacktime* dolls, but battery-powered jaws caused injuries to the hair and fingers of some children and had to be recalled. A sounder decision was purchase the next year for $737 million of Tyco Toys, the third largest US toy-maker, which had just hit the jackpot selling one million *Tickle Me Elmo* dolls that retailed for $30.

Desiring better control of distribution, Mattel started to sell *Barbie* dolls on the Internet. Unfortunately, a decision to buy Learning Channel educational software for $3.8 billion in stock after that company had taken over rival Broderbund for $400 million failed to meet expectations and the subsidiary was sold. The only reason annual company revenues topped $5 billion in 2004 was because of a licensing deal for toys based on the popular *Harry Potter* books by British author G.K. Rawlings and feature films.

Meanwhile, Hasbro built more slowly by purchasing Tiger Electronics, maker of *Furby*, which retailed for $30 but as high as $200 on the Internet as 40 million were sold in the next three years. The toy industry's number two also bought Wizards of the Coast, producing *Pokeman* collectible trading cards. Ultimately, Mattel's stronger brand names yielded higher profitability and cash flow.

Because more and more toys were made cheaply in China while demand soared, good results even for smaller companies were possible. The key, of course, was catching the fancy of the world's children. Bandai Company of Japan delighted little boys in 1993 with *Mighty Morphin Power Rangers*. Little (and big) girls went crazy about *Beanie Babies* three years later so that 100 million were sold. In 2002, privately held MGA Entertainment threatened Mattel's fashion-doll dominance with hip-hop *Bratz* dolls. Mattel's reply with *Flavas* did little to provoke excitement. As well, toys became ubiquitous in stores so that demand from toddlers to grade school kids was generated while parents shopped. TV advertisements continued to draw attention, oftentimes more than network shows.

THE ERA OF MEGA RETAILERS

The undisputed leader of toy retailing at start of the period was Toys'R'Us. After scooping up the defunct Child World and Lionel Leisure chains in 1993 and expanding beyond existing operations in the US, U.K., Germany, France, and Japan to more of Western Europe, share of the global market for toys and video games hit 13%, equal to $8 billion of sales. In the US three years later, the company strengthened its hold on one quarter of the market by taking over Baby Superstores for $376 million. The future seemed rosy. However, the advent of Wal-Mart into the toy retailing business and even failed attempts such as the Internet based e-Toys wounded profitability, as did the recession of 2001 and move by Mattel to broaden its distribution channels. Toy sales of $11.6 billion in 2003 from 800 stores and 65,000 employees were suddenly second to Wal-Mart. To boost Christmas sales and improve future profitability prospects, Toys'R'Us made an agreement with supermarket giant Albertson to put shops into 1,100 Albertson stores and then announced the closing of 182 Kids'R'Us and Imaginarium stores. When 2004 sales came in at a disappointing $11.2 billion, management put the company up for sale. Likewise, KB Toys with 1,400 outlets tried to answer Wal-Mart's challenge by upping its presence in Sears stores eight-fold to 600 shops only to teeter on the edge of bankruptcy. Other specialty toy retailers formed alliances with department stores to preserve their combined 70% share of the US market while department stores tried to inch up from just 5%.

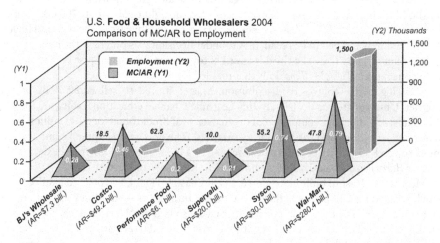

U.S. **Food & Household Wholesalers** 2004
Comparison of MC/AR to Employment

The shadow Wal-Mart cast over the retail and wholesale industries in the 1990s was just enormous. Surging from about $50 billion of annual revenue to $94 billion in 1995, generated from 2,000 stores, 240 super centers, 430 Sam's Club, and 275 international stores employing 675,000 workers, the company brought down many old and revered names, including McCrory's, Ames, Hechinger, and Montgomery Ward. After an adjustment period following the death of founder Sam Walton in 1992, Wal-Mart switched from a North American strategy that accomplished acquisition two years later of 122 Woolco stores in Canada and 96 Cifra establishments in Mexico, to global expansion. Entry into Germany, purchase of 229 ASDA Group stores in the U.K. in 1999, acquisition of a two-thirds stake worth $2 billion in SEIYU of Japan three years later, and continued growth in the US caused annual revenues to jump 275% 1997 to 2004 from 3,500 US and 1,500 foreign stores, or about 0.625% of the world economy. Controlling 30% of household products sales in the US, 19% of grocery sales, 16% of pharmacy sales, one-fifth of CD, DVD, and video sales, and maintaining powerful positions in virtually every other consumer category by carrying name brand products such as *Del Monte, Dial, Clorox, Revlon, Sony, RCA,* and others as well as discount brands, the company squeezed suppliers on costs. Annual purchase of $12 billion worth of goods made in China and restraint on wages and benefits paid to 1.5 million employees contributed to financial success. Although profit margin was only 3.5% of sales, expectation was great that Wal-Mart's tremendous economies of scale would result ultimately in greater cost efficiencies. For example, the company was extremely interested in *Radio Frequency Identification* or *RFID* chips embedded in product packaging to replace bar codes so that inventory handling could be improved and the global labor force cut.

In 1997, Woolworth could no longer stand up to the retail titan. After closing 300 stores and converting another 100 into Foot Lockers, that old and revered company with $9 billion in annual sales was replaced on the DOW Jones Average by Wal-Mart. The company subsequently in 2001 changed its name to Foot Locker. Revenue continued to flow from 3,600 stores, including Ladies Foot Locker, Kids Foot Locker, and Champs, nearly half from sale of *Nike* shoes and apparel.

Wal-Mart's roar also humbled Kmart. From twice Wal-Mart's sales in 1987, the discounter had fallen to 36% in 1995. Refocusing on core operations, the company divested 800 auto service centers, sold off the 22 book store Borders chain in 1992, and spun off two years later OfficeMax and the Sports Authority. Sale in 1997 of 127 Builders Square stores as well as Kmart Canada kept annual revenues at around $35 billion. The best thing Kmart had going for it was *Martha Stewart* products until the author of that line ran into her own problems and went to prison for five months for lying to government prosecutors about an alleged insider trading stock transaction. When the recession of 2001 hit, Kmart had to resort to Chapter 11 protection to salvage 1,500 of 2,100 stores. Sales in 2003 plunged nearly 30%.

By contrast, Sears Roebuck's contraction during the period was not so catastrophic. Peaking at nearly $60 billion of revenue in 1992, the company restructured by selling off its financial services companies. All of Allstate was dispensed with, followed the next year by Coldwell Banker, the Sears Mortgage Banking Group, and 20% of Dean Witter for $4 billion to reduce debt. Another round of consolidation came in 2001 with closure of over seven dozen poorly-performing stores.

Thus the door was opened for Kmart and Sears to be combined by Wall Street hedge fund financier Edward S. Lampert in a 2004 deal in which the former purchased the latter for $11.5 billion. The combined entity kept the Sears name, 3,500 stores, and $55 billion in annual sales.

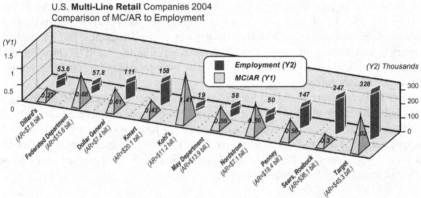

U.S. **Multi-Line Retail** Companies 2004
Comparison of MC/AR to Employment

J.C. Penney suffered a more up and down experience. Hammered by the recession of 1991, revenue declined to $16.3 billion before recovering to $18 billion the next year. When Sears temporarily gave up its catalogue business, J.C. Penney benefited. A $1 billion profit in 1994 helped fund the purchase of more drugstore chains, specifically Rite Aid and Eckerd in 1996, the latter for $3.3 billion, which pushed annual sales to $30 billion. But competition from all angles caused revenues to stall and 44 stores to be closed in 2001. With 2003 sales over $32.3 billion, MC/AR was only 0.2. The company had to cut employment 10% from its 2000 peak of a quarter million and sell Eckerd, with 45% of J.C. Penney's annual revenue, for $4.5 billion to CVS and a French company. In fact, management placed more trust in automated inventory systems for its 1,040 North American stores than people. Replacement men's dress shirts were shipped instantly by TAL Apparel Ltd. of Hong Kong, maker of one in eight dress shirts sold in the US, whenever on-shelf items were sold.

As for companies that attempted to match Wal-Mart's business model, results were mixed. CostCo expanded into Mexico and overseas to increase economies of scale in its wholesale club operations. However, penetration of only 36 states and higher benefits for employees kept revenue well below a fifth of the industry leader and profits less than 10%. Operations were considered quite lean and efficient by analysts and ready for better results with an improving economy.

Likewise, Target wrung out just about as much profitability as possible from domestic operations. Pushing Sears down into fourth place behind Wal-Mart, Home Depot, and itself, the discounter squeezed out profit margin of 4%.

Meanwhile, department store chains also lacked an overseas presence to give added economies of scale. Still, Federated nearly doubled annual revenues to over $13 billion from 330 stores in 1994 with a $4.1 billion purchase of insolvent R.H. Macy. The company went on to buy and consolidate lesser chains, for example in California the next year where the company acquired 82 Broadway, Emporium, and Weinstock department stores for over $2 billion. Unfortunately, management blundered with the purchase in 1999 of direct mail marketer Fingerhut of Minnetonka, Minnesota just as Internet sales were rising to undercut such companies.

May Department Stores did better with smaller acquisitions, including David's Bridal, the largest seller of bridal gowns with a 25% US market share, in 2000. The company's advantage was a work force half as large as Federated's. That fact made May an attractive target for Federated. The transaction was concluded in early 2005 at a price of $11 billion in stock, combining 950 department stores as well as 700 smaller retail establishments generating $30 billion in sales. Other department store chains that felt increasing pressure to combine were Dillard's and Nordstrom. All such operations were aiming to improve profitability and cash flow by re-emphasizing in-house, private brands as allegedly upscale products warranting higher prices.

As with attempts to persuade customers to use department store charge cards rather than bank credit cards, it was questionable whether the strategy would succeed. With the success of *Martha Stewart* and other affordable lines, consumers had gotten used to paying less for clothing, shoes, and accessories, albeit in a market more than doubling in the period from $175 billion of sales toward $400 billion. That was the reason that Kmart but increasingly Wal-Mart, Target, and other successful mega-sellers took greater market share. When cost-conscious shoppers wanted both lower prices and better brand names, albeit overstocks and irregulars, they frequented T.J. Maxx, whose parent TJX bought rival Marshall's to combine 1,843 stores.

The only exception to the trend of consumers using credit and debit cards to make purchases arose in conveniently located neighborhood "dollar stores" with discounts larger than offered by drug stores and supermarkets. Founded in Kentucky in 1955 and expanding over nearly half a century into a 6,000 store chain, Dollar General was the largest. Despite or perhaps because of cash only transactions, the company in 2004 rang up $7.4 billion of sales. With employment of 57,800, MC/AR descended from 1.1 the previous year to 0.9.

Dollar General, T.J. Maxx, and Marshall's stores tended to be modest size establishments in strip malls. With bigger stores, Kohl's was better positioned to sell not only popular brand clothing like *Dockers* for men and discounted brand and private brand apparel but home products. A profit margin pushing 6.3% and plans to add higher margin cosmetics from Estee Lauder pleased Kohl's investors. Estee Lauder risked, however, damaging its premium image with the connection to Kohl.

Because customers had a comfort zone in clothing stores that carried popular brand names, companies that designed and produced such apparel in a mixture of materials, colors, and styles were well regarded by investors. Such a producer was the Jones Apparel Group, which rose from being a behind-the-scenes maker of mid-price clothes for women

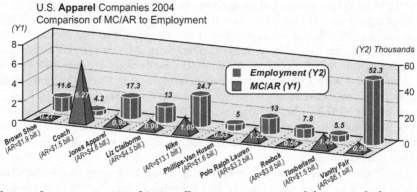

U.S. **Apparel** Companies 2004
Comparison of MC/AR to Employment

with annual revenues in 1995 of $780 million to prominence with licensing deals to make the *Polo Ralph Lauren* brand as well as *Nine West* shoes and *Gloria Vanderbilt* lines, all going into department stores and specialty chains. When Jones and Polo had a falling-out, Jones not only bought the maker of *Anne Klein* women's sportswear and *Kasper* suits for $217 million to make up three-fifths of the $550 in annual sales lost but moved to design its own *Jones Signature* line to compete with *Lauren*, *Calvin Klein*, and the products of Phillips-Van Heusen. That latter firm then bought the Calvin Klein company in early 2003 for $430 million, down from an original asking price of $1 billion, which demonstrates the impact of recessions on profits, cash flow, and market value of consumer products companies.

Reebok ellipse

Other well-thought of designers were Liz Claiborne, doing women's and men's fashion clothes and accessories, and Vanity Fair (VF). VF purchased Chic as well as other companies with popular brand names but divested itself of slower-moving, private label knit and swim wear. By contrast, sales of legendary jeans maker Levi Strauss peaked above $7 billion in 1996 only to crash toward $4 billion by 2003. Because the brand no longer generated consumer excitement and the privately held company's management was slow to sell through Wal-Mart and other discounters, employment had to be cut dramatically toward 12,000. Generally speaking, the renewed push by retailers such as Kmart and Sears, Federated and May, as well as others to combine promised to put downward pressure on the wholesale prices apparel makers could charge for their products. A better business was producing higher-end textiles and accessories with higher margins, yielding more profits and superior valua-tions. For example, maker of women's hand bags and other accessories Coach boasted profit margin over 22%. Because shoes were so easy to make and import, however, Brown Shoe had profit margin one-tenth as great.

An exception was Nike's athletic shoes, supplemented by athletic and casual-wear clothing products. The company kept profit margin over 7% in tough times with overseas production. Competitor Reebok International struggled to keep up with 30% the sales and employment. Timberland's niche in sales of hiking and other rugged foot and clothing apparel proved much more profitable.

Some specialty retailers introduced new brand names to get the public's attention. When the Gap had difficulty keeping up previous growth rates, management introduced an *Old Navy* line, which by 1997 hit $1 billion of annual sales. However, fickle teenage fashion tastes and the 2001 recession caused the 3,100 Gap, Old Navy, and Banana Republic stores operated by the chain in the US as well as 1,100 stores elsewhere to hit a rough patch. Mall locations provided strong enough sales when the economy began to turn around in 2003 to overcome the burden of high employment.

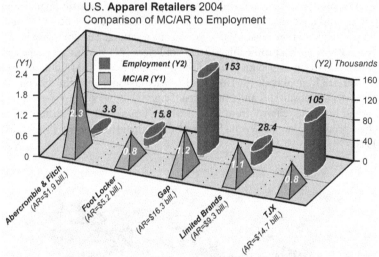

U.S. **Apparel Retailers** 2004
Comparison of MC/AR to Employment

In 1998, Limited Brands spun off Abercrombie & Fitch. Helped by selling *Victoria's Secret* lingerie over the Internet, its 2003 sales for all stores and operations netted profit margin over 8%. Meanwhile, its former unit exceeded expectations. Despite racy ads that offended the general public, Abercrombie & Fitch's profitability was proportionately as high as the Gap, which had nine times the annual revenue.

The NAFTA and WTO agreements greatly accelerated the trend of American com-panies having clothes and apparel made in Mexico, the Caribbean, Central America, and finally the Far East. From $68 billion of revenue in 1996, US textile makers contracted by over one eighth and began for the first time in over half a century to take severe losses. Employment for textiles and apparel makers went into free fall to 687,000 by end of 2004, with an expectation that resort to automation to make sheets, towels, carpets, and other low-end textiles would ultimately cut the work force below a half million. At the peak in 1973, the textile industry alone had employed 1 million persons.

Old textile mills in North Carolina started to close down or seek bankruptcy protection at an alarming rate. For example, Malden Mills, the maker of *Polartec* synthetic fleece for products sold by direct marketers Patagonia and L.L. Bean that had been founded in 1906, fell so heavily into debt that GE Finance cut off credit. Westpoint Stevens, dating from the nineteenth century and producing sheets and towels for *Ralph Lauren, Martha Stewart*, and other lines, could no longer make principal and interest payments on 1.8 billion of debt. Even a belated gamble on automation could not save Pillowtex, maker of *Charisma* sheets and *Royal Velvet* towels, from having to shut down 16 manufacturing and distribution plants. Having imprudently paid $410 million for competitor Fieldcrest Cannon in 1997, the company held out hope that Wal-Mart, the largest seller of its brands, would step in to buy the assets and update the factories. But the old contract of union workers would be null and void.

BASIC STAPLES OF THE CONSUMER ECONOMY THRIVE

With a seemingly endless multiplicity of product lines, fantastic financial and marketing power, and a singularly aggressive attitude, P&G was trying to become to the household products market what Wal-Mart was to retailing. The company increased its dominance in 1992 by high profile introduction of *Pantene Pro-V*, which became the fastest growing shampoo in the world and helped the company reach $30 billion of revenue the next year, over half from outside the US. A series of acquisitions brought the company Max Factor and Betrix in cosmetics and fragrances, Tambrands, maker of *Tampax*, the leading tampon brand in world, Clairol from Bristol-Myers Squibb for $1.6 billion in 2001, and German hair product company Wella for $5.4 billion the next year. Profit margin pushed toward 13%.

The high valuation was recognition that P&G's advertising dollars and savvy could create new niches out of nothing. After building up the *Crest Spin-Brush* electric toothbrush to $200 million of annual revenue over several years, in 2001 the company brought out *Crest Whitestrips* for teeth whitening, almost instantly doing $300 million of annual sales. In 2003, the company purchased the *Glide* dental floss line, loved by dentists because of its shred-resistant, polymer fiber material, from privately held W.L. Gore & Associates, Texas maker of *Gore-Tex* wind-stopping fabric. Management projected that wider distribution of *Glide* products would boost annual sales from $50 million annually and a 25% US share to much higher levels at the expense of market leader J&J's *Reach* product line. If the 80% of Americans who did not floss twice a day and some part of the dentally-challenged world community could be won over to this beneficial activity, sales could increase ten-fold and more. P&G relied on its clout with retailers to open more shelf space for promising products.

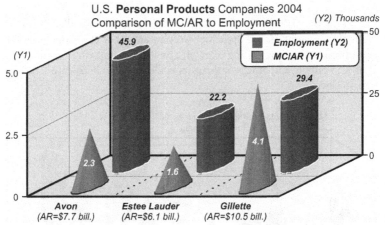

U.S. **Personal Products** Companies 2004
Comparison of MC/AR to Employment *(Y2) Thousands*

Fortunately for P&G, much of J&J's business was in pharmaceuticals and medical instruments, not household products. However, J&J did buy RoC of France in 1993 and the next year Neutrogena to boost its skin and hair care operations into a formidable business. Later in 1999, J&J took over *Aveeno* skin care products with colloidal oatmeal for itchy skin from S.C. Johnson & Son of Racine, Wisconsin. Even P&G had to be wary of taking on such a profitable competitor.

Another prime rival that P&G targeted was Kimberly-Clark. Although the company doubled in size by purchasing Scott Paper in 1995 for $9.4 billion, an attempt to create a new niche with the 2001 roll-out of *Cottonelle Fresh Rollwipes* bombed big time with the American public, which continued to prefer dry tissue. Too, Kimberly-Clark's *Huggies* brand diapers, which years earlier had seized the US market lead from P&G's *Pampers*, saw its share trimmed to less than 44% while P&G, adding *Luvs* to its line, topped 38%. Out of $19 billion of annual global diaper sales, P&G claimed $5 billion while *Huggies* generated $3 billion.

A niche in which P&G allegedly had no plans to compete — except for *Old Spice* after-shave and licensing of the *Noxema* name — was shaving products. Gillette continued to dominate after bringing out the *Mach 3* triple-blade system in 1990. A $300 million ad campaign for a *Mach 3* shaver eight years later helped boost the product line to $1 billion of annual sales. Overall company sales, including from *Duracell* batteries purchased in 1996, produced a profit margin of 14.8%. However, Energizer Holdings outraged Gillette by bringing out to great fanfare the *Schick Quatro* four-blade razor system. Gillette alleged that the new entry violated its patent on each successive blade being angled further from the skin. The company was concerned enough about the challenge to file a law suit and lay off 4,700 employees to cut costs. Management counted on its full product line, including the *Venus* non-disposable razor for women, to hold two-thirds of the market to *Schick*'s 17%. But the management of Energizer Holdings, maker also of *Energizer* batteries, believed that introduction of its *Intuition* 3 blade razor surrounded by soap for women would push annual sales even higher. Ultimately in early 2005, Gillette's management succumbed to a $56.9 billion offer from P&G—suddenly very interested in shaving products—to add another $10.5 billion and 29,000 employees to its industry leading $54 billion and 110,000. P&G's management hoped for greater leverage in dealing with Wal-Mart, source of one-fifth of its sales.

Gillette's *Right Guard* deodorants and antiperspirants for men smelled sweet even after Colgate Palmolive bought *Mennen Speedstick* to compete. That company diversified into cleaning products as well by taking over Murphy's Oil Soap. Dial, sold to Henkel of Germany for $2.5 billion, and other competitors could not match Colgate-Palmolive's size in core soap products.

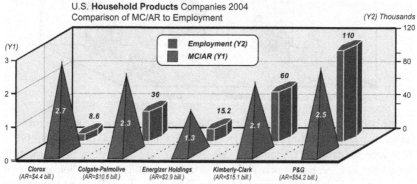

U.S. **Household Products** Companies 2004
Comparison of MC/AR to Employment

Had P&G decided to lather up soap sales, Colgate-Palmolive might not have had such a luxurious good time. However, P&G was more interested in beating back J&J's challenge in the $45 billion US and $100 billion global cosmetics and fragrances market than in putting more resources into basic products. By 2002, the company generated $8 billion in revenues from Clairol and other products in the niche. The world leader in 2004 was France's L'Oreal with $14.5 billion of annual sales. But Avon Products, after repulsing 1990 takeover attempts by AmWay and Mary Kay, rolled on to $5 billion sales by 1997 from 2.5 million independent representatives. A slowing global economy braked growth to an average of 5.5% over the next eight years.

In point of fact, any sizeable company with strong brand names in the unregulated household products industry could, with competent management and restrained employment, establish profitability and cash flow sufficient to warrant market values twice annual revenues. Clorox did so with its main bleach line supplemented by sales of *Glad* bags and wraps, *Black Flag* insecticides, as well as *STP* automotive additives.

Another growing business was lawn care. By 2004, Americans spent about $53 billion on products ranging from soil to lawn-mowers. Scotts had a strong position in lawn and garden nutritional products, including its *Miracle-Gro* line, generating $330 million annually and competing with ServiceMaster's *TruGreen* line. Half its 2004 sales of $2.1 billion came from Home Depot and Wal-Mart cash registers. However, the fastest-growing segment of the industry was lawn-care service. Scotts boosted MC/AR beyond 1.0 by increasing its 4% share of that niche, provoking a regional and national consolidation of what had always been a localized industry, and holding employment to around 4,000.

Despite FDA oversight and legal trouble for cigarette manufacturers, the food products industry was also largely unregulated. The same fundamentals as in household products therefore applied. Diversification was not necessarily essential so long as niche market share was maintained, employment controlled, economies of scale in production achieved, and distribution widened to the world market. However, bigger entities tended to have the best market value to annual revenue ratio.

That realization provoked Kraft General Foods, still owned by Philip Morris, to expand in Europe with acquisitions. Purchase in 1990 of Jacobs Suchard, Swiss maker of confectionary products and coffee, for $3.8 billion followed two years later by takeover of Splendid, largest Italian coffee manufacturer, and the next year Terry's of York, the largest U.K. confectioner, built up Kraft's old continent operation into a consolidated entity of $9 billion of annual sales and 32,000 employees. In 1993, the subsidiary also bought RJR Nabisco's cereal business, including *Shredded Wheat* products. Its ice cream business was sold for $400 million to Unilever, an Anglo-Dutch powerhouse.

Divesting itself of all agri-businesses, Unilever went on in 2000 to buy Bestfoods for $24.3 billion, creating the world's second largest food and consumer products company behind P&G, and the second largest food company behind Nestle of Switzerland. In addition to *Ben & Jerry's* ice cream and *Hellman's* mayonnaise, Unilever controlled the $1 billion plus *Bird's Eye* product line with 5% of the US market in frozen foods. Both American and world sales were impinged, however, by a trend toward healthier, fresher foods. Ironically, so was the *SlimFast* diet food business management acquired for $2.3 billion in 2001 because of the sudden popularity of the *Atkins* low-carbohydrate diet. P&G itself entered that niche after winning FDA approval of *Olestra*, a fat substitute to be used in *Pringles, Frito-Lay*, and *Nabisco* products that the company had developed over 25 years. Nestle, a company with $60 billion of revenues after purchasing 110 year old Ralston Purina, St. Louis leader in pet care, for $10.1 billion in 2001, also was interested in creating healthier variations of some of its 8,000 brands.

Meanwhile, Kraft expanded its presence in Mexico by marketing its *Crystal Light* low-calorie powdered soft drink under the *Clight* name. The company's cheese operations seemed at first so unassailable that Dean Foods, the largest US milk bottler and maker of ice cream, sour cream, other dairy, and soy milk products with annual revenue climbing toward $8 billion, did not bother to make higher value cheese products. However, grocery chains cut into sales with private branded cheese as well as gourmet offerings. The company also had to face the challenge of private label competition in snacks and *Oscar Mayer* cold cuts. One way to reply was with stepped-up advertising, which hurt the bottom line; another was brand extension to new varieties of popular products; a third

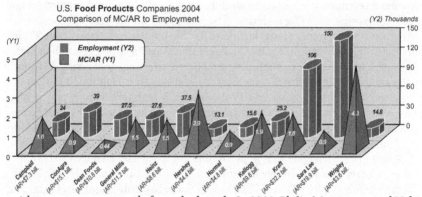

U.S. **Food Products** Companies 2004
Comparison of MC/AR to Employment

was with even stronger control of popular brands. In 2000, Philip Morris acquired Nabisco Holdings to combine *Nabisco* cookies, crackers, and snacks into Kraft. The food group's annual sales hit $21 billion, about one-third the parent company's total, including $8.5 billion from overseas sales. Employment stood at 114,000.

Half of Phillip Morris' revenues came from the sale of cigarettes, including about $19 billion in the United States. The company's dominance of the industry was so great in the early 1990s that a cut in the price of its flag-ship *Marlboro* product had forced second place RJR Nabisco to follow suit. A dark cloud on the horizon had been the 1993 proposal to fund the Clinton health care plan with higher taxes on cigarettes, cigars, and snuff as well as other unhealthful human vices. Even after Congress rejected the plan, because low-price, discount cigarettes built between 1998 and 2003 from a 3% market share to 10%, the company carried through with employment contractions and plant closings. As world-wide cigarette production lifted above 5.5 trillion, half smoked in Asia, requiring 6.3 million metric tons of tobacco, prosperity returned. Although the FDA classified nicotine as an addictive drug, an anti-cigarette campaign in the US reduced consumption only marginally.

On the other hand, law suits for covering up the known addictiveness and dangers of smoking posed a mortal threat to the industry. In 1996, the Liggett Group, the fifth largest US tobacco company with only 2% of the market, had to settle a class action lawsuit by handing over 5% of pretax earnings, capped annually at $50 million, for 25 years. That was followed in 1998 by a Master Settlement Agreement with 46 states for $206 billion on top of $40 billion tentatively agreed to 1997, albeit spread over 25 years. However, California continued to permit smokers to sue tobacco companies, culminating in a $28 billion punitive damage award on top of an $850,000 compensatory verdict by a Los Angeles jury in a lung cancer case. Fortunately for the industry, the judge reduced the punitive portion by 99%, and too, a $145 billion judgment against the tobacco industry by the state of Florida representing the claims of 700,000 Florida smokers was overturned in May 2003 because the group was too diverse. Florida's Third District Court of Appeals ruled that such a huge award would bankrupt the companies.

To pay the states, companies jacked up prices. By 2002, a pack of premium cigarettes cost $3.58, up 90% from 1997. But R.J. Reynolds Tobacco Holdings, now divested of Nabisco, had still to lay off 2,600 employees in Winston-Salem, North Carolina. Despite a 23% share of the US market for cigarettes with its *Camel* and *Salem* brands, the company's problem was that with all the taxes imposed by government, profit on 1,000 cigarettes was down to $5.79, compared to over $21 for Philip Morris. After changing its name to Altria to reflect the growing importance of its food group and to assume a lower profile for its tobacco operations, the latter company had a 50% market share. Therefore, R.J. Reynolds negotiated a merger with British American's Brown & Williamson Tobacco, maker of *Kool*, *Lucky Strike*, and other brands with a 9% market share.

Because marketing branded food products returned greater profits than non-branded, ConAgra bought Beatrice, maker of *Hunt*'s tomato paste, *Wesson* oil, and *Butterball* turkey. The company introduced *Healthy Choice* frozen dinners to supplement its *Banquet* line, and then divested itself of beef, pork, seafood, and cheese operations.

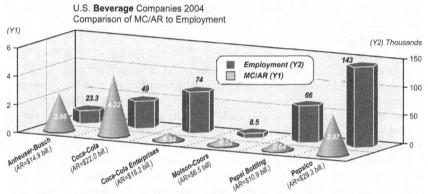

U.S. **Beverage** Companies 2004
Comparison of MC/AR to Employment

Not counting Pepsico and Coca-Cola, the next largest food company for the period was Sara Lee. Management attempted to generate more profits by strengthening clothing and household products groups, first with purchase of *Playtex* apparel, next by acquisition from SmithKline Beecham of assorted bath and body care brands. Although more acquisitions in Europe brought annual revenues to a $20 billion peak in 1998, the sprawling nature of the company's operations in Latin America, Europe, and the Philippines proved costly and unwieldy. Setbacks such as a recall of tainted deli and hot dog meat generated bad publicity and red ink. To raise cash to reduce debt, the company divested the valuable *Coach* line of apparel and accessories as well as bakery businesses in France, India, China, and the U.K. After taking over the Chock full O'Nuts coffee company, several US coffee brands from Nestle, and finally the Earthgrains Company in 2001 to triple remaining bakery sales to $3.4 billion, the comeback strategy was to refocus on core US food and beverage, global intimates and underwear, and household products groups.

Sara Lee baked goods were adversely affected by the healthy and fresh food trend, as was the General Mills *Green Giant* frozen food line. But the latter company firmed up business by purchasing *Chex Mix* snacks and *Chex* cereal from Ralcorp in 1997 and paying $10.5 billion for Pillsbury from Diageo three years later to reach an apparent $13 billion in annual sales. Unfortunately, revenue fell back with the recession to $10.8 billion. The FTC questioned the company's accounting practices. Nevertheless, *Wheaties*, *Cheerios*, *Betty Crocker*, and General Mills' other brands were too popular to be brought down by irregularities.

Boasting the even more powerful *Corn Flakes* brand but without the baggage was Kellogg. The company surged after buying Keebler Foods Company, the second largest cookie and cracker maker.

Another competitor for General Mills in canned soup and ready-to-eat meals was Campbell Foods. In the 1990s, the company broadened its global reach with acquisitions of premium canned meats, sauces, and soup products in the UK, Mexico, and Germany. But a spin-off in 1998 of Vlasic Foods International and its *Vlasic*, *Swanson*, and *Armour* brands reduced annual sales by $1.4 billion. The company no longer had to compete with Heinz, industry leader in condiments. Sale of its *StarKist* seafood line as well as pet and baby foods to Del Monte Foods also helped refocus management on core operations. In the US, Campbell sold annually 2.5 billion bowls of ready-to-eat tomato, microwavable soups, and *Swanson* chicken broths. Condensed soup products were becoming yearly more important. Campbell did retain *Pepperidge Farm* snacks, *Franco-American* gravies and pastas, *V8* vegetable juices, and *Godiva* chocolates.

By 2004, the US snack market topped $62 billion. Of that figure, $9 billion was chocolate and candy. While Nestle had a 9% share and Mars 27%, the big dog on the block was still Hershey with 43%. Since 1996, the company had fortified its position by purchasing Leaf North America, maker of *Good N Plenty* candies, *Heath Bars*, *Milk Duds*, and *Pay Day*. Hershey had also branched out to take on W.M. Wrigley Jr. Company, largest gum seller, by buying *Super Bubble* from Beatrice. After selling *Ludens* cough drops to Pharmacia, nine-tenths of Hershey's sales originated in North America. Investors liked the fact that the company was moving some production to Mexico where workers earned 10% of the prevailing US wage and the price of sugar was half. But Wrigley consolidated its market position by beating out Hershey, Mars, Nestle, and Cadbury Schweppes for the *Lifesavers* and *Altoid* brands from Kraft. The price was $1.5 billion.

Because most growth in stacks was coming from non-chocolate products, in the long run the only production Hershey, Mars, Tootsie Roll Industries, and other industry players would retain in the US would be higher-value gourmet chocolates. These products accounted for $165 million of exports to Mexico and $560 million to Canada. Too, they would be hard-pressed by more diversified food producers, including Nestle. That company's global operations generated over $74 billion of revenue and employed 250,000 people, good for an MC/AR of 1.5.

Although the Swiss company remained the largest food company in the world, it rated a distant second to Coca-Cola in soft drinks. In fact, the Atlanta legend sold as much in Europe as Nestle, Pepsico, and the fourth place company combined. That position became even more important to Coke as the US soft drink market stagnated briefly at around 183 liters *per capita* and subsequently grew at less than 2%, limiting total sales growth with price increases to roughly 3% annually. Because American consumption of soft drinks was eight to twelve times as great as on the old continent, the potential in Europe for growth was, should European appetite for wine and beer at meal-time slacken, infinitely greater.

Suddenly in the early 1990s, Snapple of New York demonstrated with over $500 million of real brewed bottled tea sales that the healthy food craze would translate to drink. In response, Coca-Cola made alliance with Nestle to market *Nestle* tea while Pepsico linked up with Lipton of Britain. On the soft drink front, a challenge arose in 1993 from Cadbury Schweppes of Britain buying A&W Brands, the sixth largest US soft drink maker, increasing its stake in Dr. Pepper Seven-Up, the third largest, and later in 2000 gaining control of Snapple to make an attempt at becoming a real threat to Coke and Pepsi. Despite the fact that Cadbury Schweppes' North American beverage sales composed about a third of that company's $8.8 billion in 2002 global sales, it was still the two industry leaders who engaged in a global Cola War. While Coke took a leading position in Latin America and the billion plus Chinese consumer market, Pepsi grabbed a one-third share in the billion plus Indian consumer market. Coke took advantage of the 1996 summer Olympics in its home base Atlanta to splurge on $500 million of advertising and marketing and jack up sales.

Chagrined that analysts put the theoretical value of the *Coke* brand at five times the *Pepsi* brand, Pepsico management decided to spin off the company's bottling operations as two separate companies. Annual revenues that had exceeded $30 billion in 1995 were split in 1997 about three quarters to Pepsico and one quarter to Pepsi Bottling. Pepsico also spun off Pizza Hut, Taco Bell, and KFC as Tricon Global Restaurants. The company bought *Tropicana* juice from Seagram for $3.3 billion the next year, introduced *Pepsi-One*, a one calorie drink, and sued Coca-Cola over allegedly anti-competitive practices in the soda fountain business, which Coca-Cola dominated with a two-thirds share by supplying McDonald's and Burger King. Further, Pepsico encouraged the French government to block Coca-Cola's proposed takeover of Orangina to prevent a monopoly in the French soft drink market. Coke recovered from the setback by purchasing the overseas distribution rights to Cadbury Schweppes' products for $1.85 billion.

In 2000, Pepsico took over Quaker Oats, owner of *Gatorade*, for $13.4 billion. After more than half a decade of strenuous effort to increase brand value, management success in condensing employment to 142,000 boosted profitability.

Coke's management, too, saw wisdom in spinning off bottling as Coca-Cola Enterprises. After wrestling away from Pepsico the contract to supply 20,000 restaurants of the privately held Subway chain, its position was even stronger. Yet, Coca-Cola and Pepsico together as well as their separated bottling operations still accounted for less than 20% of all soft drink sales, carbonated and non-carbonated beverages. The Cola War and industry consolidation would continue.

The most popular beverage in the world was beer. The global market, including bottling operations, more than doubled over the period to $382 billion, while the US market, despite increasing excise taxes to pay for sports stadiums and anti-drunk driving campaigns, shot up from $30 billion of annual retail revenue in 1990 to $78 billion in 2002. By far the largest force in America remained Anheuser-Busch with just under 50%

market share from 102 million barrels produced. Next came Adolph Coors, which merged with Molson of Canada in early 2005 to combine $6 billion of sales. Miller, acquired by South African Brewers in 2002 from Philip Morris for $3.6 billion to create SABMiller, fell to third with a declining 18.5% of the market until the low carbohydrate fad favored its *Miller Lite* brand. Imports, led by Corona from Mexico, majority controlled by Anheuser-

Busch, and family-owned Heineken of the Netherlands with nearly $12 billion of annual sales with its *Heineken* and *Amstel Light* brands, claimed 11%, up from 4.4% in 1990. The EU market was actually a quarter bigger by volume. In Germany, *per capita* consumption of beer outpaced the US nearly three to one.

By contrast, the spirits industry was dominated by a foreign-owned firm controlling both foreign and US brands. Diageo sold *Smirnoff* vodka, *Captain Morgan* rum, and *Johnnie Walker* scotch to claim 22% of the American market. All others, including Allied Domecq, marketing *Ballantine's* scotch whiskey and *Kahlua* liqueur and boasting ownership of *Baskin-Robbins* ice cream and *Dunkin' Donuts* pastry chains, Brown-Forman of the US with *Jack Daniel's* and *Southern Comfort*, Bacardi, Schieffelin & Somerset, and Jim Beam, had less than 10%. Total US sales of spirits, which had in most states to be sold in state liquor stores to insure collection of taxes, hit $40 billion in 2002, a bit less than 25% the global market.

Meanwhile, the wine industry had global sales of $100 billion, of which $14 billion was generated in the US. The industry was much more fragmented than beer and spirits, except that in California local producers dominated with two-thirds market share while foreign importers controlled one-quarter. Bottles were sold in establishments as small as specialized wine and cheese shops or as large as Wal-Mart's Sam Club warehouses. Big grocery store chains set aside areas for both wine and beer in states that permitted such sales in groceries.

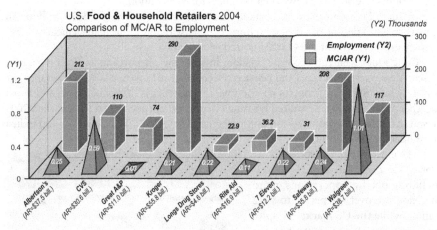

U.S. **Food & Household Retailers** 2004
Comparison of MC/AR to Employment

Briefly in 1998, Albertson's became the largest supermarket chain after buying American Stores for $8.3 billion in stock. Kroger quickly regained the lead with an $8 billion stock and $4.3 billion assumed debt takeover of Fred Meyer, which itself had $2 billion of sales after purchase of Quality Food Centers and Ralph Groceries. Also in 1998, Safeway claimed third place with the purchase of Dominick's Supermarkets. Price competition from Wal-Mart, topping 2004 grocery sales at $60 billion, was the major reason that profits, cash flow, and valuations of supermarket chains were so low.

Regional chains were even worse off. Buying 25 Thriftway stores in Ohio in 1995 and resorting to self-checkout in some stores to hold employment down, Winn-Dixie had to evacuate Texas and Oklahoma and ultimately in early 2005 filed for Chapter 11 bankruptcy protection. The worth of H.E. Butt, expanding from Texas into Mexico in 1997 to run annual revenues to $10.7 billion six years later, might have been better due to employment of only 56,000, but the company was still privately held. The value of Publix, pushing up from a strong base in Florida into South Carolina and Alabama on the way to $18.6 billion of 2004 sales and 125,000 workers, was also not public.

As for other large food sellers, Supervalu bought more regional companies such as Richfood Holdings in the Mid-Atlantic to boost its wholesaling-to-retailing connecting. The company's Sav-A-Lot subsidiary reached 1,000 stores strong in 2002.

A different business model helped privately held wholesaler C&S surge ten-fold to $13.6 billion of 2004 sales with only 12,000 employees. After building up its base in the New England area, the company in 1997 marched not only into New York, Pennsylvania, and Maryland but westward into Ohio by making an agreement to supply Tops Markets. C&S became the third largest wholesaler behind Supervalu and US Food Service, the latter owned by Royal Ahold of the Netherlands. US Food Service bought Parkway and Alliant Exchange in 2001 to reach $19 billion of sales and 34,000 employees.

A perennial problem for food retailers and wholesalers was the American love affair with eating out, or even obtaining take-out food to consume at home. The US restaurant industry generated $270 billion in the recession year of 2001, half from chains. For those who did not want to pay the tab for sit-down service, fast food chains became more numerous than ever. By 2003, there were 277,000 fast food establishments, one for every 1,050 Americans, generating $135 billion in sales, of which $100 billion came from chains.

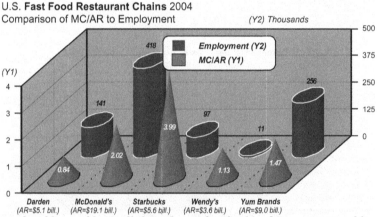

U.S. **Fast Food Restaurant Chains** 2004
Comparison of MC/AR to Employment

Battered and bruised but still the industry fast food leader was McDonald's. After a rough time in the 1990s with attacks from healthy food advocates as well as notoriously poor service, run-down installations, and uninspiring selections, the chain began offering salads and lighter meals to please the calorie-conscious. Overseas, the company continued to attract meat-eaters as geographically apart as in Germany and Brazil. Foreign sales mounted to more than a quarter of all revenues and contributed half of operating income. Competition came in Europe from local eateries but also Burger King restaurants, owned by Texas Pacific Group, an investment group started in 1993 with stakes in airlines, entertainment, food and beverage, healthcare, retail, oil and gas, telecom and technology companies. In a reviving economy, McDonald's 2004 profit margin doubled to 12%.

McDonald's and smaller competitor Wendy's of Columbus Ohio with 9,000 locations in the US and Canada remained mainly monolithic. However, Tricon, renamed Yum brands in 2003, managed 12,300 Pizza Huts, 6,800 Taco Bells, and 11,000 KFC restaurants as well as A&W Root beer stands and Long John Silvers seafood restaurants. A new star in fast food and drink in the 1990s was Starbucks. Helped by sales of decaffeinated coffee to fit with the health trend, the company went global with operations in Japan, Hawaii, and Singapore. After buying British based Seattle Coffee Company's 60 establishments in 1998, Starbucks moved the next year into China, Kuwait, Korea, and Lebanon. An agreement to open 100 shops inside Albertson stores pushed brick and mortar to 2,135 establishments. However, that was only the beginning of a huge expansion to 6,300 locations. Profit margin rose toward 8.2%.

By comparison to fast-food chains, full service restaurants had slightly more annual US sales at $140 billion but less consolidation. Not quite three in ten were part of chains. These included Darden Restaurants, combining 1,200 Red Lobster, Olive Gardens, Bahama Breeze, and Smokey Bones. Restaurant chains attached to hotels did somewhat better because of operating and marketing synergies. They were further pumped up by a US tourist industry that nearly doubled between 1990 and 1993 to $60 billion, and then doubled again by 2003 to compose a fifth of all travel and tourism spending. Specifically, the Howard Johnson chain was revived by expanding foreign operations to over 500 hotels in 14 countries hosting 15 million lodgers. Hospitality Franchise Systems (HFS), parent of Howard Johnson but a subsidiary itself of Blackstone Capital Partners, also came to own Ramada Inns, Days Inns of America, the Super 8 Motel chain, and Resort Condominiums International, an Indianapolis company founded in 1974 to invest in global resorts, vacation timeshares, and whole-ownership condominiums.

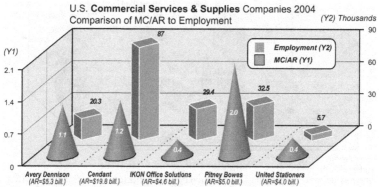

U.S. **Commercial Services & Supplies** Companies 2004
Comparison of MC/AR to Employment

In 1996, HFS also bought Avis and Coldwell Banker from Sears, and Sears' share of the Home Mortgage Network, a computerized loan origination system, to subsume in PHH Mortgage of Cherry Hill, New Jersey. The next year, the company merged with CUC International, an internet marketer of household items from toiletries to appliances that sold memberships in Shoppers Advantage, Travelers Advantage, and other discount buying clubs, to create Cendant. However, accounting troubles revealed in 1998 dropped market value. The holding company's fortunes turned around with a surge in Coldwell Banker's revenue to $10 billion from 25,000 real estate transactions, sparked by falling interest rates. Overall, Cendant produced a profit margin above 9% in 2004. The company also bought the Galileo International global information system founded in 1963 by United Airlines, British Airways, KLM, and others that connected 46,000 travel agencies to airlines, car rental companies, hotels, tour operators and major cruise lines as well in 2004 as on-line travel company Orbitz for $1.25 billion.

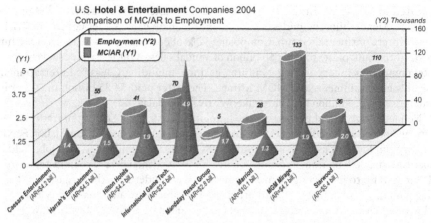

U.S. **Hotel & Entertainment** Companies 2004
Comparison of MC/AR to Employment

Coming on to surpass Cendant briefly was Marriott. In 1995, the company bought Ritz-Carlton, and two years later Renaissance Hotel Group to rise to $8 billion of sales. Investment in 146 senior living communities as well as expansion to 2,300 hotels in 63 countries, including an 8% share in the US, with 200,000 employees helped boost annual revenues to a 2002 peak of $20 billion. Spin off of the senior living group and Marriott Distribution Services cut that figure almost 55%.

Marriott's smaller competitor Starwood bought Sheraton from ITT for $9.8 billion in 1997, but then got into the high-end of the market with acquisition of The Luxury Collection of 60 fine world hotels. Purchase of Westin Hotels and Resorts Worldwide from Japanese investors followed, as did takeover in 1999 of III Corporation, which was renamed Sheraton Holding. A new high-end, boutique hotel chain with modish furnishings called W helped increase 2004 sales.

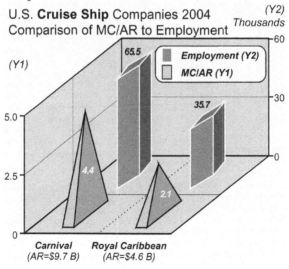

U.S. **Cruise Ship** Companies 2004
Comparison of MC/AR to Employment

In 1999, Hilton Hotels climbed to virtually the same size after buying Phoenix-based Doubletree Hotels, which had combined with Guest Quarters of Boston six years earlier. Marquee properties such as the Beverly Hilton, Hilton New York, and Paris Hilton compensated for lower profitability from Conrad, Doubletree, Embassy, and Hampton holdings. Meanwhile, the mid-scale Holiday Inn chain came under control of British owned InterContinental Group. Composing 90% of company properties, Holiday Inns provided the bulk of the roughly $6 billion of annual sales. A bit less valuable were resort hotel companies incorporating gambling casinos, including Caesar's Entertainment, Harrah's Entertainment, and MGM Mirage. The latter paid $4.85 billion in 2004 plus assumption of $2.8 billion in debt to takeover rival Mandalay.

No matter the mix of properties, the hotel industry was like the retail trade, restaurants, and other old economy service sectors heavily dependent upon manual labor. Service industry employment as a whole provided 39% of the 140.1 million civilian jobs held by Americans in 2004, up from under one quarter in 1990. Although service industry share of GDP moved up to just over 21% from a previous level under 19%, these figures included telecommunications, Internet, and other higher value New and quasi-New Economy industries. Without those sectors, share of GDP would have been significantly lower.

CHAPTER XVII. THE NEW ECONOMY REACHES CRITICAL MASS

The transformation in government policy toward Old Economy industries in the late 1970s and 1980s redounded to the benefit of emerging New Economy industries in the 1990s. The push for deregulation of the transportation sector, in particular, demonstrated that Washington had seen the error of excessive meddlesome ways and would foster technologies fundamental to the republic's success as a global competitor. Although because of the burden of social welfare programs, national security appropriations, and interest on the national debt, the House and Senate were not in a position to provide the same level of financing and other asset-based assistance bestowed upon railroad construction in the nineteenth century, roads and highways in the twentieth, the three branches of the federal government could yet create conditions wherein new technology and industry would flourish. The lion share of funding would come from private business and finance.

The resources available from non-government sources for investment were substantial and growing greater all the time. Not only would the assets of financial institutions rise 270% between 1990 and 2004 to over $35 trillion, but financial assets of non-financial businesses would more than triple to $13 trillion. Corporations might have returned more of this windfall to shareholders had not the bias against dividends built up by Washington's mid-twentieth century policy of high taxation actually increased as taxes came down. Corporate executives realized that earnings on hoarded financial assets were in many cases as important for the bottom line as earnings from continuing operations. Certainly this was the experience of the Big Three automakers as well as GE, John Deere, and many other big industrial companies. A change in dividend policy did not come until government cut taxes on those pay-outs to 15% in the new century.

The problem for companies such as Microsoft that accumulated profits was that there were a limited number of excellent options for investment that would produce the double-digit returns demanded by astute money managers. On the other hand, the first responsibility of manufacturing companies was reinvestment in continuing operations for modernization and improvement. In the context of fending off foreign imports and slashing labor costs, a strong trend emerged toward spending for automation of factories. Annual capital expenditures climbed as a percentage of all wages and salaries paid by manufacturing companies from less than a fifth in 1990 to one quarter a decade later.

Microsoft X-box

When measured in 2004 money, however, annual spending on plant and equipment remained fairly level at around $180 billion before collapsing to only $150 billion in the recession year 2001. Even when taking into consideration widespread automation of office functions with computers, most profits and cash flow were not put back into operations. Rather, a portion was used to cover principal and interest payments on debt built up to fund 1990s mergers and acquisitions. Another portion was allocated to look for other investment opportunities in industries not so oppressed by stiff competition, government regulation, and/or declining fundamentals. These opportunities could be found as well in start-up ventures and new technologies. Just as a century earlier Americans had poured money into the great inventions of electricity, photography, telephones, automobiles, and airplanes, Americans of the last decade of the twentieth century were eager to be in on the ground floor of the "next big thing."

That urge was so strong that one in sixteen Americans was classified as an entrepreneur engaged in starting up a small business for profit. Of that number 90% were so-called opportunity type entrepreneurs, not forced by job loss or other straitened circumstances to gin up income by means other than mainstream employment. The number of entrepreneurs peaked in 2000 before the stock market crash. Even after the recession of 2001, the flame of innovation burned far brighter in the US than in other western industrialized countries and Japan.

To keep the high-technology part of the economy humming, annual spending on research and development topped $200 billion in the late 1990s. Two-thirds was paid for by private industry with most of the remainder contributed by government. The result was better computers and software, a national fiber optics system, state-of-the-art telecommunication satellites, advanced digital technology, genetically improved foods and drugs, unchallengeable military weapons systems, super-efficient automobile prototypes, and stronger, more precise machine tools. Nowhere else in the world was such a variety and abundance of invention and innovation to be found.

That explains why so much money flowed from domestic and foreign sources into the US stock and bond market. This concentration of capital was a bubble in some equities double or triple what was warranted by underlying revenues and profits. As consumer spending on Internet and telecommunication services, computer hardware and software, media and entertainment, rose to unimagined heights, the New Economy took off. Products and services in these sectors came to contribute a tenth of US GDP.

THE INTERNET PHENOMENON

Aside from its own purchases of New Economy products and services, Washington's best contribution to the forward advance of technology was in creating the favorable conditions whereby invention could be turned into industry. When government regulation, albeit for legitimate purposes of protecting citizens and the public interest, became too burdensome, creativity was stifled. One of the wisest collective decisions ever taken by the three branches of the federal government was to protect and foster the development of the Internet, reaching 30 million people in 137 countries by 1993. Not only did the Clinton administration set an example of welcoming telephone-based web connections by installing e-mail capability in the White House in June, but an administration report pushed for creation of high-speed, later called broadband, transmission of information between and among businesses and household personal computers by telephone line, cable connection, and later wireless communication.

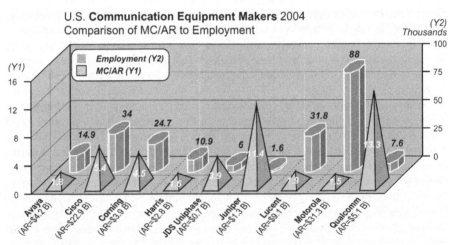

That in turn gave gusto to efforts by various companies to build the hardware infrastructure necessary for seamless operation of the World Wide Web. Early success story making Internet routing and switching equipment through wire phone lines was Cisco Systems. Already by 1992, the company reached $2 billion of annual revenue. Four years later, Cisco exceeded $5 billion of sales with 85% market share, and in 2000 approached $500 billion of market capitalization.

True high-speed Internet service would require new generation systems, however, and that meant fiber optic lines to convey digital video, audio, and text data in light waves. Companies as diverse as Dow Corning, a joint venture of Dow and house ware maker Corning of New York, Qwest Corporation, an innocuous Dallas digital microwave company until taking over SP Telecom from the Southern Pacific Railroad in leveraged buyout and beginning construction of what ultimately became a 104,000 mile fiber optic network, the Williams Communication Group, formed by the Williams Company to run fiber optic cable through decommissioned natural gas pipelines, conglomerate Tyco with an undersea fiber optic network, and AT&T were already building the system. Simultaneously, Cisco, Nortel of Canada, and others began making optical equipment, boosting US revenue from fiber optic technology from $1 billion in 1991 to $2.5 billion the next year. The US market for all advanced ceramics, about four times as large but only a small percentage of the total ceramics market, began to explode.

When in 1996 AT&T decided to raise cash to fund a new strategic plan, discussed below, management spun off its telecommunication equipment division, including the legendary Bell Labs, as Lucent Technologies. With $21.7 billion of annual revenue but 121,000 employees and over $800 billion of loss in 1995, that company went on a $46 billion acquisition binge. The big prize in 1999 was Ascend Communications for $24 billion, leader in data networking equipment for Internet Service Providers (ISPs). Peak revenue of $38.3 billion and profit margin from continuing operations over 14% drove market capitalization up to $287 billion. The future looked even brighter because Bell Labs continued to turn out wondrous inventions. The *Raman Amplifier*, for example, boosted signals in fiber optic lines by transferring energy from a powerful pump beam to a weaker signal beam.

However, it was a collection of aggressive newcomers who challenged bigger names in fiber optics. SDL, E-Tek Dynamics, JDS Fitel, Uniphase, and others competed to make subsystems for fiber optic networks. After the last two entities merged in 1999 as JDS Uniphase, that San Jose, California company offered "one-box" solutions. More acquisitions climaxing in early 2001 with purchase of SDL, E-Tek, and other rivals brought annual revenue to $3.2 billion, though market capitalization was far down from the 1999 peak of $90 billion.

Meanwhile, prospects for prosperous commercial transactions over the burgeoning Internet were greatly improved by the Supreme Court's decision in *Quill Corporation v. North Dakota* on May 26, 1992 that the 7,600 tax jurisdictions in the nation could only tax companies with a nexus in the taxing district, in other words a physical location. Internet businesses operating over the World Wide Web, as well as direct marketers using telephones, thereby obtained a price advantage over brick-and-mortar businesses equal to the state and local taxes paid by those conventional companies. Congress then codified another advantage with the Internet Tax Freedom Act of 1998 that prohibited "multiple or discriminatory" taxes that discouraged Internet use and electronic commerce for at least five years. As revised in 2001, the law eliminated exceptions for Texas and Wisconsin to tax Internet service and for several states to tax phone line digital service links (DSLs), first invented as a faster substitute for dial-up Internet service by Bell Lab scientists in 1989.

Public trust that purchases made on web sites would not prove fraudulent restrained Internet commerce until reputable ISPs as well as Internet portals (IPs) with web sites through which users entered the World Wide Web established themselves. Only then did users browse the Web with confidence through phone line connections and modems peaking at 56K speed with *Navigator* software made by Netscape or Microsoft's *Internet Explorer* to find and patronize legitimate Internet merchandisers. In 1994, AOL reached 1 million customers and expanded not only into Canada but Germany, the U.K., and France. After introducing a flat-rate $19.95 per month pricing plan in December 1996, the company overtook and outdistanced main competitors CompuServe and Prodigy. Within a year, membership surged to 10 million, driving Prodigy out of business. After peaking at 5 million subscribers and then plummeting to half as many, CompuServe was bought by AOL in 1998. By purchasing as well ICQ, an online messaging innovator, and designing its own portal page, AOL surged toward 27 million subscribers in 2000. Total US Internet subscription exceeded 80 million that year, slightly more than half the global figure.

Generation of revenue by ISPs through monthly subscription was straightforward. However, AOL's ability to sell advertisements on its portal page as well as e-commerce web services boosted sales 50% each year. Thus, 2000 revenues approached $8 billion. With operating margin touching 15%, MC/AR soared to an unbelievable 18.0. Reward for such 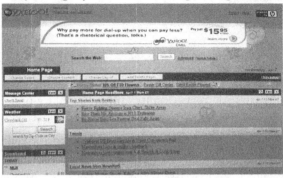 performance was the ability to take over multimedia powerhouse Time Warner in a stock merger. Founder and CEO Steve Case was briefly the man of the hour.

The economics of IP companies was more problematic but equally exciting to investors. Founded in 1994 with only 49 employees but backed by venture capital firm Sequoia Capital, Yahoo built a business model counting in the first instance on advertising dollars, next on search services to web sites, and finally on other services such as audio-video streaming, store hosting and management. Annual sales rose steadily toward a goal of $1 billion. Market capitalization touched $90 billion at its 1999 peak, when by comparison GE, with 200 times more revenue, was rising toward $400 billion.

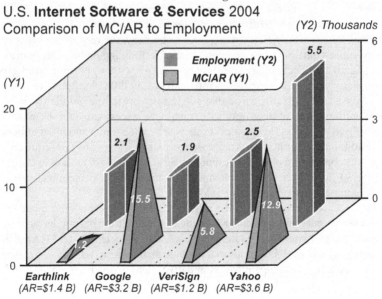

U.S. Internet Software & Services 2004
Comparison of MC/AR to Employment

Much more lucrative in the long run than merely providing ISP and IP service was Internet commerce *per se*, in other words commercial transactions by users. The first seller to make a big splash was Amazon.com, started in 1995 to sell books and later music CDs for non-Internet vendors. In order to speed shipments, the company eventually decided to build up its own inventory. Despite failing to make a profit in any quarter prior to 2002, Amazon.com was a darling of investors, reaching market capitalization of $25 billion in 1999.

For most of the last decade of the twentieth century, the greatest peril to the smooth and profitable functioning of the Internet arose from "hackers" who made a game of gaining access to web server computers of ISPs and causing systems and web sites to crash or otherwise not function properly. For example, a 15-year-old boy from Montreal, Canada with user-name *Mafiaboy* succeeded in bringing down eBay, CNN, Amazon.com, and Yahoo. Each time a system was penetrated, and particularly as the mischief morphed into substantial economic loss, business for companies specializing in Internet, web site, and data security proliferated. Two of the most successful were Sungard Data Systems and Veritas Software. Founded in 1987, the former protected NASDAQ trades passing through its systems and provided remote and on-site disaster recovery service for PCs, mainframes, and servers of large corporate clients. Veritas, on the other hand, was founded in 1989 to provide backup and storage of data based on Unix systems. After a 1997 merger with OpenVision Technologies, the company purchased two years later Seagate's Network and Storage Management Group to diversify into *Windows NT* and *NetWare*.

It turned out, ironically, that cutting-edge technology, the very element that made the Internet possible, contributed to its greatest setback. Building on Bell Labs work, Massachusetts Institute of Technology researchers came up with a photonic band gap micro cavity resonator that split light waves into as many as 100 color bands to magnify the amount of data transmittable through a single fiber optic line. Suddenly in 2000, the world's 39 million miles of fiber optics lines had 90% excess capacity. Demand for new equipment dried up just as the business cycle was heading down and inflated bubbles for Internet and telecommunication stocks were about to burst. The consequence for JDS Uniphase was contraction of annual revenue by 80% to only $676 million in the fiscal year ending June 30, 2003. Even with employment slashed a similar percentage from a high of 29,000, the company lost a cumulative $65 billion.

Likewise, Lucent crash-landed. To raise cash, the company offered a partial IPO of Agere Systems, its microelectronics business, with the intention of completing the spin-off later. Annual R&D spending at Bell Labs was cut two-thirds to $115 million and employment was reduced, but as annual revenue also contracted, those measures were woefully inadequate. The company lost cumulatively $40 billion between 2001 and 2003.

By contrast, Cisco made a dramatic recovery by laying off 11,000 workers, slashing parts and suppliers, diversifying into wireless fidelity (Wi-Fi) equipment, security devices, and other products, and making fewer but better acquisitions. In 2003, for example, management bought Linksys, on the cutting edge of home-networking equipment, to boost profit margin above 20%.

Despite ensuing stock market and recession troubles, US use of the Internet rose by fall 2001 to 115 million or about two-thirds the global total. Because AOL was late jumping on the broadband bandwagon, US market share fell below 30%. Aside from local phone and cable companies, the company also had to contend with MSN, Microsoft's ISP, and Earthlink, allied with Sprint. Into 2003, the industry innovator was able to hold the allegiance of two-thirds of its 35 million subscribers to its relatively slow dial-up service by customizing its portal page with many preset links and options, holding a monopoly on the popular "You've got mail" e-mail announcement, which inspired a 1998 feature film of the same name, and beginning to discount prices.

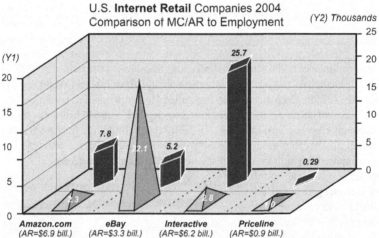

U.S. **Internet Retail** Companies 2004
Comparison of MC/AR to Employment

Another survivor was Yahoo. After a $93 million loss for 2000-2001, the Internet portal resumed its advance while cutting employment. No wonder that AOL, MSN, and other companies providing portal pages, search and other services were determined to increase market share. But it was privately held Google that came out of nowhere with a superior capability for directing browsers to the most popular of millions of web sites to grab 31.5% of the Internet search service business compared to 28.5% for Yahoo and AOL's fifth. When the company finally went public in spring 2004, market capitalization doubled to $50 billion by Christmas on $3.2 billion of ad-driven annual revenue, fewer than 2,000 employees, and superior profitability. Plans to develop software to search files on personal computers even ruffled Microsoft's feathers. A high-profile agreement to scan the holdings of major university research libraries for on-line search pushed expectations as high as Google's valuation.

For Amazon.com, the expectation that profit and cash flow must eventually flow from revenues that jumped toward $7 billion in 2004 caused market capitalization to lift. The strategic plan included a transformation into an "Online shopping mall" selling brand-name clothes, sporting goods, and other products at a discount. No matter that companies like Nike did not want to cheapen their brands, investors were enticed by the prospect of commissions as high as 20% on sales by third parties such as Toys "R" Us. That retailer already did $340 million of business through Amazon.com.

Whether Amazon.com could ever fulfill its promise was unknown. However, a programmer named Pierre Omidyar, who started eBay in 1995, had already constructed a much more profitable business model. The company's purpose was to act as a middleman connecting buyers to sellers in auction bidding and take commissions and fees on an endless variety of new and used goods. The concept was so successful in generating tens, and then hundreds of millions of dollars in annual revenues that eBay went public in 1998. Proceeds of the stock issue helped pay for the acquisition of PayPal, an Internet credit-card charging service, for $1.3 billion. Even after a side-line called Half.com failed to turn a profit and had to be closed down, core operations continued to expand. The $15 billion in merchandise bought through eBay accounted for 14% of all Internet commerce in the US and Europe. With half of all Internet sales made by Americans, e-commerce was growing 40% annually, compared to traditional retail sales of similar items below 3%.

Another successful Internet industry that relied upon commission revenue was travel services. Priceline, Expedia, Hotels.com, and Hotwire.com made their mark acting as middlemen for consumers seeking bargains on airfares, hotels, automobile rental, and other such services. Priceline in particularly was highly valued by investors after a TV advertising campaign featuring William Shatner, the actor who had played Captain

James T. Kirk on the classic science fiction TV show and movie series *Star Trek*. With an early 2000 peak of $23 billion in market capitalization, 163 times as much as annual revenues, the future seemed rosy. However, realization that Priceline, like Amazon.com, would not be profitable any time soon as well as fall-out from the September 11, 2001 terrorist attack, brought the company's stock price crashing down.

By contrast, the upside potential for LendingTree.com seemed more substantial. The company made mortgage loans and acted as a real estate agent while charging only a third of the industry standard 6% commission. Because total US mortgage loans were rising toward $3 trillion annually by the new century and real estate agents scraped in $60 billion annually in fees, the company's $167 million in 2001 revenues were set to grow. That was enough to convince Barry C. Diller, CEO of USA Networks, to include the Internet company in the acquisitions he made when putting together a new e-commerce power-house called InterActiveCorp. First, however, he bought a 64% stake in Expedia from Microsoft. When all was said and done, he grouped together as well Hotels.com, Hotwire.com, City/Search/EPI, the TV-telephone sales based Home Shopping Network, and entertainment event company Ticketmaster. InterActiveCorp's size and clout was such that investors were betting that hotel chains, anxious about the size of the discounts Diller's company was taking, would not be able to reverse the trend. Unlike Priceline, revenues were not solely dependent upon commissions.

A full resurgence for the Internet industry was predicted once the now decade-old promise of an information superhighway through service was fulfilled. Until wireless connections became available in 2003, DSLs with 256K speed competed with cable connections potentially six times as quick for market share. Contraction and collapse of early DSL innovators such as Covad Communications and NorthPoint Communications had not prevented the surviving Baby Bells as well as lesser entities from embracing and perfecting the technology. Comcast, Time Warner, Cox, Charter, Cablevision, and other cable companies with faster service including T-1, T-2, and T-3 lines for businesses wound up claiming a two-thirds market share of broadband subscriptions building toward 35 million in 2004. That level, analysts opined, was nearly double critical mass for companies to lower prices as much as 40% from the going rate of $50 per month and induce even more users to switch over. Content suppliers would then be able to sell profitably high-speed downloads of music and feature films. And in fact, several companies did in 2003 offer affordable music downloads requiring in some cases less than a minute per song. Movie downloads would require much faster connections, however, potentially by wireless transmission, all the rage in 2004.

COMMUNICATIONS EXPLOSION AND IMPLOSION

Wireless technology was well-advanced thanks to telecommunications companies. Even before the Internet hit full stride, deregulation of the phone industry, once again encouraged by all three branches of the federal government, dramatically increased the economic potential of both wire and wireless calling. The Supreme Court in 1990 supported a lower court ruling that the seven Baby Bells could own information services provided over their lines. In a severe defeat for the newspaper industry, cable TV operators, and long-distance companies, they were permitted to start offering such services immediately. A federal court ruling three years later in favor of Bell Atlantic that the 1984 Cable Act, prohibiting phone companies from selling cable TV services in areas where they provide phone service, violated First Amendment right of free speech, settled the matter once and for. However, the FCC in 1992 offset the advantage somewhat by ending the Baby Bells' monopolies on local phone service.

Cell phone towers

Until competitors could organize to take advantage of that ruling, the action centered on long distance service and wireless cell phones. In 1992, United Telecom became Sprint, the third largest long-distance company behind AT&T and MCI. Management then acquired Centel of Illinois the next year for $4.7 billion. A flat-rate long distance plan in 1995 as well as prepaid calling cards entrenched Sprint's industry position.

AT&T, meanwhile, was thinking long-term with introduction in 1992 of the first color videophone at a price of $1,500. Because functionality also required receiving parties to have videophones, the system was more appropriate for government agencies and big corporations than individual consumers. The next year, Ma Bell concluded a deal with the Chinese government in Peking to research, develop, and manufacture a phone switching and transmission system. Because China had only two phones per 100 people, versus 80 per 100 in the US, the potential market in the world's most populous country with more than four times the citizenry of the US was huge. But with 53,000 employees overseas, AT&T was already a global player. The problem was that its position at home was steadily being undermined by former dependencies.

Perhaps the most aggressive of the Baby Bells was BellSouth. Benefiting from a potential market of 36 million people in over 50 US metropolitan areas, and later a like number abroad, the company jumped right into the cell phone market in 1991 as well as fiber optic delivery of information. The recession that year was a catalyst for investment in computers at the expense of middle management, cut by 4,000. Quick reward for the company in 1993 was $5 billion of cash flow from nearly $16 billion of revenues.

Likewise, cable deliverer Comcast was determined, now that phone companies could become cable providers, to jump with both feet into wireless services and take advantage of the FCC allocating another 120 megahertz (MHz) of spectrum for the industry. The company combined its Amcell subsidiary with Metrophone to form Comcast Cellular and reach 7 million customers in the Philadelphia and neighboring areas. Further south, Fleet Call of Virginia, a company founded in 1987, went public and changed its name to Nextel. With financing supplied in part by a $1.1 billion investment by Craig O. McCaw, the carrier in 1994 bought Motorola's SMR radio licenses in the US to obtain spectrum rights in the top 50 US cities.

McCaw had the cash because he and other shareholders had just sold McCaw Cellular to AT&T for $11.4 billion. Ma Bell won crucial FCC approval for the deal by agreeing to provide equal access on its system to all long distance carriers. But Sprint, after obtaining personal communications services (PCS) wireless licenses for 29 areas in the

FCC's first license auction in 1995, which ultimately sold 500 PCS licenses on the 30 MHz broadband spectrum for $10.2 billion, proceeded in a joint venture to build up its own national system. By 1998, the company bought out all partners. Briefly, the licenses themselves escalated in value, making the holdings of even innocuous entities like NextWave valuable enough to bring offers of $16 billion when later the company went bankrupt without making use of the licenses. After the telecom bust, the licenses were reduced in value 60%.

As the leading maker of cell phones, Motorola invested in 1993 in a new concept. The *Iridium 66* satellite-linked, digital cellular phone network, developed at cost of $5 billion, 20% financed by Motorola, promised to provide not just national but global data, fax, paging, and voice services. However, development took half a decade and in the interim, Motorola lost the cell phone equipment lead to Nokia of Finland. Although for the moment, the company maintained a strong position, booking $27 billion of revenue at mid-decade, it was missing out on the wireless service component. Because of 25 million mobile phone users in the US alone, rising toward 100 million over the next five years, cell phone service revenue provided the bulk of the increase in annual wire line and wireless service sales. By 1998, the industry was ringing up $300 billion of annual revenues.

Most cell phone technology in the US came to be based on code division multiple access (CDMA), introduced by Qualcomm in 1989 after its founding four years earlier in San Diego. Because 13% of the world's 1.1 billion used phones licensing CDMA technology, by 2003 Qualcomm's revenues and profits soared.

Delighted with growth in cell phones and inspired by technological and economic advance in the freewheeling Internet industry, Republicans and many Democrats in Congress decided to move toward complete deregulation of the telecommunications industry. In February 1996, the House and Senate passed the Telecommunications Act with a goal of eventually permitting any long-distance, regional phone, and cable company to offer any service provided by the others, except that local phone companies could not carry long distance until full interconnectivity with rivals and telephone number portability was established. One method was to give away over 10,000 MHz of digital spectrum worth $30-70 billion to TV and cable broadcasters on stipulation that either by 2006 or whenever 85% of US households could tune in to digital signals, broadcasters would surrender their analog spectrum to wireless companies. The time frame to develop a digitally capable, high definition television (HDTV) system was believed to be a decade.

Another method of overhauling the telecommunications industry was to force Baby Bells to share phone lines with competitive local exchange carriers or CLECs. Although after the 1992 FCC rule change ending the Baby Bell monopoly virtually nothing had changed, within three years of passage of the 1996 act 300 CLECs came into existence, backed by $30 billion of investment dollars. A wild free-for-all ensued in which consumers made local calls through myriad companies by dialing a multiple number code prefix. To gain financial leverage to deal with the challenge, big companies naturally moved into another round of mergers and acquisitions. Ultimately, all but 70 CLECs folded under the pressure of the stock market implosion of 2000 and following recession. Survivors were worth less than one-tenth the value of capital invested. Nor did an unregulated, competitive environment result in lower fees for users. Because FCC regulation of local, long-distance, and wireless phone service was now lax, all manner and form of deceptive billing practices ensued. Likewise, Congress used the 1996 law to impose new federal fees on long-distance service to fund as much as $2.25 billion a year of phone and Internet service and investments for schools and libraries. Consumers' basic monthly phone bills doubled.

The Telecommunications Act signaled federal acceptance of a new round of combinations within and across telecommunications media. That year, for example, US West bought Continental Cablevision, the third largest cable company with over 4 million subscribers in Florida, Georgia, Michigan, Ohio, and Chicago for $10.8 billion. But the most important activity was mergers among the Baby Bells. Seven entities were fated to become four by end of the period, albeit with much broader business interests.

Now serving customers from Maine through Virginia, NYNEX was taken over in 1996 by Bell Atlantic for $24 billion. That company then subsumed GTE in a stock merger that swelled 23% to $65 billion by the time the deal was closed. Bell Atlantic became the largest US wireless provider by merging the US network of Vodafone of Britain into its system and taking over Frontier Cellular. To avoid overlapping service in some areas of the country, management had to exchange some wireless interests with ALLTEL. When in 2000 the company was renamed Verizon Communications, the wireless and joint venture with Vodafone became Verizon Wireless. Because of the telecommunications stock crash and $56 billion of debt used to fund the expansion, revenues contracted but then recovered in 2003-2004, 30% from wireless operations. Fierce competition held profit margin to under 11%. By comparison, Vodafone was the most valuable telecom company in the world with $61.8 billion of revenue, 60,000 employees, and MC/AR of 1.5.

In 1997, Southwestern Bell (SBC) of San Antonio acquired Pacific Telesis for $16 billion, creating the second largest phone company after AT&T even before adding Southern New England Telecommunications the next year. With stock values growing to their pre-crash peak, the company then took over Ameritech for $72 billion. To ease concerns by federal regulators, having second thoughts about the telecommunications consolidation, the company had to sell some Ameritech wireless businesses to GTE for $3.3 billion. Of 2004 revenue, a fifth came from Cingular Wireless operations, a joint venture agreed to with Bell South in 2000 that included Comcast Cellular, purchased in 1999 for $1.7 billion.

US West, the fourth surviving Baby Bell, suddenly lost its independence in 2000 to Qwest. That company thereby acquired local telephone lines building to 16.5 million by 2002 as well DSL services and Web-based *Yellow Pages*. Annual revenues of $19.7 billion looked impressive to investors until it was revealed that management had booked swaps as revenue and engaged in other accounting irregularities. Corrected financial data brought revenues down to only $15.4 billion in 2002 with a loss of $38.6 billion, attributable in large part to overpaying for US West. Without significant wireless operations, the company was poorly positioned for the future, even after management sold the *Yellow Pages* operation to reduce debt by more than a third to $16 billion. The SEC levied a $250 million fine for Qwest's management's misdeeds.

On another front, more companies challenged AT&T in long distance. Having previously opened wireless phone stores, ALLTEL gained the potential for greater size and competitiveness by buying in 1997 PCS licenses for 73 cities in 12 states. An acquisitions binge culminated with the $1.8 billion takeover of Aliant Communications in 1999 as well as Liberty Cellular, adding customers in Nebraska and Kansas. After the 2000 swap with Bell Atlantic-GTE, the company consolidated its position as fifth largest wireless company with 6.1 million subscribers and 95% coverage of the United States. ALLTEL was the sixth largest local telephone service provider with 2.5 million customers.

The more serious challenge to AT&T in long distance came from MCI. By 1997, the company reached $20 billion of annual revenue. Briefly, British Telecom attempted to buy the company for $21 billion, but a brief contraction in MCI revenues scared off the overseas suitor. Instead, upstart WorldCom, begun by Bernard J. Ebbers in Jackson, Mississippi in 1983 as LDDS Communications, but now boasting annual revenues of $10 billion, took over MCI in a leveraged buyout in 1998 for $36.5 billion. MCI WorldCom thus became the second largest voice carrier in the world. As telecom stocks soared the next year, management considered a merger with Sprint valued at $115 billion that would, had the FCC not objected on anti-trust grounds, have created an equal rival for AT&T. For one thing, Sprint had put together the only truly nationwide wireless PCS network, albeit fourth largest in the country. Management split the FON and PCS operations at least temporarily to issue separate tracking stocks.

U.S. **Telecom Services** Companies 2004
Comparison of MC/AR to Employment

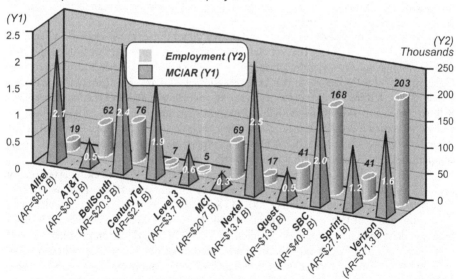

It turned out to be fortunate for Sprint that the WorldCom merger never went through. In 2002, Ebbers' company became embroiled in an accounting scandal that included labeling telephone-line and other operating expenses as capital improvements, which could only be depreciated over time, as well as personal loans from the company to Ebbers amounting to $408 million to help consolidate his debts. Despite reported annual revenues exceeding $35 billion from 20 million customers and half of all Internet traffic in the country, WorldCom's market capitalization fell from a peak in summer 1999 of $120 billion to only $335 million three years later, destroying retirement plans for thousands of employees. As the news became public that management had falsified over $11 billion of profits, assets listed at $107 billion fell in value nearly 90%, which provided insufficient collateral for $36 billion in debt. To survive, the company sought bankruptcy protection. Ebbers found himself the subject of criminal prosecution.

AT&T, with 40 million customers, including 4 million business clients, should have been in position to benefit from WorldCom's collapse, but management made a series of bad mis-steps. Strategy for dealing with competitors' cut-rate fees, rebates for switching service, and other aggressive tactics was to diversify again to gain greater size and financial clout. As well as continuing to build up McCaw Cellular into its AT&T Wireless division, the company in 1998 bought the global data network of IBM for $5 billion. The next year, management closed a deal to buy cable company TCI for $53 billion, up from an original price of $37 billion because of the surge in stock prices. That deal was swiftly topped by a $58 billion takeover of MediaOne Group after a Comcast merger with MediaOne fell through. The company became briefly the largest provider of cable TV services in the nation. When, however, the cable business proved far less lucrative than management had hoped, the stock market plunge made AT&T's $43 billion in debt weigh far more heavily on the books than anticipated. The cable division was sold to Comcast in November 2002 for $30 billion in cash and $20 billion of assumed debt, in other words a loss of tens of billions of dollars.

Along with that dose of strong medicine, Ma Bell in 2000 spun off AT&T Wireless into a separate company. Focused mainly on long distance service, management slashed employment 40% to reduce debt to $18 billion.

Hurting the company's prospects and drawing into question the decision to spin off AT&T Wireless was the fact that wireless phones in service in the US in 2004 topped 170 million, 80% as many as regular phone lines, while cell phone use in Europe was even higher at 70% of the population. With the recession of 2001, revenue from traditional local phone service fell for the first time, causing the operating margins of the surviving Baby Bells to contract to 35%, even as wireless margins ran up marginally toward 33%. Thus, Ma Bell's 1999 return to local phone service in New York with a *Local One Rate* plan did not in the short run prove as profitable as hoped. Competition in long distance from wireless companies such as Verizon further befuddled the republic's original phone giant.

On the other hand, the Supreme Court supported the FCC in blocking attempts by SBC, US West, and Bell Atlantic to offer long distance service until local phone markets were better opened to competition in 2003. AT&T hoped to complicate by court challenge the re-emergence of WorldCom, renamed as MCI, from bankruptcy with as little as $5 billion of debt and stream-lined employment of 55,000. When the attempt failed, Ma Bell was again assaulted by cut-rate charges and forced in succession to stop soliciting new local and long-distance service in seven states, layoff 7,000 more employees, and in early 2005 accept a $22.5 billion buyout offer from SBC. With revenues down to $20 billion and market capitalization under $7 billion, MCI, too, became a takeover target for Verizon and Qwest.

The US wireless industry was also extremely competitive. By 2003, Verizon with 36 million subscribers controlled just under a quarter the market, Cingular nearly a sixth, AT&T Wireless about 15%, Sprint PCS a bit more than a tenth, Nextel a twelfth, T-Mobile, owned by Deutsche Telecom, a bit less, and others (including AT&T Wireless and

Sprint affiliates) the remaining 17.8%. As AT&T Wireless' 2003 revenues increased, Cingular was induced to make an all cash bid that escalated as Vodafone entered the fray. The deal between the original suitors was ultimate closed in early 2004 for $47 billion, forming a company with 87 million customers.

The only pure wireless company with better financial prospects was Nextel. Annual 2003 revenues arising seven-eighths from US operations and the fact that the company had a higher percentage of business customers with monthly revenue per customer over $70 from its 12.3 million global subscribers pleased investors. Moreover, the annual churn rate of Nextel's business clientele was below 1.4%, as opposed to about 25% for regular wireless customers. That loyalty was jeopardized by federal rule changes going into effect November 24, 2003 permitting portability of wireless telephone numbers. Yet the company hoped to maintain and increase market share by building on a program called *Nationwide Direct Connect*, charging $60 per month unlimited "push-to-talk" service popular with construction workers and delivery drivers. Management came out with plans to let Nextel customers use long-range, digital walkie-talkies in areas where they traveled as well as connect with anyone on Nextel's national network.

Ultimately in December 2004, however, the pressure of consolidation in the $784 billion US telecommunications industry, including smaller player Alltel buying Western Wireless for $5.6 billion to unite $10 billion in annual revenues, compelled Nextel's board to accept a $44 billion offer from Sprint. The combined entity looked to the future with 35 million customers and potential to cover 85% of the US market.

Patented Motorola *iDEN* technology in Nextel phones was superior to rival push-to-talk products offered by Verizon and others. T-Mobile sought to offset this advantage by lower prices, but failed at first because of poor service. However in December 2002, Verizon moved to buy up more radio-wave licenses from a Cablevision-backed venture for $700 million. A key consideration in wireless service in the US was the fact that carriers had access to only 189.1 MHz of spectrum compared to 10,170 MHz for broadcasters, while overseas wireless carriers in Germany, Japan, and the U.K. held over 300 MHz each. The Commerce Department's National Telecommunications and Information Administration did have a plan to release an additional 90 MHz, half no longer needed by the military, for bidding under FCC supervision for use by 2008. The idea was to boost so-called 3G or next-generation wireless phones, in effect hand-held devices combining phone, computer, Internet, and even camera functions, to transmit high-speed data and full-range video. Previously, European companies had invested $150 billion in 3G licenses and infrastructure but had lost all when wireless technology for fast Internet service and swapping of audio and video files on hand-held devices had not been ready. US companies, by comparison, had invested 10% as much for wireless technology, bearing fruit as Internet use soared in 2004 to three-quarters of Americans, compared to less than half in the core 15 EU countries.

With its one-fifth stake in the *Iridium* satellite phone venture, Motorola had hoped to trump ground-based wireless systems. However, when finally offered in 1998, the clunky equipment cost flabbergasted customers $3,000 with a $3 per minute charge. Since digital cell phones introduced by Nokia did the job, albeit on a national basis with huge gaps in service, at one tenth the cost, *Iridium* attracted only 2% of projected customers and folded two years later. Motorola lost its entire $1 billion investment. Too, a soft computer chip market and failure to keep up with consumer tastes, such as for the phones with color screens brought out by Samsung of South Korea forced the company to lay off employees. Sixty thousand, or 40% of the work force, were let go through 2002. Then CEO Christopher B. Galvin, grandson of the company's founder, after failing to turn things around by buying for $11 billion in 1999 General Instrument Corporation, maker of set-top boxes delivering Internet services to TV, was forced himself to resign the next year. Annual revenues that peaked in 2000 at $37.6 billion plummeted, resulting in cuts in employment and cumulative losses of $2.5 billion.

A major reason for the collapse was that Motorola's margin on cell phones fell to 3.3% or about an eighth of Nokia's figure. Another lapse was failure to bring out cell phones with built-in cameras, introduced in Japan in 2001 and selling 65 million globally two years later, equal to 13% of the world cell phone market. NEC and Matsushita Electric Industrial of Japan profited, as did Nokia, controlling just over one-third the $60 billion mobile phone market to only 15% for Motorola. The company did hold on to a 27% share in the US. But management announced in October 2003 that not only would they miss the Christmas selling season entirely for camera phones but would have to divest the company's $4.8 billion semiconductor business to raise cash and reduce debt. Even in the $45 billion global mobile networks market, Motorola's 10% share was only half of Ericsson of Sweden and fifth behind as well Nokia, Siemens of Germany, and Lucent while the company's 15.7% share of world cell phone shipments was half Nokia's market leading total.

Post-mortems on the Telecommunications Act of 1996 focused on the mistake of government encouraging speculative capital investment and over-expansion of an industry. Those who defended the legislation pointed out that Motorola and other companies had on their own made decisions to invest $17 billion in commercial space ventures, including satellite phone communications and space imaging, which had proved costly flops. Other companies had invested more shrewdly in satellite broadcast of cable signals and direct TV signals to satellite dishes. The pace of technological change as much as human decision-making played a part in the rise and fall, or at least decline, of telecommunications giants.

The advance of a superior wireless technology was the reason that BellSouth got out of the pay phone business in 2001. Although over-capacity in fiber optics momentarily ravaged companies in the industry, a long-term comeback was in the offing over the next two decades as the Baby Bells developed plans to connect individual homes by fiber optic lines, replacement for copper wire. Such a system would permit faster Internet service, more efficient downloads of music and video, and HDTV service. On the other hand, phone calls using voice over Internet protocol (VOIP) technology, not subject to the usual telecommunication taxes and fees, threatened to undermine local phone company revenues, particularly when adopted by entire companies such as Cisco. In fact, sales of VOIP systems doubled in 2003 to 1.6 million lines, half of all business lines. Time Warner began making VOIP available to households in select areas as part of $39.95 per month unlimited local and long distance Internet phone calling plan while Comcast announced it would offer phone service to 40 million households within two years. AT&T, BellSouth, Qwest, and others were also gearing up to compete for VOIP customers, making currently 3% of all global voice phone calls. Like the Internet generally, the 6.5 million VOIP lines in place by 2004 were unregulated by government.

U.S. **Electrical Equipment** Companies 2004
Comparison of MC/AR to Employment
(Y2) Thousands

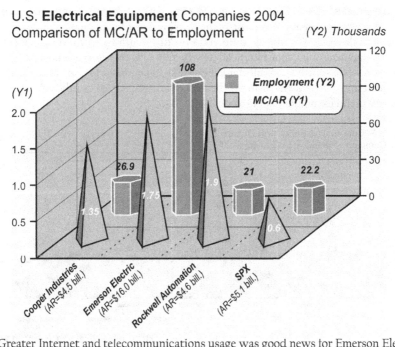

Greater Internet and telecommunications usage was good news for Emerson Electric. The company's business evolved in the 1990s to become a leader in network power systems, including backup power to protect critical data from being lost.

THE COMPUTER INDUSTRY MATURES

The early 1990s witnessed the final victory of PCs over minicomputers. Selling for a tenth as much, PC software was also much cheaper and once PC speeds and memory capability improved just as effective. But that transition to a superior technology caused IBM to lose $4.75 billion in 1992 and lay off 25,000 workers. Even after the economy recovered, competition from old and new rivals continued to take a toll.

For that reason, management decided to change strategy. Big Blue would henceforth emphasize the growing market for services such as consulting but also designing, installing, and maintaining new computer systems for major corporate clients. Although computer services grew by 2004 into a $400 billion annual industry, IBM's ascent was cut off by the stock market crash and recession. From a peak of $87.7 billion of revenue in 1999, the company contracted to just $81.1 billion in 2002 and profits of $5.3 billion. Management counted on leadership in higher-end semiconductors as well as mainframes to keep its overall industry lead. A new *z990 eServer* that had cost $1 billion to develop and made use of *Linux*-based operating software to compete with linked supercomputer servers helped IBM hold nearly a quarter of the $16 billion global market for computers costing over $250,000 as well 35% of the high-profile $20 billion US market for *Intel* and *Unix* based servers and software. Although the expensive computer market actually contracted one fifth through 2002, its importance lay in that it drove software license and maintenance sales, 25% of IBM's revenue and 45% of its profit. While investing $3 billion in a state-of-the-art semiconductor plant in New York State, management brought employment down 20% and jacked up 2004 profit margin to 8.8%. Management considered the moment opportune to unload its struggling PC division to Lenovo of China for $1.25 billion while securing a comfortable 19% stake in Lenovo, approved once the Defense Department and Congress scrutinized the deal to forestall the possibility of a transfer of technology useful for military applications.

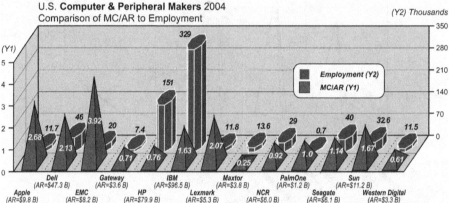

U.S. Computer & Peripheral Makers 2004
Comparison of MC/AR to Employment

Slipping behind IBM in the server business was HP with a 28% share, down from a one-third prior to the tech slump. However, the sight of the industry's number one and two computer makers butting heads was for most of the period the exception, rather than the rule. HP only got into high performance servers after buying Tandem of California in 1997. Its main effort was still in PCs and printers. *Pavilion* brand desktop and laptops from 1995 forward pushed the company toward significant market share in the former. As ink and toner sales grew into a $50 billion business by 2003, the company scored with both desk jet color printers and all-in-one machines that combined printing, faxing, copying, and scanning features. HP also carved out a lucrative niche in light emitting diodes for cars, traffic control, and other purposes. In 1999-2000, management spun off its unit that built measurement devices and components, chemical analysis machines, and medical instruments as Agilent Technologies.

CEO Carleton (Carly) S. Fiorina, highest profile of all women top executives in the nation, decided that new acquisitions were necessary to stay competitive. After buying Indigo, maker of commercial and industrial digital printers, she engineered over intense shareholder opposition a 2002 merger with Compaq for stock worth $22.7 billion. Although combined revenues topped $70 billion the next year, employment was cut by a sixth. The fact that Compaq had swallowed DEC for $9.6 billion in 1998 after that company's high-end workstation machines had already lost out to PCs made the relatively low valuation all the more bitter for shareholders to swallow. Ultimately in early 2005, HP's board of directors forced Fiorina out. Neither did her strategy of providing customers with a full range of consumer electronic devices produce the desired profitability, nor did HP keep its market share in printing technology, software, and in particular high margin ink and toner supplies above 50%.

HP OfficeJet

The third strongest US maker of servers with market share recovering to 21% in 2004 and the leader throughout the period in workstations was Sun Microsystems. Like DEC, the company watched its high-end hardware with customized, high performance software suffer at the hands of less expensive computer architecture. For a time, Sun's *SPARCstation 10*, the first multiprocessing desktop computer, and contracts with IBM and HP to standardize *Unix* based software, kept the company at the cutting edge. The company upgraded again in 1996 with a workstation family using a 64 bit *UltraSPARC* processor for multimedia, graphics, and imaging. However, big computer servers with Sun chips and software, including the 1997 *Enterprise 10000* server with the processing power of four mainframes, cost over $100,000 while cheaper systems using standardized Intel chips and running *Windows* and *Linux* software eventually were offered. When PC-based servers priced in a range from $10,000 down to $2,000 became available, the global server market contracted 28% over three years to $50 billion in 2004. Moreover, CEO Scott McNealy was slow to cut annual R&D spending from just under $2 billion and employment by a fourth to 36,000 for fear of sacrificing future innovation to present financial need. Revival plans centered on emulating competitor strategy of offering cheaper servers while boosting software and security sales for mobile laptop users.

Dell Dimension case

The sun had not altogether set on Sun but the company was definitely in eclipse, not least because of Michael S. Dell. As a college student at the University of Texas in 1984, he built and sold PCs out of his dorm room. Soon, he was well on his way to constructing a company producing custom-made computers from standardized parts for direct sale to customers by phone and after 1996 the Internet. Production in Mexico, China, and Brazil kept costs down and profits up. Annual revenue nearly tripled despite recessionary times from 2000 to 2004. Pleased by profit margin over 6%, investors gave the company an MC/AR over 2.1, albeit down from a high over 8.0 two years earlier.

Dell was not done embarrassing industry titans. In 2004, the company surged to a leading share of nearly 18% in the $175 billion PC world market, which was flat in dollar sales but rising in units sold to 177 million annually. HP slipped to second place with just under 16% while IBM controlled only 5.9%. Although the top three US producers, as well as Gateway and eMachines, accounted for less than half the global market, no other competitor had more than 4%. Industry consolidation favored the low-cost producer, and that was most emphatically Dell. Management cut costs further by developing an automated assembly line that processed orders with robots. But HP still held a preponderant 48% share of the printer market, while Dell's bid to sell *Dell* branded printers made by Lexmark of Lexington, Kentucky had just begun. The larger company also held a 15% market share to 5% hand-held computers and a nearly three to one advantage in servers. Nevertheless, two-thirds of Dell's revenues came from PCs. Because the company kept R&D expenses under $500 million, compared with ten times as much for IBM and over seven times as much for HP, its ability to compete in high-end products was limited.

Hand-held computers were an innovation evolving out of Palm's 1996 *Palm Pilot* personal digital assistant (PDA), commonly used at first to store phone numbers, addresses, and other useful information as well as keep schedule calendars and take notes. These small, battery-powered organizers then morphed into little computers with further applications. Although after being spun off by 3Com Technologies in March 2000, Palm controlled a 50% global market share and generated $1.6 billion of annual revenue, its portion was reduced by entry of HP from the computer end. Nokia, Sony Ericsson, and Motorola from the "smart phone" end, selling products that combined cell phone with PDA, camera, and Internet functions, and even Sony with $69.4 billion of sales and 162,000 of employees overawed the industry originator. With 2003 market share down to 37% and average price per hand-held in the $200 range, market capitalization collapsed from a high of $54 billion at spin-off to $400 million. Management engineered a merger with rival Handspring for $240 million to enter the smart phone market and split the company into PalmOne, making hand-helds, and PalmSource, developing new software to fend off Microsoft's attempt to dominate the PDA market.

By contrast, Apple continued to maintain viability as both a computer and software maker. Although the company's US market share was just 4.5%, its *iMac* and *Next* brand computers, the latter purchased in 1996 from Jobs, who eventually returned to the company as CEO, ran on a proprietary operating system. Because many schools and businesses did not want to bear the expense and retraining aggravation of switching over to *Windows*-based computers, Apple's position was relatively secure. A success in 2001 selling *iPod* digital music players priced at $300-500 to hold 1,000 songs in card pack size captured nearly one-fifth the US market from much bigger competitors. Further, Apple launched a *Windows* version of *iPod* in 2002 as well as an Internet music downloading service at 99 cents a song. In 2004, Jobs inked an agreement with HP to resell *iPods*, including less expensive models designed to fend off competitors, under HP's name. Apple sold 5.7 million of the devices in just three years and came to provide a quarter of the company's $9.8 billion in annual revenue.

However, it was Dell's business model that moved the PC industry toward standardization of computers and components. As chips and other parts became mass-produced and interchangeable, they were priced more like other commodities. After the market for desktop and laptop computers reached saturation, the only way computer makers could continue to boost revenues was by making machines faster, adding memory, improving monitor size and resolution, and adding capabilities for playing music, watching video, and other multi-media functions. Oversupply of semiconductors drove down prices. Room remained for wholesale distributors of computer parts and software to succeed. Ingram

Apple iPod & accessories

Micro, combining 1979 start-up Micro D of southern California with Buffalo's Ingram Software, founded 1982, grew into a global business with $25.5 billion of 2004 sales, 11,300 employees, and MC/AR of 0.12.

Between 1990 and 1995, prices for DRAMs collapsed from $12-15 per 1-megabyte memory chip, capable of storing 1,000 double-spaced, typewritten pages of text, to only $6. NEC commanded a higher price for its 1994 innovation RDRAM chips for fast data transfer at 500 MHz per second for graphics and multimedia workstations. However, the coming of 4-megabyte chips followed by 16 and 64 megabyte chips necessarily made the old size obsolete. Because the *Windows* operating system spurred another PC sales boom, global semiconductor sales surmounted the early decade recession to rise from $50 billion in 1990 to a peak of over $140 billion five years later. That included a jump of North American sales to over $25 billion in 1993 to pass slumping Japanese sales for the first time since 1985. When saturation was finally achieved at mid-decade, a drop below $130 billion of global semiconductor sales with no immediate sign of recovery forced Motorola and TI to cut their work forces.

Computer chips became multipurpose during the 1990s. For example, Motorola entered into a joint venture with IBM and Apple to make *PowerPC* 32-bit embedded microprocessors with 150-160 MHz range for use in computer peripherals such as laser jet printers as well as telecom devices, cable TV boxes, and automotive engine controls. In 1996, the company emulated the European success putting microchips in identification and health care cards by bringing out memory chips for "smart cards," that is credit cards with embedded memory. Five years later, Motorola marketed a 256 K, magneto-resistive

Inside a Dell Dimension computer

random access memory (MRAM) chip integrating multiple memory functions for use in computers, cell phones, mobile devices, cars, and other devices, which was upgraded to a 1 megabyte MRAM the next year. While management ordered construction of low-end semiconductor plants in China and Hong Kong in 1995, its $3 billion *PowerPC* chip plant was located in Richmond, Virginia. Late in 2003, the company decided to "de-asset" by selling one of its China plants for $1 billion.

IBM went on without TI in 1998 to produce a 400 MHz *PowerPC* made of carbon, not aluminum. Two years later, the speed was in the gigahertz range. Big Blue's engineers kept experimenting with different materials so that in 2003 they succeeded in combining on a single chip formerly incompatible designs used previously on silicon-germanium fast communications chips and silicon computer chips. IBM's book of patents, exceeding 3,400 in 2001, generated $1.5 billion in annual revenue.

While Motorola was investing on the Chinese mainland, Texas Instruments preferred Japan. A 1990 joint venture with Kobe Steel to make advanced semiconductors was followed by an arrangement with printing companies Canon of Japan and HP to build a chip facility in Singapore and a deal with Hitachi to develop 256 megabyte DRAMs. However, the company sold its custom manufacturing business to contract producer Solectron three years later and in 1998 dealt its DRAM operations for $800 million to Micron Technologies, the last US company that made those chips. Management focused on higher end products such as in 1992 the *microSPARC* single-chip processor for engineering workstations, a second generation Reduced Instruction Set Computer (RISC) processor, and digital signal processors (DSPs), which accomplished specific processing tasks to improve the functionality of memory boards and chips used in fax, modem, answering machines, graphics, sound, and digital wireless applications. While the company was restructuring in 1998 to abandon defense and electronics, mobile computing, software, and telecommunications systems, TI engineers succeeded in producing low power DSPs to make wireless communications, for example voice-enabled cable modems, and high speed Internet access price feasible. Together with chips for wireless phones and other consumer electronics products, these innovations helped the company generate the bulk of its revenue and profits.

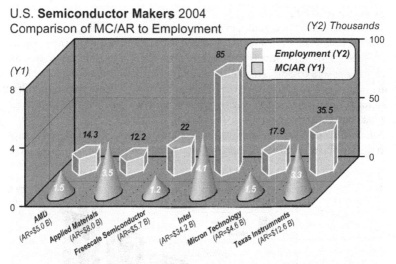

U.S. **Semiconductor Makers** 2004
Comparison of MC/AR to Employment

If TI had a lesser but still important share of annual global semiconductor sales, topping $200 billion in 2000 before slumping toward $140 billion two years later and see-sawing in 2004 back toward $213 billion, Intel by focusing on microprocessors for PCs and giving advertising dollars to PC makers to trumpet the *Intel* brand inside their products came to control nearly a fifth. The surge toward market dominance in PC chips was accelerated by introduction in 1992 of the *Pentium* microprocessor, at 66 MHz twice as fast as the 486. The extra speed was needed to make *Windows* and other multi-tasking operating systems such as *Unix* and IBM's *OS/2* work well. The *Pentium I*, followed by *Pentium II* at 300 MHz in 1997 and even faster *Pentium* versions that breached 3 GHz, became such an industry icon that neither a 1995 recall of defective chips that cost $475 million nor a challenge by Advanced Micro Devices (AMD) after its 1995 merger with NexGen could shake Intel's nearly four-fifths global market share.

In 1996, the company also made a splash with flash memory, 64 megabyte chips the size of a match-book to store images and data in digital cameras, digital wireless messaging pagers, audio voice recorders, PDAs, and solid-state hard drives. By building chip plants overseas and minimize still substantial construction costs rising from $750 million for a plant in Ireland in 1993 to well over $1 billion for a more modern facility in Malaysia, the company achieved at the 2000 stock market peak a valuation of $460 billion. Even after the technology stock crash and a quarter billion dollar judgment against the company for violating with its *Itanium* chip Intergraph's patents on parallel processing technique, equal to 25% of Intel's R&D cost on *Itanium*, investors liked the company's fundamentals. On the strength of a strategy shift to produce microprocessors two-thirds the size and energy consumption as before, for example the *Pentium* M for laptops, that figure was not considered inflated. The company announced late in 2003 that its scientists had solved, by use of new materials, the problem of electricity leakage in chips that had threatened to halt the miniaturization trend so critical for generating greater computing power and speed. New revenue would come from static random access memory (SRAM) chips with double the number of transistors, liquid crystal on silicon chips for improved flat-panel, big screen TVs, and most ambitiously *WiMax* technology for wireless Internet service up to 30 miles distance from transmitters.

Many US and foreign companies made chips around the world. Like TI, some dealt off manufacturing to contract producers when competition increased to the point at which superior return on investment was impossible. Thus NCR sold all its computer hardware manufacturing assets to Solectron in 1998. That company concentrated production in China and other Far East countries to keep labor costs low. Of course, profitability in con-tract manufacturing was hard to come by when economic times were bad. Rival Samnina-SCI also was battered, but Tech Data, founded in Clearwater, Florida in 1974 to market and distribute data processing supplies, evolved into a full-line supplier of components, networking, peripherals, software, and systems to computer resellers and retailers.

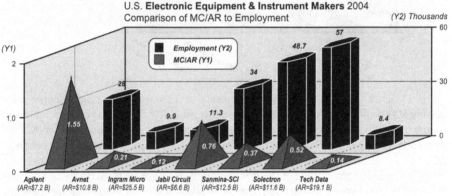

U.S. **Electronic Equipment & Instrument Makers** 2004
Comparison of MC/AR to Employment

By 2003, less than one quarter of the nearly $90 billion contract electronics good assembling business was done in the US. What remained was more likely than not to be low volume production of a high mixture of products such as done by Plexus of Neenah, Wisconsin. On the other hand, Applied Materials, a leader in manufacturing the equipment that made semiconductors, had its principal manufacturing site in Austin, Texas. The company increased annual revenues almost five-fold over a decade in part by getting into diagnostics and control equipment and manufacturing execution system software for semiconductors. Because of improving global prospects for chip production, low profitability did not discourage investors.

Still producing in the US but also around the world were two big computer memory storage companies. Seagate and EMC of Massachusetts came to control two-thirds of the global storage market. After a 1996 merger with Conner Peripherals, the former became the largest privately held disc storage company in the world. Its global market share for hard drives amounted to 30%. Technology advanced from 7,200 revolutions per minute disc drives to 15,000. Seagate's *Barracuda* 180 gigabyte hard drive in 2000 had the most capacity of any on the planet. Supplying hard drives for Microsoft *Xbox* the next year, the company went public in 2002.

EMC came later to prominence and $1 billion of 1994 revenues by introducing its *Sym-metrix* 5500, first terabyte storage system for mainframes. After adding a storage management software product, the company surpassed IBM as the largest mainframe storage leader. A system that handled 1 petabyte, equal to 1,000 terabytes, advanced revenue toward $4 billion in 1998, one quarter from Europe. Management set a goal of raising software revenue from 10% of sales toward 25% because margins were higher. As well as developing software internally, the company bought rivals Legato Systems and Documentum. That consolidation persuaded the management of Symantec, another California innovator, to purchase Veritas in 2004 for $13.5 billion. The company became second only to EMC in software storage and the fourth largest software company overall.

In point of fact, the asset value of software held by businesses in the US had been outpacing the asset value of computer hardware and peripherals such as printers since 1990. From approximate equality in 1990, software had more than tripled in value to $325 billion in 2000, over twice the value of hardware. Early recognition of the trend convinced AT&T to buy NCR for $7.3 billion in 1991 and three years later rename it Global Information Solutions. When the subsidiary was spun off in 1996, again named NCR, with plans to exit hardware entirely except for ATM and retail scanning machines, its main business was providing store automation and management software for the food-service industry as well as check-processing software through its Dataworks division.

In 2004, NCR was finishing up its twelfth decade in business. Microsoft, by comparison, had not yet finished its third. However, the Redmond, Washington company found the key to seemingly unlimited riches with its *Windows* operating system, periodic upgrades, and bundled applications programs. In 1995, for example, *Windows 95*, packaged with Microsoft's *Office* suite that featured the *Word* word-processing program, *Excel* spreadsheet, and *Powerpoint* presentation software, sold one million copies in four days. Three years later when *Windows 98* debuted with Microsoft's *Internet Explorer* web browser bundled, previous versions were already running on 375 million PCs worldwide. The company surged by end of period toward an incredible 95% share of the $9.7 billion market for PC operating system software and 49% of server software. Completely overshadowed in the former market were Apple's *Mac* operating system at 3.1% and free *Unix*-based *Linux* software of eccentric programmer Linus Torvalds of Finland at 2.4%. In the latter, *Linux* server software, pushed by IBM, HP, Dell, Intel, and Oracle, was rising fast at 25.7% of the market while *NetWare*, made by Novell of Provo, Utah, as well as *Unix* each had less than a twelfth share.

The practice of bundling applications software with operating software raised cries of unfair competition, particularly when Microsoft engineers did not spend an inordinate amount of time making rival company software work as efficiently with *Windows* as in-house programs. In one of the most notorious cases, Microsoft attempted to compel PC makers to install *Windows* web browser *Internet Explorer* instead of Mosaic's *Navigator*, launched in 1993. The Justice Department intervened in 1994 to force the company in a consent decree to desist. With the price of *Navigator* rising from $28 to $71, Mosaic renamed itself Netscape and achieved an instant IPO market capitalization of $2.7 billion. However, Microsoft's bundling of *Internet Explorer* with *Windows* turned the situation around over night. Netscape sued but had to sell itself to AOL for $4.2 billion to gain the backing of an entity with deeper pockets. Not until April 2000 did a federal court side with complainants against Microsoft's monopolistic practices and order the company split into one half running the operating system business and a second doing everything else. An appellate decision in November the next year that the trial judge went too far as well as

U.S. **Software** Companies 2004
Comparison of MC/AR to Employment

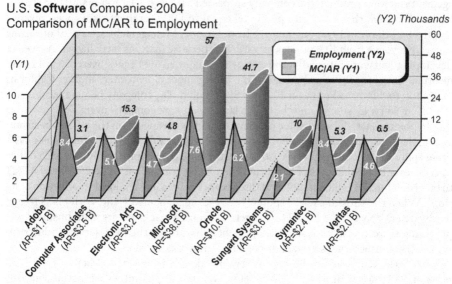

(Y2) Thousands

arrival in office of the administration of the younger Bush, more sympathetic to Big Business interests, kept Microsoft not only intact but as aggressive as ever. Newly appointed senior officials in the Justice, Treasury, and Commerce departments concluded that it was bad for business and bad for America to undercut a US profit-making marvel. However, EU regulators imposed a $612.7 million fine on Microsoft for unfair use of its market monopoly power in loading up *Windows* with its *Media Player* software and forced the company in the future to sell the operating software — at the same price, was the unhappy irony for customers — without *Media Player*.

What was at stake in the Microsoft case, beyond just the ambition of Gates to monopolize software and European angst over US economic domination, was a clash between two philosophies. While Gates advocated less complicated software that worked seamlessly together over the entire range of operating, application, and Internet functions, others favored "best of breed" specialization to perfect the finest individual software programs, and then make them work well together after the fact. Microsoft's financial results, summed up in profit margin of 30%, proved that most computer users agreed with or at least acquiesced in the first strategy. Even those who favored the second philosophy were partially mollified when a $399 *Windows XP* improvement was introduced in October 2001 to fix many of the flaws that had marred the performance of previous versions. Critics still complained with some justification that in the rush to close out rivals, Microsoft had not thoroughly corrected problems that permitted hackers to send out destructive worms and viruses over the web and onto PCs in homes and businesses. The fact remained that most best of breed software, for example Adobe's graphic, desktop publishing, and document sharing software, worked quite well with *Windows XP*.

That did not stop Microsoft from ginning up simpler alternatives for Adobe products. Gates' team even offered in 2003 as part of an improved *Office* suite, an *InfoPath* program retailing for $199 that created electronic forms and facilitated the sharing and finding of documents. That was a direct attack on Adobe's *Acrobat* reader for portable document format (PDF) files as intermediate files between layout programs and raster image processors, in essence, a one file format for print and electronic publishing. Because Microsoft had already sold 500 million copies of *Office* around the world and was likely to induce many users to upgrade over time, Adobe had to take the threat very seriously. In 2004, Microsoft flaunted its size and superiority by distributing to shareholders in a special dividend 53% of a $60 billion cash hoard. Continuing excess cash flow, including from a new deal to license software to Comcast to run TV set-top boxes, would be used to buy back $30 billion of stock over four years and double the usual annual dividend.

Although by market capitalization, annual revenue, and employment, Microsoft topped Adobe 20, 22, and 18 to 1 respectively, it still trailed other competitors in sales. Sony, for example, keeping a wary eye on Microsoft's *Xbox* alternative to its *PlayStation* for electronic games, had twice the US company's revenues. However, when in October 2003 Microsoft brought out *Office Sharepoint Portal Server* software at a retail price above $5,500, to improve productivity of groups of workers not just individuals, Gates' aspiration to vault his company onto a higher revenue plain was clear. With a *MediaPlayer* already bundled onto *Windows*, he was planning to claim a lion's share of the audio and video downloading market as well.

It had always been the purpose of database software makers to woo large corporate clients. Oracle stretched revenues toward $3 billion in 1995 focusing on that strategy. But a 350% leap by 2004 was made possible by branching out from database software into enterprise resource planning applications, modifying Oracle software to run on *Unix* and *Linux* based operating systems, and boosting capability of software and servers to support more users, more data, and higher availability.

Oracle's biggest competitor was SAP of Germany with a 20% share of the global market, compared to only 7% for Oracle. However, PeopleSoft of Pleasanton, California became a potent challenger by concentrating on human resources management software, including tracking personnel, financial accounting, and sales and marketing. When revenues climbed over $2 billion in 2003, the company offered to buy rival J.D. Edwards, which concentrated on small and medium-size customers as well as manufacturers, for $1.75 billion in stock. Oracle immediately tried to thwart the combination by making a hostile all-cash bid for PeopleSoft that was raised progressively toward $10.3 billion. Although PeopleSoft's management, while proceeding with the J.D. Edwards takeover, was adamant against falling under the control of Oracle's self-assertive CEO Larry Ellison, shareholder interest in cashing out ultimately forced the board of directors to capitulate. Microsoft opened off-and-on discussions to buy SAP but did not push hard to close the deal .

Some large companies did not want to be bothered figuring out the complexity of information technology systems and software. For them, outsourcing was the solution. Hence, GM's subsidiary EDS made a rapid rise from an entity drawing half its revenue from in-house operations to one with a majority of outside business. After multi-billion dollar, multi-year contracts with Saab Automobile of Sweden, which GM subsequently purchased, Chausson of France, an industrial firm, U.K. Departments of Social Security and Inland Revenue, Continental Airline's reservation system, and Xerox, as well as many acquisitions, topped in 1995 by purchase of A.T. Kearney, the fourth largest privately held management consulting firm in the world, revenues doubled to over $15 billion. After GM spun off EDS in 1996 as an independent company, many more outsourcing deals, including

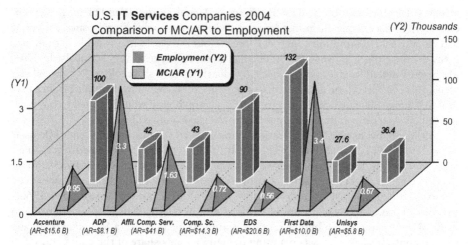

U.S. **IT Services** Companies 2004
Comparison of MC/AR to Employment

(Y2) Thousands

with Commonwealth Bank of Australia, BellSouth, and the US Marine Corps were concluded. By also web hosting over 6,000 clients world wide and managing servers at six dozen sites, the company boosted annual revenues above $20 billion 2002-2004. That was only 4% of the fragmented global IT market, which was still largely in-house. Competition from IBM, Cap Gemini Ernst and Young, which took away the UK Inland Revenue contract, and companies like Computer Sciences, which managed computer and communications facilities for clients like General Dynamics, as well as difficulties with a big contract to unify the US Navy's world-wide computer system hurt profits

OTHER HIGH TECHNOLOGY DEVELOPMENTS

Use of computers for various business and work purposes, including better forecasting of supply and demand, inventory management, consulting, and other service-related activity, helped boost US productivity markedly after 1995. Annual increase through 2000 averaged 2.6% versus a bit more than half as much in the previous 23 years. Even greater gains were made after the recession of 2001 because businesses downsized employment and up-sized expectations of what remaining workers were supposed to do. Productivity growth by 2003 was bounding along at a 5-6% pace. For each 0.5% increase in productivity, moreover, the annual income of a worker making $30,000 increased 5%. Productivity improvement averaging 4% over a decade would add another $1 trillion to the US economy.

Naturally, factory automation contributed to the upsurge. Also important was other business machines such as printers and photocopy equipment. While HP led the way with ink jet printers and higher end lasers, Xerox in 2000 tried to make an end run by purchasing Tektronix's color printing and imaging division for $925 million. Tektronix printers used wax instead of ink. Further, Xerox concluded a $2 billion alliance with Sharp and Fuji to make faster ink jet products for small businesses and home offices. However, sales of all-in-one machines hurt the copier business badly, causing a global market that had risen 33% in half a decade to $68.8 billion in 1995 to slump under $64 billion in 2000 and keep falling. After implementing a cost cutting plan that reduced employment to

67,800, three-fifths in the US, and selling off assets in China and Hong Kong for $500 million to Fuji Xerox to refocus on core strengths, including digital copiers, flat annual revenue in 2003 and 2004 of $15.7 billion generated a modest profit. MC/AR hovered around the humble level of 0.8.

Part of the problem was that Eastman Kodak had entered into the digital copier market and begun making digital continuous tone printers as well. In 1994, the company divested non-imaging health care operations to refocus on those cutting-edge products as well as core strength in cameras and film. The latter was supplemented in 1996 by professional digital cameras that captured images electronically, not on film. Management did not believe that digital cameras for the consumer mass market would cut sharply into Kodak film business until after 2000 when mega-pixel images as sharp as 35 millimeter camera pictures arrived. Nevertheless, the company cut the work force by 30,000 over the next five years. By 2002, operations generated better than a 6% profit.

However, the roof almost fell in on Eastman Kodak and its 70,000 employees. Seemingly in a blinking of an eye, US consumers began spending half as much on digital picture printing, including $3 billion on home printers, paper, and ink, as the $6.6 billion spent in 2002 on traditional camera film processing. The company's photo group watched sales drop 51% that year to just over $700 million. A 24% drop in US film sales held overall revenue virtually flat in 2003. The reason was obvious. Consumers had started to go for digital cameras in a big way. Fuji of Japan, Eastman Kodak's principal competitor in the camera and film market, had anticipated the swing and shifted its product line toward digital offerings. That company generated 15% of its $21 billion in annual revenue in the US. Moreover, when Eastman Kodak belatedly came out with *Easy Share* digital cameras retailing between $150 and $400, market leadership for 13 million units sold in the US in 2003 had already been secured by Sony and Olympus Optical, also of Japan. Only 12 million traditional cameras were sold, down from a peak of 20 million three years earlier.

Management's recovery plan focused on building up digital camera market share, boosting sales of photo ink jet paper from $100 million annually, or 20% of the half billion dollar market dominated by HP, and most controversially, making $2 billion of acquisitions as part of a move to abandon all film products over time in favor of digital products in health care imaging, cameras, and high-speed digital printing machines. A step was taken in that last direction in a joint venture with Heidelberger Druckmaschinen of Germany to take on HP's *Indigo* and Xerox's *IGEN 3* machines. Eastman Kodak also began putting retail digital mini-labs in drug stores for those consumers who did not have the ability to adjust and print out digital pictures using programs such as Adobe's *Photoshop*. Although the overall strategy was bold, institutional investors who had counted on the company being a cash cow from traditional camera and film sales, particularly overseas, were concerned enough to challenge aspects of the plan. Critics were particularly unmanned by the notion of challenging HP in the crowded ink jet printer field. The idea of making non-*Kodak* brand, heavily discounted film during the transition phase was also unappealing.

Arguing on Eastman Kodak management's behalf was the fact that the forces of rapid technology change, freer trade, globalization of markets, and increasing competition did not permit the luxury of sitting back and taking stock of the situation for very long. Even seemingly untouchable, New Economy powerhouses like Microsoft and Intel constantly scanned the horizon for fundamental consumer and corporate shifts. Though the specific strategic direction chosen by Eastman Kodak management could be argued, the necessity of doing something to salvage a proud business heritage, aside from planning to slash another 15,000 jobs through 2006, was clear. The only saving grace was that government had still not seen fit to intervene in a regulatory manner in New Economy sectors of the Internet, computer hardware and software, and related digital technology.

Quite the reverse, the government was more anxious than ever to offset a relative decline in manufacturing sector production and employment with growth in technologies. Continuing with the policy of establishing favorable conditions for New Economy endeavors, Washington set standards for Wi-Fi in 1997. That field of endeavor had been created in 1994 when the Harris Corporation of Melbourne, Florida used radio technology to beam data from one computer to another. Intersil, spun off by Harris in 1999, became the largest manufacturer in a nearly 40 million Wi-Fi chip market. However, entry of larger players into the market caused the company to sell its Wi-Fi operations for $365 million. Intel, in particular, with its *Centrino* chip for laptops used Wi-Fi as a loss leader because other products going into laptop computers were far more lucrative. By 2003, chip prices were down over three-fold to $15. Cisco decided to compete by purchasing Wi-Fi equipment maker Aironet Wireless Communications in November 2002 for $800 million, and then Linksys for $480 million the next March. The consequence of bringing order out of chaos was proliferation of Wi-Fi networks in dense areas of large cities. Wi-Fi began to pose a strategic threat to cable and DSL Internet services.

Washington was not averse to putting taxpayer dollars where Congress' mouth was. When HP and Compaq invested $600 million into a joint venture called Candescent Technologies to develop a thin cathode ray tube (CRT) flat-panel computer monitor with a picture as clear and crisp as TV, the House and Senate chipped in $45 million. However, difficulties stabilizing two thin sheets of glass within a pressurized perfect vacuum without creating spots on the glass where columns touched as well as developing a profitable mass production process foiled the enterprise. Back-lit Japanese displays trapping liquid crystals between two glass sheets for use in laptop computers took over the flat-panel computer monitor market, and soon the flat-panel under 40 inch TV market.

A related field was flat-panel, gas-plasma-filled TV screens over 40 inches, particularly for HDTV tuners that distinguished digital signals from cable and satellite providers. The government hoped that US companies could use HDTV to jump back into the $13 billion annual US TV market after three decades of Japanese domination. For that reason, Washington delayed setting HDTV standards, but the prohibitive cost of HDTV sets, still above $5,000, held sales to only 100,000 units through 2001. Thus, it was Toshiba and other Japanese companies that took the lead, albeit through Best Buy and other electronic retailers, in pushing up market penetration to over a tenth of US households. When the price of big screen, flat-panel TVs finally came down into a range that middle class Americans could afford but which still produced substantial profits, HP, Dell, Gateway, and other computer industry powerhouses moved in to compete. HDTV technology was still not integrated in most liquid crystal and gas-plasma sets.

Congress did not give up trying to accelerate the pace of change. The National Nanotechnology Initiative with an initial funding in 2001 of $500 million was intended to advance the quest for tinier, faster, and more powerful instruments. Although that was just a drop in the bucket compared to the $200 billion spent annually on all R&D efforts, even a small contribution could go a long way. The next year, Sandia National Laboratory came up with a new light bulb with a tungsten microscopic lattice instead of a filament that produced less heat and would ultimately be 60% more efficient.

Overall, the potential value in goods and services by 2015 of nanotechnology was estimated at over $1 trillion. An example was IBM's data storage breakthrough of nanometer-scale tips punching indentations into thin plastic film that could be erased and written over through techniques that coaxed heated film back into its original shape. The result would be a doubling of data storage per square inch for memory cards for cell phones, digital cameras, and computers. A postage stamp size memory card would ultimately be capable of containing data for 25 million printed textbook pages, about 20 times what was possible on hard drives currently.

When attempting to promote the general advance of science and technology, the government also continued to invest billions, not just millions. In addition to aerospace-defense contracts, the Reagan administration had proposed and won funding for an $11 billion, 54 mile circumference *SuperConducting SuperCollider* project in Texas to smash together sub-atomic particles and see what resulted. Burdened in the early post-Cold War period by still substantial national security appropriations, Congress cancelled the over-budget program in 1993. After NASA lost contact with the $1 billion *Mars Observer*, 11 months and 450 million miles into its journey toward the red planet, the space agency's spending authority too was cut. Although *Space Shuttle* missions continued right up to another disaster in 2001, it was clear to all that the high hopes of the country for a commercially viable, manned space mission program would not be fulfilled in the first decade of the new century. What was not in doubt was that Congress would persist in funding what senators and congressmen believed would be cutting edge technologies in the national self-interest.

As a direct response to the September 11, 2001 terrorist attacks, the House and Senate became interested in Directional Infrared Countermeasures. Specifically, lasers would be used to shoot down heat-seeking missiles aimed by terrorists at 6,800 US commercial airliners, foreign planes, and US military aircraft that were in the skies at any one time. The price of $2 million per laser was high, but mass production might cut the cost in half. The price of not having any defense would be infinitely greater.

Amtrak high-speed engine

Meanwhile, DOT approved in November 2002 preliminary plans for a $6 billion, high-speed train service between Charlotte and Washington. When completed by 2010, the train would cover the distance in 6 hours at an average speed of 90 mph, twice the current average. The idea was to reduce automobile and truck congestion along the heavily traveled eastern seaboard. Given Amtrak's inability to turn a profit in the Northeast, however, it was dubious that another subsidized rail line would be any more successful. Likewise, no early success was seen for a $1.2 billion, multiple year initiative announced by President Bush in 2003 to develop hydrogen fuel-cell technology. Advocates of free markets did not see the sense in weaning the country off internal combustion engines powered by cheap gasoline for a much more expensive technology.

In fact, the conclusion drawn by critics of Washington's successes and failures was that specific, non-defense related technology choices should be left in the hands of private industry. They pointed out that corporate R&D departments continued to come up with new consumer and industrial products. For example, GE scientists produced new synthetic diamonds in 1990 that conducted heat 50% better than natural diamonds, were 10 times more resistant to charge from electron beams, and absorbed 10 times more light. Further innovation by the company of Edison, including composite fan blades for jet engines, a digital X-ray detector that permitted X-rays to be read on computer screens without developed film, and high-field open magnetic resonance imaging (MRIs) to produce improved pictures of organs, tumors and other anatomical structures helped push the conglomerate's historic 10% operating margin to 15% in the last few years of the decade.

Intel facility in Hillsboro, Oregon

Other medical technology breakthroughs included pacemakers that used fiber-optic cable instead of wire so that MRIs could be done on 3 million pacemaker patients. Because the new device cost $14,000, twice as much initially as the old, the annual market for installing 600,000 pacemakers would rise to $8 billion. In dentistry $50,000 laser equipment began to replace drills, albeit in only 1% of the offices of 200,000 dentists, to vaporize gums and other soft tissue and prepare for small to medium size cavity filling. Although laser treatment took a bit longer to heal, both sides of the mouth could be treated during the same appointment, usually without anesthesia.

Far more expensive were positron emission tomography (PET) scans to detect biochemical functions such as oxygen consumption in the brain and heart after an injection of short-lived, radioactive tracer which emitted gamma rays that could be processed by a computer producing images. The capital cost of up to $2.5 million for scanners in combination with 50-ton cyclotrons (particle accelerators) at $1.5 million to produce the tracers was only reduced in 1996 after pharmacy networks agreed to supply the tracers. At $3,000, PET scans were still twice as expensive as CAT scans and MRIs. The advantage was early detection of changes in cells before formation of lesions and tumors. Thus in July 2001, Medicare approved the

Laptop PC

procedure to detect six kinds of cancer. Breast cancer was added in October 2002.

A major reason that US productivity continued to escalate in the new century was that the innovations of the 1990s were proliferated in industry. Intel built identical state-of-the-art, 200,000 square foot, $2 billion, automated chip factories to insure consistent production of 12-inch silicon wafers. Additionally, companies made incremental improvements in old technologies. IBM's *ASCI Purple* project to produce a 100 teraflop supercomputer with roughly the same calculations as the human brain but without the sophistication would give way by 2004 to a *Blue Gene* project shooting for 1,000 teraflop speed.

Although only a fifth of the patents awarded each year by the US patent office went to individuals, the number was nearly 70,000. It was still possible for some lone inventor to come up with an invention or innovation to create new economic opportunity. Because of high R&D and marketing costs, the more usual scenario was an alliance with a bigger entity with deeper pockets. Microsoft dumped nearly $500 million into developing what Gates called a Tablet PC to enable users to write in longhand on a computer screen like a child with the old *Etch A Sketch* toy. Although the company did bring out a product by 2003 that transformed sketches drawn by hand into graphical images with Corel's *Project Coligo* software, the technology was only in its infancy. Only time would tell if Microsoft had found another big revenue generator.

Chapter XVIII. Creative Content Creates Big Profits

US media and entertainment companies, with many of the same attributes as the New Economy, in particular a commitment to leading-edge technology, globalization of production and sales, restrained employment, and intangible intellectual property rights, chipped in half a trillion dollars of business revenue, which was 45% of all media and entertainment revenue world-wide. However, an absence of stifling regulation at home and overseas gave TV, radio, music, film, home video, publishing, sports, and electronic games not to mention art, theater, amusement park, and other niches an economic value more commensurate with their collective cultural, political, and social importance, which was pervasive. For that reason, the big players pushed in the 1990s to expand and merge into multi-media giants. Ironically, the hottest properties in the 1990s were in the cable industry, which Congress moved to regulate in the early 1990s.

Jack Nicholson

Revenue flowing into cable companies provided the wherewithal not only to challenge broadcast TV networks but bid to take them over. With the stock market surge, media industry CEOs paid top dollar for properties, conversely asked top dollar to be acquired. With the burgeoning number of cable networks, acquiring content as well was critical. Syndication rights to old TV programming as well as current production capabilities brought value to any deal. Too, professional, college, and even odd-ball sporting events claimed a more riveting hold on the competitive mind-set of the American public. Live entertainment events in arenas and stadiums seating tens of thousands tended naturally, therefore, to boost TV viewership rather than bring tens of millions out of their homes.

Ownership and the ability to create content was the same reason that movie studios found themselves hot properties even while suffering from broadcast and cable TV competition. The film industry also lost the attention of many children and teenagers to electronic video games. Film makers compensated for the drop in box office revenue with higher ticket prices, wider distribution overseas, VHS and DVD sales, TV syndication rights, and motion picture soundtracks. The more fragmented music industry hung on gamely with an emphasis on major recording artists putting out superb quality CDs until Internet downloading of free music capsized revenues and profits.

Most oppressed by the nation's fascination with moving images was the publishing industry. Had not books emerged as a major source of ideas for TV shows and motion pictures, the drift away from reading might have been even more pronounced. Newspaper and magazine publishers compensated with full-color pictures and web sites condensing print articles into concise summaries. Illustrated books cost more but had a decided price advantage over non-illustrated.

In fact, any entertainment or information product or service that combined two or more elements achieved a competitive advantage. Although one dimensional media such as radio continued to serve a purpose, their markets would not sustain many large players. The only question in this era of multi-media powerhouses was whether government would intervene to head off final consolidation of industries and prevent creation of monopolies. The urge for Washington to dabble, if not intervene outright, in the republic's intangible economy was almost irresistible.

CABLE REVOLUTIONIZES THE TV INDUSTRY

It was the Cable Television Law of October 5, 1992, passed over the elder Bush's veto, that authorized the FCC to set guidelines so local governments could establish reasonable prices for basic cable service and keep an eye on premium and other optional services. No longer would cable providers be granted exclusive franchises. Moreover, cable programming producers had to offer programs at "reasonable prices" so as not to squeeze cable providers into bankruptcy. On the other hand, local TV stations had the right to negotiate with cable providers for payments for re-transmitting their signals.

An FCC order the next year based on the Cable Act rolled back cable service fees to levels as of October 1992, amounting to a $1 billion reduction. US cable provider revenue would again come in around $22 billion. However, permanent price controls were not adopted. Once the cable industry embarked on a decade long consolidation, fewer cable providers existed to compete in local and regional areas.

In 1994, Comcast bought the operations of Maclean Hunter and E.W. Scripps to exceed 4 million customers and claim third place in the cable provider industry. The next year, management bought 57% of QVC to become an important supplier of content. After Microsoft in 1997 invested $1 billion in the company, Comcast had the wherewithal to buy a 40% controlling interest in E! Entertainment in partnership with Disney. Purchase the next year of Jones Intercable with 1.1 million customers, and Prime Communications with 400,000 put Comcast in position to bid for industry leadership. But a merger with MediaOne, valued in the inflated stock market at $60 billion, fell apart. Management settled for a $1.5 billion termination fee, which helped the company buy 2.7 million AT&T subscribers, Lenfest Communications' 1.3 million, and the popular Golf Channel.

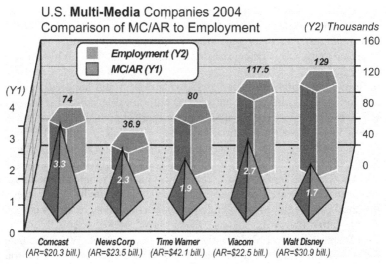

U.S. **Multi-Media** Companies 2004
Comparison of MC/AR to Employment   *(Y2) Thousands*

Comcast	NewsCorp	Time Warner	Viacom	Walt Disney
(AR=$20.3 bill.)	(AR=$23.5 bill.)	(AR=$42.1 bill.)	(AR=$22.5 bill.)	(AR=$30.9 bill.)

In 2001, Comcast merged with AT&T Broadband in what was expected to be a deal valued at $72.5 billion, including $25 billion of assumed debt, until the falling stock market and FCC delay in approving collapsed the figures by end of 2002 to $50 billion, of which $20 billion was assumed debt. The company served 21 million regular and 6.3 million digital cable subscribers, as well as 3.3 million DSL and 1.3 million cable Internet sub-scribers in 41 states with coverage of the nation's cable TV markets just under the FCC rule limit of 30%. Although takeover expenses and other costs associated with consoli-dating 82,000 employees were high, earnings from continuing operations before interest, taxes, depreciation, and amortization exceeded 8% of sales. Moreover, management sold QVC to Liberty Media for $7.9 billion to obtain cash to pay down debt. Still supplying sig-nificant content, Comcast was now entrenched as the nation's largest cable provider, with ambition to acquire a major media content company such as Walt Disney.

As previously discussed, after overpaying $55 billion for TCI and $58 billion for MediaOne in 1999, AT&T had when the stock market contracted to deal it all off to pay down debt. Management had been seduced by the rapid expansion of industry revenue toward $100 billion without an appreciation of industry fundamentals. A better business model would have included ownership of cable networks. Companies supplying content increasingly supplemented revenues based on fees charged to cable providers with adver-tising dollars amounting by 2002 to $10.8 billion.

Obtaining content was the motivation for Time Warner management buying Turner in 1995 for $7.5 billion, all stock. Ted Turner got a seat on Time Warner's board to help oversee combined annual revenues, including cable, movies, music, publishing, and TV, of $18.5 billion. As mighty as that multi-media empire appeared, the company's earnings were weighed down by $19 billion of debt. In January 2000 at the peak of the stock market bubble, the company succumbed to a landmark merger with Internet provider AOL that valued Time Warner at $165 billion while AOL's market capitalization was $185 billion. However, when the crash came, AOL Time Warner reported a first quarter 2002 loss of $54 billion from writing down the value of intangible assets, especially intellectual properties. Another whopping write-down of $45.5 billion in first quarter 2003, while not further undercutting market capitalization, forced Case to resign as chairman of the board. New leadership then dropped the AOL from Time Warner's name in fall 2003. Cable operations from 11 million subscribers, generating $7.7 billion of revenues as well as a third of the company's profits, was a prime reason the company survived in humbled but reasonable shape.

A move toward digital cable service, showing dozens and hundreds of shows and accounting for about a third of the nation's 80 million cable subscribers, also helped. Digital service brought twice the usual $500 per subscriber annual revenue. Overall, cable service drew a 50% share of the potential TV audience from all 107 million US households, up from less than 10% in the late 1980s, compared with a third for the major broadcast networks. Americans who opted to pay for expanded service and even premium service such as multiple HBO channels branching out from movies into entertainment specials and continuing series such as the smash hit The Sopranos about mafia family life, whether through analog or digital cable, enjoyed an eclectic variety of choices, increasingly controlled by powerful cable networks.

One cable empire was cobbled together in 1994 after head of QVC Diller failed in an attempt to buy CBS. Instead, he acquired Home Shopping Network and TV station owner Silver King Communications and then started building up USA Networks, centered on the USA and Sci-Fi channels. Universal Studios, controlled in 1998 by Seagram, was impressed enough by Diller's vision to combine its international TV operations with USA Networks. Vivendi of France three years later paid Diller $10.3 billion for his holding. However, the stock market decline and Vivendi's heavy debt load persuaded new management in 2003 to subsume Vivendi's film and TV properties in GE's NBC for $14 billion. GE wound up owning 80% of the NBC Universal group, Vivendi 20%, with annual 2003 revenue of $13 billion.

Woe to those cable providers who controlled little or no content, however. Cox Communications, the nation's fourth largest with 6.5 million broadband subscribers, was afflicted by some of the 27 cable networks raising fees on popular shows. For example, Disney's ESPN jacked up its per subscriber fee per month to over $3.00. Cox anted up for fear that angry customers would drop cable and sign up for satellite TV service.

The two main satellite TV competitors became DirecTV, controlled by GM's Hughes subsidiary, and EchoStar. Although tough bargaining by local TV stations for high fees complicated satellite broadcast of those signals, the former built toward 9.5 million subscribers in 2003, nearly half of all US satellite TV customers, while the latter had about 8.2 million. When the FCC rejected in October an EchoStar's proposed takeover of Hughes out of fear of creating a satellite TV monopoly, News Corp stepped in to acquire a controlling 34% stake for $3.8 billion. Murdoch's company promised the FCC that a $1.5 billion Spaceway project to supply Internet service by satellite signal would be completed by 2007. Meanwhile, Cablevision's chairman of the board Charles F. Dolan planned to spin off under his own control the company's small satellite division under the bold assumption that he could take on the big players and succeed. Cablevision's main cable operations were supplemented by ownership of the NBA New York Knicks, National Hockey League New York Rangers, and Madison Square Garden.

The ground-based cable TV industry not only had to worry about competition from satellite TV service but a resurgence by the major broadcast networks, albeit as subsid-

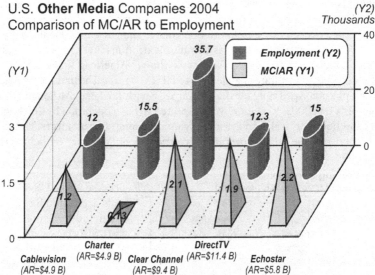

U.S. **Other Media** Companies 2004
Comparison of MC/AR to Employment

iaries of multi-media companies with much more financial clout. The new wave of consolidation started in 1995 when Walt Disney, bought Capital Cities and its ABC subsidiary for $19 billion. That prompted CBS to sell itself to Westinghouse, which changed its name to CBS in 1997 and divested itself of slower growing furniture, power-generation, and light bulb manufacturing operations. In addition to radio holdings, management in 1999 acquired King World Productions, a TV program syndicator, for $2.5 billion.

But that year Viacom, the multi-media giant controlling Paramount Studios and its UPN TV network, local TV stations in Philadelphia, Miami, Boston, and elsewhere, Blockbuster video, Simon & Schuster publishing, as well as cable networks *Nickelodeon, MTV, VH1* and later *Showtime, Country Music Television*, and others, offered to buy CBS for $36 billion in stock. By the time the deal closed in May 2000 near the peak of the stock market, the value was $50 billion.

Viacom went on to buy Black Entertainment Television for $3.3 billion. With CBS and UPN, the company controlled two of the six major broadcast networks. One problem was that CBS reached 39% of US viewers, a violation of FCC rules limiting broadcast networks to 35% coverage. However, in 2003 the FCC upped the figure to 45% until stiff congressional opposition forced an apparent compromise at 39%, which was then negated by a 2004 ruling by a US appeals court. Further, Viacom's extensive cable network holdings broadened its lead over News Corp's Fox, also with 39% broadcast coverage of the US, NBC with a bit more than a third, ABC with just less than a quarter, and Time Warner's WB network about an eighth. NBC's holding included Spanish-language Telemundo Communications with a 20% share of Hispanic American viewing, which the GE subsidiary bought in 2001 from Sony and Liberty Media for nearly $2 billion. GE also moved to correct the Peacock network's deficiency in TV production studios with the Vivendi deal. The Universal TV assets grouped with NBC included three *Law & Order* shows, rights to which NBC would have had to pay $550 million annually to keep.

Murdoch's control of Fox was an exception to US law capping foreign ownership at 20% direct and 25% indirect. Not only had he become a US citizen in 1988 but won FCC approval of his arrangement seven years later on the grounds that more competition in broadcast TV was in the public interest. By contrast, British TV and radio remained closed until a May 2002 decision by London to deregulate. The UK government's hope was to encourage the US further to open its communication markets as well as entice US investment. London wanted access to state-of-the-art American know-how and technology, for example to facilitate change over to HDTV signals. The first such broadcast in the US took place in April 1999 for the *Tonight Show* with Jay Leno. Although HDTV sets cost about $1,500 in 2003, 10 million were expected to be in operation by 2004, including flat panel and liquid crystal displays already used in computer monitors. Unlike continental EU countries, the British government worried about falling too far behind the New World republic.

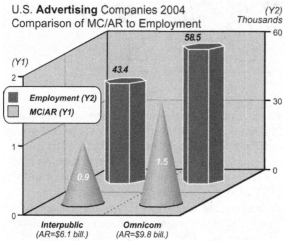

U.S. **Advertising** Companies 2004
Comparison of MC/AR to Employment

(Y2) Thousands

Because in the US, TV commercials accounted for one quarter of the advertising industry's $141 billion revenue in 2004, about 53% of the worldwide total, viewership of whatever kind was important for TV networks. The six major broadcast networks alone accounted for $22.5 billion in ad revenue, three-fifths attributable to commercials for the fall season new episode premiers, while all national advertising amounted to three fifths of the total. Key to success was commercials for big sporting events such as the NFL's Super Bowl, rising from $850,000 per 30 second spot in 1992 toward $2 million eleven years later while spots for *Friends*, the most popular TV series of NBC, topped $470,000. Local newspapers still held the top spot with $24.6 billion of ad revenue.

Speaking of big-time sports, escalating TV contracts for the major leagues, culminating in the NFL's $11.5 billion six year deal through 2010 with CBS, Fox, and DirecTV, resulted in record mergers and acquisitions. For example, Fox bought the Los Angeles Dodgers for $311 million in 1998. Viacom sold Madison Square Garden to Cablevision for nearly $1.1 billion.

Legalized gambling in casinos in Nevada, Atlantic City, Indian reservations, and riverboats as well as horse-racing betting, state and regional lotteries, video poker machines, and Internet games caused the total take from games of chance to surge to over $50 billion in annual revenue, five times the level of 1981. Following the Indian Gaming Regulatory Act of 1988, the smart money was placed on reservation casinos, generating over a third of that haul by 2004. Escalating profits for casino companies demonstrated that most gamblers' money never returned to their pockets. Smaller bets by millions of addicted gamblers also helped push prize money in horse-racing, including $5.2 million for the 1998 *Breeder's Cup* horse race won by Awesome Again, up to record levels.

Naturally, companies that created ads vied for the business of major clients such as GE, P&G, the car companies, and others. Interpublic of New York briefly took the lead in the ad industry through a series of acquisitions culminating in purchase of Chicago's True North Communications for $2.1 billion in 2001. But heavy debt taken on to fund the spree as well as difficulties consolidating companies undermined profitability. Ominously, client Coca-Cola began reviewing its contract with Interpublic as well as other companies.

Meanwhile, Omnicom Group of New York moved onward and upward. The only other big competitors of note were WPP Group of Britain with $7 billion of annual revenue and Publicis of France with $4.7 billion, both of which had MC/ARs more in line with Omnicom's than Interpublic's.

PANORAMA OF VIDEO POSSIBILITIES

The movie industry with roughly $9.5 billion in US theater ticket sales in 2002, 55% of the world total, overlapped with the TV and cable industry in falling into the hands of multi-media giants. The fundamental problem for most studios was that production costs, including salaries for major stars, were escalating so fast that a typical feature film cost tens of billions of dollars, with some exceeding $100 billion, particularly when including marketing and distribution costs. One way to reduce costs was to film away from Hollywood, including in Mexico and Canada, where non-union workers could be hired for half or two-thirds the US wage. While US film production costs amounted in 2002 to $3.25 billion, another $1.25 billion was split evenly between the NAFTA neighbors.

Regardless of production costs, the key to commercial success became big opening weekends. Positive reviews by film critics with advance screening could result in packed theaters and favorable word-of-mouth. For example, when Sony's Columbia/Tristar's *Spider Man* opened before the prime summer season on May 3, 2002 with a strong story line and wow special effects, it grossed $286.5 million in 16 days, a third of its eventual global box office take. European box office was by far the most important overseas market.

But the aftermarket for home video DVD and VHS rentals and sales was even more important. On average, they accounted for 46% of a film property's revenues. Thus, *Spider Man*'s ultimate take eventually approached $1.5 billion. Projected revenue from pay-for-view, broadcast, and cable TV distribution chipped in over time another $880 million. With all these revenue streams, even a single smash hit could, like a billion barrel oil field, propel a company to riches. Each of the major studios wanted a chunk of the annual global marketplace for film and related revenue, exceeding $50 billion by 2003.

The risk was still high. Failures such as orchestrated by acclaimed actor-director-producer Kevin Costner with his film *The Postman*, costing $100 million, which generated only $17 million of box office for Warner, could severely wound a studio. Management had to protect the interests of shareholders by seeking the protection of companies with deeper pockets. Hence in 1994, Paramount was bought by Viacom for $1.8 billion, defeating a rival bid by Diller's USA Networks and QVC. When in 1998, Paramount's *Titanic* grossed $600 million in the US and ultimately an additional $1.2 billion world wide, Viacom's acquisition was justified. The film brought more prestige to the studio by taking the Academy Award for Best Picture.

In 1996, Australia's Seven Networks acquired MGM for $1.3 billion. That studio also became more valuable after taking over Orion Pictures, just emerging from Chapter 11, for

Genealogy of Movie Industry, 1946-2004

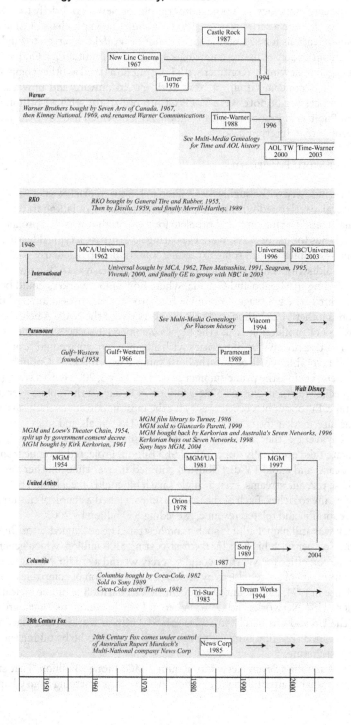

$573 million and then in 1999 buying PolyGram's film library to increase its holding to 4,100 titles, including half of Hollywood's productions since 1948. In 2004, Time Warner tried to buy MGM, independent again, for $4.6 billion but was outmaneuvered by Sony. The Japanese company took the legendary film company and its treasure trove of films for $3 billion in cash as well as assumption of $1.9 billion in debt.

Meanwhile, Twentieth Century Fox, still under News Corp, found success not only with a new trilogy of *Star Wars* prequels that promised to ring up another $1 billion in direct box office and nearly $4 billion of revenue overall but a Fox network TV show, the *X-Men*, taken to the silver screen as a feature film. Boasting over $22 billion in 2004 revenue, the parent company reaped greater profits from follow-up DVD sales of movies and TV shows than any other business line. Murdoch then decided to move incorporation from Australia to the US, whence three-quarters of the company's revenues arose. The land Down Under thus lost its largest corporation and a success story begun with a single paper in the city of Adelaide.

To secure movie content for his cable networks, Ted Turner took over Castle Rock Entertainment and New Line Cinema in 1994. Castle Rock concluded an exclusive deal with the *Showtime* network to make 50 made-for-cable movies. After Turner merged into Time Warner and AOL took that company over, New Line Cinema gambled and hit the jackpot. The 2001 film *Lord of Rings, Fellowship of the Ring*, based on the books of deceased British professor of languages J.R.R. Tolkien, sold $860 million worth of tickets as well as another $440 million of home video sales with much more expected over time. Because production and marketing costs amounted to $160 million, executives all the way up the food chain from New Line to Time Warner to AOL breathed a sigh of relief. *The Two Towers* and *Return of the King* sequels, shot simultaneously with the original in New Zealand to keep down costs, did equivalent business.

The *Matrix* movies, another trilogy, were almost as successful, albeit costing $400 million because they were shot separately. Star Keanu Reeves alone received $40 million for the three films. In a surer bet, Warner also gathered in nearly $1 billion from *Harry*

Potter and *The Sorcerer's Stone*. As many sequels as author J.K. Rawlings wrote books were planned.

The only major studio to retain its independence and become a multi-media bonanza in itself was Walt Disney. A decade of growth began in 1993 when Kodak *Cineon* technology was used to digitally re-master the *Snow White & Seven Dwarfs* classic for re-release in theaters and home video. The next year, the Magic Kingdom scored a hit with the *Lion King* animated film that grossed $312 million at the box office around the world. Through 2001, the *Lion King* franchise generated another $700 million in other revenue, including merchandising.

Production costs for the film were a hefty $50 million. However, the Lion King's success persuaded Disney executive Jeffrey Katzenberg, after a falling out with CEO Michael D. Eisner, to leave the company and join up with director Steven Spielberg and music producer David Geffen to found a new studio called DreamWorks. While Dream-Works did have conventional successes with *Saving Private Ryan* and *American Beauty*, its biggest impact was hiring away Disney animators and thus raising salaries in the industry to unheard of heights. To lower production costs for animated films and lessen the risk of flops, such as Disney's *Treasure Planet*, based on John Lewis Stevenson's classic book about pirate gold, *Treasure Island*, both DreamWorks and Disney turned to digital animation using computers. The former's 2001 hit *Shrek* as well as the latter's *Finding Nemo* in 2003 used digital animation. A new company called Pixar Animation Studios, run by Apple's Steve Jobs, more than doubled its annual revenue to $49 million by working for Disney on *Finding Nemo*. However, the greatest reward went to Disney, racking up $400 million globally from the film while DreamWorks did nearly half a billion on *Shrek*. When Disney refused to cut Pixar in for a larger share of future profits, Jobs startled Eisner by severing ties with the Magic Kingdom, thus giving legitimacy to criticism by Roy E. Disney (founder Walt Disney's grandson and top individual shareholder) that Eisner was doing a poor job.

As mentioned above, home video rentals and sales became indispensable to the economics of theatrical films. Sales of VHS tapes for play on VCRs, present in 90% of US households by the new century, soared from $12 billion in 1992 to double that figure by end of the period. About the same time in 1994 that Viacom bought Paramount, management paid $8.4 billion for an 80% stake in Blockbuster after the video rental chain put $1.85 billion into Viacom. As Blockbuster expanded into international markets, its value rose again. With the changeover from VCRs to DVDs, annual revenues built toward $6 billion in 2004. By comparison, competitor Columbia House, a direct marketer about three-fifths owned by the Blackstone Group after that private equity firm paid $410 million in 2002, only did $1 billion a year. However, as a seller of tapes and discs not a renter, Columbia House was able to adjust more swiftly to the aggressive move by Wal-Mart, Target, and others to sell DVDs near or below $10. Blockbuster, too, was forced to sell more DVDs, including discs previously used as rentals, to remain viable.

Coming fast was the video game industry, sometimes as with *Lara Croft, Tomb Raider* an inspiration for feature films. However, in the new century, hardware and software sales of video games exceeded movie theater revenues to reach $10 billion in the US in 2002 and $27 billion in the world. As well as Sony with Playstation, Nintendo with GameCube, and Microsoft with Xbox, prime beneficiary was Electronic Arts (EA Sports) of Redwood City, California. The company claimed a 10% global share by virtue of annual improvements to its *Madden NFL* and *Tiger Woods Golf* games. In 2003, management picked Sony over Microsoft as a partner for on-line Internet gaming out of fear of Microsoft's history of muscling in on the business of allies. Microsoft had tried to play hardball in negotiations by refusing to share a percentage of subscriptions for the new service.

Tiger Woods

Developers of video and electronic game software went to elaborate lengths, of course, to prevent theft of intellectual property and illegal copying of products. The Digital Millennium Copyright Act of 1998 established broader protection as well for owners of creative material ranging from books to films to music. The Copyright Term Extension Act, authored by former pop singer turned congressman Sonny Bono that same year, lengthened copyright protection from 75 years to 95 years for literature, music, movies, and other material beginning 2003. The value to current copyright holders was estimated in the billions.

Not in need of protection, of course, were one-of-a-kind items. The original manuscript of Jack Kerouac's *On the Road* sold for $2.3 million at auction in 2001. Works of art of all kinds soared in value during the 1990s because the run-up of the stock market created wealth for the well heeled. Nineteenth century Dutch painter Vincent Van Gogh's *Portrait de l'artiste sans barbe* sold for $71 million in New York City in 1998. However, after the stock market crash, Christie's and Sotheby's, the two principal auction houses, with about $950 million and $350 million in annual revenues respectively, struggled to make a profit. Price-fixing scandals also shook the art auction business.

The popularity of electronic games did not subvert sales of traditional sports products. Nike moved to generate more revenue by association with Woods and other stars. Reebok, too, went the way of celebrity endorsements to boost annual revenue. Brunswick, an old-line maker of billiard tables, fitness equipment, bowling, boats, and marine engines, generated sales the old-fashioned way, by brand awareness.

ELUSIVE PROFITS FOR MUSIC AND PUBLISHING

A lesser supplemental revenue stream from film was movie soundtracks. One reason that Geffen, after selling Geffen Records to MCA for stock in 1990 for $545 million and doubling his fortune the next year with the purchase of MCA by Matsushita Electrical Industrial of Japan, joined DreamWorks was to develop this aspect of the business. Particularly as the durable CD format, selling 300 million discs globally, finished off the old LP format, music took off. However, fickle consumer tastes and the challenge of free music downloads caused DreamWorks to sell off its music division to Vivendi Universal for $100 million in 2003.

That transaction actually united Geffen's old music company with the new one. Back in 1995, Seagrams of Britain bought 80% of MCA from Matsushita for $5.7 billion, and then subsumed it into Universal Studios. Three years later, Seagrams purchased PolyGram, a record company with extensive US holdings originally founded by Philips Electronics of the Netherlands in 1972, for $10.4 billion and combined its music operations into a Universal Music Group. When Vivendi of France took over Seagram's in 2000, Universal Music Group was included. Belatedly in 2003, Universal acquired 100% of the MCA label and put its operations under Geffen Records. Still under Vivendi, Universal Music controlled in 2002 just under a quarter of the $30 billion global music market, including about 30% of US sales.

However, the industry had taken a severe hit from the success of Napster. Founded in 1999, that company and other Internet downloaders of music distributed copied music in MP3 format for free between user members through central servers while making money from ads. US music sales, in particular, contracted 14% by annual revenue through 2003 and one quarter by volume of shipments. Although Napster was shut down by court order in 2002, Internet downloads continued between users without central servers. A move by Apple with its *iPod* portable music player to sell songs for 99 cents each was emulated by several other music industry backed companies. Better positioned as usual to take advantage of Internet related downloads, not only of music but video, was Microsoft with its *Media Player* software bundled with the *Windows* operating system.

Further roiling the waters, Universal Music Group suddenly in September 2003 cut CD prices about a third to a range of $10 to $13 to stimulate sales. Its four main competitors, Time Warner's Warner Music Group and Bertelsmann's BMG each with a sixth of the US market and under an eighth of the world, Sony Music Entertainment with a slightly smaller US share and larger global share, EMI of Britain with about a tenth of the US and an eighth of the world, as well as lesser entities with a combined 15% in the US and one quarter of the global music market were faced with a decision whether to concur or risk a consumer backlash. Warner, after a 1994 takeover of CPP/Belwin, the world's largest publisher of printed music, had as the subsidiary of Time Warner the deepest pockets. However, the parent sold the division to an investor group led by Seagram's former majority owner for $2.6 billion, giving up about the same figure in annual sales.

Free Internet downloads had no effect, however, on the drive by Clear Channel Communications to grab the radio industry by the throat. The company was helped in 1992 by an FCC rule change to allow ownership of two FM and two AM stations in a single market. By 1995, Clear Channel owned 43 radio stations and 16 TV stations in 32 markets, mostly from Texas to Florida to Virginia. The company then went overseas to take a half interest in the second largest radio network in Australia and a one third stake in the largest New Zealand network.

The Telecommunications Act of 1996 opened the door to more wheeling and dealing. Management built up the company's holdings to 1,200 stations in the US and hundreds more overseas by a flurry of large and small purchases costing tens of billions of dollars. Too, Clear Channel widened its presence in outdoor ads to 700,000 displays and bought SFX Entertainment, producer of live entertainment events. Revenues arose about 40% each from radio and live entertainment operations, as well as pre-programmed music which severely reduced the need for disc jockeys and other employees.

By comparison, the radio network CBS built up with a 1996 purchase of Infinity's radio broadcasting and outdoor advertising group for $4.7 billion, a 1997 take over of the American Radio Systems chain for $2.6 billion, and a sell-off of 17% of the Infinity holding for $2.9 billion the next year when stock values were high was far less than 10% the number of Clear Channel stations. Industry size was considered too insignificant for the FCC to intervene.

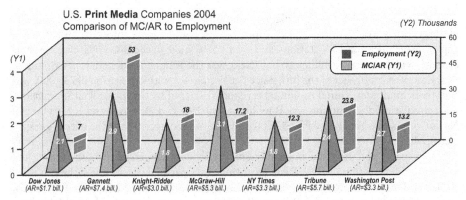

Meanwhile, newspapers and magazines not only dwarfed radio ad revenue, they generated approximately 30% more than TV. Because circulation figures for daily newspapers continued to contract in the 1990s, ad sales were the industry's lifeblood. Companies squeezed out more profit by mergers and acquisitions as well as diversification into ownership of more local TV and radio stations. The Tribune Company of Chicago even grabbed a 10% stake in AOL for $5 million in 1991. By comparison, the purchase price in 2000 for the Times Mirror newspaper and magazine group, whose managers must have been kicking themselves for failing to close a 1997 deal to acquire eBay for $40 million, was $6.5 billion. To reduce debt, Tribune sold off Times Mirror's magazines, including *Golf*, *Ski*,

Skiing, Field & Stream, and *Yachting*, to Time Warner. Its *L.A. Times* was in fourth place with 955,000 daily copies and the *Chicago Tribune* held onto eighth at 613,000.

Gannett, on the other hand, achieved even greater success with a series of acquisitions that began with outdoor advertiser and radio station owner Multimedia in 1995. The company also bought up newspapers and magazines in the U.K. After divestiture of Multimedia, management refocused on *USA Today*, the leading national newspaper with 2.25 million daily papers circulated.

By comparison, *NY Times* circulation of 1.1 million was good for third place nationally but less than a 50% share in the Big Apple. The parent company enjoyed a mix of newspapers, magazines, local TV stations, and even a 50% stake in the *Discover Civilization* cable channel, which cost $100 million to buy. Next was the Knight-Ridder chain. Washington Post Company, publisher of the fifth place *Washington Post* with circulation of 730,000, was slightly behind as measured by annual revenue. Owner of second place *Wall Street Journal* with circulation of 2.1 million was Dow Jones. The *New York Daily News* with 730,000 and News Corps's *New York Post* with 652,000 provided stiff competition in the nation's largest metropolis.

Newspaper and magazine publishers suffered from stagnated ad spending during and following the recession of 2001. Rising printing costs particularly attacked the profits of the latter. Long-term prospects were probably not helped by the $2.8 billion takeover of Moore Wallace of Canada by R.R. Donnelley & Sons to claim a twentieth of a highly fragmented $160 billion annual commercial printing industry and prepare the way for further consolidation. That company would now combined $8 billion and 50,000 employees to increase its leverage with clients such as *Sports Illustrated* and *T.V. Guide*. J.C. Penney, for whom Donnelley printed catalogues, and UPS, which always needed forms and labels, were other prominent customers. The company's economies of scale improved.

Although rising printing expenses from the cost of paper hurt book publishers, a general apathy in readership in the TV and video era was more to blame for the industry's struggles. Even so, best selling non-fiction books could approach 1 million copies while fiction best sellers sold perhaps twice as much. The fact that the US population continued to increase pushed book sales up toward $27 billion in 2002, not quite twice as much as in 1990. Because of the Baby Boom generation's procreative activities, the most consistently lucrative niche continued to be text and other educational books.

The three leaders in college textbooks became Pearson of Britain, controlling Prentice Hall and Penguin Books, Thompson of Canada, and McGraw Hill of New York. Their combined share of the English language market grew from a bit more than a third in 1990 to over three-fifths in 2004.

But the largest book publisher in the US became Bertelsmann of Germany after buying Random House for $1.5 billion in 1998 to align with its Bantam Doubleday, Alfred A. Knopf, Pantheon, and other US and overseas units. The company also took a 50% stake in a Barnes and Nobles on-line venture. Borders, generating sales from 1,200 Borders and WaldenBooks stores in the US and overseas, teaming up with Amazon.com to sell books on line, continued to compete with the Barnes and Noble chain for national bookstore leadership.

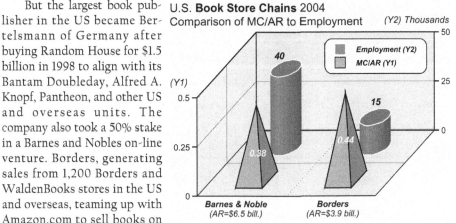

U.S. **Book Store Chains** 2004
Comparison of MC/AR to Employment *(Y2) Thousands*

Overall in the last decade of the twentieth century and first decade of the twenty-first, intangible entertainment and information content and services became more valuable than physical products. Income and profits from the New and quasi-New Economy boosted the net worth of many households and businesses. However, the cornucopia was not yet large nor well distributed enough to compensate fully for contractions in income and profits in old economy industries. Those citizens who had lost well-paying manufacturing and other jobs had to settle for lower paying service employment were particularly bewildered, frustrated, and envious of the wealth and income of the more fortunate.

CHAPTER XIX. BLENDING THE OLD ECONOMY WITH THE NEW

One of the most potent sectors of the economy in the 1990s was not part of the New Economy. The roots of health care dated back to the earliest time of the republic. However, in more modern and sophisticated times it grew to account for one sixth of GDP. It was the service counterpart to the retail trade for goods. Health expenditures were similar to consumer non-durables because medical care was as essential for living as food and other basic products. Yet dollars spent on drugs, doctor visits, and hospital stays generated no permanent wealth for the buyer.

Another way of looking at health care was in relation to the Old Economy and the New. To the degree that companies relied upon large physical infrastructures and labor forces, they were part of the Old. Moreover, a legacy of government regulation and oversight constrained business opportunities. To the issues of monopoly control, safety regulations, and employee job security and wages, much debated in transportation, energy, and other historically regulated industries, was added public outrage about excessive profits. On the other hand, to the degree that pharmaceutical makers, medical instrument companies, and even hospital chains accessed high technology and used automation to replace workers they resembled New Economy purveyors of the Internet, telecommunications, computer software, and other creative content. They needed New Economy returns on investment, moreover, to cover high R&D costs.

The reason that government maintained closer supervision of the health care system was that medical insurance premiums and expenses negatively impacted standards of living, particularly during recessions when citizens of middle and marginal means were put under the gun by rising costs. Government pressure on drug companies, insurance companies, and hospitals to make health care accessible to a larger proportion of the population diminished in more prosperous years but was never absent. Yet the large physical infrastructure of institutions, health care employment pushing past 2 million, and the republic's expectation of further medical advances prevented the federal government and states from going too far in impinging revenues and profits. As health care came to contribute more to the economy, national income, and tax revenue, more of a balancing act

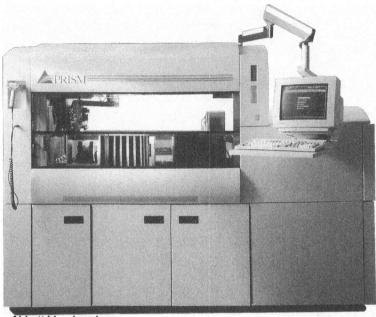

Abbott blood analyzer

was struck to moderate medical cost inflation without contracting the overall sector. Demanding quality and affordable health care almost as a God-given right, the American people never quite came to grips with the fact that "quality" and "affordable" were contra-dictory terms. Regulation and government oversight was what the American people insisted upon to keep down costs.

CLINTON ECONOMICS AND THE HEALTH CARE MAELSTROM

In the 1992 election, those voters who were most concerned about health care and other standard of living issues voted in overwhelming numbers for Bill Clinton. However, the basic economic program as set forth the next year by Chairman of the National Economic Council Robert Rubin, formerly head of Goldman Sachs and later to become Secretary of the Treasury, was not to attack specific ills inflating the cost of living, rather to cut spending and increase taxes by a combined $500 billion to eliminate the federal deficit. Budget expenditures heading toward balance with revenue would permit Greenspan, still chairman of the Federal Reserve System as he moved into his eighth decade, to cut interest rates and stimulate growth. Moderating energy costs and pressure on unions from auto-mation and the developing world labor market would also tend to reduce inflation.

The fact that actual experience with higher deficits in the 1980s had not indicated that deficits in themselves inhibited growth did not seem to matter. More attention was paid to the absolute dollar figure of deficits, amounting then annually to more than $200 billion, than to the deficit as a percent of GDP. Thus, the President persuaded the Democratic majority in Congress to pass on August 10, 1993 an Omnibus Reconciliation Act that increased taxes on wealthier persons, including those receiving Social Security, to a top marginal rate of 39.6%, up from 31% under the elder Bush and a low of 28% under Reagan in 1988. The legislation also boosted the gas tax, paid by all Americans who drove cars and trucks, and squeezed down federal spending on Medicare, Medicaid, and other health care programs by reducing reimbursements to doctors and hospitals regardless of their fees.

Robert Rubin

That latter action was merely a stop-gap measure until comprehensive health care reform, a major plank in the Democratic platform, could be debated and enacted. Some sort of overall reform plan seemed inevitable because between 1987 and 1993, *per capita* cost had risen 25% to $4,000, federal spending on health care had passed 10% of GDP, and overall health care spending finally exceeded $1 trillion. Annual double-digit health insurance premium increases in the first years of the decade swelled the number of Americans without such plans to 37 million. In combination with the 1991 recession, inflationary pressures threw more families out of the middle class.

Upon taking the oath of office, Clinton appointed a commission to look into the sector of the economy that threatened to overwhelm the finances of 100 million households. In an unprecedented and controversial decision, and contrary at least to the spirit of US law forbidding a President's relative to hold high federal office, he appointed his wife Hillary to head that investigation. After eight months of hearings, conducted to the chagrin and suspicion of health care leaders behind closed doors, the commission reported on September 22 that the republic should move to a system of managed competition. At once, the plan ran into a hailstorm of criticism. Hospitals, doctors, and other medical professionals complained that a health care system more heavily regulated by the federal government would ruin the better aspects of the system, such as patient choice of doctors, while resulting in no improvement in the worst. They railed against the calamity that would result should bureaucrats intrude upon medical decisions about who should be treated, when, and with what drugs and procedures.

In the end, Republicans mustered enough support to kill the larger plan. A general muting of inflation and enactment of specific proposals such as portability of coverage, limiting pre-condition restrictions, and patient consent to release medical records, the last measure by Executive Order in December 2000 just before Clinton left office, temporarily got the public off politician backs. However, managed care contracts signed by companies with big HMOs to limit costs, while successful between 1994 and 1999 in holding health care spending increases to an annual rate of 2.5% and a low of 13.3% of GDP, harmed the overall quality of medical care and established a combative environment between on the one hand health care suppliers and the other Medicare/Medicaid administrators and private insurance companies. As *per capita* spending on health care jumped again in the new century toward $6,000 and the number of uninsured, albeit as a lesser percent of the overall population, mounted to a new record of 46 million, the issue reemerged as a political hot-potato for which no national leader could propose a facile and workable solution.

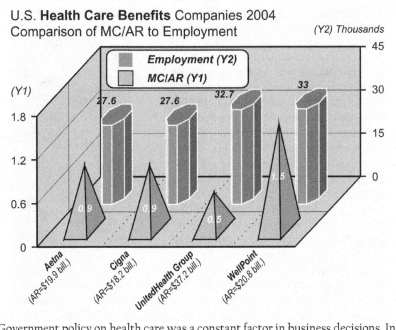

U.S. **Health Care Benefits** Companies 2004
Comparison of MC/AR to Employment

(Y2) Thousands

Legend: Employment (Y2), MC/AR (Y1)

Values: Aetna (AR=$19.9 bill.) — 27.6, 0.9; Cigna (AR=$18.2 bill.) — 27.6, 0.9; UnitedHealth Group (AR=$37.2 bill.) — 32.7, 0.5; WellPoint (AR=$20.8 bill.) — 33, 1.5

Government policy on health care was a constant factor in business decisions. In 1991, insurers were so frantic over what to expect that Aetna Life and Casualty sold its individual health book of business to Mutual of Omaha while Lincoln National got out of managed health care the next year. But four years later after the political situation stabilized, Aetna bought US Healthcare for $8.9 billion to take the lead in managed care and in 1998 paid $1 billion for the health division of New York Life Insurance. By the last decade of the century, the company was the largest health insurance company in the country. That status and rigorous application of HMO rules brought class action lawsuits charging Aetna with unfair billing policies and interference with legitimate medical decisions. The company's goal appeared unmistakably to squeeze out the last dollar of profit. That impression was reinforced by management's announcement in December 2000 of double digit increases in health premiums to offset rising claims and a net loss the next year of $280 million as well as layoff of 15,000 employees. Steady application of the controversial practice of dropping coverage on policy holders in ill health who receive more in claims than they contributed in premiums cut managed care membership from a high of 21 million to about 13 million by 2003-2004.

After the Clinton plan was rejected, Blue Cross of California formed Wellpoint Health Systems as an independent company to operate its managed care business. With Corporate America embracing ever more severe variations of the cost-cutting concept, Wellpoint re-merged with Blue Cross of California four years later under the Wellpoint name. As well, the company bought the life and health division of Massachusetts Mutual

Life Insurance and John Hancock Life Insurance. Management also gobbled up Blue Cross and Blue Shield companies in Georgia and Missouri.

Before Wellpoint took its Blue operations across state lines, Anthem in 1993 expanded from Indiana into Kentucky, and then in the next six years took over Blue Cross and Blue Shield plans in Ohio, Connecticut, New Hampshire, Maine, and Virginia. Simultaneously, the company bought other HMOs to build up overall membership to 22 million, including 18 million in managed care. Adding 15 million dental benefit members,

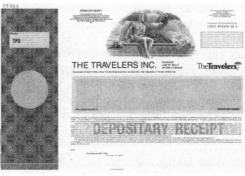

Anthem came to insure over 14% of the US population. Seeking synergies and greater leverage with customers, management in October 2003 negotiated an agreement to buy Wellpoint at a substantial premium for $15.2 billion in stock and $1.2 billion in assumed debt. Once the merger was approved, combined revenues of the company, taking Wellpoint's name, amounted to $21 billion while share of the nation's 84 million Blue Cross and Blue Shield members topped 30%.

Another company that drove the managed care bandwagon was United HealthCare. In 1994, the company sold its Diversified Pharmaceutical Services subsidiary to SmithKline Beecham of Britain for $2.3 billion and used the money the next year to buy MetraHealth, a joint venture of Metropolitan Life and Travelers for $1.65 billion. Changing its name to UnitedHealth Group in 1998, the company configured its *Clinical Profiles* data base as a marketing tool to build up its network of physicians and as a benchmark to compare clinical practices with nationally accepted standards of care. By consistent annual premium increases for 18 million members, UnitedHealth Group built revenues. Recognizing that the Mid-Atlantic region was one of the fastest growing population areas in the country, management in 2003 negotiated to buy Mid-Atlantic Medical Services of Rockville, Maryland for nearly $3 billion. The deal added another $2.3 billion in annual revenue from nearly 2 million members, and promised to boost revenue even further as United-Health imposed its premium structure. Because of the same fundamentals, UnitedHealth then purchased Oxford Health Plans the next year for $5 billion. After consolidating Oxford's financials, Americans served by its network of 400,000 physicians and 3,600 hospitals rose to 52 million while annual 2004 revenues jumped to $37.2 billion.

Next largest riser was CIGNA. In 1997, the company bought Healthsource of New Hampshire to spread its HMO business into more areas and build up by end of period to 11 million members. Deciding that global health and pension operations supplied superior return on investment, management sold off its individual life and annuity business to Lincoln National for $1.4 billion. Two years later, its property and casualty business went to ACE, a global operation with over $12.3 billion in revenues by 2004, for $3.45 billion. In 2000, remaining life insurance and accidental death policies were dealt off to Swiss Reinsurance Group. Because of the possibility of heavier government regulation in the future as well as present economic uncertainties that resulted in a loss of $400 million, CIGNA's revenue contracted, forcing management to slash its dividend by over nine-tenths in 2004 and cut 3,000 jobs.

A smaller, less attractive company for investors who followed the managed care industry was Humana. In addition to its main thrust of HMO and PPOs contracts, the company also covered Medicare and Medicaid patients, offered dental, disability, and group life insurance, and provided health care coverage to military personnel and dependents. By also making use of the Internet to sell insurance, managed care membership climbed to 6 million in 2003.

Humana's main competition in disability insurance was MetLife and niche leader UnumProvident, formed in 1993 when Colonial Life merged with Accident to make Unum, and then Unum bought Provident of Chattanooga for $4.75 billion. Whereas Accident had been a leader in group disability, Provident specialized in individual policies.

While HMOs and other health insurance companies were trying to help employers and governments hold down costs, pharmaceutical firms, now including bio-tech businesses, still wanted to maximize shareholder value. The best way to do that was by taking advantage of the patent system for prescription drugs. True, R&D expense was great and the FDA required rigorous clinical trials to test safety and effectiveness before approving new medications, but once approved even a single prescription drug could generate hundreds of millions and even billions of dollars in annual revenue. In part because managed care companies began in 1996 adding prescription drug benefits to attract members, the US prescription drug market grew from $33 billion in 1990, of which about a quarter was non-patented generics, to $122 billion in 2000. Thereafter, double-digit annual increases in demand outpacing price increases three to one caused revenues to boom toward $235 billion in 2004. On average 30% cheaper than patented prescription drugs, generics accounted for about 40%.

Back in 1992, in anticipation of the impact of health care reform, major US pharmaceutical companies started buying up generic drug companies. When the Clinton plan was announced, it contained a proposal to establish a new national health board to investigate "unreasonable" prices, force a 15% rebate on drugs paid for by Medicare after the government had already bargained down prices, and consolidate most Americans into huge health plans with more clout to encourage use of generic drugs. Before Congress' rejection of the plan in spring 1994, market capitalizations fell a third. Most big drug companies announced layoffs.

Even when the specter of severe regulation was temporarily lifted, the industry had to deal with a law suit by 20 drugstores about price-fixing and anti-trust violations. In 1995, Congress applied pressure to limit prescription drug prices to Medicare and Medicaid recipients. In reaction, companies decided to counteract the effect of price cuts on profit margins with cost-savings. The best way to do that was, of course, by greater economies of scale through consolidations. Bigger size translated ultimately into greater leverage to insist upon higher prices for new prescription drugs, hence a movement after the turn of the century by health management companies and even state and local governments to import cheaper generics and patented drugs. A nasty confrontation developed between industry leader Pfizer and others who were determined to protect their business fundamentals and government entities outside of Washington determined to secure the drugs Americans needed and wanted at more affordable prices.

DRUG COMPANIES PROSPER IN THE GLOBAL MARKET

The pharmaceutical industry and the government were not always at odds. Washington helped through the Free Trade regime of GATT and WTO in persuading the Japanese to open their market for prescription drugs so that imports claimed by 2003 a quarter of a $50 billion market. Likewise, the FDA began pressuring the EU as part of overall trade jockeying to ease price controls that kept drug prices as low as a third of US prices. By paying much higher prices for drugs, the reasoning went, American taxpayers were in effect subsidizing Europeans, paying less. Meanwhile, high prices for drugs in the US caused European drug firms to shift operations away from the Old Continent to the New World. From a one-third share of world pharmaceutical sales in 1990, the US rose to half by end of the period.

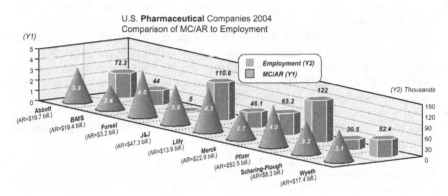

U.S. **Pharmaceutical** Companies 2004
Comparison of MC/AR to Employment

Therefore, the lion's share of the R&D burden shifted from European backs to American. In 2003, US companies spent $20 billion for R&D, nearly a five-fold increase from beginning of the period, while European companies invested only $14.8 billion, about double the 1990 figure. But pharmaceutical companies knew that R&D expenses running on average $800 million per drug and twice as high when including marketing and other overhead costs would both from a profit and a human progress point of view be worth it if major killers, led by coronary heart disease alone claiming over half a million Americans in 2004, as well as cancer and HIV/AIDs could be defeated. With a fifth of all Americans categorized as seriously overweight and a quarter of adult citizens suffering from some reproductive or related ailment, drugs to reduce obesity and sexual problems, too, would prove lucrative for companies and beneficial for society.

Merck's strategy for bearing an R&D burden building toward $2 billion annually by 2004 continued to be joint ventures to spread the risk. For example, a licensing agreement with J&J in 1995 to distribute an over-the-counter (OTC) version of *Pepcid AC* captured a large part of the OTC heartburn drug market. Another long term development program was finding promising drugs overseas. A decision in 1988 to license *Fosamax* for osteoporosis from the Instituto Gentili of Pisa, Italy paid off seven years later when the FDA approved the drug for introduction into the US and annual sales rose steadily to $2.8 billion.

New home-grown drugs also helped the bottom line. After research showed that a cocktail of protease inhibitor *Cirxivan* with older anti-virals reduced HIV in blood systems to insignificant levels, the company had a difficult time keeping up with world demand. *Singulair*, a one-day asthma and allergy medicine generating annually nearly $1.4 billion that went off patent in 2001 actually experienced sales growth to over $2 billion. Anti-hypertensive drugs *Cozaar* and *Hyzaar* contributed over $3 billion annually.

In 1993, Merck bought Medco Containment Services, a pharmacy benefits manager with $2.5 billion of annual sales that was renamed Medco Health Solutions. By providing drug benefits for 62 million Americans, including members of United HealthGroup, that subsidiary came in 2002 to increase revenues 13 times. But it was *Zocor*, the company's powerhouse drug to reduce cholesterol and fight heart disease, which not only provided by 2002 over 10.5% of Merck's $50 billion plus revenue but a disproportionate share of $7 billion of profits. The drug was set to go off patent in 2006 with no prospects large enough to plug the expected revenue short-fall. Thus, management spun off Medco in 2003, sacrificing $33 billion of annual sales but only $9.4 billion of market value. Employment was reduced by over 13,000.

Suddenly in 2004, Merck's strategy and value were undermined by news that its *Vioxx* drug for osteoarthritis increased the risk of heart attack. Management decided to withdraw the product entirely from the market at cost of $2.5 billion in annual sales, 5,100 jobs, and one-third of the company's market capitalization. Medco, by comparison, boosted its fortunes by purchasing Accredo Health of Memphis for $2.2 billion to combine $4 billion in annual revenue selling specialty pharmacy products and services. Distribution of drugs to treat multiple sclerosis, hemophilia, and other niche health problems had higher margins than distribution of bigger market drugs.

Meanwhile, Pfizer's strategy for growth in the 1990s was more exclusive. After the Clinton health care mess was cleared away, the company jacked up annual R&D expense from $1 billion in 1994 to $2.5 billion four years later. Big successes with *Zoloft* for depression, *Norvasc* for high blood pressure, and the antibiotic *Zithromax* carried the company until *Viagra* for erectile dysfunction was ready. Selling 500 million pills in five years, the *Viagra* product line eventually generated about $1.7 billion in annual revenues, or nearly 5.3% of the company total. But more than a third of Pfizer's sales came from its Warner-Lambert division, acquired for $90.3 billion in 2000 and including products as diverse as *Halls* cough drops and *Lubriderm* lotion, *Chiclet* chewing gum and *Zantac* acid reducing tablets. Pfizer also gained control of anti-cholesterol *Lipitor*, the best selling drug in the world with nearly $8 billion of sales, and then in 2004 purchased Esperion Therapeutics, a maker of cardiovascular treatments, for $1.3 billion.

A third huge pharmaceutical company was also created by mergers. After Pharmacia succeeded at long last in 1992 in getting FDA approval for its *DMPA* injectable contraceptive and started distribution overseas through the USAID program, the company took over Upjohn three years later for $7 billion. That brought control of the popular non-prescription *Motrin* drug for pain relief, *Cortaid* steroid cream for itching, *Halcion* for sleep, and *Rogaine* for hair loss. The only negative was the fact that a *Halcion* side-effect brought on depression in some and the possibility of law suits. Management moved on to buy chemical-maker Monsanto in 2000 to take over its G.D. Searle pharmaceutical subsidiary. Everything but the drug division was spun off under the Monsanto name two years later.

It was then that Pharmacia, now in possession of a significant portfolio of non-prescription drugs, attracted the attention of Pfizer. The latter's management made a successful bid to buy the former for around $60 billion in stock in 2003. With dominance of

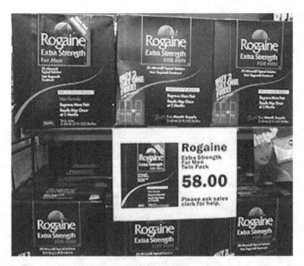

the $16 billion global market for *Lipitor*-like statins or their substitutes, and *Viagra's* potential market of 30 million US men and hundreds of millions of others around the globe who might benefit, the company was well positioned for the future. Moreover, Pfizer had first refusal to co-develop and market other promising drugs, such as *ApoA-1 Milano*, developed by Esperion Therapeutics of Ann Arbor, Michigan to reduce plaque build-up in arteries, which company Pfizer then bought for $1.3 billion.

Abbott Labs, too, succeeded with its drug pipe-line of new products and mergers. In the 1990s, the company marketed *Clarithromycin* antibiotic, useful it turned out for stopping infections in AIDs patients, *Norvir* protease inhibitor of HIV, *Depacon* for epilepsy, *Prevacid*, in combination with *Clarithromycin* combative of small intestinal ulcers, and *Depakote*, surpassing lithium for treating mania and later in extra strength preventing migraines. But a light calorie version of its *Ensure* nutritional supplement, an improved version of *Similac* infant formula, and other non-pharmaceutical products provided 45% of revenues, keeping the R&D budget down to around $1.1 billion annually. The company was able to afford a series of acquisitions that included BASF of Germany and Knoll Pharmaceuticals. Abbott was anticipating $750 million more in annual revenue from its *Kaletra* anti-AIDSs drug as well as new revenue from its test for *Herceptin* treatment for women with metastatic breast cancer and a 400% increase in *Norvir's* price to $265 per month, still less than half as much as *Kaletra* and other drugs with which it beneficially interacted.

Another drug company heavily involved in the fight against AIDS and cancer was Bristol-Meyers Squibb. Its HIV treatment called *Videx* or *ddI* competed with the better known *AZT* from Glaxo-SmithKline.

In 1993, the company discovered that *Taxol*, made from endangered Pacific Yew trees, was effective against breast, ovarian and lung cancer. Two years later, the company introduced *Pravachol* to reduce the risk of heart attacks for patients with cholesterol problems or chronic heart disease. Although in 1998, Bristol-Meyers Squibb expanded its OTC headache sales with *Excedrin Migraine*, the overall strategic plan was to reduce non-prescription drug operations. In 2000, management divested both *Clairol* hair care products (to P&G for nearly $5 billion) and Zimmer orthopedics. That brought cash to help conclude the purchase of DuPont's pharmaceutical division for $7.8 billion, including *Crystalline*, a leading prescription anti-coagulant. Despite lowering the cost of its HIV/AIDs drugs in Africa and failing to break even in 2002, a big jump in revenues pushed profit margin back up above 15%.

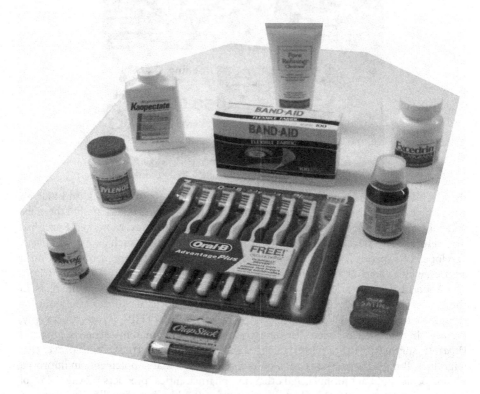

AHP also moved in the direction of beefing up pharmaceutical products at the expense of other operations by purchasing in 1994 American Cyanamid, maker of the OTC multivitamin *Centrum*. As *Premarin*, a drug bringing relief to women from menopausal symptoms, built toward $1 billion of annual sales, management contemplated a takeover of Monsanto. But that $35 billion deal was canceled in 1998 because of clash of corporate cultures. AHP branched out into bio-technology with a genetically engineered blood-clotting protein called *BeneFix Coagulation Factor IX* as well as bio-medications for hemophilia and a joint venture with Immunex of Seattle to fight rheumatoid arthritis. After spinning off American Cyanamid's old agricultural products division and changing its own name back to Wyeth in honor of the company founder, the company pushed profit margin over 21%. Several billion dollars were set aside to cover diet drug liability claims from a class action lawsuit.

Personality conflicts also scuttled a cross-Atlantic merger between AHP and Smith-Kline-Beecham. That British company had bought Eastman Kodak's OTC drug unit for nearly $3 billion in 1994 only to deal off the North American part to Bayer for $1 billion. Thus, Bayer recovered ownership of *Bayer Aspirin*, confiscated and sold off by the Wilson administration during the First World War. Eastman Kodak's prescription drug division, worth $1.7 billion, was sold to Sanofi of France.

Even more successful than Wyeth was Eli Lilly. That company rode its *Prozac* anti-depression drug, doing $3 billion of sales annually, as well as its *Zyprexa* anti-psychotic drug, claiming 37% of a $10 billion annual market. However, when the company announced in 2000 that *Prozac*'s patent would end in 2003, two years earlier than expected, its stock value dropped nearly a third. Because employment was held steady, and despite $2 billion in annual R&D expenses, the company still made 13% profit on 2004 sales. *Cialis*, a competitor for *Viagra* that featured a 36 hour effectiveness window, rather than 4 hours, was imminent. Another new drug called *Cimbalta* would when approved by the FDA for depression and urinary incontinence generate $2 billion a year. However, *Zyprexa* was threatened by Bristol-Meyers-Squibb's new *Abilify* as well as report of a few severe diabetic reactions. Eli Lilly hoped to maintain market share with an injectable form of the drug.

One company that was hurt badly by the end of patent protection for its drugs was Schering-Plough. First, its *Intron A* anti-viral, anti-cancer recombinant drug bringing in nearly $1.5 billion in annual revenue went off patent in 2002. Next, Roche Holding of Switzerland carved out an over 50% of the market for hepatitis C drugs fighting the virus that causes liver cancer, formerly a Schering-Plough mainstay. Finally, the company's *Claritin* anti-allergy pill, generating twice as much sales, was thrown open to generic competition in 2003. The company tried to salvage what it could in the anti-allergy market by introducing an OTC version of *Claritin* as well as a slightly different patent-protected drug called *Clarinex*. Schering-Plough banked on a new anti-cholesterol pill called *Zetia*, developed in a joint venture with Merck, which was considered promising because it interfered with the absorption of cholesterol in the small intestine.

Besides a proposed FDA rule change to hasten generics to market and patents running out, the future for major US pharmaceutical companies was made more difficult to predict by a number of factors. Competition from foreign firms with ready access to the US market was growing stiffer as overseas companies merged for greater economies of scale. In 1998, Astra of Switzerland combined $14 billion of annual revenue with Zeneca of Britain. Astra-Zeneca's heartburn medicine *Prilosec* with $6.3 billion of global 2000 sales was momentarily the best selling prescription drug in the world. Even when the patent ran out in 2002 and sales plummeted 27%, the company struck a deal with P&G to distribute an OTC version backed by Wellpoint, distributing samples. That was a direct threat to Merck and J&J's alliance with *Pepcid* OTC.

Also a problem for big US drug-makers was new US competition. In 2000, P&G made a deal with Aventis to market its *Actonel* treatment and prevention of post-menopausal osteoporosis. Aventis had been formed two years earlier from a merger of Rhone-Poulenc of France and Hoechst of Germany. At that time the second largest pharmaceutical company in the world, Aventis also made a joint venture with Merck to distribute vaccines in Europe.

By 2004, the other big foreign players were Sanofi of France, which merged with Aventis, Bayer, Novartis of Switzerland, formed in 1996 by a merger of Sandoz and Ciba Geigy, and Glaxo Welcome-Smith-Kline Beecham, assembled in final form in 2000 in a $75 billion merger. Bayer was best known to the American public because of *Bayer Aspirin* as well as the powerful anti-biotic *Cipro*, generating $1.75 billion of annual revenue in 2001. When after the anthrax terrorist scare of October 2001 and before it was technically due to go off patent the next year the company sold the drug to the US government at half price, favorable publicity helped alleviate a fiasco with its *Baycol* anti-cholesterol drug that had caused 31 deaths. Glaxo, too, wanted to make itself a household name by taking on *Viagra* and *Cialis* with *Levitra*, developed jointly with Bayer. New revenue would make up for losing patent protection on its $2 billion annual revenue *Augmentin* drug for fighting bacterial sinusitis and pneumonia and $1.3 billion *Flovent*, a fast-acting inhaler to relieve asthma.

Another strategic threat was posed by smaller US companies. Determined to find help for a son suffering from depression who was not helped by leading medications *Prozac*, *Zoloft*, and Glaxo's *Paxil*, CEO Howard Soloman of Forest Laboratories came upon a drug in the Netherlands subsequently distributed in the US as *Celexa* starting in 1998. It quickly accounted for 70% of Forest's 2004 revenues. With profit margin pushing 30%, the company's strategy continued to be finding little-known European drugs to license for the American market.

Less of a peril than the advent of new drugs was outright patent violation. Such theft became more likely as populations grew desperate to acquire critical drugs that either cost too much or were in short supply. Thus, the government of Brazil authorized import of generic versions of still patented AIDS drugs owned by Abbott, Merck, and Roche. The companies had refused an additional 40% discount on top of other large discounts already granted that had lowered the annual cost to $2,000 per person compared with six times as much in the United States. Brazil complained that only a third of its 500,000 HIV positive citizens were receiving medication. Rather than risk spread of AIDS to a larger percentage of its 180 million people, the government would take matters into its own hands.

In 2003, the FDA proposed new rules to permit generic-making companies like Sicor of Irvine, California, purchased by Teva Pharmaceuticals Industries of Israel for $3.3 billion in 2003, as well as Mylan Laboratories, ironically buying King Pharmaceuticals for $4 billion the next year to boost its line of branded products, to sell drugs that were slightly different than patented drugs before the patent period ran out without having to repeat costly clinical trials. Late in November, Congress incorporated that change into a bill to expand Medicare to cover part of the cost of prescription drugs at an estimated cost over ten years of $400 billion officially but as much as 50% higher unofficially. Fundamentally, the government would as a stop-gap measure permit seniors to buy a discount drug card, and then in 2006 implement a permanent plan. Medicare beneficiaries would either sign up for a prescription drug plan with a $35 monthly premium, $250 deductible, 75% of costs covered up to $2,250, none covered thence to $3,600, and 95% coverage thereafter or join a private health care plan with a similar drug benefit. Companies that decided to keep prescription drug benefits for their retirees would be subsidized $86 billion over ten years by the federal government to keep down premiums. Another provision introduced means testing for doctor visits outside of hospitals so that instead of paying 25% of premiums for that portion of Medicare insurance (Medicare B), wealthier beneficiaries would pay a sliding scale topping out at 80% for those with annual incomes over $200,000.

Prior to 2006, the law halted construction of new specialty hospitals, limited the expansion of others, and permitted a 1.5% increase over two years of payments to doctors. In essence, those provisions kept the *status quo* for the nation's health care system. However, as an indication of how high Congress believed federal health care expenses might go over time, the law required the House and Senate to review Medicare spending once the program consumed 45% of all general revenue funds in the federal budget. Although the new law would, barring certification by the Department of Health and Human Services, continue to ban drug imports from Canada and forbid the government from negotiating drug discounts, it would speed the introduction of generic drugs. Therefore, it was unclear whether drug company revenues and profits would be helped or hurt by the change. Much would depend on the specific language adopted by the FDA to govern the procedure wherein generic-making companies side-stepped patent protection.

More difficult, but not impossible, for generic-makers to replicate would be many of the bio-engineered drugs coming onto the market in increasing numbers. The global market for such substances had grown during the period from only a few billion dollars to more than $41 billion annually, half in the US. Although companies wanted to emulate the success of big pharmaceutical makers with blockbuster medications generating over $1 billion of sales annually per drug, smaller niches about a tenth the size could still make money. New Economy emphasis on high margins, global markets, and more productive, if fewer, employees using better equipment combined with an investor expectation of patent-protected profits offset the danger of tightening government regulation and translated into impressive market capitalizations.

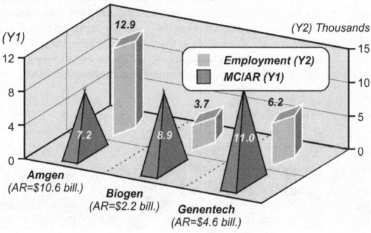

U.S. **Bio-Tech** Companies 2004
Comparison of MC/AR to Employment

The fastest rising bio-tech company was Amgen of Thousand Oaks, California. Management grew sales over seven-fold 1993 to 2004 by genetically engineering drugs to help cancer patients. In 1997, *Neupogen* was introduced to prevent infection resulting from damage to the immune system from undergoing chemotherapy and *Rituxan* was offered to battle non-Hodgkin's lymphoma (blood cancer) in 50,000 cases a year. Two years later, *Epogen* counteracted anemia in children on kidney dialysis. Purchase of Immunex for $11 billion in 2002 and a further $1.5 billion capital investment to upgrade plant facilities in Rhode Island gave impetus to *Embrel*, Immunex' drug aimed at rheumatoid arthritis and other ills, to capture 40% of the market, compared to 50% for arch-rival J&J's *Remicade*. *Embrel*'s revenue doubled in 2003. Despite a loss in 2002 of nearly $1.4 billion, profits turned around.

Genentech, majority owned by Roche, also made itself an investor favorite by targeting cancer. In 1995, a $500 million investment in phase three clinical trial for *Herceptin* paid off in remission for 30% of breast cancer patients and for the company in annual sales of the drug ascending toward $400 million. The company had high hopes that *Avastin*, 15 years in development to cut off the blood supply to colon cancer tumors, would win quick FDA approval and generate as much as $2 billion in sales annually.

Other bio-tech players large and small coveted investor dollars. J&J was actually one of the leaders in the field with *Remicade* and other drugs, giving an important boost to its stock price. Bio-engineered drug treatments for lung cancer were available from Genentech, ImClone, and AstraZeneca. Hyland came out with the first genetically manufactured *Factor VIII* product for hemophiliacs back in 1992.

Four years later, Biogen's *Avonex* for multiple sclerosis was approved by the FDA. Because the drug accounted for virtually all the company's $1 billion plus revenue, management decided to broaden its product line by acquiring Idec Pharmaceuticals. That company contributed half a dozen drugs targeted at cancer and auto-immune diseases that generated $500 million of annual revenue. A stock merger valued Idec at a 20% premium over market capitalization of $5.4 billion. Too, Biogen concluded an arrangement with

Elan Pharmaceuticals of Ireland to market its *Tysabri* drug to use in combination with Avonex. However, news in early 2005 that two patients had developed a rare neurological disease from *Tysabri*, causing the death of one, forced withdrawal of the product.

Similar in the 1990s to the surge in bio-tech drugs was proliferation of genetically engineered foods. In 1992, a company called Vindicator opened a $7 million plant in Mulberry, Florida to irradiate citrus, strawberries, tomatoes, and other local produce for longer preservation. However, it was Monsanto which moved to the forefront in the industry by acquiring several cutting-edge innovators, including in 1997 DEKALB Genetics, second largest US seed company. Management counted on bio-engineered drugs to reduce the company's heavy dependence on the *Roundup* herbicide, accounting for half of all annual sales. With new *Roundup* versions targeted to protect canola, cotton, soybeans and finally corn, the product line was still of extreme importance. When, however, the patent for *Roundup*'s glyphosate molecule ended in 2000, Dow, DuPont, and other competitors quickly captured 30% of the market.

Thus, management targeted bio-engineered foods more so than ever. After buying Cargill's international seed operations, Monsanto acquired Plant Breeding International Cambridge Limited, a leader in bio-engineering in Europe, from Unilever for $525 million. However, that subsidiary failed in a bid to make hybrid wheat sell on the Old Continent. After in 1998 the EU slapped a moratorium on $250 million of annual US bio-engineered food imports, particularly beef containing growth hormones, European consumers became convinced that tampering with the natural food chain was dangerous. Although the US eventually won a WTO protest over the beef ban, Old World public opinion remained rigid. Monsanto's management sold off fermenter Kelco Biogums for $685 million and its *NutraSweet* product line for $440 million, and then accepted a buyout offer from Pharmacia. That company spun off Monsanto without G.D. Searle. Despite great hope for new

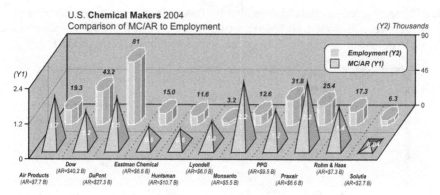

U.S. **Chemical Makers** 2004
Comparison of MC/AR to Employment

products, such as an artificial hormone for cows to increase production of milk up to twelve pounds per day per cow, profitability was thin.

What was needed in the politically risky bio-engineered foods field was deeper pockets. In 1999, DuPont entered the fray by purchasing Pioneer Hi-Bred International, a company started in Des Moines, Iowa back in 1926 by Henry Wallace, future Vice President under FDR. In the 1970s, Pioneer had developed genetically engineered seeds to provide bumper crops for corn farmers. The company fit in with DuPont's operations because DuPont used corn sugar to make *Propanediol*, an ingredient in the *Sorona* polymer that made softer fibers with superior stretching and recovery properties. Two years later, DuPont introduced with partner Bunge Limited the *Solae* brand soy protein, used in food, beverage, and meat products. *Solae* was not only highly digestible and lactose-free but had the same 90% protein score as meat, egg, and milk protein. Thus, its benefits included lowering cholesterol, reducing the risk of heart disease and certain cancers, and strengthening bones in women. The bottom line for DuPont was another profitable product line.

Overall US exports of bio-engineered foods topped $12 billion by 2002. Even with the EU ban, demand for genetically altered and improved soybeans, cotton, and corn was growing in Japan, China, the Middle East, and Southeast Asia. Nor would the US government remain content that Europe held itself aloof. Even if the French, Germans, and others refused to admit products of the new industry for fear of harmful contamination, Washington did not want their opinions to contaminate the potential of other markets.

As previously discussed, European governments had much less objection to normal, everyday, chemically composed US pharmaceuticals so long as prices could be controlled. The pressure for discounts built up in the US as well so that drug distributors had to combine for greater economies of scale. Cardinal Health became the largest of all drug wholesalers after a series of acquisitions beginning in 1991 to serve the Ohio valley, Dixie, and South Central parts of the country. At mid-decade, management bought Medicine Shoppe International, the largest franchiser of retail pharmacies, to go beyond distribution. Subsequently, the company acquired physical therapy systems, medical surgery, and automation companies, for example to track drugs from hospital pharmacies through use by doctors, nurses, and other medical personnel. Although a 1997 offer to take over Bergen Brunswig for $2.8 billion fell through, revenues from health care products and services on five continents made Cardinal ultimately the world's largest drug wholesaler. However, the regulatory squeeze overseas, Canadian drug imports, and further direct-to-consumer marketing through the Internet all hurt profitability.

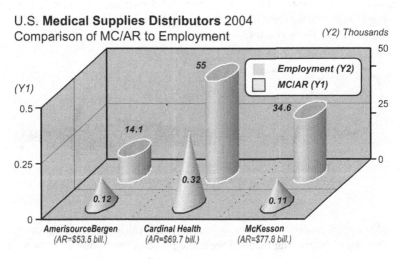

U.S. Medical Supplies Distributors 2004
Comparison of MC/AR to Employment

Other competitors were even worse off. After buying HBOC's hospital network in 1999 and becoming a full line health care company, McKesson of San Francisco could manage profit margin of only 1% in 2003 and lost money the next year. Although Alco Standard went public in 1995 as Amerisource Health Corporation of Valley Forge, Pennsylvania and thickened annual revenues toward $14 billion in 2000, a merger the next year with Bergen Brunswig yielded disappointing results. Revenues distributing pharmaceutical products and services to hospitals, alternative care facilities, and pharmacies did push up, but profit margin was lower than McKesson's. Complaints that AmerisourceBergen sold counterfeit drugs, fixed prices, and engaged in other illegal practices worried investors. In a reverse of usual fundamentals, the company's modest workforce compared favorably with McKesson and Cardinal but did not help the bottom line.

Also caught up in the forces attacking pharmaceutical profits were retail drug store chains. Although in 1996 the FCC had no problem with J.C. Penney buying Eckerd for $3.3 billion, the commission did block Rite Aid's proposed takeover of struggling Revco for $1.8 billion for fear of driving up prices in the Midwest and Southeast. Instead, Rite Aid  bought Thrifty PayLess Holdings, the leading west coast chain, for $2.3 billion in stock and assumed debt. In 1997, CVS grabbed Revco to compete in all areas east of the Mississippi. In fact, that company's holding of 4,100 stores was second only to Walgreen's 4,600 until management purchased over 1,200 Eckerd stores from J.C. Penney. Because 70% of sales came from prescription drugs, increasingly vulnerable to generics, Internet sales by Drugstore.com and discounted imports, investors liked Walgreens' operations with 60%

of revenue from prescription drugs, more than CVS business. Moreover, Walgreens boasted bigger stores, drive-through pharmacies, and one hour photo processing. Rite Aid 3,400 stores were one-tenth as attractive to investors.

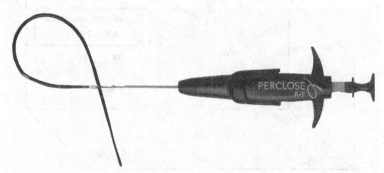

In addition to demand for pharmaceuticals, the health care industry had also to absorb the cost of improving medical technology. Sometimes, however, new devices actually saved money. One example was stents, tiny metal scaffolds invented for cardiologists in 1994 to prop and keep open arteries to avoid the necessity of by-pass surgery. While pressure from Washington cut Medicare reimbursements for by-passes 50% to $1,850, the stent procedure cost about $1,000. However, the arrival in 2003 of drug-eluting stents to prevent reclogging of arteries boosted potential revenue for each procedure roughly three-fold. The annual US market for all stent procedures would thereby double to as much as $5 billion.

A loss for high-paid cardiac surgeons was a gain for J&J. Its medical division made the *Cyper* drug-eluting stent, priced at $3,195. Even a discounted price for rival products cost patients $2,600. The stent business looked so lucrative that Abbott Labs bought a maker of stents in 2002 to combine with its Perclose subsidiary that made the *Closer* vascular closing device.

Another major force in stents as well as implantable defibrillators was Guidant. The company was spun off from Eli Lilly in 1994. In 1998, management bought Cook, a privately held maker of cardiovascular devices, for $3 billion. However, a subsidiary making stent-grafts and other aortic-aneurysm devices was hit with allegations that 12 deaths had resulted from its products. Potential liabilities, as expensive perhaps as the $3.2 billion Dow Corning paid in 1998 to settle silicone breast implant injuries, could not undermine favorable developments based on events such as a Medicare rule change to cover the $40,000 total cost of defibrillators, rather than just two-thirds. Because not only the current 45,000 patients but an additional 10,000 would be affected, Guidant expected to take a healthy chunk of the $1 billion increase in the US market. But its larger competitor Medtronic of Minneapolis also made defibrillators, pacemakers, and other cardiac products to account for over half its annual revenue. Faster growth in spinal and diabetes equipment and therapies pushed up profits.

Yet another company that competed in stents was Boston Scientific. In addition to catheters, coils, and sponges, the company was coming out with a drug-eluting stent called *Taxus* that would be priced at $1,800. After a series of acquisitions, management built up annual revenues. Investors liked the company's 19% profitability and productive work force.

Baxter competed in cardiovascular devices until spinning off those operations as Edwards Lifesciences in 2000. The company continued to lead in blood products with its *HomeChoice* dialysis machine, a compact device introduced in 1994 to cleanse blood overnight, as well as blood-cell separators, and I.V. solutions. By the new century, the company was shipping 1 billion units of its *Factor VIII* anti-hemophilia medicine from its Thousand Oaks facility.

Because prices of medical devices, as opposed to pharmaceuticals, were likely to remain unregulated, J&J decided to become a major force. In addition to stents, the company bought makers of orthopedic devices. It was the 1998 takeover of DePuy for $3.7 billion that made it an industry leader. In the next five years, the company's position became so strong that it was first, in a move to stop counterfeiters of prescription drugs, to order that wholesalers buy all J&J products directly from J&J. Management then negotiated a 2004 deal to buy Guidant for $25 billion. The idea was to combine J&J's coated stent technology with Guidant's more flexible stent product, but at the last moment in 2005 Boston Scientific swooped in to snatch Guidant away from J&J with a better $27 billion offer.

U.S. **Medical Equipment** Companies 2004
Comparison of MC/AR to Employment

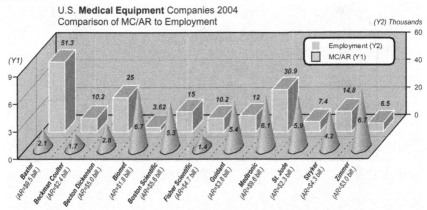

J&J's main competitors in orthopedic devices were Stryker and Zimmer. After the former grew over seven-fold by acquisitions in the US, the latter in 2001 was spun off from Bristol-Myers-Squibb to continue making hip, shoulder, and elbow replacements. However, Zimmer's low employment boosted profitability over 20%. When the company won a bidding contest to take over Centerpulse of Switzerland for $3.2 billion, three times annual revenue, its global market share in orthopedics surpassed J&J's and Stryker's.

Likewise, GE looked for superior rates of return in the health care field. By 2003, its medical division approached $10 billion of annual revenue. Although the EU had two years earlier shot down GE's proposed $42 billion takeover of Honeywell, the company's $2.3 billion bid for Instrumentarium of Finland, a medical instrument maker, was approved once management agree to divest its Spacelabs subsidiary, making patient monitoring machines. Management followed up that success with a $9.5 billion deal to acquire Amersham of Britain, producer of contrast agents for medical scanning, and thus combine $14 billion of sales and 42,000 employees under GE's UK-based GE HealthCare. That acquisition fit nicely with GE's operations as the world's largest maker of medical scanners. The overall plan was to build up the medical division to contribute one seventh or more of the company's $151 billion in annual 2004 revenues. As the share of double-digit profits generated by interest rate dependent GE Finance was thereby reduced from half to a lower level, MC/AR would rise despite the burden of employment for 305,000 from around 2.5 to a better figure.

Another major US corporation that increased its stake in medical products was Tyco. Adhering to its strategy of adding high-quality but cost-competitive and lower-tech products to its portfolio of businesses, the big conglomerate began buying up companies, headed by Kendall International in 1994, that made disposables such as dressings, bandages, elastic support, adult incontinence, disposable diapers, and sutures. By contrast, Air Products bought American Homecare Supply, a privately held maker of respiratory therapy and home medical equipment, to add to its medical equipment line. Management boosted profitability above 7%.

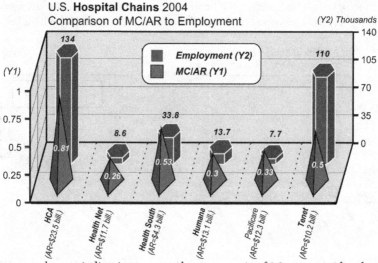

U.S. **Hospital Chains** 2004
Comparison of MC/AR to Employment

Even a market capitalization to annual revenue ratio of 1.0 was considered excellent for investor-owned hospital chains, struggling as the managed care agenda weighed heavily on lucrative elective surgeries such as hip and knee replacements. While embarking on a new round of consolidations and divestitures, they struggled in the face of regulatory pressures to earn superior returns. One of the most active was HCA. After Columbia Hospital in 1993 took over Galen Health Care, formerly Humana's hospital operations, HCA the next year obtained Columbia to combine 320 hospitals. Almost immediately, management acquired Medical Care America to peak at $20 billion of annual revenues and 285,000 employees working in 350 hospitals, 145 outpatient surgery centers, and 550 home care agencies. The next year, management bought HealthTrust to reconsolidate former HCA hospitals. The *status quo* was maintained until 1999 when Columbia/HCA spun off Triad and LifePoint, renamed itself HCA, and retained 180 hospitals and 80 other facilities in the US, England, and Switzerland that employed 126,000 people. Because of a continuing threat of lawsuits from unsavory past practices, MC/AR eroded.

Also under investigation by government for unnecessary heart surgeries and other unscrupulous acts were Tenet and HealthSouth of Birmingham. Stretching from Massachusetts to Dixie, Pennsylvania to Nebraska, the former's investor owned hospital network suffered a small loss. The latter used acquisitions to become by 1995 the nation's largest provider of rehabilitative services, including sports medicine. After buying Horizon/CMS Healthcare in 1997 to get to 875 outpatient and 30 inpatient facilities, HealthSouth began a selective overseas expansion into Australia, Puerto Rico and Saudi Arabia. Had not CEO and founder Richard M. Scrushy ordered profits to be overstated by $2.7 billion over several years, MC/AR would have been much higher. Annual 2002 revenues of $4.3 billion placed HealthSouth technically ahead of Triad Hospitals of Texas and Universal Health of Pennsylvania, but the company only narrowly avoided bankruptcy while stabilizing revenue the next two years.

Chapter XX. A Republic Richer than Croesus

Accumulation of currency and coin was comparable to acquisition of cars, appliances, and other depreciable assets in that the value of savings did not immediately result in a decline in wealth, rather eroded with the effect of inflation over time. Financial assets that earned interest and capital gains were more like investment in housing because wealth was not only preserved but increased. However, the service and intangible nature of banks, insurance companies, accounting firms, investment, and other operations held down labor costs so that a one-fifth share of GDP for finance by the new century required only one twentieth of the workforce. With fewer employees and physical assets to support, profits for financial services companies soared.

Alan Greenspan

Therefore, it was in the taxing interest of the United States government to protect and advance the fortunes of such firms. Because to compete successfully in financial services it became not merely advisable but necessary to participate in a variety of national and global investment opportunities, Washington moved to deregulate the industry. Although oversight was maintained by federal officials, participation in the global marketplace tended to supersede national regulation and control. As with other industries, financial service multinationals achieved enormous economies of scale by offering products overseas.

In the final analysis, financial entities are but empty shells without clients to charge commissions and fees for managing financial assets. As in the 1980s, public reaction to abuses and poor management undercut companies and businesses as much as or more so than government sanction. If national leaders judged correctly in the 1990s that the marketplace itself would best regulate success and failure, it was still necessary to establish the overall business environment. Even before the transformation was accomplished, the financial service sector blossomed.

FREEING THE GOLDEN GOOSE OF FINANCIAL SERVICES

It was only natural after the stock market boom of the 1980s, resulting in fantastic accumulations of wealth as well as shocking examples of greed, for the government to review its position on financial service industry regulations. Most important was protecting the money supply composed of $2.5 trillion in bank deposits, about 46% of all bank assets, and circulating currency of $300 billion from malfeasance and inflation. Granted, annual price increases ceased to be much of a factor after victory in the Persian Gulf War, the recession of 1991, and the movement toward a global labor force, but Congress gave authority to the FDIC anyway to tighten up control by boosting the premiums banks and S&Ls paid to insure their deposits. A savings rate that peaked at 8.7% of disposable income in 1992 and drifted down gently to 6.1% two years later insured that bank assets would double in the period.

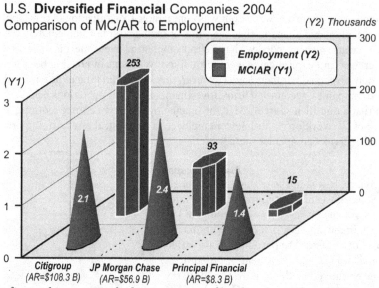

U.S. **Diversified Financial** Companies 2004
Comparison of MC/AR to Employment

But financial institutions had gotten a taste of headier times. Their CEOs argued that more efficient markets and better internal controls warranted a loosening of federal regulations. Ambitiously, they wanted Congress to repeal parts of the old Glass-Steagall law so that financial holding companies could own commercial banks, securities underwriters, and other entities. Their philosophy was that all things within reason should be allowed to well-managed companies that were "well capitalized." In that manner, US financial institutions could more effectively compete with international holding companies. Big Japanese banks in particular had when the *yen* was flying high in the 1980s and real estate in downtown Tokyo was the most valuable in the world accumulated more assets that any other competitors.

The imperative of gaining greater size and strength was so urgent that US banks did not wait for Washington to act. While avoiding the forbidden field of investment banking, they built up alternative streams of revenue. For example, Citibank surged to the lead in US credit card and charge card issuance by 1993, and then expanded its credit card presence in Europe and Asia. By 2004, credit card debt in EU countries ran about 50% of the US total of $950 billion.

Revenue from credit card operations flowed in the first instance from charging customers annual fees. However, fierce competition soon eradicated those front-loaded charges in favor of back-loaded interest compiled on monthly balances. To maximize profits, some banks even revoked the cards of customers who did not charge enough to warrant the administration costs of servicing accounts. Customers who paid off balance statements each month to avoid interest charges were prized as excellent credit risks so long as their conservatism was balanced by a percentage of higher risk customers who did not.

The other source of revenue from credit cards was fees charged to businesses that accepted such cards for the payment of goods and services. While credit card volume built toward $1.2 trillion in the US in 2002, rates remained typically between 2% and 4% of the charged amount. By contrast, the fee on debit cards, introduced in 1996 to deduct funds directly from checking accounts, was as low as 25 cents per transaction, as high as $1.50. Volume accelerated in the new century toward $500 billion annually. For that reason, MasterCard and Visa were able to manipulate the system to defraud Wal-Mart, Sears, and other large retailers. In 2003, the former was forced to pay a $1 billion settlement to satisfy claims while the latter chipped in twice as much.

First Data consolidated its position as leader in the field of consumer money wire transfer services through paper, plastic, wire, and the Internet as well as credit card transaction processing by purchasing in 1995 Atlanta's First Financial Management, including subsidiary Western Union, for $6.7 billion. However, the company was forced by federal regulators to divest MoneyGram. Subsequently, a surge in debit card transaction processing pushed revenue up. Management attempted to purchase the next year Concord EFS to gain control of the *Star* network handling half of all debit transactions in the country, but the Justice Department blocked the bid temporarily on the grounds that First Data would thereby gain monopoly control of the system over which consumers bought $150 billion of goods and services annually. Additional negative fall-out of the stalled deal was decisions by Wells Fargo and Wachovia to switch debit card transaction contracts to Visa. First Data finally was able to close the deal for $6.9 billion in early 2004.

In 1995, banks in Florida, Connecticut, and other states gained the right to sell annuities. Because that change infringed on the business of big insurance companies, renewed impetus was given to the idea of breaking down all barriers between components of the financial service industry. Already in 1993 consumer lending and investment company Primerica bought Shearson Lehman Brothers from American Express to combine with its Smith Barney subsidiary. That year Primerica also took over Travelers Property and Casualty but assumed the Travelers name.

Another wave of big bank consolidation washed over the industry beginning in 1996. Chase briefly became the largest bank holding company by gobbling up Chemical Bank, which had bought Manufacturers Hanover five years earlier. Too, Wells Fargo Capital grabbed First Interstate Bancorp only to merge into Norwest two years later for $34.4

billion. With a strong presence in the West and Midwest, the combined company kept the famous Wells Fargo name. After up-and-comer NationsBank of Charlotte acquired Barnett Bank in 1997 for $14.8 billion and Bank of America the next year for $61.6 billion, it subsumed itself in the latter's name and legacy. Pressure on Congress to revise Glass-Steagall to get ahead of the financial sector evolution curve became intense.

Travelers umbrella symbol
New York headquarters

Jumping onto the consolidation bandwagon, Citicorp acquired Salomon Brothers for $9 billion in 1997 to compete in Treasury securities as well as take on Travelers' Smith Barney, formerly a unit of Salomon. However, deciding that cooperation was better than confrontation, management agreed the next year to Travelers' offer to combine the two companies under a holding company called Citigroup, with Citicorp's value set at $72.6 billion. A subsequent takeover of The Associates, with operations in insurance, commercial loans, and truck leasing, made the company an even more diversified entity. In 2002, Citigroup spun off the Travelers' property and casualty insurance division, which now included an operation Citicorp had acquired from Aetna in 1995, for $16 billion.

Still the largest financial institution in the world, Citigroup serviced about $1.2 trillion of assets with a quarter million employees. As the economy improved, the company grew even bigger with a $31.8 billion purchase of Sears' credit card unit. Number of credit card accounts was boosted 75% to 176 million, including 15 million outside the US. Not even a $2.6 billion fine, topping the $2 billion J.P. Morgan Chase paid, imposed by the government for failed due diligence in selling WorldCom stocks and bonds to investors at a time when that company was about to implode could seriously tarnish the company's patina of success.

By comparison, GE Capital had about 100 million credit card accounts. That subsidiary announced in August 2003 acquisition of the finance units of Dutch insurer Aegon for $5.4 billion. While bulking up commercial and consumer finance operations, management decided late in 2003 to spin off its mortgage-insurance and life-insurance operations, sacrificing $13 billion of annual revenue but only $1.1 billion of profit out of $15 billion for the parent company. GE Capital's assets therefore declined from $425 billion.

In 2000, at the apex of the economic boom, Congress in the Gramm-Leach-Biley bill acted to permit holding companies to control both commercial and investment banking operations in separate subsidiaries. That action opened the door to a takeover of J.P. Morgan, focusing on investment banking after selling off other operations in 1996, by Chase for $35 billion. The resulting J.P. Morgan Chase became in 2001 the second largest financial institution with assets pushing $800 billion.

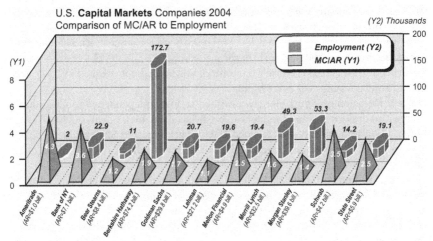

U.S. **Capital Markets** Companies 2004
Comparison of MC/AR to Employment

Congress' abandonment of Glass-Steagall on the eve of the 2001 recession was a heavy blow to investment banking firms. The industry had enjoyed a golden era of wide-open wheeling and dealing after a congressional fight over funding for the SEC in 1994 had forced the agency to cut back on oversight and supervision. In fact, the number of merger and acquisition deals by Morgan Stanley, Goldman Sachs, and other leading firms rose from 3,500 worth $400 billion in 1995 to 9,000 worth $1.4 trillion four years later and 10,500 worth nearly as much the next year. Sparked by 1,100 tech companies going public between 1995 and 2000, or one-third the total, the IPO market also brought in big profits. At its peak, the average IPO underwriting size for tech companies was $1 billion.

However, the telecom and Internet stock crash as well as the recession reduced initial valuations ten fold. The US mergers and acquisition market fell below $450 billion in 2002, less than in Europe, before exceeding $550 billion the next year and $777 billion in 2004. The contraction would have been worse had not companies resorted to spin-offs to rid themselves of heavily indebted subsidiaries and divisions. Investment banking firms also contended with the practice by commercial banks of "tied loans," in which lower interest rates were offered to companies in exchange for other business such as underwriting stock and bond issues. Although such tactics were technically illegal, banks were permitted by law to consider their overall relationship with customers before deciding to make loans. Therefore, bank managers cut interest rates to win the comprehensive business of corporate customers.

Nevertheless, the resources of pure investment banking companies to combat competition from Citigroup, J.P. Morgan Chase, and other diversified financial services entities were not insubstantial. Attending the merger and acquisition boom had been a run up in corporate securities underwriting business. By 2002, corporate debt levels amounted to nine-tenths of annual revenue. The higher risk associated with the burden widened the interest rate gap between medium-quality corporate securities and Treasury securities to 2.7%.

The period got off to a formidable start in 1991 with a record $580 billion in corporate security placements, up from the previous year's $312 billion. The greatest beneficiary was Merrill Lynch, a company with brokerages and other diversified activities. The company placed $100 billion of securities, up from $56 billion. Once the ensuing recession ended, business vaulted again to triple that level by 1998, good for a one sixth share of the US market. A quarter share the next year in the fast-rising $33 billion debt convertible securities market also enhanced the firm's reputation. When the boom peaked in 2000, Merrill Lynch had annual revenues of $44.8 billion.

Except for Salomon Smith Barney, destined to lose independence to Citigroup, the next largest underwriter was Morgan Stanley. By securing major deals such as DuPont's $4.4 billion IPO spin off in 1998 of Conoco, the firm accumulated $220 billion of business. Four years later, management purchased Dean Witter to diversify into the brokerage business.

Focused on bonds, Goldman Sachs increased underwriting over five fold to $210 billion in 1998. Privately held until the next year, the company suffered only a 5% contraction in revenue in 2001 before bouncing back. Another force in bonds gained independence when American Express spun off Lehman Brothers in 1994. Although Lehman fell behind other competitors in securities as well as mergers and acquisitions, management rejuvenated investment banking activities by increasing operations in Western Europe.

Facilitating and financing the buying and selling of companies was the main activity of investment banking firms. Configuring mergers and acquisitions on balance sheets and income statements for optimum impact on profitability and taxes was the province of major accounting firms. In the 1990s, the outsourcing market for such services was captured by limited liability partnerships with national and global interests. After further consolidation and upheaval related to accounting scandals, only four remained.

The largest was Deloitte Touch Tohmatsu with 115,000 employees and $16.4 billion of revenue, about 40% from US operations. Next stood PriceWaterhouseCoopers, created in 1998 with the merger of Price Waterhouse with Coopers & Lybrand. Privately held like the others, that firm used business from mergers and acquisitions as well as other corporate accounting contracts to lift 2004 revenue to $16.3 billion, a 12% increase over the previous year. Employment was 7,500 more than Deloitte Touch Tohmatsu. Third was Ernst & Young after getting into real estate investment and development by acquiring Kenneth Leventhal & Company of Cleveland as well a tax preparation company in Canada. Despite selling off consulting operations to Cap Gemini of France, partners managed to generate over $14.6 billion of revenue to support a workforce exceeding 100,000. Finally, KPMG finished 2004 with $13.4 billion of revenue. Employment contracted to 94,000.

There was a fifth big accounting firm until 2002. Arthur Anderson went under because of complicity in the misdeeds of high executives in Enron, WorldCom, and other companies. To curb such excesses, Congress passed the Sarbanes-Oxley Act establishing the Public Company Accounting Oversight Board to set guidelines for corporations in installing new financial controls as well as management checks and balances. The big four survivors counted on consulting work from putting in place those systems to generate over time billions more in revenue.

The possibility that small competitors could cobble together the strength to challenge the major accounting firms was remote. However, a large company might move in from a related sector. For example, after buying rival AutoInfo, and GSI of Paris in 1995 to become a global player in payroll services, ADP acquired payroll, human resources, accounting services operations in Brazil as well as auto collision estimates business in Switzerland. After taking over Advantage Payroll Services, Paychex served 50,000 small and medium size businesses, reaching 505,000 clients in 2004, more than a ten fold increase in nine years.

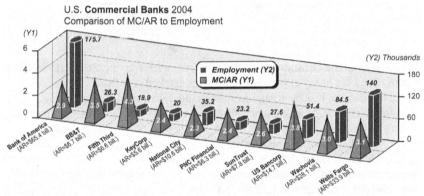

U.S. **Commercial Banks** 2004
Comparison of MC/AR to Employment

Meanwhile, Bank of America's management took dead aim on becoming the largest consumer bank in the country. The plan was facilitated ironically when the recession of 2001 dried up corporate and commercial loans because the company, matching Citigroup with $82 billion of credit and debit card volume, was much better positioned with a strong system of bank branches to generate consistent results. Although revenues contracted from $57 billion in 2000 to below $50 billion in 2003, profit margin soared toward 33%. An October agreement to buy FleetBoston for $43 billion, created in 1999 from the takeover by Fleet Financial of BankBoston for $15.9 billion, was forged. The 67% premium for Fleet-Boston's 33 million customers, 2.5 million business clients, and $25 billion of credit and debit card volume did give pause to some investors. However, the new Bank of America combined $933 billion assets and 5,700 branches, 6.5% of the national total, to cover all parts of the country except the Midwest.

No other bank could boast such geographic spread. Wells Fargo owned nearly $400 million of assets and 4,900 locations in 23 states mostly west of the Mississippi as well as Canada and some Latin American countries. Profit margin reached 33%. The company placed eighth in home loans while credit and debit card volume hit $35 billion.

Washington Mutual became the nation's second largest seller of home loans by purchasing Great Western Financial in 1997 for $6.6 billion and then its nearest S&L competitor H.F. Ahmanson for $9.9 billion in stock. By 2003, the company serviced $287

U.S. **Thrifts & Mortgage Financers** 2004
Comparison of MC/AR to Employment

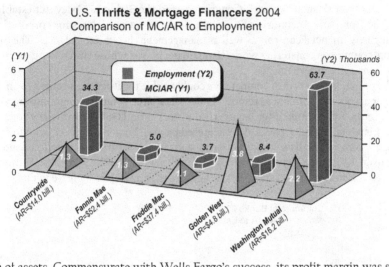

billion of assets. Commensurate with Wells Fargo's success, its profit margin was strong enough to overcome heavy exposure in mortgage-backed securities and customer complaints of bogus fees, lost mortgage payments, mistaken credit reports, and generally sloppy administration. Management continued a strategy of building up a nationwide network of branches.

One key market Washington Mutual attacked was Chicago. BankOne was the big player after blowing into the Windy City in 2002 to take over First Chicago NBD for $29.6 billion and combine $290 billion of assets. Over-aggressiveness in building up an industry leading $134 billion in credit and debit card volume increased defaults. Concentration of 1,800 branches in the Midwest and Southeast and a spread of mutual funds attracted J.P. Morgan Chase's interest in a 2004 acquisition valued at $58 billion, a 20% premium over BankOne's market value.

Another player in the Midwest and West, Firstar of Milwaukee, bought US Bancorp of Minneapolis for $21.1 billion in 2000 but took the US Bancorp name. The company's nearly 40% profit from $189 billion of assets as well as $54 billion of credit and debit card volume in 24 states thrilled investors. Likewise, Wachovia of Charlotte, controlling Prudential Securities, also pushed the profit envelope after a 2001 merger with First Union. Revenues from $388 billion of assets and $14 billion of credit and debit card volume lifted profit margin to 27% and made possible a 2004 purchase of SouthTrust for $14.3 billion.

As banking industry leaders had argued, size and economies of scale were critical to profits. For banks and financial institutions that could not reach critical mass, the consequence was sometimes loss of independence. After feeling the heat from Washington Mutual and exiting consumer branch banking as well as life insurance in 1995, Household invested in sub-prime auto financing by purchasing Transamerica Financial Services. Although the company built toward $15 billion of 2002 revenues from $120 billion of assets by acquiring Beneficial Corporation of Britain, an MC/AR of only 0.75 convinced management to sell out to HSBC of London.

Meanwhile, Bankers Trust of New York City lost half a billion dollars in Russian and other international loans. Management's acceptance of a takeover bid by Deutsche Bank for $10 billion made the German company briefly the largest bank in the world. By contrast, Countrywide Financial tried to remain a player in home mortgages by entering into a joint venture with Woolwich of Britain. Profit margin lagged that of other competitors.

The possibility of earning lucrative commissions and fees on consumer credit cards attracted more non-banks. In 1992, GM's EDS subsidiary launched the *GM MasterCard* so successfully that 2.8 million customers received cards in 3 months. The hook was earning a 5% rebate that could be applied to GM cars and trucks, up to a maximum of $5,000. Although the program did generate profits as well as car sales, some potential customers were put off by having their choice limited.

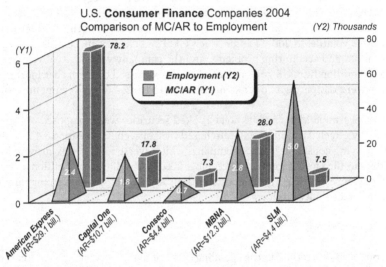

U.S. **Consumer Finance** Companies 2004
Comparison of MC/AR to Employment

By contrast, aggressive entities such as Capital One, founded in McLean, Virginia in 1995, won more adherents by offering cards with no strings attached. The company came by 2002 to offer credit and debit cards with $43 billion of annual volume to Americans, often with less than impressive credit ratings. Higher default rates kept profitability down below the industry average for banks. In 2005, management decided to gain a foothold in retail banking with purchase of Hibernia of New Orleans with branches in Louisiana and Texas for $5.3 billion.

By comparison, more judicious but still aggressive selection of customers by MBNA of Delaware, handling $60 billion of credit and debit card business, pushed up profit margin toward 20%. At nearly $12 billion, revenues in 2004 were sufficient to qualify the company as a large cap stock.

In addition to the benign eye cast by federal regulators on bank mergers and acquisitions, another factor boosting the fortunes of banks was the rise of mortgage backed securities. Fannie Mae and Freddie Mac had since 1981 packaged home loans as debt instruments for sale to investors with interest and principle flowing from payments by home owners on their loans. By purchasing as well mortgages from Wells Fargo, Washington Mutual, and other institutions, Fannie Mae's assets increased between 1990 and 2003 seven fold to $930 billion while Freddie Mac's went up 27 times to $600 billion. Their rise contributed to a relative fall by banks and S&Ls from holding 40% of credit instruments in 1982 to about one quarter two decades later.

In the new century, a plunge in the 30 year mortgage rate toward 5.25% prompted a tripling of annual re-financings between 2000 and 2003 to $600 billion. That was a sixth of all mortgage loans made that year. Fannie Mae and Freddie Mac owned or guaranteed a third of the total $6.5 trillion mortgage loans outstanding. Despite employing in aggregate just 12,000 persons, profitability was thin. Had not Fannie Mae's securities been heavily exposed to mobile home loans with a 9% default rate, results might have been better. An embarrassing accounting scandal for Freddie Mac in which management manipulated revenues, including limiting profits so no one would notice a strategy of using derivatives to offset interest rate shifts and hedge against ups and downs of loans' values, was considered even more serious. The practice actually made interest rates in the broader mortgage market more volatile. In 2004, Fannie Mae's CEO and chief financial officer were forced out over fraud and accounting problems, and the company was eventually compelled to pay a $400 million fine. US government officials expressed concern that mortgage loan holdings were dangerously over-concentrated in these two government-sponsored entities.

Many of Fannie Mae's mobile home backed securities were composed of loans made originally by Green Tree Financial, purchased by Conseco in 1998 for $6.4 billion. That once high-flying consumer finance company, which averaged over 40% growth for more than a decade, filed for Chapter 11 in December 2002 after piling up $51 billion of liabilities. However, Conseco re-emerged the next year as strictly an insurance company selling health, life, and annuity products.

An Investor's Market

Republicans liked the Clinton spending cuts but not the tax increases. After they won control of both houses of Congress and 30 governorships in the 1994 election and rendered politically impossible any further major change in the economic *status quo*, a more stable and predictable environment was created for investors. With the booming economy, corporate profits thickened. The percent of US households directly or indirectly involved in the stock market rose from a third to 60% by the new century.

Specifically, stocks held by households quadrupled to $7.5 trillion at their 2000 peak. Mutual fund holdings increased six fold to $3.1 trillion, about half of all such US assets and a tenth of the global total. Although pensions built more evenly from $3.4 trillion to $9.1 trillion, in combination with stock and mutual funds they accounted for half of all household financial assets, up from one quarter in 1990. After the dollar began a prolonged rise in 1995 *vis-a-vis* foreign currencies, NYSE stocks valued ultimately at $13 trillion and US debt securities reaching $16 trillion, one quarter mortgage-backed securities and one sixth US Treasuries, attracted not only domestic investment but funds from Europe, Japan, and even struggling Russia. Net private foreign capital invested in the US jumped as a consequence from $20 billion in 1996 to $254 billion the next year. The peak was the recession year of 2001 with $455 billion when foreigners gambled and lost a bet that US stocks would recover sooner rather than later from their steep decline.

The greatest bull market of all was in NASDAQ tech stocks. In the decade long period ending in summer 2000, NASDAQ's market capitalization soared a fantastic 1,300%

toward $6 trillion. The advantage of being listed and publicly traded was highlighted by the fact that the asset value of businesses and professions that remained privately held climbed only 50% to $4.8 trillion. The run up in stock values created a "wealth effect" that convinced Americans to drop the savings rate for disposable income to a low of only 1.0% in 2000.

The range of investment opportunities for wealthy clients and corporations was much broader than for households, of course. Companies such as Johnson & Higgins and the Sedgwick Group of Britain catered to high earners. Acquisition of both by insurance broker Marsh & McLennan in 1997 helped that company generate three-fifths of 2003 revenue from its Putnam Investment subsidiary. Putnam was caught up in a "market timing" scandal that illegally gave big clients the ability to trade mutual fund shares after hours. Having already lost 45% of assets under management from a $450 billion peak in 2000, Putnam hemorrhaged another 10%. Ultimately, Marsh & McLennan and other companies were investigated by New York state attorney general Eliot Spitzer for cheating corporate clients by rigging bids and throwing business to insurers in exchange for fees. After chairman and CEO Jeffrey Greenberg resigned, 3,000 other employees lost their jobs, the company paid an $850 million fine, and Spitzer announced he was running for governor of New York.

The mutual fund scandal of 2003 was one in a series of misdeeds that plagued the financial services industry in the period. Earlier in 1998, a hedge fund called Long Term Capital Management (LTCM) with capital of $4.8 billion had gone bankrupt after running up borrowing capacity to $200 billion and ultimate theoretical exposure in derivatives to a staggering $1.25 trillion. Because the hedge fund industry, built up after 1996 by a pro-

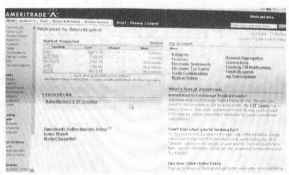

vision in the National Securities Markets Improvement Act that increased the number of investors permitted into new hedge funds from 99 to 499, would have collapsed with LTCM's fall, the Federal Reserve Bank of New York rallied leading financial institutions to take over the entity with a $3.5 billion infusion. Reviving interest in hedge funds eventually pushed the total to 600 entities with an average value of $1 billion. Wall Street also received a black eye in 2003 from conflict-of-interest charges that brokers in subsidiaries of Citigroup, First Boston, Merrill Lynch, and other companies unduly touted to investors the stocks of companies for whom personnel in other subsidiaries were conducting investment banking services. Fines amounted to $1.4 billion.

Unprecedented market capitalizations in new economy stocks enticed individual investors to pick up the slack caused by institutional investor caution. A new breed of day-traders who made their living buying and selling stocks advanced the fortunes of Schwab. By 1998, that company became the second largest brokerage behind Morgan Stanley, which had acquired Dean Witter after that company was spun off by Sears in 1993, by charging discounted fees of $29.95 for trading up to 1,000 shares. Schwab's *supermarket of mutual funds* concept placed it ahead of PaineWebber, Merrill Lynch, and other big name brokerages that charged higher fees. However, implementation of Electronic Communications Networks trading over the Internet permitted even lower discounted trades for under $10 through E*Trade, Ameritrade, which took over E*Trade, and a host of other competitors.

Another attractive investment vehicle was REITs. Not taxed in the trust, they generated predictable income flows without the illiquidity of bond investments. Even after a change in the law in 2003 to tax dividends at a 15% rate induced more corporations to pay out dividends, REITs held their combined market capitalization of about $200 billion. Some REITS could be bought and sold like stocks.

For the broader class of investors, it was privately held Fidelity of Boston, grouping 342 funds under a holding company called FMR that perpetually led the mutual fund pack. Assets under management by 1996 of $500 billion doubled through the stock boom, generating after the tech bust $9.2 billion of 2003 revenues and employing 29,000. By comparison, second largest fund manager Vanguard of Malvern, Pennsylvania (founded 1975) built up by 2003 to 150 funds and $750 billion of assets, 10,000 employees, and $2 billion of annual revenue. Schwab and Merrill Lynch were the next nearest competitors. With almost three times the employment as Vanguard but without Merrill Lynch's diversified clout, Fidelity needed to win big contracts, such as a five year deal with GM handling the auto maker's pension plan for 700,000 active and retired employees. After beating out

MetLife and EDS to administer GM's health and welfare plan for 1.2 million retirees and dependents, the company's benefits outsourcing business covered 15 million current and former employees at 12,000 companies, including IBM, BP, and Monsanto.

Meanwhile in 1996, Merrill Lynch went on a global spree of acquisitions, joint ventures, offices expansion, and trading. Assets under management topped $1 trillion the next year while employment eventually soared over 50,000. Japan, where households hoarded $10 trillion in low-yield savings and personal assets, appeared to be ripe for penetration, but failure to induce conservative investors to take on more risk for greater gain resulted in a $500 million loss. Because of the recession, annual revenues crash landed in 2003 before bouncing back in 2004.

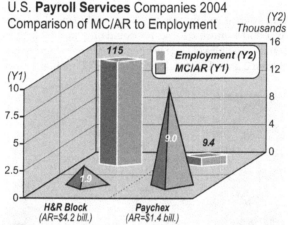

U.S. **Payroll Services** Companies 2004
Comparison of MC/AR to Employment — (Y2) Thousands

H&R Block (AR=$4.2 bill.)   Paychex (AR=$1.4 bill.)

Banks supplying depositors with a range of services were in theory more conservative at fund management than Wall Street's leaders. In 1994, Mellon of Pittsburgh bought Dreyfus to become the largest bank manager of mutual funds. As Dreyfus rose by 2002 to $180 billion of assets in 190 funds, Mellon exceeded $500 billion of assets under management. By comparison, State Street derived revenue from managing over $600 billion of assets and keeping under custody ten times as much.

Although banks had come a long way in diversifying their portfolio of investments, they remained wary of putting capital directly into companies not traded publicly because of the difficulty of establishing valuation. Even venture capital fund managers put only 6.5% of the $164 billion in new investment dollars they attracted in 2000 into private companies. Caution proved wise when the estimated average valuation of such companies declined three-fifths over the next two years to only $60 million. New investment in private companies collapsed, as a consequence, to $1.7 billion.

Investment in publicly traded companies declined as well during the economic slowdown but not by as great a percentage. US companies remained more attractive on average than those in Western Europe, Japan, and other developed economies. Despite the fact that the EU launched its Euro single currency on January 1, 1999, European investors continued to put four-fifths of all foreign direct investment into the US, which peaked in 2000 at $308 billion before contracting to $131 billion newly invested the next year and down toward $100 billion in 2002. Foreigners came by 2003 to hold two-fifths of the securities issued by the US government.

No wonder that H&R Block decided in 2002 to diversify into investment services. Supplementing its core tax preparation business, the company founded a brokerage and offered annuities, mutual funds, and IRAs.

American Express also made a late entry into fund management. In 2003, management bought Threadneedle Asset Management Holdings of Britain from Zurich Financial for $567 million. Most of the company's employees were still focused on travel services and credit card operations, however.

Bringing More Variety to Insurance

Threadneedle was subsumed in American Express Financial Advisors. That division also offered insurance and annuities. Banks too could offer insurance through subsidiaries to create synergies and economies of scale in operations. Bank One, for example, purchased Zurich Life in 2001 from Zurich Financial Services for $500 million.

The key advantage of whole life as well as a new product called universal life with a guaranteed minimum death benefit or cash value and an additional return dependent upon the performance of insurance company investments was that like any financial investment it preserved and increased value. Premiums paid on term life, medical, disability, auto, property and casualty, and other types of insurance typically did not. For that reason, life insurance assets rose from $1.3 trillion in 1990 toward $3.9 trillion in 2004 and continued to compose the overwhelming majority of all insurance assets. Other types of insurance assets, including medical savings accounts, jumped over six-fold to $750 billion to claim a bigger percentage piece of the pie.

Although the insured could borrow against the cash value of life insurance policies, the relative illiquidity of the instrument, the fact that benefits after death went to someone else, albeit tax-free, as well as the burgeoning stock market were reasons that Americans opted increasingly for other investments. In such a mature industry, moreover, the percentage of income-earners with dependents who already owned life insurance policies was high. Therefore, agents and companies searched about for a new way of selling life insurance to make it more attractive as an investment. They came up with a concept called corporate owned life insurance (COLI) that companies could buy on the lives of employees in which they had an "insurable interest." The idea in full flower was that by taking out policies on several thousand people and borrowing money to pay the premiums, corporations could get an immediate tax deduction for interest on the loans and then receive a tax free stream of income as employees, ex-employees, and retirees died off at a predictable rate. Over time, COLIs would produce superior returns. Eventually, the product proved so compelling to management that COLIs came to account for as much as one-third of all life insurance contracts. A big breakthrough came in 1995 when Wal-Mart bought $20 billion worth of face COLI value on 325,000 employees.

One problem was that "insurable interest" was usually defined by courts as only applicable to employees with rank of manager. An attempt by some sellers and buyers to turn COLI into "janitors' insurance" on ordinary workers who did not even know a bet on their collective life expectancy was making money for their employers drew fire from Congress. In 2003, American Electric Power of Columbus, Ohio lost a janitor insurance, federal court case in which management had bought COLI on 20,000 lives. The plan was ruled to be a tax dodge scheme, forcing the company to pay income tax on its death benefit gains.

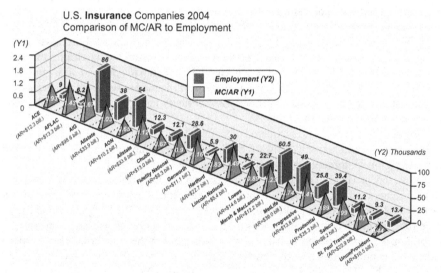

U.S. **Insurance** Companies 2004
Comparison of MC/AR to Employment

In addition to AIG, the biggest players in life insurance continued to be MetLife, Prudential, Hartford Financial Services, John Hancock, and AFLAC. MetLife built up revenue after taking over New England Life seven years earlier and then Travelers Life & Annuity from Citigroup for $11.5 billion in early 2005. Prudential, with more diversity of products and services, was held down by continuing uncertainties about Congress attacking the tax breaks and other advantages of life insurance and COLIs. Spun off in 1995 after a quarter century under ITT, Hartford also offered more diversification of products, including CNA's group life, disability, and accident business, purchased for $500 million late in 2003. John Hancock, however, lost independence when purchased by Canadian Manulife for $10.3 billion. As for AFLAC, the company nearly quadrupled annual revenue between 1997 and 2004 by popularizing its supplemental health insurance side-line with somewhat annoying AFLAC duck, name-recognition commercials.

Behind MetLife in the US but the top insurer around the world was AIG. The company's global operations included a strong presence in China, where state-owned China Life controlled half the market but where AIG alone of foreign insurers had the right to possess wholly owned subsid-  iaries. AIG also competed in India, where competition came from Prudential, Allianz of Germany, and big state-owed companies, Eastern Europe, and Japan. In 2003, the company bought GE Edison Life Insurance, a GE subsidiary operating in that latter country for $2.5 billion. Management also controlled 20th Century's auto insurance business, purchased in 1994, as well as other non-life insurance lines. To improve overall profit margin and reduce uncertainty and cyclicality, AIG wanted to sell its financial guarantee insurance business, investment groups, and life-reinsurance portfolio.

Lincoln National Insurance got out of HMO excess-of-loss reinsurance in 1999 for the same reason. The company had already moved into the individual life and annuity business by purchasing a division of Cigna for $1.4 billion.

Lincoln also divested its American States Financial subsidiary in 1997 for $2.8 billion. Safeco bought that operation to offer insurance for small to medium size businesses. Safeco also picked up Washington Mutual's life insurance division to distribute annuities through Washington Mutual's banking network. The company derived 30% of revenue from life insurance operations. However, management planned to sell its life insurance and investment businesses to focus on property and casualty insurance. The bigger players in the former fields were just too strong.

Property and casualty was rendered more problematic in the 1990s because of a series of costly natural and man-made disasters. In 1992, Hurricane Andrew did $15 billion of damage in Florida, forcing many companies to cease insuring homeowners in the state. That year, too, rioting in Los Angeles in reaction to the acquittal of police officers in the Rodney King beating case destroyed more than $1 billion of property. Two years later in the City of Angels, an earthquake of 6.6 on the Richter Scale killed 34 people and caused seven times as much damage. But floods in the Midwest in 1993 generated claims totaling $17 billion, 6.8% of all property liability premiums paid in the world that year. Property and casualty companies had to build up significant strength to survive even worse disasters such as Hurricane Katrina in 2005 that flooded New Orleans and neighboring low-land areas, destroyed tens of thousands of homes, and caused 300,000 people to flee, generating hundreds of billions of dollars in direct and indirect costs.

Thus, in 1995 CNA Financial, still a subsidiary of the Loews Corporation that employed 25,800 people and also owned hotels, Lorillard Tobacco, Bulova watches, and Diamond Offshore Drilling, acquired Continental Corporation for $1.1 billion. CNA provided at $12.3 billion three-quarters of the parent company's 2003 revenue. But profit margins had been undercut by the recession, resulting in a loss of nearly 5%. To improve profitability, the subsidiary increased deductibles, imposed tougher standards for filing claims, eliminated coverage for high-risk problems such as mold in houses, and sold off its group benefits and individual life insurance divisions. Overall in the industry, in the first year of the new century when US property and casualty companies suffered through a cumulative $16 billion loss on $53 billion of claims and $37 billion of investment earnings, 700,000 of the industry's 60 million homeowner policies were dropped.

By contrast, St. Paul was twice as successful. After the company merged in 1998 with USF&G and four years later exited the medical malpractice and reinsurance fields, profit margin topped 10%. Late in 2003, management proposed a take over of the Travelers to gain a more comprehensive line of property and casualty products for businesses and wider national geographic coverage. The price was $16.4 billion in stock.

Chubb, on the other hand, was far more global in its operations. By supplementing employees spread over 31 countries with 5,000 independent brokers and agents, the big marine insurance company with many other property and casualty lines pushed profit margin over 7.3%.

Despite being spun off to shareholders by Sears in 1995 in a deal valued at $10 billion, AllState remained throughout the period the leader in auto insurance. Its position was strengthened two years later by entering the Canadian and German market and even selling life insurance in Asia, beginning with South Korea and Indonesia. By 2004, the company's *Good Hands Network* of direct telephone and Internet sales, selling predominately in big urban areas, built annual revenues back up toward $34 billion. The company's biggest competitor was State Farm Insurance of Bloomington, Illinois, a mutual insurer owned by policy-holders that was founded in 1922. Not publicly traded, the company in 2003 boasted 72,000 employees and annual revenues of $56.1 billion.

Progressive mounted a challenge to the industry giants. In 1992, management launched a toll-free number shopping service to compare rates. The next year, the company changed strategy to move beyond non-standard insurance to a less risky portfolio of auto insurance including good drivers. Profit margin jumped toward 10%.

Warren Buffett

One reason Progressive moved away from non-standard car insurance was the rise of Geico, an aggressive on-line seller of policies. The company was controlled by Berkshire Hathaway, the 40 year old holding company two-fifths owned by billionaire Omaha, Nebraska investor Warren Buffett with stakes as well in Coca-Cola, American Express, Gillette, and Wells Fargo. After Berkshire Hathaway bought General Reinsurance for $22 billion, revenues leaped over $74 billion in 2004. Profit margin settled below 9%.

Annual revenue generated in 2002 by insurance companies ranked in the top 900 US corporations approached $180 billion. By comparison, banks boasted about $290 billion, diversified financial holding companies over $450 billion, and real estate services about $15 billion. In total, financial services provided by companies in the top 900 chipped in 4% of the approximately $23.2 trillion in revenues generated by all US businesses. All 900 big businesses generated about $6.8 trillion of revenue.

However in the recovery year of 2003, Fortune 500 companies alone generated $7.5 billion of revenue. Despite the fact that the country boasted 5 million incorporated entities, as opposed to over 18 million sole proprietorships and not quite 1.9 million partnerships, it was these large companies that at nearly $450 billion of combined earnings captured 70% of after tax profits. Just over one fifth of that figure was claimed by big financial services companies. No other sector, not even technology, could boast profit margins so high. While the average for the financial sector was comfortably in double figures, big health care companies profited less than 10% of revenues while car and car parts makers struggled in the low single digits. The obvious conclusion was that making money from money, rather than from the sale of goods, had become the best way to accumulate wealth in America.

CHAPTER XXI. COMPETITION FOR WEALTH AND INCOME

Accumulating national wealth and improving standards of living have always been the general goals of American leaders in government and the private sector. However, they have been guided by Jefferson's statement in the Declaration of Independence that all men have the unalienable right to "life, liberty, and the pursuit of happiness," rather than "life, liberty, and property," as asserted by English philosopher John Locke in 1690 in *Two Treatises on Government*. Even to the most enlightened eighteenth century mind, society appeared to have a natural stratification based on wealth. Whether the product of talent, intellect, good luck, or happenstance, wealth bestowed upon those who possessed it a disproportionate say in the affairs of law and government, particularly to insure that order and stability be maintained.

Not until the Founding Fathers passed away did thinking evolve to extend the franchise, and trust, to property-less men. A heavy bias remained in society in favor of protecting property and those who owned it against those who did not. Of course, wealth in itself facilitates a person's ability to mobilize economic, legal, political, and societal forces on his own behalf. Despite guarantees written into the Constitution and law that opportunity in equal measure is available for all, from a practical point of view the poor have always been at best unequal citizens.

In the late nineteenth century, the republic's economy expanded sufficiently to raise living standards more broadly and distribute a portion of the fruits of industrialization and big business combinations to a growing middle class as well as skilled tradesmen. Semiskilled and unskilled workers only started to participate in the national abundance during the Progressive era, Roaring '20s, and FDR's New Deal. American global ascendancy following the Second World War not only restored losses from the Great Depression but increased the republic's wealth more rapidly. By the 1950s, a majority of Americans became relative haves as opposed to relative have-nots.

Because of government sympathy with the basic aims of unionism, pressure for a more equitably leveling of material circumstances increased. Challenged by Soviet Communism, American Capitalism was not about to succumb to a Socialist revolution. Even at the peak of Johnson's attempt to foster a Great Society of plenty for all citizens, social welfare and

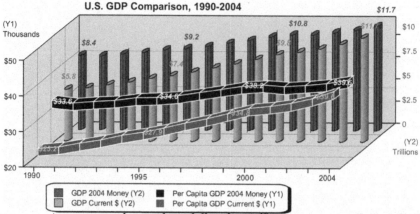

U.S. GDP Comparison, 1990-2004

(Legend:)
GDP 2004 Money (Y2)   Per Capita GDP 2004 Money (Y1)
GDP Current $ (Y2)   Per Capita GDP Current $ (Y1)

income security programs that used tax dollars from affluent citizens to alleviate the distress of the unfortunate never threatened the basic hierarchy of wealth. Dependent in the last analysis upon private business success, government in the last quarter of the twentieth century permitted the free enterprise system to recover much of the autonomy compromised in the first three-quarters. Organized labor's efforts to win an increasing share of national income for working men and women not only stalled but because of automation, globalization, and other forces beyond their control collapsed. Tens of million of middle class families, too, were buffeted by these changes.

The irony is that at the turn of the twenty-first century, Americans in absolute terms had far more wealth than ever before. Invention and innovation had through mass production and the mass market put into the hands of citizens, rich and poor, myriad number of products. Services, free and at cost, were plentiful to improve health and day-to-day living. In comparison to most peoples of the world, Americans of even marginal means lived like kings.

Why then did so many citizens consider themselves disadvantaged? Why, in a republic with 2004 GDP exceeding $11.7 trillion, *per capita* GDP pushing $40,000, assets not counting disposable inventory, personal effects, and other valuables building toward $150 trillion, and national net worth approaching $69 trillion, was not all serious distress relieved? Why with all the resources of technology and education at the country's disposal could better progress not be made in turning the US into a Great Society of material prosperity and plenty?

The new century recession that sent unemployment up to 6.4% of the working population undoubtedly cast a pall over the usually buoyant optimism of Americans. Widening disparities in wealth and income made the plight of the middle and working classes seem more tenuous than they actually were. But a broader answer to the above questions arises from the nature of wealth itself and in the distinction between how wealth is accumulated in a modern society and how it is used. American anxiety about the future was not perhaps unwarranted.

Wealth can be created in four basic ways: by sale of an existing asset for a profit above and beyond what was paid for that asset, by renting the use of an asset for income over time, by building something new which has a value greater than the sum of its parts, and by selling one's labor, ingenuity, and talent for salary, wages, and/or other compensation.

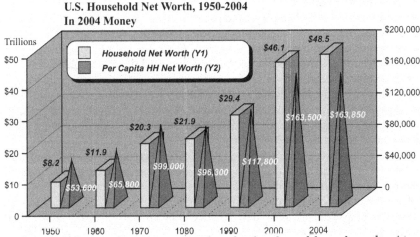

U.S. Household Net Worth, 1950-2004
In 2004 Money

From the point of view of a consumer, on the other hand, wealth can be utilized in two ways: to create more wealth or to buy a wasting asset or service. For example, when a contractor gathers land, material, and labor to build a house, the end product has a value to him greater than the sum of its parts. The consumer not only exchanges money of equal value for the property but benefits as the value of his home appreciates over time, as has almost always been the case in the US except in depressions and severe recessions. However, when a consumer purchases goods and services, he acquires something that will not retain or increase in value in perpetuity. Money spent, say, for an automobile may be salvaged in part by reselling the vehicle, typically for the original price less depreciation, but wealth equal to the depreciation has been lost just as surely as if the consumer goes to the store to buy food or household products for immediate consumption.

Much more calamitous is an event that destroys wealth. Although destruction can occur by intention, such as when a property owner tears down an existing structure to clear land for alternative use, the usual method is accident or natural disaster, such as a fire that destroys a house and everything in it or an earthquake that levels parts of a city. Government, society, and individuals take elaborate precautions to prevent calamities but are generally powerless to avoid acts of God. The development of the insurance industry was on the whole a successful attempt to compensate for wealth-destruction incident with a countervailing wealth-creating investment, or at least a plan to transfer wealth back to the insured in the event of a wealth-destroying catastrophe.

If governments, businesses, or households create more wealth than they transfer or have destroyed, they are better off. If they transfer or have destroyed more than they create, they are the reverse. However, scale is important too. Accumulation of wealth in excess of use is to no avail if sufficient wealth is not created in the first instance to pay for all the material and service advantages required to be successful in a modern society.

For example, a person who lives like a pauper on $10,000 and saves 5% may continue to provide for his existence but is in no way as well off materially as an investor with an annual income of $10 million who consumes all but 1%, and then reinvests that $100,000. Further, the wealthy man has the wherewithal to engage in more and greater wealth-creating activities to increase his advantage, whereas the pauper must sell his labor, ingenuity, and/or talent to entities usually controlled by other members of the affluent class. It is in the material interest of employers to pay the lowest wage possible, albeit without causing disgruntlement that affects production and profits. Particularly when the bargaining leverage of working men and women is weak, they receive pay insufficient to maintain standards of living, and consequently cannot find the disposable income to buy higher-value products and services offered by their employers. In other words, what they earn they spend predominately on wealth-transferring activities. They buy food and clothing, pay for education for their children, cover insurance and medical expenses, make existing car, car repair, and gasoline payments, and fork over taxes to government without any expectation of a wealth-creating return to themselves.

For most Americans, the primary wealth-creating activity is and has always been investing in home-ownership. In 2004, approximately 6.7 million existing and 1.2 million new homes were purchased while over 69% of all US households owned homes. Median price for existing homes was around $189,000 compared to an average price of $242,000. The median and average prices for new homes climbed toward $200,000 and $282,000 respectively.

However, those statistics obscure the fact that a concentration of meaningful net worth has not occurred for all 75 million home-owners. As the figures for national assets and net worth indicate, much wealth is highly leveraged by debt. Particularly on the individual level, when mortgage payments relative to annual income become excessive and cost of repair, utilities, and property taxes escalates, the wealth-creating experience of buying a home can turn into a wealth-transferring albatross. When recession brings unemployment, less family income, and other straightened circumstances, whatever net worth exists for families of marginal means can swiftly be lost. And in fact, after the peak of national wealth in year 2000, $5 trillion of net worth was lost even as assets increased $5 trillion. A chunk of the $40 trillion in household net worth that remained in 2002, recovering to $48 trillion two years later, is at risk not only because of debt but because the salaries and wages paid by businesses are in many cases no longer growing at a pace in excess of inflation.

Although the private sector has reclaimed much freedom of action to power the economy, government retains authority, actual and potential, to intervene for the benefit of citizens and groups. Naturally, the President and Congress as well as state and local government are interested in creating more wealth and seeing that it is adequately distributed to build up the middle class as well as a well-off working class. The problem is that one man's wealth creation is another man's wealth transfer. The basic tension between buyer and seller, business and consumer, employer and employee continues to exist. Thus, lower prices for goods and services reduce the cost of living, but lower profits impair what businesses can pay workers. The imperative of satisfying investor expectations for high rates of return limits job-creation no matter the success of businesses. Union leaders want to negotiate the best wage and benefit package possible but risk replacement of their members by machines or cheaper labor at home and abroad if they demand too much. Even when they bargain merely to preserve what they have, management chafes at work rules that inhibit freedom of action to cut costs, improve efficiency of production, and respond to marketplace changes.

Even in this era of deregulation and risk-taking, government has intruded in private sector affairs to save US jobs and production. Farm subsidies and steel tariffs are good examples. However, tariffs and subsidies risk foreign retaliation as well as entrenchment of inefficient ways. Most economists now agree that carrying the doctrine of comparative advantage to its logical if ruthless conclusion will provide a greater overall economic pie than piecemeal application of the concept.

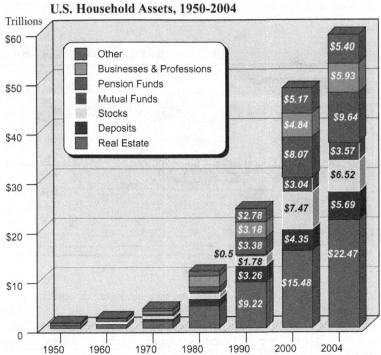

As for redistributing wealth and income by confiscatory tax policy, Washington has moved away from that concept in favor of policies favorable to business for the very same reason. Federal, state, and local governments prefer to use tax-dollars to employ 28 million people themselves, or about 19% of the workforce rather than to tip the scales of "economic justice," as some call it, to balance out wealth and income. In fact, Adam Smith's ideal world in which buyers and sellers, businesses and consumers, employers and employees dicker, negotiate, and compete in a virtually free market is closer to fruition than not. That state of affairs is as much a source of satisfaction for some as it is a catalyst for protest from others.

Big Buildup of Wealth—and Debt

In the last decade of the twentieth century and first few years of the twenty-first, the bedrock of American wealth remained holdings in real property. Although the bull market in stocks caused household real estate to decline from 27% of household assets in 1990 toward 23% in 2000, after the tech stock bust, that share climbed again by 2004 toward 31% of the $59 trillion total. With home values rising considerably faster than the historical average, mortgage debt as a percent of household real estate declined from half in

1990 to a low of only 42.7% in 2000. More lenient mortgage terms in the new century and a splurge of re-financings to take advantage of rock-bottom interest rates caused that figure to rise again. In fact, banks permitted home buyers to borrow on average over two-thirds of a home's purchase price, up from two-fifths 20 years ago when mortgage debt as a percent of household real estate was only three dollars in ten. Nearly half of all home-owners who refinanced in 2002 used a cash-out option to remove an average of $31,000 of equity.

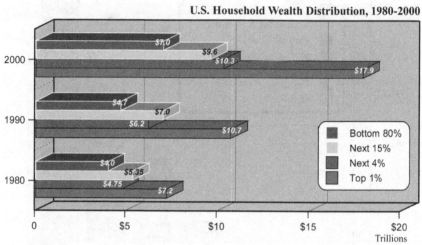

U.S. Household Wealth Distribution, 1980-2000

In the 1990s, median US household income rose 8% faster than inflation to nearly $43,150. After the 2001 recession, it fell 2.2%. Although because of a decade of low inflation and high productivity national DPI of $7.85 trillion was nearly double 1990's figure, the savings rate plunged to nearly zero. Despite stock market losses peaking at $8 trillion in 2002, home value increases of $3 trillion cushioned the blow.

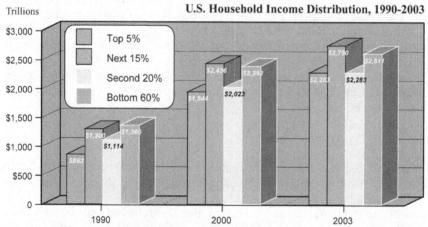

U.S. Household Income Distribution, 1990-2003

In bigger cities, the spread between home price increases and income increases reached 5% or greater. That discrepancy meant that new home buyers in particular were harder pressed to make mortgage payments. Home prices relative to household income in the priciest markets reached a level double or more the benchmark of 3.0 considered safe by housing industry analysts. By 2003, mortgage payment delinquencies for first time home buyers with loans insured by the FHA climbed to a record one in eight. When considering that these are average figures, the plight of lower income Americans can better be understood. African-Americans, for example, earned 75% as much as white Americans while possessing net worth one-tenth as much.

Nevertheless, it was the vaulting of consumer debt above $2 trillion and other liabilities toward $1 trillion, rather than mortgage debt, which reduced household net worth as a percentage of total household assets to a low of 83%. Credit card debt alone, not backed like auto loans by some asset, reached $8,800 per household in 2004. As credit card companies gathered in $7 billion annually on late fees from 58% of card users in the recession year of 2001, well over a third of credit-card loans were in the sub-prime category considered highly risky. Only in 2002 did the pace of credit card borrowing brake to a 1.6% annual increase from 11.5% in 2000.

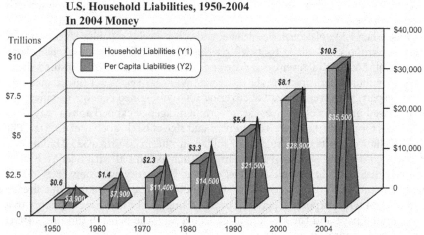

U.S. Household Liabilities, 1950-2004 In 2004 Money

Household debt hit a record 103% of DPI that year. A steady 14% of DPI was used to pay principle and interest. Because the richest fifth of households averaged 120% debt to DPI, the ratio for the other 80% was at four dollars of debt to five dollars of DPI not so extreme. Still, personal bankruptcies topped 1.5 million, motivating a movement in Congress to tighten up bankruptcy law.

All US private sector borrowing consumed $2.4 trillion or three-fifths of debt raised globally. In addition to home mortgages, all that borrowing financed the purchase of a hoard of consumer durables valued in 2002 at $3 trillion. Actual cumulative annual investment in consumer durables through 2003 was on the order of $15 trillion, however, because even automobiles depreciate by half in three years. That explains why the fixed asset value of cars and other light vehicles only climbed from $95 billion in 1990 toward $155 billion in 2000 when annually Americans were buying anywhere from 12 to 16 million units. In other words, four-fifths of the value of investment in consumer durables in the period was used up. By comparison, Americans pumped in about $4.75 trillion in new investment in housing and land while value appreciation accounted for another $3.7 trillion.

As substantial as was the increase in tangible assets, the surge in intangible assets was even greater. Household financial assets crested near $34 trillion in 2000 before falling back a couple trillion with the recession and thickening again with the stock market recovery of 2003. Nearly half of the total was attributable to pension funds and stocks. All retirement assets peaked a year earlier in 1999 at $11.4 trillion before sliding down to $10.9 trillion in 2002. Half the nation's 140 million man workforce at the turn of the century had no employer-sponsored pension, rather relied on Social Security or personal savings. Even workers with pensions began to worry when unfunded pension liabilities of US corporations more than quadrupled with the stock crash and 2001 recession to $111 billion, and then virtually tripled again to $300 billion in 2003.

For example, GM spent $5 billion annually for retirees and active employees, but was at one point when investments were down nearly $30 billion under funded. That shortfall was 50% as great as the company's market value. The reason investors were not unduly panicked was that pension assets would increase as the economy and stock prices recovered. They knew that pension liabilities were unsecured, though so too were their own equity stakes.

Thus, when LTV, National, Bethlehem, and other steel companies failed in the new century, bankruptcy and sale of assets left retirees and laid-off workers without a claim on the buyers of those assets' revenues and profits. Only because the PBGC insured the pensions of 45 million Americans were the retirement years of so many not turned into impoverished despair. However, instead of covering 100% of defined benefits calculated by a formula based on years of service, the government agency capped annual pay-outs at $43,977, less for people under 65. The number and size of bankruptcies caused the PBGC with $39 billion of assets to go from a $7.7 billion surplus in 2002 to a $23.2 billion deficit in 2004. A continuing peril that big airliners, such as United with over $6 billion in unfunded pension liability, would go under exposed the agency, with only $800 million of annual premium, to a bill it could not pay without a bail-out by Congress. But already in 2003 and 2004 with corporate operating profits rising for the first time in history to a $1 trillion annual pace and the stock market recovering, the pension funding situation showed marked improvement.

Equaling as troublesome from a retirement income perspective as pension funding and benefit woes was that fact that 13 million Americans had borrowed against their 401(k) plans. Proceeds up to 50% of the value or $50,000, whichever was smaller, had been used to pay off credit card debts, buy consumer durables, and even fund vacations. Thus, the purpose of 401(k) plans as a supplement for Social Security payments was compromised. Even $2.5 billion accumulated in IRAs might be tapped at need.

As for Social Security, although the full faith and credit of the federal government was not immediately in question, the present value of total projected government benefit payments for retirement purposes exceeded the present value of projected revenue by $7.5 trillion. Infinitely more frightening, the present value of government payments for Medicare/Medicaid and other health care benefits was by worse case scenario over $60 trillion more than the present value of projected revenue. Deferred taxes on the $11 trillion building up in IRAs, 401(k)s, and traditional pensions might over time cover a few trillion of the shortfall, but young Americans did not believe that promised funds would be available in their retirement years. The performance of other investments and savings loomed as all the more important.

Through the 1990s, the aggregate value of those holdings more than doubled from $5 trillion to $11.8 trillion. The composition of the accounts swung from not quite two-thirds bank deposits in 1990 to more than three-fifths stocks in 2000. At their peak in March 2000, all stock holdings by households, businesses, and foreign investors amounted to $17 trillion, including more than $6 trillion in NASDAQ technology stocks and virtually all the rest in NYSE issues. When telecom and Internet stocks began to crash in March 2000, initially money flowed into Dow Jones industrials and other traditional stocks, bringing those more reliable securities backed by predictable revenues to a peak value in August of $12.9 trillion.

However, as the recession came on, corporate profits were far too little to support the valuation bubble. A more general stock market contraction cut total NYSE and NASDAQ valuation down to $10 trillion by summer 2002. Not less than $2 trillion was lost in telecom stocks alone, as well as half a million jobs. A ruthless weeding out of Internet stocks eliminated those with faulty business models, which was an overwhelming majority. Globally, too, stock values fell like stones. In Europe, the value of the top 1,200 publicly listed companies contracted from $9.5 trillion to $4.5 trillion.

Before the crash, three out of five US households were invested in some manner in stocks. Afterward, that figure slipped below 50%. The only saving grace from a societal standpoint was that average loss of $63,500, double that in some locales, was mostly paper loss and concentrated in households with the wherewithal to absorb them without significant change in living standards. US stocks still accounted for roughly 56% of the total market capitalization of stocks in the world. Then in 2003, stock values rose again to $12.5 trillion, of which nearly 78% was NYSE valuation. While the average portfolio size for the 54 million US households invested in some manner in stocks was $240,000, the median portfolio was only $34,000.

That was pocket change to Bill Gates, the world's richest man. Although a decline in the price of Microsoft stock cut his fortune in half, he still had $46.5 billion left in 2004. Other new economy entrepreneurs such as Microsoft co-founder Paul Allen with $21 billion, Oracle's Larry Ellison with $18 billion, Michael Dell with $16 billion, and Intel co-founder Gordon Moore with $5 billion had gigantic fortunes. Savvy investors such as Warren Buffett at $44 billion, takeover artist Carl Icahn at $8 billion, and Russian immigrant George Soros at $7 billion prospered without shining in the glow of a single star. But it was the four offspring of Sam Walton who collectively at $82 billion controlled 75% of the republic's greatest private legacy. The Rockefeller fortune, by comparison, had long since been dispersed among many heirs.

By 2000 a re-concentration of wealth, due in part to the stock market surge, in part to reduced taxes on high incomes, in part to decrease in estate and gifts taxes and increases in estate and gift tax exclusions to $1 million in 2001, permitted the top 1% of households to claim for the first time since 1930 more than a two-fifths share of wealth. While the top 5% climbed above a 64% share by 2003, the next 15% actually fell over three percentage points to a 21% share while the bottom four-fifths of all households saw their share of wealth contract to 15%.

In dollar figures, the average net worth of the top 1% of households nearly doubled in the 1990s to $15.6 million, the top 5% experienced a similar rise to $4.9 million, the next

15% rose from $195,000 to $560,000, and the bottom four-fifths went from $44,560 to $75,760. Correcting for inflation, the bottom 85 million households saw their wealth increase at an annual pace of 2.6%, a big improvement on the 0.3% pace of the 1980s. However, the bottom 50% of American households had only 2.8% of household net worth, or about $1.17 trillion. That was $8,000 per person.

Moreover, in the midst of the greatest wealth increase in history, the number of impoverished peaked at 39 million in 1994, fell to about 31 million in 2000, and then climbed again toward 35 million. This population was disproportionately composed of African, Hispanic, and Asian-Americans and women. Their plight was somewhat alleviated by annual charitable contributions climbing by 2001 to $212 billion, of which $9 billion came from corporations. Charitable institutions themselves were substantial non-profit businesses with total assets the next year of $486 billion, over ten times higher than in 1981.

LeBron James

Another factor permitting wealthy households to claim a greater share of wealth was dramatic increases in the annual income of highly paid people in all professions. For example, top movie actors secured contracts calling for $10 million a picture, and then $15 million, and then $20 million. In TV, morning talk show host Katie Couric was signed by NBC in 2001 for $60 million over 5 years. Stars of popular TV series received as much as or more than movie actors. In professional sports, 18 year old high school basketball star LeBron James not only received a three year package worth $13 million from the Cleveland Cavaliers of the NBA but signed a $90 billion shoe endorsement contract with Nike. Under union agreements guaranteeing players a fixed percent of attendance and TV revenues, even mediocre talent among professional athletes in the NBA, NFL, and Major League Baseball received million dollar salaries. In government, the President made $400,000 annually while Congress voted in November 2002 to raise the pay of congressmen to $154,700. Members of the first Congress, arguably more productive than the current 108th Congress, received a *per diem* of $6 when in session. In 2004 money, the pay of a representative in 1789 was about one sixth the pay of today's representatives.

But it was the realm of corporate compensation that created the most new multi-millionaires. After Congress passed a 1993 law limiting business deductions for executive salaries exceeding $1 million, boards of directors turned to stock options to put "golden handcuffs" on the most valuable employees. As stock prices soared during the decade, options granted for large blocks of shares were exercised at low prices to permit execu-tives to cash in. The amount of wealth so transferred by Fortune 500 companies between 1995 and 2000 was $30 billion. Only after the stock market crash wiped out the retirement income of rank and file employees of Enron, WorldCom, and other fraudulently managed companies did a backlash develop and FASB propose that stock options be expensed by corporations beginning in 2006. With a median total compensation package peaking in 2001 at $2.4 million and an average package of $36 million, CEOs were being paid 400 times the average pay for production worker, nearly ten times the ratio as in 1981.

In addition to stock options, CEOs also were awarded deferred compensation packages in which corporations set aside pretax dollars for investment, typically with a guaranteed double-digit rate of return, for pay-out prior to retirement. That was a device used to transfer millions of dollars to discredited Enron executives, for example. But no matter the compensation method, the highest paid CEOs, in command of top corporations, were sometimes paid as richly as if they were the original founders of the business. When Jack F. Welch, Jr. of GE retired in September 2001 after 20 years at the helm, $250 million of his net worth of $456 million was composed of GE stock.

LABOR AS A GLOBAL COMMODITY

Despite the large and growing disparities in wealth and income between the segments of society that the Census Bureau typically divides into fifths, the real determinant of satis-faction or dissatisfaction for citizens has been whether they possess the economic where-withal to attain and preserve the material part of the American Dream. Perspective as to what that dream entails varies by individual, but generally speaking most middle and working class families aspire to enough income to afford not only basic food and household products but home ownership and modern appliances, automobiles and con-sumer electronics, comprehensive medical and dental care, quality education for their children, and the electricity, gasoline, natural gas, water, and other raw materials required to make utilities function. They want further to enjoy weekly or monthly entertainments and vacation travel at home or abroad. The topper is accumulation of a secure nest egg to pay for a dignified retirement.

As has been amply described in previous chapters, the principal agencies available to provide a comfortable standard of living are businesses as well as government agencies. Unions, as direct representatives of working men and women, have applied pressure to apportion corporate and government revenue more equitably. Despite the PATCO strike disaster of 1981, unions continued in the 1990s to employ job actions to press demands. A March 1990 strike by Greyhound employees accompanied by vandalism and service can-cellations won concessions from the country's intercity bus company but alienated the public and temporarily put Greyhound into bankruptcy. Likewise, a 1994 strike by the Teamsters against 22 trucking firms over recruiting part-time, lower wage drivers to deliver to multiple locations opened the door for independent truckers to take business and income from union drivers. A strike that year by the URW against Bridgestone's Fire-stone subsidiary backfired so badly when the company hired replacement workers that the URW had to merge with the USWA to survive. Another failed strike was the walk-out from Caterpillar plants by 14,000 UAW members, working without a contract for three years, which extended through 1995. The company's use of 4,000 temporary workers,

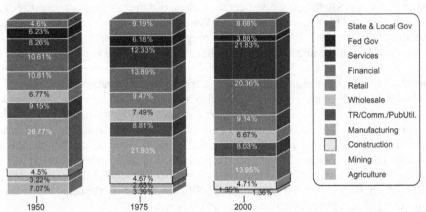

Sector Contribution to U.S. GDP, 1950-2000

former employees, and administrative personnel to man production lines with no loss of revenue forced the union to order its members back under the humiliating condition that they would have some jobs, but not necessarily the ones they had formerly performed.

More successful was the August 1997 Teamster strike against UPS to force the company to upgrade 10,000 part-time drivers receiving $11 per hour wages to full-time status and wages of $17.50, albeit shy of the $20 average. UPS also agree to hire 10,000 more full-timers through expansion and consolidation, and provide annual wage increases in a new five year contract. The key factor in management's decision to make those concessions was UPS' domination of the industry. Market share of 56%, or 12.5 million parcels delivered daily, permitted rate increases to be passed along to businesses and consumers. After a huge $5.5 billion IPO in November 1999, both UPS and its employees prospered. However, pressure from FedEx and other competitors threatened to reopen the issue of less than full-time employees.

Although the Clinton administration paid lip-service to unions, the Bush administration dispensed with all pretense. When the Pacific Maritime Association of owners locked out 10,500 west coast dock workers of the International Longshoremen and Warehouse Union (ILWU) on September 29, 2002, the President persuaded a federal judge to invoke the Taft-Harley Act 80-day cooling off period. The ILWU had engaged in a work slowdown to prevent the owners from computerizing operations to eliminate clerk jobs paying $118,000 annually and generally reduce labor costs. An agreement in November protected the income of current employees but did not prevent automation. Gone forever were the days of the 1950s when 100,000 ILWU workers were needed to off-load ships and cargoes. Only a dwindling few thousand would hereafter be employed to handle the 14 ships and 215 cargo containers per day that arrived from East Asia.

In a population growing from 250 million in 1990 to 296 million in 2004, and a national workforce half as much, the labor movement's fundamental problem was ironically one of leverage. Composing a fifth of all American workers as late as 1983, union membership fell to less than 14%. While over one quarter of government workers remain unionized, the share of private sector employment claimed by unions crumpled from one in

six in 1983 to less than one in eleven. Included in those figures were out-of-work union members.

The unemployment rate varied in the period from just over 5% in 1990 to a peak of 7.8% in the recovery year of 1992 to 4% at the end of the decade to 6.4% in summer 2003 and down to 5.4% after the 2004 election. However, many of the 9.2 million self-employed were largely idle while millions more were under-employed workers staffed out by Manpower, Kelly Services, and other temporary worker companies and over 2 million others were in jail. Although lower skilled workers typically compose a disproportionate share of the job-less, the share of national employment claimed by the manufacturing sector, still a union stronghold, fell from 15.6% at beginning of the period toward 12.3% when the younger Bush took office. In the first three years of the new century, nine-tenths of the net job loss of 2.4 billion was in manufacturing. Although the stock market slump, the recession of 2001, and the impact of terrorism and war were blamed, longer term trends toward automation and job export were more fundamental.

Because of "foreign outsourcing" of jobs and a drop in manufacturing's share of GDP from 18% to 14%, the National Association of Manufacturers (NAM) warned that the republic was in danger of losing "critical mass" in manufacturing. Every dollar of spending to make goods was important because it generated another 67 cents in manufacturing as well as 76 cents of non-industrial spending. In absolute terms, however, output increased 50% to over $1.5 trillion. Productivity climbed even as the total number of manufacturing jobs declined 10% to 17.2 million. Capital improvements generally and the use of better technology specifically made the nation's production workers more efficient than larger factory workforces in past eras. Particularly where higher skills and more specific plant know-how were required, American manufacturing workers excelled. No wonder that the average manufacturing wage remained 20% higher than the national average for all wages. As heavier use of personal computers translated into a reduction in front office workers, percent of employees in manufacturing companies involved directly in production actually rose from 64% at its nadir toward three-quarters while percent of payroll taken by production workers climbed from half toward three-fifths.

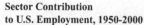

**Sector Contribution
to U.S. Employment, 1950-2000**

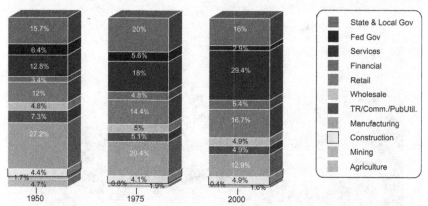

The real problem with manufacturing's relative decline was not job loss itself but the difficulty of replacing higher paying wage incomes supporting families at standards of living necessary to maintain the material American Dream. Not only were production workers paid more than workers in non-manufacturing industries, but they worked longer hours, 40.7 in an average week supplemented by 4.1 hours of overtime. The national average for all workers was just over 34 hours. As manufacturing jobs were lost, as wages and hours worked declined, households had by necessity, not choice, to rely upon two incomes.

Even when manufacturing jobs remained in the US, higher wages were no longer a given. In union-strong automobile and related industries, companies outsourced parts to non-union plants paying less wages and fewer benefits. Such was the decision in 1993 of the management of Briggs & Stratton, a Wisconsin company with $1.6 billion of annual revenue making small gasoline engines for lawn mowers. To keep open a plant at reduced employment, union leaders were forced to accept a starting wage for new hires of $11 per hour and no retiree health-care benefits instead of the regular wage of $16 per hour. But for national and multinational firms with leeway to move production around the country and world, no amount of concessions would do. Ford, for example, built a $1.2 billion factory in Brazil to turn out mini-SUVs. Just as successive US administrations had insisted that the Japanese and other foreign car makers build production facilities in the US, so now did Brazil, China, and other countries want American auto makers to locate auto plants on their soil. That decision was as sound on labor and transportation cost grounds as on political rationale.

Even while conceding that automation and globalization were inevitable, union leaders in heavy industry fought rear-guard actions to preserve past advances rather than take the offensive to secure new wage, benefit, and working condition concessions as well as unionize new industries. The UAW was particularly determined to insure that average pay for automobile assembly line workers, up to $37,000 annually by mid-decade plus $11,000 overtime, did not contract. However, UAW strikes in 1996 over GM's outsourcing of anti-lock brakes from Robert Bosch of Germany that cost the company sale of nearly

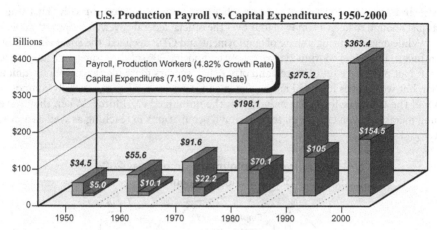

U.S. Production Payroll vs. Capital Expenditures, 1950-2000

100,000 vehicles and $1 billion only stiffened management's resolve to emulate what Ford and Chrysler first did back during the auto recession of the early 1980s. Although three year contracts signed that year by the UAW with the Big Three auto makers did provide a 3% increase in base wage to keep pace with inflation and guarantee that 95% of UAW jobs would be protected from cuts due to outsourcing, management freedom of action to automate and make other productivity improvements was not officially impaired. Thus in 1998 when GM changed work rules at its Flint, Michigan stamp and die plant, 190,000 UAW members struck in protest. Company officials simply shifted production from Flint to another location.

The new century's economic slump brought further parts outsourcing, automation, and employment reductions to the US auto industry. By 2003, employment in the US at GM, Ford, and Chrysler was down to a quarter million. Equally as troubling as the jobs contraction, GM's former parts subsidiary Delphi and Ford's Visteon as well as other unionized parts companies now employed less than a quarter of workers in the auto parts sector compared with 55% in the late 1970s. In a three year contract signed that year with all those companies, the UAW had to agree to freeze base assembler pay for two years at $25.63 per hour, though workers did receive a $3,000 bonus the first year, a bonus equal to 3% of the previous year's earnings in the second, and an increase in pension benefits. In exchange for pressuring suppliers like Dana to permit the UAW to organize thousands more workers in those companies who earned about $14 per hour, the Big Three won the right to slash employment by another 50,000 workers through attrition or buyout packages.

Fundamentally, the UAW was sacrificing the income of future workers for the prosperity of current workers and retirees. Given that the alternative was a showdown with auto and parts makers that would, barring government intervention, result in transfer of production to the South where transplants such as Mercedes Benz in Alabama paid as low as $10 per hour, the compromise can be better understood. Unlike the jobs of coal miners that paid $19.40 per hour and construction workers who brought home $17.40 per hour, auto manufacturing jobs could more easily be exported. From a labor supply and demand point of view, nothing really stood in the way of management squeezing down wages to the average of $10.80 earned by textile workers but political pressure. One step below the textile industry wage was retail positions that paid $9.30 or $18,860 annually. That wage was just enough to keep a family of four over the official federal government poverty line.

While manufacturing's share of employment and GDP declined, the share claimed by non-financial services continued to rise, now composing 30% of the former and 22% of the latter. Not only were retail, hotel, and other such sectors more likely to hire non-union labor, but workforces included more women and minorities. Women generally composed 45% of the US labor force but only 15% of the unionized workforce. When they were union members, women tended to hold down occupations in teaching as well as autos, steel, and shipping.

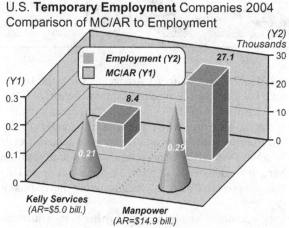

U.S. **Temporary Employment** Companies 2004
Comparison of MC/AR to Employment

Kelly Services (AR=$5.0 bill.)   Manpower (AR=$14.9 bill.)

Except for government, the largest employer of women was Wal-Mart. For reasons varying from the fact that some women preferred part-time work to blatant discrimination, alleged in a class action law suit involving 1 million former and 600,000 current female American employees, women at Wal-Mart earned around 10% less than 340,000 male employees. Because many Wal-Mart employees did not work full day schedules, average pay for sales clerks of about $8.30 per hour translated into an average annual wage of less than $14,000. The company provided health care benefits for only 43% of its workers.

Another way for companies to cut labor costs within the US was to import workers. Because about 20% of the world's 6 billion people, including 200 million Chinese, lived on approximately $1 per day, there was no lack of candidates for immigration. But the nation was shocked in 1996 to learn that undocumented Thai workers had been working in sweat shot conditions at a clothing factory in El Monte, California. The illegal immigrants were slaving away to pay off the cost of passage to the United States.

Meanwhile, the number of illegal Mexican immigrants crossing into the US more than doubled to 4.2 million annually by the new century and in aggregate 8-12 million at any one time. An agreement Washington made with Mexico City to expand a temporary worker program to allow many undocumented Mexicans to gain permanent legal status was canceled after the September 11, 2001 terrorist attacks. That did not dissuade Tyson Foods officials from smuggling Mexican workers into US meat processing plants, for which indiscretion the company was fined. JDS Uniphase escaped all but public contempt for paying female Chinese immigrants in fiber-optics plants less than the industry average $12 per hour and then outsourcing other work to companies using Vietnamese immigrants working at home for as little as $4 per hour.

Sweat shop wages and conditions could not be imposed upon higher-skilled workers, of course. However, under the *H-1B* visa program, companies were permitted by the Department of Immigration to bring in foreign professional workers. When a temporary tripling of annual visas to 195,000 resulted in job loss for US workers, Congress in 2001 banned use of *H-1B* visas to fill vacant jobs in the US and forced employers to pay *H-1B* visa workers prevailing US wages. Dell, the Germany electronics firm Siemens, and other multinationals cleverly switched to more loosely regulated rules governing *L-1* intra-company transfers, particularly of information technology workers. Thus, a move by Congress in October 2003 to cut back the *H-1B* visa quota to 65,000 annually was already negated. *L-1* workers soon equaled the 400,000 or so *H-1B* workers in the country. Since many *L-1* workers originated in India and were willing to accept salaries one-third prevailing US pay, the potential for undercutting high-paying US employment was high. Foreign companies in the $250 billion US information technology industry held a rapidly rising 3% share.

Yahoo call center in Bangalore, India

In the global economy, the House and Senate did little to prevent multinationals from exporting jobs. The $6.75 billion of software services provided in 2003 to the US by persons in India was growing by leaps and bounds. Time Warner opened a call center for customer service employing 1,500 people making $2,500 annually in Bangalore, India—the Silicon Valley of that country—while laying off 420 such workers in the US earning $20,000. AT&T Wireless planned to lay off 10% of the company's workforce of 30,000 and out-source those customer service and other jobs to the sub-continent. On the other hand, Verizon's management calculated that technology-related improvements would permit downsizing its 203,000 workforce by one-third without any job export. Because 78,000 workers employed in wire-line phone service operations had job security and better pay through a union contract, generous early retirement packages had to be offered.

Earthlink, Yahoo, J.P. Morgan, Texas Instruments, and IBM were other high-profile companies that contributed to the flood of 200,000 service jobs, most in information technology, that were sent overseas to US-controlled foreign subsidiaries in the first three years of the new century. The trend was likely to continue at a pace of about 100,000 per year or more because salaries in India even for accounting, engineering, financial analysis, graphic design, chip design, and software averaged 20% of pay in the US. GE Capital, for example, already employed 15,000 in India, while Citigroup, American Express, and other big financial services companies believed that relocating 10% of their workforces to regions where educational and skill level did not necessarily translate into substantial compensation made good business sense. India's particular advantage over other populous countries was that much of the population spoke passable English.

Higher paying finance and information technology jobs had been viewed as part of the replacement for high wage manufacturing jobs. While 7.8 million Americans remained employed in the former sector and 6.5 million in the latter, the longer term prospect for those and other computerized positions not requiring a physical presence in a specific location no longer looked so bright. No matter the language and job, foreign labor almost always cost less than American. While in the US the minimum wage rose from $3.80 per hour in 1990 to $5.15 per hour by 2004, the unskilled wage came up to $7 per hour, and the national average approached $15 per hour, US factories employed 1.4 million people in Mexico receiving $3.00 per hour. However, the basic wage rate in China was around 50 cents per hour. For that reason, US companies were not only exporting jobs to the Far East but beginning to close down Mexican plants. Only final assembly of GE side-by-side refrigerators, Ford automobiles, and other such bulky items with high transportation costs were not typically moved. Job losses to East Asia and the fact that US agricultural products were undercutting the livelihood of millions of peasant farmers worried the Mexican government and brought the southern neighbor's long-term fidelity to NAFTA into question.

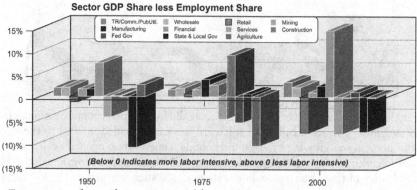

Exaggerating the gap between US and foreign labor costs was the fact that health and pension benefits composed about 28% of total US labor costs. By 2004, the average employee health care cost to corporations was $6,680, 86% higher than in 1997. Rising expenses caused the percent of businesses with fewer than 200 workers that covered health care to fall to less than two-thirds. While 98% of companies with 200 or more workers still did offer coverage, the trend was to pass along more of the costs to employees as well as reduce or drop coverage for retirees. Those among the 160 million workers and their family members who were covered by businesses such as Wal-Mart that emphasized a philosophy of providing catastrophic medical coverage for cancer and other life-threatening illnesses but not comprehensive care were, therefore, little better off on a day-to-day basis than the 45 million Americans who had no health insurance.

More typical was the practice of GE. The company did provide comprehensive health insurance but sought to cut its $4.2 billion health care bill, $1.3 billion for prescription drugs alone, for 300,000 current workers as well as 900,000 dependents, retirees, and retiree dependents by boosting co-pays on emergency room visits, increasing deductibles, and making other changes. The long-term goal was to require employees to contribute the national average of 30% of the cost, up from 17% currently. After tough negotiations with 24,000 union workers in the company's appliance, airplane engines, power, medical systems, and industrial systems divisions, management got employee health care contribution up to 20% while holding wage increases to an average annual rate of 2.8% over three years. Given that GE's union wage was about $21.50, the contract was not unfavorable to employees. However, only 15% of the company's US workforce was covered by the agreement.

Even more under the gun were heavy industry titans like GM. The company's $3 billion a year health care bill was made more burdensome by the fact that 460,000 retirees and their spouses outnumbered current employees over three to one. In 2003, the present value of GM's promised medical benefits exceeded an incredible $63 billion. Because a quarter of the retiree population had been salaried workers not protected by union contracts, management was ironically freer to impose upon them higher premiums, deductibles, and co-pays. Nationally as annual out-of-pocket medical expenses per person zoomed toward $2,500, retiree payments, particularly for older persons in poorer health, reached much higher levels. Retirement income would have to be redirected to cover health care costs.

Americans were on firmer legal ground with regard to pensions. By 2001, GM was obligated to pay an average annual pension of $14,000, with an aggregate present value liability of $6.3 billion. Some companies like Delta tried to reduce pension plan expenses for current employees by changing from defined benefit plans to cash benefits. In essence, they wanted to pay out only what contributions actually earned as opposed to pensions calculated according to some formula, which might be higher than actual fund earnings. However, the likelihood was that courts would block changes to current pension plans. In August 2003, in fact, a US district court judge ruled that IBM's attempt to switch to a defined contribution plan for current employees amounted to age discrimination under the Employee Retirement Income Security Act of 1974 because the effect would be to diminish pensions for older workers while increasing them for younger, and required IBM to pay $300 million in compensation.

As has been previously discussed, the pension benefit burden for employees of companies that went bankrupt or sold assets to dissolve operations was shifted onto the PBGC. Health and life insurance benefits, however, were not covered at all. That raised a question whether the government would continue to sit idly by in the face of a benefit crisis that threatened to wipe out a significant portion of the nest egg counted on by American workers to fund a dignified retirement or resume an activist role. The issue boiled down to how Washington would craft policy to keep the material part of the American Dream intact for a majority of citizens.

GOVERNMENT'S SHIFTING POLICIES

In the last quarter of the twentieth century but in particular the last decade, government policy evolved from direct intervention in the economy on behalf of well-defined groups of citizens toward facilitating the growth of the overall economy and relying on private business enterprises to supply the jobs and incomes necessary for higher standards of living. The fact that Washington continues to provide employment for 4.1 million people, including 1.3 million military personnel, is as much a legacy of bygone days as requirement for running a huge federal establishment. State and local governments, by contrast, have continued to increase their workforces toward 23.5 million people, nearly 3 million more than in 1990 and a 16% share of the national total. Because their employment share exceeds their GDP share by 7.7 (16 less 8.3) while the federal employment share is exceeded by its GDP share by 1.0 causes some to charge that state and local government is particularly wasteful and tax addictive. However, the non-financial service and retail sectors also have an excess of employment share over GDP share just under 8.0. The excess of financial services GDP share over employment share in the range of 15.0 is the factor that makes all other sector differentials appear worse than otherwise would be the case.

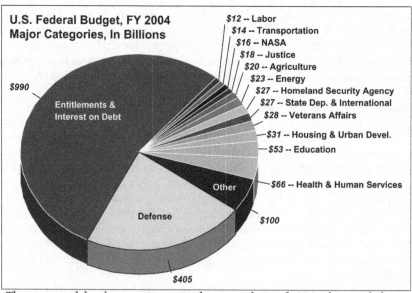

The state and local government employment share of GDP share imbalance has actually improved since its post-war peak of 12.2 in 1955. Because Eisenhower' New Look defense strategy for smaller conventional forces and heavier reliance on nuclear weaponry had not yet been implemented, that was a relatively fat year too for the federal government with employment share topping GDP share by 0.9. Although the Vietnam War draft once again boosted military personnel deployments, US withdrawal from Southeast Asia in the 1970s followed by Ronald Reagan's commitment to smaller government bureaucracy caused federal GDP share to exceed employment share. The end of the Cold War and the Clinton administration's restrained fiscal policy insured that Washington would henceforth keep the differential positive. However, the federal workforce is supplemented in effect by 4.5 million contract employees from private corporations utilized in defense manufacturing and services as well as energy. The Bush administration would like to privatize another 850,000 federal jobs, but is being blocked by Democrats in Congress.

The major tool used by Reagan to put more money back into the pockets of citizens and build up the capital investment base required for entrepreneurial activity, new ventures in technology, and other wealth-creating enterprises was tax cuts. Still on the books was the right to deduct mortgage and consumer interest from taxable income. Although the infrastructure inherited from the New Deal and Great Society eras remained to fund Social Security and Medicare through employer and employee contributions and assist households of moderate and low income to cover the cost of wealth-transferring expenses and otherwise supplement their income, in the 1990s Washington's failure to enact comprehensive health care reform signaled for Democrats an inability, for Republicans an unwillingness to take a more active role in social welfare. The small increase in the top individual tax rate to 39.6% and corporate tax rate to 36% proposed by Clinton and passed by Congress in 1993 was insufficient to generate enough revenue to implement any other major new program. Even when the economy boomed, the watch-words were fiscal responsibility and balanced budget. By 2000, federal taxes on citizens peaked at 20.8% of GDP before falling with the economic slowdown and Bush's tax cuts toward 16%.

Taxpayers continued to pay an even larger chunk of their salaries and wages because of state and local income taxes, property taxes, sales taxes, and other impositions increasing from under $690 billion in 1990 above $900 billion in 2004. Combined state and local government general revenue budgets amounted to $1.3 trillion. Like the federal government, states were saddled with an increasing social welfare burden. On their plate was $300 billion of annual Medicaid expense, including double-digit prescription drug cost increases for 47 million poor people, 15 million at their discretion, $250 billion of education costs for the Baby Boom generation's children covered by nearly $300 billion in property taxes, and 26 weeks of unemployment benefits, costing nearly $11 billion, for the nation's 8.8 million out-of-work, supplemented by Washington paying for at least 13 additional weeks. No wonder that state and local tax increases cancelled out the federal government's attempts at restraint. The topper was that virtually all state governments were required by law to balance their budgets.

Thus, when the energy crisis, recession, and slow-down in capital gains tax revenue put California $25 billion in the red for the 1999-2003 period, Governor Gray Davis and the state legislature raised taxes and fees on individuals and businesses. A citizen backlash resulted in his recall in November 2003 and election of the actor Arnold Schwarzenegger as governor to terminate the deficit. By contrast, voters in Oregon approved new state payroll and personal income taxes to raise $20 billion to cut the average family health care bill more than in half to $2,200. The shortfall would be covered by higher business taxes. Meanwhile in Alabama, state officials started to rethink tax abatements that had brought $11 billion of additional capital investment, including foreign owned car plants, as well as 72,000 new jobs but reduced overall revenue. Just about every state in the Union was annoyed that 290 Fortune 500 companies escaped paying state income taxes by incorporating in Delaware, which had no such tax, no personal property and inventory taxes, low real property taxes, and many tax breaks for businesses.

Arnold Schwarzenegger
In the absence of a shift-the-burden plan by Washington, and because of the wealth and income discrepancies discussed above, the only way for a majority of households to improve standards of living in the 1990s was to take on more debt. This they did by working hard, investing in the stock market, and pushing household liability as a percent of household assets to 15.6% in 1995. The only reason the trend was reversed during the second half of the decade to a nadir of 15.1% was because of the stock market bubble and run up in the value of homes. After the bubble burst and the recession took hold, the figure went up above 18%.

The election of the younger Bush in 2000 heralded at first another dose of Reaganism. The new Republican President intended to cut taxes to stimulate the economy and restrain federal spending. With the help of a Republican and conservative Democratic majority in Congress, he accomplished the first objective, phasing down the top four individual tax brackets from 39.6%-31%-29%-28% to 35%-33%-28%-25% by 2006 while keeping the 15% bracket intact and introducing a new 10% bracket for low income earners. The second objective was disrupted by the September 11, 2001 terrorist attacks. Not only did Washington have to spend billions to help clean up the destruction of the World Trade Tower complex and bail out the airline industry, but projected tax revenue was undercut by economic uncertainties reducing GDP by hundreds of billions and pushing the country into recession. Tens of billions of dollars more were spent on wars in Afghanistan and Iraq. The recession drove several hundred public companies into Chapter 11 bankruptcies, further adding to the federal burden in covering pensions and paying unemployment benefits. Overall loss to the economy might have been as high as $500 billion, and for the world three times as much.

To help the economy recover, in May 2003 Bush proposed and the House and Senate agreed to accelerate reduction of the top marginal tax rate to 35%, speed up as well as increase the child credit for low-income families with three or more children first enacted by Congress in 1997 as an alternative to raising the minimum wage, to $1,000, cut the capital gains tax to 15%, and slash the tax rate on dividend income from the same rate as income taxes to 15%. Other changes permitted small businesses to write off a maximum of $100,000 in capital expenditures, up from $25,000, increased federal aid to states for Medicaid and other expenses by $20 billion over 18 months, and made adjustments in tax brackets to reduce the so-called marriage penalty, the increase in taxes couples had to pay by filing jointly rather than separately and claiming separate deductions. Because the estimated cost to the Treasury over ten years ranged from $350 billion to $810 billion, of which about 30% would remain in the pockets of the richest 1% of households while the poorest 20%, who paid no taxes in the first place, would get nothing, Democrats decried the unfairness of the law. The economy surged late in the summer, however, above an 8% annualized pace, boosting GDP for the year by about 4% and a similar increase in 2004. That improvement came too late to prevent a record federal deficit of about $500 billion. As a percent of GDP, however, the figure was about 4.2%.

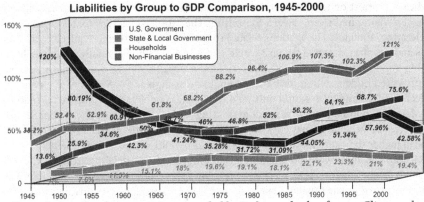

Liabilities by Group to GDP Comparison, 1945-2000

Nevertheless, fiscal conservatives, now led by Rubin and other former Clinton administration officials, complained that annual red ink, pushing the total public debt above $8 trillion, was a drag on the economy. They calculated that for every $200 billion of tax cuts implemented by Congress, long-term interest rates rose by about 0.15%. Thus, the $1.4 trillion in tax cuts already implemented by the Bush administration and their supporters would over 10 years raise long-term rates about 1.15%. The economy would be 0.7% less than otherwise would be the case, or $30-60 billion per year. However, Bush's economic team replied that the shortfall would only be one-third that amount and would be more than compensated for by faster economic growth stimulated by the tax cuts. In any event, the deficit would remain a small fraction of GDP.

Undermining Rubin's argument was the fact that as the federal budget turned from a $200 billion plus surplus in 2000 to a $100 billion plus deficit in 2001, the Federal Reserve began a series of cuts in the Federal Funds Rate from 6.5% to 1.75%. Subsequent cuts brought the rate down to 1% in June 2003, the lowest since 1958. Rather than increasing, long-term interest rates also declined dramatically so that 30 year home mortgage rates plummeted toward 5% before settling around 5.5%. When the general inflation rate, despite oil price instability caused by the Iraq War, fell below 1.5%, Greenspan and the Federal Reserve began to worry about *deflation* such as plagued Japan for most of the 1990s rather than inflation and pushed the Federal Funds Rate back up to 2.5% by early 2005.

Were deflation to take hold, business revenue would decline, making it difficult to pay down debt. Worker wages would have to be cut. However, higher productivity from automation and computers averaging 3.5% from 1995 to 2003, with a surge to 5.5% for 2002-2003, permitted higher wages because fewer workers could produce more; in fact, 1% of productivity increase required 1.3 million wage earners. As consumers enjoyed flat and falling prices for cars, computers, DVD players, TVs, and other electronics made by cheap labor in East Asia, those white and blue collar workers with well-paying jobs found that their standards of living had been enhanced. What cost more were homes, prescription drugs, educational books, energy, and services such as cable TV, car repair, child care, college tuition, dining out, entertainment tickets, and health care. The fall-out from the terrorist attacks undercut demand and rates on air fares, hotel rates, and rental cars.

Aside from the stimulative effect of the federal government spending more than it took in, government programs were either widely popular or widely recognized as necessary. About 45% of the $2.2 trillion budget for FY 2004 was allocated for Social Security, Medicare, interest on the debt and other obligations. Because the cost of maintaining one combat division had risen toward $15 billion, the purchase of high tech weaponry was accelerating, and global obligations related to the War on Terrorism required extra munitions and supplies, national defense would exceed $400 billion annually. Admittedly containing appropriations for "pork," discretionary programs topped $780 billion. Although the projected budget deficit for FY 2004 might go as high as $525 billion, as a percent of projected GDP the figure would only be 4.6%. If the economy picked up faster than projected and individual income taxes contributing 45% of federal revenue, Social Security, Medicare, and other such payroll taxes at 37%, and corporate income taxes around 9.3% came in higher than anticipated, the budget deficit would narrow substantially.

Rubin and other Clinton administration officials liked to claim credit for the 1990s economic boom. Their policies merited praise, but other factors played an equal role. These included a turn in the business cycle, technology and productivity advances, and freer trade around the globe. The most important factor was still consumer spending, coaxed by 0% auto financing and credit card rates toward a 70% share of GDP in the new century.

In fact, the public's insatiable appetite for borrowing against future income for present prosperity shifted the overall national debt burden away from Washington and toward households and businesses. Overall US debt to GDP skyrocketed from 564% in 1995 to around 700% in 2004 while all US liabilities as a percent of all US assets hovered above 73%. Clearly, the American public agreed with the old adage that "it takes money to make money." Whether continuation of such a strategy was tenable for the future was less certain. Nevertheless, the overall tangible and intangible resources of the nation had never before been so great. Another century of economic progress, or decades of decline, might depend on how those resources were applied to create wealth, transfer it, or destroy it.

CHAPTER XXII. LEGACY OF THE PAST INSPIRES A CHALLENGE FOR THE FUTURE

To say that the United States has been blessed by God and nature with economic success is almost understatement. Right from the beginning, four hundred years ago, the first colonists were presented with a secluded, untapped, and under-populated continent overflowing with animal, vegetable, mineral, and water resources. Making liberal use of free and indentured labor, they cleared land along the Atlantic coast, moved up the river valleys, and penetrated deep into the wilderness. Under the protection of a great empire, they developed an agricultural and commercial economy that became the envy of the colonial world. Although native peoples could not be harnessed to the plough, African slaves were. Farms became plantations for production of commodities required for the growth of towns into cities and generation of export income. Basic industries of construction and ship-building, iron forging and textiles then laid the foundation for a more diversified economy. After a century and a half of tightening mercantile controls, Americans were ready to take control of their own destinies.

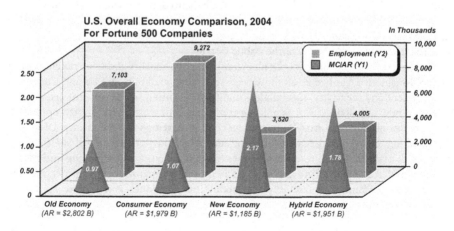

Economically, the Revolution was almost a foregone conclusion years before the Shot Heard Round The World. However, independence with material advantage seemed likely to end in fragmentation and internal conflict until common sense produced a remarkable Constitution amenable to property and business interests. The political genius of the Founding Fathers was not so much that they innovated with democracy as that they synthesized in pragmatic form a republican government with checks and balances on power. The success of the US in retaining and extending the prosperity of colonial times arose in the first instance from re-establishing trade ties with the mother country, in the second in establishing a *laissez-faire* business atmosphere. In the nick of time, economic, political, and social theory coalesced into a concept of Free Market democracy anchored on a cooperative relationship between private enterprise and government. Because men of property organized and dominated the republic, personal and national economy was foremost in the public mind.

Britain's experience with finance, manufacturing, and trade set a good example for development of a modern economy, but the first true American contribution to economic progress was thinking on a much bigger scale than anything that had been attempted before. This was true even before the US acquired the fiscal resources to impose its will on neighbors. Both Hamilton's program and Jefferson's Louisiana Purchase laid the foundations for development of a huge domestic market. By funding a national transportation and communication infrastructure, throwing open the country to new immigration, and encouraging westward expansion, Congress brought that vision to fruition sooner rather than later. Home-grown inventions such as the cotton gin as well as adoption of machines invented abroad, in particular steam engines, helped agriculture and industry reach size and strength. In combination with government largesse and foreign investment, the republic's banks assembled sufficient capital to finance new ventures and to speculate.

Indian wars, the war with Mexico, and the show-down between the states sorted out the issue of whether an indissoluble United States would be dominant in North America or some European-like hodge-podge of greater and lesser states. Aided by government contracts, bigger and more successful businesses developed railroads, oil fields, steel mills, lumbering operations, and other heavy industry. Using cut-throat tactics to build up monopoly power, captains of industry crushed competition, squeezed suppliers, and maximized revenues and profits. A broadening class of corporate executives, office workers, government officials, and even skilled tradesmen benefited from boom times. But farmers, immigrants, ex-slaves, and others who provided the bulk of the work force saw no sustainable rise in living standards. Belatedly, the government stepped in to restrain self-made men from running roughshod over the public interest.

In the last quarter century of the nineteenth century, another and more potent dose of good old-fashioned Yankee know-how, assisted in no small measure by importation of foreign talent and creativity, turned ideas and theories into practical inventions, innovations, and new industries. Even as holding companies and trusts were broken up, potentially greater monopolies arose in telephone communications and electricity. Discovery that food and household brand name products, backed by economies of scale in production, distribution, and retailing, might translate into premium pricing and higher revenue guided the marketing and sales strategies of companies catering to a growing affluent class. Automobiles, assembly line production techniques, and more technological advances, including the airplane, made the republic an economic great power. Presidents, congressmen, and bureaucrats suddenly realized that the US could swing a Big Stick at the western hemisphere and the world. The republic emerged from a war with Spain in possession of a far-flung island empire.

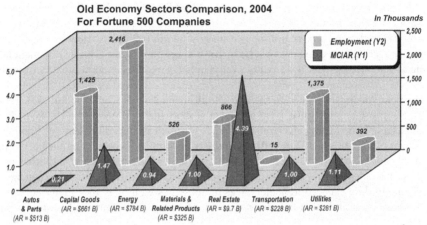

Old Economy Sectors Comparison, 2004
For Fortune 500 Companies

A sudden fervor in Washington and state capitals to use government power for progressive purposes ended the brief infatuation with imperialism and benefited at last the broader mass of working people in their employment, homes, and day-to-day living. Because Henry Ford paid a living wage to his workers and because of general population increase and burgeoning industrial production, a mass consumer market began to take hold. Government pointed the way to a quantum leap in economic potential by borrowing against future tax revenue as well as taxing the incomes of individuals and businesses for the wherewithal to fight the First World War. American consumers in the 1920s adapted the strategy to their own purposes by borrowing against future income to buy durable goods and stocks. Even citizens of marginal means were enticed to overindulgence by clever advertising in newspapers, on billboards, and over the new medium of mass communications, radio. Although the vices of hedonism and materialism backfired most disastrously in 1929, they set the stage for what would become in succeeding generations the major strategy for accelerated economic growth.

However, the chasm of the Great Depression had to be spanned first. When private enterprise could not build the bridge alone, Washington jumped in with economic assistance and regulation on an unprecedented scale. The *laissez faire* business environment became entangled and constrained in a cobweb of government agencies and programs. More taxes were taken from Big Business and the wealthy to sustain the majority and pump-prime the economy. The stimulus was insufficient to surpass the prosperity of the past until the imperative of preventing dangerous enemies from conquering Europe and Asia required full mobilization of the military power and industrial might of the United States. Because the Second World War was fought for the most part in the Eastern Hemisphere, the homelands of other Great Powers were reduced to rubble even while American soil remained untouched.

Diminishment of foreign competition, pent-up demand for housing and consumer products and services, a larger hoard of financial resources, and a new burst of technology both for civil and military purposes that included TV and the atomic bomb made the US economy the envy of the world. With easy access to the oil, coal, iron, wood, and other raw materials of domestic and distant regions, the American industrial machine cranked up production of machinery, motor vehicles, and electrical equipment, shipment of consumer durables and non-durables, and construction of buildings big and small to record levels. Using new fertilizers and feeds to increase crop yield and herd sizes, American farmers fed the country and saved tens of millions around the world from starvation. Ironically, the triumph of agriculture came even as the sector was eclipsed in the economy by manufacturing and services so that fewer and fewer people derived a livelihood directly from the soil.

Instead, Americans looked to the sky. The airline industry became Big Business in the 1950s. Mainframe computers, soon using transistors instead of vacuum tubes, proved indispensable in providing electronic guidance for nuclear-tipped rockets, jet bombers, and shorter range missiles. The military-industrial complex became another important sector of economic growth. Back on earth, copiers, electric typewriters, and other new business machines increased the production of white collar workers. In the golden age of television, middle class contentment was increased as well by books, magazines, and newspapers, sport and other live entertainment, and creative content in film, fine art, and music.

Government sympathy and legal protections for unions finally fulfilled the promise to working men and women in older industries of higher wages and benefits, better working conditions, and material comforts. As hard fought had been the victory for labor, harder still would be holding on to the American Dream. To survive competition at home and abroad, corporations pushed for more economies of scale in production. Automation threatened the long-term viability of assembly line workers. For the moment, however, industrial union members came into the material mainstream of the republic. Two cars in family garages became the norm for both the middle and working classes.

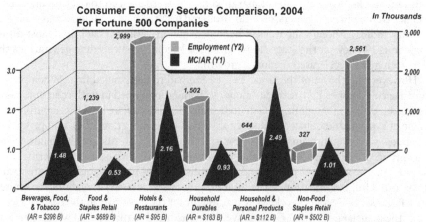

In the 1960s, economies of scale in retailing, wholesaling, restaurant, grocery, and hotel chains, and other service sectors brought down prices for brand name food and household goods. Living standards were broadly higher than ever before. When reduction of income taxes spurred new economic growth for big businesses, more national income for citizens, and more overall revenue for the federal government, the time seemed right to expand Washington's role yet again. The goal was a Great Society in which the vast majority of the American people, now including African-Americans with full civil and political rights, could partake of the mass market for goods and services. Hence, another cobweb of agencies and programs, rules and regulations bent business operations, employment, and revenue in directions of Washington's choosing, not that of management and shareholders. The benefit to the majority of expanded health and other social services was offset by a situation in which government interference paralyzed the decision-making authority of corporate leaders just at the moment when Communist advances in Vietnam and other Third World areas obscured the challenge of reviving economies in Western Europe and Japan. Thus, when in the 1970s the US was hit with oil embargoes and increasing foreign import competition, American business and industry could not respond effectively. Wedded to over regulation and price controls, government had the wrong formula for success.

In the 1970s, citizens howled at high inflation, high interest rates, and high unemployment. Stagnating living standards among working class and even middle class households mandated two family incomes. In combination with advances made by African-Americans under Civil Rights laws, the feminist revolution that encouraged middle class women to seek independent careers, and a new burst of immigration from overseas and Latin America, the consequence was a glutted labor market. Except where union contracts and seniority protection prevailed, wages, benefits, and working conditions eroded. The malaise that settled over the republic was caused as much by realization that the Great Society might never be achieved as actual economic dislocations and distress. Government bowed to the inevitable logic of free markets and began to deregulate transportation and communication industries.

For a third time in a hundred years, technological innovation came to the rescue. In the 1980s, personal computers sparked a boom that carried over to printers, storage devices, and other peripheral equipment and supplies. More valuable in the long run was the software that made the hardware work. Together with the rising stock market and successes with media, information, and entertainment, the intangible part of the economy rose up to equal the tangible. Government got on the bandwagon by easing restrictions in banking and finance. A new concentration of capital for investment and speculative ventures then increased the potential of computers, telecommunication, and other cutting edge areas such as bio-technology. Direct assistance from Washington also put together the Internet superhighway. A grimmer consequence of the boom was restructuring in heavy industries, contraction of higher paying wage jobs, and export of manufacturing capacity by US multinational companies. Union membership began a precipitous decline.

In the last decade of the twentieth century, leaders in both major political parties committed to globalization not only of goods and services but labor markets. However, Free Trade agreements lessened government's ability to direct and regulate the economy, put pressure on US and foreign corporations to balance revenues and profits with the public interest, and redistribute a portion of wealth and income from society's wealthy to have-nots. In the midst of a bull market, differences in wealth and income between affluent and have-not households widened to a chasm. After New Economy sectors failed to replace all the jobs and income lost by workers in Old Economy sectors, the bulk of employment shifted to lower-paying service sector work. Only then was Washington's relative impotence to boost living standards deeply felt. The principal method in which state and local governments aided the American people was by using tax dollars to provide public employment as well as services.

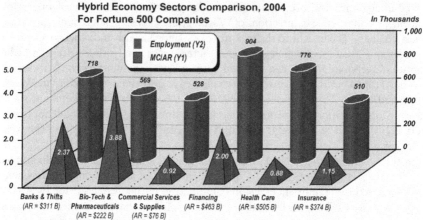

Implosion of Internet, telecommunication, and other technology stocks in the new century betrayed not so much a temporary blip in the economic juggernaut of cutting edge businesses as a Roaring '20s speculative bubble. By blending New Economy emphasis on high technology, smaller labor forces, and more intangible assets with Old Economy reliance on economies of scale, distribution to mass markets, and monopoly domination of industries, most big US businesses survived the downturn. However, a trend toward foreign outsourcing of production and jobs reduced the prospects for tens of millions of middle and working class Americans. Particularly since the majority does not possess a lasting store of wealth, the challenge for government of spurring another sustained period of growth that encompasses most citizens without interrupting the basic Free Market economy becomes more difficult.

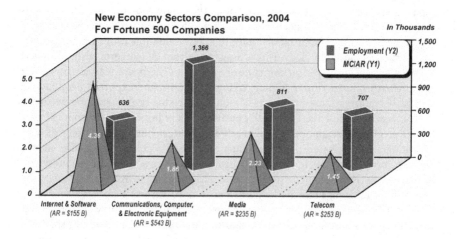

The ill-concealed secret of Capitalism is that overall economic success does not require the affluence of all citizens. The size of the US population, combined with those of other developed and developing nations, is great enough to sustain a mass market for goods and services without including the least prosperous half. However, leaving out have-nots adds to the structural burden on the American and world economy of supporting the living standards and expectations of lower income households. Political and social strife generated by discontentment can undermine prosperity as rapidly as adverse economic developments, over-regulation by government, and mistakes by business leaders. Therefore, it is in the self-interest of Americans rich and poor to support actions and policies that reinvigorate the material part of the American Dream for the vast majority. Although tax cuts are an indispensable tool for stimulating the economy, although a perpetual war on America's enemies may be good in the short run for aerospace and defense industries, Washington's focus needs to be broader and more imaginative. This is particularly the case since leading politicians rest assumptions about economic growth all too blithely on past performance. Even the great engine of US material success may falter one day if not oiled, serviced, and tuned up periodically to run better in the long run than would be the case by neglect.

It has been the author's purpose in this book to provide a comprehensive history of the American economy and Big Business without injecting too frequently personal opinion. However, in a different forum a debate about the direction the republic can take to promote a greater and more general prosperity can and should be joined. Perhaps not in this generation but the next the inherent conflicts and danger of a Have versus Have-Not society may reach a crisis point. The ascent of the American Republic, founded in large part on the rise of its economy and the initiative of its people, must not be considered a foregone conclusion.

INDEX OF NAMES

Index of Companies, Products, and Services

G

693